10-08

Leathernecks

Leathernecks

An Illustrated History of the U.S. Marine Corps

Merrill L. Bartlett and Jack Sweetman

NAVAL INSTITUTE PRESS

Annapolis, Maryland

This book has been brought to publication with the generous assistance of Marguerite and Gerry Lenfest.

Naval Institute Press
291 Wood Road
Annapolis, Maryland 21402

Library of Congress Cataloging-in-Publication Data

Bartlett, Merrill L.
  Leathernecks : an illustrated history of the United States Marine Corps / Merrill L. Bartlett, Jack Sweetman.
        p. cm.
Includes bibliographical references and index.
ISBN 978-1-59114-020-7 (alk. paper)
1. United States. Marine Corps.—History. I. Sweetman, Jack, 1940- II. Title.
VE23.B368 2008
359.9'60973—dc22

                          2008015582

Printed in the United States of America
15 14 13 12 11 10 09 08   9 8 7 6 5 4 3 2
First printing

Creative direction and book design: Chris Onrubia, Fineline Graphics LLC

To the memory of our mothers

Amelia Schirman Bartlett

(1910–1990)

and

Bertha Michael Sweetman

(1910–2005)

Contents

Maps

Foreword

Yes, we have another illustrated history of the Marine Corps, one of the most photogenic subjects in the military genre to judge by the number of similar works that have appeared over the years. Much sets this one apart, starting with two highly readable, award-winning authors noted for their past publications on related subjects—the Marine Corps and the Navy. Skip Bartlett and Jack Sweetman served as history professors at the Naval Academy thirty years ago, and from this friendship the reading public has benefited many times over. To name just a few of their books, Skip's *Lejeune: A Marine's Life* and *Pete Ellis: An Amphibious Warfare Prophet* (with Dirk Anthony Ballendorf) remain the definitive biographies of these unforgettable and greatly influential Marines. Jack Sweetman's equally impressive contributions include *American Naval History: An Illustrated Chronology of the U.S. Navy and Marine Corps* and perhaps his best-known book, for many years the premier gift to all visiting dignitaries at the Naval Academy, *The U.S. Naval Academy: An Illustrated History*. Their previous works clearly influence this rich history of the Marine Corps and, as the reader will see, give it a taut, professional flavor rarely found in the efforts of less seasoned authors. They have striven—successfully—to achieve what their preface describes as a "concise narrative, balanced in terms of both chronological and topical content . . . [with] a generous selection of art." They have exhaustively researched and uncovered numerous unpublished and perhaps unknown visuals of every description: portraiture, contemporary art, combat art, sketches from *Harper's Weekly* and the *Illustrated London News*, among others, and best of all, modern combat art that heretofore has appeared only in shows to which the public had limited access.

The photographs are an entirely separate subject. Some will be recognizable by historians and the general public, but others are rare indeed and often give a totally different view of events and the people involved, all thought to be well known. As the former director of Marine Corps History and Museums with control over all combat art, photographs, and other visuals, I have been pleasantly surprised to encounter such images. The authors are also to be commended for their use of maps, and for the construct of the maps themselves—not too busy, easily understood, and well placed in relation to the accompanying story. Stingy use of maps can easily ruin (and often does) the very best of otherwise excellent histories.

There is also something to be said of the synergy sparked by the teaming of a prominent Marine Corps historian, Skip Bartlett, and an equally prominent naval historian, Jack

Sweetman. Together they emphasize the naval flavor of the Marine Corps that has existed since its inception and continues as strongly as ever today. All Marines understand and celebrate the power—massive power—that can come only from the continued teamwork and unparalleled support our Navy provides. Whereas the Marine Corps and the Navy both exist in the Department of the Navy as separate services, we are brothers in the truest sense, as the authors make clear.

The reader will see that this is no chest-thumping treatise about the smallest, but perhaps the best known worldwide, of our nation's armed services. That the Marine Corps has carved out its own reputation, predominantly in battle, over its more than 230-year existence is unmistakable. What Bartlett and Sweetman have done here is to take one along that path, revealing the events that shaped our Corps, the personalities involved—some of whom have received scant recognition in the past—and the decisions—not always good ones—that have brought the U.S. Marines into the world's collective consciousness as a premier, if not *the* premier, fighting force.

Almost fifteen years ago I made a statement to a group in St. Louis that has reverberated many times over and is now attributed to several other speakers: "There are only two types of people who understand Marines: Marines and the enemy." This book does an excellent job of showing the reader why this is true.

Col. John W. Ripley, USMC (Ret.)

Tell It to the Marines

Some time during the reign of Charles II (1649–85), no less a luminary than Samuel Pepys, Secretary of the Admiralty, recorded the following exchange in the King's court. Apparently, the monarch had granted an audience to the captain of a ship that he just returned from a voyage to the Indies. The master of the vessel sought to belabor the royal ears with descriptions of the many strange things he had seen. But when the mariner told of seeing fish that flew through the air like birds, the monarch expressed incredulity. "Fish that fly through the air!? Sir, such a thing is beyond believing." King Charles II turned to Colonel Sir William Killigren who commanded the newly-formed maritime regiment of Marines. "What say you, sir, to a man who tells for truth that he has seen fish that fly through the air?"

Philip N. Pierce, "Tell It to the Marines," Marine Corps Gazette 36 (March 1952): 34.

"I should say, your majesty," replied Colonel Killigren, "that he hath sailed in southern waters. When your majesty's business carried me thither of late I did frequently see such a sight." The king searched the weatherbeaten colonel's face to ascertain if his senior marine officer spoke in jest, but found his manner sincere. His majesty turned to Pepys and remarked: "From the very nature of their calling, no class of our subjects has as wide a knowledge of the seas and lands as the officers and men of our loyal maritime regiment. Henceforth, whenever we cast doubt upon a tale that lacketh likelihood we will tell it to the Marines. If they believe it, it is safe to say that it is true."

In the Age of Sail, sailors loathed the marines because of their role as shipboard policemen and tended to denigrate their status in the ship. In response to a sailor's exclamation of utter nonsense, he might be chastised by a messmate to "go tell it to the Marines." On Thanksgiving Day, 1944, Radio Tokyo waxed eloquent on a variety of matters concerning the Marine Corps. After expounding at length on the subject of the disreputable ancestry of America's Leathernecks, he referred to them as "a bunch of roughnecks who don't give a hang about their lives, which is the reason they fight so recklessly." The Son of Nippon added that the "Marines are so ignorant that they will believe what you tell them when the general public will not." "Hence," he said, "came the expression 'tell it to the Marines' which means the same thing as 'don't be silly.'"

The Marines' Hymn

From the halls of Montezuma
To the shores of Tripoli,
We fight our country's battles
In the air, on land, and sea.
First to fight for right and freedom,
And to keep our honor clean,
We are proud to claim the title
Of United States Marines.

Our flag's unfurled to every breeze
From dawn to setting sun;
We have fought in every clime and place
Where we could take a gun.
In the snow of far off northern lands
And in sunny tropic scenes,
You will find us always on the job—
The United States Marines.

Here's health to you and to our Corps
Which we are proud to serve;
In many a strife we've fought for life
And never lost our nerve.
If the Army and the Navy
Ever look on Heaven's scenes,
They will find the streets are guarded
By United States Marines.

Preface

The history of the U.S. Marine Corps is among the greatest military success stories of all time. It is the story of how a service that throughout its first hundred years seldom exceeded the strength of an infantry regiment not only overcame repeated challenges to its existence but eventually attained a strength exceeding that of some armies. At the same time, it consistently demonstrated an extraordinary level of combat effectiveness and acquired what is arguably the world's most potent military mystique. It should surprise no one that its members, past and present, argue that there are only two types of people in the world, Marines and those who wish they could have been Marines.

Under such circumstances, it is scarcely surprising that the Corps has become the subject of an abundant literature. This literature includes a number of illustrated histories. By and large, these works concentrate on the Corps in combat since World War I, which makes for stirring reading and viewing, but which leaves many aspects of its corporate life unaddressed and relegates the first, highly eventful—one might even say formative—century and a quarter of its existence to little more than a prelude; furthermore, none of these works has been the product of trained historians. For these reasons, it seemed to us that there was room for a new illustrated history in which a reasonably concise narrative, balanced in terms of both chronological coverage and topical content and buttressed by fresh, historically accurate research, would be complemented by a generous selection of art. This book is the result.

Like that of all military organizations, the Corps' history has two major motifs, the operational and the institutional. The operational is the investigation of how it has performed its assigned missions, especially in battle. The institutional is the examination of the evolution of those missions, the changes in its structure, its internal politics, and its relations with its sister services and civilian authority. Within the limitations of space, we tried to develop both motifs, but because any armed service's fundamental reason for being is to fight, we were particularly attentive to the operational.

Of course, the history of any organization, military or otherwise, is the product of the actions of the individuals who compose it. Therefore, we have profiled the services of some of the Marines who made exceptional contributions to the Corps' heritage. A number of them—Smedley Butler, Pappy Boyington, and Chesty Puller, for example—will be known to every student of American military history. Others, such as Archibald Henderson, Henry

Clay Cochrane, and Dan Daly, will be familiar only to the cognoscenti of the Corps. We believe the reader will enjoy making, or renewing, the acquaintance of them all.

The illustrations are for the most part contemporary to the subjects they portray. A number have never been published, and others have not been reproduced since their original appearance in periodical literature a century or more ago. Of the later works upon which we drew, usually in the absence of contemporary art, most are taken from the collection of carefully researched studies executed under the auspices of the Marine Corps University's History Division (Reference Branch) or Museums Division (Art Collection) and the Alfred M. Gray Research Center, Quantico. Other illustrations and photographs were located in the holdings of the National Archives and Records Administration, Archives II, College Park, Maryland; Naval Historical Center, Washington Navy Yard; Navy Art Collection, Washington Navy Yard; and Photographic Archives, Library of Congress.

Other useful repositories included the U.S. Naval Academy Museum; the Beverley Robinson Collection, U.S. Naval Academy Museum; Franklin D. Roosevelt Library and Museum, Hyde Park, New York; Defense Visual Information Center, March Air Force Reserve Base, California; AKG-Images, London; Alinari, Rome; Fitzwilliam Museum, Cambridge; Harry Ransom Humanities Research Center, The University of Texas, Austin; Boston Athenæum; Wadsworth Atheneum, Hartford; U.S. Naval Institute Photo Archives; the Mariner's Museum, Newport News, Virginia; Photographic Archive, the Florida State Archives; and Getty Images. Unaffiliated artists James Dietz, Ted Wilbur, and Charles Waterhouse contributed works from their private collections.

Finally, we would like to emphasize that this is in no sense an official history. The views expressed are our own and do not necessarily represent those of the Navy Department or either of the naval services. The authors met and conceived the idea of this book while they taught history at the U.S. Naval Academy.

Acknowledgments

We are indebted to a lengthy list of archivists, photographic specialists, librarians, and art curators. Without them, this book would never have been brought to fruition. It is our pleasure to record our thanks.

Research for the textual portions was assisted by the Reference Branch, Histories Division (HD), Marine Corps University (MCU), in the persons of Danny J. Crawford, Robert V. Aquilina, Annette Amerman, Kara Newcomer, and Sheila Boyd. The late Benis M. Frank, and then Lt. Col. Gary D. Solis, USMC (Ret.), provided access and guidance to the HD's Oral History Collection. Dr. Jack Shulimson, former head of the HD's Vietnam histories project; Charles R. Smith, the HD's specialist on Marines in the formative years; and Col. Jon T. Hoffman, USMCR (Ret.), former deputy director of the HD, gave freely of their time to answer queries on a variety of minutiae. Evelyn A. Englander, the HD's long-time librarian, located several out-of-print of books that proved invaluable.

The staff at the Library of Congress furnished guidance in searching the stacks for long-out-of-print volumes and made available its invaluable manuscript collections. At the National Archives and Records Administration, the staffs at both NARA I and NARA II provided unfettered access to primary source materials. The Suzallo Library, University of Washington; King County Library and its branch on Vashon Island; and the Seattle Public Library assisted in the location of reference materials not available locally. The staffs of the New York Historical Society, Herbert Hoover Presidential Library, Franklin D. Roosevelt Presidential Library, Dwight D. Eisenhower Presidential Library, and the Nimitz Library at the U.S. Naval Academy facilitated research on matters germane to the Marine Corps. The late Thomas S. Butler graciously allowed access to the personal correspondence of his famous father, Smedley D. Butler.

In the quest for photographs and illustrations, especially materials contemporary to the scenes they depict, we owe a debt of thanks to a multitude of imagery specialists, art curators, and historians as well as individuals who had exclusive access to materials sought. These include Owen L. Connor, Curator for the Uniforms and Heraldry Section, National Museum of the Marine Corps; Lena M. Kaljot, Photographic Historian, Reference Branch, HD-MCU; Maj. Jack Dyer, USMCR (Ret.), former Art Curator and his replacement, Charles G. Grow (former sergeant and combat historian, USMC), along with the Assistant Art Curator, Joan Thomas, Museums Division, MCU; Edwin C. Finney Jr., Photographic Historian, Naval Historical Center; Holly Reed and Rutha Beamon, Still Photographic Branch, NARA II; Kathy Vinson,

Department of Defense Visual Information Center; Michelle M. Frauenberger, Franklin D. Roosevelt Museum; Renée Klish, Art Curator, U.S. Army Center for Military History; and Ivey Photo of Seattle. Joe McCary, Photo Response Studio, located and copied misfiled photographs at the Still Photograph Branch, NARA II. Elizabeth S. Bingham authorized the use of a daguerreotype of her gallant ancestor, Capt. John D. Simms, USMC and CSMC; Dr. Vernon L. Williams loaned his personal copy of an early photograph of Littleton W. T. Waller; and Mary Ripley contributed the portrait of her distinguished father. At the U.S. Naval Academy Museum, its administrative assistant, Dolly Pentalides, and the curator of the Beverley R. Robinson Collection, Sigrid Trumpy, assiduously searched for images we sought held by the museum. Debora Wynne, archivist, Florida State Historical Society, and Patricia S. Robertson, Florida State Archives, traced the photograph of Lt. David Raney.

Other people assisted us in a variety of matters. Matt Deines, Col. George F. Spires, USAF (Ret.), and Gregory Falconer, a former Marine, shared their expertise in computers. David M. Sullivan opened his storehouse of knowledge on the Marines in the Civil War. Lt. Col. Kenneth W. Estes, USMC (Ret.), and Lt. Col. Brendan Greeley Jr., USMC (Ret.), commented on chapter 15. Col. John W. Ripley, USMC (Ret.), graciously contributed the foreword. Capt. Gordon Peterson, USN (Ret.), provided us with the latest Marine Corps casualty figures for the Vietnam War.

We appreciate the help and encouragement of various members of the staff at the U.S. Naval Institute. Fred L. Schultz, senior editor of *Proceedings* and *Naval History*, was always helpful. Shepherding this production to completion has been the untiring effort of Susan Brook, without whom *Leathernecks* would be even further behind schedule. We are grateful to Susan Corrado, Christine Onrubia, Marla Traweek, and other members of the Naval Institute Press staff who produced this volume. While they are no longer with the Institute, Mark Gatlin, Dawn Stitzel, Jennifer Wallace, Linda O'Doughda, Dave Hofeling, and Craig Triplett also deserve our thanks. And we would like to acknowledge our excellent copy editor, Patti Bower.

Finally, our wives, Blythe W. Bartlett and Gisela A. Sweetman, have endured more distraction and mood swings from their husbands than deserved. To them, we are indebted for their unflagging encouragement and support.

Abbreviations

More than one observer of military and naval life has suggested that any member of the Armed Forces, past or present, is capable of speaking at length without using words common to any civilized tongue. Often, the speech used by Marines tends to puzzle civilians because of its mixture of soldierly vocabulary enriched with the lexicon of those who serve at sea. The abbreviations that punctuate everyday military and naval speech make it difficult, if not impossible, for the lay listener or reader to fathom the content of any discourse. Your authors have attempted to keep the acronyms in the text to a minimum, but consider the following list of common abbreviations and terms essential to the narrative.

AAV	amphibious assault vehicle
AEF	American Expeditionary Forces
amtrac	amphibious tractor
ANGLICO	Air and Naval Gunfire Liaison Company
ARVN	Army of the Republic of Vietnam (South Vietnam), also a soldier of that army
AWOL	absent without leave
BLT	battalion landing team
CAP	combined action platoon
CENTCOM	Central Command
CINCLANT	Commander-in-Chief, Atlantic
CINPAC	Commander-in-Chief, Pacific
DMZ	demilitarized zone
FLEX	fleet exercise
FMF	Fleet Marine Force
FMFPac	Fleet Marine Force, Pacific
FOB	forward operating bases
FSB	fire support base
GOSP	gas and oil separation platform
HMH	Marine heavy helicopter squadron
HMM	Marine medium helicopter squadron
HMR	Marine helicopter transport squadron
HMX-1	Marine Helicopter Experimental Squadron
HQMC	Headquarters Marine Corps
IED	improvised explosive device
JCS	Joint Chiefs of Staff

LAR	light armored reconnaissance battalion
LCM	landing craft, mechanized
LCVP	landing craft, vehicle and personnel
LPH	amphibious assault ship
LST	landing ship, tank
LVT	landing vehicle, tracked
MAAG	Military Assistance and Advisory Group
MAB	Marine amphibious brigade
MACV	Military Assistance Command, Vietnam
MAF	Marine amphibious force
MAG	Marine air group
MAU	Marine amphibious unit
MAW	Marine air wing
MEB	Marine expeditionary brigade
MEF	Marine expeditionary force
MEU	Marine expeditionary unit
MPS	maritime prepositioning ship
NATO	North Atlantic Treaty Organization
NCO	noncommissioned officer
NVA	North Vietnamese Army, also a member of that army
ONI	Office of Naval Intelligence
OSS	Office of Strategic Services
PDF	Panamanian Defense Force
PLO	Palestine Liberation Organization
RCT	regimental combat team
ROK	Republic of Korea
RPG	rocket-propelled grenade
SOC	special operations capable
STO/VL	short take off/vertical landing
TF	task force
TOW	tube-launched, optically tracked, wire-guided (missile)
VC	Viet Cong or Vietnamese Communist
VMA	Marine attack squadron
VMAQ	Marine tactical electronic warfare squadron
VMF	Marine fighter squadron
VMFA	Marine fighter attack squadron
VMF(N)	Marine fighter squadron (night)
VMO	Marine observation squadron
VMSB	Marine scout bombing squadron
WMD	weapons of mass destruction

Leathernecks

CHAPTER 1

Marines through the Ages

The simplest definition of a marine is also the most traditional: a soldier of the sea. In the case of the U.S. Marine Corps, whose primary mission is amphibious assault and whose most famous battles have been fought on land, it might seem more accurate to say soldier *from* the sea. The Corps' specialization is a relatively recent development, however. Marines of centuries past were neither expressly trained nor principally employed as amphibious forces. Although they participated in operations ashore, as a rule it was merely as the most proficient element of naval landing parties. For the first twenty-five hundred years of their existence, marines fought the majority of their battles at sea.

Until the mid-nineteenth century, when the introduction of explosive shells and long-range, rifled guns made it possible to sink a ship without coming near her, every naval engagement was potentially a boarding action. The role of marines, often simply embarked soldiers, was to spearhead such actions. There were marine detachments aboard the Greek galleys that shattered the Persian fleet at the Battle of Salamis in 480 BC, the climax of the first naval campaign in

recorded history. Each of the Athenians' 180 vessels, for example, carried four archers and fourteen infantrymen protected with brass body armor and armed with a short sword and an eight-foot-long spear. The Greeks called their marines *Epibatoe*—heavy-armed sea soldiers. Their superiority in close combat over their Persian counterparts, mainly archers protected only by quilted tunics, was an important ingredient of the Greek victory.

The names of the first two marines known to history emerged from the Battle of Salamis. One belonged to the contingent from the Greek city-state of Aegina, the other to that from Troezene. The galleys in which they were serving were cut off and captured by the Persians shortly before the battle. The Troezenian marine, Leo, was chosen for his good looks to be sacrificed to the Persian gods. His comrade was more fortunate. Herodotus reports:

> The ship of Aegina gave the Persians no small trouble, a certain Pytheas, who was a fighting man thereon, bearing himself very bravely. For when the ship was taken, he did not cease to contend with the enemies, until he fell, being covered

Opposite: Greek marines in action on the decks of their galleys at the Battle of Salamis in 480 BC. Peter Connolly's recent painting reflects the latest research on the construction and appearance of the vessels engaged. (AKG-Images)

with wounds from head to foot. But the Persian soldiers, finding that he was not dead . . . made much of him, seeking to keep him alive. His wounds they dressed with myrrh and bound with bandages of cotton; and when they came back to their encampment they showed the man to the host, admiring him and dealing with him kindly.

Happily, the Persian vessel was among those captured at Salamis and Pytheas regained his freedom.

Two centuries later, the Romans owed the transformation of the Mediterranean into *Mare Nostrum* to the strong arms of their *milites classiarii*—soldiers of the fleet. Purely a land power at the commencement of her imperial career, Rome was compelled to become a sea power as well when the extension of her influence to the island of Sicily brought her into conflict with the maritime empire of Carthage. In the opening naval actions of the First Punic War (261–241 BC), the Romans quickly discovered that they lacked the skill to counter the ram-and-run tactics of their seafaring antagonists. The only way to offset the Carthaginians' seamanship,

they reasoned, was by finding a means to get their marines aboard the enemy vessels. Their solution was the invention of the *corvus* (raven), a heavy fenced gangway, about eighteen feet long and four feet wide, that was secured in an upright position in the bow of each Roman galley. Attached to the underside of the upper end of this gangway was a great iron hook; the lower end was fastened into a swivel in the deck. When a Carthaginian galley approached to ram, the Romans released the tackle holding the *corvus*. The impact of the free-falling gangway embedded the hook in the enemy's deck, the marines charged across two abreast, and that was that. Although the Carthaginians carried marines of sorts, they were no match for Rome's sea-going legionnaires. In time, the Romans learned to handle their ships expertly enough to do without the *corvus*, but they continued to rely on boarding actions to win battles.

The fragmentation of political authority in Western Europe following the collapse of the Roman Empire in the fifth century AD spelled an end to regular naval and marine forces but did nothing to affect the tactics of war at sea. Throughout the Middle Ages, boarding action by soldiers embarked for

Medieval marines clash in a miniature from an English manuscript of AD 1271. (The Fitzwilliam Museum, Cambridge, England)

that purpose remained the decisive element of Mediterranean galley warfare. Often ships of a squadron were actually lashed together to create a floating battlefield. If enemy boarders gained a foothold on any one vessel, reinforcements from neighboring ships were fed into the fray to repulse them. At the Battle of Lepanto in 1571, where the Christian League's fleet defeated that of the Ottoman Empire in the last great galley action, twenty-five to thirty vessels crowded into a space of approximately 250 by 150 yards to support the engagement between their respective flagships, each of which carried several hundred men-at-arms.

The boarding action also retained its primacy in northern European waters, where high-sided sailing ships called "cogs" began to be used in combat early in the thirteen century. Elevated "castles" were built fore and aft as fighting platforms for men-at-arms, and archers, crossbowmen, and stone throwers took position in the crows'-nest. Sometimes the ship's boat was slung halfway up the mast to accommodate additional missile men. Normally, the side that established fire superiority would seek to postpone boarding until its projectiles

had cut down most of the opposing fighting men. Grappling hooks were used to prevent an enemy from disengaging and, as in the Mediterranean, friendly ships often roped or even chained themselves together.

In the sixteenth century, the age-old format of war at sea was broken by a revolutionary weapon system created by the integration of two technological innovations, both of which had appeared approximately one hundred years earlier. They were the three-masted, square-rigged ship, an ocean-sailing vessel of unprecedented efficiency; and the single-piece, cast-bronze cannon, the first reasonably reliable gun. When such guns were positioned to fire broadside along the length of such ships, it became readily possible to disable an opposing vessel without coming into physical contact with her. This potential gave birth to a new age of naval tactics destined to last into the twentieth century, in which the gunnery duel supplanted the boarding action as the principal mode of combat.

The defeat of the Spanish Armada in 1588 signaled this change. Both the English and Spanish fleets consisted almost entirely of broadside-firing ships; but the towering Spanish galleons were much less

AN OFFICER
OF THE
DUKE OF YORK AND ALBANY'S MARITIME REGIMENT OF FOOT
(THE LORD HIGH ADMIRAL'S REGIMENT.)

A SOLDIER
OF THE
DUKE OF YORK AND ALBANY'S MARITIME REGIMENT OF FOOT
(THE LORD HIGH ADMIRAL'S REGIMENT.)

maneuverable and their cannon were mostly short-range, heavy-caliber ship-smashers intended to soften up the enemy for boarding, a tactic to which the Spanish remained committed. Finding that their handy vessels could easily evade the Spaniards' attempts to close, the English kept out of their grasp while maintaining a galling fire that reduced the Invincible Armada to a mob of fugitive ships.

But the advent of the gunnery duel did not end the usefulness of marines. Battles were still fought at very close quarters. As late as the War of 1812, the maximum effective range of naval guns was no more than four hundred yards. Serious engagements usually opened at two hundred yards and a captain with strong nerves might hold fire until half that. In these actions, marines on their ship's deck or aloft in her fighting tops would rake the enemy with musketry. Their fire began to become effective at two hundred yards and increased in accuracy as the range fell until, at one hundred yards or less, an average marksman could hit a man-sized target more often than he would miss. The distance

between Lord Nelson, the most illustrious victim of ships' small arms fire, and the unknown Frenchman who put a musket ball through his spine from the mizzen-top of the *Redoubtable* at the Battle of Trafalgar was approximately fifteen yards.

Marines also joined in the boarding actions that, despite the ascendancy of the gun, often formed the last act of such close combat. In contests between ships of comparable sizes, the side that found itself getting the worst of the gunnery duel would frequently attempt to reverse the tide of battle by boarding. Conversely, the side that dominated the gunnery action might try to board and capture a beaten ship rather than batter her to pieces.

In addition, marines stiffened the parties their ships sent ashore in landings and raids. This had always been one of their functions, but its importance increased as the expansion of Europe, made possible by the ship and the gun, extended the interests of the Atlantic powers to the four corners of the earth. The colonial and maritime conflicts that ensued did more than give marines active employment, however. In the sixteenth and seventeenth centuries the spoils of these struggles contributed to the rise of governments that could afford to maintain their own full-time, professional armed forces, institutions absent from the Western world since the fall of Rome.

The first regularly constituted marine formation in modern times, the French regiment *la Marine*, was founded by Cardinal Richelieu in 1627 to guard the country's ports and "form the garrison" of ships. Richelieu embodied a second marine regiment, the *Royal Vaisseaux*, in 1635, and later in the century his successors organized two others. Meanwhile, Great Britain had established The Duke of York and Albany's Maritime Regiment of Foot—commonly called the Admiral's Regiment, for the duke was Lord High Admiral of England—by an Order in Council of 28 October 1664 that directed "twelve hundred Land Souldjers be forthwith raysed . . . to be distributed into his Ma^ts Fleets prepared for Sea Service." The United Provinces of Holland followed suit by the creation of their *Korps Mariners* on 10 December 1665. Peter the Great founded the Russian marines—technically, naval infantry or *Moraskaya Pekhota*—in the midst of the Great Northern War with Sweden on 16 November 1701.

The evolution of British marine forces was naturally the most relevant to the military experience of the American colonists. The Maritime Regiment of Foot was disbanded in 1690 after active service afloat and ashore in the Anglo-Dutch Wars, the Low Countries, and North Africa; one company

had also done two years' peacekeeping duty in Virginia. The reason for the regiment's dissolution was probably its presumed sympathy for its first colonel, the Duke of York, who, having ascended the throne as King James II in 1685, had been driven off it by the Glorious Revolution of 1688. That the value of marines was not an issue is indicated by the fact that the two new units, the 1st and 2nd Regiments of Marines, were organized later in 1690. Detachments of both entered combat almost immediately. In 1698 the two regiments, apparently much reduced in numbers, were consolidated and three infantry regiments were converted into marines. But by then the country was, for once, at peace, and all four regiments were disbanded in 1701.

The peace was short-lived. In May 1702 Britain intervened in the War of Spanish Succession, and in June Queen Anne called for the formation of six regiments of marines. These units served with distinction throughout the conflict, taking part in the destruction of a Spanish fleet at the Battle of Vigo Bay, the capture and subsequent defense of Gibraltar, the capture of Barcelona, and numerous other campaigns along the coasts of Spain and France and in the Mediterranean.

All six regiments were also represented in the assault on the French base at Port Royal (afterward renamed Annapolis Royal), Nova Scotia, in 1710, an undertaking in which they were joined by colonial American forces. Although this was not the colonists' first amphibious operation—they had already mounted several expeditions against the French in Canada and the Spanish in Florida—it was the first in which they

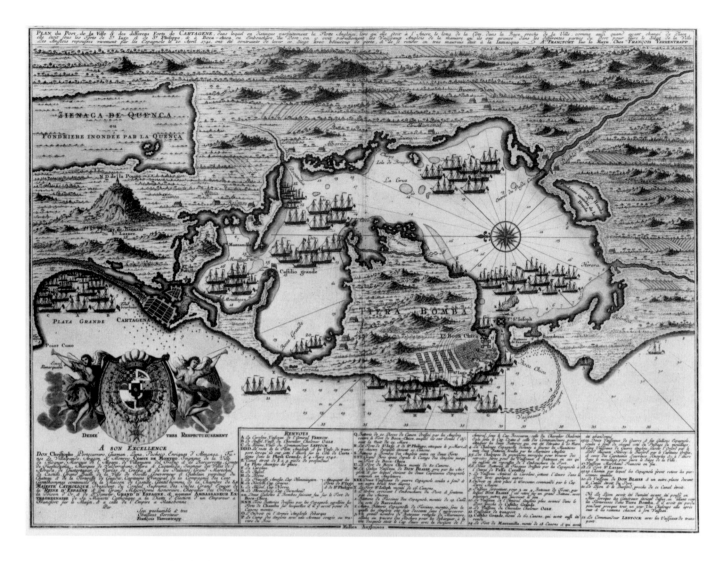

fought beside British troops. The landing force consisted of fourteen hundred regular infantry, six hundred marines (one hundred from each regiment), fifteen hundred American militia (two battalions from Massachusetts, one from Connecticut, and a composite battalion from New Hampshire and Rhode Island), a detachment of Indians, and some guns. Arriving off Port Royal on 23 September, the expedition suffered its only reverse the next day, when thirty men were drowned in the wreck of a transport. Otherwise, everything ran smoothly. The troops landed on 25 September, laid siege to the fort the next day, and received its surrender on 2 October. An American company formed a cordon on either side of the gate that the French marched out, and afterward the British officers gave a farewell breakfast to the ladies of the garrison.

In the military cutbacks following the peace of 1713 the British marines were again disbanded, three regiments being transferred to the army and three paid off. The same fate befell ten regiments raised at the outbreak of the War of Jenkins' Ear in 1739 and retained through the War of Austrian Succession but disestablished with restoration of peace in 1748. Seven years later the onset of war with France prompted another—the century's third—revival of marines, of which the Admiralty organized fifty independent companies. The uninterrupted existence of the Royal Marines (a title granted in 1802) begins with this force, which, unlike its forerunners, was not dissolved once the shooting stopped.

Among the amphibious campaigns of the preceding conflicts were several undertaken wholly or in part by American forces. The War of Jenkins' Ear consisted mainly of seaborne assaults on Spanish possessions in the New World. In 1740 militia units from Georgia and South Carolina and five hundred Indians under the command of Gen. James Oglethorpe invaded Florida, captured two Spanish posts on the St. Johns River, and laid siege to the Castillo de San Marcos at St. Augustine. The old fortress proved superior to the colonials' siegecraft; after two months outside its coquina walls, they withdrew. A second attempt on the fortress in 1743, also led by Oglethorpe, proved equally unsuccessful.

Meanwhile, the first authentic American marines had shared in a debacle that might stand as a model of everything an amphibious operation ought not to be. After reestablishing its own marines in 1739, the British government decided to raise four additional battalions in North America, whose inhabitants were presumed to be better suited than Britons for campaigning in the Tropics, where the deadliest foe was always disease. Some thirty-six hundred men were enlisted and organized into one very large regiment. As was customary in British forces, the unit took the name of its commander, Col. William Gooch, lieutenant governor of Virginia, and was called Gooch's Marines. With the exception of about thirty British younger sons, the officers came from the upper levels of colonial society. The rank and file came from the nethermost, the majority of the colonies having filled their quotas with criminals, debtors, and derelicts.

Sailing from New York in October 1740, Gooch's Marines joined eight thousand British troops—six regiments of marines and two of infantry—being assembled at an advanced base in Jamaica. Early in March 1741 the combined force set out in a fleet of 138 sail to attack Cartagena, on the coast of present-day Colombia. The city stood at the northern end of a harbor that could be entered only through a narrow channel commanded by forts on both sides. The expeditionary force secured a beachhead on 9 March. The forts covering the channel were captured on 25 March and, on 5 April, fifteen hundred troops landed in the inner harbor to attack Fort St. Lazar, the last fortification outside Cartagena.

Unfortunately, by then British leadership had become its own worst enemy. The naval commander, Adm. Edward Vernon, was a most impatient man; the land force commander, Brig. Gen. Thomas Wentworth, a very deliberate one. The stately pace of preceding operations ashore had convinced Vernon that Wentworth was a dolt, and of the interservice cooperation vital to amphibious warfare there was no trace. When the general asked the admiral to land additional troops for the assault on Fort St. Lazar, Vernon declined to do so. Wentworth's remonstrance finally caused him to relent, but Vernon refused to provide naval gunfire support for the attack, insisting that the harbor was too shallow in that area, an opinion shared by few others. For his part, Wentworth made no attempt to emplace his own artillery, the only officer believed capable of constructing a battery having been killed. The result was summarized by one of the century's great novelists, Tobias Smollett, who served in the campaign as a naval assistant-surgeon: "A resolution was taken . . . to attack the place with musketry only. This was put into execution, and succeeded accordingly; the enemy giving them such a hearty reception that the greatest part of the detachment took up their everlasting residence on the spot."

The plan called for simultaneous pre-dawn assaults to be made on the fort's northern and southern faces by columns that were to move inland from the beach at 0400. The northern column consisted of five hundred grenadiers; the southern, of a thousand British marines. Behind both came parties of American marines carrying extra hand grenades, scaling ladders, and wool-packs to fill the ditches surrounding the fort. The columns lost their way in the darkness and suffered heavy casualties storming the fort's outworks, some of which they had been told to expect and some of which they had not. Eventually the Spanish were driven into the fort, but the break of day found the British at the foot of its walls. The commander of the northern column, Colonel Grant of the 5th Marines, was mortally wounded there. He is reputed to have expired with the words, "The general ought to hang the guides and the king ought to hang the general."

The conduct of Gooch's Marines may charitably be characterized as prudent. To quote a contemporary account: "The Americans finding that they were knocked down without any arms to defend themselves, threw down their ladders, etc., and retired to their camp. Three only were brought up to the trenches, upon which about ten of our Grenadiers and a Sergeant mounted the walls of the fort, but being unsupported, were immediately cut to pieces except for the Sergeant who saved himself by jumping down again."

Recognizing the futility of further sacrifice, Wentworth ordered a retreat. Together the two columns had lost forty-three officers and six hundred men killed and wounded. Shortly thereafter Vernon conceded defeat, and in May the expedition withdrew. In the course of the siege, battle casualties and disease, especially the latter, had reduced its strength to four thousand men. Only twenty-seven hundred remained alive to make an abortive landing in Cuba in August, and three months there finished most of them. The arrival of three thousand British reinforcements in February 1742 simply swelled the expedition's cemetery. By midsummer, the great offensive against the Spanish colonies had literally died away.

One thing that had been accomplished was to reveal the error of the assumption that North Americans would flourish in the tropics, for only 10 percent of Gooch's Marines survived them. However else it might be esteemed, there is no gainsaying Allan Millett's conclusion that, "As an experiment in social purification, the regiment was a success." Among the handful who came home was Capt. Lawrence Washington. A company commander in the Virginia contingent, he had a great respect for Admiral Vernon—so great, in fact, that he named his estate after him. When Washington succumbed to a disease contracted at Cartagena, Mount Vernon was inherited by his young half-brother, George.

The last expedition of the decade in which Americans took part ended, quite unlike Cartagena, in victory. Moreover, it was basically an American affair. In 1744, France officially entered the War of Austrian Succession in which Britain had intervened

several years earlier. The colonial extension of the conflict was called King George's War. The French had just completed the construction of a great fortress at Louisbourg, on Cape Breton Island at the northern tip of Nova Scotia, to guard the mouth of the St. Lawrence River, the umbilical cord of New France. Hostilities opened when a detachment from Louisbourg seized a New England fishing base at Canso in Nova Scotia. Gov. William Shirley of Massachusetts thereupon proposed launching an assault on Louisbourg.

It was an audacious initiative. The British government promised to furnish naval support, and a force of four thousand Massachusetts, Connecticut, and New Hampshire men was organized under the command of Col. William Pepperell, a fish merchant by trade. Sailing from Boston in its own transports, the expedition reoccupied Canso on 1 April 1745. Three weeks later

a Royal Navy squadron appeared to cover the landing on Cape Breton and the New Englanders invested Louisbourg. Amateur soldiers though they were, their conduct of the siege was highly creditable. On 17 June, the largest coastal fortification on the continent hauled down its flag. Acclaimed as "the severest blow that could have been given the Enemy, and in the tenderest part," the capture of Louisbourg was the major event of the war in North America.

To its conquerors' dismay, the fortress was returned to France by the peace of 1748, so Canada was as well defended as ever when the French and Indian War broke out six years later. In the long struggle that followed, the New England colonies again mounted an amphibious operation of their own, sending 2,000 militia bolstered by 250 British regulars to seize two French Canadian outposts in 1755. They also contributed troops to several

The capture of Louisbourg by New England forces in 1745 was celebrated by a print published soon afterward in London. (Beverley R. Robinson Collection, U.S. Naval Academy Museum)

British expeditions. The army that retook Louisbourg in the summer of 1758 included a battalion of five hundred New England rangers. A slightly larger contingent was present at the capture of Quebec in 1759.

By then, the contest for Canada had become merely one of the theaters of the Seven Years' War (1756–63), in which Spain improvidently aligned itself with France in 1761. Already having made close to a clean sweep of the French overseas empire, the British promptly laid plans for an attack on Havana, the supposedly impregnable capital of Spanish Cuba. Some four thousand men were recruited in Connecticut, New Jersey, New York, and Rhode Island to take part in the campaign. Mindful that many Americans recalled the fate of Gooch's Marines, the British disingenuously declined to specify the expedition's objective, promising only the prospect of "very agreeable" service.

The first fourteen hundred colonials joined the army besieging Havana on 28 July 1762. The British, ashore since early June, had almost overcome the city's defenses, but yellow fever, malaria, and dysentery had so depleted their ranks—the mortality rate approached 50 percent—that the newcomers were a welcome reinforcement. Havana surrendered on 11 August. Only seven Americans had been killed or wounded in action, but nearly half of the others died of disease before they were withdrawn in October. This was the last amphibious operation in which Americans served as subjects of the British crown.

Thus, by the close of the Seven Years' War, the employment of marine forces and the practice of amphibious warfare had become part of the American military experience as well as the British. Furthermore, Britain's marines had begun to assume an important new responsibility that would later become and would long remain one of the principal functions of the United States Marines as well: the maintenance of order or, more bluntly, the prevention of mutiny aboard ship.

The Royal Navy's need for an internal security force arose from its recruiting methods. At least in wartime, about half the seamen in an average crew had been kidnapped by naval press gangs, and the nature of life within Britain's wooden walls was not calculated to reconcile men to their lot. As early as 1690 an English writer had observed that "the whole body of seamen on board the Fleet, being a loose collection of undisciplined people and (as experience shews) sufficiently inclined to mutiny, the Marine Regim^ts will be a powerful check to their disorders, and will be able to prevent the dangerous consequences that may thence result."

After being put on a permanent footing in 1755, British marines began to serve precisely that purpose, greatly to the satisfaction of generations of sea officers and the disgust of generations of seamen, who viewed their red-coated shipmates as seagoing police. It was, in fact, to honor its members' steadfast support of authority during the unrest in the Mediterranean Fleet between 1798 and 1800 that the corps was granted its "Royal" title. But all this lay in the future in the victory year of 1763, when Britain, having extinguished the French threat in North America, seemed to have secured an empire that would soon be lost.

CHAPTER 2

The Continental Marines, 1775–1783

Late in May 1780, Capt. James Nicholson's Continental frigate *Trumbull* stood to sea from New London, Connecticut, on her first cruise in the War of Independence. No record exists of her exact dimensions, but she must have measured approximately 125 feet from stem to stern and displaced seven hundred tons. She carried thirty guns, most of them along the single gun-deck characteristic of frigates, and two hundred men. The latter included a detachment of thirty Marines commanded by Capt. Gilbert Saltonstall and two lieutenants, Jabez Smith Jr. and David Starr. Also aboard were two unattached officers serving as volunteers, Capt. John Trevett and Lt. David Bill.

The *Trumbull* was some three hundred miles north of Bermuda around 1030 on 1 June when lookouts spotted a sail on the horizon. As the ships closed to within hailing distance, the other vessel revealed herself to be the 32-gun British privateer *Watt*. Saltonstall described the engagement that followed in a letter to his father on 14 June:

We saw a sail from mast-head directly to windward; as soon as she discovered us she bore down for us; we got ready for action, at one o'clock began to engage, and continued, without the least intermission, for five glasses [two-and-a-half hours], within pistol shot. It is beyond my power to give an adequate idea of the carnage, slaughter, havoc, and destruction that ensued. Let your imagination do its best, it will fall short. We were literally cut all to pieces; not a shroud, stay, brace, bowling, or any other of our rigging, standing. Our main top-mast shot away; our fore, main, mizzen and jigger masts gone by the board; two of our quarter deck guns disabled; thro' our ensign 62 shot, our mizzen 157, mainsail 560, foresail 180, our other sails in proportion; not a yard in the ship but received one or more shot; six shot through her quarter above the quarterdeck, four in the waste; our quarter, stern and nettings full of langrage, grape [types of scattershot made up, respectively, of scrap iron,

nails, bolts, flints, and shot weighing
from eight ounces to four pounds] and
musket ball. . . . After two and a half
hour action, we hauled her wind. Her
pumps going, we edged away; so that it
may fairly be called a drawn battle.

Both ships had fought well. Of the
Trumbull's people, thirteen had been killed
or mortally wounded and eighteen others
hit. Among the dead were four Continental
Marines: three officers and Sgt. Ezekial
Hyatt. Lieutenant Bill was killed early
in the action when a piece of langrage
took off the top of his head. "Lieutenant
Starr," wrote Saltonstall, "was wounded
in the later part of the engagement with a
grape shot, which went in just above the
right hip bone and was cut out behind. He
lived until four o'clock Monday morning
following, when he died without a groan or
struggle. I was with him most of the time."
Lieutenant Smith lingered on until 28 June.

The surviving officers also contributed
to the *Trumbull*'s casualties. Trevett
received two wounds, one of which
cost him an eye. Saltonstall had "eleven
different wounds from my shoulder to my
hip, some with buckshot, others with the
splinters of the after quarter-deck gun. I
had some shot through the brim of my
hat; but was not so disabled as to quit the
quarter-deck until after the engagement."

The *Watt* had suffered even more
severely than the *Trumbull*, losing thirteen
men killed and seventy-nine wounded. At
one time the inrush of water through hits
the *Trumbull* scored below her waterline
threatened to overwhelm the one pump that

had not been disabled. As Saltonstall told
his father in a follow-up letter of 19 June:

Though we were cut to pieces [the *Watt*]
has nothing to boast of should she get
in—her sides were damaged as much as
our sails and rigging—her maintop mast
was hanging over the side just ready
to go as well as her mainmast—her
sails and rigging were not damaged as
much as ours—as we fired principally at
her hull, whence we concluded we did
more execution than they, though they
did well enough. Had we a sufficiency
of langrage, I think we should have
carried her—our wads [bundles of rope
yarn that were tamped down the bores
of muzzle-loading canon to keep the
powder charges in place; their flaming
remnants were expelled with enough
force to travel a short distance] set her
netting on fire on her larboard quarter,
which they cleared themselves of by
cutting part of their nettings away.

The range at which the *Trumbull* and
Watt engaged, never more than eighty
yards and usually fifty yards or under, was
so close that they ignited the hammocks
stowed between the rope screens—
netting—that ran along a wooden warship's
gunwales. In battle, the netting served to
reduce the sprays of splinters that were
among the deadliest features of sea fights in
the Age of Sail. Saltonstall continued:

We saw them heave sundry of their men
overboard during the action. Their wads
set our nettings afire on our starboard

bow—our main and quarter-deck guns expended 388 rounds, 86 of which were fired on the quarterdeck; the Marines fired pistols during the engagement exclusive of which they fired near 1200 rounds. Upon the whole there had not been a more close, obstinate, and Bloody engagement since the war.

Limping home their separate ways, the *Watt* reached New York on 11 June; the *Trumbull* anchored off Nantasket, Connecticut, on the fifteenth. Their encounter was unique in that in Saltonstall's letters it produced the most detailed account of a sea battle known to have been written by a Continental Marine. Otherwise, it was a representative if exceptionally ferocious example of the type of

action American Marines fought during the War of Independence.

The corps to which Saltonstall belonged had been founded in November 1775. The revolution was then six months old. Congress had taken the first steps towards creating a navy in October, authorizing four vessels to be outfitted to attack British supply ships. The foundation of the Continental Marines did not follow from this legislation, however. The impetus was provided by the good citizens of Passamaquoddy, Nova Scotia, who petitioned Congress "to be admitted into the association of North Americans, for the preservation of their rights and liberties."

In the deliberations of the five-man committee appointed to report on this

request, the pleasing prospect of carrying liberty to Passamaquoddy was soon overshadowed by the still more appealing idea of capturing the big British naval base at Halifax. The report on Passamaquoddy's petition was therefore a recommendation to raise two 550-man Marine battalions from Gen. George Washington's army outside Boston in preparation for a landing on the coast of Nova Scotia in December. Even if Congress were to deem the operation impractical, the committee urged it to approve the organization of the Marines, who would be of "utmost service, being capable of serving either by land or sea." Agreeable to both ideas on Friday, 10 November 1775, Congress

voted to propose the Nova Scotia project to Washington and further resolved: "That two battalions of Marines be raised, consisting of one Colonel, two Lieutenant Colonels, two Majors & Officers as usual in other regiments, and that they consist of an equal number of privates with other battalions. . . . That they be distinguished by the names of the first & second battalions of American Marines."

These battalions were never raised. Informed of the resolutions, Washington replied with remarkable restraint that he doubted the wisdom of weakening the army besieging Boston in order to invade Nova Scotia, and that the stipulation that Marines were to enlist for the duration of

Top: Maj. Samuel Nicholas, as portrayed in a contemporary miniature by an unknown artist. (Marine Corps Art Collection)

Left: *The First Recruits, December 1775*, by Col. Charles Waterhouse, USMCR, shows Capt. Samuel Nicholas, 1st Lt. Matthew Parke, and a scowling sergeant with prospective Leathernecks on the Philadelphia waterfront. (Marine Corps Art Collection)

the war would make them difficult if not impossible to recruit. Congress deferred to his judgment and on 30 November notified him that the Marines would be raised separately from the Army. It had already begun appointing Marine officers.

The earliest commission, a captaincy dated 28 November, went to Samuel Nicholas, a thirty-one-year-old Philadelphia Quaker whom the U.S. Marine Corps honors as its first commandant. Nicholas himself never used that title and apparently gave only a single order to a unit outside the Philadelphia area, but he remained the senior officer of the Continental Marines and as such served as the "muster master" to whom the corps' strength reports were

forwarded. Relatively little is known of his private life. The son of a prosperous blacksmith, he attended the Academy of Philadelphia, a precursor of the University of Pennsylvania. From it he emerged into the elite of Philadelphia society, a status attested by his membership in two prestigious clubs, the Schuylkill Fishing Company and the Gloucester Fox Hunting Club. After the Revolution he was a tavern keeper at the Sign of the Conestoga Wagon, which may have been his prewar occupation as well, although according to one report he was a ship-owner's agent in the merchant marine.

Another nine officers were commissioned within days and began raising five

Map 1, bottom:
The New Providence Raid

Right: The landing on New Providence
Island, 3 March 1776, recreated in a modern painting by V. Zveg. Fort Montagu is visible in the left background. The two sizeable
ships in the foreground are the *Wasp* (left)
and *Providence*. (Naval Historical Center)

companies to serve in the little fleet of
converted merchantmen being equipped
by Congress. Following the custom of
the day, gaily caparisoned drummers
were sent parading through the streets
to attract recruits, ending their rounds
at a "rendezvous," usually a tavern,
where an officer waited to enlist the
men who followed them. Legend has it
that the Marines' principal rendezvous
was Tun Tavern, at the corner of Tun
Alley and King Street (now South Water
Street) in Philadelphia. Unfortunately for
legend, proof is lacking. Robert Mullan,
commissioned a captain of Marines in
June 1776, was probably the proprietor
of Tun Tavern; if so, its association with

the Corps may have begun the previous
year, but existing records allow a variety of
interpretations. In any case, five companies
of Leathernecks had been recruited by the
end of December.

Nonetheless, the legends surrounding
Mullan as the Corps' first recruiter endure.
Supposedly, he promised those men who
answered his call to the colors a sumptuous
daily ration: a pound of beef or pork,
a pound of bread, and ample supplies
of flour, raisins, butter, cheese, oatmeal,
molasses, tea, and sugar; a pint of wine or
half a pint of rum would accompany the
repast. Mullan claimed that "the single
young man, on his return to port, finds
himself enabled to cut a dash on shore with

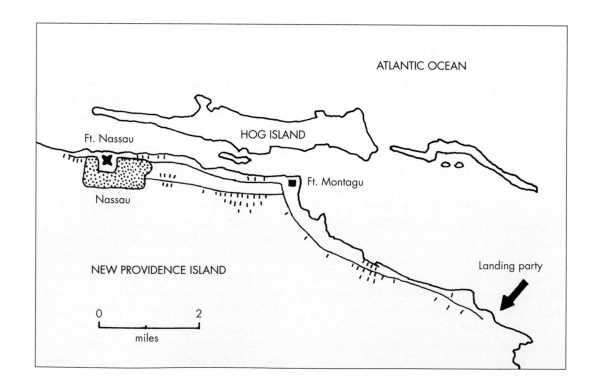

his girl and his glass that might be envied by a nobleman."

The men who enlisted that month were not actually the first Marines of the revolution. On two occasions earlier in the year soldiers had been detailed to act as Marines in vessels operated by the Army. Continental troops served in two ships that patrolled Lake Champlain from the capture of Fort Ticonderoga in May until the invasion of Canada in October, and in the schooner Washington sent to raid British shipping in September, a month before the foundation of the Continental Navy. But these men remained soldiers and as such are not considered forerunners of the U.S. Marine Corps. In addition, many of the two thousand or more American privateers that put to sea during the war carried their own, private marines and most of the eleven known state navies included marine forces.

The fleet to which the Philadelphia Marines were assigned put to sea on 17 February 1776. Commanded by Commo. Esck Hopkins, a Rhode Island merchant skipper, it numbered eight vessels: Hopkins' flagship, the *Alfred*; the ship *Columbus*; the brigs *Andrew Doria* and *Cabot*; the sloops *Hornet* and *Providence*; and the schooners *Fly* and *Wasp*. All except the *Fly* carried Marines. The largest detachment and the only one in uniform was the sixty-two-man company under Captain Nicholas in the *Alfred*. On the fleet's second day at sea a serious collision occurred between the *Hornet* and *Fly*. The *Hornet* was forced to return to port and the *Fly* dropped behind. This accident reduced the force with which Hopkins had resolved to seize Nassau, capital of the Bahamas, to six ships carrying 580 seamen and 234 Marines.

There was no mention of Nassau in Hopkins' instructions from Congress. They specified that he was to clear the Chesapeake Bay and central seaboard of British naval forces, but they contained the usual loophole, through which he shaped course for the Caribbean. His decision probably stemmed from knowledge of a secret report to Congress that the military stores at Nassau included a large quantity of gunpowder, a commodity of which Washington's army was in dire need. Whatever the commodore's reasons, they led to the first landing of the Continental Marines.

Nassau stood on the northern side of New Providence Island, along the shore of an elongated harbor between it and Hog Island (now Paradise Island). The eastern and western entrances to the harbor were guarded by two small masonry works, forts Montagu and Nassau, respectively. A small British garrison had been withdrawn months earlier, which left the island's defense to its militia.

Arriving off Nassau at dawn on 3 March, the fleet anchored six miles east of the settlement and began offloading Nicholas' Marines around noon. The addition of fifty seamen to his command raised its strength to 284 officers and men. The governor of the Bahamas, Montfort Browne, had known of the Americans' approach since 1 March, when a whaler reported sighting the fleet off Great Abaco Island, but he had not acted on the information and the landing was unopposed. The ships' appearance finally started Browne's adrenalin flowing, and by 1400, the hour at which Nicholas' troops began moving down the coast toward Nassau, 140 militiamen had been sent to garrison Fort Montagu. When scouting parties scurried back with the news that the Americans were coming, Browne became apprehensive that they would swing inland around the fort to occupy the town and ordered his men to fall back to Fort Nassau. For the sake of appearances, before leaving he had three cannons fired in the direction of the Marines.

These harmless shots proved to be the only ones fired in defense of Nassau. Finding Fort Montagu deserted, Nicholas decided to rest his men there overnight and sent a message informing Hopkins of its uncontested occupation. This report apparently encouraged Hopkins to believe that the operation could be completed without bloodshed, for he immediately issued a proclamation to the citizens of New Providence, announcing that his objective was "to take Possession of the Powder and Warlike Stores belonging to the Crown and am I not Opposed . . . the Persons and Property of the Inhabitants Shall be Safe." Nicholas' men put this manifesto into circulation among the residents of eastern Nassau.

Hopkins' assurances, coupled with the self-evident impossibility of defending the town from its far side, undermined Browne's hopes of making a fight. At a council of war he held in Fort Nassau that evening, the majority of the militia officers and local notables voted for surrender. They did agree to transfer 162 barrels of powder stored in the fort to two merchant ships, which then slipped out the western end of the harbor, Hopkins having contented himself with blockading the eastern end. All of the powder might have been saved, but Browne felt that it would be politic to let the Americans capture a little. Thereafter the militia melted away. At dawn, Nicholas' advance from Fort Montagu was met by an emissary bearing word that Fort Nassau would not be defended.

Despite Browne's success in spiriting away most of the powder, the New Providence raid reaped a rich haul: fifty-eight cannon, fifteen mortars, more than sixteen thousand shot and shell, and assorted other hardware. It took Hopkins' men almost two weeks to load the booty aboard their ships. The governor spent this period under guard of a Marine detachment, whose members, he afterwards complained, helped themselves to his liquor. On 17 March, the fleet sailed for home.

Most of the return voyage was uneventful, but off the coast of Rhode Island the sea suddenly filled with enemy shipping. Two small naval vessels and several mer-chantmen were gobbled up on 4 and 5 April, and at 0100 on the sixth, the fleet encountered HMS *Glasgow*, a 20-gun frigate admirably commanded by Capt. Tryingham Howe. The three-and-a-half hours' running battle that ensued revealed that, whatever Hopkins' merits, he was not up to controlling a fleet in action. Engaged in awkward succession by the *Cabot* (fourteen guns), *Alfred* (thirty guns), and the *Columbus* (twenty-eight guns), the *Glasgow* beat off their attacks and, although heavily damaged, made good her escape. American casualties were nine dead and sixteen wounded. They included two Marine lieutenants, John Fitzpatrick

of the *Alfred*, the first Marine officer killed in action, and John Hood Wilson of the *Cabot*, who was mortally wounded. The *Glasgow*'s losses—one man killed and three wounded—were inflicted by Marine musket fire. After this disappointing encounter, the fleet continued on course for New London, where it dropped anchor on 8 April 1776.

The New Providence expedition appeared to augur well for the institutional integrity of the Continental Marines. Even though the landing force consisted of independent companies, it had functioned as a battalion of the sort envisioned by the Corps' founding legislation and in the type of amphibious operation that legislation anticipated. The expedition's two failures—missing the gunpowder and allowing the *Glasgow* to escape—could hardly be blamed on the Marines. Congress indicated its satisfaction with the performance by promoting Nicholas to major, a rank he was the only Continental Marine to attain.

But these auguries were illusionary. New Providence was the last as well as the first operation in which the Continental Marines participated as an integral corps. In the seven years of war ahead there were fewer than seven occasions when as many as three companies saw action together, and only one, the Penobscot expedition, was an amphibious assault. Otherwise, the history of the Continental Marines is an episodic account of independent companies whose fortunes followed those of the ships in which they served.

The decentralization of Marine operations reflected the practice of the

British Marines, who were organized in independent companies. Even if Americans had been inspired to ignore precedent, however, the conditions of the conflict would have made the maintenance of a unified corps impractical. The key factors in the naval war were, first, the overwhelming preponderance of the Royal Navy and, second, the extreme difficulty experienced in manning the Continental Navy, small as it was. The New Providence raid was the only time the Continental fleet operated as such. Never again could enough seamen be collected for it to put to sea as a unit. Only in rare instances did as many as three ships sail together, and single-ship cruises were the rule. The problem was not a shortage of seafarers. America had plenty of sailors, but they preferred to serve in privateers, which offered the prospect of far greater financial reward than the navy.

Considering the odds, the dispersion of the American naval effort was, on the whole, a good thing. For the Continental Navy to have operated as a fleet would have been a good way to lose the Continental Navy. At the onset of the conflict the Royal Navy had 268 vessels in commission; thereafter, its numbers increased. Granted that its entire strength could not be committed to the American war, still there was no possibility that the Continental Navy could win command of the sea. From necessity its operations took the form of commerce raiding, a weaker navy's usual resort, and attempting to punch an occasional hole in the British blockade of the American coast, either by driving blockaders away from a particular port or by shepherding

a convoy home from the West Indies. These activities, plus chance encounters with enemy warships, set the stage for the Continental Marines' battles at sea.

In December 1775 Congress had appropriated funds to build thirteen frigates. None got to sea in 1776, but two merchant brigs whose conversion was approved that March, the *Lexington* and the *Reprisal*, were soon ready for action. The *Lexington* sailed that month; the *Reprisal* did so in July. Six of Hopkins' vessels also made successful single-ship cruises in 1776, capturing several small British warships and numbers of merchantmen. At year's end, there were approximately six hundred Marines in service.

Meanwhile, the Army had raised another force of freshwater Marines. The American conquest of Canada had come to grief outside Quebec in December 1775. British reinforcements sailed up the St. Lawrence the following spring, and in June an eight-thousand-man army pushed down the Richelieu River into New York. Realizing that the enemy advance through the wilderness was dependent on water transport, Gen. Benedict Arnold—prior to his treason, among the ablest Continental commanders—began building ships to contest the control of Lake Champlain. The British were compelled to halt and do likewise. Eventually Arnold's fleet counted fifteen vessels manned by nine hundred soldiers, seamen, and Marines. It was obliterated by a more powerful British force at the Battle of Valcour Island in mid-October 1776. But Arnold's defeat turned out to be a victory, for the British concluded that winter was too close to continue the campaign and withdrew to Canada. "Gentleman Johnny" Burgoyne's renewal of the advance the next spring ended in his army's surrender at Saratoga, which persuaded France to come into the war on the American side. Her intervention would prove decisive.

Yet France would not officially enter the war until June 1778. In the meantime, the revolution was to pass through its darkest days. Those days began in August 1776, when the British launched a campaign to pacify the central colonies by capturing New York City. By the onset of winter they had advanced as far as the Delaware River.

Conscious of the need to revive his countrymen's flagging morale, Washington conceived plans for a bold attack on the British outpost line in New Jersey. Among his troops were three Marine companies, numbering at most 130 men, that had been recruited to serve in the frigates being built near Philadelphia. Organized into a small battalion under Nicholas and sent to reinforce Washington early in December, they were subsequently incorporated into a Philadelphia militia brigade commanded by Brig. Gen. John Cadwalader.

Cadwalader's troops were unable to get over the icy Delaware to share in Washington's victory at Trenton on 26 December but managed to cross a day later. On 2 January 1777 the brigade fought in the delaying action at Assunpink Bridge, where it helped hold off a superior enemy force moving to support the threatened garrisons, and on 3 January it was roughly handled in the opening minutes of the battle in which Washington scattered three British regiments outside Princeton. The role Nicholas' Marines played in these engagements is unknown, but only eighty were left to enter the army's winter quarters at Morristown, Pennsylvania. One company was detached to escort British prisoners to Philadelphia in February. Another returned to the city in April, and the remnant of the third was dissolved.

The British capture of Philadelphia in September 1777 again involved Marines in the war inside America. To deny the enemy the advantage of access to the sea, American forces sought to hold forts Mercer and Mifflin, which commanded the Delaware a few miles below the city. Six Continental ships, including the *Andrew Doria* and the new frigate *Delaware*, both of which carried Marines, and the entire Pennsylvania state navy were committed to the defense. The *Delaware* ran aground and was captured while engaging a British battery at Philadelphia on 27 September. Four days later a British squadron working upstream reached the American positions, and seven weeks of heavy fighting took place on the Delaware and along its banks.

Finally, the pressure on the forts became overwhelming. Mifflin was evacuated on 15 November. Mercer fell on the twenty-first and the ships that had helped defend the river were burned to keep them out of enemy hands. The British army would winter in the comforts of Philadelphia; Washington's men, in the misery of Valley Forge.

These operations notwithstanding, Marine activities continued to center on the war at sea. The scale of the Continental

naval effort increased in 1777. Four new frigates—the *Boston, Hancock, Raleigh,* and *Randolph*—made their first cruises, as did the sloop-of-war *Ranger,* while three smaller vessels were outfitted in France. All carried Marines. Shortly after the *Randolph* sailed, Capt. Samuel Shaw's company quashed a mutiny by a group of English sailors in her crew. This was the first of several instances in which Continental Marines suppressed attempted mutinies.

In the course of the year Continental vessels captured more than fifty merchantmen and privateers and one frigate (which was soon recaptured). The price of these prizes was four ships and three Marine detachments: the *Cabot,* whose men escaped when she beached herself upon being overhauled by an enemy vessel twice

her strength; the *Reprisal,* lost in a storm with all hands except her cook; and the *Hancock* and *Lexington,* forced to strike in actions with British ships.

American losses were heavier in 1778. The first occurred on 7 March, when the 32-gun frigate *Randolph* blew up while audaciously engaging—and apparently getting the better of—the 64-gun ship-of-the-line *Yarmouth* until an unlucky shot touched off her magazine. Shaw and his Marines perished with their ship, from which there were only four survivors. Three other vessels—the *Alfred, Columbus* (all of whose people escaped ashore), and the new frigate *Virginia*—were captured or destroyed that same month, and the *Raleigh* was driven aground while engaging two British warships in September. However, these losses were more than offset by ships that got to sea during the year: five new frigates, the *Alliance, Confederacy, Deane, Providence,* and *Warren*; the *Queen of France,* an old frigate purchased in that country; and the prize brigantine *General Gates.* Each had Marines, as did the frigates *Boston* and *Trumbull* and the sloops *Providence* and *Ranger.* Thus at year's end, eleven detachments remained afloat.

In addition to their services on the high seas, in 1778 Marines conducted a daring amphibious landing and an unsavory riverine operation. The latter was the brainchild of James Willing, a well-connected young Philadelphian who had drunk his way through his patrimony after setting himself up in business in Natchez, Mississippi. Returning home in 1777, Willing persuaded the Commerce Committee of Congress to entrust him with command of an expedition whose objective was to seize control of the Mississippi from the confluence of the Ohio to the Spanish colonial frontier at Manchac (near present-day Plaquemine), Louisiana. He was also authorized to seize British property encountered along the river, an instruction in whose fulfillment he showed exemplary zeal.

Commissioned a captain in the Navy, Willing proceeded to Fort Pitt, Ohio, where he raised a Marine company of two officers and thirty-four men from the garrison. On 10 January 1778 the expedition set off down the Ohio in the 10-oared barge *Rattletrap*. On the way south Willing augmented his force by recruiting ten river ruffians, including George Girty, one of the notorious renegade brothers. (Willing made him a lieutenant, but he deserted anyway.) By the time the expedition reached New Orleans in March, it had well and truly pillaged the loyalist plantations along the Mississippi, burning houses and crops, slaughtering livestock, and making a haul of movable property from silverware to shirts.

At New Orleans, Willing quickly antagonized the city's capable Continental agent, Oliver Pollock, and the Spanish governor, Bernardo de Galvez. Forces from British West Florida captured the garrison he had left at Manchac, substituting one of their own, and by mid-April Willing's dubious achievements had been undone. He lingered in New Orleans until August, having in Pollock's opinion "only thrown the whol[e] river into confusion and created a Number of Enemies and a heavy Expense

which would not have happened had [the expedition] been otherwise Governed."

The year's amphibious assault was made on New Providence Island. In contrast to Commodore Hopkins' large-scale landing, it was carried out by a solitary frigate, Capt. John Peck Rathbun's *Providence*, and a twenty-eight-man Marine detachment commanded by Capt. John Trevett. The idea originated with Rathbun, who seems to have been motivated mainly by the desire to capture the British privateer *Mary*, which he had learned was being overhauled at Nassau. His sailing master had been killed in a brush with her in 1777, and he intended to settle the score. Trevett, a veteran of the first New Providence expedition, realized the risks of attempting to duplicate it with so diminutive a force, but agreed to try. In his diary he wrote, "I have had A long time to think of What I am A Going to undertake but I am Very well satisfied that we Are in a Good Cause & we are a fiting the Lords Battel."

The plan called for the Marines to land under cover of darkness and seize Fort Nassau by surprise. Once in possession of the fort, they could hold the town hostage to its guns. Around midnight on 27 January 1778, the *Providence* anchored off Hog Island and Trevett, Lt. Michael Molton, and their twenty-six Marines rowed into the night. From his previous visit, Trevett remembered that one of the stakes had been missing from the fort's palisade. It was missing still, and he led his men through the gap and up their scaling ladder into the fort. To his great relief, he found that the garrison consisted of a pair of night watchmen who were overpowered before they could give the alarm. At dawn Trevett hoisted the American flag and informed Nassau's startled residents that he had occupied the fort with thirty officers and two hundred men from a fleet anchored off Abaco Island. His orders, he continued, were to seize the *Mary* and other "warlike stores." The persons and property of the inhabitants would be respected.

Trevett's bluff worked to perfection. Concluding that resistance might entail "the disagreeable consequence of the destruction of the Town," the town council elected not to oppose the occupation. Although a few tense moments intervened, Trevett held Fort Nassau for four days, the time Rathbun needed to ready the *Mary* and four captured American vessels found in the harbor for sea. On the morning of 1 February, Trevett and his men returned to the *Providence*, having accomplished one of the war's most audacious undertakings.

By this time Continental naval forces had expanded their activities to European waters. Extended operations there were made possible by the cooperation of France, which even before her official entry into the war allowed American warships to use her ports as bases. The first cruise from France was made by the *Reprisal* in January 1777. Of the many others that followed, the most famous were those of John Paul Jones in the *Ranger* (April–May 1778) and the *Bonhomme Richard* (August–October 1779).

The *Ranger* carried a small Marine detachment commanded by twenty-three-year-old Lt. Samuel Wallingford, a judge's son from New Hampshire. When on the night of 22–23 April, Jones took two boat parties to set fire to the shipping in the British port of Whitehaven, he gave Wallingford command of the second boat. It was the first time since 1667 that a foreign foe had set foot on English soil. Although the townsfolk extinguished the fires before much damage had been done, the moral effect of the raid was tremendous.

On 23 April, Jones included Wallingford in the party he landed at St. Mary's Isle to kidnap the Earl of Selkirk, whom he intended to hold hostage for the good treatment of American prisoners in British hands. To Jones' chagrin the earl was absent, although his spirited, very pregnant young wife was at home. Worse yet, Sailing Master David Cullam and Wallingford proposed looting the Selkirk mansion; after all, the British were looting New England homes. Jones reluctantly consented to the liberation of the Selkirk's silverware (which he later restored to them at his own expense) and returned to the boat landing. Cullam and Wallingford told Lady Selkirk to have her servants collect the silver, which was soon done. Afterwards she gave the officers a glass of wine. Informing her husband of these events, she wrote that Cullam "seemed by nature a very disagreeable & one may say a bad man," with "a vile blackguard look," but the junior officer, "a civil young man . . . seemed naturally well bred and not to like his employment."

The next day the *Ranger* captured the British sloop *Drake* after an hour's action. Among the dead were the *Drake*'s commanding officer, Cdr. George Burden,

John Paul Jones' Raid at Whitehaven by Charles Waterhouse depicts the Marines serving in the sloop *Ranger* as they row ashore to raid Whitehaven on St. Mary's Isle off the southwestern coast of Scotland. (Marine Corps Art Collection)

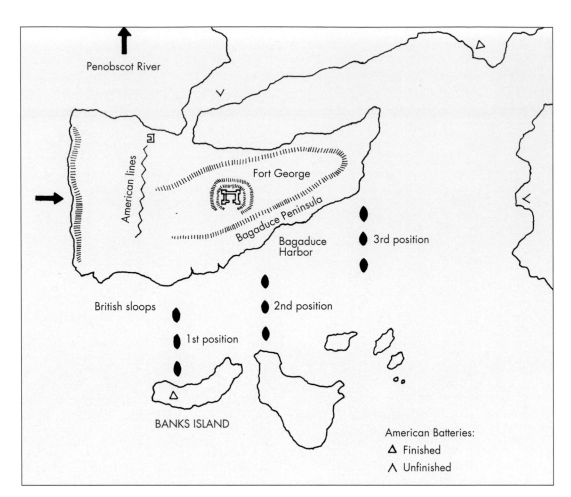

Map 2, left: The Penobscot Expedition, July–August 1779.

Right: Charles Waterhouse's *Fighting Tops, 29 May 1781,* specifically relates to the engagement between the frigate *Alliance* and the British sloops *Atalanta* and *Trepassey,* but it typifies the activities of the Leathernecks who fought aloft in all the Continental Navy's actions. (Marine Corps Art Collection)

and Wallingford, both of whom were shot through the head by enemy marines. In reply to Jones' letter promising that his silver would be returned, the Earl of Selkirk noted that "we were all sorry afterwards to hear that the younger officer . . . had been killed, for he in particular showed so much civility."

There were 137 Marines aboard the *Bonhomme Richard* in her epic engagement with HMS *Serapis* on 23 September 1779, but they were red-coated acting-Marines of the French army's Infanterie Irlandaise, Regiment de Walsh-Serrant. Their musketry made an important contribution to Jones' victory, preventing the British from cutting the lines to the grappling hooks that pinned the *Serapis* to the *Richard* and driving the enemy seamen and Marines out of her fighting tops. This achievement made it possible for William Hamilton, a Scots seaman, to shinny out on a yardarm and

begin dropping grenades on the deck of the *Serapis.* One of them fell through an open hatch and exploded amid a pile of powder sacks on the gun deck below, killing twenty men and injuring many others. Still later the French helped discourage an enemy attempt to board. When the *Serapis* surrendered after almost four hours' fighting, 150 men had been killed and wounded out of the *Richard*'s complement of 325. The number of Infanterie Irlandaise in the former figure is not known, but it must have been substantial. American Marines served in another ship of Jones' little squadron, the *Alliance,* commanded by the psychotic Frenchman Pierre Landais; but, aside from pouring three broadsides into the *Richard,* she took no part in the action.

In 1779, Marines assisted in the capture of more British vessels than in any previous year. During this same year, however, Continental naval forces suffered

the first of two blows from which they would never recover. On 15 June, 640 British regulars under Brig. Gen. Francis McLean landed on the Bagaduce peninsula on Penobscot Bay, Maine, then part of Massachusetts and now the site of the town of Castine. The objects of the occupation were to establish an advanced naval base for operations against American privateers and to provide support for local loyalists.

Informed of the enemy's presence, the government of Massachusetts—accustomed since colonial days to mounting amphibious operations—resolved to expel the British before they could become entrenched, and an expedition was quickly assembled. Massachusetts committed the three brigs comprising her navy and chartered a dozen privateers and twenty-three merchantmen for use as transports; the Continental Navy contributed the *Warren*, sloop *Providence*, and brig

Diligent with their Marine detachments; and New Hampshire furnished a chartered privateer. Only 873 of the 1,500 militiamen summoned actually appeared; this number, added to the 227 Marines of the Continental and Massachusetts navies, gave the landing force a strength of 1,100 men. Command was divided between Continental Navy captain Dudley Saltonstall and Brig. Gen. Solomon Lovell of the Massachusetts militia.

The wooded Bagaduce peninsula lay on the northern side of a harbor of the same name. Approximately two miles long and one wide, it was connected to the mainland by a narrow isthmus midway its northern face. To the south it was roughly paralleled by several islands along the southern side of the harbor. Arriving on the scene on 25 July, the Americans discovered that the British were constructing a log fort (Fort George) in the center of the peninsula

and had established a battery on Banks Island. Fire from the fort and the battery overlapped to cover the entrance to the harbor, which was also defended by three British sloops. Taken together, these were the elements of an amphibious equation the Penobscot expedition failed to solve.

Operations began on 26 July 1779, when Marines led by Capt. John Welsh, the expedition's senior Marine officer, seized lightly defended Banks Island and opened fire on the British sloops, which withdrew up the harbor to an anchorage off Fort George. Having accomplished this much, the expedition's commanders disagreed on what to do next. Lovell wanted to land on the southern side of the peninsula, where there was a good beach. First, however, Saltonstall would have to enter the harbor and dispose of the sloops; but he balked at sending his ships into "that damned hole" before Lovell captured the fort. After a day's debate, they settled on a less suitable landing site on the precipitous western end of the peninsula.

The assault, supported by fire from four ships, was made at dawn on 28 July. Welsh's Marines formed the right wing of the landing force. They met the toughest resistance. Taken under musket fire while still in their boats by British troops on the headland, once ashore they found that their beach lay at the foot of a slope so steep that they had to grasp shrubs to pull themselves up. Welsh was killed almost immediately. Lt. William Hamilton fell mortally wounded, and thirty-two other men were hit. But their comrades pressed ahead and drove the British back to Fort George. Following in their footsteps, a company of Massachusetts marines reached the edge of the clearing around the fort. As yet its walls were barely a yard high. Inside them General McLean stood by the flagstaff, ready to haul down his colors as soon as a few shots were fired for honor's sake against the attack he was sure would come.

None did. Fearful of exposing his men to the fire of the sloops, Lovell called a halt. "Our general," a Marine veteran recalled, "was said to be *a very good sort of man*, but these good sort of men seldom make good Generals. . . . Mr. Lovell would have done more good . . . in the deacon's seat of a country church, than at the head of an American Army." In succeeding days Lovell undertook the methodical procedures of eighteenth-century siegecraft, building earthworks, blockhouses, and batteries, all the while entreating Saltonstall to go after the sloops. Fearful of exposing his ships to the fire of the fort, Saltonstall

with equal persistence refused.

By 13 August, the American lines had inched to within half a mile of Fort George. That afternoon a British fleet hurrying to the rescue was sighted entering Penobscot Bay. During the night the American troops ashore were reembarked. The next morning, after essaying to form a line of battle across the entrance to the harbor, the American ships suddenly and simultaneously fled up the Penobscot River. The British pursued, and by the afternoon of 15 August every vessel afloat at Penobscot two days earlier had been captured or destroyed. Although many of its members escaped through the wilderness, the Penobscot expedition had ceased to exist. Estimates of personnel casualties range as high as five hundred.

The offensive fiasco in Maine was followed by a defensive disaster in South Carolina. Having failed to pacify the central colonies, late in 1779 the British adopted a "southern strategy" intended to extinguish the revolution in the region where loyalist sentiment was believed strongest. The campaign opened with an assault on Charleston. In anticipation of the attack, Congress dispatched four ships—the frigates *Boston, Providence,* and *Queen of France* and the sloop *Ranger*, with their Marines—to bolster the defense. This deployment proved a mistake. In February 1780 a vastly superior British amphibious force trapped the ships in Charleston harbor and landed troops whose fire drove the American fleet up the Cooper River, effectively out of the battle. The *Queen of France* was scuttled to obstruct the river channel and all four ships' complements were plugged into the American lines ashore. The Marines joined Army artillerymen manning five waterfront batteries. They had been committed to a losing fight. Outnumbered almost three to one, Charleston's 5,400 defenders surrendered on 12 May. It was the greatest American defeat of the war.

It was also nearly the swan song of Continental naval forces. The vessels lost at Charleston left only five others—the *Alliance, Confederacy, Deane, Saratoga,* and *Trumbull*—and their Marine detachments afloat. Moreover, they were a wasting asset. Congress was finished building ships, which were expensive and all too clearly subject to loss; besides, the French fleet posed a greater challenge to the Royal Navy than Congress could aspire to mount. The Continental war at sea was winding down.

Nevertheless, a few hard battles remained to be fought. The *Trumbull* took on the *Watt* in June 1780; and the *Alliance,* 36 guns, captured the British sloops-of-war *Atalanta,* 16, and *Trepassey,* 14, in an equally grueling encounter on 29 May 1781. At the beginning of the action the air was too still for the *Alliance* to maneuver. By using long oars called sweeps, the lighter British vessels reached positions athwart her bow and stern, where few of her guns could return their fire, and pounded the hapless frigate for nearly three hours. The casualties she suffered during this period included Marine lieutenant Samuel Pritchard, mortally wounded by a 6-pound shot; Lt. James Warren Jr., a Harvard graduate who received a wound that cost him a leg; and Sgt. David Brewster, drilled through the head by a British Marine. Finally, a breeze sprang up, allowing the *Alliance* to bring her broadsides to bear, and her tormentors were quickly battered into submission.

The *Alliance*'s victory was more than balanced by the loss of three frigates and their Marines in 1781. The *Saratoga* went down with all hands in a Caribbean gale in March, the *Confederacy* surrendered to two Royal Navy vessels in April, and in August the *Trumbull* was taken in an action with three enemy ships. These reverses reduced the effective strength of the Continental Marines to the detachments in the *Alliance* and the *Deane.*

By the end of 1781, however, the condition of Continental naval forces had ceased to matter. In September Britain's southern strategy reached a catastrophic climax when American and French forces commanded by General Washington and Comte de Rochambeau closed around Gen. Charles Cornwallis' army at Yorktown, Virginia. A French fleet fended off the Royal Navy's rescue attempt, and on 19 October Cornwallis surrendered. The War of Independence had been won.

But it was not over. A year and a half would pass before the peace was settled; in the meanwhile, the war at sea continued. Checkered as its career had been, the Continental Navy went out in style. Both the *Alliance* and *Deane* (later renamed *Hague*) made successful cruises in 1782 and 1783. Continental Marines fired their last shots in an engagement between the *Alliance* and the British frigate *Sybil* on 10 March 1783.

With the conclusion of peace, Congress ordered the two ships laid up—later to be sold, and their complements discharged. Lt. Thomas Elwood of the *Alliance* was the last Marine to be retained on active duty. His release in September 1783 brought the history of the Continental Marine Corps to a close.

From first to last, 131 officers and approximately 2,000 noncommissioned officers and men had served in the Continental Marines. Although surviving documentation is too sparse to permit an exact reckoning, they had suffered heavy losses. Of the officers, for whom records are fairly complete, 15 had been killed in action, died of wounds or gone down with their ships, 1 had fallen overboard and drowned, 3 are known to have been wounded, and 22 captured: a casualty rate of 33 percent. Enlisted casualties must have been in the neighborhood of 500 (25 percent).

Of the estimated five thousand African Americans who fought against the British in the Revolutionary War, scanty records reveal that at least three served as Continental Marines. The officer commanding the Marines in the *Reprisal* recruited a slave, John Martin or "Keto," without his owner's permission. After capturing five British merchantmen, the *Reprisal* floundered in a gale and Keto drowned with all but one of the brig's crew. Two other African Americans, Isaac Walker and a man known only as "Orange," were enlisted for service in Nicholas' battalion and crossed the Delaware with it to fight with Washington at Princeton on Christmas Eve 1776.

Clearly, the Continental Marines had done their share to win America's independence. The little navy in which they served had been unable to do much more than nip at the heels of its mighty adversary, but they had contributed to its successes and helped maintain its discipline. Even more important, perhaps, they had made Marines part of their new country's military heritage.

CHAPTER 3

The Early Years, 1798–1820

For nine years following the sale of the last Continental warship, the new nation did without a navy. The weak government provided by the Articles of Confederation simply could not support one. Authority to "provide and maintain" a navy financed by taxation was among the powers vested in Congress by the Constitution adopted in 1789, but a stalemate between the Federalist and Republican parties prevented this power from being put to use. The Federalists argued that a navy was needed to protect maritime trade and uphold national interests. The Republicans insisted that a navy would ruin the country's finances and stir up needless wars.

The impasse was broken by Algiers. For centuries, the four Barbary powers on the coast of North Africa—from west to east: Morocco, Algiers, Tunis, and Tripoli—had derived most of their income by charging seafaring nations an annual fee to abstain from attacking their shipping. Though the United States had been dutifully paying this "tribute," in 1793 it bridled at the amount Algiers demanded. The United States Navy was created in consequence.

The Navy Act of 27 March 1794 called for the acquisition of six frigates, cruising vessels able to outsail any enemy they could not outfight. To satisfy Republican scruples, it included a proviso that the program would be cancelled in the event a diplomatic settlement was reached before the ships entered commission. Algiers did in fact come to terms while the ships remained under construction, but the Federalists negotiated a compromise that saved the infant navy from being stillborn. Three vessels would be completed; the others would be placed "in ordinary," the equivalent of today's "mothballs."

A new source of maritime friction arose shortly thereafter. Britain and France had gone back to war in 1793. Each claimed the right to suppress neutral trade with its enemy, a potentially serious threat to the American merchant marine. It first seemed that the menace might not materialize. In 1794 Jay's Treaty brought about an understanding with Britain, and for several years France forebore from molesting American commerce. In July 1796, however, the French government announced that henceforth any vessel found to have been trading with Britain or carrying

Opposite: Robert Salmon showed Captain Carmick's Marines in the cutter (right) on their way to spike the Spanish fort's guns in his early-nineteenth-century painting of the capture of the *Sandwich* at Puerto Plata, Santo Domingo, on 12 May 1800. (Boston Athenæum)

any article of British manufacture in her cargo would be subject to seizure. By the end of 1797 approximately three hundred American merchantmen had fallen prey to French ships—a few naval vessels and scores of privateers—based on their country's West Indian colonies.

These losses spurred the newly-elected Federalist administration of President John Adams to take action. On 27 March 1798, Congress resolved that the three finished frigates should be readied for service. Authorizations for the acquisition of additional vessels and the completion of the other frigates followed in succeeding months. The Navy Department was founded on 30 April. On 24 May, the *Ganges*, a converted merchant ship carrying twenty-six guns,

Maj. Daniel Carmick, one of the Corps' original officers, served with distinction in the Quasi-War with France and the War of 1812. (National Archives)

became the first U.S. naval vessel to put to sea. The government initiated the purely naval Quasi-War with France on 28 May, instructing American men-of-war to attack

French armed ships. On 7 July, the 20-gun sloop of war *Delaware* became the first of the navy's ships to enter action, capturing the 14-gun French privateer schooner *Croyable* off the coast of New Jersey. Four days later Congress formally established the United States Marine Corps.

There had never been any question that the naval service would include a Marine Corps. The Navy Act of 1794 had specified that each of the six frigates would carry a Marine guard: an officer and fifty-four men on the four 44-gun ships, and an officer and forty-four men on the two 36s. Eight officers had received Marine commissions before there was a Marine Corps, and one of them, 1st Lt. Daniel Carmick, had taken a detachment of two dozen men to sea in the *Ganges* in May. The Corps created in July was to number 33 officers (a major, 4 captains, and 28 lieutenants) and 848 NCOs and men, including 32 "drums and fifes." Unfortunately, Congress failed to provide much in the way of remuneration to attract good men: a major earned just fifty dollars a month with four rations per day; a second lieutenant, eighteen dollars a month plus two rations a day; and a private earned a miserly four dollars a month and only a single ration a day. Not quite eight months later, the Act of 2 March 1799 increased the Corps' authorized strength to 41 officers and 1,044 other ranks. The effect of the change was slight. Unlike the Army and Navy, the Marine Corps was not allowed to offer enlistment bounties, and during the opening decade of its existence its actual strength probably never exceeded 600. The enlistment of the first Marines included the Corps' first sergeant major, Archibald

Summers, who assumed his duties on 1 June 1801. When he left the Marine Corps after just a year, Alexander Forest replaced him as sergeant major; the dour Scot served until 1832, when he reached his seventieth birthday.

To command the new Corps, President Adams personally selected forty-year-old William Ward Burrows, a wealthy Philadelphia lawyer and businessman with strong Federalist ties. Burrow's appointment dated from 12 July 1798. His duties included those of both paymaster and quartermaster, staff appointments that Congress failed to authorize until a year later. A South Carolinian by birth, Burrows had studied and practiced law in London before the Revolution. Returning home in 1775, he may have served an inconspicuous stint in the state militia during the war. In any event, it was clearly not for his military experience that Adams chose Burrows for the post. It was because of his managerial and social skills, and his political connections. Described by Washington Irving as "a gentleman of accomplished mind and polished manner," he would prove the president's confidence well justified.

Major Burrows opened Marine Corps headquarters at Philadelphia, then the national capital, on 23 August 1798. A Marine camp was set up outside the city a few days later. From the start, Burrows sought to establish the Corps as a separate sea service and to define a distinctive role for its guard detachments at sea, where many naval officers were inclined to treat Marines as supernumerary seamen. He understood that the achievement of these aims would require the Corps to establish a glowing image with Congress and the public at large.

Burrow's program was an ambitious one for an embryonic organization, but under his leadership much of it was accomplished. Officers were assured of their commander's support in resisting attempts by Navy officers to misuse Marines to perform seamen's duties. This support was demonstrated in November 1799, in the aftermath of an altercation on board the *Ganges*. Navy lieutenant Allen McKenzie had put a Marine in irons without consulting the guard detachment's commander, 1st Lt. Anthony Gale. When Gale demanded an explanation, McKenzie called him a rascal and struck him. The ship's captain brushed off the incident, but as soon as the cruise ended Gale challenged McKenzie to a duel. McKenzie chose pistols, and Gale shot him dead. Burrows heartily approved. "It is to be hoped," he wrote in a letter to Gale, "that this may be a lesson to the Navy officers to treat Marines as well as their officers with some more Respect." A year later, Burrows virtually ordered 2nd Lt. Henry Caldwell to challenge a naval officer who had struck him; "Without you wipe away this insult offer'd to the Marine Corps, you cannot expect to join our officers." Bloodshed was averted by the offender's apology. Finally, in August 1801, Burrows persuaded Secretary of the Navy Robert Smith to issue a circular setting forth the duties to which Marines were and were not subject aboard ship.

To promote the Corps' public relations, Burrows took advantage of its allowance of thirty-two "drums and fifes" to form a regular band. Late in 1798, he circulated a memorandum to his officers: "[The] officers here [at headquarters] have agreed to advance 10 dollars each to enable the regiment to procure music and I hope will be agreeable to [other] officers . . . to advance the same sum." With a second lieutenant's monthly pay averaging about eighteen dollars, not every young officer heeded the commandant's entreaty. Determined, Burrows followed up his solicitation of funds in June 1799 with orders to each recalcitrant on his lineal list, informing them that those who had not "forwarded their 10 dollars are expected to do it." A year later, Burrows wrote directly to the last holdout, Lt. John Hall: "You must . . . charge yourself 15 dollars [the rate had increased] for the Music Fund already paid by every officer but yourself." However disgruntled the Corps' officers felt, their money proved to be well spent. Beginning with its public début at a Fourth of July celebration in Philadelphia in 1800, the Marine Band became an immediate success. The band played for President John Adams on New Year's Day, 1801. In 1805 Congress authorized public funds to support the band and the program of obtaining "voluntary donations" from the Corps' officers ended.

Of course, Burrows' main responsibility was to provide guard detachments in the ships that sailed to fight the Quasi-War. One of these units formed prior to the foundation of the Corps had been in the *Delaware* under the command of 1st Lt. James McKnight when she captured the *Croyable* in July. The former privateer was commissioned in the U.S. Navy as the *Retaliation* and given a Marine guard under 1st Lt. Simon W. Geddis. In November the tables were turned. The *Retaliation*, mounting fourteen guns, fell in with two French frigates mounting a total of seventy-

six. Her captain surrendered without offering resistance, and Geddis and his men became the first U.S. Marines taken prisoners of war.

All of the Navy's other meetings with French ships ended in the enemy's capture or flight. Marine guards were present at most of these encounters. Detachments commanded by 1st Lt. Bartholomew Clinch fought aboard Capt. Thomas Truxtun's frigate *Constellation* in the two major actions of the war, the capture of the frigate *Insurgente* on 9 February 1799 and the defeat of the *Vengeance* on 1 February 1800. The close combat both engagements included gave the *Constellation*'s Leathernecks the opportunity to perform the traditional Marine function of directing small arms' fire at enemy personnel. Clinch's men made an especially valuable contribution to the second victory, a brutal night battle in which their musketry and lobbed grenades helped beat off an attempt by the *Vengeance*, a larger ship with a bigger crew, to board the *Constellation*. Other detachments' musketry played a role in the capture of the frigate *Berceau* by the *Boston* on 12 October 1800 and in the sometimes sharp actions smaller U.S. vessels fought with French privateers.

Marine guards also demonstrated their worth in several clashes with the barge pirates who were preying on American shipping in the Bight of Léogâne, off the west coast of Haiti. The biggest fight occurred on New Year's Day 1800, when twelve barges, some mounting light cannon, manned by more than five hundred Haitians, attacked a becalmed convoy of four merchant vessels escorted by a 12-gun schooner, the *Experiment*, carrying a crew of seventy and a fourteen-man Marine guard. Second Lieutenant Nathan Sheredine commanded the Leathernecks. Between 0700 and 1600, the pirates made three distinct assaults on the convoy, returning to base after the first and second to unload their dead and wounded and to take on replacements. At the end of the day, they succeeded in taking two merchantmen that had drifted away from the convoy; but two barges had been sunk, and the *Experiment*'s grapeshot and musketry had smashed every effort to grapple with her. Edward Stevens, an American diplomat who happened to be on board, attributed this outcome in part to the "great steadiness and activity" of Sheredine's Marines.

The Quasi-War also engendered the U.S. Marine Corps' first two landings on foreign soil. The earliest took place at Puerto Plata, on the northern coast of Santo Domingo, on 11 May 1800. A French privateer, the 8-gun schooner *Sandwich* (a captured British vessel whose name had been retained), lay at anchor under the guns of the little Spanish fort there. Informed of her presence, Commo. Silas Talbot, commanding the USS *Constitution*, conceived a plan for cutting her out. An innocuous American trader, the *Sally*, would be sent into the harbor with a few men visible above deck and eighty-five other seamen and Marines packed into her hold. Once the *Sandwich* had been seized, the Leathernecks would go ashore and spike the fort's guns to preclude any interference from the Spanish during the hours it would take to get the ship rigged and ready to catch the evening breeze off the island. In overall command of the expedition Talbot placed the *Constitution*'s first lieutenant, Isaac Hull. Capt. Daniel Carmick and 2nd Lt. William Amory led the Marines.

Talbot's plan worked smoothly. The Americans boarded the *Sandwich* unopposed, and within moments her twenty-three startled crewmen were confined below deck. The next day Carmick wrote a friend that

the only disagreeable part of the business was being cooped up in a small vessel for 12 hours. . . . It put me in mind of the wooden horse at Troy. . . . The men went on board like devils and it was as much as the first lieutenant and myself could do to prevent blood being spilt. I believe it was not half an hour after the ship was taken that I had possession of the fort and all the cannon spiked and returned again on board. . . . I presume [the Spanish] were rather surprised. . . . By six o'clock [PM] the lieutenant had everything in order and the men stationed at the cannon, ready with my marines to oppose all their force, which we understood was about 500 men. They sent several flags of truce making different requests, to which we answered that we had only executed the orders of our commander. . . . [The Spanish commandant] concluded we must have been pretty determined before we undertook the business, as we had no other alternative but to die or succeed. He however remained very quiet, and we came out in the morning and joined our commodore.

For his part, their commodore was pleased as punch. "Perhaps no enterprise of the same moment was ever better executed," Talbot declared, "and I find myself under great obligations to Lieutenant Hull, Captain Carmick, and Lieutenant Amory . . . for the handsome manner and great address with which they performed this daring adventure."

The second Marine landing occurred at Willemstad on Curaçao, a Dutch possession that was invaded by a force of fifteen hundred French from nearby Guadeloupe early in September 1800. On the twenty-second of that month two U.S. sloops of war, the *Merrimack* and *Patapsco*, appeared off the island in response to an appeal for help from the American consul. By then the four hundred Dutch defenders—and a number of American volunteers from the merchant ships trapped at Willemstad—had retired into Fort Amsterdam, overlooking the entrance to the harbor. The next day the 24-gun *Patapsco* silenced the batteries the French had erected to cover an assault on the fort, and on the twenty-fourth she landed seventy seamen and Marines to reinforce the defenders. Their intervention proved unnecessary. Convinced by the *Patapsco*'s bombardment that it would be impossible to storm the fort in the face of the ships' fire, the French withdrew from the island that afternoon.

Less than a week later, on 30 September 1800, the Convention of Mortefontaine brought the Quasi-War with France to an end. Neither side had ever really wanted the war, and both were glad to be out of it, even if the terms of peace did not represent a triumph for either. At sea, the conflict was clearly a triumph for the U.S. Navy, which had captured eighty-five French privateers and two government frigates at the cost of a single

vessel, the little *Retaliation*. Marine guards had rendered valuable services in a number of engagements—most importantly, perhaps, the *Constellation*'s action with the *Vengeance* and the *Experiment*'s convoy battle. The cost to the Corps was six men killed or died of wounds and eleven wounded. No Marine officer was either killed or wounded, but 2nd Lt. Dyre S. Wynkoop became the first to lose his life in the line of duty. He and his detachment were among the 340 men who perished when the ex-French frigate *Insurgent* went down with all hands some time after sailing for the West Indies from Norfolk in August 1800. At the conclusion of the Quasi-War, Congress ordered a large reduction in the size of the Army; the Marine Corps benefited from the legislation by accepting the best of the discharged soldiers into its ranks.

Meanwhile, the seat of government had moved to the new "federal capital" at Washington, D.C. Lieutenant Colonel Commandant Burrows—a rank and title he acquired in April 1800—and Marine Corps headquarters followed that summer. He took the Marine Band along, of course. In March 1801, it played at the inauguration of President Thomas Jefferson, just as it has at every subsequent presidential inauguration; thereafter, it was heard at the White House so often that it soon became known as the "President's Own." That same month the commandant and the president, who were personal friends, rode out together to select a site for the Washington Marine Barracks. They considered sites at Bladensburg, Georgetown, and Washington before deciding on the block between Eighth and Ninth and G and I (Eye) Streets, Southeast, not far from the Washington Navy Yard. Among the buildings put under construction at the site was the commandant's house, of which Burrows' successor became the first occupant. A small Federalist mansion, it has been the home of every succeeding commandant and is today the oldest public building in use in Washington except for the White House.

In March 1804, ill health and financial problems forced Burrows to resign from the Corps he had served so well. His departure occurred toward the close of a war in the climax of which a tiny Marine detachment would play a vital role. In May 1801, Yusef Karamanli, the pasha of Tripoli, declared war on the United States, which he had decided was paying him insufficient tribute. The United States responded by sending an annual succession of squadrons to blockade the port city of Tripoli. The first squadron, dispatched upon reports of the pasha's discontent, reached the Mediterranean in July.

Combat operations began on 1 August, when the 12-gun schooner *Enterprise* fell in with the enemy's 14-gun *Tripoli*. Battles between wooden ships were usually over within an hour; theirs lasted for three. The Barbary corsairs favored boarding tactics, but the *Tripoli*'s repeated attempts to close were repulsed by broadsides from the *Enterprise*'s well-served battery and the musketry of 2nd Lt. Enoch S. Lane's Leathernecks. Of the *Tripoli*'s eighty crewmen, fifty were killed or wounded. The *Enterprise*'s ninety-four seamen and Marines did not suffer a single casualty.

This spirited affair proved to be the last of its kind. American squadrons lacked sufficient shallow-draft vessels and adequate charts to conduct a very effective blockade of Tripoli's dangerous coast, and it had never been Tripolitan policy to seek engagements with enemy warships. There was not another ship-to-ship action in the entire war, and not another action of any sort until boat parties totaling fifty sailors and Marines, the latter under Lane, landed near Tripoli on 21 June 1803 to destroy some coasting vessels that had been forced to beach themselves. The Americans succeeded in setting fire to the ships at a cost of fifteen killed and wounded, but following their withdrawal the Tripolitans extinguished the flames.

The tempo of operations increased after Commo. Edward Preble assumed command in the Mediterranean in September 1803 with the firm intention of winning the war. His prospects of doing so suffered a severe setback the following month when the frigate *Philadelphia*, one of his two big ships, ran hard aground while chasing a blockade runner and was surrounded by a covey of Tripolitan gunboats. Concluding that resistance would be futile, her captain surrendered the ship without a fight. First Lieutenant William S. Osborne and his 42 Marine guards were among the 307 Americans made prisoner. Two days later, abnormally high tides enabled the Tripolitans to refloat the *Philadelphia* and tow her into port.

The naval part of the enormous problem this created was solved on the night of 16 February 1804. Reprising the ruse employed to cut out the *Sandwich*, seventy-four volunteers under Lt. Stephen Decatur entered Tripoli harbor on board an innocent-looking coastal trader, overpowered the *Philadelphia*'s caretaker crew, set the frigate ablaze, and

Michel F. Corné painted *The Battle of Tripoli, 3 August 1804* for Commo. Edward Preble. Six gunboats of Leathernecks and Bluejackets advanced to engage a flotilla of eighteen Tripolitan gunboats. The large vessels in the foreground are, from left to right, the *Enterprise, Nautilus, Argus, Syren, Vixen,* and *Constitution.* (U.S. Naval Academy Museum)

escaped without the loss of a man. Seven Marines led by Sgt. Solomon Wren took part in the exploit, which Britain's renowned Adm. Horatio Nelson praised as "the most bold and daring act of the age." The diplomatic difficulties stemming from the fact that Yusef Karamanli retained 307 American bargaining chips persisted throughout the conflict.

That spring, Preble decided that the best way to compel the pasha to come to terms would be by bombarding his capital. The American squadron lacked the types of vessels needed for a close inshore attack, but the Kingdom of the Two Sicilies, which was also at war with Tripoli, agreed to supply six gunboats and two bomb vessels. These craft would be supported by the fire of Preble's flagship, the frigate *Constitution*, and six smaller American vessels.

The first bombardment of Tripoli took place on 3 August. The Tripolitan flotilla—

eighteen gunboats and two galleys—came out to drive off the small craft, and a division of three gunboats commanded by Decatur soon became engaged in a fierce melee. Decatur personally led boarding parties that captured two gunboats. Sergeant Wren, who had been with him in the destruction of the *Philadelphia*, was among the wounded.

Lt. John Trippe, commanding *Gunboat No. 6*, also called away boarders and leaped from his vessel to the deck of an enemy gunboat. A moment later the two craft drifted apart, leaving Trippe, Midn. John D. Henley, Sgt. Jonathan Meredith, and eight seamen and Marines to contend with thirty-six Tripolitans. Trippe engaged their captain, from whom he quickly received eleven saber wounds about the head and shoulders. Another Tripolitan circled around to strike him from behind. Meredith bayoneted the man, while Trippe succeeded in plunging his boarding pike into his opponent's chest. Within moments, more than half of the Tripolitans had been killed or wounded; the others laid down their arms. Besides Trippe, three members of the boarding party, two of them Marines, suffered wounds.

Four days later Preble renewed the attack on the city. This time the Tripolitan vessels made no move to close. Ships as well as shore fortifications returned the American fire, however, and either an enemy shot or accident touched off the magazine of *Gunboat No. 9*. Sixteen of the twenty-eight men on board became casualties; the dead included gallant Sergeant Meredith.

Unfortunately, neither of these bombardments nor three others conducted in following weeks, nor an attempt to blow up the vessels in Tripoli harbor with a powder ship that exploded prematurely, induced the pasha to reduce his demands. Late in September Preble rotated home thinking himself a failure, only to discover that his aggressiveness had made him a national hero.

In the meanwhile, another American had been thinking of a way to win the war: William Eaton, a forty-year-old Revolutionary War veteran, sometime schoolteacher, and former U.S. Army captain who had become familiar with Barbary politics while serving as U.S. consul at Tunis. Yusef Karamanli had become pasha of Tripoli by shooting his oldest brother, Hassan, and driving his older brother, Hamet, into exile. Eaton believed that the ideal solution to the Tripolitan imbroglio would be to restore Hamet to the throne. Returning to the United States in the summer of 1803, Eaton eventually lobbied a dubious Jefferson administration into approving

the project. In July 1804 he sailed for the Mediterranean to carry it out.

Finding Hamet, who had taken refuge in Egypt, and making preparations for the campaign turned out to be a lengthy process, but on 8 March 1805 "General" Eaton (as he styled himself in a treaty with Hamet) was ready to set out from Alexandria on a six-hundred-mile desert march to the Tripolitan frontier. All told, his little army numbered approximately 400 men: 325 Arabs; a

Lt. Presley O'Bannon carried the American flag to the shores of Tripoli. This miniature is the work of an unknown artist. (National Archives)

mercenary company of 35 Greeks; another mercenary company, also Christian, of 22 cannoneers; and 9 Americans—a midshipman and seven Marines under 1st Lt. Presley N. O'Bannon.

A twenty-nine-year old Virginian, O'Bannon had entered the Marine Corps

in 1801 and had already served a tour in the Mediterranean. In a letter to the commandant during that deployment, his ship's captain described O'Bannon as "one of the Happiest fellows Living," adding, "he has just returned from spending the evening with a Brilliant Circle of Spanish Ladies, & by way of Consolation for the loss of their company, Philosiphy & the fiddle is called to his aid, on the latter he is now playing, Hogs in the Cornfield." Ashore in North Africa the carefree fiddler would show himself to be, as Eaton recorded, an "intrepid, judicious, and enterprising Officer."

The long march across the desert was grueling. Provisions ran short, and on several occasions O'Bannon's Leathernecks, supported by the Christian mercenaries, had to face down threatened mutinies by Hamet's Arab followers. Finally, on 25 April, the army reached the heights overlooking the Tripolitan frontier city of Derna. The next day Eaton sent the governor a polite request to allow him free passage. "My head or yours," came the reply.

Eaton attacked on 27 April. A number of Arab horsemen had joined the expedition since it left Egypt, giving him upwards of six hundred combatants more or less under command. He deployed them for a two-pronged attack. Hamet's cavalry would swing inland to threaten Derna from the south while the Marines, the Christian mercenaries with the army's solitary cannon, and a few Arab foot soldiers stormed the barricade screening the city's eastern face. Three of the Mediterranean Squadron's smaller warships were on hand to furnish fire support.

At first progress was slow. The naval bombardment silenced the city's battery, but the enemy gunners reinforced the infantrymen behind the barricade. Seeing the mercenaries beginning to waver, Eaton decided that "our dernier and only resort" was to charge. In his words:

We rushed forward against a host of Savages, more than ten to one. They fled from their Coverts, irregularly, firing in retreat from every Palm tree and partition wall in their way. . . . Mr. O'Bannon accompanied by Midshipman [George] Mann of Annapolis, urged forward his Marines, Greeks, and such of the Cannoneers as were not necessary to the management of the field piece, passed through a shower of Musketry from the walls of houses, took possession of the Battery, planted the American Flag upon its ramparts, and turned its guns upon the Enemy.

In a half hour Eaton's forces were in undisputed control of Derna. One Marine private was killed and two wounded, one mortally, in its capture. Eaton himself was shot through the left wrist, and the mercenaries suffered ten casualties. The general made no record of Arab or hostile Tripolitan casualties, but the governor escaped with his head.

Eaton's scheme did indeed bring the Tripolitan War to an end, though not in the way he had imagined. Hamet's presence in Derna prompted Yusef Karamanli to rethink his position. On 3 June he concluded a treaty with U.S. negotiator Tobias Lear agreeing to free the *Philadelphia*'s company and waive all claims to future tribute in exchange for a one-time payment of sixty thousand dollars—by Barbary standards, a bargain-basement price. Eaton protested angrily that he and Hamet had been betrayed, but there was nothing he could do. The Americans, Hamet and his retinue, and the Christian mercenaries were evacuated from Derna on board the *Constellation* on 12 June.

In the United States, Eaton and O'Bannon were hailed as heroes. Congress honored them and the other Americans who fought at Derna with a joint resolution of thanks; Eaton's native Massachusetts awarded him a huge land grant; and Virginia presented O'Bannon with a costly Mameluke sword (on which it misspelled his name "Priestly"), traditionally believed to have been modeled after one given him by Hamet Karamanli.

Sadly, a Marine Corps with only four captain's slots could do little to reward first lieutenants, and in 1807 O'Bannon resigned his commission. In civilian life he made a good marriage, settled in Kentucky, became a large landowner, and served several terms in the state legislature, dying at the age of seventy-four. But while he spent only six years in the Marine Corps, Presley O'Bannon became one of its icons. The exploits of his tiny detachment would often be cited to refute the arguments of those who questioned the Corps' usefulness, and its officers still carry the elegant Mameluke sword (officially adopted in 1826) that came into fashion because of him.

The Marine Corps had fought the last year of the War with Tripoli under a new commandant. On 7 March 1804, a day after Lieutenant Colonel Burrows resigned, thirty-six-year-old Capt. Franklin Wharton, the Corps' senior officer, was appointed to replace him. A member of one of Philadelphia's most prominent families, Wharton had obtained one of the Corps' original captaincies in 1798 and served afloat during the Quasi-War with France. Since then he had commanded the Marine guard at the Philadelphia Navy Yard.

In many respects, Wharton proved to be an excellent commandant. Like Burrows, he understood the relationship between

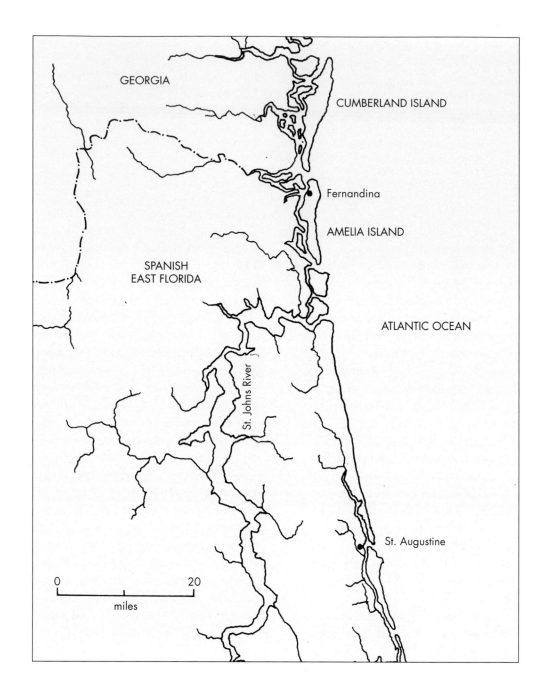

esprit de corps, public relations, and political capital, and the role spit and polish could play in fostering all three. Significantly, the Corps' first uniform regulations were issued within a month of his appointment. The items of apparel they prescribed included the traditional broad leather stock, intended both to resist cold steel and improve the wearer's bearing, that gave the "Leathernecks" their name. Wharton also introduced the hand salute and made Marine Barracks, Washington, "the school where young officers and recruits are to be instructed in the various duties which they may be called upon to perform." He continued Burrows' support of the Marine Band, which had become a feature of Washington social life. The urbane commandant himself became one of the capital's civic leaders. Unlike Burrows, however, Wharton was an astute financial manager. Under his stewardship the Corps established the reputation for accountability and frugality that it has taken care to maintain to the present. Yet at the critical moment of his career Wharton acted in a manner that many deemed disgraceful.

Map 3, left:
The Patriots' War

Right: *Swamp Ambush*,
by Col. Charles
Waterhouse, depicts
the Spanish attack on
Captain Williams'
supply train on
12 September 1812.
(Marine Corps Art
Collection)

The first few of Wharton's years as commandant were mostly quiet. In 1809 the threat of war with Spain prompted Congress to raise the Corps' authorized strength to 46 officers and 1,823 men, but it was unable to recruit more than 1,100 of all ranks. By that date the Corps was supplying guards for the Navy yards at Norfolk, Boston, Brooklyn, Charleston, and New Orleans as well as Washington and Philadelphia. In January 1811 the New Orleans detachment, commanded by Major Carmick since 1809, participated in an expedition against "Negro insurgents"—presumably bands of escaped slaves—in the wilderness north of the city. To Carmick's disgust, the insurgents fled after a brief exchange of fire; "they gave us but little opportunity to put ourselves in danger," he grumbled.

A year later, another Marine unit became involved in a deadlier struggle resulting from a covert attempt to annex Spanish East Florida: the so-called Patriots' War. The scenario called for a group of American "Patriots"—civilians promised land grants in reward for their services—to seize the town of Fernandina and proclaim the Republic of Florida, which they would immediately cede

to the United States. Then, with the support of U.S. forces pre-positioned on nearby Cumberland Island, Georgia, they would push south to capture the Spanish provincial capital of St. Augustine. The town of Baton Rouge had been filched from Spanish West Florida by a similar scheme in 1811.

At first all went well. The Patriots occupied Fernandina on 17 March 1812, and within a month the U.S. Regiment of Riflemen joined them on the outskirts of St. Augustine. There the operation began to go sour. The Americans lacked the artillery needed to assault the city's formidable Castillo de San Marcos, and in June they made a disastrous error by rebuffing the Seminole Indians' offer to take their side. The Seminoles then turned to the Spanish, who did not repeat the invaders' mistake. Soon, Seminole war parties began raiding the American lines of communications. In July a company of Marines under forty-six-year-old Capt. John Williams was ordered forward from Cumberland Island to convoy supplies to the front.

Bound by the kind of rules of engagement that would madden Marines in future "twilight wars," Williams found his assignment frustrating. In a letter written to the Corps' adjutant on 6 September, he complained, "I wish you . . . would find out the reason of the U.S. Troops being kept in this province without the liberty of firing a gun unless we are fired upon. Our situation is an unpleasant one."

Six days later, the forebodings that underlay the captain's letter were realized. Twenty Leathernecks and Patriots under his command were ambushed by fifty to sixty Seminoles and Spanish black troops while escorting a wagon train through a swamp. The attackers were beaten off, but one

Marine was killed and scalped, and eight other men wounded. The latter included Williams, who was shot eight times. Game to the end, he dictated a report of the action for the commandant, adding, "You may expect I

am in a dreadful situation, though I yet hope I shall recover in a few months." On 29 September he died.

By then the difficulty in bringing up supplies had caused the Americans to pull back from their position outside St. Augustine. Yet Williams' death did not go unavenged. In February 1813 Marines commanded by his replacement, Lt. Alexander Sevier, took part in a punitive expedition that burned the villages of the Seminoles who had ambushed him. But the little war in East Florida was a sideshow the United States could ill afford in view of the big war it had begun with Great Britain. In April, Washington ordered U.S. forces to evacuate Spanish territory.

Anglo-American relations had deteriorated steadily since 1803, the year Britain and France resumed their long struggle after the short-lived Peace of Amiens. Charged with conducting a blockade that eventually embraced the continent of Europe, the Royal Navy not only seized American ships but also impressed thousands of American seamen to fill its crews. The ill will these practices created was aggravated in 1811 by the discovery that British forces in Canada were supplying the Indian tribes resisting American settlement of the Ohio Valley. The obvious solution to that problem was congenial to the spirit of expansionism current in American society and politics, and on 18 June 1812 the United States declared war with the aim of expunging British power from North America.

The war's supporters assumed that the conquest of Canada would be, as Jefferson once prophesied, nothing more than "a matter of marching." Senile generals,

unreliable troops, poor planning, and an energetic enemy combined to confound that expectation. All three of the U.S. invasions of Canada in 1812 ended in failure. During that same year, however, the U.S. Navy covered itself with glory (and saved the national psyche) by startling victories in three consecutive frigate actions. In each case, the U.S. ship had the advantage of the heavier broadside—as would be true of the winner in all but two of the twenty-five single-ship engagements with Royal Navy vessels on the high seas. But that was beside the point. In the wars with France and her allies, British ships routinely beat opponents with heavier broadsides. In this war, they did not. Ship for ship and man for man, the U.S. Navy had shown itself second to none.

Marine musketry contributed to two of the Navy's three opening victories. In the first,

the *Constitution*'s battle with the *Guerrière* (19 August 1812), the British captain and both his first and second lieutenants were hit by small arms' fire. But the carnage was not wholly one-sided. The commander of the *Constitution*'s Leathernecks, 1st Lt. William S. Bush, had promised a friend, "Should an opportunity be afforded for boarding the enemy, I will be the first man on his deck." As the two ships crashed together, he climbed to the *Constitution*'s rail and shouted to the captain, "Shall I board her, sir?" An instant later, one of the *Guerrière*'s Royal Marines drilled him through the head.

The *Constitution*'s guard may have included the first woman to serve in the U.S. Marine Corps, at least if any credence is placed in an alleged autobiography originally published in 1815 as *The Adventures of Louisa Baker: A Native of Massachusetts,*

Who, in Early Life having been shamefully Seduced, Deserted her Parents, and Enlisted in Disguise, on Board an American Frigate, as a Marine Where, in Two or Three Engagements, She Displayed the Most Heroic Fortitude, and was Honorably Discharged Therefrom a few Months Since, Without a Discovery of her Sex Being Made. In later editions, more pointedly entitled *The Female Marine,* the author confessed that Louisa Baker was a *nom de plume* and identified herself as Lucy Brewer, which modern research suggests was still another *nom de plume.* In any case, Lucy's jaunty narrative records that in each of the *Constitution's*

actions she was in the maintop, "busily employed . . . plying my faithful musket with the best success, whenever the smoke would permit me to see a blue jacket of the enemy."

The introduction to a recent, scholarly edition of *The Female Marine* contends that the work was a hoax. Among the reasons offered is that, the author's explanation notwithstanding, a woman would not have been able to conceal her sex in the exceedingly communal circumstances of life aboard ship; and yet there are a few well-documented instances of women who did succeed in passing for men in eighteenth- and nineteenth-century navies and armies. Perhaps the most reasonable answer to the arguments pro and con the existence of the female Marine is the Scots verdict: "Not proved."

The war's second frigate action, between the *United States* and the *Macedonian* (25 October), was won outside musket range. In the next, the *Constitution* with the *Java* (29 November), the antagonists again came to close quarters, and the *Java*'s captain was mortally wounded by a musket ball. The fourth action broke the string of American victories, but there was none in which Marines displayed more valor.

The defeat occurred on 1 June 1813, when Capt. James Lawrence, only ten days in command, took the *Chesapeake* out of Boston harbor with an untried crew to engage HMS *Shannon*, which, after six years in command,

Capt. Philip Vere Broke had made probably the most formidable frigate in the Royal Navy. Broke planned to capture the *Chesapeake* by boarding. To make that feat easier, he positioned carronades—the artillery equivalent of sawed-off shotguns—to sweep the American vessel's forecastle and quarterdeck, and specifically instructed his Royal Marines to aim for her officers. The battle lasted barely a quarter of an hour. By the time Broke led his boarders over the *Chesapeake*'s bulwarks, British fire had made a bloody shambles of her deck. Every exposed officer had been shot at least once, and many seamen had fled below. The commander of the ship's Marine detachment, 1st Lt. James Broome, was down with a mortal wound, but the NCOs and men still on their feet put up the only organized

resistance the British encountered. Fourteen of the *Chesapeake*'s forty-four Leathernecks were killed or died of wounds, and twenty (including both sergeants) were wounded—a casualty rate of 77 percent, more than twice that of the ship's company.

Subsequently, Marine guards played a conspicuous role in three of the U.S. Navy's ten remaining victories at sea. At the climax of the engagement between the sloop of war *Wasp* and the British brig *Reindeer* (28 June 1814), the *Reindeer*'s captain, William Manners, already twice wounded, called away boarders and climbed into his ship's rigging, sword in hand, to lead them. As he did so, two Marines in the *Wasp*'s maintop put bullets through the top of his skull. The Americans then boarded and captured the *Reindeer*. Neither side tried to board during the *Constitution*'s double victory over the smaller frigate *Cyane* and sloop of war *Levant* (20 February 1815), but the battle opened at so close a range that the *Constitution*'s Marines were engaged almost from the beginning. Afterward, the ship's captain commended them for their "lively and well-directed fire." In the action between the sloops of war USS *Hornet* and HMS *Penguin* (23 March 1815), the latter's captain was picked off as he closed with the intention of boarding. His first lieutenant succeeded in laying the *Penguin* alongside the *Hornet*, but the British seamen, apparently impressed by American musketry, ignored the call for boarders. The *Penguin* surrendered minutes later.

The war also included the first and last naval battle in which a Marine commanded the American ship engaged. In February 1813, Capt. David Porter took the frigate *Essex* around Cape Horn to attack the British whaling fleet in the South Pacific. Over the next few months the *Essex* took so many British vessels that Porter ran short of Navy officers to use as prize captains, and in May he assigned his Marine officer, First Lieutenant John Marshall Gamble, to command the *Greenwich*, a whaler armed with ten guns. "I had much confidence in the discretion of this gentleman," Porter wrote in his journal. "To make up for his want of nautical knowledge, I put two expert seamen with him as mates, one of whom was a good navigator." On 14 July the *Greenwich* defeated the 14-gun British whaler *Seringapatam* while within sight of the *Essex*—and a nervous David Porter. In a letter written to Gamble a few days later, a friend in the frigate told him that

> Capt. Porter chewed as much tobacco and kept his poor spyglass as constantly employed as ever I knew him to. At one time, when the *Seringapatam* tacked, Capt. Porter became more anxious than ever; fearful you would tack at the same time and receive a raking shot, he exclaimed, "Now, Mr. Gamble, if you'll only stand on five minutes and then tack, I'll make you a prince." You stood on a while, when he again exclaimed: "Now is your time;" just when we observed your ship in stays [in the process of tacking], which gave you the raking shot that did the enemy so much injury. So now, my dear fellow, you stand a chance of being princed, knighted, or something else. The Captain was much pleased.

Not all naval actions took place on the high seas. The two of greatest strategic significance, both American victories, were fought on inland waters: the battles of Lake Erie (10 September 1813) and Lake Champlain (11 September 1814). By winning control of Lake Erie, Commo. Oliver Hazard Perry undermined British plans to block American expansion into the Ohio Valley; by defeating the British attempt to win control of Lake Champlain, Commo. Thomas Macdonough repulsed the major enemy offensive of the war, an invasion from Canada by ten thousand veteran troops. Thirty-four Leathernecks served in Perry's ships at Lake Erie. Four were killed in action or died of wounds, and another fourteen suffered wounds. Among the dead was their commander, 2nd Lt. John Brooks. Mangled by a British cannon ball, he begged for someone to put him out of his misery before

succumbing to shock or loss of blood. There were no Marines in Macdonough's squadron at Lake Champlain, but the Army detailed soldiers to perform their duties.

The invasion from Canada was only one element of the offensive that the wind-down of the war with France enabled Britain to mount against the United States in 1814. The other was the dispatch of an amphibious striking force—fifty-four hundred men under Maj. Gen. Robert Ross—to raid American cities with the aim of diverting troops from the invasion front and undermining support for the war. Convoyed by a squadron stronger than the entire U.S. Navy, Ross' army landed at the Patuxent River town of Benedict, Maryland, on 1 August and marched north toward Washington.

The forces available to Brig. Gen. William H. Winder to defend the capital consisted of approximately fifty-five hundred militia, a single regiment of regular infantry, and a naval brigade led by Commo. Joshua Barney. As commander of the Chesapeake gunboat flotilla, Barney had vainly contested the British advance up the Patuxent. Once the action passed him by, he struck out overland for Washington with the flotilla's 420 seamen and Marines and five guns, plus a detachment of 103 Marines that Wharton had sent from the Washington Barracks under the Corps' adjutant and inspector, Capt. Samuel Miller, to support the flotilla's operations.

The armies made contact on the west bank of the Eastern Branch of the Potomac (today's Anacostia River) opposite the village of Bladensburg on 24 August. There were, in effect, two battles of Bladensburg. The first, and the only one the Americans had any possibility of winning, had been lost by poor generalship and panicky militia before the naval brigade, which Winder had neglected to order forward, reached the field.

Barney formed a front along a ridge that crossed the Washington Turnpike approximately a mile behind the original American line. Two 18-pounders under Barney's personal command were sited to fire directly down the pike; the three 12-pounders, assigned to Miller, were wheeled into a field to the right. The seamen and Marines not detailed to serve the guns deployed into a firing line. Other late-coming units aligned on the brigade's flanks: militia on the right, the regular infantry regiment and more militia, including a battery of five guns, on the left.

Flushed with their easy victory in the battle's opening round, the British attacked straight down the pike. The artillery and musket fire that slammed into their ranks from the ridgeline drove them back in surprise. Quickly reforming, they came on again, only to be repulsed again. A third assault, bravely mounted minutes later, met the same fate. Barney seized the moment to counterattack, and the bloodied British regiments to his front gave ground to the brigade's seamen (shouting "Board 'em! Board 'em!") and Marines.

Hurrying to the scene with reinforcements, Ross ordered his troops to work around the American flanks. He need not have bothered. Almost simultaneously Winder, intent on saving whatever he could of his army, directed the units there to retire. Inexcusably, he neglected to notify Barney. Soon the naval brigade found itself under fire from three directions. Barney took a bad wound in the thigh. Miller, himself handling a musket, was hit in the arm by a British soldier with whom he was trading shots. Seeing that the situation had become hopeless, Barney gave the order to spike the guns and retreat. Both he and Miller were captured.

Upon meeting Barney, Ross complimented him on his command's gallant stand. The compliment was well deserved. Of the 249 British casualties at Bladensburg, nearly all had occurred during the second phase of the action. The same was true of the approximately 150 American casualties, the Marines' share of which was 8 dead and 14 wounded. In a sense, it had been for nothing. There was never any chance that the naval brigade and the neighboring units could hold off Ross' army. Yet in a larger sense, the fight they put up achieved a great deal. It did not save the national capital, but it saved the national honor.

Lieutenant Colonel Commandant Wharton had remained at the Marine barracks. When it became known that the redcoats were coming, he collected his headquarters detachment, the Marine Band, and the Corps' records and pay chest, and marched to the Washington Navy Yard. Despite an order from the secretary of the navy to withdraw to Frederick, Maryland—the designated refuge of the fleeing government—Wharton volunteered to assist Commo. Thomas Tingey in the yard's defense or destruction. Tingey declined the offer, and Wharton proceeded to Frederick. He was, of course, only following orders, but a number of the Corps' fire-eating young officers found his failure to do something more inexcusable.

After burning Washington's public buildings (but not, for unknown reasons, the Marine barracks and the commandant's house), the British army returned to its ships. Its next objective was Baltimore. Among the ten thousand defenders—again, mostly militia—hurriedly concentrated in anticipation of the attack was a thousand-man naval brigade including the Marines who had fought at Bladensburg and detachments from several nearby ships and stations. The British landed southeast of the city on 12 September, but no new Bladensburg ensued. The militia they encountered stood firm; an American sniper killed Ross; and their ships' fire failed to subdue Fort McHenry at the entrance of the harbor. On 14 September, the invaders withdrew.

Following this check, the British assembled an even more powerful amphibious force for their next operation. This time the target was New Orleans. The expedition anchored off the Louisiana coast on 8 December. Rather than sail upstream against the strong Mississippi River current, the British chose to approach the city via Lake Borgne, an arm of the Gulf of Mexico. Five U.S. gunboats, embarking 147 seamen and 35 Marines, contested their passage. On 14 December these vessels were carried in hand-to-hand fighting by British boat parties numbering nearly a thousand men, but Maj. Gen. Andrew Jackson used the time they had bought him to strengthen the defenses of New Orleans.

Ashore, Major Carmick's Marines took part in each of the ensuing actions: Jackson's night attack on the British advance guard on 23 December; British exploratory attacks on 28 December and 1 January 1815; and the British grand assault, which was shot to pieces on 8 January. But after 28 December the Marines were no longer led by Carmick. Before the battle, he had been placed at the head of a battalion of New Orleans volunteers. There, an observer recorded, "he was struck by a rocket, which tore his horse to pieces, and wounded the Major in the arm and head." The Leathernecks completed the campaign under the command of 1st Lt. F. B. de Bellevue. Carmick died in 1816, perhaps because of his wounds. The *Washington National Observer* lamented his passing with a fulsome tribute, noting that, "[the nation] was thus deprived of the experience, discipline, and gallantry of this valuable officer." At the time, he was the senior Marine officer next to Wharton. Had he lived, he would no doubt have succeeded him as commandant, and thereby spared the Corps the embarrassment of Anthony Gale.

Tragically, all the deaths resulting from the Battle of New Orleans were unnecessary. U.S. and British negotiators meeting in Belgium had signed a peace treaty restoring the prewar status quo on 24 December.

In the War of 1812, U.S. Marines cemented the reputation to which they had laid claim in earlier conflicts as first-class fighting men. If overall casualties had not been heavy—46 dead and 66 wounded—they were proportionate to those suffered by the seamen and soldiers with whom Marine detachments served. Congressional approval of the Corps' performance was evident in two acts passed in 1814. One raised its authorized strength to 93 officers and 2,622 men, an increase of more than 60 percent. The other made Marine officers eligible for brevet promotions for "gallant actions or meritorious conduct" or after having spent ten years in grade. The 6 officers who received brevets during or for the war included Capt.

Samuel Miller, the hero of Bladensburg, and the commander of the *Constitution*'s Marines during her action with the *Cyane* and *Levant*, Capt. Archibald Henderson.

Operationally, the years following the War of 1812 were relatively quiet for the Corps. Marine guards sailed in the two squadrons sent to the Mediterranean in 1815 to chastise the Barbary Powers, which (Morocco excepted) had taken advantage of the navy's wartime absence to begin misbehaving, but after four U.S. ships gobbled up an Algerine frigate the offenders peaceably acceded to American demands. Nearer home, in Spanish East Florida, Marine detachments took part in expeditions that destroyed pirate lairs on the Apalachicola River in 1816 and Amelia Island in 1817. More than three hundred Spanish Negro troops had attacked the Florida patriots on the island in September of that year, but were beaten off. On 22

The Battle of Lake Borgne was painted by T. L. Hornbrook within a few years of the action. British boat parties are already boarding the American gunboat in the center. (U.S. Naval Academy Museum)

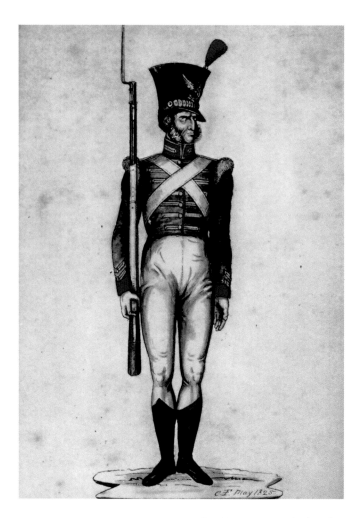

A contemporary engraving based on a sketch by 2nd Lt. Charles R. Floyd, USMC, shows a Marine private in the green "coatee" (short coat) prescribed by the uniform regulations of 1819. The color of the coat reverted to blue in 1824, returned to green in 1834, and changed back to blue for once and all in 1839. (Marine Corps Art Collection)

December, the United States took formal possession of the area by accepting the surrender of the Spanish force. The Marine Guard in the frigate *John Adams* served ashore with the Army during the engagement.

In March 1817 Congress imposed the first of what would become the routine postwar cutbacks on the Corps, passing a Peace Establishment Act that reduced its authorized strength to 50 officers and 942 NCOs and men. The act specified the number of officers at each rank: 1 lieutenant colonel commandant, 9 captains, 24 first lieutenants, and 16 second lieutenants, but failed to provide for any in the rank of major. The detailed legislation included the number of enlisted men at every rank as well. A year later, the drum major of the Marine Band resigned, and the lieutenant colonel commandant posted an advertisement for a replacement in the *Washington National Intelligencer*: "Wanted. For the Marine Corps of the United States. A sober, steady man, in the capacity of drum major. He must be a master of his profession, and capable of playing well on the clarinet."

Institutionally, the postwar years were anything but quiet. A number of Marine officers considered Wharton's failure to take the field against the British an act of rankest cowardice. None was more disgusted than Bvt. Maj. Archibald Henderson. In 1817 he preferred charges that brought Wharton before a court-martial. There were two specifications: neglect of duty and conduct unbecoming an officer and a gentleman, in that he had declined to take steps to silence criticism of his actions in 1814 "so highly injurious to his own character and of great disadvantage to the Corps." The court acquitted him of both charges. But the commandant did not have long to savor his vindication. The following year he sickened and on 1 September he died.

With Wharton's demise, fifty-seven-year-old Bvt. Maj. Anthony Gale, the duelist Burrows had commended for shooting Lieutenant McKenzie, became the Corps' senior officer. Irish by birth, Gale joined the Marines in September 1798, served afloat in the Quasi-War and the War with Tripoli, commanded the Philadelphia Barracks, and took part in the defense of Baltimore. His brevet rank had been awarded in 1814 by virtue of ten years in grade.

As seniority alone generally governed promotions and appointments in the U.S. armed forces, it might have been expected that Gale would be named to succeed Wharton as promptly as Wharton had been to succeed Burrows. Instead six months passed, during which Henderson served as acting commandant. The delay was clearly caused by the doubts raised by Henderson and Bvt. Maj. Samuel Miller regarding Gale's fitness to occupy the Corps' premier post, for which they considered themselves eminently qualified. Henderson stood second on the seniority list; if Gale was passed over, he would have the strongest claim to the appointment. Miller, whose efforts to promote his own candidacy permanently alienated Henderson, was sixth on the seniority list, but he had Bladensburg and at least one highly-impressed Congressman in his favor. The uncertainty culminated in a court of inquiry convened in February 1819 to investigate updates of two charges

of which Gale had been cleared by a court-martial in 1816: misuse of government funds and "conduct unbecoming" by being drunk on duty. At the close of its hearings the court ruled that neither charge had been upheld, and on 3 March Anthony Gale was appointed Lieutenant Colonel Commandant of the Marine Corps.

Lamentably, the accusation of intemperance was all too well justified. In the summer of 1820 Gale came to cross purposes with Secretary of the Navy Smith Thompson, who granted some Marine Corps officers furloughs without consulting him. Gale thereupon wrote to the secretary seeking to clarify their command relationship. Thompson responded by countermanding two of the commandant's officer personnel assignments. This frustrating situation set Gale off on a colossal and highly indiscreet jag, during which he was arrested by the police at about 2100 one night, clad only in his nightshirt and slippers, beating on the door of a bordello that refused him admittance. A court-martial ensued, and on 19 October, Gale was dismissed from the Corps. He died in obscurity in rural Kentucky. Today, unhappy Anthony Gale is the only deceased commandant of the Marine Corps whose gravesite is unknown and of whom no likeness is known to exist.

CHAPTER 4

The Era of Archibald Henderson, 1820–1859

The Gale affair did not shake official faith in appointment by seniority, and effective 17 October 1820 Archibald Henderson became commandant of the Marine Corps. Samuel Miller could not have been surprised by his new commandant's ready acceptance of his resignation of the post of adjutant and inspector, but he must have been chagrined when Henderson appointed a mere first lieutenant to the post.

Born at the village of Colchester, Virginia, a few miles from present-day Quantico, in January 1783, Henderson had begun his career as a second lieutenant at the age of twenty-three. He was then a slender, red-haired, soldierly, and extremely ambitious young man. Both before and after the War of 1812, dissatisfaction with his prospects for advancement had caused him to seriously consider leaving the Corps. His efforts to oust Wharton from the commandancy and prevent Gale from ascending to it have been recounted. Now Henderson had attained his goal, and in the nick of time. Although the Corps retained a reservoir of good will from its performance in the War of 1812, the problems that had surrounded the office

of commandant ever since the Battle of Bladensburg had undermined the authority of its headquarters. Strong leadership was urgently needed. Archibald Henderson provided it for the next thirty-eight years.

Henderson acted swiftly to restore the authority of Marine Corps headquarters, insisting on the sanctity of the chain of command. When in 1822 Samuel Miller moved President Monroe to countermand an order from Henderson sending him to sea, Henderson responded to the presidential intervention by offering to resign. Soon Washington officialdom as well as the Corps' officers came to realize that this was a commandant who could not be ignored.

Henderson took an abiding interest in the Corps' personnel. He was especially concerned with increasing the quality and professionalism of its officers, many of whom owed their commissions to political patronage rather than martial aptitude. This goal could be accomplished, he believed, by recruiting graduates of the U.S. Military Academy; but his repeated requests for permission to do so were denied. Refused that remedy, Henderson carefully monitored the accession of applicants from civil life

Opposite: Archibald Henderson was painted from life by an unknown artist about 1820. Harriet Trimble Smith made this copy for the Marine Corps Art Collection. (Marine Corps Art Collection)

and continued the practice of ordering all newly commissioned officers to Washington Barracks for orientation and training. He was also prepared to eliminate the unfit. Under his predecessors, a Marine officer had been cashiered or dismissed on the average of once every four and a half years; under Henderson, the frequency of such actions nearly doubled.

Stern as he was with the Corps' officers, Henderson showed much sympathy for the Spartan lot of its NCOs and men. To make enlisted service less onerous—and thereby, he hoped, reduce the chronically high desertion rate and facilitate recruiting—he made Sunday a day of rest; abolished flogging ashore two decades before the Navy abolished it afloat; provided better barracks; and secured at least modest increases in pay and allowances for fuel, clothing, and rations. Though these measures must have been appreciated by long-service Leathernecks, they failed to produce the anticipated institutional benefits. Desertion remained rampant, and even by bending regulations the Corps was never able to enlist the number of men Congress authorized.

In addition to the steps Henderson took to retain men already on board, he ceaselessly campaigned for authority to recruit more. He scored a major victory in 1825 by persuading the Board of Navy Commissioners—a panel of three senior officers, then under the presidency of Commo. William Bainbridge, that advised the secretary of the Navy on professional matters—to propose what became known as the Bainbridge Scale for ships' guards. This was simply the rule applied to the Royal Marines that stipulated that the strength of a guard detachment should equal the number of its ship's guns, which would have sent virtually the entire Marine Corps to sea. Though the Navy Department never officially adopted the Bainbridge Scale, it gave Henderson a useful talking point. At first Congress turned a deaf ear, but eventually his persistence began to be rewarded. By the time Henderson died in harness, the Corps' establishment stood at 63 officers and 2,010 NCOs and men, more than double its strength at the date he had become commandant.

What Henderson viewed as these men's bread-and-butter missions were the same ones Marines had been performing at the time he entered the Corps: providing security for the Navy's yards and furnishing ships' guards to discourage mutiny, scour enemy decks with musket fire, and contribute a contingent of trained light infantry as the backbone of naval landing parties. Yet in another respect, Henderson was an innovator. Throughout his years as commandant, he maintained a battalion—because of the constant manpower crunch, a very small battalion—at Eighth and Eye as a standing force in readiness, capable of deploying at a moment's notice. This practice was to pay rich dividends in terms of both service to the country and the renown of the Corps.

The Corps' renown was of great concern to Henderson, not merely as a matter of institutional pride but also of existence. While Americans no longer questioned their nation's need for a navy as well as an army, some regarded its Marine Corps as an extravagance that should be absorbed by one of the larger services. Henderson understood that his Leathernecks' survival would depend upon the esteem in which they were held by members of the public—at least, those with political influence—and in the halls of Congress. He overlooked no opportunity to enhance that esteem.

Like his predecessors, Henderson encouraged the activities of the Marine Band, which became even more popular following the appointment of Francis Maria Scala, a Neapolitan clarinetist, as bandmaster in 1845. In other exercises of public relations, Henderson held biweekly dress parades at Washington Barracks and personally hosted frequent receptions on the grounds of the commandant's house, especially after his marriage at age forty to a young lady of

twenty, who would give him nine children. But Henderson never forgot that, in the final analysis, the Corps' reputation rested on Marines' performance in battle. The United States engaged in two major conflicts—the Seminole War and the Mexican War—while he was commandant. He took steps to see that Marines had the chance to enter battle in both.

Aside from operations in the course of those conflicts, Leathernecks made more than forty landings during Henderson's decades at their head. The earliest occurred in the Caribbean, where in the 1820s the U.S. Navy and the Royal Navy collaborated to suppress the piracy that still flourished off the coasts of Cuba, Puerto Rico, and Central America. At the peak of the American effort, in 1823–24, three hundred Marines served in the ships of the West India Squadron. A number of minor actions occurred afloat and ashore, but the pirates proved no match for regular naval forces, and the Corps' participation in the campaign, virtually concluded by 1826, passed almost unnoticed.

In contrast, the suppression of the Massachusetts State Prison revolt of 1824 by Marines from the Boston Navy Yard brought the Corps a public relations bonanza. An account of the incident caught the attention of Williams Holmes McGuffey, who found in it an illustration of the virtues promoted by his ubiquitous *Readers*. The result was to make a Marine officer an exemplar of courage, coolness, and compassion to three-quarters of a century of American schoolchildren.

The trouble began when prison officials announced that 3 inmates were to be flogged

Left: Robert D. Wainwright, shown in this painting by an unidentified artist, was commissioned in 1807 and served until his death in 1842. He was the Corps' acting commandant for six months in 1836–37 when Archibald Henderson went to Florida "to fight the Indians." (Marine Corps Art Collection)

Right: The attack on Quallah Battoo in 1832 was tidied up in this contemporary woodcut. (National Archives)

for violating regulations. In protest, 283 prisoners armed with hammers, chisels, and other tools from the prison workshops seized control of the dining hall and declared that they would not disperse until the sentence was remitted. After the guards' attempts to persuade the convicts to return to work had been rebuffed, they sent a message to the commander of the Marine barracks, Bvt. Maj. Robert D. Wainwright, requesting his assistance in restoring order. A veteran of seventeen years in the Corps, Wainwright soon arrived at the head of a detachment of Marines. The prison authorities suggested that he have his men open fire on the convicts through the dining hall's high windows, at first with powder only, and, should that prove unavailing, ball cartridge. Wainwright demurred. Instead, he led the Leathernecks into the dining hall and informed the prisoners that he had been instructed to quell the insurrection. They replied that they were ready to die where they stood. *McGuffey's Reader* continued:

> Major Wainright now ordered his Marines to load their pieces, and that they might not be suspected of trifling, each man was told to hold up to view the bullet that he afterwards put into his gun. This only caused a growl of determination, and no one blanched. . . . They knew that their numbers would

enable them to bear down and destroy the handful of Marines, after the first discharge.

> The Marines were ordered to take aim; their guns were presented; but not a prisoner stirred, except to grasp more firmly his weapon. Still desirous, if possible, to avoid such a slaughter as must follow the discharge of the guns, the major advanced a step or two, and spoke even more firmly than before, urging them to depart. Again . . . they declared their intention of fighting it out. The intrepid officer then took out his watch and told his men to hold their pieces aimed at the prisoners, but not to fire till they had orders. Then, turning to the convicts, he said, "You must leave this hall. I give you three minutes to decide. If at the end of that time a man remains, he shall be shot dead. I speak no more."

> No more tragic situation that this can be conceived: at one end of the hall a fearless multitude of desperate and powerful men waiting for the assault; at the other a little band of well-disciplined Marines, waiting with leveled muskets . . . and their tall commander holding up his watch to count the lapse of the three allotted minutes. For two minutes not a

person or a muscle moved; not a sound was heard except the labored breathing of the infuriated wretches. . . . At the expiration of the two minutes, . . . two or three of those in the rear, and nearest to the further entrance, went slowly out; a few more followed their example, dropping out quietly and deliberately; and before half the last minute was gone, every man was struck by panic, and crowded for the exit, and the hall cleared as if by magic. Thus the steady firmness of moral force, and the strong effect of deliberate determination, cowed the most daring men, and prevented a scene of carnage which would have instantly followed the least precipitancy or exertion of physical force.

The potential value of such publicity became fully apparent in December 1829, when President Andrew Jackson sent Congress a message recommending that the Marine Corps should be merged into the Army. The president's action was provoked by a treasury audit that found that although the Corps was about the same size as an infantry regiment, it cost at least two and a half times as much a year to maintain, between $185,000 and $220,000 vice $75,000. The difference was to a considerable extent due to officer pay and allowances. By 1829, for example, the Corps included no fewer than five brevet lieutenant colonels, "who," the president acidly noted, "receive the full pay and emoluments of their brevet rank, without rendering proportionate service."

Jackson's proposal became the subject of hearings in both houses of Congress the following year. Testifying in its favor before the Senate Naval Affairs Committee, Secretary of the Navy John Branch candidly presented the results of an informal survey of senior Navy officers revealing that some believed Marines were no longer needed on board American warships, but others considered them invaluable. The president's recommendation died in committee.

That was not the end of the matter, however. Late in 1831 a new secretary of the Navy, Levi Woodbury, renewed the contest by proposing that the Corps should either be abolished or absorbed by the Army or the Navy. Congress again declined to act, but the Corps' future remained clouded when, a few months later, a landing party of Bluejackets and Leathernecks became engaged in the most spirited action fought by U.S. naval forces since 1815.

On 7 February 1831 Malays from the settlement at Quallah Battoo (Kuala Batu) on the northwestern coast of Sumatra plundered the trader *Friendship*, out of Salem, Massachusetts, and murdered three of her crewmen. Immediately upon receipt of the news, the 44-gun frigate *Potomac*, then in New York harbor under the command of Commo. John Downes, was ordered to proceed to the scene and exact retribution. She sailed on 27 August.

The *Potomac* dropped anchor off Quallah Battoo on 5 February 1832. That afternoon a group of officers made a close inshore reconnaissance in one of the ship's boats. The landing party, 286 seamen and Marines under the ship's executive officer, Lt. Irvine Shubrick, disembarked early the next morning. Organized and drilled on the long voyage out, the force consisted of three divisions of seamen armed with pistols and cutlasses, each headed by a Navy lieutenant, and the *Potomac*'s Marine guard carrying rifles with fixed bayonets, led by 1st Lt. Alvin Edson and 2nd Lt. George H. Terrett—a young man destined to see as much combat as any Leatherneck of his generation—plus an artillery detachment of sailors, hauling a 6-pounder affectionately known as Betsy Baker.

Landing shortly before dawn, the party fanned out to attack the three forts that had been identified by the afternoon's reconnaissance. These were substantial works, with citadels built on elevated platforms mounting small cannons. Shubrick took the first and third seaman divisions to assault the largest fort. The second division and the Marine detachment were each assigned to storm one of the others. The Malays proved themselves formidable adversaries, "fighting with . . . undaunted firmness," wrote a member of the landing party, "and displaying such an utter carelessness of life as would have been honored in a better cause."

The two lesser forts were quickly carried, but the principal work continued to hold out even after the Leathernecks and the second seaman division joined Shubrick's force outside its walls. Eventually their combined fire, augmented by Betsy Baker's grapeshot, cut down most of the defenders, and the citadel was carried by a rush. A fourth, previously unobserved fort at the edge of the jungle then opened fire but was promptly overrun by seamen and Marines. After putting the torch to the forts and the village, the landing party withdrew. Three of its members had been killed and 14 wounded, including 4 Marines. The Malays were estimated to have lost 150 dead, among them Rajah Po Mahomet, whom American traders considered the area's chief malefactor. Later that day the *Potomac* bombarded the ruins of Quallah Battoo, and in the afternoon a Malay delegation paddled to the frigate and professed the desire to establish amicable relations with the United States.

The action at Quallah Battoo soon became nationally known. As the *Potomac* remained in the Pacific, the first news of the affair to reach the United States was carried by American traders returning from the Indies. Their sometimes exaggerated accounts stirred up so much press criticism of the "unmerciful attacks" that President Jackson had Secretary Woodbury order Commodore Downes to forward a detailed report at once. Age of Sail communications being what they were, Downes' report was not received until the spring of 1833, but its effects proved to be everything the administration could have desired. From a cause of embarrassment, Quallah Battoo was transformed into a

source of pride. It even came to be celebrated by a broadside verse, "Printed at the request of Williams, York, Tucker, and others of the crew of the Potomac," the tenor of which is indicated by the stanza:

> To revenge the sad wrongs which
> our friends and the nation,
> So oft have sustained from these
> demons of hell,
> Our work we commenced, and the
> bright conflagration
> Left but few of our foes the sad story
> to tell.

For his part, Archibald Henderson did not neglect to remind Secretary Woodbury that "the attack of the Malays found the Marine Guard fully sufficient for the perilous duty assigned it."

To what extent Congress was influenced by reports of Marine prowess at Quallah Battoo can only be conjectured, but in June 1834 it quashed the Jackson administration's ongoing challenge to the Corps by the passage of an act that enjoyed Archibald Henderson's blessing, "for the better organization of the Marine Corps." Until that date Marines had been subject to the army's Articles of War while ashore and Navy Regulations while afloat. The act's most important feature eliminated this anomaly by defining the Corps as an individual sea service, distinct from the Navy but within the Navy Department and governed by Navy regulations—a status it retains today. Other provisions raised the rank attached to the office of commandant to colonel and increased the Corps' authorized strength to 63 officers and 1,224 NCOs and men. Inevitably, trade-offs accompanied the legislation. Marine officers were made subordinate to naval officers of equivalent rank, even if the latter were junior in date of rank, and the practice of granting officers brevet promotions after ten years in grade was discontinued; henceforth, brevets would be awarded solely for distinguished conduct under fire. Finally, the act expressly confirmed the power previously vested in the president to attach the Marine Corps to the Army in time of need.

Two years later, Henderson took advantage of this provision to commit the Corps to a land campaign. In 1830 Congress passed the Indian Removal Act, which directed the government to encourage and assist tribes residing in the eastern United States to move west of the Mississippi. Seven chiefs representing the Florida Seminoles subsequently consented to the removal. Afterward several of them claimed to have signed the treaty under duress, and by the time the exodus was scheduled to begin, the majority of the Seminoles were strongly opposed to leaving Florida. War broke out on 28 December 1835, when a party of Seminoles destroyed two companies of troops under Maj. Francis L. Dade on the march from Fort Brooke (the site of present-day Tampa) to Fort King, one hundred miles to the northeast. Although Seminole warriors numbered at the most fourteen hundred, their canny tactics and superb field craft, coupled with the support of numerous escaped slaves and the difficulties of the terrain, made the

conflict the longest and most costly Indian war the United States ever waged.

The following spring, three bands of Creek Indians went on the warpath in southern Georgia and eastern Alabama. Marines were already serving in the Seminole War: ships' guards had gone ashore to reinforce Fort Brooke following the Dade Massacre, and others continued to take part in the Navy's patrol of the Florida coast. But with the spread of hostilities Henderson concluded that the Corps could do more. In May 1836, he volunteered to muster a regiment of Marines to serve with the army in the Creek campaign. On the twenty-third of the month, President Jackson accepted the offer.

Using the force he maintained at Eighth and Eye as a nucleus, Henderson was able to assemble a four-hundred-man battalion ready to take to the field in just ten days. Washington's *National Intelligencer* must have been almost embarrassing in its praise of the deployment, which it called "another striking evidence of the great value of this arm of the national defense; it has shown itself as prompt to defend its country on the land as on the water." On 1 June, the battalion began its movement to the theater of war with Henderson at its head. As second in command he took his old bête noire, Bvt. Lt. Col. Samuel Miller. Legend holds that Henderson posted a note on his office door: "Gone to fight the Indians. Will be back when the war is over." A second battalion of 160 men drawn from northeastern Navy yards followed within days.

Henderson's battalion spent the summer in a camp named for its commander fifteen miles south of Columbus, Georgia. Despite aggressive patrolling, it failed to make a firm hostile contact before the recalcitrant Creeks were subdued. The second battalion proceeded to Fort Mitchell, Alabama, but was soon transferred to northern Florida. Henderson's battalion joined it there in late August, and the two were consolidated into a six-company regiment that sailed from Apalachicola to Fort Brooke in October. Of the regular troops in Bvt. Maj. Gen. Thomas S. Jesup's Army of the South at the end of November, Leathernecks numbered 18 of 76 officers and 303 of 1,681 NCOs and men.

On 22 January 1837, the army advanced eastward into central Florida from a position near the Dade battleground. Jesup had placed Henderson in command of one of its brigades, a force consisting of a mounted battalion of Alabama volunteers, a battalion of friendly Creeks, and a company of mounted Marines (the original "horse Marines") under Capt. John Harris. On the morning of the twenty-seventh, scouts found numerous Indian signs on the prairies west of Hatcheelustee Creek, not far from today's Disney World. Jesup ordered Henderson's brigade forward to reconnoiter. The result was the only battle in which a serving commandant of the Marine Corps has exercised tactical command.

Henderson's advanced guard soon struck a Seminole camp, capturing five Indian women and children, nineteen runaway slaves, and more than one hundred ponies. The remainder of the Indians had fled into the nearby Big Cypress Swamp. The troops plunged into it after them. As was invariably the case when Seminole camps were taken by surprise, the warriors' only interest was

in delaying the pursuit long enough to allow their families to escape. A quarter of a mile inside the swamp they made a stand behind the Hatcheelustee, a deep creek twenty to twenty-five yards wide bridged by two fallen trees. Henderson deployed his men to the right and left to establish a crossfire on the enemy bank, and Harris and three other officers scrambled across the trunks, followed by their men. Seeing another officer swim the creek, Henderson set out to do the same, but quickly concluded that he had better use a tree trunk.

Deeper inside the Big Cypress the Seminoles made another brief stand. From that point their trail led out of the swamp and through a pine woods before doubling back to reenter the swamp three-quarters of a mile away. Henderson and his men followed. Twice more the warriors paused to exchange fire with their pursuers, breaking contact when the troops came too close. A black family of three was captured shortly after the last of these encounters. By then it was 1600 hours, and Henderson decided to regroup his scattered command.

During the day's fighting, the troops passed the bodies of one Seminole and two blacks. Otherwise, hostile casualties were unknown. All of Henderson's losses were Leathernecks: two dead and four wounded, and all of the wounded soon died. In his after-action report Henderson praised the conduct of his entire command, but he could not resist paying especial tribute to the Marines. "The killed and wounded show where they were," he wrote.

Few Seminoles lost their lives or freedom at the Hatcheelustee, but the battle

In 1840 the *U.S. Military Magazine* published this lithograph of a Marine on sentry duty on the Capitol grounds. The monument behind him, in memory of the Navy officers killed in the War with Tripoli, was later moved to the U.S. Naval Academy. (National Archives)

gave them a considerable shock. Within a week their chiefs entered negotiations that, though ultimately unsuccessful, caused many persons, Jesup and Henderson included, to believe that the war as good as over. Furthermore, Henderson felt that it was time to be getting back to Eighth and Eye. Jesup granted his request with a gracious commendation, and late in May Henderson set out for Washington with four of his six companies. The other two, organized as a little battalion under Samuel Miller, remained at Fort Brooke. In July, Miller was relieved by Capt. William Dulany. Dulany's detachment served in Florida until April 1838.

Marine operations on the Florida mainland were not over, however. In April 1839 the Navy detached the assortment of small craft and open boats being used to patrol the lower peninsula from the West India Squadron and established an autonomous Florida Expedition ("for the Suppression of Indian Hostilities"), promptly dubbed the Mosquito Fleet, based on Tea Table Key. By that date, most of the Seminoles who had not been killed or captured had retired into the watery fastness of the Everglades. Lt. John T. McLaughlin assumed command of the Mosquito Fleet in January 1840 with a fierce determination to penetrate that refuge. The 622 officers and men that his force numbered at peak strength included two companies of Marines, successively commanded by first lieutenants George H. Terrett (who had also served in Henderson's regiment) and Thomas T. Sloan.

Beginning in April 1840, the men of the Mosquito Fleet made numerous expeditions into the Everglades and waterways to the north, frequently in concert with Army units. On 31 December 1840 a party of 150 seamen and Marines under McLaughlin's personal command left Fort Dallas (where downtown Miami now stands) to become the first whites to cross the Everglades, emerging on the Gulf Coast on 19 January 1841. McLaughlin crossed the swamp again in November 1841, and detachments were constantly on patrol between December 1841 and March 1842. Although few Indians were encountered in these forays, many cultivated fields, dwellings, and canoes were destroyed. Losses to hostile action were next to nil, but disease and extreme exertion often incapacitated as many as a quarter of the members of an expedition.

The Seminoles never surrendered, but by May 1842 fewer than four hundred were believed to remain at large. U.S. forces simply suspended operations. Three Marine officers were awarded brevets for their services in

the struggle: Henderson to brigadier general and Harris to major, both for gallant and meritorious conduct, and Dulany to major for meritorious conduct.

The Seminole War was Miller's last campaign. At age seventy, he volunteered for active service upon the outbreak of the Mexican War. By then he had become the Corps' lieutenant colonel, but Henderson decided that he was a little old for field soldiering. The hero of Bladensburg died, still in uniform at eighty, in 1855.

By the start of the Seminole War the U.S. Navy had established six overseas squadrons: the Mediterranean Squadron (reestablished in 1815), the Africa Squadron (1820), the West India Squadron (1821), the Pacific Squadron (1821), the Brazil Squadron (1826), and the East India Squadron (1835). None was very sizeable; at times one might consist of no more than a pair of ships. Nevertheless, they enabled the Navy to act in what contemporaries considered an expeditious manner to protect American commerce, lives, and property—and to retaliate for attacks upon them—in potentially difficult or dangerous parts of the world.

The Navy's nearly global presence was reflected in the geographical range of the landings in which Leathernecks participated from 1835 to 1846. Of these operations, one took place in South America (1835), one in the East Indies (1839), four in the South Pacific (two each in 1840 and 1841), one in the Mexican province of Upper California (1842), five on the west coast of Africa (1843), one in China (1844), and one in Vietnam (1845). Six—in the East Indies, the South Pacific, and one in Africa—were punitive in nature, usually involving an action with native warriors and invariably climaxing in the burning of one or more villages; the others passed off peacefully. All but three were undertaken directly or indirectly in support of American trade. The exceptions were the short-lived seizure of Monterey, California, by the commodore of the Pacific Squadron, Thomas ap Catesby Jones, under the erroneous impression that war had broken out with Mexico (a miscue that cost him his command); a landing in west Africa, where a local tribe was menacing the American black settlement of Liberia; and a confused attempt to rescue a French missionary from his Vietnamese captors.

Catesby Jones had jumped the gun, but three years to the month after he relinquished Monterey, the Marine Corps was represented, in the redoubtable person of 1st Lt. Archibald H. Gillespie, in the onset of the real war with Mexico. In March 1845 Congress voted to annex the Republic of Texas, which Mexico regarded as a wayward province. Whether the outrage this action engendered in Mexico City would result in war was uncertain. Yet the expansionist administration of incoming President James K. Polk was not content with Texas. It also harbored designs on California and a lively apprehension that Britain did the same.

In the fall of 1845, Polk decided on a policy calculated to lead to the acquisition of California without overtly involving his administration in an act of aggression. Americans in the province should secretly be encouraged to revolt against Mexico and discouraged from accepting the protection of any power other than the United States. The

next step was to communicate this policy to the man would presumably be responsible for carrying it out, Thomas O. Larkin, U.S. Consul at Monterey. Of course, instructions could be and were sent by ship, but the long voyage around Cape Horn might take nine months. The fastest way to get a message to California would be for its bearer to make two much shorter voyages by proceeding overland across Mexico from the Gulf port of Veracruz to the Pacific port of Mazatlán. In view of the contents of this particular message, that was not an itinerary for the faint of heart. Lieutenant Gillespie set out on his journey early in November.

Gillespie had received his instructions at a secret meeting with Polk in the White House on 30 October. He was also charged with delivering a packet of personal letters to Army captain John C. Frémont, the son-in-law of powerful Senator Thomas Hart Benton, then leading an exploring expedition to the Pacific. An energetic, red-bearded thirty-three-year-old, Gillespie had served briefly as an enlisted Marine before being commissioned. Nine of his thirteen years' service since then had been spent afloat. He had yet to see combat. How Polk came to select him for this mission is unknown. Gillespie was fluent in Spanish, obviously an important qualification, but other Spanish-speaking officers and officials were available.

Whatever his reasons, the president had made an excellent choice. Traveling in the guise of a salesman for MacDougal Distilleries, Ltd., of Edinburgh, Gillespie crossed Mexico without undue incident—he had prudently burned his instructions after committing them to memory en route to Veracruz—and reached

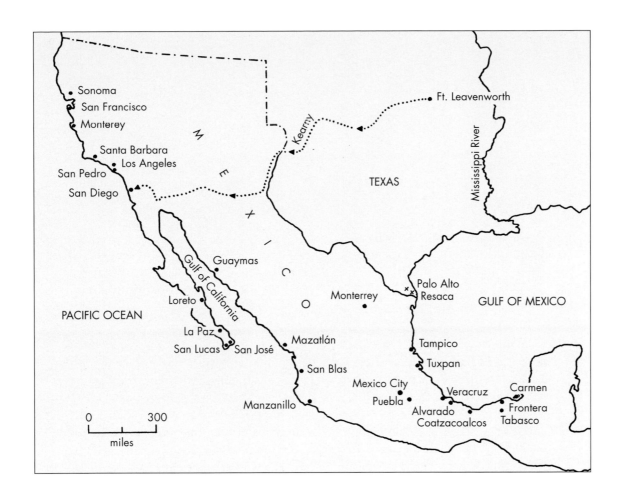

Monterey on 17 April 1846. The ship carrying the duplicate dispatches did not arrive for another three months.

After conferring with Larkin, Gillespie rode north in search of Frémont. They met at Klamath Lake, Oregon, on 9 May. Neither man ever recorded exactly what passed between them, but the course of ensuing events makes clear that Gillespie gave Frémont a briefing on Polk's policy as well as his letters. That night the Marine officer received his baptism of fire in helping to beat off an Indian attack that left three of Frémont's sixty men dead. The next day the party headed south.

American settlers in California were already restive under Mexican rule. The return of Frémont's expedition, which had been ordered out of the province earlier in the year, spurred them to take action. On 4 July, a gathering at Sonoma proclaimed the independence of the Bear Flag Republic. Frémont responded by organizing the California Battalion, 230 men strong.

Gillespie accepted the appointment of captain and second in command.

The critical moment was clearly at hand. As early as 31 May the commander of the Pacific Squadron, ailing old Commo. John D. Sloat, had received unofficial reports that fighting had broken out between U.S. and Mexican forces in Texas, but, mindful of his predecessor's gaffe, he had waited to receive official notification before committing himself. The news that Frémont had thrown in with the Bear Flaggers convinced him he could wait no longer. Between 7 July and 6 August ships of the Pacific Squadron landed parties that peacefully occupied Monterey, San Francisco, Santa Barbara, and San Pedro, peeling off a few Marines to garrison each site, and had deposited the California Battalion at San Diego. On 8 August Frémont advanced on the provincial capital of Los Angeles with 120 men, leaving Gillespie with 50 others to hold San Diego. Three days later vigorous Commo. Robert F. Stockton, who had replaced Sloat on 30 July, marched

out of San Pedro at the head of 360 seamen and Marines bound for the same place. Both forces entered Los Angeles unopposed on 13 August. The handful of Mexican troops nearby surrendered the next day. California had been conquered in less than six weeks.

The conquest came undone just as quickly. Stockton divided California into three military districts. To command the southern district, with headquarters in Los Angeles, he installed Gillespie. This was a mistake. Gillespie's robust administration so antagonized Los Angeles' citizens that they rose in revolt. On 23 September

Gillespie, with sixty Bear Flaggers, found himself besieged by several hundred irate Californians. Six days later he negotiated a capitulation that allowed his command to evacuate the town and march under arms to board ship at San Pedro. The American garrisons also withdrew from Santa Barbara and San Diego.

The first attempt to recapture Los Angeles followed almost at once. During the siege, one of Gillespie's men had slipped through Mexican lines carrying an appeal for help to Monterey. In response, Capt. William Mervine arrived at San Pedro in the frigate *Savannah* on 6 October. Gillespie's garrison was still on board an American merchant ship in the harbor. Mervine decided to launch an immediate counteroffensive. Gillespie urged him not to act rashly. Most native Californians, feeling little love for the Mexican government, had sat out the original occupation, but now they were up in arms. Mervine ignored his advice. The next day 225 seamen and Marines from the *Savannah* marched on Los Angeles. The Leathernecks formed the column's advanced guard; Gillespie's riflemen covered its flanks. On 8 October the Americans encountered some 130 mounted Californians possessed of a field piece, of which they had none. After three charges failed to capture the gun, which the Californians withdrew each time their adversaries approached, Mervine concluded that it was no go. Gillespie's detachment covered the retreat. It was then transported to San Diego.

In succeeding weeks Commodore Stockton made plans for a convergent advance on Los Angeles by a naval force under his command and Frémont's California Battalion. The former would set out from San Diego; the latter, from Santa Barbara. Before the commodore's preparations were completed, a courier reached San Diego with startling news. Brig. Gen. Stephen W. Kearny, whose Army of the West had recently occupied New Mexico, had entered California with an escort of only one hundred dragoons with four guns, having heard that the territory was at peace. In less than two hours, Gillespie was riding east with thirty-nine men to guide Kearny to San Diego.

Gillespie joined Kearny on 5 December. Late that afternoon they learned that a troop of Californian cavalry was camped outside the nearby village of San Pasqual; the next morning, the Americans attacked. Unfortunately, their attack was disjointed, and although the Californians were outnumbered two-to-one, the lances they carried proved far superior to the Americans' swords in the hand-to-hand combat that followed. Gillespie was unhorsed by a thrust that struck him in the back while he was parrying one in the front. Before he could get to his feet, he received another, deeper thrust in the back and a glancing blow to the mouth. He finally escaped from the melee and fired one of the cannons, perhaps as a result of which (as Gillespie insisted) the Californians retired. Nineteen Americans had been killed and fifteen wounded. One Californian was captured and about a dozen wounded. That night another messenger slipped away to San Diego, and on 10 December a relief column reached the battered command.

Meanwhile another apparently unconnected revolt had broken out in the north. To put it down Capt. Ward Marston, twenty-seven years a Marine, marched out of San Francisco with thirty-four Leathernecks, sixty-seven volunteers, and one gun. On 2 January 1847, he defeated a slightly stronger Californian force near Mission Santa Clara. The next morning the Californians' leader appeared under a flag of truce and accepted an armistice that restored peace to the region.

A few days later, Stockton and Kearny fought the decisive battle in the war for California. They had advanced from San Diego with a highly heterogeneous collection of 607 men—Leathernecks, sailors, dismounted dragoons, elements of the California Battalion, and volunteers—on 28 December. The convalescent Gillespie commanded one of the four divisions into which these groups were organized.

On 8 January the column encountered the Californian army, a mounted force of approximately equal strength, posted on high ground beyond the San Gabriel River. The Americans formed square—the standard formation for infantry confronting cavalry—and forded the stream under fire from two guns. Just beyond the bank they unlimbered their own more powerful battery, which soon forced the enemy artillery to withdraw. Its shot also checked a body of 100 to 150 lancers that started toward the left face of the square. Stockton then ordered the advance to resume. While most of the Californians slowly gave ground, the band of lancers who had earlier been repulsed made a wide circuit of the square and charged its rear face, where Gillespie commanded, only to be repulsed by his men's musketry. Still, the Californians were not ready to concede defeat. Half a mile from their original position they rallied and brought their guns back into action. The fire superiority Stockton's artillery again established finally convinced them to call it a day. Both sides had suffered about a dozen casualties.

One more battle remained to be fought. Several hours after breaking camp the next morning the Americans found the Californian army, reduced by desertion to some three hundred men, deployed to oppose their advance across La Mesa, the broad plain south of the Los Angeles River. The action was essentially a repetition of its predecessor, on a smaller scale. The American guns overpowered the Californian artillery, and the lancers who charged the square were stopped eighty yards from its face. The following day, Archibald Gillespie was given the honor of hoisting the same flag he had hauled down in September over Los Angeles' Government House. Frémont reached the town on 14 January. En route he had stopped to negotiate the surrender of the remnant of the Californian army.

Following the reconquest of California, the Navy turned its attention to Baja California and the Pacific coast of Mexico. Beginning in March 1847 parties of seamen and Marines were landed long enough to raise the flag, conclude conventions acknowledging American authority, and/or spike the guns at San José del Cabo, San Lucas, La Paz, and Loreto in Baja, and Guaymas, San Blas, and Manzanillo, Mexico. In July two companies of New York volunteers went ashore from the Pacific Squadron's storeship to occupy La Paz, the capital of Baja California, and in November the Navy seized Mazatlán, Mexico's second-largest port.

None of these operations was opposed, but Baja did not remain quiet. In early November rumors of an impending revolt led to the landing of two dozen Marines under 1st Lt. Charles Heywood at San José. The rumors proved to be true. The New Yorkers beat off three attacks on La Paz that month, and at San José Heywood withstood two sieges, the first from 19 to 21 November 1847 and the second from 22 January to 14 February 1848. An offensive by the reinforced garrison of La Paz crushed the revolt in March. Leathernecks also took part

in four clashes between naval landing parties and Mexican units in and around Guaymas between November 1847 and March 1848.

Despite the vast territory at stake, from a military standpoint the operations in the Californias and on the Pacific coast of Mexico were strictly a sideshow. President Polk expected the war to end not far from where it began, just inside the Rio Grande, with Maj. Gen. Zachary Taylor's victories at Palo Alto and Resaca de la Palma in May 1846. After the receipt of additional transport and reinforcements Taylor advanced into Mexico and captured Monterrey, the capital of Nuevo León, in September. Successes such as these, together with the blockade the Navy's Home Squadron clamped on the Mexican coast, were supposed to convince the enemy that the sensible thing to do was make peace. The Mexicans' refusal to accept that conclusion obliged the Americans to revise their strategy. Apparently it would be necessary to carry the war to Mexico City. For Taylor's army to cross the four hundred miles of difficult, barren terrain separating it from that objective was deemed impractical even by Taylor. His view clinched Polk's decision to

adopt a plan proposed by Maj. Gen. Winfield Scott to execute an amphibious end-run to Veracruz, only two hundred miles east of the Mexican capital, and advance on it from there. In November, the president entrusted Scott with conducting the campaign.

In the meantime, the Home Squadron had launched the first in a series of smaller amphibious operations in which its Leathernecks would see action along the Gulf Coast. Attempts to take Alvarado in August and October failed when the steamers towing the landing party's boats proved unable to cross the bar at the mouth of the Alvarado River. Later in October a force under the squadron's second in command, Vice Commo. Matthew C. Perry, captured Frontera and Tabasco (Villahermosa) on the Tabasco (Grijalva) River, though it did not occupy either. Prior to the expedition, Perry had arranged to have the squadron's guard detachments concentrated in a two-hundred-man landing battalion under Capt. Alvin Edson, the Leatherneck commander at Quallah Battoo. On 14 November the battalion took part in the unopposed occupation of Tampico, the port selected to serve as a base for the assault on Veracruz.

The Home Squadron put Scott's army of eighty-six hundred men ashore in an uncontested landing a few miles south of Veracruz on 9 March 1847. Scott attached Edson's Leathernecks to the 3rd Artillery during the siege of the city, which surrendered on the twenty-seventh. Three days later Congress, somewhat belatedly anticipating the expiration of the one-year enlistments of the many volunteer units serving with Scott, authorized the raising of ten new Army regiments and a wartime increase of twelve officers and a thousand men in the strength of the Marine Corps. Archibald Henderson took this as his cue. Once again, as at the time of the Creek uprising, he volunteered to furnish a Marine regiment to serve with the Army. The president and secretary of war welcomed his overture, and on 21 May the secretary of the Navy authorized the deployment.

A battalion of 22 officers and 324 NCOs and men sailed within a month. In Mexico,

it was to be joined by the Home Squadron's Marine battalion to form a six-company regiment. Henderson, now sixty-four, stayed home this time. As regimental commander he selected Bvt. Lt. Col. Samuel E. Watson, a veteran of thirty-five years in the Corps. The Leathernecks reached Veracruz on 1 July.

During the intervening months, the Home Squadron had been busy buttoning up the Mexican coast. Alvarado was rather embarrassingly captured by a single small gunboat sent ahead of a major expedition at the end of March. Immediately afterward Commodore Perry, who had assumed command of the squadron that month, organized a naval brigade of two thousand men, including Edson's Marines, to be employed in amphibious operations. The Leathernecks and several of the Bluejacket battalions in this force made their first hot landing on 18 April to capture the defended port of Tuxpan.

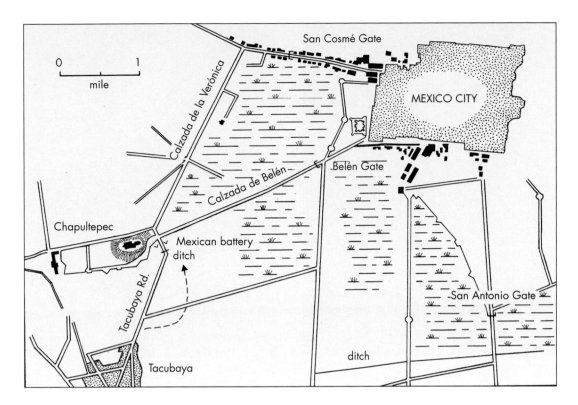

Map 5, right:
The Battle of Chapultepec

No resistance was offered to the seizure of Coatzacoalas and Carmen the following month, but members of the brigade saw action again in June when Perry decided to make a second expedition up the Tabasco River to occupy the town of that name. The Mexicans had strengthened Tabasco's defenses since his last visit by throwing up several additional earthworks along the river below it. At a bluff called Seven Palms, about four miles below the town, Perry landed at the head of 1,173 men with seven guns. The successive Mexican works were either outflanked, stormed, or overcome by ships' fire, and by mid-afternoon and at the cost of five wounded the American flag was floating over Tabasco.

Perry's amphibious interests frustrated Archibald Henderson's designs. Upon the arrival of Watson's battalion at Veracruz, the commodore refused to surrender more than a handful of his squadron's Leathernecks. On 16 July, the battalion that would not become a regiment set off in company of other troops for Puebla, seventy-five miles from Mexico City. Scott had been awaiting replacements for his time-expired men there since mid-May. Joining his army on 6 August, the Marines were assigned to the 4th Division, commanded by Brig. Gen. John A. Quitman, and linked with the 2nd Pennsylvania Volunteers to form a brigade of which Watson was given command. Maj. Levi Twiggs, a burly Georgian who had fought the British, the Creeks, and the Seminoles, took over the Marine battalion. Scott marched on Mexico City the next day.

The American army entered the Valley of Mexico only eight miles southwest of the capital on 17 August. Detailed to guard the baggage train, Quitman's division played no part in the first three battles that followed—Contreras, Churubsco, and Molino del Ray. In the next, it would see all the action its most ardent member could have craved.

On 10 September, three days after Molino del Rey, Scott decided to make a full-scale assault on Chapultepec Castle, which screened Mexico City's western face. Formerly the residence of the Spanish viceroys and now the site of the Mexican military academy, the castle crowned a volcanic outcropping two hundred feet high and eighteen hundred feet long. Both the castle and the ridge itself were enclosed by high stone walls. No intelligence was

available as to the strength of the garrison. In fact, it numbered approximately a thousand, including the military academy cadets.

The operation opened with a day-long bombardment on 12 September. Three of the army's four divisions were to attack the next morning. Brig. Gen. Gideon J. Pillow's 3rd Division from the west, and Quitman's division from the south, along the road extending from the village of Tacubaya. Brig. Gen. William J. Worth's 1st Division would support Pillow. The 2nd Division, commanded by Brig. Gen. David E. Twiggs (a relative of the Marine major) was split in two. One of its brigades was sent to support Quitman while the other staged a demonstration against the southern face of the city. The stakes were high. Wastage and casualties had reduced Scott's army to seventy-two hundred effectives. His opposite number, Gen. Antonio Lopez de Santa Anna, had at least three times as many at his disposal. The Americans could not afford a defeat.

Each of the attack divisions was to be preceded by a storming party. On Scott's orders, Twiggs supplied Quitman with a detachment of 250 men to serve in that capacity. Loath to have his assault spearheaded by strangers, Quitman also organized a second, volunteer storming party from his division, 120 men whom he placed under the command of Major Twiggs. A 40-man pioneer storming party equipped with scaling ladders, pickaxes, and crowbars was entrusted to another Marine, Capt. John G. Reynolds. The Marine battalion, Quitman's only regular unit, was to follow at the head of Watson's brigade and give the storming parties covering fire.

At dawn on 13 September, the American batteries resumed their bombardment. The infantry started forward at 0800. Quitman's storming parties had reached a point about 250 yards from Chapultepec's outer walls when the fire from a battery directly ahead forced them and the Marine battalion to take cover in a ditch that had been dug across the road to impede an advance. As soon as the situation was reported to Quitman, he directed the Pennsylvania regiment and his other brigade to turn off the road before reaching the point where the storming party had been checked and sent the brigade on loan from Twiggs to swing wide to the right to protect his flank. Watson was ordered to hold his position.

A lively firefight between the Marines and soldiers in the ditch and the Mexicans in the battery to their front and the castle grounds to their left continued for some time.

Presently Twiggs, favorite shotgun in hand, climbed out of the ditch onto the roadway, apparently intent on getting things moving. Reynolds joined him. They exchanged a few words and Twiggs was shot through the heart. Reynolds carried his body behind a stone wall. There he found Watson and Bvt. Maj. William Dulany. They were concerned about the expenditure of ammunition. Reynolds urged Watson to renew the advance, but the colonel was unwilling to move without orders.

Meanwhile, Pillow's and Worth's divisions had broken through the Mexican defenses on their front and were storming Chapultepec Castle; the units Quitman had sent to the left had begun entering breaches in the outer wall; and Twiggs' brigade, having completed its swing to the right, was about to envelop the batteries at the end of the Tacubaya road. Quitman now sent the storming party orders to charge.

Captain Terrett had been aching for just such a command. That it did not pertain to the Marines was a detail he dismissed. Without a moment's hesitation, he led his sixty-some officers and men up the road and overran one of the Mexican batteries. The rest of the battalion remained behind, performing its assigned mission of providing the attackers with covering fire. After the charge, it joined Quitman's other units inside the walls of Chapultepec, where it captured some dispirited Mexicans. Terrett took his little company in search of new adventures.

From the northeastern face of Chapultepec two divergent causeways ran toward Mexico City: the Calzada de Belén to the Garita de Belén, a fortified stone police and customs station, and the Calzada de la Verónica to the Garita de San Cosmé, farther north. The Americans called the *garitas* "gates," although neither actually included any such structure. Strangely, Scott's plans did not extend beyond the capture of Chapultepec, and some time passed before the army was ready to exploit its victory. Pillow having been wounded, Quitman enterprisingly attached two of his colleague's regiments to his division. The combined force, including the Marine battalion, then advanced to attack the Belén Gate, which was occupied after heavy fighting at 1320. Six leathernecks were killed and two wounded in the capture and subsequent defense of the work.

At the same time that Quitman's division started down the causeway toward the Belén Gate, Worth's division, reinforced by one of Pillow's brigades, began moving up

The Storming of Chapultepec was painted by an American eyewitness, James Walker, an artist marching with Scott's army. This lithograph of his work was published by the New York firm of Sarony & Major in 1848. (Library of Congress)

the Calzada de la Verónica—along which Terrett's company and a number of small Army detachments led by junior officers with the bit in their teeth were already fighting their way. Terrett would later defend his arguably excessive initiative by stating, "What Colonel Watson's orders were, whether to enter the gate of the Castle or not, I am ignorant, as I did not receive from him any order or direction, and in going forward, deemed I could not be wrong, so long as the Enemy in large numbers were ahead."

In their advance along the causeway, Terrett's men supported three pieces of horse artillery in breaking up a counterattack by Mexican infantry and cavalry. The guns then retired to replenish ammunition, but the Leathernecks pushed ahead, forcing another body of enemy troops to abandon a barricade by turning its flank. Two miles north of Chapultepec, at the point where the causeway met the San Cosmé road, they were halted by an entrenched gun and infantry firing from housetops. Soon they were joined by about two dozen members of

the 4th Infantry, among them 1st Lt. Ulysses S. Grant. Making a reconnaissance to the west of the causeway, Grant discovered that, by moving behind two sides of a walled garden, the Americans could outflank the entrenchment. A company of infantry that had just come up reinforced the movement while the Leathernecks and soldiers who remained in front charged. The Mexicans retreated, and the Americans, in hot pursuit, overran a second barricade halfway between the intersection and the San Cosmé Gate. What happened next is debatable.

According to almost every history of the Corps, the Marines pressed forward from the barricade and seized the San Cosmé Gate, making them the first American troops to set foot in the Mexican capital. Fifteen minutes later, hearing bugles sound the recall, they withdrew. Most works add that Grant's detachment accompanied the Leathernecks on their lunge into the city.

The problem is that these accounts contradict the one contained in Grant's *Memoirs*. According to Grant, the advance

Commodore Perry's Marines parade on the temple grounds at Shimoda, Japan, 8 June 1854. Shimoda was one of the two Japanese ports opened to American ships by the treaty Perry negotiated. Artists Eliphalet Brown and William Heine, from whose work this contemporary lithograph was produced, accompanied the expedition. (R. B. Griffin Collection, Naval Historical Center)

did not proceed beyond the second barricade. The detailed histories of the war written by Roswell S. Ripley and Cadmus M. Wilcox, officers in Scott's army, agree. The undisputed fact that this barricade was abandoned soon after being overrun suggests that somehow it became confused with the San Cosmé Gate. Yet however far Terrett's company advanced, it was far enough for glory.

Worth's division captured (or recaptured) the gate for once and all about 1800 that evening. The Mexican army evacuated the city during the night, and the Americans occupied it the next morning. General Quitman, appointed military governor, sent the Marine battalion to evict a mob of looters that had invaded the Palacio Nacional, and Leatherneck 2nd Lt. A. S. Nicholson became the first man to raise the American flag over the halls of Montezuma.

Prolonged peace negotiations resulted in the signing of the Treaty of Guadalupe Hidalgo on 2 February 1848. The war it officially ended had cost the Corps eleven dead and forty-seven wounded. More than half of these casualties had been suffered at Chapultepec, but there is no truth to the legend that the red stripe that Leathernecks began to wear on their trouser legs not long afterwards is a "blood stripe" to commemorate the losses there.

Shortly after the Marines returned to Washington, the capital's citizens presented the Corps with a handsome new flag featuring an eagle and anchor, with a motto that would, with a little editing, become famous: "From Tripoli to the halls of Montezuma." No fewer than twenty-seven Marine officers earned brevets for the

Mexican War, fourteen of them at Chapultepec. Archibald Gillespie received not one but two brevets, captain for the defense of Los Angeles and major for San Gabriel. He resigned his commission in ill health in 1854, settled in (where else?) California, and died in San Francisco in 1873.

In the following decade Marines took part in more than twenty landings abroad and one at home. The latter occurred in January 1856, when the sloop-of-war *Decatur* sent her guard and some seamen ashore to drive off a band of Indians that was threatening the little settlement at Seattle, Washington. This action turned out to be the Leathernecks' last experience of Indian fighting.

Seven of the foreign landings occurred in Central and South America. Six were made to protect American lives and property during revolutions or riots—at Buenos Aires, Argentina (twice in 1852); Greytown (now San Juan del Sur), Nicaragua (1853); Montevideo, Uruguay (1855 and 1858); and Panama City, in what was then New Granada (1856). Aside from a skirmish with a mob of looters in Buenos Aires in February 1852, the only deployment to involve the use of force was the bombardment and destruction of Greytown by the sloop-of-war *Cyane* on 13 July 1854 in retaliation for the refusal of municipal authorities to make amends for having forcibly detained the U.S. ambassador overnight.

All the other landings occurred in or across the Pacific. Six officers and two hundred men served in the East India Squadron during Commodore Perry's momentous expedition to open relations with Japan. Aware that his reception would

depend in part on the show he put on, Perry used his Marines to help create a scene of martial pageantry in his meetings with Japanese officials at Uraga in July 1853 and Yokohama in March 1854. At the latter the entire squadron's guard detachments were organized into a battalion under Perry's senior Marine officer, Bvt. Maj. Jacob Zeilin. The Japanese were highly impressed by the Leathernecks' precision drill.

The following year reports of the mistreatment of American traders in the Fiji Islands prompted Cdr. E. B. Boutwell to proceed there in the sloop of war *John Adams*. Lt. John L. Broome's Marine guard took part in each of the four landings Boutwell ordered in September and October 1855. The first three eventuated in peaceful palavers or demonstrations intended to induce the islanders to mend their ways. The fourth was a return visit to Vitia Levu, where King Tui Viti had reneged on the engagements into which he had been dragooned. It eventuated in a brisk little battle and the burning of three villages.

Marines made four landings in China, then in the throes of the great Taiping Rebellion. When in April 1854

government troops began to encroach on the International Settlements at Shanghai, the sloop of war *Plymouth* landed 60 seamen and Marines, who together with 150 of their British counterparts and 37 American and British volunteers dispersed the interlopers at the cost of a dozen casualties. A recurrence of the threat to the settlements led to the landing of the frigate *Powhatan*'s Leathernecks in May 1855, but on this occasion there was no fighting. That August, the *Powhatan* collaborated with HMS *Rattler* in a boat attack on a Chinese pirate fleet in Ty-Ho Bay, near Hong Kong. Seventeen junks were captured in a day's combat. By a grim coincidence, the allied forces each lost two Marines and two Bluejackets killed in action. The appreciative British commemorated the outcome of the foray by erecting a granite monument in Hong Kong's Happy Valley.

The final action in Chinese waters involved the heaviest fighting in which Marines had engaged since the Mexican War. On 15 November 1856 the Barrier Forts on the Pearl River below Canton—four modern, granite-faced works designed by European engineers—began firing on ships and boats of the East India Squadron, apparently

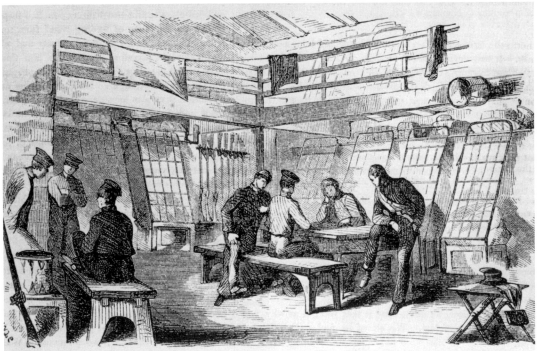

in an outburst of xenophobia inspired by difficulties with the British. The next day, the 20-gun *Plymouth* returned the compliment. Neither her shot nor an attempt to open negotiations produced any effect, and on 19 November her captain, Cdr. Andrew Hull Foote, the senior officer present, resolved to storm the forts. A landing party had already been organized from the seamen and Marines of the *Plymouth*, the 22-gun sloop of war

Levant, and the frigate *San Jacinto*, which remained downstream at Whampoa. Early the following morning, while the *Plymouth* and *Levant* laid down covering fire, Foote led its 287 men ashore. The Marine contingent numbered 2 officers and 50 men under Bvt. Capt. John D. Simms.

By the afternoon of 22 November, the landing party had captured the four Barrier Forts and their 176 guns, plus a 6-gun

battery, and repulsed three counterattacks by 3,000 Chinese troops from Canton. American casualties were 7 dead and 22 wounded, 6 of the latter being Marines. Foote estimated Chinese losses to be about 250. Simms' men played a conspicuous role in all three days' fighting, spearheading the advance on the forts—in two of which the Leathernecks' standard bearer, Cpl. William McDougal, was the first man to plant the American flag—capturing the battery, and beating off two of the Chinese counterattacks. "It may be seen," Foote wrote in his after-action report, ". . . how efficient our marines are in the services of this kind; and the inference is inevitable that an increase of . . . the number of officers and men attached to our ships, would tend to insure success in like expeditions."

Despite the passing of the years, Henderson's warrior spirit remained keen as ever. He displayed it once again during the election-day riots in Washington on 1 June 1857. The Know-Nothing Party, a violence-prone populist group, had imported a gang of Baltimore hoodlums called the Plug-Uglies to take control of the city's polling places. The Plug-Uglies brought with them a brass cannon. When the police were unable to preserve order,

Mayor William Magruder asked President James Buchanan to call in the Marines from Eighth and Eye. A two-company battalion under Capt. Henry B. Tyler, the Corps' adjutant and inspector, marched to the city hall. Henderson accompanied the detachment in civilian clothes.

On their way through the city, the Marines encountered a mob of Plug-Uglies. The rioters followed them, dragging along the cannon and shouting threats. From the city hall the mayor accompanied the battalion to one of the polls that had been forced to close. Upon reaching the scene, the Leathernecks halted and ordered arms. The Plug-Uglies responded by trundling their cannon forward and sending a party to tell Tyler that they would open fire unless his force withdrew at once. At that moment, seventy-four-year old Henderson stepped forward to block the cannon's mouth with his body. "Men," he said, "you had better think twice before you fire this piece at the Marines."

To take up the account in the next day's *Washington Star*:

[Henderson] informed the crowd that the [Marines'] pieces were loaded with ball cartridge, and warned them repeatedly;

warned the citizens to leave the spot. The general, finding that the piece would be fired unless captured immediately, crossed over to Captain Tyler, and gave the order for ten or fifteen Marines to take it. During this time a number of pistol-shots were fired at General Henderson, some of the parties standing within a few feet of him. One platoon charged the piece on the run. Those in charge of the piece instantly retreated, and a dozen or more revolvers were discharged at the platoon, which had laid hold of the gun and were taking it away. . . .

A man ran up to the general within two feet of his person, and was about to discharge his pistol, when a private with his musket struck his arm causing the weapon to fall; at the same time the general seized the villain and marched him off to the mayor, into whose hands he placed him. The pistol-shots now rattled around like hailstones, and the officers had great difficulty in restraining their men from returning the fire. General Henderson and all the officers were constantly admonishing the men not to fire until the order was given.

Nevertheless, the Marines—sixty of them green recruits—finally did fire before the order was given. The *Star* reported that the men reached the breaking point after several

Top: The 1859 *Uniform Regulations of the United States Marine Corps* were illustrated by a series of colored plates produced by Charles Desilver of Philadelphia. This one shows the summer dress uniforms authorized for the Corps' officers. From left to right: colonel commandant, major, captain, and first lieutenant. (Marine Corps Art Collection)

Bottom: Another plate depicted the officers' duty uniforms. From left to right: lieutenant colonel, captain, first lieutenant, and second lieutenant. The captain's red shoulder sash indicates that he is serving as officer of the day. (Marine Corps Art Collection)

Top: Desilver posed the figures displaying the Corps' enlisted uniforms aboard ship. From left to right: first sergeant, corporal, private, and private in undress uniform. (Marine Corps Art Collection)

Bottom: The Marine Corps Band's distinctive uniforms were also illustrated. From left to right: sergeant major, chief musician, drum major, and musician. (Marine Corps Art Collection)

An artist for the *Illustrated London News* sketched these officers and men aboard the U.S. steam frigate *Susquehanna* in 1857. Four of the figures are Marines accoutered according to the regulation of 1839. From left to right: private, undress; corporal, dress, with the cap and eagle-and-anchor cap device adopted in 1846; another enlisted man, viewed from the rear; two Navy officers; and a Marine officer wearing an undress coat and fatigue cap, with the thin scarlet trouser stripe authorized in 1849. (Beverly R. Robinson Collection, U.S. Naval Academy Museum)

had been struck by stones and a private received "a dreadful wound" from a shot in the face. Conversely, a Marine officer present insisted that discipline had held firm and the firing resulted from a misunderstanding; seeing the private shot, Mayor Magruder cried out, "Why don't you fire?" and the men had taken the last word as a command.

Although the volley sent the Plug-Uglies scuttling down the street in disarray, they soon stopped to regroup. Scattered shots continued to ring out, and presently a Marine was hit in the shoulder. Tyler then ordered the battalion to prepare to fire. That was sufficient. The Plug-Uglies took to their heels.

The remainder of the era of Archibald Henderson passed quietly. Following the election-day riot no Leatherneck fired another shot in anger until October 1858, when forty seamen and Marines from the sloop-of-war *Vandalia* landed on Waya in the Fiji Islands to avenge the murder of two American traders. Exactly three months later, on 6 January 1859, Archibald Henderson returned home from headquarters and lay down on the sofa for his afternoon nap. He never awakened. His funeral was attended by President Buchanan and the members of the cabinet.

This time there was no struggle for the succession. Only two days after Henderson's death, the president appointed sixty-eight-year-old Lt. Col. John Harris commandant. The Corps' senior officer, Harris had been commissioned in 1814, led the horse Marines at Hatcheelustee, commanded a Marine battalion sent to Mexico too late to engage in hostilities, and spent twenty years at sea. Unfortunately, by 1859 the fire had gone out of his belly. Indeed, it had ebbed as early as 1847, when the prospect of being ordered to Mexico to serve under an officer of the same rank led him to advise Henderson that "I would rather stay at home than go second to an officer of my own grade. . . . I have no desire to go," although "if you think the good of the service requires it, I shall not hesitate to do so."

Nonetheless, Harris' devotion to the good of the service remained strong. In less troubled times, he might have made an unexceptionable if unenterprising commandant, but he was hardly the man to lead the Corps through the national convulsion that broke out two years later. Symbolic of the change at Eighth and Eye, the uniform regulations of 1859 replaced the Mameluke saber Henderson had authorized for wear by Marine officers and NCOs in 1826 with the straight sword carried by their counterparts in the U.S. infantry.

CHAPTER 5

Marines in Blue and Gray, 1859–1865

While Archibald Henderson was creating a professional Marine Corps, the nation it served drifted toward civil war. The Corps played a key role in a harbinger of the bloodbath to come when the abolitionist John Brown and twenty-one followers seized the federal arsenal at Harpers Ferry, Virginia, before dawn on 16 October 1859. Brown believed that his action would spark a slave uprising. Events revealed his error. There was no uprising, the townsmen and the militia sprang somewhat gingerly to arms, and after a few fusillades in which men died on both sides, the raiders withdrew into the arsenal's sturdy brick firehouse. With them they took eleven hostages, including Col. Lewis Washington, a great-grandnephew of the first president.

Virginia's governor John Letcher requested federal assistance the next morning. The nearest regular troops were the Marines at Eighth and Eye, and that afternoon the officer of the day, thirty-five-year-old 1st Lt. Israel C. Greene, set out with eighty-six NCOs and men and two 12-pounder howitzers on the train to Harpers Ferry. Handpicked by Archibald Henderson to add an artillery course to the instruction given at Marine Barracks, Washington, Greene was one of the Corps' best and brightest. Accompanying him in an advisory capacity was Maj. William W. Russell, the Corps' paymaster, who had fought in the Mexican War, but as a staff officer lacked command authority.

Reaching Harpers Ferry around midnight, the Marines met the Army officer who had been put in command of the operation, Col. Robert E. Lee, and his aide, 1st Lt. J. E. B. Stuart. At sunrise, Lee moved to bring the incident to a close. Stuart approached the firehouse under a white flag with a note from Lee calling on Brown to surrender. When Brown refused, Greene led a storming party of twelve Marines forward to break down the building's sturdy double doors. After failing to make an impression with sledgehammers, they used a ladder as a battering ram to punch a hole through which a stooping man could scramble. To reduce the danger to the hostages, Lee had ruled out the use of firearms; the Leathernecks would rely on cold steel.

Greene, sword in hand, was the first man inside. Close behind him came Russell, unarmed except for his rattan cane. The third man to enter the building, Pvt. Luke Quinn, was mortally wounded by a bullet through the stomach. The next, Pvt. Matthew Ruppert, was shot in the face.

Meanwhile, Greene had reached the rear of the firehouse and encountered Colonel Washington, who pointed out a kneeling figure in the act of reloading a carbine as John Brown. Greene slashed at the man's head. Brown tried to dodge the blow and was sent sprawling when it sliced into the back of his neck. Greene followed with a thrust at Brown's heart, but the point of his dress sword failed to penetrate and the blade bent double. Only then did he see that Brown was unconscious. Two other raiders were impaled on the fixed bayonets of the Marines who had continued to plunge through the shattered door, and the survivors surrendered. None of the hostages had been harmed. Greene noted that the entire action had taken not quite three minutes.

Tried and convicted of treason, John Brown was hanged at Charleston, Virginia, on 2 December 1859; nevertheless, as the "Battle Hymn of the Republic" put it, his spirit went marching on. The raid on Harper's Ferry did nothing to improve relations between North and South, and in

November 1860 the election of Abraham Lincoln, whom many Southerners regarded as a closet abolitionist, brought the sectional crisis to a head. On 20 December 1860, South Carolina became the first state to secede from the Union. Six others joined it to form the Confederate States of America by 12 April 1861, the day the bombardment of Fort Sumter signified the commencement of the Civil War. Four more states, including Virginia, seceded between that date and June in reaction to President Lincoln's call for seventy-five thousand volunteers to suppress the rebellion.

On 2 November 1860 the Marine Corps had numbered 63 officers, 252 noncommissioned officers, 113 musicians, and 1,347 privates, for an aggregate of 1,775 men, slightly more than 10 percent of the strength of the regular Army. Almost a third of the officers cast their lot with the Confederacy, but hardly any of the Corps' other ranks imitated their example. Nevertheless, there were few old hands available for the battalion Colonel Harris consigned with "feelings of great anxiety"

to the Union army that marched south from Washington to win the war on 15 July 1861. The battalion commander, Maj. John G. Reynolds, was at age sixty a seasoned campaigner with service dating back to the Seminole War, but of his 11 officers and 342 men, only a handful had been in uniform for any length of time and fewer still had ever heard a shot fired in anger. Among the exceptions was Bvt. Maj. Jacob Zeilin, who volunteered to take command of one of Reynolds' four companies. Acutely aware that he was leading green troops, Reynolds took advantage of every halt during the advance into Virginia to exercise them in battalion drill and the manual of arms.

Six days later, fate placed the Marine battalion at the very fulcrum of the Battle of Bull Run, on the rolling terrain of the Henry House Hill, where the Union advance was halted by a brigade commanded by a certain Thomas J. Jackson, ever afterward known as "Stonewall." The guns of Griffin's battery, which the Leathernecks had been directed to support, changed hands three times in the seesaw struggle that ensued. Major Reynolds' drills had not been in vain. Each time the Marines were pushed off the hill, they obeyed their officers' orders to rally and return to the fight. Finally, around 1600, two fresh Confederate brigades broke the deadlock, and the Union army went streaming back toward Washington. Even then, about two-thirds of Reynolds' men remained in the ranks until they reached the bridge over Cub Run. There the combination of Confederate artillery fire, a bottleneck formed by abandoned vehicles, and rumors of advancing cavalry sparked a contagious panic; like the Army

units around it, the Marine battalion dissolved. Late that night, Major Reynolds led seventy men he had waited to collect at the Long Bridge over the Potomac back to Eighth and Eye.

In his report to Secretary of the Navy Gideon Welles, Colonel Harris declared that Bull Run was "the first instance recorded in [the Corps'] history where any portion of members turned their backs to the enemy." Although Harris was clearly chagrined, Reynolds felt that for a force composed largely of raw recruits, his battalion had fought well, a contention its casualties—forty-four killed, wounded, or

missing—would tend to support. Major Zeilin was among the wounded.

Bull Run was the only overland campaign in which the U.S. Marine Corps fought during the Civil War. All its other field service occurred within the naval and amphibious framework of the strategy known as the Anaconda Plan. This plan called upon the Navy to isolate the agrarian South from the industry of the outside world by blockading its coast and closing its ports and, in conjunction with the army, to cut it in two by seizing control of the Mississippi River. For its part, the Army was to maintain a relentless pressure on the Confederate land frontiers.

A month after Bull Run, Marines participated in the landing at Hatteras Islet, North Carolina, the first of the advanced bases established to support the blockade. This detachment consisted of ships' guards, but in September Flag Officer Samuel F.

Du Pont, who had learned the value of Leatherneck landing parties during the Mexican War, requested the assignment of an integral battalion to an expedition being organized under his command to seize another advanced base at Port Royal Sound, South Carolina. Accordingly, Harris furnished a battalion of 347 men under the indefatigable Major Reynolds. The expedition sailed from Hampton Roads, Virginia, on 29 October 1861. Three days later, the transport carrying the Marines sank in a storm. Although all but 7 of them survived, none reached Port Royal in time to aid in its capture. Anticlimax continued to dog the battalion in succeeding months. Sent to attack Fernandina, Florida, in March 1862, the battalion arrived to find that the city had already surrendered. The same thing happened two weeks later at St. Augustine, and at the end of the month the battalion was disbanded.

Its misadventures notwithstanding, the battalion's mere existence appeared to augur a significant role for the U.S. Marine Corps in the amphibious operations instrumental to the Anaconda Plan. The appearance proved deceptive. Of the five Marine battalions that saw amphibious service after the Port Royal expedition, all except one were improvised by combining a squadron's guard detachments for a specific undertaking, at the conclusion of which they returned to their ships.

Four other battalions were assembled for miscellaneous duties ashore. One took over the security of the recently recaptured Norfolk Navy Yard in May 1862. Seven months later, another was sent to establish a Marine barracks at Mare Island Navy Yard near San Francisco, California. Small battalions were also included in the naval brigades deployed by the Brooklyn Navy Yard to help maintain order during the draft riots of July 1863, and by the Philadelphia Navy Yard to guard the railroad bridge at Havre de Grace, Maryland, at the time of Gen. Jubal Early's raid in July 1864.

The battalion ordered to California, 112 officers and men under Maj. Addison Garland, underwent the Corps' most embarrassing Civil War experience. On 7 December 1862, Capt. Raphael Semmes' Confederate cruiser *Alabama* captured the entire unit aboard an unarmed passenger steamer off the east end of Cuba. Semmes had the Marines sign paroles—promises not to bear arms against the Confederacy until properly exchanged—and sent them on their way. (The insult did not go unavenged. In June 1864 a sergeant's guard participated in the engagement in which the *Alabama* was sunk by the USS *Kearsarge*.)

The limited role the Corps played in the war was to an extent dictated by its numbers, despite the fact that they were doubled soon after the outbreak of hostilities. On 25 July 1861 Congress raised the Corps' manning level to 93 officers and 3,074 men, and later President Lincoln took advantage of an existing law allowing the chief executive to substitute Marines for landsmen aboard naval vessels to increase its authorized strength by another 1,000 men. At the height of the Union naval effort in 1864, however, Marine guards served in a hundred ships and provided security at nine navy yards. Such commitments would have made it difficult to maintain a sizeable amphibious force.

At the same time, Harris and his senior officers continued to view the Corps' primary mission as the performance of the same shipboard duties it had fulfilled in the War of 1812. If the lengthening range of rifled cannon threatened to eliminate the opportunity to deliver small arms' fire during naval engagements, the growing interest in ramming tactics promised to preserve it. Furthermore, the Corps had already established a fallback position, a Navy general order of June 1859 having authorized guard detachments to man some of their ships' big guns. The institutional weakness of this expedient was that it merely duplicated an activity performed mainly by seamen. For Marines to serve as gunners was a task; it was not a reason for being.

In contrast, the Confederate States Marine Corps soon formed a battalion that served as both a key component of the defenses of Richmond and a source of immediately deployable detachments for operations elsewhere. Though this unit's inception owed to accident rather than design, its retention led Ralph W. Donnelly, the pioneer historian of the CSMC, to conclude that "in many ways, the Confederate States Marine Corps was the true connecting link between the Marine philosophy of Commandant Archibald Henderson and the U.S. Marine Corps of today."

The grayback Corps was established by the Confederate Congress at Montgomery, Alabama, on 16 March 1861. This legislation provided for a Corps of six companies, each to consist of a captain, a first and second lieutenant, eight noncommissioned officers, two musicians, and one hundred men. On 20 May 1861, following the Confederate capital's removal to Richmond, another act increased its strength to 46 officers and 944 NCOs and men—the equivalent of a ten-company regiment—including a headquarters composed of a colonel commandant, a lieutenant colonel, a major, an adjutant, a paymaster and a quartermaster (all holding staff rank as major), a sergeant major, a quartermaster sergeant, and two principal musicians. Finally, an act of 24 September 1862 authorized another forty NCOs and forty more musicians. Probably as a result of recruiting laws that favored the Confederate Army, the Corps never attained its prescribed strength and peaked in 1864 at about six hundred officers and men.

A nucleus of trained officers was available in former members of the U.S.

Marine Corps. Of the sixty-three officers on active duty in early 1861, twenty "went South" in the course of the year. Nineteen took commissions in the Confederate Corps; the twentieth entered the Army. Their loss was even more damaging to the USMC than their numbers would suggest, for they included a disproportionate share of its ablest officers. Among them were its adjutant and inspector, Maj. Henry B. Tyler, a veteran of thirty-eight years' service; the commander of Marine Barracks, Washington, Capt. George H. Terrett, who had stolen the show at Chapultepec; three officers who, like him, had won brevets for gallantry in the Mexican War—captains Algernon A. Taylor and Robert Tansill, and Bvt. Capt. John D. Simms Jr., who had commanded the Marines in the assault on the Barrier Forts; and 1st Lt. Israel Greene of Harpers Ferry fame.

Tyler became the Confederate Corps' lieutenant colonel. Terrett was appointed its major of the line, and as such held its principal operational command throughout the conflict. Taylor became its quartermaster, Simms its senior company commander, and Greene its adjutant. Only Tansill jumped ship, resigning from the Corps in February 1862 to enter the Confederate Army, in which he attained the rank of colonel. Tyler and Terrett served stints of detached duty as acting brigadier generals in the Army, as did another former U.S. Marine, Capt. John R. F. Tatnall. Tatnall seems to have spoken for all three when he declared that he would rather command a company of Marines than a brigade of volunteers.

From the first to last, a total of fifty-eight officers accepted commissions in the Confederate States Marine Corps. Ironically, the thirty-nine with no prior Marine experience included its colonel commandant, Lloyd J. Beall. A West Point graduate (class of 1830), he probably

owed his position to an old acquaintance with President Jefferson Davis, another West Pointer (class of 1828) and onetime regimental comrade in the 1st Infantry. Beall had subsequently transferred to the 2nd Dragoons, but in 1844 he accepted a staff appointment as a paymaster major, the rank he resigned in 1861. The management of the Confederate Marine Corps indicates that he was a capable administrator. In operational matters, it seems probable that he relied on the advice of Terrett and Greene.

Other than its commandant, only three men who had not belonged to the U.S. Marine Corps were commissioned above the rank of lieutenant in the Confederate States Marine Corps: Richard T. Allison, a former U.S. Navy paymaster appointed its paymaster major; and two of its original captains, Reuben T. Thom, who had served as an infantry officer in the Mexican War, and Alfred C. Van Benthuysen, the Confederate Marine Corps' most colorful character. Just twenty-four when he raised one of its first three companies, Van Benthuysen had already fought in the Taiping Rebellion in China in 1857–58 and served as a staff officer with Garibaldi's Red Shirts in the Italian campaign of 1860. Amiability was not among his virtues. Twice in 1862 courts-martial sentenced him to be dismissed from the Corps in consequence of altercations with brother officers, once while in his cups. On both occasions his punishment was commuted to suspension from duty and pay. That he was a nephew-in-law of President Davis could not have hurt him. But he was a fighter, and in 1864 he commanded the Confederate Leathernecks in one of their finest hours.

The remaining thirty-five officers were commissioned as first or second lieutenants. Among them was Archibald Henderson's son Richard, who had been practicing law in Washington at the approach of war. All except eight of the officers had served as enlisted men in the Confederate Army, but none came from the ranks of the Confederate Marine Corps. Not a single Confederate Marine officer was killed in action, but up to the fall of Richmond,

twelve company-grade officers had been wounded or captured—in four cases, both—for a casualty rate slightly in excess of 20 percent. Seven other officers were dismissed, four as a result of what was politely termed intemperance, and one deserted.

The Confederate Marine Corps enlisted its first men at Montgomery in late March 1861. Recruiting then moved to New Orleans, and by late July three companies (A, B, and C) had been raised and concentrated at Pensacola, where Confederate forces ashore and Union troops on Santa Rosa Island were exchanging occasional artillery bombardments and raiding one another's shipping. In addition, the Corps had furnished guard detachments for the commerce raider *Sumter*, which ran the blockade of the Mississippi River on 30 June, and the river defense gunboat *McRae*. Confederate Marines had also seen their first action, fifty-five men under Captain Thom having taken part in an expedition (5–9 July) that occupied Ship Island in the

gulf below Biloxi, Mississippi, and drove away a Union blockader.

The concentration at Pensacola proved short-lived. In September, Company A was ordered to Savannah; in November, Company C was sent to Norfolk; and in February 1862, Company B went to Mobile. Captain Thom's Company C drew the most eventful assignment: to provide guards for the principal vessels of the James River Squadron, the wooden gunboats *Patrick Henry* and *Jamestown* and the ironclad ram *Virginia*, which was being built on the hull of the U.S. frigate *Merrimack*.

All three ships carried Marine guards into the two days' Battle of Hampton Roads on 8–9 March 1862. Fifty-four Marines under Captain Thom served in the *Virginia;* twenty-four under 1st Lt. Richard Henderson (the commandant's son) in the *Patrick Henry;* and twenty under 1st Lt. James R. Y. Fendall in the *Jamestown.* In the first day's action, an attack on the wooden ships of the blockading squadron anchored in the roads, the *Virginia* rammed and sank the sloop-of-war *Cumberland* and destroyed the frigate *Congress* with shell fire. Returning the next morning intent on adding the grounded frigate *Minnesota* to her score, she encountered the USS *Monitor*, which had arrived on the scene around midnight. The two ironclads then fought to a draw in the first battle between ships of their kind.

Thom commanded two of the *Virginia*'s eight broadside guns on both days. What part his men played is unclear. A militia unit manned one of Thom's guns, so it seems reasonable to assume that the other was served by some of his Marines. In any case, Thom's conduct earned the approbation of the *Virginia*'s commander, Flag Officer Franklin Buchanan, a hard man to please. In his report of the first day's battle, Buchanan wrote, "The Marine Corps was well represented by Captain Thom, whose tranquil mien gave evidence that the hottest fire was no novelty to him."

Thom was not the only Marine officer commended for his conduct at Hampton Roads. Both the Union ships destroyed the first day carried guard detachments, and twenty-two-year-old Capt. Charles Heywood, whose father had defended San José del Cabo, fired the sinking *Cumberland*'s last shot. Her captain's report that Heywood's "bravery . . . won my highest applause" prompted the Corps to award the young officer the brevet of major. Fourteen of his forty-four Leathernecks went down with the ship. The *Congress*' guard, sixty-two strong, suffered nine casualties.

The *Virginia* and her consorts returned to Hampton Roads to offer battle on several occasions in April and May. The *Monitor* had orders to stand on the defensive, however, and the ironclads did not meet again before the approach of Union troops compelled the Confederates to evacuate Norfolk on 9 May. Efforts to lighten the *Virginia* enough to allow her to withdraw up the James River were unavailing. Early the next morning, her officers blew her up to keep her from being captured.

By that date, Capt. Julius E. Meiere, a prewar U.S. Marine at whose November 1860 wedding President-elect Lincoln cut the cake, had succeeded Captain Thom in command of Company C, and a second company of Confederate Leathernecks had reached Norfolk, Captain Van Benthuysen's Company B having been transferred from Mobile in March. These units' retreat upstream ended at a steep promontory on the south bank of the James River seven miles below Richmond, where an artillery captain named Augustus Drewry had just emplaced three guns to oppose a Union advance up the river. Situated at the start of one of the many bends through which the James twists toward the city, Drewry's Bluff offered its defenders a picture-perfect field of fire for a mile straight downstream. The Confederates quickly set about enhancing the position's natural strength. Army engineers threw up earthworks on its crest while members of the James River Squadron manhandled five of their ships' guns up the slope to reinforce Drewry's battery and sank the *Jamestown* and several smaller vessels to obstruct the river channel.

A Union squadron consisting of the ironclads *Galena* and *Monitor* and three

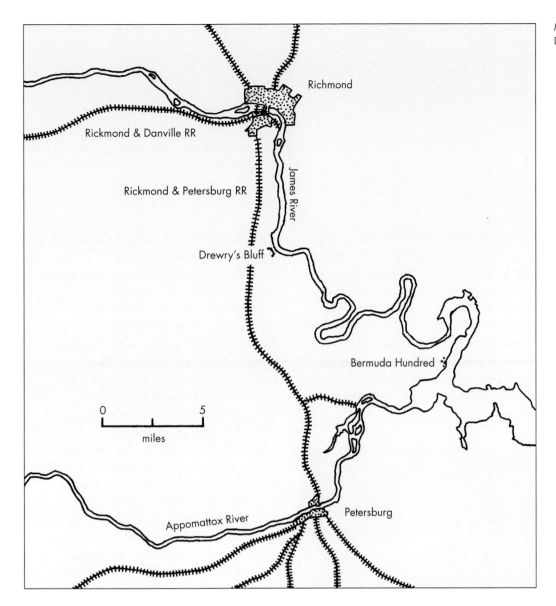

Richmond

Rickmond & Danville RR

Rickmond & Petersburg RR

James River

Drewry's Bluff

Bermuda Hundred

0   5

miles

Appomattox River

Petersburg

gunboats appeared below the bluff at about 0730 on 15 May. The gunboats halted at a respectful distance, but the *Galena*, followed by the *Monitor*, closed to approximately six hundred yards, anchored to present her broadside to the battery, and began returning its fire. At the same time, Confederate riflemen in pits on both sides of the river started sniping at anyone who showed himself above her bulwarks. The Marines, organized as a little battalion under Captain Simms, occupied a line of bluffs only two hundred yards from the nearest Union vessels. "We immediately opened a sharp fire on them," Simms reported, "killing three of the crew of the Galena certainly, and no doubt many more. The fire of the enemy was

materially silenced at intervals by the fire of our troops."

It soon became evident their elevation gave the gunners on the bluff an advantage over their opponents on the river below. The Union ironclads nevertheless maintained the contest for almost four hours. In its course, Cpl. James Mackie, commanding the *Galena*'s guard detachment, became the first Marine to earn the Medal of Honor, which was established in December 1861 to reward enlisted members of the sea services for extraordinary heroism in the line of duty. In the words of his citation, "As enemy shell fire raked the deck of his ship, Corporal Mackie fearlessly maintained his musket fire against the rifle pits along the shore and, when ordered to fill vacancies at guns by men wounded and killed in action, manned the weapon with skill and courage." But bravery could not cancel ballistics. By 1300, the thin-skinned *Galena* had taken more than forty hits, thirteen of which pierced her armor. Thirty-three of her crewmen had been killed or wounded, and she was almost out of ammunition. The Union ships retired.

Without at first realizing it, the Confederate Marine Corps had found a home at Drewry's Bluff, which now became a naval link in the chain of defenses around Richmond. Company A was ordered there from Savannah a few months after the battle, joining B and C to form a three-company battalion under Major Terrett. This force remained in being throughout the war. The Marines at Camp Beall, as their bivouac came to be called, spent the summer of 1862 under canvas, but at the approach of winter the colonel commandant obtained funds enabling them to build cabins. The Confederate States Naval Academy opened aboard the *Patrick Henry* on the James in October 1863, and Drewry's Bluff quickly acquired the amenities of an established naval station, with married quarters, flowered walks, kitchen gardens, a post office, a chapel, and a cemetery.

For the Confederate Corps, Camp Beall served much of the purpose Archibald Henderson had envisioned for Marine Barracks, Washington, maintaining a force in readiness for instant deployment and providing training and orientation (including spit and polish) to newly joined officers. "Everything is so different from the Vol. Army to which I have been accustomed," wrote one such officer, 2nd Lt. Ruffin Thomson, in a letter to his dear pa. "Here all the formalities & etiquette of the Regular Service are rigidly enforced."

Meanwhile, the implementation of the Anaconda Plan had brought about the war's greatest naval action—the Battle of New Orleans. Marines of both navies took part. All told, there were 333 U.S. Marines in guard detachments serving in the ships of Flag Officer David Glasgow Farragut's fleet when, on the night of 23–24 April 1862, it fought its way up the Mississippi past forts Jackson and St. Philip and smashed the Southern naval forces beyond them, breaching the defenses of the Confederacy's most populous city and principal port. Twenty-seven Marines were killed or

wounded in the engagement, and three of their officers received brevet promotions. The Confederate States Marine Corps was represented by a sergeant's guard of about twenty men aboard the gunboat *McRae*. The detachment appears to have been taken prisoner after its ship sank as a result of battle damage a few days later.

Anchoring off New Orleans on 26 April, Farragut sent officers ashore to demand the city's surrender. When three days of meetings with local authorities produced no result, he directed his fleet marine officer, Capt. John L. Broome, to form a landing battalion. Together with a detachment of seamen, Broome's battalion formally took possession of the city on the twenty-ninth. An army of occupation began to arrive on 1 May.

The Battle of New Orleans marked the end of the Confederate Marines' participation in the Mississippi campaigns. In contrast, U.S. Marine guards continued to see action along the river until the fall of

Vicksburg in July 1863 cut the Confederacy in half. Later still, guard detachments served in the unsuccessful Red River Expedition.

The measures put under way to strengthen the defenses of other Southern ports soon led to an expansion of the Confederate Corps' sphere of activity. Guards were assigned to the ships of the Mobile Squadron in August 1862; the Charleston Squadron probably received its first Marines around the same time; and early in the winter of 1862–63 a detachment was sent from Mobile to form a guard for the newly commissioned ironclad *Atlanta* at Savannah. In October, Beall ordered Captain Meiere to take command of the Marines at Mobile. This unit was subsequently designated Company D. Tatnall commenced recruiting Company E at Savannah in January 1863, and beginning in April Meiere raised Company F at Mobile. A little more than a year later, Company F was dissolved and its members transferred to Camp Beall.

Altogether, the Confederate States Marine Corps supplied guards for twenty-six warships and two floating batteries in home waters, plus the three commerce raiders—the *Sumter*, *Tallahassee*/*Olustee*, and *Chickamauga*—that put to sea from Southern ports. No detachments were furnished for the raiders outfitted in Europe, but the *Shenandoah*'s commander, Lt. James I. Waddell, organized one at sea from the members of his crew. Also, individual Leathernecks served in at least six other combatants at home or abroad.

In the spring of 1863, persistent rumors that Union forces were planning to move against Charleston prompted the dispatch of a battalion of two hundred Marines under Captain Simms from Camp Beall to aid in the defense of the city. On 7 April an attack on the harbor fortifications by eight Union ironclads was repulsed. Weeks of quiet followed, and at the end of the month the battalion returned to Drewry's Bluff.

Yet the capture of Charleston, the cradle of secession, remained high on the Union wish list. Operations to take the city by siege began on 10 July with the landing of three thousand troops on Morris Island, on the south side of the main ship channel into Charleston harbor. The next morning the Union advance was checked by Battery Wagner, a Confederate earthwork at the north end of the island. A week later, the work's defenders beat off another major assault. Rear Adm. John A. Dahlgren, who had been placed in command of the South Atlantic Blockading Squadron expressly to prosecute the naval side of the siege, put his ships' guards ashore as an ad hoc battalion to support the struggle for Battery Wagner and requested additional Marines.

Thus, for the second and last time in the war, the Corps assembled an integral battalion for amphibious service. The new unit, three hundred men under Zeilin, reached Morris Island on 10 August. On Dahlgren's orders, it combined with the battalion already ashore to form a Marine regiment with Zeilin at its head. Unfortunately, illness quickly invaded the unit's ranks. An ailing Zeilin was replaced by that apparently indestructible old campaigner John Reynolds, but there were not enough indestructible old campaigners to go around. By the time the Confederates

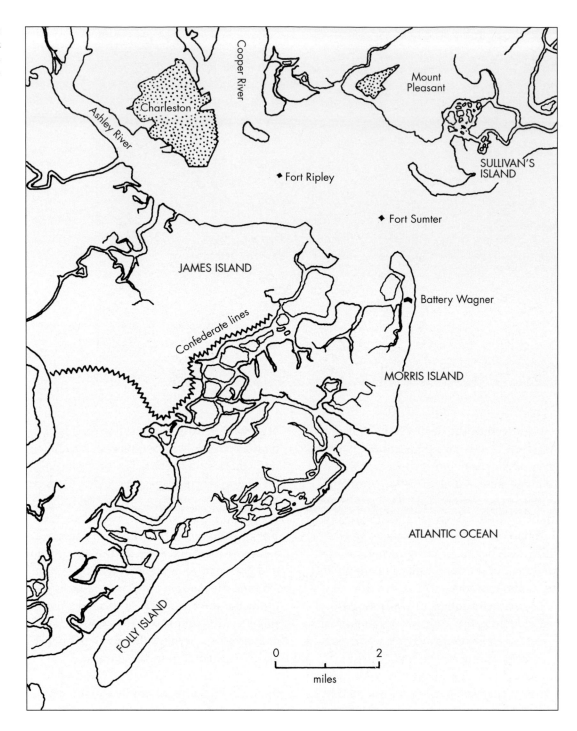

evacuated Battery Wagner on 7 September, Marine strength on Morris Island had dwindled to a small battalion.

Dahlgren decided to follow up the occupation of the battery with an assault on Fort Sumter, in the mouth of the harbor, the very next night. Although Union bombardments had silenced Sumter's guns and savaged its brick walls, the fort was still held by a Confederate garrison of unknown strength. The admiral's plan called for the formation of five assault divisions, four from the seamen and Marines of his squadron and one composed of Marines from Morris Island, each numbering approximately ninety men. After a tug had towed the force's boats as close as possible to the fort, the naval divisions would row forward to carry the work under covering fire from the Marines.

Neither the officer named to lead the expedition, Cdr. Thomas H. Stevens, nor the commander of the Marine division, Capt. Charles G. McCawley, thought much of the idea. Stevens expressed his misgivings to Dahlgren. The admiral dismissed them with the promise: "You have only to go and take possession. You will find nothing but a corporal's guard to oppose you."

That night the junior officers' forebodings proved well founded. The corporal's guard at Fort Sumter numbered 320 men; the crowd of small boats seen calling on the flagship and the Confederates' unsuspected ability to read the fleet's signal code put the defenders on the alert; and, probably owing in part to the haste with which the operation had to be mounted, most of Stevens' subordinates misunderstood his instructions. He intended to send one division forward to make a feint that would trick the defenders into revealing their strength. As soon as it started to pull for the fort, most of the other divisions, assuming that the order to advance had been given, raced after it. Stevens tried to recall them. They kept going, and he unhappily ordered the boats that had remained under control to follow.

Chaos ensued. A rocket soared into the sky above Sumter, and a moment later the batteries on nearby James and Sullivan islands and the ironclad *Chicora* (which carried an officer's guard of Confederate Marines) began to sweep the area with shrapnel and canister. Simultaneously, Sumter's parapets filled with riflemen who took the expedition's boats under a brisk fire. The parties that pushed ahead to land beneath the fort found themselves unable to scale its walls. They also found themselves exposed to a rain of hand grenades, bricks, and debris from above. Soon the men whose boats remained intact withdrew; those whose boats had been smashed or swamped had no alternative to surrender. In the confusion, McCawley tried to rally several boats that retreated past his own before the futility of prolonging the agony became evident. In twenty minutes, it was all over.

This disaster cost the attackers 124 casualties, most of whom were captured. The latter included 2 Marine officers (1 mortally wounded) and 39 NCOs and men. McCawley and 5 other officers present received brevet promotions for gallantry. Shortly afterwards, the Marine battalion was moved to Folly Island, south of Charleston. In 1864 it was dissolved.

Confederate Leathernecks also took part in a number of special operations. Early in 1864, plans were made for a combined assault on the enemy enclave on the Neuse River at New Bern, North Carolina. While army units attacked the Union lines, boat parties would deal with any gunboats—three of which were active in the area—that might come to the garrison's aid. The naval contingent was commanded by the redoubtable John Taylor Wood, a kind of freelance aide to President Davis, at once colonel, CSA, and commander, CSN, who had conducted several similar expeditions in Virginia waters. His party consisted of 115 officers and men from the James River Squadron, 10 midshipmen from the naval academy, and 25 Company C Marines under Capt. Thomas S. Wilson from Camp Beall.

The Confederate ground attack miscarried on 1 February. Wood resolved to carry on with the naval part of the program, and shortly after 0230 the following morning he and his men captured the gunboat *Underwriter* in hand-to-hand combat off New Bern. A Union lookout spotted the raiders three hundred yards from the ship, so the last part of their approach had to be made in the face of a stinging small arms' fire from her deck. Wilson's Leathernecks, who had been distributed among the expedition's boats for just that purpose, returned the Union fire. Afterwards a Southern midshipman recalled the "conspicuous . . . conduct of the Marines . . . [who] rose and delivered their fire, taking accurate aim, [and] reloading still under the heavy fire from the enemy." They then joined the fighting aboard the gunboat. One Marine lay among the five Confederate dead, and four were in the eleven wounded. Of the *Underwriter*'s crew, nine were killed and nineteen wounded; twenty-three escaped. When the force ashore began shelling the gunboat, her captors set her afire and withdrew.

The Confederate Congress honored the expedition's members with a joint resolution of thanks. In a letter to Colonel Beall, Wood recorded his satisfaction with "the fine bearing and soldierly conduct of Captain Wilson and his men . . . As a body they would be a credit to any organization, and I will be glad to be associated with them . . . at any time."

Confederate Marines were also assigned a major role in what would have been an even more audacious undertaking: the liberation of the fourteen thousand Confederate prisoners of war confined at Point Lookout, Maryland, where the Potomac flows into the Chesapeake Bay. The operation was proposed by Gen. Robert E. Lee on 26 June and approved by President Davis, who entrusted its execution to John Taylor Wood. The latter quickly assembled a party of approximately 150 seamen from the James River Squadron and 130 Marines from Camp Beall and the guards at the two Richmond navy yards under Capt. George Holmes, the commander of Company A. With this force Wood planned to sail from Wilmington, land at Point Lookout, overwhelm the camp guards, and lead the ex-prisoners north around Washington into Virginia. Rifles enough were collected to arm two thousand of them, and Gen. Jubal Early, whose army crossed the Potomac into Maryland on 5 July, was told to be ready to detach a cavalry brigade to screen their march. Security leaks caused Davis to telegraph Wilmington canceling the expedition as it was putting to sea on the evening of 10 July.

By then war had returned to Drewry's Bluff. On 5 May, Union major general Benjamin F. Butler, one of the war's outstandingly incompetent political generals, landed 30,000 men at Bermuda Hundred on the James River roughly ten miles southeast of the bluff and twelve miles northeast of Petersburg. At that moment, the back door to Richmond was guarded by fewer than 4,000 men. These troops included at most 350 artillerymen

and Marines at Drewry's Bluff, whose defense had been entirely a Marine Corps' responsibility since March, when a manpower shortage had necessitated the withdrawal of the seamen stationed there. (In light of this development, Terrett was granted the additional commission of temporary colonel, CSA.)

To Richmond's relief, Butler failed to exploit his opportunity. Not until 12 May, after several timid probes toward Petersburg, did he advance on Drewry's Bluff. In the intervening week the Confederates had concentrated twenty thousand men around it. During a day's skirmishing in which Camp Beall's adjutant recorded that Terrett was "in the trenches" with his Leathernecks, the Union advance ground to a halt. Four days later the Confederates counterattacked, drove Butler back to Bermuda Hundred, and proceeded to pen up his army behind a line of entrenchments, where it remained for the rest of the war.

The U.S. Marine Corps' commandant, Col. John Harris, died at age seventy-three on the day Butler attacked Drewry's Bluff. Not long before, he had performed what was perhaps his greatest service to the

Corps as its commandant. Anticipating yet another Congressional resolution to transfer it to the army, he had shrewdly solicited testimonials from a galaxy of admirals extolling the Corps' value as a branch of the naval service. These statements helped squash the measure that emerged soon after his death.

Harris' demise left Secretary of the Navy Welles embarrassed for a successor. The most likely candidate might have seemed to be John Reynolds, whose record of service was second to none, but he had ruined his chances in 1862. That spring Reynolds had become convinced that, despite the tradition barring staff officers from command, Paymaster Major Russell was conniving to position himself to become the Corps' next commandant, and that his schemes enjoyed Harris' blessing.

Reynolds thereupon favored the commandant with a barely intelligible but unmistakably sharp open letter of protest. While this may have cooked Russell's goose, it certainly scorched Reynolds' gander. An outraged Harris court-martialed him on charges of drunkenness and disrespect. There was probably something to the first of these specifications. In his diary Welles recorded that privately Reynolds acknowledged the failing, and a young officer who admired him wrote, "Colonel Reynolds always has everything about him in order, and, drunk or sober, duty must be carried on right." Nevertheless, the court found him innocent on both counts. Reynolds celebrated his acquittal by filing charges against Harris, at which point an exasperated Secretary Welles brought the matter to a close by sending both men letters of reproof. The affair represented merely another untoward incident in Reynolds' controversial career.

In 1822 his obstreperous behavior had led to his dismissal from the U.S. Military Academy. Like many young men found wanting at either West Point or Annapolis in the decades preceding the Civil War, he soon obtained a commission in the Marine Corps. His drunken behavior and frequent disagreements with his superiors made him the most litigious Marine officer of his era.

So it seems no wonder that following Harris' death, Welles wrote grimly of his problems in naming a new commandant. The higher class of Marine officers are not the men who can elevate or give efficiency to the Corps. To supersede them will cause much dissatisfaction. Every man who is [passed over] and all of his friends will be offended with me for what will be deemed an insult. But there is a duty to be performed." On 10 June he retired all four officers in the Corps above the age of sixty—as a consolation, they were allowed to remain on duty for the duration of the war—and fifty-seven-year-old Major Jacob Zeilin became the seventh commandant.

Although Welles' diary suggests he was less impressed by Zeilin than unimpressed by his seniors, the new commandant possessed good credentials. A near graduate of the West Point Class of 1826 who was dismissed for academic failings, he had been commissioned into the Marine Corps in 1831, won a brevet for gallantry during in the Mexican War, and served as Commodore Perry's senior Marine officer in the expedition to Japan. So far in the Civil War, he was the only Marine besides Reynolds to command a battalion at the front. Neither Welles nor anyone else expected Zeilin to promote any major changes in the Corps, and he did not surprise them.

In contrast to their Union counterparts, most Confederate Marine officers would have been delighted to have the Army

adopt their Corps. Apparently convinced that the Navy Department lacked sufficient influence to advance the Corps' interests—and no doubt frustrated by the limitations its size imposed on promotions—nearly all of them signed a petition to President Davis late in 1864 proposing that the Marine Corps should be transferred to the Army and enlarged to a brigade of three regiments. One regiment was to be designated "Marine Infantry" and furnish ships' guards; the other two presumably

would have consisted of Marine artillerists employed to garrison coastal fortifications. A resolution calling for the Committee on Naval Affairs to investigate the expediency of transferring (though not enlarging) the Corps was, in fact, introduced in the Confederate Senate on 6 February 1865, only to be tabled two days later.

The battered Confederacy of February 1865 would have had little use for Marine artillerists, in any event. Most of the ports they would have defended had already been

lost. At the beginning of June 1864 Mobile, Savannah, Charleston, and Wilmington remained in Confederate hands, and the first and last were havens for the swift gray steamers that still ran the blockade. Within eight months, all four ports had been captured or closed.

The process began at the Battle of Mobile Bay, an action in which both Marine Corps participated, on 5 August 1864. As at New Orleans, only this time in broad daylight, a Union fleet under Admiral Farragut had to fight its way through a narrow channel under fire from two masonry forts (Gaines and Morgan) with Confederate warships waiting to engage its leaders as they emerged. Farragut's force included four monitors and fourteen wooden sloops and gunboats. Adm.

Franklin Buchanan's Mobile Squadron consisted of the ironclad ram *Tennessee* and three gunboats. The U.S. Navy did not assign Marines to monitors, but guard detachments served in the other Union ships. All the Confederate vessels except the *Selma* carried officer's guards, and Captain Meiere collected two officers and twenty-five NCOs and men from the Marines serving ashore to join a provisional battalion rushed to reinforce Fort Gaines.

The battle lasted barely three hours. Only a single Union vessel, the monitor *Tecumseh*, which strayed into a minefield, was lost during the passage of the forts. Inside the bay, the others quickly disposed of the Confederate gunboats. The *Selma* struck her colors, the *Gaines* ran aground, and the *Morgan* retreated to Mobile.

Left to carry on alone, the *Tennessee* was hammered into submission by Union gunfire after a wild melee. Her guard of thirty-three Marines was captured with her. Meiere's detachment followed them into captivity when Fort Gaines surrendered three days later. Union casualties totaled 315 killed and wounded, 8 of whom were Marines. Farragut's senior Marine officer, twenty-four-year-old Bvt. Maj. Charles Heywood, who had been in the *Cumberland* at Hampton Roads, won the brevet of lieutenant colonel and the sobriquet "the boy colonel." Sent to post a guard in the *Tennessee*, he could not resist remarking to Admiral Buchanan that they had met before. The other 2 Marine officers present also received brevet promotions, and 8 enlisted Marines earned the Medal of Honor. Mobile remained a Confederate city, but with Union ships in Mobile Bay it ceased to be a Confederate port.

Savannah's turn came next. On 15 November 1864, Gen. William T. Sherman set out from Atlanta on his March to the Sea. To facilitate his advance by complicating enemy troop movements, the South Atlantic Blockading Squadron organized an expedition of seamen, Marines, and assorted Army units to push up the Broad River from Port Royal, South Carolina, with the objective of cutting the Savannah-to-Charleston railroad. The Marine contingent, formed from ships' guards, consisted of 182 men under 1st Lt. George C. Stoddard, the squadron's sole Marine officer. Though the Leathernecks distinguished themselves in a series of

sharp little actions and Stoddard won a brevet captaincy, the defenders stopped the expedition short of the tracks.

The Southerners' success was ephemeral. On 10 December, Sherman's army of sixty thousand appeared outside Savannah, where the Confederates had been able to assemble only a quarter of that number to face them. Marines of Tatnall's Company E served in the trenches during the skirmishing that preceded the evacuation of the city on 12 December. That night, most of the company boarded the railroad to Charleston while a sergeant's guard in the ironclad *Macon* started up the Savannah River to Augusta.

Wilmington was now the eastern Confederacy's only open port, and the Union had already initiated measures to close it. The city stood ten miles from the sea on the east bank of the Cape Fear River, the entrance to which was defended by an enormous earthwork named Fort Fisher. Located near the tip of a peninsula curling down from the north, the fort was built in the shape of a capital T, minus the right half of the crossbar. The left half bisected the peninsula above the high water mark, a distance of approximately half a mile, and was called the land face. It mounted twenty heavy guns positioned one and two each in individual chambers connected by heavy traverses. The upstroke of the T, called the sea face, extended for more than a mile along the shore and mounted twenty-four guns in similar chambers. About fifty feet in front of the land face the peninsula was again bisected by a palisade of sharp-pointed logs, some five hundred feet in

advance of which the defenders had laid a field of electrically detonated mines. To the left of the upstroke, at a landing on the river side of the peninsula, was Battery Buchanan, a detached work armed with four guns manned by naval personnel. Its purpose was to prevent enemy vessels from entering the river to attack the fort from the rear and, should the fort fall, to serve as a strong point to which the garrison could retreat and from which it might be evacuated.

The first Confederate Marines had come to Wilmington from Camp Beall to furnish guards for the ironclads *North Carolina* and *Raleigh* in January 1864. Capt. Alfred Van Benthuysen assumed command of these detachments in June, shortly after the expiration of the sentence imposed by his second court-martial enabled him to return to active duty. In November, an officer's guard was assigned to Battery Buchanan, and when an enemy armada anchored off the coast on 23 December, Van Benthuysen took his Wilmington Marines to join Fort Fisher's garrison.

As it turned out, there was no need of them. For a day and a half, a powerful Union fleet commanded by Rear Adm. David Dixon Porter subjected the fort to a heavy but not especially accurate fire. Two thousand men, almost a third of Maj. Gen. Benjamin Butler's expeditionary force, landed the second afternoon. A close look at the fort led their commanders to conclude—probably with good reason—that it had not been damaged enough for an assault to succeed. On 26 December, the troops reembarked and the fleet withdrew.

Undeterred by this setback, Union leaders promptly organized a second Fort Fisher Expedition. Porter retained his command, but Butler was replaced by Maj. Gen. Alfred H. Terry and the Army contingent was increased to eight thousand men. The new armada appeared in sight of Fort Fisher late on 12 January 1865. Van Benthuysen's seventy-some Marines were among the seven hundred reinforcements that reached the fort via Battery Buchanan over the next thirty-six hours, raising the strength of the garrison to fifteen hundred men. They were in for the fight of their lives.

This time the fleet's fire proved extremely accurate. Starting on the fourteenth, it was seconded by batteries emplaced by the troops who had begun landing the day before. By 1500 on the fifteenth, the hour chosen for the assault, all except one of the guns in Fort Fisher's land face had been silenced, the underground wires to the minefields severed, and gaps opened in the palisade.

The Union plan called for simultaneous assaults to be made against both ends of the fort's land face. The western attack, along the river bank, would be delivered by Terry's infantry; the eastern attack, along the seashore, by a naval brigade from Porter's fleet. The latter consisted of sixteen hundred seamen organized into three divisions led by their ships' officers and an improvised battalion of four hundred Marines under Capt. Lucian L. Dawson. In overall command Porter placed his fleet captain (chief of staff), Lt. Cdr. Kidder R. Breese.

According to the instructions Dawson received from Breese, the Marines were to advance by stages to occupy three successive lines of rifle pits being dug by naval working parties, the last only two hundred yards from the fort. In this position they would provide covering fire for the naval divisions, which had been armed with pistols and cutlasses. Upon the order to attack, the sailors would charge through them and, as Porter quaintly put it, "board the fort on the run in a seamanlike way." Once the sailors had passed, the Marines would follow.

Things began to go wrong almost at once. Dawson was still in process of sorting out his battalion when Breese ordered him to bring it to the front. Hardly had the Marines reached the second line of rifle pits than a new order arrived. Breese had discovered that the incline where the beach sloped down to the sea furnished "splendid

cover." He ordered Dawson to move his Marines there. Soon the entire brigade was lying in a long column beside the water's edge, with the Leathernecks abreast and inland of the second naval division. The next order Dawson heard was the shout "Charge! Charge!"

With a cheer, the brigade sprang up and dashed down the beach toward Fort Fisher, some six hundred yards away. Fire from riflemen on the fort's parapet halted the head of the column fifty yards short of its goal. A few sturdy souls managed to get inside the palisade. Most of their comrades threw themselves to the ground, where, in the words of an officer present, "they were packed like sheep in a pen, while the enemy was crowding the ramparts . . . and shooting into them as fast as they could fire." Dawson had just caught up to his leading company after a hard run through the sand when the sailors broke to the rear. Seeing panic spread throughout the column, he shouted to the Marines to "Lie down and fire at the parapet!" Most of the men in the first two companies obeyed him; most of those in the last two joined the stampede. As soon as the brigade was out of range, he ordered the men who had stayed with him to retire by squads. Dawson himself and a number of officers remained outside the fort until nightfall.

All told, the naval brigade suffered 351 casualties, among them 57 Marines: 16 killed or missing and 41 wounded. Dawson and 7 of his officers won brevets for gallantry. Six enlisted Marines earned Medals of Honor ashore at Fort Fisher (plus one for heroism aboard a ship on the

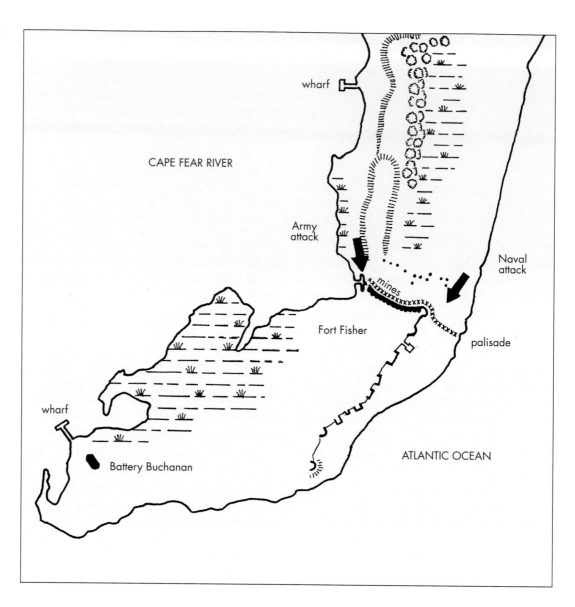

CAPE FEAR RIVER

wharf

Army
attack

Naval
attack

mines

Fort Fisher

palisade

wharf

Battery Buchanan

ATLANTIC OCEAN

firing line), the last of seventeen awarded to Leathernecks during the Civil War.

Yet these honors lay in the future. In the immediate aftermath of the attack, Breese ungraciously affixed the blame for its rout on "the absence of the marines from their [assigned] position." Although Breese graciously added that he attributed their failure to insufficient time to organize "so many small squads of men from the different vessels" and "not . . . to any want of personal valor," Dawson's detailed reports make clear where the fault really lay. Unfortunately, most Navy officers took Breese's view, thereby creating a point of dissension that would trouble

Navy–Marine Corps relations for the next thirty years. The fundamental error, as the leader of one of the naval divisions commented years later, "was in expecting a body of sailors, collected hastily from different ships, armed with swords and pistols, to stand against veteran soldiers armed with rifles and bayonets." Future admiral George Dewey, who watched the assault from the deck of his ship, summed it up nicely: "Such an attempt was sheer, murderous madness."

Well merited as these strictures were, the charge had one positive albeit unintended consequence. It served as an admirable diversion for the army's assault. No more than 500 of Fort Fisher's defenders were involved in its repulse, but this left only 250 to hold the western land face, a late reinforcement of 350 men who had been ordered there declining to depart the bomb-proofs in which they had taken refuge. Furthermore, the attack absorbed the attention of both the fort's dynamic young commander, Col. William Lamb, and his superior officer, Maj. Gen. W. H. C. Whiting, the Wilmington district commander, who had felt honor-bound to join the garrison. Thus, glancing at the opposite end of the land face after the naval brigade had been beaten off, they were astonished to see three Union flags waving over it.

Calling on the men nearby to follow, Whiting rushed along the parapet toward the enemy. He soon went down with wounds to which he would eventually succumb, but his charge checked the Union advance. For the next five hours, Fort Fisher was the scene of some of the most intense combat of the war as men fought, often with clubbed rifles, through the traverses between the land-face gun chambers. Lamb built up a front to contain the Union brigades pushing into the work from the west; Porter's fleet shifted its fire from the sea-face batteries to the struggle under way in the interior of the fort; and the sea-face batteries that could be brought to bear did the same. To his dying day, Lamb believed that had he not been disabled by a shot in the hip at the moment of launching a counterattack for which he had scraped up every available man, he could have driven its assailants out of Fort

Fisher before sunset. Exactly where the Confederate Leathernecks were engaged is unknown, but that they were heavily engaged is evident from the fact that four of their six officers were wounded. Eight of the sixty-six enlisted Marines who survived had also been wounded, three mortally. Several weeks later, a midshipman who had been stationed at Wilmington recorded having heard that "our men, as a general thing, behaved well. The company of marines fought splendidly."

Around 2100, the arrival of a fourth Union brigade caused the defense to crumble. Captain Van Benthuysen, himself wounded in the head, decided that the time had come to evacuate Whiting and Lamb. A squad of his Marines carried the two officers toward Battery Buchanan. The remnants of the garrison, some four hundred men, soon followed. A terrible disappointment awaited them. The naval officer commanding the battery, a work erected in part to support a garrison in such a situation, had spiked its guns, withdrawn its men, and taken everything that could float. Fort Fisher's defenders had been abandoned to their fate.

The capture of Fort Fisher completed the Anaconda Plan's amphibious agenda. As of 16 January 1865, the eastern Confederacy was isolated from the world beyond. In the words of Rear Adm. Raphael Semmes, "The anaconda had, at last, wound its fatal folds around us." Although ships' guards continued to serve in blockaders off the Southern coast and participated in the capture of the city of Mobile, for the U.S. Marine Corps the war was as good as over. It had seen its last significant Civil War combat.

This was not the case with the Confederate States Marine Corps, whose most trying times lay just ahead. On 17 February 1865 Sherman's army, striking north from Savannah, forced Charleston's defenders to evacuate the city after a siege of 567 days. Commo. John R. Tucker, commanding the Charleston Squadron, destroyed his ships and led their seamen and Marines north on a circuitous journey to Richmond. There his command was combined with the Marine battalion at Drewry's Bluff to form a unit known as Tucker's Naval Brigade. Tatnall's Company E withdrew into the interior of North Carolina, where it remained until the end of the war.

The end was not long in coming. Before dawn on 2 April, Union forces enjoying an overall numerical superiority in excess of two to one punched through the overextended Confederate lines south of Petersburg. Later that morning, Lee advised Davis that the army would have to evacuate Richmond. Tucker's Naval Brigade, almost five hundred strong, was assigned to a scratch corps commanded by Lt. Gen. Richard S. Ewell and accompanied Lee's army as it retreated to the west. An order was also sent to Semmes, commanding the James River Squadron, to join Lee with its five hundred officers and men, but by the time they had destroyed their ships and reached Richmond, the army had withdrawn and the "last train" had departed. Putting together a train of its own at the railroad depot, the little

force proceeded to Danville, Virginia, just above the North Carolina line, to which Semmes had been informed Lee planned to withdraw.

Lee hoped that his army would be able to shake off its pursuers. His hopes were in vain. Union cavalry tore at the flanks and rear of the shrinking Confederate columns, sometimes slowing them sufficiently for enemy infantry to come up and engage them. Terrett was among a number of Leathernecks captured in the rear-guard action at Amelia Court House on 5 April. The next day enemy pressure compelled Ewell's corps to halt and give battle on the wooded heights overlooking a stream called Saylor's Creek.

Tucker's Naval Brigade was posted between Ewell's two divisions. The artillery continued its retreat. Following a preliminary bombardment to which the Confederates could not reply, two Union divisions deployed into a single line, waded the creek, and advanced up the slope. As they neared its crest, Ewell's men surprised them with a counterattack that hurled the Union center back in disorder. All accounts agree that the Marines, now commanded by Captain Simms, distinguished themselves in this action. In his official report, a Union division commander recorded that "the Confederate Marine Battalion fought with particular obstinacy." A Confederate soldier said it more simply: "Those marines fought like tigers and against odds of at least ten to one."

But the effort was in vain. Other Union forces quickly enveloped both Confederate flanks, and Ewell's divisions

were obliged to lay down their arms. Not
so the naval brigade. Unaware of the
disaster befalling its neighbors, it retired
into a densely wooded ravine where it
remained undisturbed. Near dusk, a
Union general investigating rumors that a
Confederate formation was lurking there
unwittingly rode into its lines. Narrowly
escaping with his life, he returned under
a flag of truce and acquainted Tucker
with the hopelessness of his situation.
The commodore then agreed to surrender.
Afterwards he told a friend that, never
before having been in a land battle, he had

thought "everything was going on well."
An incomplete return shows that Simms,
six other Marine officers, and forty-five
NCOs and men were captured with him.

A few other Leathernecks somehow
managed to slip away. For the next three
days these gallant men soldiered through
the death throes of the Army of Northern
Virginia. Four officers and twenty-five
men were present to surrender with
it at Appomattox Court House on 9
April. Among them was 1st Lt. Richard
Henderson. One suspects that his father
would have been proud.

Semmes' command spent that fateful April week in Danville. Detraining around midnight on the fourth, it found the Confederate government already established in the little town. The next morning Semmes was commissioned brigadier general, CSA, and the seamen and Marines of the James River Squadron were organized into an artillery brigade that, together with two infantry battalions, formed the garrison of the Confederacy's temporary capital. That responsibility ended the day after Appomattox, the news of which caused the government to flee south. Subsequently attached to the Confederate Army in North Carolina, the brigade surrendered at Greensboro on 1 May. The remnants of Company E had stacked arms there three days earlier.

The last Marine unit to serve under the Stars and Bars was Company C, which had been partially reconstituted following its near destruction in the Battle of Mobile Bay. Between 27 March and 11 April, its members served afloat and ashore in the unsuccessful defense of Mobile against a Union offensive along the eastern side of the bay. The city fell on 12 April, and the Mobile Squadron retreated some thirty miles up the Tombigbee River to Nanna Hubba Bluff. At the time of its surrender on 10 May, the guard detachments in the gunboats *Nashville* and *Morgan* numbered three lieutenants and twenty-four NCOs and men.

The American Marines' Civil War thereby came to an end. In the course of the conflict the U.S. Marine Corps had lost 148 men killed in action or died of wounds, 131 wounded, and 108 captured; 257 died of causes unrelated to combat. Aside from the approximately 250 men who are known to have been captured, the lack of records precludes a comparable determination of Confederate States Marine Corps casualties.

CHAPTER 6

At Sea in the Postbellum Years, 1865–1898

Most historians of the Marine Corps have been faintly embarrassed by its performance in the Civil War, attributing its failure to cultivate an amphibious capability to a lack of institutional vision. At the restoration of peace, however, nearly everyone in high places in the Corps, the Navy, and indeed, the government as a whole was well pleased with the part it had played. This became obvious as an ironic result of a Congressional resolution introduced in June 1866 that directed the House Naval Affairs Committee to investigate the feasibility of disbanding the Corps. Lifting a leaf from his predecessor's book, Colonel Zeilin collected encomiums to its service from no fewer than fourteen of the war's foremost admirals, including Farragut, Porter, Dahlgren, and Du Pont. Farragut, the most famous of the Navy luminaries, exclaimed that "a ship without Marines is like a garment without buttons." The outcome was a triumph for the Marines and their supporters. Reporting adversely on the resolution in February 1867, the committee asserted, "From the beginning, this Corps seems to have satisfactorily fulfilled the purposes of its organization,

The Marine Corps recruited boys as musicians during the Civil War and through-out the decades leading up to the Spanish-American War. William Crawford, age thirteen, appears in this photograph taken in 1866. He enlisted as a fifer that year and reen-listed in 1870, 1874, and 1878. (National Archives)

and no good reason appears for either abolishing it or transferring it to the Army; on the contrary, the Committee recommends that its organization as a separate Corps be preserved and strengthened . . . [and] that its commanding officer shall hold the rank of brigadier general."

The Senate's approval of the latter recommendation made Jacob Zeilin the first Marine to attain regular rank as a general officer, Archibald Henderson having attained the rank of brigadier general by brevet. At least for the time being, the Marines also escaped the usual postwar cutbacks. Whereas the Army had enlisted most of its men "for the duration" of the war, the Corps had continued to sign up its recruits for four years. Unless they could obtain substitutes, Marines were required to serve out that period.

Eventually, of course, the axe fell. It did not fall on the Leathernecks alone. Most Americans, their absorption in domestic affairs only rarely interrupted by fleeting war scares, saw no reason to spend large sums on armed forces for which they foresaw no need. By 1870, the number of the Navy's active ships had dwindled from a wartime peak of nearly seven hundred to barely fifty, and a few years later, the size of the Army was cut from fifty-four thousand to twenty-seven thousand. The Corps' turn came in 1874, when its enlisted force was reduced by a third, from three thousand to two thousand men; the strength of its officer corps was capped at seventy-five; and, although General Zeilin kept his star, the rank attached to the office of commandant was rolled back to colonel.

Compared with the two larger armed services, the Marines had gotten off lightly. Because the Corps was so small to begin with, however, it found the cuts particularly painful. For the next quarter century it operated in a condition of chronic overstretch. On only a handful of occasions would as many as two hundred Leathernecks assemble in any one place. The effects of the ceiling set on the officer corps were equally unfortunate. There were years—sometimes, years in succession—when the Corps could

not commission a single second lieutenant. At the same time, promotion practically ceased, especially for the bloc of company-grade officers who had answered the call to the colors during the Civil War.

The experiences of Henry Clay Cochrane, who had escorted President Lincoln to Gettysburg, may serve as a case in point. Cochrane had been commissioned in September 1861 and promoted to first lieutenant in August 1865. Thereafter he waited nearly fourteen years for his next promotion, and at the opening of the Gay Nineties he had yet to receive another. No wonder that in a plaintive, not to say pathetic, letter written as a white-bearded captain to Secretary of the Navy Hilary A. Herbert in 1894 he lamented that "the years are rapidly passing, my vision is fading, my

hair and teeth are going, and it has dawned on me that I am on the down hill side of life and yet doing practically the same duty that I did more than a quarter of a century ago."

Just as the Civil War has often been viewed as far from the Corps' finest hour, the thirty-three years that intervened before the war with Spain have generally been considered its nadir. Such an interpretation requires qualification. While it is true that the decades in question were devoid of big battles, they included no fewer than twenty-nine landings, one of which (Korea, 1871) was a sizeable operation by the standards of the times. On more than a dozen other occasions, Marines were deployed in support of the civil authority within the United States. Their activities in this role ranged from escorting revenue agents in raids on illegal stills in a turbulent neighborhood known as Irishtown near the Boston Navy Yard (1867,

1868, and 1871) and helping maintain order in Baltimore, Philadelphia, and Reading during the great railway strike of 1877 to guarding a quarantine camp established at Sandy Hook, New York, when cholera was discovered aboard immigrant ships (1892).

Thirteen of the landings, including all three in which shots were fired, took place on Zeilin's watch. The first was a punitive expedition against the aborigines—"savages" in the less-nuanced language of the day—inhabiting the southeastern tip of Formosa (Taiwan) in retaliation for the massacre of the shipwrecked crew of the American bark *Rover* in March 1867. This deployment turned out to be one of the few nineteenth-century operations in which a landing party found that it had bitten off more than it could comfortably chew.

On the morning of 13 June, the screw sloop *Hartford*, flagship of the Asiatic

Squadron, and the screw sloops *Plymouth* and *Wyoming* anchored off the landing site. From their decks officers with long glasses could see small groups of aborigines in breechclouts, their bodies painted red, musket barrels glinting in the sun, gathering on hilltops two miles away. At 0930, the *Hartford*'s skipper, Cdr. George E. Belknap, led a force of 181 men ashore. Included in this number were 43 Marines under Capt. James Forney, who had earned two brevet promotions for gallantry during the Civil War. Pushing inland under a blazing sun, the expedition tried in vain to come to grips with the Formosans. The Asiatic Squadron's commander, Rear Adm. H. H. Bell, recorded the party's frustration: "As our men marched into the hills, the savages, knowing the paths, boldly decided to meet them, and, gliding through the high grass and from cover to cover, displayed a stratagem and courage equal to our North American Indians. Delivering their fire, they retreated without being seen by our men, who, charging upon their covers, frequently fell into ambuscades. Our detachments pursued them, in this harassing manner, out of sight of the ships, until two o'clock p.m."

At that time, Belknap called a halt to rest the men, many of whom had begun to show signs of heat prostration. So far the force had burned a few huts, but that was the extent of its accomplishments. Half an hour later, while the main body remained inert, Belknap's second-in-command, Lt. Cdr. Alexander S. Mackenzie, was killed leading the advance guard into a thicket from which shots had been fired. Mackenzie's death and the battalion's exhaustion convinced Belknap that it would be wise to fall back to the beach where its boats remained under guard. The additional exertion brought the expedition close to collapse, and by 1600 it was back aboard ship. Three years later, Forney received a third brevet for his part in the affair. No other Marine officer obtained that distinction between 1865 and 1898.

The next contested operation was smaller in scale but more successful: the seizure and burning of the piratical steamer *Forward* by six boats of Bluejackets and Leathernecks from the screw sloop *Mohican*

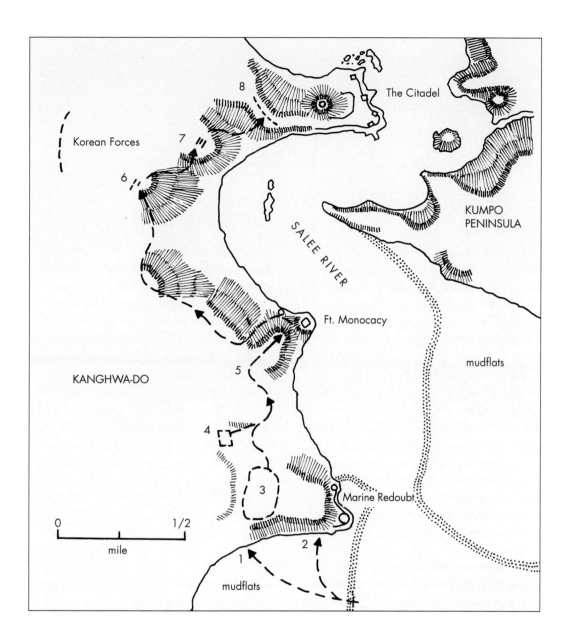

The Citadel

Korean Forces

SALEE RIVER

KUMPO PENINSULA

Ft. Monocacy

mudflats

KANGHWA-DO

Marine Redoubt

0   1/2

mile

mudflats

in the Teacapan River on the Pacific coast of Mexico on 17 June 1870. The last such operation, also successful, included the largest-scale combat in which Leathernecks participated in the three decades following the Civil War. This was the Korean Expedition of 1871.

On 23 May of that year, five vessels of Rear Adm. John Rodgers' Asiatic Fleet—the frigate *Colorado*, sloops *Alaska* and *Benicia*, and gunboats *Monocacy* and *Palos*—entered Roze Roads on the west coast of Korea not far from Chemulpo (modern Inchon). Aboard Rodgers' flagship, the *Colorado*, was Frederick F. Low, U.S. Minister to China, who had been sent to open diplomatic

relations with the Hermit Kingdom of Korea. Contact was made with the local inhabitants, and on the thirty-first a small delegation of low-ranking Korean officials appeared. Low refused to receive them and directed his secretary to explain that the presence of first-rank officials qualified to conduct negotiations was required. In the meantime, the Koreans were informed that the Americans desired to chart the Salee River, as the channel of the Han River between Kanghwa-do (island) and the Kumpo peninsula was then called. As the Han led to the capital city of Seoul, the Koreans might have been expected to consider such an act provocative, American assurances of good will notwithstanding, but they raised no objections. Twenty-four hours were allotted for them to notify the appropriate authorities.

Accordingly, at noon on 1 June, four steam launches followed by the *Monocacy* and *Palos* set out to begin the survey. As they came abreast of the fortifications on the heights of Kanghwa-do, the Koreans opened fire. The surveying party replied with gusto, shelling the forts into silence, and returned to the fleet's anchorage. American casualties numbered two men wounded.

Rodgers waited nine days for an apology or better tides. The former was not forthcoming, and on 10 June a punitive expedition entered the river with the mission of capturing and destroying the errant forts. The landing force numbered 686 officers and men, including 109 Marines organized into two little companies and a naval battery of seven 12-pounder howitzers. Fire support would be provided by the gunboats and four steam launches mounting 12-pounders in their bows. Cdr. L. A. Kimberly was placed in command of the landing force. The Asiatic Fleet Marine Officer, Capt. McLane Tilton, led its Leathernecks. Tilton was one of those unconventional characters for whom the Corps has always seemed to exercise an attraction. (Writing his wife from a Mediterranean deployment, he reported that when he first went on deck each day, "If anyone asks me how are you old fellow, I reply, 'I don't feel very well; no gentleman is ever well in the morning.'")

Three forts, each with a walled water-battery, overlooked the shore of Kanghwa-do. In the course of the operation, the Americans christened them the Marine Redoubt, Fort Monocacy, and the Citadel. The *Monocacy* took the first two under fire shortly after noon. Both had been silenced by the time the *Palos* appeared with the landing party's boats in tow about an hour later. The boats cast off half a mile below the nearest fort, and at 1345 that afternoon, the Bluejackets and Marines began struggling ashore across a broad, knee-deep mud flat, "crossed by deep sluices," a disgusted Tilton noted, "filled with softer and still deeper mud." Some men left their shoes, socks, leggings, and even trouser legs behind, and the howitzers bogged down to their barrels. Fortunately, the Koreans did not attempt to oppose the landing.

The Leathernecks had been selected to serve as the expedition's advance guard. Tilton deployed them into a skirmish line as soon as they left the boats. Once both companies reached firm ground, Kimberly ordered Tilton to lead them toward the fort, an elliptical stone redoubt with walls twelve feet high. Most of the sailors remained behind to manhandle the guns out of the muck. Upon the Marines' approach, the fort's white-robed defenders fled, firing a few parting shots. The work mounted fifty-four guns, but all except two were insignificant brass breechloaders. Tilton halted his men until the main body came up, "when we were again ordered to push forward," he wrote, "which we did, scouring the fields as far as practicable from the left of the line of march, the river being on our right, and took a position on a wooded knoll . . . commanding a fine view of the beautiful hills and inundated rice fields immediately around us." At this point he received orders

to hold for the night. It was 1630 before the guns had been dragged ashore, and too few hours of daylight remained to demolish the captured fort and tackle the next. The seamen bivouacked half a mile to the rear.

The landing force moved out at 0530 the next morning. Its fire support had been reduced by the withdrawal of the *Palos*, which had hurt herself on an uncharted rock while the landing was in progress, but that available from the *Monocacy* and the launches would prove more than sufficient. The second fort, a chipped granite structure about ninety feet square, stood on a bluff a mile upstream. Tilton's men found it deserted. While a Marine bugler amused himself by rolling thirty-three little brass cannon over the bluff into the river, other members of the expedition spiked the fort's four big guns and tore down two of its walls. Then the march resumed.

The track between the first two forts had been relatively easy going, but beyond the second it became extremely difficult, "the topography of the country being

indescribable," Tilton reported, "resembling a sort of 'chopped sea,' of immense hills and deep ravines lying in every conceivable position." Presently the column came under long-range musket fire from a Korean force estimated to number from two to five thousand among some hills beyond the Americans' left flank. Five guns supported by three companies of seamen were deployed to hold this body in check and the remainder of the party continued its advance. On two occasions the Koreans made a rush toward the detachment, but a few artillery shells turned them back each time.

The Americans called the last and strongest of the Korean fortifications the Citadel. It consisted of a stone redoubt crowning a steep, conical hill on a peninsula some two miles upstream from its neighbor. The *Monocacy* and the steam launches opened fire on it at about 1100. At noon, Kimberly halted his command six hundred yards from the fort to give the men a breather. By that time, the parties of Koreans seen falling back on the Citadel and the forest

Korean dead inside the Citadel. (Naval Historical Center)

of flags in and around it left no doubt that the position would be defended.

After signaling the *Monocacy* to cease fire, the storming party, 350 seamen and Marines with fixed bayonets, dashed forward to occupy a ridge line only 120 yards from the fort. Although Tilton's men were still armed with the Model 1861 muzzle-loading Springfield rifle musket (in his words, "a blasted old *Muzzle-Fuzzel*"), they quickly established fire superiority over the fort's defenders, who were armed with matchlocks, a firearm that had disappeared from Western arsenals two hundred years before. "The firing continued for only a few minutes, say four," Tilton wrote, "amidst the melancholy songs of the enemy, their bearing being courageous in the extreme."

At half past twelve Lt. Cdr. Silas Casey, commanding the Bluejacket battalion, gave the order to charge. "And as little parties of our forces advanced closer and closer down the deep ravine between us," Tilton continued, "some of [the Koreans] mounted the parapet and threw stones etc., at us, uttering all the while exclamations seemingly

of defiance." The first American into the Citadel, Navy lieutenant Hugh W. McKee, fell mortally wounded by a musket ball in the groin and a spear thrust in the side. The spearman also stabbed at Lt. Winfield Scott Schley, who had followed close behind McKee. The point passed between Schley's left arm and chest, pinning his sleeve to his coat, and he shot the man dead.

Tilton was among half a dozen officers who led their men into the fort moments later. The Koreans stood their ground, and the fighting became hand to hand. Clambering over the parapet, Pvt. Michael McNamara encountered an enemy soldier pointing a matchlock at him. He wrenched the gun from the Korean's hands and clubbed him to death with it. Pvt. James Dougherty closed with and killed the man the Americans identified as the commander of the Korean forces. Tilton, Pvt. Hugh Purvis, and Cpl. Charles Brown converged on the Citadel's principal standard, a twelve-foot-square yellow cotton banner emblazoned with black Chinese characters signifying "commanding general." For five minutes, the fort's interior

The Korean commanding general's flag and its captors aboard the *Colorado*. From left to right: Cpl. Charles Brown, Pvt. Hugh Purvis, and Capt. McLane Tilton. Brown and Purvis won the Medal of Honor in the storming of the Citadel. (National Archives)

was a scene of desperate combat. Then the remaining defenders fled downhill toward the river, under fire from the Marines, a seaman company, and the two howitzers that had accompanied the attackers; there, the defeated Koreans slashed their own throats or drowned themselves for failing to successfully resist the interlopers. The landing force located twenty wounded defenders, but the island's governor refused to accept them, and they were left on the beach for nature to take its course.

A total of 143 Korean dead and wounded were counted in and around the Citadel, and Lieutenant Commander Schley, the landing force's adjutant, estimated that another 100 had been killed in flight. Forty-seven flags and 481 pieces of ordnance, mostly quite small but including 27 sizeable pieces—20-pounders and upward—were captured. The storming party lost 3 men killed and 10 wounded, with a Marine private in each category. Tilton was pleasantly surprised by his survival. In a letter home a few days later, he wrote, "I never expected to see my wife and baby any more, and if it hadn't been that the Coreans can't shoot true, I never should." He retired as a lieutenant colonel in 1897. Nine sailors and six Marines earned the Medal of Honor. They included Corporal Brown and Private Purvis, who had rendezvoused with Tilton at the Citadel's flagstaff. In his official report, Commander Kimberly paid the Leathernecks a fulsome tribute: "To Captain Tilton and his Marines belongs the honor of first landing and last leaving the shore, in leading the advance on the march, in entering the forts, and in acting as skirmishers. [The Marines

were] chosen as the advanced guard on account of their steadiness and discipline and looked to with confidence in case of difficulty, their whole behavior on the march and in the assault proved that it was not misplaced."

Of the Marines awarded the Medal of Honor, only Coleman and Purvis completed a full-service career, the latter transiting the promotion ladder from private to corporal and back. Brown deserted during the squadron's first port visit after the action in Korea, Dougherty was discharged as "worthless" because of his drunken behavior, Owens left the Corps because of medical problems precipitated by alcohol abuse, and McNamara completed his enlistment and then disappeared into obscurity.

The landing force reembarked early the next morning, leaving the Citadel in ruins. "Thus," wrote Rodgers, "was a treacherous attack upon our people and an insult to our flag redressed." Successful as it had been from a military standpoint, however, the operation was not a masterstroke of diplomacy. Subsequent communications with Korean authorities, conducted by messages tied to a pole on an island near the anchorage, were entirely unproductive, and on 3 July the fleet withdrew. A treaty with Korea was not negotiated until 1882.

The view that the Corps spent the years from 1865 to 1898 in suspended animation must also be modified to take into account the reform movement that developed among its company-grade officers. Perhaps the most articulate of the reformers was Henry Clay Cochrane, whose promotion problems have already been noted. In a pamphlet printed for confidential circulation among

his brother officers in 1875, Cochrane asserted that the Corps, "neither respected nor respectable," stood in need of "a resuscitation or a funeral." The best thing might be for it to acquire a new name and mission as the U.S. Naval Artillery, with the task of manning the country's coastal fortifications. That idea found scant support among Cochrane's colleagues, most of whom cherished the Corps' link to the Navy as its key to salvation, but the remainder of his program reflected the progressive consensus. Its objective was to transform the Corps into a military elite. The progressives hoped to accomplish this goal by improving the quality of its officers and men; providing professional education for all ranks; rationalizing its organization as a brigade composed of permanent regiments; and, especially after the cutbacks of 1876, increasing its authorized strength.

The officer corps would be upgraded by restricting commissions to graduates of the service academies, instituting physical and professional examinations for promotion, and lowering the mandatory retirement age to sixty-two. In addition to their purely professional benefits, the first and second of these measures would reduce the effects of the political influence all officers deplored, at least when exerted by others. The second and third, by eliminating the unfit and infirm, would enhance the opportunities of the able, which was a highly attractive prospect to captains who, studying the Corps' lineal list, could expect to remain captains for twenty years.

The progressives hoped to raise the caliber of enlisted Marines by similar means.

These measures included more selective recruiting, improving the conditions of service and the quality of barracks' life, the institution of orderly avenues of advancement to noncommissioned rank, and the standardization of drill and training, still largely at the whim of the barracks commanders. Reformers believed that these initiatives would not only promote discipline but would also discourage desertion, which hovered around an embarrassing 20 percent per annum, the highest in the armed forces.

Contrary to what Cochrane's pamphlet implied, Zeilin had been neither an inactive nor a reactionary commandant. Like the reformers, he remained acutely concerned about the quality of the enlisted force. In fact, he coined a phrase that would serve generations of Marine recruiters, asserting that "a few good men are preferable to a number of . . . inferior material." An at least moderately progressive outlook was further evidenced by his adoption of a tactical manual embodying the lessons of the Civil War, Maj. Gen. Emory Upton's *Infantry Tactics*, and the dispatch of Capt. James Forney on a year's tour to study and report on the organization and activities of European Marine forces.

Zeilin also exerted a long-lasting influence on the Corps' insignia and accouterments. In 1868 he convened a board of officers that produced the eagle, globe, and anchor cap device that, with some stylistic revision, remains in use today, and in 1875 he approved his officers' request for the return of the Mameluke sword; the Army sword was retained for NCOs. The same set of uniform regulations also eliminated the high

Opposite: Dress and duty uniforms prescribed by the regulations of 1876 as depicted in a twentieth-century watercolor by Col. Donald L. Dickson, USMCR. From left to right: private, undress; lieutenant colonel, full dress; captain, mess dress; second lieutenant, fatigue; first sergeant, full dress; corporal, fatigue; drum major, full dress. (Marine Corps Art Collection)

The Marine guard in the sloop *Lancaster* parades for captain's inspection, circa 1883. (Naval Historical Center)

leather stock that had chafed Marine necks for nearly a century.

Nevertheless, there is no question that Zeilin's view of the Corps was fundamentally conservative. The changes in which he had interested himself did not extend much beyond keeping it operationally up to date. As if in response to the reformers' more far-reaching aims, his last annual report included the almost defiant declaration that "the present organization of the Marine Corps is the best that can be devised."

On 1 November 1876 Jacob Zeilin retired, having spent forty-five of his seventy years in Marine uniform, and Charles G. McCawley became the Corps'

eighth commandant. Zeilin had established McCawley as his heir apparent by appointing him commanding officer of Marine Barracks, Washington, and director of recruiting in 1871, and the transition was tranquil. The only Marine officer to have been brevetted for gallantry in both the Mexican and Civil wars (at Chapultepec and Fort Sumter, respectively), McCawley had been associated with the Corps since boyhood; his father was a Marine captain who had died on active duty in 1839.

Although at forty-nine McCawley was too old to be counted among the reformers, he shared a number of their goals. Perhaps because of his years in recruiting, he was especially interested in improving the conditions of enlisted service. He planned to provide better food; monthly, rather than quarterly, pay periods; more livable barracks with recreational facilities; and higher status for NCOs. McCawley also hoped to persuade Congress to increase the Corps' strength by four hundred men, and to restore the rank of brigadier general to the office of commandant. He eschewed any notion of organizing the Corps into permanent units but directed an increased emphasis on standardizing drill and training.

The results of McCawley's efforts were mixed. The professional potential of the enlisted force was enhanced by requiring recruits to demonstrate that they could read, write, and speak English. Examinations on professional subjects became mandatory for promotion to corporal and sergeant. Two barracks were built, and Congress agreed to institute a pension for thirty years' faithful service, a benefit not extended to the Navy's enlisted men until the end of the century. Contrary to all expectations, however, the desertion rate remained as high as ever. The commandant's campaigns to obtain more men and a star were also unavailing.

As it transpired, the most important reform of the McCawley years was accomplished courtesy of the Navy. One of the points upon which the commandant and the reformers agreed was that the best way to improve the quality of the officer corps would be to fill its openings with graduates of the service academies. Journalists had been sniping at the Corps' junior officers ever since the Civil War. One suggested that "USMC" stood for "Useless Sons Made

Comfortable," a reference to the patronage that often figured in appointments. Another member of the fourth estate alleged that "the Marine Corps officer wears corsets, and parts his hair in the middle. He also has a pedigree and a sword. He carves out his career with his pedigree." Obtaining all new officers from the academies promised to infuse some starch into the Corps' commissioned ranks. This would require a change in existing legislation, which reserved the graduating classes of both institutions to their school's parent service. In 1880 and again in 1881, McCawley sought permission to recruit graduates of the Military Academy. Congress declined to act on his requests, but on 5 August 1882 it passed a naval appropriations bill containing a clause, inserted on the Navy's initiative, that authorized the Corps to commission Naval Academy graduates.

The Navy's motives were not altogether altruistic. By 1882, the personnel of the shrunken fleet included one officer for every four enlisted men. To check the influx of unneeded officers, the House Naval Affairs Committee drafted a bill, sure to pass, limiting the number of appointments made each year to the number of vacancies that had occurred the year before. For the foreseeable future, many if not most academy graduates would be surplus to requirements. Allowing some of them to enter the Marine Corps would not only increase the government's return on investment but would also—so it was hoped, and so it proved—promote homogeneity among the officer corps of the sea services.

While the Act of 5 August 1882 did not restrict the Corps' intake of officers to

Annapolis graduates, that was its predictable effect. Every one of the fifty-two second lieutenants commissioned from 1883 to 1897—later to be rounded off as the "Famous Fifty"—was an alumnus of the Naval Academy. Their number included five successive commandants: George Barnett, class of 1881 (1914–20); John A. Lejeune, class of 1888 (1920–29); Wendell C. Neville, class of 1890 (1929–30); Ben H. Fuller, class of 1889 (1930–34); and John H. Russell, class of 1892 (1934–36), plus thirteen other general officers. These men's influence on the Corps' evolution would be immense.

Two of McCawley's internal initiatives made major contributions to the Marine Corps' heritage, however. The first was the reinvigoration of the Marine Band, which had undergone a marked decline following Francis Scala's retirement in 1871, by the appointment of young John Philip Sousa to be its leader in 1880. The son of a sometime Marine bandsman, Sousa had originally joined the band as a thirteen-year-old "music boy" in 1868 and had gone on to conduct light opera companies. A tireless drillmaster

and prolific composer with a superb sense of theater, he quickly pulled the band out of the doldrums. In 1892 Sousa resigned his position to enter show business, in which he became famous as the international "March King," but by then the Marine Band had attained new heights of popularity. Seven years later President McKinley signed legislation that doubled the size of the band, raised the pay of its members, and authorized a first lieutenant as its leader and a sergeant major as its second leader. Despite his superlative performance, Sousa had not advanced beyond the rank of sergeant major.

By the time Sousa relinquished his baton, the rousing strains of "The Marines' Hymn," first performed shortly after the Civil War, had become a mainstay of the band's repertoire. The origin and the author of the lyrics are unknown. The melody is similar to that of the "Gendarmes of the Queen" duet in the Offenbach opera *Geneviève de Brabant*, originally staged in Paris in 1859. The tune may also have its origins in a Spanish folk song. Whatever its source, the piece did not receive "official" adoption by the Marine Corps until it was copyrighted in 1929 as "The Marine Corps Hymn." The verses have remained sacrosanct since then, beginning with Mexico and ending up in Heaven, despite more than a few feeble attempts to change them. The *Navy Book of Songs* provides a sailor's lyrics, sung to the same tune:

> *It was out there on the* Albany
> *In the Asiatic Fleet.*
> *The Marines were so damned lazy*
> *They could only sleep and eat.*
> *From eight bells to the dogwatch*
> *On deck they're never seen,*
> *Oh the question that we ask you is:*
> *Why the Hell is a Marine?*

McCawley's other lasting contribution to the Corps' heritage, made in 1883, was the adoption of what was destined to become the most famous American military motto: *Semper fidelis*—Always Faithful. It replaced *Per mare, per terram* (By Sea, By Land), which General Zeilin had appropriated from Britain's Royal Marines. As McCawley may or may not have been aware, the British connection continued, for *semper fidelis* was also the motto of the Devonshire Regiment. Five years later, when John Philip Sousa composed the official Marine Corps march, he used the new motto as the title.

Operationally, the fourteen years and three months McCawley served as commandant were among the quietest Marines have ever experienced. On only six occasions did disturbances ashore lead to landings, and all except one of them were minor operations involving no more than a ship's guard. The exception, however, grew into the largest deployment the Corps had yet made. The trouble began in January 1885, when Colombia withdrew its garrison from the province of Panama to combat a revolution at home. The troops' departure was a signal for two local leaders to launch revolutions of their own, sparking a three-way civil war between their followers and Colombian loyalists.

Although the United States considered transit of the isthmus a vital interest, guaranteed by treaty since 1846, the new Democratic administration of President Grover Cleveland was determined to avoid becoming entangled in Panamanian affairs. It underwent a change of heart upon learning that on 1 April 1885, one of the rebel bands had burned the city of Aspinwall (now Colón), the Atlantic terminus of the transisthmian railroad.

On the morning of 2 April, the Marine barracks at Boston, Philadelphia, and Portsmouth, New Hampshire, were instructed to rush detachments to the New York Navy Yard to constitute a battalion for expeditionary service. A force of 213 officers and men under Bvt. Lt. Col. Charles Heywood, the "boy colonel" of Civil War days, sailed for Panama at 1700 the next afternoon. A second battalion, 250 strong, with a six-gun naval battery attached, followed on the seventh. With it went the Navy officer who had been chosen to command the forces ashore, Cdr. Bowman H. "Billy Hell" McCalla.

Heywood's battalion reached Aspinwall, where landing parties from several U.S. warships had already gone ashore, on 11 April.

Reporting to Rear Adm. James E. Jouett, the commander of the North Atlantic Station, Heywood was ordered to take his battalion across the isthmus in an armored train and protect Panama City, the railroad's Pacific terminus. The second battalion arrived four days later. McCalla kept it at Aspinwall. At the same time, however, he directed Heywood to organize the two battalions and the naval battery—an aggregate of 796 officers and men—into the first brigade the Corps had ever mustered. In addition to garrisoning Panama City, Aspinwall, and two villages on the railroad line, the Marine brigade furnished guards for the trains that, as Jouett was pleased to report, continued to run on schedule.

The intervention proved to be an unmitigated success. Despite a few tense moments, the landing force maintained order without the need to fire a shot. At the end of the month, Colombian troops landed at Panama City and the rebels melted away. A phased withdrawal of American forces was completed on 27 May. Later, some historians viewed the Corps' performance in the Panamanian intervention as a precursor of the rapid deployment role it would assume in the twentieth century. At the time McCawley pointed with pride to the "extraordinary dispatch" with which the two battalions had been organized, outfitted, and embarked, but perhaps because of the alacrity with which the movement had been improvised, no steps were taken to facilitate similar operations in the future.

McCawley reached the statutory retirement age of sixty-four in January 1891. To no one's surprise Charles Heywood, whom the commandant had brought to Washington two years earlier to command the Marine barracks, was selected to succeed him. At fifty-one the "boy colonel" remained an unmistakably martial figure, six feet tall, trim, and broad-shouldered, with strong features adorned by a majestic mustache. A member and favorite of the Corps' reformers, he immediately and energetically set out to implement their agenda. In this endeavor, he would attain considerable success.

Within four months of his appointment, Heywood achieved one of the reformers' key goals by persuading Secretary of the Navy Benjamin F. Tracy to sanction the establishment of a School of Application for newly joined second lieutenants and recently promoted noncommissioned officers at the Washington Barracks. Organized by Capt. Daniel Pratt Mannix, an ex-enlisted Civil War veteran who had spent four

years on detached duty teaching at the Chinese naval academy, the school provided instruction in seven departments: infantry, artillery, administration and sea service, law, torpedoes, engineering, and military art. Also in 1891 Heywood laid down the requirement that the commanders of Marine formations and installations write an annual fitness report—today's "fitreps"—on each of their officers. The following year he secured congressional consent to institute both professional and physical examinations for officers as a prerequisite for promotion, another of the progressives' highest priorities. Of course, the new commandant did not have everything his way. His early requests for additional manpower met the same rejection as had those of his predecessors.

Top left: Marines halt on the Panama Railroad during the intervention of 1885. This sketch by Thure de Thulstrup appeared in *Harper's Weekly* for 30 May 1885. (Beverley R. Robinson Collection, U.S. Naval Academy Museum)

Bottom Right: Colonel Commandant Charles Heywood (center) at Marine Barracks, Boston, in 1884. Seated beside him are Maj. Robert Meade (left), who would briefly command U.S. forces in north China during the Boxer Rebellion, and Capt. F. C. Harrington, who would command a company at Guantánamo during the Spanish-American War. Like Heywood, both were Civil War veterans. (National Archives)

Congress' unwillingness to grant the Corps even a small increase contrasted with the generosity with which it was funding the Navy's expansion. A naval renaissance had begun modestly enough in 1884 with an appropriation for the first state-of-the-art warships—three cruisers and a dispatch vessel—built since the Civil War. Produced by a combination of national aspirations and concerns quickened by the gospel of sea power proclaimed by Capt. Alfred Thayer Mahan, the most influential navalist of the era, the buildup continued at an accelerating tempo throughout the 1890s. Before the turn of the century, America's long negligible Navy had become one of the four or five strongest in the world.

During these same decades, the naval revolution precipitated by the Machine Age culminated in the appearance of heavily armored, steam-driven steel battleships and cruisers carrying their main armament in centerline turrets housing breech-loading, rifled guns with ranges measured in thousands of yards. Clearly, Marines would not be called upon to contribute small-arms fire to battles between ships such as these.

The institutional implications were obvious. To remain fully relevant to the New Steel Navy, the Corps needed to identify a new combat mission its guard detachments could perform in place of the one technology had superseded. The solution it espoused was to have them man some of the 6-inch and smaller guns of their vessels' secondary batteries. Ships' captains had been authorized to have guards double as gun crews in 1859, and many had done so, but the matter was left entirely at their discretion. By the late 1880s, Marine progressives had concluded

that the Corps must seek to have this practice made mandatory.

In the meantime, the Navy's own progressives had conceived another, very different new mission for the Corps. They advocated reorganizing it into an amphibious force in readiness for the seizure and defense of the advanced bases that would be required by a coal-burning fleet operating outside its home waters, along with other expeditionary service as needed. The Corps' reaction was cool. Though Marines took pride in their ability to improvise rapid deployments, their receptivity to the idea of specializing in them was constrained by the fact that it usually came coupled with a demand for the elimination of the ships' guards that comprised the Corps' traditional reason for being.

Most naval progressives viewed Marine guards as an insulting anachronism. They might concede that there had been a need for guard detachments in the days when U.S. warships were manned by polyglot crews recruited mostly from among the riffraff populating waterfront neighborhoods in seacoast cities. Now that the Navy was deliberately and successfully recruiting adequate numbers of native-born Americans, however, the presence of a seagoing police had become an affront to the competence of its officers and the character of its men. It was also alleged to inhibit recruiting. Marines did not find these arguments compelling.

Both sides took their stand shortly before Heywood became commandant. In 1889 he and Captain Mannix prevailed upon Colonel McCawley to submit a proposal calling for the mandatory assignment of guard detachments to secondary batteries to the Navy's Board of Organization, Tactics, and Drill headed by Commo. James A. Greer. To their dismay, the Greer Board not only rejected the idea but also recommended removing Marines from the Navy's ships and transforming them into a purely expeditionary force. Although Tracy ignored these recommendations, they signaled the opening of a controversy that would percolate into the next century.

In 1890 and again in 1896 the Greer Board's findings were given new life by articles in the influential *Proceedings* of the U.S. Naval Institute, a private professional association founded in 1873. The author, a veteran of the board, was Lt. William F. Fullam, the number one graduate of the Naval Academy Class of 1877, whose long crusade to rid the fleet of Marines would cause a generation of their officers to regard him as the Annapolitan antichrist. The letters that flowed into the *Proceedings'* lively "Comment and Discussion" department in response to Fullam's articles indicated that his views were widely shared among the Navy's officers. Some correspondents also revealed an antipathy to the Corps exemplified by one's observation that the name *Marine* had become "a synonym for idleness, worthlessness, and vacuity of intellect."

Despite such fulminations, Marines had no reason to worry as long as their commandant enjoyed the confidence of Congress and the secretary of the Navy, which Heywood clearly did. In the summer of 1896, shortly after the appearance of Fullam's second article, he achieved the aim

it protested. Upon his urging, Secretary of the Navy Herbert amended naval regulations to stipulate that, whenever practical, Marine guards would be detailed to man their ships' secondary batteries. A few months later, Congress rewarded Heywood's persistent appeals for more men by authorizing him to enlist another five hundred, the first significant increase the Marines had received in more than twenty years. The boy colonel was proving to be the Corps' most effective advocate since Archibald Henderson.

Heywood did his best to diffuse the simmering imbroglio over the issue of Marine guards serving in ships of the fleet. When the new battleship *Indiana* was about to be commissioned, her prospective commanding officer, Capt. Robley D. "Fighting Bob" Evans, asked that no Marine guard join his ship. Just as forthrightly, Heywood objected, and the secretary of the Navy denied Evans' request. Earlier, Evans had declared that "the more Marines we have, the lower the intelligence of the crew." In hopes of promoting good relations with the ship's officers, Heywood chose Capt. Lincoln Karmany to command the Marines.

Karmany's credentials were outstanding. A graduate of the Naval Academy Class of 1881, Karmany had ranked high enough among his peers to have obtained a commission in the Navy if he had so chosen. Unfortunately, he was inclined to drunkenness and womanizing; his off-duty antics must have scandalized the *Indiana*'s wardroom. Worse, he outraged his messmates by constant references to Evans as "Frightened Bob."

One consequence of Eighth and Eye's interest in naval ordnance was the institution in 1899 of a rank that remained unique to the Corps: gunnery sergeant, which soon became the familiar "Gunny." Selected for their proficiency in handling ships' guns, the seventy-two gunnery sergeants originally authorized became the Corps' best-paid NCOs. Much has changed in the intervening century. Gunnies are no longer required to be ordnance specialists, nor are they relatively so well paid, but they are assigned to every type of unit and their rank has become a symbol of the savvy, tough professionalism of the Corps' noncommissioned leadership.

Between Heywood's accession to the commandancy and the middle of February 1898, Marine detachments made ten minor landings on foreign soil. Another, novel deployment took place between April and October 1891, when the commandant ordered three officers and forty men under Capt. Henry Clay Cochrane to a small U.S. squadron sent to the Bering Sea to help enforce an international agreement to check the slaughter of fur seals. Of the landings, five occurred in the Caribbean or Central America, one in South America, three in East Asia, and one in the Pacific. Four were made to protect U.S. diplomatic offices during wars, revolutions, or riots; the remainder, to safeguard American lives and property—the same sort of missions that the Corps had been performing for close to a century.

In 1895 Cuban patriots launched the latest in a series of revolutions against Spanish colonial rule. Most Americans sympathized with the Cubans, but neither outgoing President Grover Cleveland nor incoming President William McKinley believed that the United States should intervene in the conflict. Even after the rebels purloined and publicized a personal letter in which the Spanish ambassador

Top Left: The Marine reformers' goal realized: members of the *Massachusetts'* guard detachment manning the 6-inch guns of their ship's secondary battery. The wooden tub caught the particles of unburned powder that had to be swabbed out of the bore after each shot. (Detroit Collection, Library of Congress)

Bottom Left: The Marine guard presents arms for captain's inspection in the cruiser *San Francisco* in the mid-1890s. (Detroit Collection, Library of Congress)

Right: This sketch of a landing force of Marines deploying ashore at Alexandria, Egypt, in 1882 appeared in an illustrated magazine of the era. (National Archives)

called McKinley "a small-time politician," the president contented himself with urging Spain to reach an accommodation with her unwilling subjects.

Early in 1898, in an attempt to improve relations between the United States and Spain, an exchange of naval goodwill visits was arranged. The United States dispatched the second-class battleship *Maine* to Havana (where, not incidentally, she would be in position to protect American interests in the event of disturbances) while Spain prepared to send the armored cruiser *Vizcaya* to New York.

The *Maine* anchored in Havana harbor on 25 January. The *Vizcaya* was still en route to New York when, at 9:40 on the evening of 15 February 1898, the battleship's forward magazine exploded, probably as a result of a fire in an adjacent coal bunker, peeling back her armored deck like the lid of a sardine can. Twenty-eight members of her Marine guard were among the 266 officers and men—exactly 75 percent of those serving in the *Maine*—who perished. Stumbling from his cabin through the pitch darkness and dense smoke that instantly filled the ship's passageways, Capt. Charles B. Sigsbee literally bumped into his Marine orderly, Pvt. William Anthony. A veteran of fourteen years in the Corps, Anthony was equal to the occasion. "Sir, I have to inform you that the ship has been blown up and is sinking." His grace under pressure made Private Anthony the first popular hero of the War with Spain—a war that catapulted the United States onto the world stage and created the conditions for the emergence of a modern Marine Corps.

CHAPTER 7

Colonial Infantry, 1898–1917

On 25 April 1898 the United States declared war on Spain. Less than a week later the nation was electrified by the news that Commo. George Dewey's Asiatic Squadron had annihilated its Spanish counterpart at the Battle of Manila Bay in the faraway Philippines. Interest then turned to the Atlantic, into which an enemy cruiser squadron under Rear Adm. Pascual Cervera had vanished after departing the Cape Verde Islands on 29 April.

Earlier that month, in anticipation of war, the commander of the U.S. North Atlantic Squadron, Rear Adm. William T. Sampson, had requested the dispatch of two Marine battalions to Key West, Florida, for service with the fleet. On the sixteenth, Colonel Heywood was instructed to make the necessary arrangements, and within four days 450 Leathernecks had been assembled at New York. In the meantime, the Navy Department had decided that the force should be mustered as a single big battalion. Heywood quickly collected another 200 men, and on 22 April the 1st Battalion of Marines sailed for Key West. Its 23 officers and 621 NCOs and men—a quarter of

the prewar Corps—were organized into five companies of infantry and one of artillery. Heywood named Lt. Col. Robert W. Huntington, a veteran of the first Battle of Bull Run, as the battalion commander. The fifty-seven-year old Huntington chose another Civil War veteran, Maj. Percival C. Pope, as his second in command. When Pope came down with fever, Huntington reluctantly replaced him with fifty-six-year-old Henry Clay Cochrane, who had finally been promoted to major in February after spending nineteen years as a captain. Well known throughout the Corps for his eccentricities, he had once court-martialed a Leatherneck returning from liberty drunk, charging him with attempting to smuggle alcohol aboard government property— inside himself. Years earlier, Huntington and Cochrane had come to blows while serving on a promotion board, and their animosity continued throughout the battalion's deployment. None of their company commanders was below the age of fifty.

Huntington's Battalion, as it soon came to be known, reached Key West the same day Cervera left the Cape Verdes. It remained there for more than a month, impatient to see action. The Army provided spoiled rations and undrinkable coffee, and an epidemic of measles spread through the squalid camp. Most of the Marines threw away their heavy woolen clothing and the ornate Prussian-style helmets. They reappeared in blue flannel shirts, khaki trousers, sturdy canvas leggings, and campaign hats. The rescue of Huntington's Battalion from its tedium and frustration came not at the hands of the Army, but from the Navy.

Foreseeing that the Spanish squadron would make for Cuba, Sampson sought to intercept it at the end of its voyage across the Atlantic. He was unsuccessful, and on 28 May Cervera's cruisers were discovered in port at Santiago de Cuba. To blockade Santiago, the U.S. fleet required a sheltered anchorage to use as a coaling station. Sampson selected Guantánamo Bay,

forty miles east of the city. On his orders, Huntington's Battalion sailed from Key West to undertake the Corps' first advanced base mission on 7 June.

"Billy Hell" McCalla, who had commanded in Panama in 1885, was put in charge of the operation. Fire from his ship, the cruiser *Marblehead*, had driven the Spanish from the vicinity of Guantánamo Bay by the time Huntington's Battalion arrived on 10 June. Landing unopposed on a headland on the eastern side of the bay, the Leathernecks entrenched a camp on a little hill some two hundred yards from shore. Tactfully, Huntington christened it Camp McCalla. Heavy growths of cactus and chaparral stood a bare thirty yards away. Although Spanish forces closed around the battalion, nothing untoward occurred during its first day ashore.

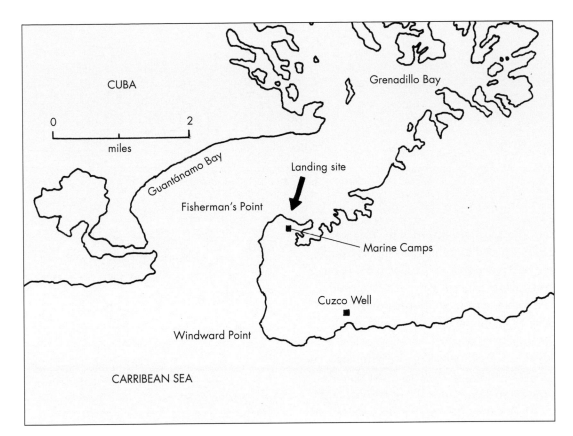

The American intrusion did not remain unopposed, however. The next afternoon two Marines were ambushed on outpost duty, and that night the camp came under heavy fire from Spanish troops in the dense brush around it. While the Spanish never attempted to storm the perimeter, the battalion surgeon and a sergeant were killed and two men were wounded before the enemy retired at the approach of dawn. That afternoon, amid sporadic sniping, Huntington shifted the campsite to a less exposed position nearer the bay. By the time of the move, nervous strain and sleeplessness had begun to take a toll on the middle-aged men commanding the 1st Battalion of Marines. Cochrane recorded that some company commanders advocated withdrawing. Cochrane himself argued against it; Huntington kept his own counsel. According to Cochrane, when Huntington mentioned the possibility of an evacuation to McCalla, Billy Hell retorted: "You were put there to hold that hill and you'll stay there. If you're killed, I'll come and get your dead body." The Spanish returned

after dark, and the battalion sergeant major died in the sporadic firing that continued throughout the night.

Then the Leathernecks' luck changed. Cuban insurgents reported that the Spanish forces—several hundred regular troops and loyalist guerrillas—were based near Cuzco Well, the only source of fresh water in the area, on a ranch approximately two miles southeast of Camp McCalla. On 14 June, Huntington sent two companies accompanied by fifty Cubans to destroy the well. With them went a dapper, tubercular young war correspondent named Stephen Crane, who had won precocious fame three years earlier as the author of *The Red Badge of Courage*. The officer in charge, Capt. W. F. Spicer, was among a number of Leathernecks toppled by sunstroke, and command devolved upon the youngest of the battalion's company commanders, fifty-one-year-old Capt. George F. Elliott.

Taking cover along the crest of a ridge overlooking the ranch, the Marines opened fire. The Spanish replied vigorously from the cover of a thicket in the valley. With the outcome of the action in the balance, Elliott decided to call in fire support from the armed dispatch vessel *Dolphin*. No one had a signal flag, but Pvt. John Fitzgerald tied his neckerchief to his rifle barrel and, silhouetted on the ridgeline, an inviting target for the enemy riflemen below, wigwagged Elliott's request to the ship. Unfortunately, the *Dolphin*'s first shells flew over the Spanish position to impact on a hill recently occupied by Marine reinforcements. Lanky young Sgt. John H. Quick responded to Elliott's shout for a signalman. Knotting his neckerchief to the tip of a long stick, Quick stood in full view of the Spanish to relay the captain's fire corrections to the ship—not once, but on three separate occasions. Stephen Crane watched in awe. Afterwards he wrote,

> As I looked at Sergeant Quick wigwagging there against the sky, I would not have given a tin tobacco tag for his life. . . . It seemed absurd to hope that he would not be hit. I only hoped that he would be hit just a little, in the arm, or the shoulder, or the leg.

> I watched his face, and it was as grave and serene as that of a man writing in his own library. . . . There was not a single trace of nervousness or haste. . . . I saw Sergeant Quick betray only one sign of emotion. As he swung his clumsy flag to and fro, an end of it once caught on a cactus pillar, and he looked sharply over his shoulder to see what had it. He gave the flag an impatient jerk. He looked annoyed.

The *Dolphin*'s fire did the trick. After a few minutes, the Spanish broke to the east. By midafternoon the Leathernecks had occupied their objective, wrecked the well, and burned the ranch buildings. Only a single Marine had been hit. Elliott conservatively estimated Spanish losses at five men killed and wounded. Cuban insurgents captured another eighteen. Spanish forces never seriously disturbed Camp McCalla again.

Eight days after the fight at Cuzco Well the V Army Corps, seventeen thousand men under Maj. Gen. William R. Shafter began landing fifteen miles east of Santiago. Admiral Sampson had requested its deployment to capture the shore batteries covering the minefields that prevented his ships from entering the channel to attack the Spanish cruisers. However, neither operation proved necessary. The governor-general of Cuba ordered Cervera's squadron to make a suicidal sortie, and on 3 July it was destroyed in a running battle with the U.S. fleet. Santiago surrendered on the seventeenth. An armistice went into effect on 12 August; Spain signed a peace treaty five months later.

The Spanish-American War cost the Corps seven dead and twenty-one wounded. Fitzgerald, Quick, and thirteen other Marines won the Medal of Honor, one for gallantry at the Battle of Santiago and twelve for serving in boat parties that dredged up and cut the Spanish undersea telegraph cable off Cienfuegos under a heavy fire from shore. The profusion of awards resulted from the fact that no other decoration for valor was available to American servicemen until World War I. Eleven officers received brevet promotions for the actions at Guantánamo and two for Santiago.

Huntington's Battalion returned home soon after the signing of the armistice. It received a warm welcome. The stories Stephen Crane and other correspondents filed from Guantánamo had made Huntington's Leathernecks heroes. Probably for the first time, the average newspaper reader became aware that the United States had a Marine Corps—and one of which every American could be proud. On 22 September the battalion paraded through Washington to the tunes of "The Marine Hymn" and "A Hot Time in the Old Town Tonight."

In terms of its duration and human cost—114 days and 379 men killed in action—the Spanish-American War was a very minor conflict, but its consequences were immense. In the summer of 1898 the United States emerged as a world power. By year's end it was also a colonial power, having claimed the Philippines, Guam, and Puerto Rico from Spain, annexed the Hawaiian Islands, and established a virtual protectorate over Cuba. The fact that this insular empire would require a great navy to safeguard it and the proof its acquisition presumably offered of Mahan's theory of sea power confirmed the course and quickened the tempo of the American naval renaissance. During the ensuing decade, the United States laid down an average of two battleships a year.

A bigger Navy gave promise of a bigger Marine Corps. In May 1898 Congress approved a wartime-only addition of 1,640 men to the Leathernecks' ranks and authorized the president to issue temporary commissions to qualified applicants from civilian life and—for the time—meritorious NCOs. Altogether, forty-three such commissions were granted, three of them to NCOs. Even if the accessions had been permanent, however, Heywood believed them far too small to meet the demands that would result from the nation's naval expansion and imperial commitments. Late in 1898, he proposed what would have been unthinkable a year earlier: a six-thousand-man Marine Corps. An exuberant Congress proved amenable, and the Naval Act of 1899 increased the Corps' strength to 201 officers and 6,062 NCOs and men. It also raised the rank attached to the office of commandant to brigadier general and allowed for five colonels and five lieutenant colonels of the line—which allowed Henry Clay Cochrane, who had taken thirty-six years to reach the rank of major, to progress to colonel in two.

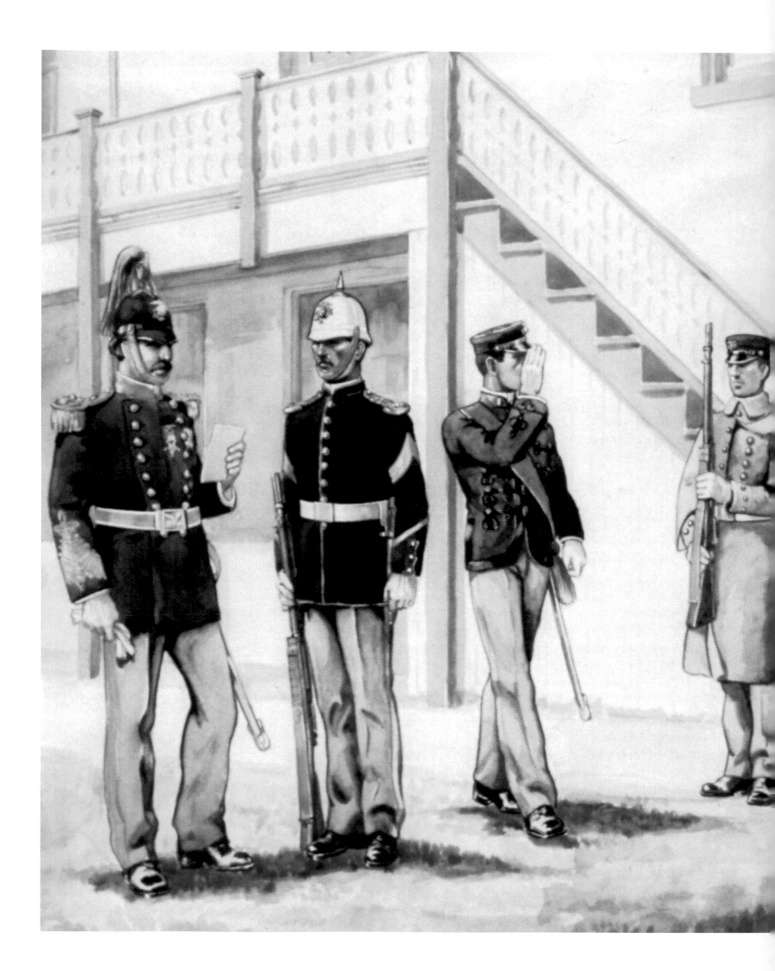

Veteran Marine Corps artist Donald L. Dickson prepared this plate illustrating the uniforms worn in 1900. From left to right: colonel, special full dress with epaulets; sergeant, full dress with white summer helmet; lieutenant, undress, with shoulder sash showing that he is officer of the day; private, undress, with overcoat and detachable cape. The lieutenant's coat, which had been known as the fatigue coat, was redesignated the undress coat in 1891. The Prussian-style helmet worn by the colonel and the sergeant was discarded in 1902. (Marine Corps Art Collection)

Still, Heywood did not regard the act as more than an interim measure. Asserting that in five years the Corps would need at least ten thousand men to keep pace with the Navy's growth, he continued to press Congress to reinforce its ranks. In 1902 it obliged him with another 750 men as well as a personal promotion to the rank of major general. This made the erstwhile boy colonel the first Marine ever to wear two stars. The following year the legislators allowed the Corps another 77 officers and 720 men.

But the Marine Corps acquired more than additional manpower as a consequence of the Spanish-American War. It also acquired two new missions. One was to develop the advanced base capability that had been under discussion for a decade; the other was to serve as colonial infantry, policing the peripheries of the American empire. Regrettably, they were conflicting.

The advanced base mission was assigned to the Corps by Secretary of the Navy John D. Long upon the recommendation of the General Board of the Navy in November 1900. Earlier that year Long had established the General Board, a panel of nine senior officers, to advise him on naval strategy and policy. Although the board lacked executive authority, its conclusions carried great weight, and Long and his successors often transformed them into orders. Among the board's chief concerns was the defense of America's overseas possessions, which it foresaw might require the fleet to operate hundreds if not thousands of miles from its nearest permanent base. The occupation and defense of advanced bases would be imperative. The misunderstandings that

had developed between Admiral Sampson and General Shafter during the Santiago campaign made it appear unwise to rely upon the Army to conduct such operations to the Navy's satisfaction. That was where the Corps came in.

Heywood's response was lukewarm. He agreed to give his Leathernecks training in advanced base activities—emplacing big guns, constructing field fortifications, laying minefields, and so on—and furnished a battalion that had undergone such training to take part in the fleet's annual winter maneuvers in the Caribbean in 1902–3. Conversely, he declined to form the permanent units that the General Board believed should comprise an advanced base force. Too many Marines were already committed to the Corps' other new mission.

In contrast to the advanced base duty with which it had been formally tasked, the Corps' employment as colonial infantry was the child of circumstance. The American Empire was basically the Navy's concern, and the Corps was the Navy's force in readiness. Thus, while Marines continued to make traditional, small-scale landings for brief periods to protect American lives and property, they were also called upon to carry out politically motivated interventions that might absorb a thousand men or more for months and sometimes years. These deployments would hamper the development of an advanced base capability for a third of a century. Of course, as naval progressives never tired of pointing out, manpower sufficient for both missions could have been assembled by withdrawing Marine guards from the Navy's ships, but that idea remained anathema to the Corps.

The Leathernecks' service as colonial infantry began in the Pacific. In February 1899 the Filipino leader Emilio Aguinaldo launched an insurrection against American rule, and a month later a native revolt broke out in the Samoan Islands, which were jointly administered by the United States, Great Britain, and Germany. The major action of the Samoan Uprising took place on 1 April, when a patrol of 118 American and British Bluejackets and Marines was ambushed in thick brush outside Apia, on Upolu Island. The column's machine gun jammed, both contingents' commanders were killed, and the seamen fell back in disorder. Twenty U.S. Marines under 1st Lt. Constantine M. Perkins covered the retreat. Three members of his little detachment were awarded the Medal of Honor.

This reverse notwithstanding, the Samoan Uprising had been suppressed by the end of month. The Philippine Insurrection was a different matter. It would last more than three years and involve 125,000 troops, 4,200 of whom were killed in action—eleven times as many as in the Spanish-American War.

A Marine battalion, requested by Dewey to garrison the naval station at Cavite on Manila Bay, reached Luzon in May. Before the year's end it had been joined by two others to form a provisional regiment.

For the most part, the Leathernecks' war was limited to skirmishes fought by patrols from the installations they guarded. An exception occurred on 8 October 1899, when a 376-man battalion under George F. Elliott, a lieutenant colonel now, was detailed to cooperate with the army in a pincers movement on Novaleta, an *insurrecto* village at the base of the Cavite peninsula. The Marines were to storm the village; the soldiers, to intercept its fleeing defenders. Geography precluded tactical finesse. Elliott's Leathernecks carried their objective in a frontal assault along a narrow causeway and through waist-deep marshes and paddies. Surprisingly, only twelve of them were hit, three fatally. Afterward, Elliott had his men gather in the shade of a giant mango tree and led them in singing "America." Two lieutenants earned brevets for their gallantry in the engagement.

Left: First Lieutenant Constantine M. Perkins, in whites, and his Marines guard the residence of U.S. Consul Osborne at Matautu Point, Apia, Upolu Island, during the Samoan Insurrection of 1899. (National Archives)

Right: Henry L. Hulbert, shown in this photograph as a sergeant major, earned the Medal of Honor as a private at Samoa in 1899. During World War I, he advanced from gunner to first lieutenant before falling mortally wounded at Blanc Mont. (National Archives)

The buildup in the Philippines brought into contact two of the most remarkable warriors ever to wear the globe and anchor: Smedley Darlington Butler, then a nineteen-year-old first lieutenant, and forty-four-year-old Maj. Littleton Waller Tazewell Waller, whose friends called him "Tony." Butler never forgot his first sight of Waller, "a little fellow with a fiery mustache and a distinguished bearing" that made him seem to tower over taller men. A descendent of several prominent Virginian families, Waller had entered the Corps in 1880. Two years later he landed in a detachment under Henry Clay Cochrane to help restore order after the British bombardment of Alexandria, Egypt, and somehow attached himself to the British army for the start of the ensuing campaign. During the Spanish-American War, he commanded the Marine guard in the battleship *Indiana* during the Battle of Santiago. Dashing, indomitable, a magnificent campaigner, at heart a romantic, full of war stories featuring himself, he made a lasting impression on the young men who served under him. Years after Waller's death

had ended their long association, Butler characterized him as "the greatest soldier I have ever known." Another officer of Butler's generation who met Waller in the Philippines recalled, "The U.S. Marine Corps was his God. He never let you forget it."

Like Waller, Butler was descended from several prominent families—in his case, of Pennsylvania Quakers. His father, Republican representative Thomas S. Butler, sat in Congress from 1896 until his death in 1928. At the outbreak of the Spanish-American War, Smedley had added more than a year to his age and, with his parents' reluctant consent, obtained one of the Corps' temporary commissions a few months before his seventeenth birthday. The fighting was as good as over by the time he joined Huntington's Battalion at Guantánamo, but the experience whetted his martial appetite. In 1899 he secured a regular commission, passing second in an examination of thirty-two candidates. A slight, wiry man with a great beak of a nose, Butler relished the challenge of combat. Caught in a nasty night ambush in Haiti in 1915, he exclaimed, "Isn't

this great?" ("Great, hell!" a subordinate retorted. "We're all going to be killed.") By that date Butler had come to disdain what he considered the "over-educated" element of the Marine officer corps, to which he consigned most Annapolis graduates. "If you have too much education," he explained, "you are acutely conscious of the risks you run and are afraid to act. . . . I never went to any military school, and so perhaps I wasn't trained to know danger when I saw it." But if Butler liked to think of himself as a simple fighting man, he was a sensitive one. Wherever he served, his sympathies were with the downtrodden, and inwardly he questioned the motives behind the interventions that brought him fame.

In June 1900 Waller and Butler shared the bleak prospect of spending several years on Guam, generally considered the Corps' dreariest post. Waller had been detailed to form a detachment to take over the Marine barracks there, and Butler was one of five officers who agreed to accompany him. At the last moment, a change of orders came as what both regarded as a reprieve. The detachment was diverted to China to fight the Boxers.

"Boxer" was the occidental abbreviation for a member of the Fists of Righteous Harmony, a peasant movement provoked by the Western penetration of China. First tolerated, then encouraged, and finally supported by the imperial government, the Boxers aimed to purge China of foreign influences by eliminating those who bore or succumbed to them, beginning with Chinese Christians. By the late spring of 1900, two years after its inception, their sanguinary crusade had reached the outskirts of Peking, seat of the eleven foreign legations to the Manchu court.

On 28 May the eleven ministers wired a joint request for guards from the warships that the troubles ashore had drawn to the mouth of the Pei-Ho River. A force of 337 men representing seven nationalities entered Peking on 31 May. The American contingent consisted of 48 Leathernecks and 5 Bluejackets under Capt. John T. "Handsome Jack" Myers, whose father had been the Confederacy's quartermaster-general. Eighty-nine more European sailors arrived on 3 June.

Subsequent events having cast doubts on the sufficiency of this little force, on the ninth the ministers appealed for additional troops. Within twenty-four hours, an international expedition of 2,130 men headed by British admiral Sir Edward Seymour, the senior allied officer present, set out by rail for Peking from Tientsin, a treaty port on the Pei-Ho River eighty miles to the southeast. Included in it were 112 American Bluejackets and Marines. The telegraph line to the legations went dead that same day. Damage to the railroad and attacks by both Boxers and Chinese army units slowed Seymour's projected dash to Peking to a crawl, and on the thirteenth the expedition disappeared into the limbo that enshrouded the legations after the Boxers seized control of the railroad behind it. A day later the Foreign Settlements at Tientsin, garrisoned by 2,400 mostly Russian troops, were besieged by many times their number of Chinese. The single encouraging development in a week replete with alarming ones occurred on the morning of the eighteenth, when the allies captured the Taku Forts guarding the

mouth of the Pei-Ho, thereby ensuring a bridgehead into northern China.

This was the situation when Waller's minute battalion—7 officers and 131 men— landed at Tangku early on the twentieth. That afternoon, unknown to the outside world, the Chinese launched their first attack on the hastily fortified legations at Peking. By then, the Leathernecks had begun advancing

Top Left: Col. Charles Waterhouse's *Red Pants at Noveleta* depicts the Leatherneck assault on the *insurrecto* position near Cavite on 8 October 1899. (Marine Corps Art Collection)

Bottom Right: Maj. Littleton W. T. Waller in tropical service dress about the time of the Philippine Insurrection. (Courtesy Vernon L. Williams)

Map 11:
Marine
Operations
in the Boxer
Rebellion,
May–August
1900

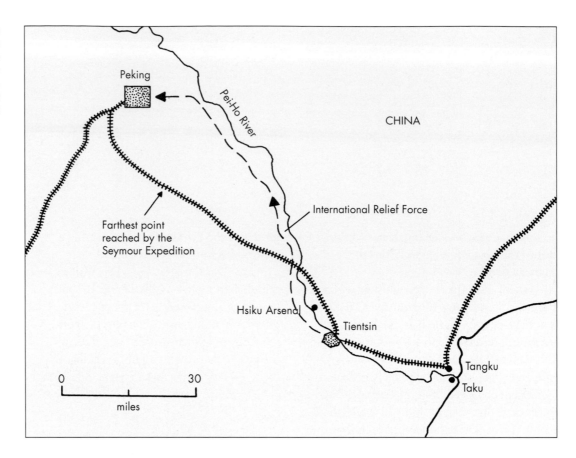

along the railroad to Tientsin. Twelve miles from the city they encountered a battalion of 440 Russian infantrymen whose commander Waller browbeat into joining in an attempt to break through to the Foreign Settlements the next morning.

The attempt did not succeed. Nearing Tientsin, the combined force came up against several thousand imperial troops in entrenched positions, and after an hour's fight, the Russians began to make their way to the rear. Waller turned to Butler. "I hate to give the order," he lamented, "but if we don't retire at once, we'll be cut off."

"I vote to run," Butler interjected.

"Marines never run, my boy," said Tony Waller.

The conclusion of a long rear-guard action found the battalion back at its starting point. Thirteen Leathernecks had been killed or wounded. More new arrivals, mainly Russian and British, came up from Tangku that evening, raising the strength of the allied forces outside Tientsin to 2,300 men. They moved forward on the twenty-

third and entered the Foreign Settlements after what Butler described as "a terrible march in the face of a sand storm, and very severe fighting." Clearly in the mood for a drink, Waller concluded one of his after-action reports with a terse request: "Send more whiskey."

The following day a Chinese courier slipped into the settlements with news of the Seymour Expedition. After losing contact with Tientsin, it had pushed on toward Peking until, on the nineteenth, mounting opposition compelled it to abandon its trains and begin a desperate retreat along the banks of the Pei-Ho. Burdened by more than two hundred wounded who could not be left to the mercy of the Boxers, the expedition appeared in imminent danger of being surrounded and destroyed. "It often occurred to me," Admiral Seymour recalled, "what a very curious scene such an international holocaust would be."

Providentially, before dawn on the twenty-second, the battered column stumbled upon and succeeded in capturing the Hsiku Arsenal, a massive fortification six miles from Tientsin. It was from there that the courier had come. A relief expedition including Waller's battalion started for the arsenal the next day. The Chinese did not seriously oppose its advance, and on the twenty-sixth it escorted Seymour's force back to the Foreign Settlements.

Waller's pride in his Leathernecks' performance knew no bounds. In his official report of the week's operations, he wrote: "Our men have marched ninety-seven miles in five days, fighting all the way. They have lived on about one meal a day for six days, but have been cheerful and willing always. They have gained the highest praise from all present, and have earned my love and confidence. They are like Falstaff's army in appearance, but with brave hearts and bright weapons."

A pause ensued while the forces in the Foreign Settlements awaited reinforcements to storm the city of Tientsin. Among those they received were another battalion of Marines and two of the 9th Infantry from the Philippines. Accompanying these units was Marine colonel Robert L. Meade, a veteran of the boat attack on Fort Sumter, who assumed command of U.S. forces ashore.

The ad hoc American regiment, one thousand men strong, was among the sixty-eight hundred allied troops who delivered a poorly planned assault on Tientsin on 13 July. Meade, whose rheumatism had flared up, entered action with his hands and feet swathed in bandages. He and his men spent a miserable day pinned down in rice paddies by fire from the city's forty-feet-high walls. Finally, at 0300 the next morning, the Japanese contingent blew in Tientsin's

South Gate, and the attackers poured into the streets. During the battle and throughout the remainder of the campaign, the Leathernecks served beside a battalion of the Royal Welch Fusiliers, with whom they developed a friendship that continues to the present; on St. David's Day, Wales' national holiday (1 March), and the Marine Corps Birthday (10 November), the commandant of the Corps and the colonel of the Royal Welch exchange the traditional watchword, ". . . and Saint David."

Another pause followed the capture of Tientsin while the allies gathered strength for the advance on Peking. A third Marine battalion, hastily organized at the Washington Barracks under Maj. William P. Biddle, and another infantry regiment arrived at the end of July to reinforce the Americans, who also received a flinty new commander, Maj. Gen. Adna R. Chaffee. Poor old Meade had been invalided home by then, and Biddle, five months senior to Waller, assumed command of the Marines.

Finally, on 4 August, a relief force numbering 18,600 troops from eight nations marched from Tientsin. The 2,500-man U.S. contingent included two Marine battalions with a strength of 482 officers and men. Evidently no friend of the Corps, Chaffee left the third battalion behind with the garrison at Tientsin and assigned one of the others to guard his baggage train, leaving only Waller's battalion to share in the glory at the front. As always, Waller strove to gather as much of it as possible, and his Leathernecks played a respectable part in the actions culminating on 14 August in the capture of Peking.

The relief force was delighted to find that after fifty-five days under siege the legations were still holding out. Myers' Marines had distinguished themselves in the defense, manning a breastworks on the broad Tartar Wall that bounded the south side of the legation quarter. Myers also led the defenders' only important offensive undertaking, a night attack by thirty of his own men, twenty-six Royal Marines, and fifteen Russian sailors on a bastion in which the Chinese had erected a tower overlooking the American barricade. The bastion was captured and thirty-six of its garrison killed. Allied casualties were two dead, both U.S. Marines, and three wounded, including Myers. U.S. Minister Edwin Conger called the action "the bravest and most successful event of the whole siege." Some years later a monument to the Royal Marines

was erected outside the British Admiralty. One of its panels depicts Handsome Jack Myers leading the sortie on the Tartar Wall.

Seventeen Marines—more than a third of those present—were killed or wounded in the defense of the legations, and about twice that number in the operations leading to their relief. Thirty-three earned the Medal of Honor: eighteen for the defense of the legations, three for the Seymour Expedition, and twelve for the fighting around Tientsin. Ten officers, including Meade, Waller, Myers, and Butler (who had helped rescue a wounded man under fire) were honored by brevet promotions.

In October the Marines returned to the Philippines, and the units there were organized into a brigade. The insurrection still thrived, a bitter guerrilla war having developed after the dispersal of Aguinaldo's conventional forces, but soon the Army's increasingly aggressive counterinsurgency began to gain the upper hand. Aguinaldo was captured in March 1901. In April he urged his supporters to give up the struggle. Thousands complied, and in July President Theodore Roosevelt proclaimed the war at an end.

The proclamation proved somewhat premature. Two pockets of resistance remained: a province of Luzon and the island of Samar. The vigor of the insurrection on Samar became terribly evident on 28 September when a company of the 9th Infantry garrisoned at Balangiga, on the south coast, was almost wiped out by a Sunday morning surprise attack in which the townsfolk joined.

Reaction to the Balangiga Massacre was swift. Brig. Gen. Jacob H. "Hell-Roaring Jake" Smith was given the task of pacifying Samar. The Navy offered to help with a battalion of Marines, and on 22 October Tony Waller sailed from Cavite with fourteen officers and three hundred men. The verbal instructions he received in a conference with Smith the next day were at least unambiguous: "I want no prisoners. I wish you to kill and burn, the more you kill and burn the better you will please me. I want all persons killed who are capable of bearing arms in actual hostilities against the United States." In response to a question from Waller, Smith defined such persons as everyone aged ten years and above. Waller was appalled. Repeating Smith's orders to his officers, he added: "But we are not making war against

women and children. . . . Keep that in mind no matter what other orders you receive."

The military subdistrict assigned to the Marines embraced six hundred square miles of unmapped jungle on southern Samar. To cover it, Waller stationed two companies at the coastal town of Basey, where he established his headquarters, and his other two companies thirty miles east at Balangiga. Small punitive expeditions immediately began to push out from both bases, burning villages, destroying foodstuffs and livestock, and killing or capturing able-bodied men. Between 31 October and 10 November Waller's Marines burned 255 homes and 30 boats, destroyed a ton of hemp and half a ton of rice, and killed thirty-nine Filipinos while capturing another eighteen.

The campaign climaxed at Sohoton Cliffs on 17 December. A supposedly impregnable stronghold occupied by several hundred *insurrectos*, the cliffs towered more than two hundred feet above the Cadacan River sixteen miles north of Basey. The *insurrectos* had carved caves that could be reached only by long bamboo ladders into the cliffs' soft stone face, from which they had suspended cages full of rocks that could be cut loose to cascade down on an assailant. Young Capt. David Dixon Porter, a grandson of the admiral and reputedly the handsomest man in the Corps, was to approach the cliffs overland from the east with 125 men. Waller himself would come up the Cadacan with 75 men in boats towing a raft to which he had lashed a 3-inch field gun. Waller's plan called for the two columns to storm the cliffs together at first light.

Company H, 1st Battalion, of the Marine brigade stationed in the Philippines posed for this photograph outside Olongapo in 1901. Leathernecks sent to the islands served tours of two to two-and-a-half years. (National Archives)

As it happened, the plan did not survive the first light. Upon reaching his position, Porter decided that Waller's detachment would be shot to pieces and attacked at once. To guarantee the quality of its covering fire, he entrusted the column's machine gun to GySgt. John H. Quick—"one of the most competent, intelligent men I ever met in the Corps, officer or otherwise." Pvt. Robert LaKaye swam the river under fire and brought back a boat in which the command began crossing. Porter and Capt. Hiram I. "Hiking Hiram" Bearss led their men up ladders the *insurrectos* had been too surprised to withdraw while the sweep of Quick's machine gun kept anyone from getting near the rock cages above them. By the time Waller's column appeared, the battle was over. Thirty insurgents had been killed and substantial caches of gunpowder and rice as well as forty small bronze cannons captured. Leatherneck casualties were nil. The insurrection on southern Samar had been dealt a mortal blow. Years later, after officers had become eligible for the decoration, Porter and Bearss were awarded Medals of Honor for their heroism at Sohoton Cliffs.

Triumph was soon followed by disaster. On 28 December, following instructions from General Smith, Waller left Lanang, an army base on the east coast, to survey the route for a telephone line to Basey, a distance of thirty-five to forty miles. His party consisted of fifty-five officers and men, two Filipino scouts, and thirty-three native bearers. They carried four days' rations, which Waller calculated would suffice to reach a supply depot inland from Basey.

Army officers at Lanang had warned Waller that he would need supply depots along the way, and they were right. Waller had miscalculated. Hacking their way through almost impenetrable jungle, clambering over the rocky ridges of the Sohoton Mountains, crossing and recrossing meandering streams in a drenching monsoon rain, and maddened by sucking leeches and biting ants, the Leathernecks traversed three or four miles for every one they advanced. Despite the dramatically swift deterioration of the party's physical condition, Waller was forced to cut rations and cut them again. After five days, the slim supply of rations ran out. Finally, two detachments of the most fit men set out to bring help—one led by Waller to Basey and the other by Captain Porter to Lanang. The remaining thirty-three Marines were left under the command of 1st Lt. Alexander S. Williams. By the time a relief column reached them on 18 January 1902, ten Marines had died of exhaustion and exposure. An eleventh succumbed shortly thereafter.

The survivors told a tale of treachery. As they had grown progressively weaker, their bearers had become increasingly unreliable, refusing to help gather firewood, keeping the sweet potatoes and other edibles they harvested from the jungle for themselves and, according to a private who understood some of the Visayan language, plotting to kill the enfeebled Americans. When Lieutenant Williams drew his revolver to enforce an order, a bearer snatched it away from him and another struck him several times with a bolo before Williams succeeded in wrenching the knife out of his hands.

Porter, Williams, and, on being asked for his opinion, Sergeant Quick, recommended that nine bearers and a scout who had idly

watched the attack on Williams be shot. Waller, down with a raging fever after exertions that had prostrated men half his age, promptly ordered all ten executed, along with a bearer who had tried to steal his bolo one night. From this comfortable distance, it is easy to conclude that the Marines overreacted, but their response to any hint of treachery was conditioned by the memory of the Balangiga Massacre. The Marines carried out the executions on 20 January. Waller reported them to Smith by a telegram that opened: IT BECAME NECESSARY TO EXPEND ELEVEN PRISONERS.

Waller was astounded by what happened next. Embarrassed by reports of American atrocities, General Chaffee, now commanding U.S. forces in the Philippines, ordered him court-martialed for murder. Waller defended himself on the grounds that, first, the executions were justified, and, second, he had the authority to order them under the martial law then prevailing on Samar. Despite strong command pressure for conviction, the court acquitted him by a vote of eleven to two. Hell-Roaring Jake, whose "kill and burn" order came out at the trial, did not fare as well. He was court-martialed and forced into retirement.

Still, Waller had been hurt. At home the anti-imperialist press seized the occasion to brand him the "Butcher of Samar," a calumny he never quite lived down. But the officers of the Marine brigade understood what Waller's battalion had undergone and achieved. Whenever one of its veterans appeared in their messes, the toast was raised: "Stand, gentlemen, he served on Samar."

By April 1902 the pacification of Luzon and Samar was complete. Twenty-six Leathernecks had been killed or wounded in the insurrection, and six were awarded the Medal of Honor. The Marine brigade remained in the Philippines until 1914, one regiment stationed at Cavite and another at Olongapo. In the rapid unfolding of events in Cuba, the Philippines, and China twenty-four officers received promotions by brevet, the last to be authorized since Congress created the award in 1814.

In addition to major deployments, the Corps made ten small landings in the opening years of the century: six in the Colombian province of Panama (1901–2), two in Honduras (1903), one in Santo Domingo (1903), and one at Beirut, then in the Turkish province of Syria (1903). All were undertaken to protect U.S. citizens and their interests at times of actual or threatened disorders.

As required by regulations, Heywood retired upon reaching age sixty-four in October 1903. His successor had already been selected. In June, the president announced that George F. Elliott, a captain at Cuzco Well just five years earlier, would become the Corps' brigadier general commandant. An academic drop-out of the Military Academy Class of 1872, Elliott had spent thirty-three of his fifty-seven years in the Marines. Like Heywood he was an imposing figure, broad-shouldered, wasp-waisted, and ramrod straight. Smedley Butler, who served in his battalion in the Philippines, considered Elliott "one of the kindest men in the world," despite his gruff manner and explosive temper. A first-rate field soldier, Elliott was a little too impulsive to operate with maximum efficiency in the highly political environment in which his new duties placed him. But to his credit, he steered the Corps through the most serious political challenge it had faced since the presidency of Andrew Jackson.

Elliott's policies were an extension of his predecessor's. As the Navy grew steadily larger, he appealed for corresponding additions to the Corps' strength. In 1905 and again in 1908 Congress gave him more men, establishing the ten-thousand-man Marine Corps Heywood had foreseen, and in the latter year it acknowledged the Leathernecks' increasing importance by raising their commandant's rank to major general. Yet during the same period the number of battleships in commission rose from twelve to twenty-six. This increase more than doubled the need for fleet Marines, and the creation of an advanced base force continued to hang fire. The advanced base mission was not altogether ignored, however. Officers of both sea services learned valuable lessons in exercises at Subic Bay in the Philippines in 1904 and 1907, and in 1910 the establishment of an Advanced Base School at New London, Connecticut, institutionalized training for such operations.

Two sizable interventions took place under Elliott. The first occurred within three months of his appointment. In January 1903 the United States had negotiated a treaty with Colombia, granting it a one-hundred-year lease to build and operate a canal across the Isthmus of Panama in exchange for

$10,000,000 cash on the barrelhead and an annual subsidy of $250,000. In August, the Colombian senate unexpectedly rejected the treaty on the grounds that these sums were insufficient. Thereupon an outraged Theodore Roosevelt apparently entered into a secret understanding with Philippe Bunau-Varilla, a Frenchman with a financial stake in the start of an American-owned canal. From his suite in the Waldorf-Astoria Hotel in New York, Bunau-Varilla arranged for the Panama City Fire Department to revolt against Colombia.

Panamanian independence was proclaimed on 2 November. On 3 November, five hundred Colombian troops came ashore at Colón to quell the uprising. Within hours the captain of the gunboat *Nashville* landed fifty seamen and Marines and, aided by the American superintendent of the Panama Railroad, contrived to keep the Colombians from proceeding across the isthmus to Panama City. On 4 November, an eight-thousand-dollar bribe from Bunau-Varilla's Panamanian confederates persuaded the Colombian commander to reembark his men. A Marine battalion that happened to have sailed from Philadelphia under Maj. John A. "Gabe" Lejeune on 25 October reached Colón the next day. The United States recognized the independence of Panama on 6 November. A canal treaty was signed twelve days later.

As relations between the United States and Colombia soured, three more Marine battalions were ordered to Panama. Elliott, a veteran of the 1885 intervention, accompanied the last two. Landing at Colón on 7 January 1904, he organized the Leathernecks on the isthmus into a provisional brigade. This would be the only occasion in the twentieth century on which a serving commandant assumed personal command in the field. Happily, the crisis soon passed. Most of the Marines were on their way back to their barracks by the middle of February, but they left behind a battalion that would be garrisoned in Panama until 1914.

The other big intervention was in Cuba. Upon the dissolution of the American military government in 1902, the United States had dictated the insertion in Cuba's new constitution of a clause giving it the right to intervene to preserve Cuban independence, discharge treaty obligations, and maintain "a government adequate for the protection of life, property and individual liberty." When in 1906 a rigged election ignited a civil war that threatened the extensive American investments on the island, Roosevelt reluctantly decided to exercise that right. Early in October a fifty-four-hundred-man Army of Cuban Pacification sailed from the United States.

The Marines got there first. A battalion reached Havana on board the transport *Dixie* on 16 September. Reinforcements followed quickly, and on 1 October Tony Waller, now a colonel, began organizing them into a brigade. At peak strength later that month his command numbered approximately twenty-nine hundred men.

The intervention accomplished its objectives without fighting. An American provisional government assumed control of Cuban affairs, and the warring factions were persuaded to surrender their arms. The Marines began withdrawing in a matter of days, but, as in the case of Panama, the movement was incomplete. A regiment remained with the Army until the end of the occupation in 1909.

A number of minor landings took place as well. At the turn of the year 1903–4 nineteen Leathernecks under Capt. George C. Thorpe escorted a diplomatic mission through hundreds of miles of dangerous territory to and from Addis Ababa, the capital of Ethiopian emperor Menelik II. In January 1904, an anti-American demonstration in Seoul prompted the dispatch of one hundred

sailors and Marines to guard the U.S. legation. A month later, a Japanese army occupied Korea in the opening moves of the Russo-Japanese War, and part of the legation guard stayed on until the restoration of peace late in 1905. Meanwhile, in May 1904, the

Moroccan bandit chief Raisouli kidnapped a naturalized U.S. citizen, Ion Perdicaris. Roosevelt responded by cabling a demand to Sultan Abdul Aziz IV: "Perdicaris alive or Riasouli dead." To underscore the president's message, Handsome Jack Myers led the cruiser *Brooklyn*'s guard ashore at Tangier. The outcome was Perdicaris alive.

Nearer home, a revolution in Santo Domingo (as Americans persisted in calling the Dominican Republic) occasioned four landings in 1904. In 1907 a Nicaraguan invasion of Honduras prompted a gunboat to put her corporal's guard ashore there, and two subsequent deployments were undertaken in consequence of events within Nicaragua itself. In October 1909 the Conservative Party launched a revolt that enjoyed American favor against the Liberal regime of President José Santos Zelaya, whose ambitions had annoyed Central America for more than a decade. To safeguard American interests should the need arise, a provisional regiment including the Panama Battalion, then commanded by Maj. Smedley Butler, was kept on a transport off Corinto from December 1909 to March 1910. The need did not arise, but by the time the Leathernecks were recalled, U.S. diplomatic pressure had forced Zelaya into exile. The Liberal government retained power, however, and in May its army pushed the Conservatives' dwindling forces back to Bluefields, on the Atlantic coast. Fearful that the city would become a combat zone, the U.S. consul called for Marines. Two gunboats promptly put landing parties ashore, and Butler's battalion was rushed to the scene. Though privately Butler deplored American involvement in what he saw as the senseless

U. S. MARINES
"SOLDIERS OF THE SEA"

For Full Information Apply
RECRUITING STATION

bloodshed of the Nicaraguan civil war, he also saw where his duty lay. At Bluefields he informed the leaders of the opposing forces that he would not allow fighting around the city. His reluctant intervention saved the revolution from certain defeat. Disheartened, the government army withdrew, and the reinvigorated Conservatives began an advance that carried them to the presidential palace in August. Butler's Leathernecks returned to Panama a month later. For a decade thereafter, Nicaraguan mothers quieted unruly children with the admonition, "Hush, hush! Major Butler will get you!"

The challenges the Corps confronted in these diverse deployments paled in comparison to one it encountered in Washington. On 16 October 1908, Rear Adm. John E. Pillsbury, Chief of the Bureau of Navigation (really, of personnel), wrote Secretary of the Navy Victor H. Metcalf to recommend what many Navy officers had long advocated: that Marine guards should be withdrawn from the Navy's ships. Metcalf concurred and forwarded the proposal to Roosevelt, who gave it the presidential stamp of approval. After protesting the decision to Metcalf, General Elliott appealed directly to the chief executive. He found the president inflexible; the guard detachments would have to go, and he was not to make trouble over it. On a happier note, Roosevelt agreed to put the Corps' future on a firm footing by allowing Elliott to prepare a formal statement of its duties for his consideration. The president signed the resultant document into law as Executive Order 969 on 12 November. Mention of ships' guards was conspicuous

by its absence. Soon the fleet began sending its Marines ashore.

Elliott thought he had achieved everything possible under the circumstances. That satisfaction was soon dispelled by reports that the president wanted to do more than take the Marines off ships: he wanted to merge them into the Army. The reports were true. In conversation with his military aide, Army captain Archie Butt, Roosevelt declared: "[The Marines] have augmented to themselves such importance, and their influence, which they have gained by pandering to every political influence, has given them such an abnormal position for the size of their corps that they have simply invited their own destruction. . . . No vestige of their organization should be allowed to remain."

Elliott now went to action stations. For once the sea services showed a united front; even naval progressives were aghast at the prospect of losing the Marines altogether. From 7 to 15 January 1909 a subcommittee of the House Naval Affairs Committee under the friendly chairmanship of Smedley Butler's father investigated the removal of guard detachments from the Navy's big ships. Elliott, his senior staff officers, Waller, and others delivered predictably impassioned testimony in favor of their retention. The House found the Marines' arguments persuasive. On 3 March, it attached what was called the Butler Rider to the Naval Act of 1910. This stipulated that none of the monies allocated to the Marine Corps should be spent unless the ships' guards were restored. With only days left in office and otherwise satisfied with the contents of the act, Roosevelt chose not to continue the contest. The Marines returned to the fleet.

As Elliott approached retirement, most observers assumed that he would be succeeded by Waller, the officer the Corps itself undoubtedly would have chosen. There were other contenders, but none could match Waller's record of service. As expected, Secretary Meyer recommended his appointment to President William Howard Taft. The president in turn told Archie Butt that he intended to name Waller to the post—"and this in spite of the fact," Butt wrote his sister-in-law, "that Waller was court-martialed for shooting a few of the little Brown Brothers in the Philippines. . . . But Waller is the idol of the Corps and certainly the only man in the entire body who has any fitness for the position at the present time."

At this point Pennsylvania's influential senior senator Boise Penrose paid the president a call. Penrose's message was blunt. His candidate for commandant was Col. William P. Biddle, a member of the prominent Philadelphia family. Unless Biddle received the appointment, Penrose would withdraw his support for Taft's legislative program. "In five minutes," Butt noted sadly, "Waller was sidetracked and Colonel Biddle elevated to the place of command. . . . Presidents have always used the army and navy for trading stamps, but I had hoped that the President would throw down the glove to Penrose or rather pick up the one Penrose threw at his feet; but it was not to be." On 10 February 1911 Biddle became the Corps' eleventh commandant.

A veteran of almost thirty-six years' active duty, Biddle had been Dewey's fleet Marine officer at Manila Bay, led the Leathernecks in the march on Peking, and later commanded the brigade in the Philippines. This rather impressive résumé notwithstanding, most contemporaries found the new commandant lacking in drive. In China his staff dubbed him "Sitting Bull," having concluded, as one of its members wrote, "that Major Biddle's dominant characteristic was love of a comfortable chair." Josephus Daniels, the second of the navy secretaries under whom Biddle served, described him as "an agreeable gentleman . . . not noted for vigor and initiative."

Whatever Biddle's energy level, his years as commandant were eventful. In March 1911, less than a month after his appointment, the threat that the opening spasms of the Mexican revolution posed to American residents led to the formation of an expeditionary brigade under Waller at the U.S. base at Guantánamo, Cuba, ready to intervene at a moment's notice. The call to do so never came, and in a few months the brigade was disbanded, but its brief existence had an important consequence.

Concerned about the recent exhibitions of hostility to the Corps in high places and unhappy with the selection of Biddle as commandant, the brigade's officers met on 26 April and established the Marine Corps Association, an unofficial, self-supporting organization with the mission of representing their corporate interests and stimulating their professional development. Two years later the association received a written charter, and in 1916 it commenced publication of the *Marine Corps Gazette*, which it defined as "a periodical journal for the dissemination of

information concerning the aims, purposes and deeds of the Corps, and the interchange of ideas for the betterment and improvement of its officers and men." The *Gazette* has discharged those duties ever since.

A new outbreak of violence led to the deployment of another expeditionary brigade to Cuba in May 1912. This time the trouble was in Cuba itself, where the government's refusal to allow the organization of a political party along racial lines provoked the Negro Rebellion. The Leathernecks guarded towns, railroads, and American properties, freeing the Cuban army to search out the rebel bands. Fighting had ended by mid-July, and the brigade was dissolved later that month.

During the deployments to preserve order and *yanqui* interests in Cuba after 1911, a group of disgruntled officers composed new verses for "The Marines' Hymn":

> *From the Pest Hole of Cavite*
> *To the Ditch at Panama,*
> *You will find them very needy*
> *Of Marines—that's what we are;*
> *We're the watchdogs of a pile of coal*
> *Or we dig a magazine,*
> *Though he lends a hand at every job,*
> *Who would not be a Marine?*

> *From the School of Application*
> *To the Shores of Subig Bay,*
> *We've avoided exertion*
> *In the most ingenious way;*
> *Admiration of our mattresses*
> *It is the finest thing we've seen,*
> *For it answers to the question,*
> *Why the Hell is a Marine?*

The Nicaraguan kettle also continued to boil. In July 1912 Gen. Luis Mena, an erstwhile ox-driver who had become minister of war in the Conservative government, launched a revolt against President Adolfo Díaz. Highly pleased with Díaz and apprehensive about the danger to American citizens and investments, the United States intervened. On 4 August the gunboat *Annapolis* sent one hundred seamen and Marines to guard the U.S. legation at Managua. Butler's Panama Battalion reached the capital ten days later. By the end of the month naval landing parties had gone ashore at Bluefields, Corinto, and San Juan del Sur, and the 1st Provisional Regiment, 780 Leathernecks under portly, bespectacled Col. Joseph H. "Uncle Joe" Pendleton, was on the way from Philadelphia. One of the Naval Academy's "Famous Fifty" Marine graduates, Uncle Joe was among the best-loved officers in the Corps' history. Even Butler, who had no use for Annapolitans, was pleased to call "that sturdy old soldier and genial companion" a friend. Arriving at Corinto on 4 September, Pendleton assumed command of the Marines ashore in western Nicaragua.

The campaign was waged along the railroad that ran in a southeasterly direction from Corinto through León, Managua, and Masaya to Grenada on Lake Nicaragua. At the beginning of the intervention, all except Corinto and Managua were in rebel hands. Butler kept going throughout the ensuing operations despite an attack of malaria that sent his temperature soaring to 104 degrees. His feverish, bloodshot stare inspired his men to give him the enduring nickname "Old Gimlet Eye."

The decisive action occurred on 4 October. By then Butler had talked Mena into surrendering, but another rebel general, Benjamin Zeledón, remained in arms. Just north of Masaya, the railway ran between two hills, Coyotepe and Barranca. Coyotepe, an elevation of about five hundred feet, was the higher and steeper. Zeledón held both summits with approximately a thousand men in trenches protected by barbed wire and supported by a few small field guns. Following his rejection of Pendleton's summons to surrender by 0800 on 3 October, two Marine batteries shelled the rebel positions throughout the day. At 0515 the next morning the Americans attacked Coyotepe: Pendleton with 600 Bluejackets and Marines from the east and Butler with

250 Marines from the southeast. Exactly thirty-seven minutes later and at a price of four dead (all Marines) and five wounded they were in possession of the hilltop. Twenty-seven Nicaraguans had been killed and nine captured. Barranca's defenders decamped when the Americans on Coyotepe took them under fire. The Nicaraguan army, which had prudently awaited the outcome of the fight, captured Masaya that same day.

Another American force occupied León on 6 October. Mopping-up operations ended on 2 November, and, except for a hundred-man legation guard, the Leathernecks were withdrawn by the end of the month. All told, the Nicaraguan intervention cost the Corps thirty-seven casualties. This was the first time Marines had been committed to combat to uphold or install a Latin American government of which the United States approved. It would not be the last.

Meanwhile, the Corps had finally begun to take serious steps toward developing the capability to perform its advanced base mission. Much of the impetus for its new interest was from external sources. By 1910, the General Board had become highly dissatisfied with the spasmodic efforts that had been made to create an advanced base force during the past decade. So, too, were the Navy reformers, most notably the Corps' old scourge, William F. Fullam, now a captain who had attained an influential position as an aide to Secretary Meyer. Yet it seems clear that Headquarters Marine Corps was not merely reacting to outside pressures. While Biddle had never been an exponent of the advanced base mission, he was clearly more receptive to it than his predecessors had been. This receptivity was reflected by his appointment of Maj. Eli K. Cole, arguably the foremost advocate of that mission, to the newly established post of assistant to the commandant, with special responsibility for readiness and training. Within a year, one or more permanent companies had been organized at every Marine barracks, and the Advanced Base School relocated to Philadelphia, where Biddle set an enrollment of 250 officers and men. By the end of 1912, almost a fifth of the Corps had passed through it.

Biddle also evidenced an openness to innovation by approving 1st Lt. Alfred A. Cunningham's request for permission to attend the Navy's fledgling flight school in Annapolis. Cunningham's reporting date, 22 May 1912, would become the official birthday of Marine aviation. A second Marine, 1st Lt. Bernard L. Smith, also earned his wings that year, and a third,

2nd Lt. William M. McIlvain, in 1913. Together with seven ground crewmen, Smith and McIlvain formed the Aviation Detachment, Advanced Base Force, in the fleet maneuvers of 1913–14, which proved to be a watershed in the evolution of the modern Marine Corps.

Planning to have the maneuvers include a major advanced base exercise had begun in January 1913. The experience gained at Subic Bay in 1907 had convinced the Corps that an advanced base force should consist of two regiments: a fixed defense regiment to man the base's big guns and fortifications, and a mobile defense regiment with field artillery and machine guns to deal with any enemy forces that succeeded in getting ashore. Because of the usual manpower shortage, the regiments formed for the exercise numbered eight hundred rather than the approximately thirteen hundred men they were to count at full strength.

First Lt. Alfred A. Cunningham (left), the Corps' first pilot, cranking up the trainer known as Noisy Nan at Philadelphia in 1911. He became interested in aviation while assigned to the Advanced Base School a year before obtaining his orders to flight school. (National Archives)

The Leathernecks began to ship out from Philadelphia on 27 November, and the 1st Advanced Base Brigade was formally constituted on 23 December. Its mission was to hold Culebra, a small island off the coast of Puerto Rico, against an assault by an enemy—"Black"—fleet. Col. George Barnett, who commanded the Philadelphia Barracks, was selected as the brigade commander. From 10 to 18 January 1914 the brigade dragged its guns into position, built emplacements and entrenchments, strung wire, laid minefields, and otherwise prepared the island for defense. After two days of mock bombardments, the Black fleet began landing a force of twelve hundred seamen and Marines before dawn on 21 January. Within hours the chief umpire, Navy captain William S. Sims, ruled that the attackers had failed to crack Culebra's

defenses. The Corps had demonstrated the feasibility of advanced base operations to the Navy and itself.

Biddle's tour as commandant ended the following month. In March 1913 newly elected Democratic president Woodrow Wilson had named Josephus Daniels, an energetic southern newspaper editor possessed of an ardent streak of egalitarianism and a penchant for micro-management, to serve as secretary of the navy. Determined to destroy what he considered the undue influence of officers who homesteaded positions in Washington, Daniels announced that henceforth such assignments would be made for a single, four-year term. Some months thereafter Biddle put in for retirement. Daniels ascribed the commandant's decision to the introduction of the single-term policy, which would have prevented his reappointment, but it may well be that Biddle was loath to spend another year, much less face another four, under the iconoclastic secretary.

Biddle's action presented the Wilson administration with an unexpectedly early opportunity to install a commandant of its own choosing. Once again, most observers thought that Waller, still the Corps' favorite, enjoyed the inside track. But once again, most observers were wrong. This time Waller was undone by the shadow of Samar. Daniels decided that his appointment would be incompatible with the administration's policy of promoting cordial relations with the Philippines. In his memoirs, Daniels acknowledged Waller's "high qualities as a man and an officer." Nevertheless, he recalled, "It seemed to me unwise to appoint as head of the Marine Corps an officer who was alleged to have needlessly caused the death of Philippine soldiers [sic], though in the trial he had been acquitted. . . . Except for my intense hostility to the war upon the Filipinos and my zeal that they be given the right of self-government, I would have favored him."

On 25 February 1914, President Wilson announced that he had selected George Barnett as the major general commandant of the Marine Corps. Despite the disappointment some Leathernecks felt over his selection, the polished and charming Barnett proved to be an effective commandant. Whereas his predecessors had accepted the advanced base mission, with either tepid enthusiasm or benign neglect, Barnett embraced it. In testimony before Congress he declared, "The fortification and defense of naval advanced or temporary bases for the use of the fleet has been made the principal wartime mission of the Marine Corps." To ensure that this was well understood, Barnett emphasized the importance of the Advanced Base School and detailed the captains and majors who had interested themselves in advanced base operations to serve as instructors-evangelists at the Naval War College.

Unfortunately, the Corps' rival mission repeatedly frustrated Barnett's efforts to implement more than doctrinal change. On assuming his duties, Barnett planned to establish the permanent brigade the General Board had decided would be needed for advanced base duty in time for the next fleet maneuvers. The intervening occupation of Veracruz, Mexico, prevented him from carrying out that intention. In 1915 he was able to organize the fixed defense regiment, but the following year the Caribbean claimed it, too.

Trouble had been brewing between the United States and Mexican governments since August 1913, when Gen. Victoriano Huerta shot his way into power, only to be challenged by a revolution that President Wilson applauded. To increase its chances of success, Wilson refused to recognize Huerta and declared an arms embargo of Mexico. He also deployed naval forces to protect American interests along the Mexican Gulf coast. On 9 April 1914, the tension was brought to a head by Mexican troops who briefly detained a party of U.S. seamen at Tampico. Although Huerta apologized for the incident, he refused to fire the twenty-one-gun salute the United States demanded without an assurance that it would be returned. Wilson

found the reservation unacceptable. On 20 April, the president asked Congress for authority to use armed force in Mexico, but the Senate adjourned without taking action on the measure.

At 0230 the next morning Wilson was awakened and informed that the German steamer *Ypiranga* was expected to dock at Veracruz that day with a huge shipment of American-made arms and ammunition. The president decided that her cargo must not reach Huerta. Orders were sent to Rear Adm. Frank F. Fletcher, commander of the naval forces off Veracruz, to seize the city's customs house and intercept the arms as they were landed.

In an attempt to avert bloodshed, Fletcher notified the military commandant of Veracruz, Gen. Gustavo Maass, and the municipal authorities of his orders and urged them not to offer resistance. For his part, Huerta replied to Maass' request for instructions with orders to withdraw peaceably, but it was too late. The general had already sent an officer to exhort, arm, and release the inmates of the city jail and dispatched one hundred regulars to the harbor area to "repel the invasion." Their efforts to carry out his order would be supported by the cadets of the Mexican Naval Academy, policemen, members of the home guard, and ordinary Veracruzanos who took up arms in defense of their city.

The landing party came ashore at 1130. It numbered 787 men—285 seamen from the battleship *Florida* and 502 Marines, made up of the understrength 2nd Advanced Base Regiment, which had remained on call since the Culebra maneuvers, and a provisional battalion composed of the guard detachments from the *Florida* and her sister ship, the *Utah*. The Bluejackets were to occupy the customs house, and the post and telegraph office; the Leathernecks, the railroad terminal, roundhouse, and yard, the cable office, and the power plant.

The Mexicans did not oppose the landing, but as the Americans marched into the city they were greeted by a fusillade of small-arms and machine-gun fire from street corners, windows, and parapet roofs. Suddenly, Veracruz became a battleground. While the forces ashore slowly fought their way forward, Fletcher landed the *Utah*'s 384-man Bluejacket battalion, the only other unit at his disposal. By midafternoon the Americans had occupied all of their objectives. Fletcher then called the advance to a halt, initially in hopes that it would be

possible to arrange a cease-fire. It was late in the day before those hopes faded, and he instructed the landing party to remain on the defensive pending the arrival of reinforcements.

Five battleships and two cruisers reached Veracruz during the hours of darkness. The battleships' seaman battalions were organized into a regiment twelve hundred strong, and their Marine detachments into a three-hundred-man battalion. After another vain attempt to contact Mexican officials, the advance got under way at 0745. Street fighting was as much a novelty to the Leathernecks as to the sailors, but they quickly adapted. Smedley Butler, who landed about midnight, recalled that "stationing a machine gunner at one end of a street as a lookout, we advanced under cover, cutting our way through adobe walls from one house to another with axes and picks. We drove everybody from the houses and then climbed up on the flat roofs to wipe out the snipers." By noon Veracruz had been secured, although scattered sniping persisted for several days.

American losses totaled seventeen dead and sixty-three wounded; four of the former and thirteen of the latter were Marines. Mexican casualties must have numbered upward of five hundred.

The 1st Advanced Base Regiment, originally ordered to Tampico, went ashore that afternoon. A third provisional regiment assembled at Philadelphia disembarked on the twenty-ninth, and on 1 May, Tony Waller arrived to assume command of what now was an entire brigade of Leathernecks consisting of 3,141 officers and men. By then the sailors and fleet Marines had returned to their ships and an Army brigade had landed. Leathernecks and soldiers garrisoned the city until the U.S. withdrawal on 23 November. Huerta had entered exile in July.

Nine Marines, including Butler, were among the fifty-five men awarded the Medal of Honor for Veracruz. All of the Marines and most of the others were officers, who finally became eligible for the honor in March 1915. Butler returned his medal to the Navy Department, protesting that he had done

Left: A Marine
mounted patrol
sets out into *caco*
territory with a
Haitian guide in
1915. (National
Archives)

Map 13, right:
The Haitian
and Dominican
Campaigns,
1915, 1916,
and 1919–22

nothing heroic. He was told that he would keep and wear it.

Seven months after the evacuation of Veracruz, the Corps was committed to an occupation destined to last almost two decades. In a region wracked by what Theodore Roosevelt called "the revolutionary habit," Haiti held the revolutionary record. Between December 1908 and July 1915, seven presidents had been either overthrown or assassinated. The U.S. State Department took a dim view of such high jinks, fearing that sooner or later they would cause Haiti to precipitate an international crisis by defaulting on her foreign loans.

Nevertheless, the American intervention was unplanned. When on 27 July 1915 a mob tore an eighth president quite literally to pieces, 330 Bluejackets and Marines were landed at Port-au-Prince to preserve order. Once the capital had been occupied, however, Wilson was unable to resist the temptation to take matters in hand. Five companies of Leathernecks plucked from Barnett's fixed defense regiment disembarked at Port-au-Prince on 4 August, and on the fifteenth Tony Waller came ashore with a full regiment

and organized the Leathernecks into the 1st Provisional Marine Brigade, then numbering 2,029 men. Rear Adm. William B. Caperton, the senior U.S. officer present, stage-managed the Haitian National Assembly's acceptance of a hand-picked new president and a treaty effectively transforming the country into an American protectorate. Waller set about to eliminate the bane of the Haitian political process, the *cacos*.

Named for an indigenous bird of prey, the *cacos* were bandits who inhabited the mountains and jungles of northeastern Haiti. They eked out their livelihood by shaking down the peasantry and by helping presidential aspirants realize their ambitions "for a certain sum," as Waller put, "to be paid out of the Haitian treasury . . . [and] also the privilege of looting some of the towns on the way down." To induce the *cacos* to disband, Waller offered a subsidy of one hundred Haitian *gourdes*—about twenty dollars—to each chief who would turn in himself and his weapon, and ten *gourdes* to each rank-and-file *caco*. At the same time, he began to push combat patrols inland from the coastal towns in American

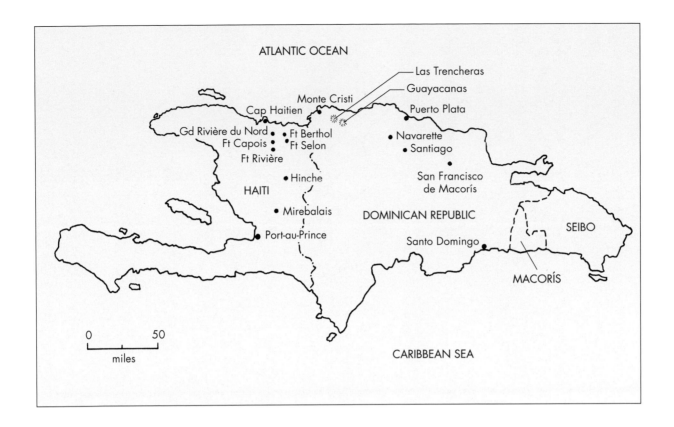

hands. Several skirmishes ensued, and by early October, the remaining *cacos* had retired deep into the interior.

Butler was delighted to have Waller give his battalion the task of penetrating their refuges. On 22 October, Butler set out to locate a *caco* stronghold called Fort Capois with a mounted patrol of forty men including GySgt. Dan Daly, who had won the Medal of Honor at Peking. After nightfall on the twenty-fourth, the patrol was ambushed by a force Butler estimated at four hundred *cacos* while fording a river in a heavy rain. A pack horse went down, but the Marines made it across the river. Butler called a halt upon reaching high ground a mile from the ambush site and set about organizing a defensive perimeter. He ordered Sergeant Daly to break out the patrol's machine gun. "It was lost in the river, sir," Daly replied.

Butler masked his disappointment with a casual remark and moved on. An hour later, Daly approached him. "I've set up the machine gun, major," he reported. Acting on his own initiative and alone, Daly had slipped through the *caco* band to the ford, found the dead pack horse, retrieved the machine gun and ammunition, and returned to the perimeter before anyone realized that he was gone.

Repeatedly shifting positions to avoid being submerged by the *caco* rushes, the Leathernecks survived the night. At first light, Butler divided his command into three squads and ordered each to charge outwards. The result of this unconventional tactic was a rout in which the Marines not only put the *cacos* to flight but also went on to capture their base, Fort Dipitié, which dawn revealed lay several hundred yards away. Two Leathernecks suffered wounds in the affray; the *cacos* lost eighteen killed and wounded. On Butler's recommendation, two of his officers received the Medal of Honor, and Sgt. Dan Daly became the first Marine to be awarded a second.

In the following weeks Butler's columns captured and destroyed Fort Capois and two lesser fortifications, Selon and Berthol, with little or no opposition. His final objective was Fort Rivière, an old French masonry work some two hundred feet square crowning the remote summit of Montagne Noir. The *cacos* considered the position impregnable,

and some Marine officers believed that its reduction would require a regiment supported by field artillery. Butler chose to tackle it with about one hundred men divided into four companies with two machine guns each.

On three sides, the ground dropped away from the fort too sharply for an assault to be possible. The only practical approach was along the slope extending to the sally port on its western face. At 0730 on 17 November, Butler led a company up the slope while the expedition's machine gunners laid down covering fire. Arriving at the sally port with his orderly, Pvt. Samuel Gross (real name: Samuel Marguiles), and Sgt. Ross L. Iams, Butler discovered that it had been bricked up. The only way into Fort Rivière led through a drain four feet high, three feet wide, and

fifteen feet long into the mouth of which a *caco* was firing.

For a few seconds the Marines flattened themselves against the wall, Butler on one side of the drain, Iams and Gross on the other. Then Iams said, "Oh, hell, I'm going through," and ducked into the opening. Gross shouldered Butler aside to follow directly behind Iams. The *caco* snapped off a shot, but somehow his bullet missed all three men. Iams' aim was better, and the Leathernecks emerged from the drain to find themselves confronted by a mob of screaming *cacos*. Iams and Gross each shot one of the leaders, and Gross also dropped a giant, club-wielding *caco* who was about to brain Butler.

In the meantime, other Leathernecks had begun scrambling out of the drain.

"Hand to hand fighting, even with rocks, was going on," one recalled. "It was Sergeant Grimm, I believe, who exchanged rock for rock with some unknown *caco*; the two of them pitching big stones at each other over a wall gave a comical twist to the otherwise confused mêlée of bayonets and machetes." In a quarter of an hour, it was over. More than fifty *cacos*, including several *gros chefs*, died in the struggle. Not a single American was killed or seriously wounded. Butler, Iams, and Gross were awarded Medals of Honor, and this time Butler accepted his without complaint. He and Dan Daly remain the only Marines to share the remarkable distinction of having won the medal twice.

Even before the capture of Fort Rivière signaled the pacification of the *cacos*, the Marines had undertaken their other major mission: the creation of a national constabulary, the Gendarmerie d'Haiti, to replace the disbanded Haitian army. Until adequate numbers of native aspirants could be trained, the Gendarmerie would be officered by Marine officers and NCOs seconded to the Haitian service at a higher rank than they held in the Corps. On 3 December, Butler became its first major general commandant. Originally the force's numbers were fixed at 53 officers and 1,530 gendarmes. Under Butler's energetic leadership, progress was rapid. In February 1916 the Gendarmerie formally assumed the responsibility of policing the country, relegating the Marine brigade to a supporting role, and in August a supplementary U.S. agreement with the Haitian government increased its authorized strength by 60 percent.

Haiti's Hispaniolan neighbor, the Dominican Republic, passed under American control the following year. As usual, the intervention came about in reaction to a revolution. This one was provoked by President Juan Isidro Jiménez's dismissal of a political rival, Gen. Desiderio Arias, as minister of war. Arias responded by having his troops seize control of Santo Domingo, the country's capital.

Well content with Jiménez, who had recently accepted an American plan for reforming the republic's finances and army, the United States attempted to negotiate an end to the confrontation. On 14 May 1916 Arias agreed to evacuate Santo Domingo, where the first Marines had landed nine days earlier, and withdrew ninety miles north across the mountains to Santiago de los Caballeros. In the interim, Jiménez had resigned office rather than accept American assistance against his countrymen, but that solved nothing. In common with many other Dominicans, including a majority of the National Assembly, Arias opposed the reforms the United States wanted made. To allow his revolution to succeed, even by default, would hardly be compatible with American aims. If Dominican authorities declined to act against Arias, very well: the United States would act alone.

The job was given to Uncle Joe Pendleton, whose 4th Marine Regiment was ordered from San Diego to the Dominican Republic on 4 June. Pendleton set out for Santiago from Monte Cristi, on the northern coast, with about 850 men on the twenty-sixth. The same day a smaller column jumped off from Puerto Plata, fifty miles to the east. The two

forces were to unite at Navarette, twelve miles from Santiago.

Pendleton's column fought two actions during its advance. Like the engagement at Coyotepe, both called for assaults on entrenched hilltops. The first took place at Las Trencheras on 27 June. After the Leatherneck artillery gave the summit a good pasting, the infantry stormed it with fixed bayonets. The second clash occurred at Guayacanas on 3 July. This time dense brush impeded emplacing the artillery, but the rebel position was hosed down by machine gunners, two of whom won the Medal of Honor for their work. Marine casualties in these encounters totaled two killed and twelve wounded. The American columns met at Navarette on 4 July. A surrender delegation from Santiago appeared the next day.

During the following months the 2nd Provisional Marine Brigade, as Pendleton's command had been designated, established garrisons in ten cities; disarmed the Dominican army; and, as in Haiti, paid private citizens to turn in their firearms, eventually collecting fifty-three thousand guns

of various sorts. These activities precipitated several small shootouts and a daring coup in Pacificador Province, where Governor Juan Perez refused to recognize American authority. Apprehensive that Perez would free and arm the hundred convicts being held in the *fortaleza* at San Francisco de Macorís, 1st Lt. Ernest C. Williams, the commander of the company stationed there, decided to take charge of their custody. On the evening of 20 November, Williams led twelve picked men in a rush for the gate. The fort's forty-man garrison greeted them with a burst of fire. Eight Leathernecks fell wounded, but Williams and the others succeeded in pushing their way through the gate before it could be closed. Two Dominicans died in a point-blank exchange of shots inside the fort, and the remainder laid down their arms. The exploit earned Williams the Medal of Honor.

U.S. officials had hoped that the reforms they envisioned could be carried out with the cooperation of the Dominican government. By November it was obvious that such cooperation would not be forthcoming, and on the twenty-ninth the United States reluctantly announced the installation of a military government headed by Navy captain Harry S. Knapp. Pendleton became minister of war and the navy, the interior, and police. As in Haiti, the American intervention had become indefinite; but also as in Haiti, the Marine brigade was quickly charged with creating its replacement. On 7 April 1917, Knapp directed Pendleton to raise and train a force to which the maintenance of order could one day be relinquished, the Guardia Nacional Dominicana. Like the Gendarmerie d'Haiti, it would initially be officered by Marine volunteers.

Open-ended though it was, the occupation of Hispaniola did not threaten to impose as great a strain on Marine manpower as it would have two years earlier. In 1916, influenced by the Great War under way in Europe, President Wilson asked Congress to approve a great construction program calculated to produce a navy "second to none." To man the 157 ships to be built in three years would require the number of personnel to jump from 50,000 to 75,000. Arguing that the Marines' manning level should be a fifth as large as the Navy's, the commandant appealed successfully for a proportionate increase. The Naval Act of 1916 provided for a Marine Corps of 597 officers and 14,981 men and upgraded its rank structure to include eight brigadier generals. Tony Waller, Uncle Joe Pendleton, and Gabe Lejeune were among the colonels who pinned on stars as a result. Of great long-term significance, the act also created the Marine Corps Reserve.

The Naval Act of 1916 probably marked the passing of the Old Corps. Prior to the colonial infantry era, the Leathernecks numbered barely two hundred officers and six thousand enlisted men. Most knew the officers and senior NCOs personally, or at least by name and reputation. The troops smoked or chewed rank cigars, claiming that cigarettes were for women and children. They drank anything containing alcohol, including

hair tonic, and called the beer sold in canteens at naval bases or at taverns ashore "horse piss." Especially, Marines savored Caribbean rum. They could hike and fight on meals consisting of only strong black coffee, jerked goat meat, and beans or rice.

Liberty ashore often resulted in periods of absences without leave (AWOL), and the Marines of the Old Corps accepted the harsh punishments that accompanied spurts of AWOL and drunkenness as a necessary

Left: Leatherneck transport in the Dominican campaign extended from burros to Model Ts requisitioned from Santo Domingo's Ford agency. (Photograph album, Robert H. Dunlap Papers, Alfred M. Gray Research Center, Quantico)

Right: Who wouldn't want to join the Marines after encountering Sgt. Michael Fitzgerald at the recruiting station on 23rd Street in New York City in 1916[?] (National Archives)

accompaniment to the rough-and-tumble profession they had chosen. The quest for horizontal refreshment resulted in scandalous incidents of venereal disease, but their seniors viewed them without undue alarm, leaving the suffering to suffer. Many career Leathernecks traveled up and down the promotion ladder with regularity. Veterans considered a corporal with only one hash mark barely more than a recruit. Buck sergeants usually wore three, and senior NCOs sported hash marks up to the elbow. Even at the height of the colonial infantry era, the Marine Corps counted only four sergeants-major. But the Marines of the Old Corps knew their weapons and how to use them. To veterans of the Old Corps, the quantum increase in the numbers wearing forest green in 1916 swept away much that was unique about the smaller of the naval services.

Another of the act's provisions empowered the president to augment the Corps by 2,515 officers and men in event of war. That event was guaranteed by Germany's resort to unrestricted U-boat warfare in February 1917. But even then, the Caribbean made another claim on the Corps' resources. Defeated in a corrupt election, the Cuban Liberal Party launched an insurrection in which a number of American-owned sugar plantations were promptly torched. The first Marines committed to the Sugar Intervention landed on 25 February. Others followed, and from August 1917 to August 1919 at least one and usually two regiments were stationed in Cuba. As they had during the Negro Rebellion, the Leathernecks performed guard duties while the Cuban army operated in the field. The last Marine outposts would not stand down until 1922.

CHAPTER 8

Over There, 1917–1918

At the time America entered the world war on 6 April 1917, the Corps numbered only 511 officers and 13,214 men. The possibility that Marines might serve in France did not seem likely. Except, that is, to Maj. Gen. Commandant George Barnett, who realized that the absence of Leathernecks from the American Expeditionary Forces (AEF) would give a hollow ring to the Corps' cherished recruiting slogan—"First to Fight." Barnett

pressed his case on Capitol Hill, and when the naval appropriation bill for 1918 became law, it included provisions for an increase in the number of men wearing forest green to more than thirty thousand; by war's end, that figure would double.

Close on the heels of the declaration of war, Barnett approached Secretary of the Navy Josephus Daniels with the request that he offer a brigade of combat-ready Marines to Secretary of War Newton D.

The children of Menaucourt cheer as the 5th Marines arrive to enter cantonment there in June 1917. (National Archives)

Baker. At first, Daniels appeared reluctant to accompany the commandant to see Baker. He may have suspected that Barnett wanted the additional commitment to justify his persistent requests for personnel increases. On second thought, Daniels sagely concluded that the addition of a few Marines to the AEF could bring political dividends to the Navy in its annual budgetary battle with the Army.

At the War Department, Barnett, Daniels, and Chief of Naval Operations William S. Benson found Baker loath to allow the Marine Corps to insinuate itself into what his constituency insisted should be a purely "U.S. Army show." Baker made it clear that a token force of Marines would be an administrative and logistical embarrassment. He quizzed Barnett on details of uniform and equipment, stressing the necessity for commonality among U.S. ground forces in the interests of economy of supply. In each instance, Barnett agreed to the necessary changes, leaving Baker no excuse to refuse his offer. Even the organization of the Marine contingent had to be modified. Because Army regiments numbered twice as many men as the Marine equivalent, the Corps had to muster the proposed two-regiment brigade (5th and 6th Marines) into a single regiment—the 5th—in order to have an Army-style regiment ready to join the first troops leaving for France.

To give the outfit polish and grit, Barnett ordered eight companies of veteran Leathernecks home from the Caribbean to form the backbone of the regiment. Among the 5th Marines' fledgling officers was a twenty-five-year-old platoon leader from Texas, 2nd Lt. John W. Thomason Jr.,

whose writings were destined to make him the Kipling of the Old Corps. Thomason noted that the regiment included men from every part of the country and every walk of life: store clerks and lumberjacks, farmhands and college grads. But at the same time he observed that there were "Diverse people who ran curiously to type, with drilled shoulders and bone-deep sunburn, and a tolerant scorn of nearly everything on earth. Their speech was flavored with navy words, and words culled from all the folk who live on the seas and ports where our warships go. They were the old breed of American regular, regarding the service as home and war as an occupation; and they transmitted their temper and character and viewpoint to the high-hearted volunteer mass which filled the ranks."

The force sailed from New York in June 1917, arriving at St. Nazaire, France, at the end of the month. By 3 July, the entire Marine regiment was under canvas ashore and on 15 July joined the 1st Division to be reviewed by the AEF's commander-in-chief, Gen. John J. "Black Jack" Pershing. The sharp-eyed Pershing was mortified to note that the intrusive Leathernecks seemed better trained and looked more military than the soldiers of his beloved regular Army. This discovery notwithstanding, he assigned the Marines to military police duties along the lines of communications while the soldiers began training for front-line service. At the same time, he moved to forestall the assignment of additional Leathernecks to his command. In a terse cablegram to Washington, Pershing cited his concern for commonality, arguing that Marines did

Opposite: Howard Chandler Christy, famous for his trademark "Christy girl," put her in uniform for this recruiting poster. Painted in 1915, it was updated for World War I by the addition of Marines wearing the dishpan helmets with which U.S. forces were equipped during the conflict. (Marine Corps Art Collection)

not assimilate well into the organizational anomalies of the AEF. Finally, he asked that "no more Marines be sent to France."

To Pershing's dismay, the War Department informed him that President Wilson had already directed the deployment of more Marines to France; in fact, another regiment of Marine infantry and a battalion of machine gunners would soon sail to join the AEF. Then Brig. Gen. Henry P. McCain, the adjutant general of the Army, dictated their organization in an order that must have made Pershing bridle: "This regiment [6th Marines] to combine with the other one [5th Marines] to a brigade in the 2nd Division commanded by a Marine Corps general about to be nominated, and will be part of the Army under your command."

Back home, eager enlistees underwent a strict regimen of training that ensured that every Leatherneck scheduled to go "over there" was fit. For most of the nineteenth century, the training of Marine recruits had been left to the whims of the various barracks commanders. By the time America entered the world war, however, it had been standardized and localized on an isolated island off the coast of South Carolina. Parris Island became a name synonymous for military toughness, providing an experience that thousands of young men would never forget. One alumnus captured the essence of the ordeal in a letter home: "The first day at camp I was afraid I was going to die. The next two weeks my sole fear was that I wasn't going to die. And after that I knew I'd never die because I'd become so hard that nothing could kill me."

Descriptions of Leatherneck recruit training and its record of making a man out of a boy spread quickly. Finding herself unable to cope with an undisciplined son, a mother sought help from the Marine Corps Recruiting Station in Buffalo, New York: "I am the mother of a very unruly boy. . . . I would like very much to enlist him in the Marines at once. I must do something before it is too late. He just came home to me drunk and my heart is broken. I can't see this sorry [situation] any longer; he is getting

Top Left: Off-duty Leathernecks befriend a French farm girl at Menaucourt in the summer of 1917. (National Archives)

Top Right: Marine recruits perform physical training at the newly acquired training camp at Parris Island, South Carolina. (National Archives)

Bottom Right: On the way to France in November 1917, members of the 6th Machine Gun Battalion crowd the rails of the *Von Steuben* as another transport, the *Agamemnon*, steams past. (National Archives)

worse every day. Can you send a man here that could enlist him?"

Barnett also established an advanced-combat training program at the newly acquired base at Quantico, Virginia. Every Leatherneck slated for duty in the AEF received additional weeks of rugged indoctrination to life on the Western Front, including valuable instruction from veteran British and French officers. In addition, candidates seeking a commission had to complete the demanding program of officer candidate school. With such a program to ensure preparedness, no one should have been surprised to find that the Leathernecks appeared more polished than the Doughboys.

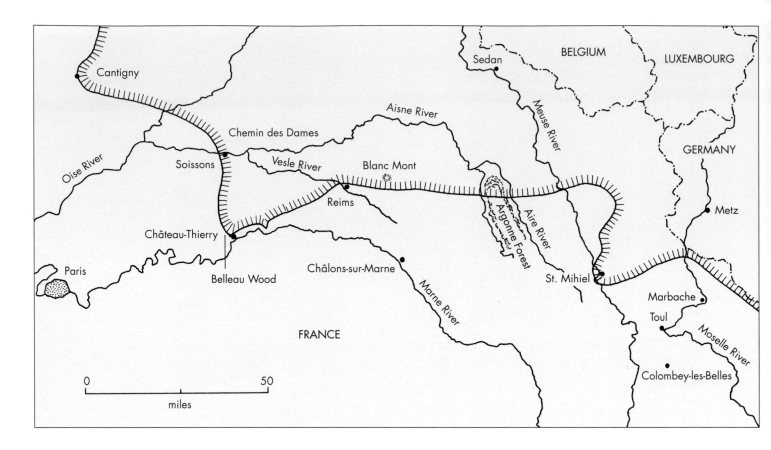

By February 1918, the 6th Marines and the 6th Machine Gun Battalion had joined the 5th Marines to form a brigade under Brig. Gen. Charles A. Doyen, Barnett's Naval Academy classmate. Doyen appealed to Pershing to allow the unit's name to reflect its parentage: thus, the 4th Brigade (Marine), 2nd Division, AEF, was born. Each AEF division contained two infantry brigades of two regiments each, a brigade of artillery, and a regiment of combat engineers, plus support and headquarters elements. The strength of these formations averaged 25,500 men, more than twice the number in a British, French, or German division.

In May 1918, Doyen became ill and AEF Headquarters sent him home, along with a message that no replacement was required. Command of the Marine Brigade passed to an Army officer, Brig. Gen. James G. Harbord, an old friend of the AEF's commander. On giving Harbord the Marines, Pershing supposedly told him, "You are to have charge of the finest body of troops in France, and if they fail to live up to that reputation I will know whom to blame." The first

test for Harbord and his Marines—an elite force of 280 officers and 9,164 NCOs and men—lay ahead at Belleau Wood.

By then the war had reached its climacteric. Having knocked out Russia in late 1917, Germany resolved to make a desperate double-or-nothing gamble to achieve victory in France before the reservoir of American manpower could be tapped. The German spring offensive opened on 21 March 1918 with a mighty blow that sent the British Expeditionary Force staggering back some forty miles. For a few days, the Allies were brought face-to-face with disaster, but in the end they managed to seal the breach. Unwilling to concede the defeat this foreboded, on 9 April the German high command launched a second, slightly less formidable assault on the British front. It, too, scored substantial gains, but eventually it, too, was contained.

Still determined to force the war to a triumphant conclusion—unlikely as that had become—the Germans turned their attention to the French. On 27 May, the third of the German spring offensives

Map 14, left: Marine Operations on the Western Front line as of 9 June 1918.

Right: The 55th Company, 5th Marines, rests in a village on the way to the front before the Battle of Belleau Wood. (NARA)

struck surprised French forces north of the Aisne, previously thinned to reinforce the British sector, and achieved a stunning breakthrough. By 31 May, the Germans had reached the Marne at Château-Thierry—barely forty miles northeast of Paris—and had driven a twenty-five-mile-wide wedge into the Allied front. Not since 1914 had the enemy stood so close to the French capital. Although in fact the losses sustained in its previous offensives had severely weakened the German Army, to the Allies the crisis of the war appeared at hand.

Previously, Pershing had steadfastly resisted Allied appeals to integrate American formations into the French and British armies. In accordance with his instructions from President Wilson, he was determined to retain control of his troops until enough reached France to form a "separate and distinct" American army. The German onslaught caused him to relent, and on 28 March he offered to place all American combat troops in France—approximately four divisions—temporarily at the disposal of the French high command. A regiment of

the 1st Division entered action at Cantigny on 28 May, the same day the 2nd Division moved forward to help stem the German advance below the Marne.

Harbord ordered Col. Albertus W. Catlin's 6th Marines to take up positions along the Paris-Metz highway, just south of a little forest called Belleau Wood. His instructions left no doubt as to the seriousness of the situation: the Marines and the soldiers of the 9th Infantry on their right were to dig in and hold at all costs: "No retirement will be thought of on any pretext whatsoever." No one had thought to issue entrenching tools, so the Leathernecks and Doughboys used their mess kits and bayonets to burrow into the ground. Meanwhile, retreating French troops streamed past on their way to the rear. Capt. Lloyd W. Williams marched his company through shattered Meaux, twenty-five miles northeast of Paris, on 1 June. A French officer proceeding in the opposite direction invited Williams and his Marines to join the dispirited column. The gallant Leatherneck responded tersely: "Retreat? Hell! We just got here."

Left: GySgt. Dan Daly wearing the Medals of
Honor he won in China and Haiti, and the
Distinguished Service Cross he earned in France.
(National Archives)

Right: The savagery of the Battle of Belleau
Wood is evoked in this painting by Frank
Schoonover. (Marine Corps Art Collection)

A day later, German forces approached the American position. Allowing the columns of *feldgrau* infantry to advance to within one hundred yards of their lines, the Marines cut them down like ninepins with well-aimed rifle fire. For two days the Kaiser's troops attempted to pierce their front, to no avail. By 5 June, the German offensive had stalled.

Then, on the afternoon of 6 June, the Marines received orders to eject the Germans from Belleau Wood. Their objective stood on a fold of rocky ground in the midst of rolling farm country, extending approximately a mile and a half from north to south and one half mile from east to west. Colonel Catlin described it as "a typical piece of well kept French woodland." The trees, tall but averaging only five to six inches in diameter, grew so close together that in places visibility was limited to fifteen or twenty feet. Inside, the wood bristled with machine-gun nests.

Since the initial contact, the Germans had learned that they faced American regulars. The German high command did not consider Belleau Wood of great strategic significance, but it decided to assert a moral superiority over the new enemy by repulsing the American assault. The stage was set for the fiercest battle the Corps had ever fought.

A short, savage artillery barrage preceded the Leathernecks' attack. At 1700 waves of Marines fixed bayonets and crossed wheat fields dotted with poppies. As withering German fire tore through their ranks, the Americans wavered but continued to advance. GySgt. Dan Daly, the only enlisted Marine to have been awarded two

Medals of Honor, swung his rifle toward the enemy lines and shouted to his platoon, "Come on, you sons-of-bitches! Do you want to live forever?" (After the battle, he would be cited for three separate acts of heroism, recommended for a third Medal of Honor, and awarded both the Navy Cross and the Army Distinguished Service Cross.) Catlin, watching the attack through his field glasses from a little rise three hundred yards from the woods, took a bullet through the right lung. "I suffered but little pain and I never for a moment lost consciousness," he recalled, "nor did any thoughts of death occur to me. I was merely annoyed at my inability to move and carry on." Lt. Col. Harry Lee assumed command.

By nightfall, Leatherneck blood dotted the landscape, matching the color of the poppies, but the Marines had a foothold in the woods. Later, a battalion commander declared that "the only thing that drove

these Marines through those woods in the face of such resistance was their individual, elemental guts, plus the hardening of the training." That night, Sgt. Maj. John H. Quick earned a Navy Cross and a Distinguished Service Cross to wear beside the Medal of Honor he had earned during the Spanish-American War. Learning that a battalion on the edge of the woods was low on ammunition, Quick and 2nd Lt. William B. Moore, a Princeton football hero, drove one of Henry Ford's tin lizzies through a curtain of fire to resupply it. The butcher's bill for the day numbered 1,087 Leatherneck casualties, more than the Corps had lost in all the other battles it had fought since 1775.

The next morning the advance continued in the face of bitter opposition. By the close of 12 June, the Americans held the entire wood except a small area along its northern fringe. At dawn, the Germans counterattacked behind a barrage of artillery and mustard gas. Although the gas alone caused 450 Marine casualties, the brigade held its ground in a desperate day's fighting. Late on 15 June, depleted Marine columns moved to the rear, leaving it to the U.S. 7th Infantry Regiment and French forces to mop up the remaining Germans. But the Leathernecks' battle for Belleau Wood had not ended. When the Germans reinforced the defenders, the Allied attack stalled. On 23 June, the Marines returned to the scene with newly replenished ranks. Three days later Maj. Maurice Shearer, commanding the 3rd Battalion, 5th Marines, reported with characteristic Leatherneck bravado: "Woods now U.S. Marine Corps entirely."

From first to last, the tactically insignificant forest had cost the Marine Brigade 5,183 killed and wounded, a casualty rate of more than 50 percent. Among the dead were Captain Williams, who had declined the French officer's invitation to join the retreat, and Capt. Edward C. Fuller, the son of a future commandant. A grateful France announced that Belleau Wood henceforth would be named Bois de la Brigade Marine. In a petulant gesture, AEF Headquarters altered the name to Bois de la Brigade des Americains. Just as forthrightly, the French changed it back. And the French were not

the only ones impressed by the prowess and élan of the Marines; the Germans began to refer to them as *Teufelhunden*—"Devil Dogs."

Along with the victory came an outburst of interservice acrimony that persisted throughout the war and for a generation thereafter. Although Pershing had issued orders that American war correspondents should not identify specific units in their dispatches, those covering the Battle of Belleau Wood reported the attacking units to be Marines. Then Floyd Gibbons of the *Chicago Tribune* fell gravely wounded while accompanying Dan Daly's platoon. Earlier, the intrepid journalist had approached Col. Wendell C. Neville to ask for permission to accompany the 5th Marines during the assault. The taciturn Leatherneck granted his request with a cautionary note: "Go wherever you like. Go as far as you like. But I have to tell you, it's damn hot up there."

Believing his wound mortal, friends among the censors at AEF Headquarters allowed Gibbons' "last," particularly vivid dispatch to go through unaltered. Because tiny Belleau Wood was unknown to his readership, Gibbons used the name of the entire region—Château-Thierry—for the site of the encounter. Thus, to the consternation

of every soldier in the AEF—especially the Doughboys of the 1st and 3rd Divisions fighting gallantly to stem the German offensive—the Marines became the beneficiaries of a public relations bonanza. For the remainder of the war, soldiers taunted them with a musical doggerel, sung to the tune of "Mademoiselle from Armentières," which resulted in its share of black eyes and broken noses:

> The Marines have won the Croix de
>   Guerre, parlez-vous?
> The Marines have won the Croix de
>   Guerre, parlez-vous?
> The Marines have won the Croix de
>   Guerre,
> But the sons-of-bitches were never there.
> Hinky dinky parlez-vous?

The Army's resentment was also evidenced in official snubs. After the capture of the woods, a beaming French president Georges Clemenceau visited the headquarters of the 2nd Division. Neither Harbord nor any of his Marines were invited to meet him. At home, Barnett exacerbated the Army's discomfiture by touting the record of the Leathernecks at Belleau Wood to any congressman or journalist who might offer an ear. Deeply moved, Secretary of the Navy Daniels composed a new stanza to "The Marines' Hymn":

> *As we raised our flag at Tripoli*
> *And again in Mexico;*
> *So we took Château-Thierry and*
> *The forest of Belleau.*
> *When we hurled the Hun back*
> *   from the Marne,*
> *He said we fought like fiends,*
> *And the French rechristened Belleau Wood*
> *For United States Marines.*

Despite the terrible losses the Germany army had already suffered, its high command launched another offensive on 15 July. The blow fell on the French front in Champagne. This time the Allies were prepared. Intelligence had obtained complete details of the enemy plans and in most areas the offensive was stopped in its tracks. Only eight of the forty-seven divisions committed to the operation succeeded in crossing the Marne, and on 17 July the Germans called off the attack.

Profiting from the enemy's discomfiture, the Allies immediately counterattacked. Their principal objective was to cut the highway from Soissons to Château-Thierry, used to supply German forces in the salient. The high command assigned the key role in the assault to the French XX Corps, consisting of the 1st and 2nd Divisions, AEF, and a French Moroccan division. Harbord had taken over the 2nd Division by then, Pershing having sacked its original commander and Neville succeeded Harbord in command of the Marine Brigade.

The Leathernecks moved into the pocket south of Soissons on 18 July with fixed bayonets. Once again, they attacked into a wood, the Forêt de Retz, which Lieutenant Thomason thought "was like Dante's wood, so shattered and tortured and horrible." He remembered that "machine-guns raved everywhere . . . it was every man for himself, an irregular, broken line, clawing through the tangles, climbing over fallen trees, plunging heavily into Boche rifle-pits." Mostly, Thomason recalled the dying as the gallant Marines took position after position: "Some guns were silenced by blind, furious rushes that left a trail of writing, khaki figures, but always carried two or three frenzied Marines into the emplacement; from whence would come shooting and other clotted unpleasant sounds and then silence."

In two days of bitter fighting, the brigade suffered 1,972 casualties, of which the 6th Marines took two-thirds. During the hours of desperate combat one young company commander, 1st Lt. Clifton B. Cates, sent a runner to his battalion commander to report: "I am in an old abandoned French trench, . . . I have only two men left out of my company and twenty out of other companies. . . . I have no one on my left, and only a few on my right. I will hold." On the evening of the nineteenth, the Germans pulled back across the Marne. With their withdrawal, the initiative passed to the Allies, who never relinquished it.

Two Central European sergeants in the same company of the 5th Marines, Louis Cukela and Matej Kocak, earned the Medal of Honor on 18 July. Kocak, Slovakian by birth, personally captured an enemy machine-gun nest and then led twenty-five stray Moroccans in an attack that overran another. Cukela, a Serb, had joined the U.S. Army in 1914 and had been stationed in the Philippines. Two years later the news that the Germans had captured his native village inflamed his indignation to the point that he purchased his discharge and returned to the United States with the intention of enlisting in the Canadian Army, which was already fighting in France. But like many another belligerent young man, he was seduced by the slogan "First to Fight" and reached France in June 1917 as

a U.S. Marine. According to the citation for his Navy Medal of Honor, when his company's advance was checked: "Sergeant Cukela advanced alone. . . . Disregarding the warnings of his comrades, he crawled out from the flank under a heavy fire and worked his way to the rear of the enemy position." Cukela then "[rushed] a machine gun emplacement, killed or drove off the crew with his bayonet, bombed the remaining part of the strong point with German hand grenades, and captured two enemy machine guns and four men."

Cukela, then a gunnery sergeant, had already had been recommended for the Medal of Honor for Belleau Wood, but the recommendation failed to gain approval at AEF Headquarters. Shortly after Soissons, Cukela was granted a battlefield commission. He became a well-known character in the Corps between the wars, retiring with the rank of major in 1940. Never exactly at home in his adopted language, he was apt to express his dissatisfaction by exclaiming, "Next time I send a goddamn fool, I go myself."

Late in July, command of both the 2nd Division and the Marine Brigade changed again. Pershing appointed Harbord to straighten out the muddle behind the lines in the Services of Supply (SOS). Harbord proved a success as the chief of the SOS, but his assignment left the 2nd Division without a commander. The division counted three brigadier generals: two Army and one Marine Corps, the latter of whom ranked as the most senior. Barnett had sent John A. Lejeune to France in June in hopes that he could persuade Pershing to approve the

formation of a Marine division in the AEF. When Black Jack Pershing pole-axed that notion, a decision supported strongly by the Army Chief of Staff, Lejeune went on to serve briefly as commander of an Army infantry brigade, and then took over the Marine Brigade from Neville.

A grizzled Cajun whose down-home manner masked a shrewd intelligence, Lejeune was placed in temporary command of the division while Pershing looked for a successor to Harbord. After a few days,

Pershing decided to leave him in the job, and in August Lejeune pinned on his second star. He was the first Marine Corps officer ever to lead a unit larger than a brigade in combat. His selection was undoubtedly influenced by the fact that he was one of a handful of Marines to have attended the Army War College, where he made many friends among classmates and faculty who now occupied important positions in the AEF. At the same time, Pershing and senior Army officers probably concluded that by giving

Lejeune command of the 2nd Division, it might stifle entreaties by Barnett and the Navy Department for the formation of a Marine division within the AEF. Even as these important changes were being made, Pershing and Brigadier General McCain, Adjutant General of the Army, exchanged secret cablegrams on the subject; they concluded that the AEF could do without more Marines, especially an entire division of them, whom most senior Army officers probably regarded as publicity-seeking adventurers. Neville, given his first star, resumed command of the Marine Brigade.

In early August the 2nd Division occupied a quiet sector around Marbache in the Moselle valley, readying itself for the next push. In August the Marine Brigade was inspected by Assistant Secretary of the Navy Franklin D. Roosevelt, who had just visited the battlefield of Belleau Wood. Deeply impressed by what he had seen there, Roosevelt declared that, effective immediately, the right to wear the Marine Corps' collar emblem, previously restricted to officers, was extended to enlisted men. No doubt he would have agreed with a German intelligence report prepared around the same time that explained that "the Marines are . . . a sort of elite Corps. . . . Prisoners . . . consider their membership in the Marine Corps to be something of an honor. They proudly resent any attempt to place their regiments on a par with other infantry regiments." Marines themselves relished the story of the philanthropic American lady who visited a French field hospital. Spying a clean-shaven face among the rows of bewhiskered French casualties, she exclaimed, "Oh, surely you

are an American?" "No, ma'am," came the answer, "I'm a Marine."

On 20 August the 2nd Division assembled at Colombey-les-Belles, south of Toul, in preparation for the Saint-Mihiel offensive. This battle was the payoff of Pershing's repeated refusals to allow his units to be frittered away as fillers for French and British formations: an operation conducted by an American field army—the First Army, officially constituted on 10 August—under American command. Its objective was the elimination of the Saint-Mihiel salient, a wedge-shaped indentation in the Allied front, sixteen miles deep and twenty-five miles wide at its base, that had been occupied by the Germans since the beginning of the war. Besides displaying the AEF's capabilities to friend and foe, the reduction of the salient would open important rail communications to Allied use. To carry out the operation, Pershing assembled nineteen U.S. divisions— including the 2nd—and borrowed four from the French.

At 0100 on 12 September, Allied artillery began an intense bombardment of the German lines. For four hours, American and French gunners blasted the enemy's trenches and dugouts. Pershing's men pushed into the salient from east and west at 0500. By chance, the Germans were in the process of evacuating their positions. The attacking forces encountered relatively little resistance, and by nightfall on 13 September the occupation of the salient was complete. The fruits of victory included 16,000 prisoners and 443 artillery pieces. By the horrific standards of the Western Front, American casualties were light, just under 7,000; the

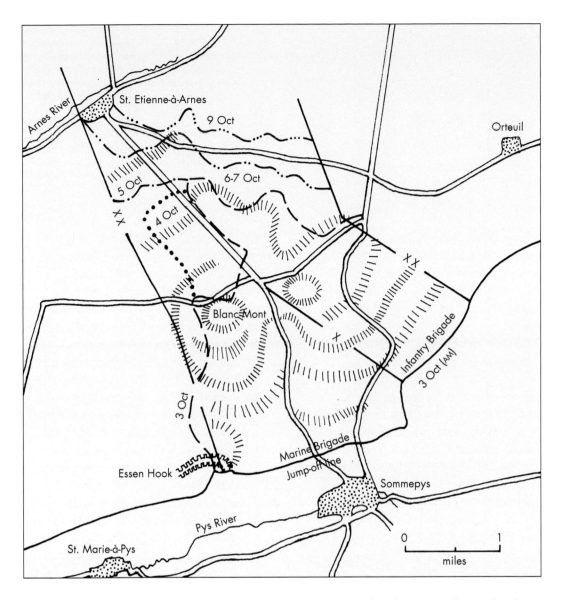

Map 15. The Battle of
Blanc Mont, October
1918

Marine Brigade's share totaled 132 dead and
574 wounded.

The Saint-Mihiel offensive proved that an
American army could fight effectively under
American command. The AEF had little time
to savor its triumph, however, for ten days
before the attack, Pershing had pledged that
it would be ready to join in an Allied general
offensive no later than 25 September. In the
north, the British would push east toward
Cambrai; in the center, the French would
thrust across the Aisne; and in the south,
the Americans would strike north through
the wooded heights of the Meuse-Argonne
toward Sedan with the objective of severing
the Metz-to-Bruges railroad, which linked the
northern and southern wings of the German
army on the Western Front. Should the Amer-

icans succeed in disrupting this vital rail
line, the enemy would find it difficult if not
impossible to conduct an orderly withdrawal
from France and Belgium. As the AEF's next
battleground lay forty miles west of Saint-
Mihiel, two weeks were consumed by the
complex task of moving 600,000 American
troops to relieve the 220,000 French in the
lines there.

The 2nd Division did not participate in
this redeployment. Together with the 36th
Division, it was loaned to the French to
reinforce an offensive in Champagne between
the Argonne Forest and Reims. From 24 to
30 September, the Marine brigade traveled
by rail with its parent division to take up a
position behind the French Fourth Army. The
keystone of the German front in this sector

was Blanc Mont Ridge, a heavily fortified eminence that dominated the last natural defensive position south of the Aisne, some sixteen miles to its rear. Its capture would compel the enemy to fall back all the way to the river.

Lejeune met his new commander, one-armed, red-bearded Gen. Henri Gouraud, at Châlons-sur-Marne on 25 September. Lejeune formed an excellent opinion of the French officer, but two days later he was shocked to hear rumors that Gouraud planned to feed American units piecemeal into the sagging lines of his poilus. As Pershing had done on so many similar occasions, Lejeune bridled. The 2nd Division, he argued, should be kept

intact. "General," he promised, "if you do not divide the Second Division, but put it in line as a unit on a narrow front, I am confident that it will be able to take Blanc Mont Ridge, advance beyond it, and hold its position." He would soon be called upon to make this promise good.

The Fourth Army had begun its attack on 26 September, the same day on which the AEF launched the Meuse-Argonne offensive. During the opening days of the attack, French troops advanced three and a half miles, but by 28 September the XXI Corps had ground to a halt against German trenches and concrete pillboxes on the desolate, chalky ground at the foot of Blanc Mont. After another conference with Lejeune, Gouraud decided to

give the 2nd Division a chance to show what it could accomplish. During the night of 1–2 October, the Americans entered the front line.

Spearheaded by the 2nd Division, the XXI Corps renewed its attack on 3 October. The 4th Brigade (Marine) attacked on the left and the 3rd Brigade on the right. A company of French tanks supported each brigade. The artillery barrage began at 0545. Thomason recalled that "the heavens seemed roofed over with long, keening noises—sounds like the sharp ripping of silk, magnified, running in swift arcs from horizon to horizon. . . . Almost, one expected to look up and see them, like swift, deadly birds, some small, some enormous, all terrible." Following the barrage within 330 yards of the first objective, by midmorning units of the 2nd Division had advanced three and a half miles. Two Leathernecks and a Doughboy earned Medals of Honor during the day's fighting, all for the single-handed destruction of machine-gun nests.

The Yanks resumed the advance on 4 October. Unfortunately, the French units on the Marines' left failed to keep pace, which required the brigade to beat off repeated German counterattacks on its exposed flank. Murderous enemy machine-gun fire from the exposed flank inflicted heavy casualties on the 5th Marines. At 0600 the next morning, the 6th Marines and the French 17th Infantry reported the capture of the machine-gun strongpoint on Blanc Mont, taking more than two hundred prisoners and sixty-five machine-guns and trench mortars. The next day, the Marines pushed over the crest of the ridge into the hasty fortifications beyond. Lejeune's promise had been kept.

On the night of 6 October, the 2nd Division was relieved by the U.S. 36th Division. The battle had cost the Marines 2,538 men killed and wounded; the dead included Matej Kocak and Henry L. Hulbert, both of whom had already earned the Medal of Honor. The grateful French presented two thousand Croix de Guerre to the officers and men of the division and appointed Lejeune a Commander of the Legion of Honor. Pershing later praised

the victory as having been won "against a persistent defense worthy of the grimmest period of trench warfare." Nonetheless, he refused to name the offensive to take Blanc Mont as a separate campaign, insisting to the consternation of Lejeune and his senior officers that the assault merely constituted part of the Meuse-Argonne campaign.

However impressive its resistance appeared, the German army was approaching exhaustion. Although Lejeune's troops had been opposed by elements of eight divisions, the German high command considered only two of those divisions fit for combat. By mid-October, the Central Powers had

begun to disintegrate. Bulgaria surrendered on 29 September; the German government dispatched the first of a series of armistice notes to President Wilson on 4 October; Turkey dropped out of the war on 31 October; Austria-Hungary, on 3 November; and on 7 November, the mutiny of the German High Seas Fleet sparked a revolution ashore. Yet even with the inevitable end in sight, the combatants continued to flail away at each other with deadly results.

Following the battle of Blanc Mont, the 2nd Division rejoined the AEF to take part in the final phase of the Meuse-Argonne offensive. Between 26 September

In the Argonne, two Leathernecks man a 37-mm gun, an infantry close support weapon, while riflemen push forward with fixed bayonets—at least, according to one of the two identifications of this photograph. The other holds that the troops shown are Doughboys from one of the 2nd Division's infantry regiments. In any case, it is arguably the most dramatic image of the AEF in action. (National Archives)

and 16 October, when the First Army was compelled to halt to reorganize, Pershing's troops advanced ten of the thirty-five miles they needed to cover to reach the railroad upon which the maintenance of the German front depended. Assigned to V Corps in the left center of the American front, the 2nd Division occupied a two-and-a-half-mile-wide sector west of the Meuse River facing the Hindenburg Line. As the AEF wheeled into position for the final battle of the war, it numbered more than a million Americans fighting in twenty-six divisions, plus eight French divisions placed under Pershing's command.

At 0530 on 1 November, the American Army attacked in strength, with the Marines moving forward on the left of the 2nd Division. The next day, the division's 3rd Brigade took the lead. In a daring thrust on the night of 2–3 November, soldiers of the 9th Infantry followed by the 3rd Infantry and a battalion of the 5th Marines marched for six-and-a-quarter hours in total darkness and driving rain to surprise sleeping German units four miles behind the front. The Americans did not suffer a single casualty. The intrepid Doughboys and Leathernecks missed capturing a German general and his headquarters by a bare fifteen minutes.

Although rations ran short, the advance continued. Marines foraged for discarded German rations, scrounged food from French civilians, and even devoured the remnants of a cabbage patch planted by the retreating enemy. Lejeune ordered another night march similar to the earlier one; it, too, brought spectacular results. By 6

November, the AEF was close enough to the vital railroad to take it under artillery fire. But while the enemy's resistance crumbled, it never collapsed. In the last eleven days of the war, the 4th Brigade (Marine) counted 273 killed and another 1,263 wounded.

When the Armistice went into effect at 1100 on 11 November 1918, most of the combat-weary Leathernecks and Doughboys sat down in numb disbelief. Warming fires appeared in the shell-pocked meadows, and the patriotic songs that had been the emotional staple of fighting men on both sides could be heard across the scarred landscape. More than a decade later Lejeune recalled the emotional impact of the cease-fire: "A few minutes before eleven o'clock, there were tremendous bursts of fire from the two antagonists and then—suddenly—there was complete silence." He thought "it was the most impressive celebration of the armistice that could have possibly taken place. There was a solemn and an earnest joy in the hearts of every man at the front. . . . We were happy because fighting, death, and destruction had ceased. I offered up a prayer of thanksgiving to Almighty God."

For soldiers and Marines alike, hope for a swift passage home proved fleeting. AEF Headquarters had other plans. Fearful that with the cease-fire America's volunteer army would unravel, Pershing chose the units for occupation duty in Germany carefully. He included the 2nd Division. In mid-November, the bone-weary troops began the long, cold march to the Rhine. Hiking along muddy roads for ten hours a day, Lejeune's men wound their way through France,

Belgium, and Luxemburg to the German border. Upon reaching the Rhine, the officers of one Leatherneck battalion marched in formation to the water's edge and urinated in it. On 1 December 1918, after a grueling march of two hundred miles, the 2nd Division crossed the bridge at Remagen and moved upriver to Koblenz. The 5th Marines took up a position in the Wied Valley while the 6th Marines occupied the towns across the Rhine. A docile populace accepted the inevitable, and the occupation proceeded without serious incident. Marines and soldiers became tourists, fought boredom, and complained about the inadequate delousing facilities. Peacetime routines of training, more training, and endless inspections filled their days.

At long last, the order came to return home. In midsummer 1919, the division boarded railway cars for Camp Pontanezen, near Brest on the Atlantic coast of France. The men of the 2nd Division marched together for the last time on 9 August when they paraded through the streets of New York to the thunderous acclaim of its citizenry. En route to Quantico, the 4th Brigade (Marine), AEF—never to be called that again—marched past the White House to be reviewed by President Wilson. Reservists and wartime-only enlistees returned to civilian pursuits, and regulars took up old duties at familiar posts and stations.

Few Leathernecks would ever forget the thrill of their first step onto the soil of France or their first time under fire. For others, the anguish of old wounds or the sear of gas-scared lungs lingered as painful reminders. The cost of being "First to Fight" had been heavy: 11,981 casualties.

Of the Marines who served in France, 1 out of 6 was wounded; 2,461 made the supreme sacrifice. The Germans managed to capture only 25 Marines. Six Marines were awarded the Medal of Honor, and 744 earned the Navy Cross or the Army Distinguished Service Cross. In addition, the citations the 2nd Division had received in the French Army's orders of the day entitled the members of its units—present and future—to wear the green and red fourragère of the Croix de Guerre. The 5th and 6th Marines wear it still. Of the 78,839 men who belonged to the Corps during the war, approximately 32,000 served in France.

Sadly, a second brigade of combat-ready Marines failed to see action. Early in 1918 Barnett had ordered the organization and training of the 5th Brigade at Quantico; composed of the 11th and 13th Regiments and the 5th Machine Gun Battalion, it went to France under the command of Brig. Gen. Eli K. Cole in September. Pershing had accepted one brigade of Marines, but he made it clear that he could do without another. To its members' dismay, the 5th Brigade was broken up and assigned to rear-area duties or used as replacements for the 4th Brigade. Both Cole and Brig. Gen. Smedley D. Butler received orders to command AEF depot divisions or processing facilities. Butler managed to straighten out the problem-ridden Camp Pontanezen, but he felt left out. To his congressman father, Butler fumed: "For over twenty years, I worked hard to fit myself to take part in this war . . . and when the supreme test came my country did not want me." But at least Butler made it to France. His idol, Waller, spent his war commanding the skeleton of the Advanced Base Force at Philadelphia and retired a major general in 1921. Three future commandants, Ben H. Fuller, John Russell, and Alexander A. Vandegrift, also failed to receive orders to France and served in posts in the Caribbean.

Butler blamed Headquarters Marine Corps (HQMC) for his failure to gain a combat assignment. Others believed that the friction that had developed within the AEF was the result of anti–Marine Corps prejudice by senior Army officers. One of Lejeune's regimental commanders went as far as to refer to the Marines as "a bunch of adventurers, illiterates, and drunkards" in official correspondence. Another senior Army officer declared that the letters "USMC" stood for "Useless Sons-of-Bitches Made Comfortable." The seeds of intense interservice rivalry had been sown on the Western Front, and the fruits of this controversy would ripen during the interwar years.

Like the Corps' ground forces, its newly hatched aviation community had to overcome major obstacles to take an active part in the war. American intervention found the 1st Aviation Company located in Philadelphia with the Advanced Base Force. Renamed the 1st Marine Aeronautical Company, from October through December 1917 it flew antisubmarine patrols from Cape May, New Jersey. On 9 January 1918, the company deployed to Ponto Delgada on Saõ Miguel Island in the Azores to patrol the waters of the Eastern Atlantic with a force of eighteen single-engine seaplanes. Its operations were generally uneventful and most of the aviators yearned to join the fight in France.

Senior Marine Corps officers wanted to see Leatherneck aviators in France. The problem, predictably, was that AEF Headquarters wanted no part of naval aviation. In February 1918, however, the Navy Department decided to form a unit, designated the Northern Bombing Group, to attack the German submarine pens along the Belgian coast. The group would consist of a Navy night wing and a Marine day wing.

The Corps' pioneer pilot, Capt. Alfred A. Cunningham, received permission to cull sufficient Navy pilot trainees from the pool at Pensacola to man the four squadrons of the newly established 1st Marine Aviation Force. Eager to join the fight, the Navy pilots—mostly wartime-only reservists—applied for transfers and accepted commissions in the Corps. Cunningham and his band of 149 aviators disembarked at Brest on 30 July 1918, only to discover that their bombers had been shipped to England. Rising to the occasion, Cunningham worked out a deal with the British to trade him bombers for American-built aircraft engines, at the rate of one for three, and, until he had enough planes to commence operations, to allow his men to gain experience by flying missions with the Royal Air Force. It was 14 October before eight DeHavilland (DH)-4 bombers—lumbering, single-engine two-seaters with a top speed of 120 miles per hour—from Squadron 9 climbed into the air on the first all-Marine raid. By then the Germans had abandoned the submarine pens, so the Marines attacked the railway yards at Thielt, Belgium.

One plane was piloted by 2nd Lt. Ralph Talbot, who had become a Navy pilot

after completing his freshman year at Yale. He accepted Cunningham's invitation to transfer to the Corps. On the return flight, Talbot became separated from the formation and German fighters jumped his aircraft. His gunner, Cpl. Robert G. Robinson, shot one down before being hit in the arm, stomach, and hip. Talbot downed another German with his forward-firing machine guns and, with Robinson unconscious in the rear seat, shook off his pursuers by a steep dive, skimming over enemy trenches at an altitude of fifty feet to land his gunner at the nearest hospital. Both men were awarded the Medal of Honor. Ironically, the riddled Robinson

lived to wear his medal, but Talbot died in a crash during takeoff eleven days later.

By the end of the war, the Marine aviators had flown fifty-seven missions—forty-three with the RAF and fourteen on their own—dropping fifty-two thousand pounds of bombs and scoring four confirmed victories and eight others claimed. Four were killed in action or died of wounds, and, in addition to the two Medals of Honor, they earned another twenty-eight decorations.

Much to his men's dismay, Cunningham requested an early return home for the 1st Aviation Force. After the signing of the

Armistice, there seemed little reason for Leatherneck aviators to remain in France—especially because the AEF did not want them. An officer of vision, Cunningham believed that "we could accomplish much more at home, getting our aviation service

established under the new conditions of peace." In December 1918, the 1st Aviation Force sailed for the States. Some senior Marine officers were disappointed that the aviators did not have the opportunity to join their comrades-in-arms in an air–ground combat team, and they questioned the utility of an aviation arm for the Corps.

In terms of public relations, the Corps' service with the AEF hit the bull's-eye. In fact, less than half of its men had reached France. Yet to most Americans, the Marines' claim to be the "First to Fight" rang solid and true. The legionary romance that had enveloped the Corps during its campaigns in tropic climes was complemented by the glory of having beaten the Kaiser's crack troops in the greatest European war in a century. In the postwar decade this shining image would be kept bright by popular works such as Thomason's *Fix Bayonets!*, a narrative of the 4th Brigade's battles, and *What Price Glory?*, a hit Broadway play by a disabled Marine officer, Capt. Laurence Stallings.

Yet most of the men who served in the Corps in 1917–18 never got "over there." In making his pitch to send Marines to France, Barnett had promised to meet the Corps' traditional naval commitments as well. Throughout the war, Leathernecks continued to serve in small detachments in the Navy's warships; naval stations at home and overseas kept their trusty Marine sentries; weak brigades remained in Santo Domingo, Cuba, and Haiti; and three regiments stayed in the States to constitute an Advanced Base Force or guard vital oilfields along the border between Texas and Mexico.

The requirement for expeditionary duty also involved the Corps in the periphery of the Russian Revolution. In June 1918, the Czech Legion, an anti-Bolshevik army of freed prisoners of war that had fought its way east along the Trans-Siberian Railroad, seized the port of Vladivostok on the Pacific Coast of Siberia. Leathernecks and Bluejackets from the flagship of the Asiatic

Top Left: In the early fall of 1919 Maj. Gen. Commandant George Barnett (left) accepted the return of the unit colors of the 4th Brigade (Marine), AEF. Lt. Col. Thomas Holcomb, 6th Marines, a future commandant, is the second officer to Barnett's right. (Barnett Papers, Alfred M. Gray Research Center, Quantico)

Bottom Left: Marinettes and Yeomen (F) at their mustering out ceremony after World War I. In the center (bareheaded) is Secretary of the Navy Josephus Daniels; to his left is Assistant Secretary of the Navy Franklin D. Roosevelt; to Daniels' right is Chief of Naval Operations William S. Benson. (National Archives)

Right: Immediately after the war, Laurence Stallings, a Marine who had lost a leg serving in France, wrote a popular Broadway play based loosely on his experiences during the war. Subsequently, it appeared as a Hollywood movie in 1952 starring James Cagney, Corinne Calvet, and Dan Dailey. (Marine Corps Art Collection)

Fleet, the cruiser *Brooklyn*, joined landing parties from British and French ships to maintain order in the city. Most of the Marines were withdrawn in August, but a detail stayed behind to guard a Navy radio station on an island in Vladivostok Bay until November 1922.

Another body of Marines was never intended to enter the firing line. On 12 August 1918, the egalitarian Secretary of the Navy Josephus Daniels authorized the enlistment of women reservists into the previously all-male Corps. Mrs. Opha M. Johnson became the first of 277 "Marinettes" to don forest green, freeing combat-trained Leathernecks from clerical duties to join their comrades in France. While HQMC limited the women Marines to administrative assignments, a barrier had been broken. *Leatherneck* magazine waxed appreciatively, if a bit condescendingly, "Everyone is proud of the Marine girls. They carried themselves like real Marines . . . and proved they were ready to go anywhere and conduct themselves with honor to the Marine Corps." As the Marinettes mustered out of uniform, Secretary Daniels paid them a memorably maladroit tribute. "We will not forget you," he declared. "As we embrace you in uniform today, we will embrace you without uniform tomorrow."

CHAPTER 9

Between the Wars, 1919–1941

For most Americans, the Armistice signified the return of peace. This was not the case for the Marines who, in the midst of demobilization, found themselves with two guerrilla wars to fight. At the same time, scandal and a political dogfight buffeted the Corps. Together these events made its transition into the postwar world a stormy passage.

The guerrilla wars began even before the Great War ended. Both took place on Hispaniola, where the effectiveness of the brigades occupying Haiti and the Dominican Republic had been diminished by the flow of troops to France. In Haiti, the calm that had prevailed since 1915 was shattered when a band of one hundred *cacos* led by Charlemagne Masséna Péralte attacked the Gendarmerie post at Hinche on 17 October 1918. The French-educated son of a prominent local family, Péralte had recently escaped from a humiliating sentence of five years' hard labor imposed for his implication in an attempted robbery of a Gendarmerie payroll. Although the assault failed, in Péralte the *cacos* had found a leader—and, as a Marine officer recalled, "a damned good one." Furthermore, resentment of the *corvée*

forced labor program—suspended, too late, in the summer of 1918—and rumor that the whites planned to reintroduce slavery gave him a broad base of support. Soon the insurrection spread throughout central and northern Haiti; several thousand full-time *cacos* were active in various bands; and Péralte began signing himself, "Chief of the Revolutionary Forces Against the Americans on the Soil of Haiti."

At first, Col. Alexander S. Williams, major general commandant of the Gendarmerie, tried to meet the emergency with the forces at his disposal. These proved unequal to the task and, in March 1919, he requested the help of the 1st Marine Brigade. Reinforced by six companies of infantry and an observation squadron of thirteen biplanes, the Leathernecks launched a campaign of combat patrols deep into the interior. A new command team also arrived, with Lt. Col. Frederick M. "Fritz" Wise relieving Williams as commandant of the Gendarmerie in July and Col. John H. Russell taking over the brigade in September.

The tempo of operations increased throughout the year, from fewer than forty hostile contacts from January through June

Opposite: James Montgomery Flagg's fanciful recruiting poster featuring a chipper Marine, an enraged jaguar, and some tropical greenery emphasized the Corps' service in the banana republics. Flagg was among the best-known illustrators of his day. (Marine Corps Art Collection)

to more than eighty from July through September. The first instance of a coordinated air–ground attack, later to become a Marine Corps specialty, occurred in August, when a Curtiss Jenny and a DH-4 cooperated with an infantry company to surprise a large *caco* camp on a mountain near Mirebalais. The planes' bombs drove the startled *cacos* off the mountaintop into ambushes set by the ground forces, which killed or wounded more than two hundred. Marine aviators also began to develop dive-bombing techniques that enabled them to place their ordnance even in the confined target areas of jungle clearings.

Despite mounting losses, the rebels remained in arms. On 7 October, three hundred of Péralte's *cacos* delivered an audacious attack on Port-au-Prince. Forewarned of the action, the Marines and gendarmes beat them off without difficulty. By that time, Fritz Wise had concluded that the only way to wind up the war would be, as he put it, to "get Charlemagne." He recognized that this represented "a pretty big order," requiring as it did the removal of one heavily guarded individual constantly on the move through a population of several millions, largely sympathetic to him, in a country the size of the state of New York.

Wise's order was carried out by Herman H. Hanneken, a twenty-four-year-old Marine sergeant serving as a Gendarmerie captain in command of the post at Grande Rivière du Nord. A native of St. Louis, Hanneken had enlisted in the Corps in 1914 after brief stints as a divinity student and cowpoke. In Haiti he learned to speak the native patois as fluently as any *papaloi*. John W. Thomason described him as "long-legged, with big bones and a square, powerful frame. . . . He has high cheekbones and lean jaws, . . . and the feature most men notice is his eye. It is an eye singularly direct, deep-set, pale, and cold, like a cat's."

With the cooperation of two Haitian agents, Hanneken concocted an elaborate scheme to entice Péralte into attacking Grande Rivière, where a warm reception was prepared. The *caco* chieftain took the bait, assembling seven hundred men for the operation, but at the last moment elected to remain behind himself. Informed of this development by one of their agents,

Hanneken and his second-in-command, Gendarmerie first lieutenant (Marine corporal) William R. Button, decided that if Péralte would not come to them, they would go to him. The agent agreed to guide them. Faces blackened with burnt cork, after nightfall on 31 October they led sixteen handpicked gendarmes through six *caco* checkpoints to Péralte's camp. As they approached the circle of firelight, the guide pointed out Péralte. Hanneken drew his .45 and put two slugs through the Chief of the Revolutionary Forces. An instant later, a *caco* camp follower threw a blanket over the fire, Button sprayed the area with his Browning Automatic Rifle, and Péralte's surviving supporters departed in haste.

The next morning, after the assault on Grande Rivière had been shattered, Hanneken brought Péralte's body into town. To dispel any doubts of the *caco*'s demise, the Marines photographed the corpse and exhibited prints throughout Haiti. Péralte was then given a Christian burial—beneath the Marine sentry post at the entrance to the headquarters of the Department of the North.

Both Hanneken and Button were awarded the Medal of Honor and Haiti's highest decoration, the Médaille Militaire. A few months later, Hanneken earned the Navy Cross for the elimination of another guerrilla chief, Osiris Joseph. Button died of fever at Cap Haitien in 1920. Hanneken, commissioned the same year, went on to command a regiment at Peleliu and retired a brigadier general.

Péralte's mantle fell briefly on the shoulders of his principal lieutenant, Benoit Batraville, but only one sizeable engagement remained to be fought. It took place on 15 January 1920, when Batraville replicated Peralté's attack on Port-au-Prince with the same lack of success. He achieved a small triumph in April with the capture of Gendarmerie lieutenant (Marine sergeant) Lawrence Muth, who had been badly wounded and left for dead by his men. Following the prescription of a voodoo wizard, Batraville cut out and ate the young officer's heart and liver in order to absorb his courage and wisdom, and smeared Muth's brains on his men's rifles to improve their accuracy. These precautions proved unavailing. On 19 May, he was killed in an action with a Marine patrol led by Gendarmerie captain J. L. "Si" Perkins.

Batraville's death rang down the curtain on the *caco* rebellion. The Marines estimated that approximately two thousand insurgents had been killed in the course of the conflict: 35 in 1918, 1,881 in 1919, and 90 in 1920. The Gendarmerie lost approximately 75 officers and men killed and wounded, while the 1st Brigade suffered 23 casualties.

The campaign had a sensational aftermath. In 1919, Russell court-martialed three enlisted men, including a private serving as a Gendarmerie lieutenant, on charges of shooting a prisoner "just for excitement." All were found guilty, but in scanning the trial transcripts General Barnett was shocked to read that an officer defending one of the men had asserted, in extenuation of the crime, that "indiscriminate killings of natives by Marines were commonplace." The commandant thereupon wrote Russell that indiscriminate killings must cease. In 1920 his order became public knowledge, provoking the predictable outcry. An American journalist who hurried to Haiti did nothing to calm the furor by reporting that, "I have heard officers wearing the United States uniform [Marines seconded to the Gendarmerie] talking of 'bumping off gooks' as if it were a variety of sport—like duck-hunting." Critics of "bayonet rule" in the Caribbean seized on the issue as an example of Yankee imperialism at its worst.

That summer, Secretary Daniels dispatched Lejeune and Butler to Haiti to investigate the allegations of Marine atrocities. They returned to report that cases of misconduct had been few and had resulted in long prison terms. A naval court of inquiry convened a few months later reached the same conclusion, as did a Senate Select Committee that visited Hispaniola in 1921 and 1922. Perhaps the best summing up was offered by Col. Frederic M. "Fritz" Wise, who noted in his memoirs that "there was no question that some rough stuff had been pulled in Haiti. . . . But that was all over now. Haiti was at peace. Haiti had been brought to peace by men fighting and living amid conditions that people back home could never even picture."

The trouble in the Dominican Republic was less an insurrection than a persistence of banditry in the unruly eastern provinces of Macorís and Seibo. Intelligence estimates placed the combined strength of the bands involved at from six hundred to one thousand men. Real battles were few and Marine casualties light, but firefights were frequent. In 1918 the 2nd Brigade's patrols made forty-four serious contacts, losing five men killed and thirteen wounded. When the incidence of violence increased early in 1919, Brig. Gen. Ben H. Fuller, who had relieved Pendleton the previous October, asked for more troops. The 15th Marines arrived in February 1919, and an observation squadron joined it in March, raising the brigade's strength to more than one hundred officers and twenty-five hundred men. The deployment marked the formation of the first task-organized Marine air ground team. As in Haiti, the aircraft—six Jennies—proved a valuable asset in the campaign: the pilots reported hostile movements, supported Marine columns in the field, and experimented with dive-bombing techniques. That year, Marine units were involved in more than 150 skirmishes. Casualties were low (three dead and four wounded), but the *banditos* remained active.

Rumors arose of Marine atrocities in the Dominican Republic, but they never attracted the attention given to reports of misdeeds in Haiti. The potential for major embarrassment was avoided by the suicide of Capt. Charles F. Merkel, a German-born ex-enlisted man who had clearly gone beyond the pale to acquire the sobriquet of "The Tiger of Seibo." Arrested and confined to quarters awaiting trial for the torture and murder of a prisoner, Merkel shot himself in October 1918 with a pistol that, according to the official account, he had hidden on his person. Scuttlebutt held that he was visited by two fellow officers who left him the traditional alternative to disgrace: a pistol loaded with a single round.

By 1919 President Wilson had begun to reconsider the wisdom of the occupation of the Dominican Republic. Late in 1920 his outgoing administration announced plans to withdraw the Marines as soon as practical. The military government was charged with executing this decision in an orderly manner. It responded by initiating a vigorous program to train the hitherto neglected Guardia Nacional Dominicana (soon renamed the Policia Nacional) and redoubling its efforts to pacify Macorís and Seibo. A combination of intensive patrolling, the screening of virtually the entire male population of the two provinces, and an offer of amnesty finally accomplished the latter, and by May 1922 the country was at peace. In August 1924, the Marines finally began an exodus from Santo Domingo; the last Leatherneck departed on 16 September 1924.

The Corps' first major postwar political controversy arose in June 1920, when Secretary Daniels ousted Barnett as commandant and replaced him with Lejeune. Barnett's Republican supporters cried "foul!" and rallied to prevent Lejeune's confirmation. Daniels believed that the redoubtable Mrs. Barnett had goaded her husband to dig in his heels. Privately, he said that if the commandant was an Indian, his name would be "Man-Afraid-of-His-Wife." Publicly, Daniels claimed that when he reappointed Barnett in 1918, the commandant promised—like each of the Navy's bureau chiefs—to step down after the war. Barnett denied it. When the secretary tried to explain his policy of limiting the tenure of senior officers in Washington to single four-year tours, even his most strident supporters had difficulty stifling yawns. Then Daniels began to argue that he believed in rewarding men "who had been at the cannon's mouth." Lejeune had the requisite tropical sweat stains and powder burns on his uniform to meet that criterion. The new secretary of the navy, Edwin H. Denby, accepted Lejeune as commandant. Denby also secured the return of Barnett's second star and put at least one controversy to rest.

But Barnett did not go quietly. According to one of the indignant general's aides-de-camp, on the morning that Lejeune appeared at headquarters for the change of command, Barnett greeted him not with a handshake but with the words: "General Lejeune, I am still the commandant of the Marine Corps, and will be until 12 o'clock noon. Stand at attention, sir, in front of my desk. I have something to tell you." Convinced as he was that Lejeune had conspired with Secretary Daniels, Smedley Butler, and Congressman Butler in his ouster, what Barnett had to tell him was not all complimentary. Then, at the stroke of noon, Barnett arose from his chair with the words, "General Lejeune, you are now the commandant of the Marine Corps." The ousted commandant asked his aides-de-camp to each remove a star from his shoulder straps. As the furious Barnett marched out of the building, Smedley Butler sat in a car parked across the street to relish in the scene.

The new commandant took the reins of the Corps firmly. In an open letter to its officers, Lejeune left no doubt as to the standards he expected: "I want each of you to feel that the Commandant of the Corps is your friend. . . . At the same time, it is his duty to the Government and to the Marine Corps to exact a high standard of conduct, a strict performance of duty, and a rigid compliance with orders on the part of all officers." He added that "you are the permanent part of the Marine Corps, and the efficiency, the good name, and the esprit of the Corps are in your hands. You can make it or mar it."

As those sentiments suggest, Lejeune was deeply concerned with the efficiency of the Corps' commissioned ranks. His experiences in France had convinced him that Leatherneck officers would benefit from a comprehensive program of professional education. While commanding at Quantico in 1919 he made the wartime training camp for incoming officers a permanent facility, soon renamed The Basic School (TBS), and as commandant he approved the organization of two more schools, one for company-grade officers and the other, modeled after the Army Command and General Staff College, for field grades. Naturally, the topics addressed at the Quantico schools included the conduct of counterinsurgencies such as the Corps found itself fighting in the Caribbean basin. The first textbook for this subject, *The Strategy and Tactics of Small Wars*, appeared in 1922. Subsequent revisions culminated in 1940 with the publication of the Corps' classic *Small Wars Manual*. More than six decades later, Marine officers combating the Iraq insurgency would testify to the enduring relevance of the principles it propounds.

Lejeune also gave his attention to the overpopulation of officers. At the beginning of the world war, the Corps' officers numbered only 341; at the end, they exceeded 2,400. To fill the leadership billets, headquarters had offered temporary commissions to meritorious noncomissioned officers (NCOs) and both permanent and reserve commissions to applicants with a college degree. Many of the ex-NCOs and young reservists sought to remain in uniform, leaving five successive commandants with the distasteful task of deciding who should remain and who should go.

Barnett had taken the first step in 1919 by convening a board headed by Colonel Russell, a graduate of the Naval Academy Class of 1892, to recommend retention or discharge for officers with temporary or reserve commissions. When Russell submitted the board's report in August, it shook the Corps to its foundations. Many officers with distinguished combat records in France or long years of expeditionary service found themselves defrocked or placed on the lineal list below contemporaries who had never heard a shot fired in anger. Disappointed contenders and their patrons charged that the board had concentrated on the applicants' social and academic qualifications rather than their martial performance. Russell, it was claimed, had advised the board to choose officers and gentlemen "who they would invite into their quarters and whom their daughters might marry." Disappointed observers, led by the irrepressible Smedley Butler, charged that the recommendations of the Russell Board represented an attempt by the Annapolis clique to maintain control of the Corps' officer ranks. Three days after assuming the commandancy, Lejeune ordered a second board to examine the credentials of officers desiring retention. Maj. Gen. Wendell C. Neville, with an impressive record of tropical campaigning and combat in France, chaired the board. All of its members were seasoned campaigners. Thus, when the Neville Board issued its report in May 1921, the results surprised few Marines. Officers who had demonstrated leadership and courage under fire received preference for retention and promotion.

A generation of officers argued over the outcome. While the Russell Board appeared to have ignored combat records in favor of pedigree and education, the Neville Board overcompensated in favor of experience in the banana wars or on the Western Front. Many of the officers it recommended for retention were too old or lacked the education necessary for professional growth. The controversy underscored the need for a system of selection boards to examine officers for promotion at each rank to replace the sacrosanct scheme of seniority.

Throughout the nine years of his commandancy, Lejeune argued in vain for such a system. With the support of Congressman Butler, Lejeune's proposal moved swiftly through the House Naval Affairs Committee during each session of Congress, but it never cleared the Senate Naval Affairs Committee, where skeptics argued that a system of promotion based on examination by a selection board offered the potential for a misuse of administrative power. The fact that both the Army and the Navy promoted their officers through such a system was simply brushed off. It would be up to Lejeune's successors to convince civilian superiors that the Corps would have better leaders if its officers were promoted on merit rather than seniority.

Lejeune did not need to consult Congress to alter the traditional focus of Headquarters Marine Corps (HQMC). Since the founding of the Corps, designated staff officers had guided the day-to-day functioning of HQMC while the commandants mostly tended to political or ceremonial duties. Lejeune believed that HQMC should be involved in planning and organization for expeditionary duty and war, not merely "housekeeping." While serving as assistant to the commandant, Lejeune had convinced Barnett to establish a planning section. Now he took his vision a step further. On 1 December 1920 Lejeune expanded the Planning Section into the Division of Operations and Training (DOT) to manage all matters relating to operations, training, education, intelligence, and aviation. To serve as DOT's intelligence officer, he brought in a protégé and friend dating from his tour in the Philippines more than a decade before, Lt. Col. Earl H. "Pete" Ellis.

A lanky Midwesterner, Ellis had enlisted in the Corps, aged twenty, in 1900 and obtained his commission a year later. His effulgent intellect and boundless energy impressed everyone with whom he came in contact. As a junior captain he had served with distinction as an instructor at the Naval War College. In France, Ellis performed brilliantly as the adjutant of the Marine Brigade from July 1918 until the end of the war, supervising its staff work so ably that he was generally regarded as

Earl H. "Pete" Ellis as a lieutenant colonel in France in 1918 while serving as adjutant of the 4th Brigade (Marine), AEF. (Courtesy Dorothy Ellis Gatz)

the man most responsible for the efficiency of its operations. Supposedly Lejeune even entrusted him with the task of planning the 2nd Division's assault on Blanc Mont, but that claim cannot be verified.

Tragically, Ellis' professional performance caused his superiors to overlook the fact that he was an alcoholic of exceptional instability whose recorded eccentricities included bringing a dinner party to a close by blasting the plates off the table with his pistol. By 1920, acute alcoholism had seriously undermined his health. During his sober interludes, however, he became intrigued with the prospect of a conflict in the Central Pacific. At the end of the world war, Japan had been given League of Nations mandates over the formerly German islands in the region—suzerainty, in effect, under the Empire of Japan. Ellis began a monumental study of the potential for amphibious operations should war break out with Japan.

On 23 July 1921, Ellis submitted the results of his labors to Lejeune: a thirty-thousand-word plan for "Advanced Base Operations in Micronesia, 1921." Anticipating the loss of the Philippines, Ellis' plan called for an amphibious advance northward across the Japanese-held islands in the Central Pacific, beginning with the establishment of an advanced base in the Marshalls. To an uncanny extent, the tactics and procedures Ellis prescribed—the use of underwater demolition teams, the organization of assault forces, and the role of naval air and gunfire support—foreshadowed the techniques that would actually be employed during the war in the Pacific. Even in specifics, his projections often proved accurate; the four thousand troops who seized Eniwetok Atoll in the Marshalls in February 1944 closely corresponded to the number he allocated to the operation.

The events that transpired after the completion of Ellis' prophetic study have become enshrouded in myth. Well before completing his study, Ellis approached Lejeune with a request for permission to visit the Central Pacific to see firsthand what fortifications the wily Japanese had constructed in the Mandated Islands. The commandant offered the services of Ellis to the Office of Naval Intelligence (ONI), which yearned for answers to the same questions. Although the terms of the mandates prohibited the Japanese from fortifying their islands, it was widely—albeit erroneously—assumed that they were. ONI provided a fund to support Ellis, thereby documenting its complicity in the amateurish undertaking after it went awry. As a bachelor, he would not need to account for his movements to anyone except the commandant because HQMC carried him on the muster rolls as an "officer on leave." Lejeune approved his proposal. Ellis gave him an undated letter of resignation to be used if needed and the commandant assisted him in establishing a fake identity as a representative of a New York firm owned by a retired Marine officer. In the summer of 1921, Ellis set out on his lonely mission.

Traveling to Japan and then on to the Central Pacific, Ellis died at Koror in the Caroline Islands on 12 May 1923. The Japanese government notified the American Embassy, and arrangements were made for Chief Pharmacist's Mate Lawrence Zembsch to travel in a Japanese ship from Yokohama to Koror to retrieve Ellis' ashes. When the vessel returned to Japan in mid-August 1923, the American assistant naval attaché found Zembsch in a catatonic state. Taken to the U.S. naval hospital in Yokohama, by the end of the month he had recovered sufficiently to report that the Japanese had known Ellis was an American agent. Before Zembsch could elaborate on this story, the hospital was leveled by the great Kanto earthquake of September 1923; he died in its ruins.

Here were the ingredients of a first-rate mystery. Friends believed that Ellis had been killed by the Japanese secret police. After World War II, the Marine Corps tried to solve the puzzle. An investigating officer interviewed a number of people who had known Ellis on Koror, including a native woman with whom he had lived. From their testimony it appears that, although the Japanese suspected Ellis to be a spy, they did not kill him. In all probability, he simply drank himself into the grave. The contribution of the Japanese authorities to Ellis' death consisted of simply allowing a chronic alcoholic to continue purchasing the beverages that destroyed him.

Informed of Ellis' death, Lejeune declined to use his friend's letter of resignation and instead issued a terse statement that Ellis had been absent without leave. His disavowal of official responsibility for Ellis' activities averted the threat of a scandal. The affair could easily have mushroomed into a cause célèbre because the Navy Department, through ONI, had supported, if not actually concocted, the risky venture. Lejeune's fault lay in allowing an unstable alcoholic to

undertake the ill-conceived mission even with the enthusiastic support of ONI.

Lejeune also interested himself in the Corps' newest component. At the end of the world war, the Marine air branch numbered 282 officers and 2,180 men. Its future remained highly uncertain. Many senior officers, disgusted that the 1st Aviation Force had not been deployed in support of Leatherneck operations in France, saw no point in maintaining air units, especially during a period of minuscule defense appropriations. As resourceful in peace as he had been in war, Alfred E. Cunningham met the opposition on its own terms, conceding that the only justification for aviation was to assist ground forces and arguing that it had great potential to do so. Those sharing his views included Lejeune, who declared that "a modern force without aviation is inconceivable." In the outcome, the progressives prevailed. The manning levels established for the Corps by Congress in 1920 authorized an aviation force of 1,020 men, and in October of that year Lejeune ordered the establishment of four squadrons: two at Quantico, one in the Dominican Republic, and one in Haiti.

To ensure that America did not forget its Marines, Lejeune—supported by the indefatigable Butler, commanding at Quantico—kept Leatherneck prowess in a variety of activities in the public eye. The first opportunity came with the annual interservice rifle and pistol matches, which Marines had dominated since 1910. In the first postwar competition, Leatherneck "dingers" swept the events. Beginning in the fall of 1921, Butler took his Quantico-based expeditionary brigade into the field to join National Guard troops in annual reenactments of Civil War battles. The first of these events took place near Chancellorsville, Virginia. More than three thousand Marines marched to the battlefield in a column five miles long. Trucks, aircraft, balloons, armored cars, searchlights, tractors, and artillery pieces added to the display.

The performance drew giant crowds of the curious and the influential. President Harding and Secretary Denby attended, giving the spectacle an official stamp of approval. Besides being great public relations, these events provided fun-filled physical fitness training for the Quantico-based Marines. Butler added to his legend in the process: the hawk-beaked warrior's favorite ploy was to take a straggler's rifle and pack and carry them along with his own gear. "Old Gimlet Eye" was then thirty-nine years old and weighed less than 140 pounds. Following this success, the Quantico Marines returned to the field for two further reenactments before the expense of other commitments caused Lejeune to cancel the annual pageants.

When not on maneuvers, Quantico Marines supported a series of superb athletic teams that contributed to the Corps' can-do image. Inspired by Butler, in four seasons the football team won thirty-eight games, tied two, and lost two against the other services, colleges, and the service academies. To the spectators' delight, Butler acted as head cheerleader, supported by the post band blaring away in the background.

The publicity generated by the reenactments, athletic achievements, marksmanship

awards, and businesslike management of the Corps' meager budget lent a rosy hue to the early 1920s. In 1921 a dramatic increase in armed robberies of railway mail cars gave the Marines another opportunity to be of service to their country—and, in the process, add luster to an already glowing image. Alarmed by the growing number of mail robberies, the postmaster general asked the president for the assistance of federal troops. Harding responded by directing Secretary of the Navy Denby to "send in the Marines." In their first stint at guarding the mails, fifty-three officers and twenty-two hundred enlisted men began their new duties on 8 November, carrying with them the secretary's stirring words: "If attacked, shoot, and shoot to kill." The colorful Denby added that if the mail did not get through, "there must be a Marine dead at the post of duty." The robberies promptly ceased and after four months the Marines were withdrawn. Five years later, a new rash of attacks on the mails led to the reintroduction of Marine guards, with equally gratifying results.

Yet as the Corps undertook this new mission, Congress continued to slash at its strength. Near the end of the Congressional session in 1919, budget cutters pruned the smaller of the naval services to 1,093 officers and 27,400 enlisted Marines. By 1921 these numbers had dropped to 962 officers and 16,085 men. Lejeune promised to reduce expenses by 40 percent that year and by 50 percent the next. He ordered two-thirds of the recruiting stations closed, and the minimum age for enlistees raised to twenty-one. For a while, the Corps was obliged to cease recruiting altogether and accept only applicants for reenlistment.

While meeting existing obligations and assuming new commitments, the Corps sought to develop its stillborn specialty of amphibious warfare and to correct short-comings evident in fleet maneuvers. The consensus of military opinion regarded this effort as a waste of time. Instructors at Army schools asserted that opposed landings offered little chance of success. As proof, they pointed to the failure of the largest amphibious operation of the world war, the British assault on Turkey's Gallipoli peninsula in April 1915. Although the attacking forces had managed to fight their way ashore, the defenders quickly sealed the beachheads, and after eight ghastly months the British withdrew. Unopposed landings, on the other hand, need not be naval in character. The Army could easily absorb such a mission.

The fleet exercises of 1922, held at Guantánamo Bay and Culebra, differed little from the Advanced Base maneuvers of 1913–14. As before, Bluejackets ferried Leathernecks to the beach, where the latter wrestled huge naval guns ashore and built emplacements. A year after this uninspiring exercise, Lejeune ordered the name of the organization changed from Advanced Base Force to Expeditionary Force. The mission to defend advanced bases for the fleet remained the same.

When the fleet put to sea for the next set of maneuvers, from December 1923 to February 1924, the amphibious play increased markedly. This time, the entire East Coast Expeditionary Force—more than thirty-three hundred Marines—embarked under the command of Brig. Gen. Eli K. Cole and Col. Dion Williams, senior officers with intelligence and vision. But the landings in the Caribbean underscored the problems that had plagued the practice of amphibious warfare since the Gallipoli fiasco. Forces still landed on the wrong beaches, naval gunfire support remained sporadic and inadequate, and supplies that had been improperly loaded were unloaded in similar fashion. Cole and Williams returned to Quantico with much to report and correct.

In 1925 Marine units participated in the fleet maneuvers conducted in the Hawaiian Islands. Lejeune managed to cobble together a contingent of fifteen hundred Marines from Quantico, Mare Island, and ships' detachments. They included the faculty and students of the Quantico schools, who arrived to operate in the field as an ad hoc staff. As part of the "Blue" force, the

Marines assaulted "Black" defenders in the islands. For a welcome change, the fleet provided sufficient gunfire support. Although a radical improvement over the clumsy attempt in the Caribbean the year before, the exercise identified additional problems: ordinary ship's boats did not appear suitable for amphibious operations; naval air and shore-based air support remained inadequate to support a major landing; troops required extensive training

Top Left: Problems evident in interwar fleet exercises, such as this one at Culebra in 1924, led to the development of amphibious doctrine and equipment used in World War II. (National Archives)

Bottom Right: For unabashed swagger, nothing could surpass Pfc. Curtis W. Knight of the Mounted Platoon, U.S. Legation Guard, Peking, in 1933. Peacetime promotions were notoriously slow, and Knight most likely made private first class after reenlisting. (National Archives)

in at-sea transfer to facilitate ship-to-shore movement; and effective communications equipment required development, existing apparatus having proven unfit for amphibious employment.

Unfortunately, increasing commitments abroad precluded significant participation by the Corps in fleet maneuvers for almost a decade thereafter. In 1927, however, the Joint Board of the Army and Navy confirmed the Marines' responsibility for the conduct of amphibious warfare. Thus, although responses to day-to-day problems kept most Leathernecks busy overseas, the Corps retained its amphibious mission.

One of the new commitments arose across the Pacific. When Generalissimo Chiang Kai-shek and the Chinese Nationalist Party, the Kuomintang, broke ranks with the communists and set out to unify China in the mid-1920s, foreign lives and properties once again appeared to be threatened. In July 1926, the Kuomintang army began to advance north into the Yangtze valley. Landing parties of Bluejackets and Leathernecks from the Asiatic Fleet streamed ashore in answer to the pleas of missionaries and businessmen. As the situation worsened, the secretary of state advised President Calvin Coolidge to take stronger action.

Late in January 1927, Coolidge approved the assembling of the 4th Marines in San Diego; on 3 February the unit sailed for Shanghai. A brigade headquarters, two more battalions for the 4th Marines, an artillery battalion, a tank platoon, and aviation elements followed three weeks later. Smedley Butler was placed in command. The year before, Butler had brought charges against Col. Alexander S. Williams—his second in command at San Diego—for drunken behavior. Recalling that incident and Butler's strident prohibitionist views, Will Rogers provided a pungent observation: "Smedley Butler has arrived in China. The war may continue but the parties will stop."

At Shanghai and Tientsin, the 3rd Brigade contributed to the maintenance of order by sheer presence. Realizing that his men's real mission was to look imposing, Butler gave his instinct for showmanship free rein, staging what amounted to a continuous military pageant enhanced by imaginative if nonregulation touches such as having the brigade's machine guns, mortars, and antitank guns nickel-plated. During one exhibition of America's military might, an aircraft buzzed the grandstand and then performed a daring roll. Unfortunately, the maneuver sheared both wings off the aircraft, which crashed into a nearby lake. As the pilot floated to the ground in front of the crowd, a lady spectator was heard to remark: "Trust Smedley, he always puts on a wonderful show." Soon young officers who had hoped to see action began quipping that the "China expedition" should have been named the "China exhibition." Butler did not share their bellicosity. To Lejeune he wrote, "General, it is all shadow boxing. There is nothing to hit. It will positively do no good to shoot a lot of Chinese coolies."

Late in May, the newly reconstituted 6th Marines and the 1st Battalion of the 10th Marines reinforced the units in Shanghai and Tientsin. By then the center of American concern had shifted to northern China, where the political situation provoked fears of another attack on the legations at Peking, and in June the bulk of the brigade moved to Tientsin. There Butler organized a mechanized "emergency flying column" of two thousand men ready to set out for the capital on two hours' notice. The call never came, and early in 1929 Butler and most of the force returned to the States. Although the apparent triumph of Chiang Kai-shek's Kuomintang promised to initiate an era of stability in China, the 4th Marines remained to assist in the protection of the International Settlements at Shanghai.

One of the Corps' most charming traditions, the Mess Night, had its origins in China. While serving as the adjutant of the 4th Marines in 1927, Capt. Lemuel C. Shepherd Jr. developed a friendship with a British officer. Shepherd and his commanding officer, Col. Henry C. Davis, received an invitation to attend a mess night as guests of the 2nd Battalion, Scots Guards. More than half a century later, Shepherd shared his reminiscences of the event to one of the authors of this volume: "It was an impressive evening. The battalion had brought out its beautiful silver to adorn the dinner table, which was lighted with handsome candelabra. During the evening, the pipe major played Scottish ballads on his bagpipe and a Guardsman danced the Highland fling and other Scottish dances." Shepherd was not the only Marine impressed. The next morning, Davis instructed him to arrange a similar event and to invite the officers of the Scots Guards, stipulating that the ceremonial procedure follow that which had been observed the previous evening. The China Marines had given birth to the Marine Corps Mess Night.

While the exhibition force was conducting its imperial tattoo, nearer home the Corps became engaged in the last and longest of the banana wars. The timing was ironic, for the United States had almost wound down its Caribbean empire. The last company of Marines had sailed from the Dominican Republic in September 1924. Not quite a year later, in August 1925, the one-hundred-man legation guard was withdrawn from Managua, Nicaragua. The only country in which Marines remained was Haiti, which the State Department did not expect to be ready for self-government—at least, by American standards—until around 1935.

To facilitate the achievement of that goal, the position of U.S. High Commissioner to Haiti, with both civil and military authority, had been created in 1922. Lejeune recommended Butler for the assignment, but the Department of State considered him too controversial and the assignment went to Brig. Gen. John H. Russell, the 1st Brigade's commander. Under Russell's proconsulship, Haiti made steady progress toward independence throughout the remainder of the decade. Russell emphasized the development of the Gendarmerie (renamed the Garde d'Haiti in 1928) into an efficient, apolitical force capable of preserving order after the end of the American protectorate.

The pattern of disengagement was interrupted by developments in Nicaragua. Later an American author calculated that, following the departure of the legation guard, three weeks, four days, and thirteen hours passed before civil war broke out between the Conservative Party in power and its Liberal opponents. In May 1926, the Marine detachment of the cruiser *Cleveland* occupied Bluefields for a month to protect the American colony from the conflict. Leathernecks and Bluejackets returned to establish a neutral zone around the city in August, and in October another detachment landed at Corinto to keep peace during an abortive, American-sponsored meeting between Liberal and Conservative leaders.

So far, U.S. involvement in the Nicaraguan imbroglio had been limited to little more than the traditional defense of American lives and property. In November, an event occurred which led to large-scale intervention. Concluding that it would be impossible to remain in power without American support, President Emiliano Chamorro resigned in favor of another Conservative, Gen. Adolfo Díaz, who was to hold office until an election scheduled for 1928. Intent on promoting the restoration of peace in Nicaragua, the Coolidge administration decided to support this solution, as the president explained to Congress in January 1927. By March, more than two thousand Marines, including Maj. Ross E. "Rusty" Rowell's Observation Squadron 1 (VO-1M), had landed in Nicaragua. Designated the 2nd Marine Brigade and placed under the command of Brig. Gen. Logan Feland, this force assumed responsibility for the defense of Managua, the security of the railway from Corinto to the capital, and the maintenance of neutral zones around major cities.

Although the Leathernecks did not join in the fighting, their presence clearly worked to the advantage of the Díaz regime. Yet the revolution showed no sign of subsiding, and in April Coolidge dispatched former secretary of war Henry L. Stimson to negotiate a settlement between the Nicaraguan antagonists. A man of great ability, Stimson did just that. According to the terms of the Peace of Tipitapa, concluded on 4 May 1927, the warring factions agreed to lay down their arms, disband their forces (to include the Nicaraguan army), and abide by the outcome of an American-supervised election in November 1928. In the meanwhile, the Marines would maintain order and begin training a national constabulary, the Guardia Nacional de Nicaragua, which Stimson believed would stabilize the country's political process by deterring presidential hopefuls from trying their hand at revolution.

Endorsed by the chiefs of both the Conservative and Liberal parties, the occupation proceeded with only one serious incident—a bandit raid on a railway town in which two Marines were killed. True, one relatively minor Liberal leader, thirty-two-year-old Augusto C. Sandino, denounced the Tipitapa agreement and led a band of 150 intransigents into the jungles of remote Nueva Segovia Province, on the Honduran frontier. But negotiations were under way to persuade him to surrender. By the end of June, the strength of the 2nd Brigade had been reduced to fifteen hundred men. To all appearances, the situation was well in hand.

Appearances were deceptive. Augusto Sandino would soon emerge as by far the most formidable of the Corps' Caribbean adversaries. A dapper, diminutive mestizo who indulged an irreverent sense of humor by penning cheeky letters to the Marines, he was the illegitimate offspring of a member of the land-owning elite and an Indian servant girl. Keenly aware of the weight of public opinion, he cultivated good relations with the press. One of his greatest successes was an interview with an American correspondent in which he compared himself to George Washington and his followers to the Continental Army.

As a result of such coverage, Sandino soon became an international symbol of resistance to yanqui imperialism and the beneficiary of fund-raisers held in Manhattan as well as Mexico City. To most Marines, though, he was just another bandit.

That Sandino meant to fight became clear shortly past 0100 on 16 July 1927, when he led eight hundred men in a determined assault on thirty-seven Marines and forty-seven *guardias* garrisoning the little town of Ocotal, capital of Nueva Segovia. The fighting was still going on at 1435 that afternoon, the moment at which Rusty Rowell appeared overhead with five World War I–era DH-4s from Managua, each carrying four fragmentation bombs. Unaccustomed to aerial intervention, the Sandinistas neglected to take cover and were decimated in probably the first sustained dive-bombing attack in history. At the end of the action, the Marines collected fifty-six bodies and calculated that the retreating enemy had carried off twice that number of dead and wounded. The garrison had lost one man killed and four wounded.

Some officers believed that this debacle would be the last heard of Sandino. They were wrong. At 0100 on 16 September, a

band of his followers attempted to storm a barracks occupied by forty-six Marines and *guardias* at Telepaneca, a village ten miles from Ocotal. The defenders repulsed the attack and the Sandinistas withdrew at dawn, having suffered an estimated fifty casualties. Two Marines were killed and one *guardia* wounded.

Thus far, the honors belonged to the Leathernecks; but Sandino learned quickly. Never again would his forces hurl themselves against a fortified position. Instead, they would employ the less costly tactics of ambush and evasion. The opportunity to put these into practice came early in October, after engine failure forced a Marine reconnaissance plane down on Sapotillal Ridge in the wilds of northern Nueva Segovia. Later the same day, a twenty-man patrol advanced from the nearest Marine outpost to rescue the two aviators. Surprised by several hundred Sandinistas as it approached the ridge the next morning, the Americans were forced to fall back, leaving behind three dead. Toward the end of the month—by which time the airmen had been captured and hanged—a second patrol reached the ridge but was immediately

attacked and pinned down until the arrival of a third patrol two days later. During the return march, the combined column was again ambushed by a sizeable Sandinista force.

These events naturally focused attention on Nueva Segovia. On 23 November, one of Rowell's reconnaissance flights located Sandino's stronghold, a fortified mountaintop called El Chipote twenty-six miles from the Honduran border. Upon receiving this intelligence, Col. Louis M. Gulick—who had relieved General Feland in August—made plans to carry the war to Sandino. Unfortunately, they were not very good plans. Grossly underestimating Sandinista capability, Gulick committed fewer than two hundred men to the offensive. Two columns, one of 115 men, the other of 65, were ordered to advance from Marine outposts, rendezvous at the deserted village of Quilali, establish a base there, and push on to capture El Chipote. This scenario did not survive ambushes sprung by more than a thousand Sandinistas on 30–31 December. The badly battered columns fought their way to Quilali, where they were surrounded, having lost eight men

killed and thirty wounded, including both column commanders.

Aviation saved the day. The Marines in Quilali cleared the grass-grown main street and 1st Lt. Christian F. "Frank" Schilt, a thirty-two-year-old ex-enlisted pilot in Observation Squadron 7, volunteered to land on it. Between 6 and 8 January 1928, Schilt made ten flights into Quilali, hauling out eighteen badly wounded men and bringing in fourteen hundred pounds of supplies and a new commanding officer. Every landing and

takeoff was made under fire on a runway so short—barely five hundred feet—that men on the ground had to dash out and grab Schilt's plane to prevent it from hurtling into a ravine at the end. Relieved of the burden of their wounded, the Leathernecks withdrew. Schilt was awarded the Medal of Honor. Like so many junior officers who won their spurs in Nicaragua, he went on to a distinguished career in the Corps, retiring in 1957 a lieutenant general after serving his final tour of duty as chief of Marine Corps aviation.

Stung by this setback, Gulick concentrated a battalion to go after Sandino. It occupied El Chipote later in January; as was to be expected Sandino had decamped. No doubt now remained of the seriousness of the insurgency. Feland returned to resume command of the 2nd Brigade, quickly brought up to a strength of thirty-seven hundred men, and Lejeune came to make a personal tour of inspection. The mission of driving the rebels out of Nueva Segovia was assigned to the newly arrived 11th Marines. Although they had accomplished that trying task by the start of summer, Sandino simply shifted his area of operations to the eastern lowlands. Marine forces there responded by thrusts deep into the interior, most notably a forty-six-man expedition led by Capt. Merritt A. "Red Mike" Edson that paddled dugout canoes four hundred miles up the Coco River to seize an enemy base camp at Poteca. All of these operations ended in what soon became

a frustratingly familiar pattern, with the Sandinistas fading into the bush.

Conversely, if the Marines were unable to grasp the will-o'-the-wisp, the will-o'-the-wisp was unable to shake their control of the country. The American-supervised election of November 1928 was acclaimed as the most honest ever held in Nicaragua and produced the first peaceful transition of power in its history. The Liberal candidate, Gen. José M. Moncado, won handily. In hopes that this outcome would satisfy Sandino, American authorities promised him amnesty if he would disband his followers. He spurned the offer, vowing to remain in arms as long as U.S. troops remained in Nicaragua.

Thus no end of the intervention appeared in sight when Stimson reentered the play as secretary of state in the Hoover Administration in 1929. At that date five thousand Marines—nearly a third of the Corps—were serving in Nicaragua. Stimson considered this commitment excessive; but he also believed that to complete the stabilization of that country it would be necessary to supervise the election of 1932. Immediately upon assuming office, he initiated a program of disengagement in which the war against Sandino was gradually transferred to the Guardia Nacional. By midsummer the strength of the 2nd Brigade had been reduced to twenty-five hundred men, and at year's end it stood at eighteen hundred.

Few Marine officers were disappointed by Stimson's decision. Most had come to regard the war as a stalemate. Despite their numerical advantage over the Sandinistas, usually no more than one thousand to fifteen hundred strong, the Marines lacked the

manpower both to garrison settlements and field patrols of the force and frequency needed to harry the enemy from his sanctuaries. In any event, hard-pressed Sandinistas could slip over the border into Honduras. Finally, the Marines realized that they did not possess the support of the civilian population, over whom they had no jurisdiction. As one officer wrote, "the shifting of the *guardias* into the bandit area was acclaimed as a probable solution to the difficulty, as they could control the civil population and force them to cooperate."

Turning the war over to the Guardia, almost wholly Marine officered in the beginning, proved a ticklish business. Commanding Nicaraguan troops called for a high order of leadership. No fewer than seven

Marines were killed by their own men in mutinies between 1927 and mid-1932. Such setbacks notwithstanding, the Guardia's efficiency increased from year to year, as did its complement of Marine-trained Nicaraguan officers. In 1932, it assumed full responsibility for offensive patrolling. The election held that November resulted in the victory of the Liberal candidate, Dr. Juan B. Sacasa. His inauguration took place peacefully on 1 January 1933. The remnant of the 2nd Brigade was dissolved the next day. In five-and-a-half years of conflict, forty-seven Marines had been killed in action or died of wounds and sixty-six others wounded.

Sandino, still in arms when the Marines withdrew, accepted the Liberal government's offer of amnesty a few months later. In 1934 he was assassinated on the order of the *jefe* of the Guardia, Col. Anastasio Somoza, who then overthrew Dr. Sacasa and erected a family dictatorship that endured for almost half a century. Despite its clouded outcome, the Nicaraguan campaign brought two benefits to the Corps. Firstly, it promoted the development of the Marine air–ground team. In Col. Robert D. Heinl Jr.'s deft summation: "Most of the things done by Marine aviation in Nicaragua had been done or experimented with before. But never before had they been done simultaneously and routinely, and never before had combat and logistic air support been woven into the fabric of a campaign."

Secondly, the Sandino chase provided a generation of officers with valuable experience in jungle warfare and small-unit tactics. Among them was a pugnacious, pipe-smoking Virginian destined to become a legend in the Corps, Capt. Lewis Burwell "Chesty" Puller. A cousin of George Patton, Puller had joined the Marines in June 1918, at the end of his freshman year at VMI. Selection for NCO and then officers' school kept him from getting to France and in June 1919, two weeks after earning a reserve commission, he was discharged because of postwar reductions. Not daunted, he reenlisted as a private for service in the Gendarmerie d'Haiti. The *caco* rebellion was then at its height. Before it was over, Puller had been in twenty actions, risen to the rank of captain in the Gendarmerie (and corporal in the Corps), and won the first of his lifetime total of twenty-two decorations. In 1924, he obtained a regular commission as a second lieutenant, USMC. Glancing at his new gold bars, he told a friend, "Well, I've got 'em. Now, all I need is a war." He found his war in Nicaragua, where in two tours as a Guardia company commander, he fought in another score of actions, earned two Navy Crosses, and cemented his reputation as an exceptionally able and aggressive combat officer.

Left: In Nicaragua, Marines airlifted supplies to remote garrisons in Fokker trimotors, the Corps' first transport plane. These two were photographed at Ocotal in 1929. (U.S. Naval Institute Photo Archives)

Right: First Lieutenant Lewis B. "Chesty" Puller, with pipe, was serving as a captain in the Guardia Nacional de Nicaragua and GySgt. Willis Lee as a first lieutenant when this photograph of them and two of their NCOs was taken in the field in 1931. (National Archives)

Meanwhile, the leadership of the Corps underwent a succession of changes. In February 1929, General Lejeune announced that he would not seek reappointment the following month. Privately, he loathed facing the defense cuts promised by newly elected President Herbert Hoover. Few were surprised when Maj. Gen. Wendell C. Neville got the nod as his replacement. A Naval Academy graduate like Lejeune, Neville shared his predecessor's commitment to a Corps tied to the needs of the fleet. Veteran Marines referred to him as "Whispering Buck" because on the battlefields of France his booming voice supposedly eliminated the need for a field telephone. Butler, who heartily approved of Neville's appointment, was not forgotten. In June 1929 he received his second star, making him, at age forty-

eight, the youngest major general in the American armed forces.

After barely a year in office, Neville suffered a debilitating stroke and died in July 1930. Many Marines expected Butler, the Corps' ranking major general, to become the fifteenth commandant. But the cantankerous Quaker had accumulated too many enemies; moreover, his powerful congressman father had died in 1928. To head the Corps, President Hoover and Secretary of the Navy Charles F. Adams chose sixty-year-old Brig. Gen. Ben H. Fuller, who had been running HQMC since Neville's incapacitation. Apparently, Hoover and Adams concluded that Fuller would be a better team player in the administration's plans for drastic defense reductions. Fortunately for the Corps, their prediction proved wrong.

Controversial as this decision has remained, it was probably for the best. Butler's view of the Corps' role was still basically that of colonial infantry, fighting little wars on the frontiers of American influence. For all his ability, he represented the past. It is difficult to imagine Butler working constructively with the admirals he loathed to develop the Corps' big war, amphibious mission. Fuller and his successors represented the future.

Deeply disappointed, Butler remained in uniform for less than a year. In January 1931 the secretary of the navy threatened him with a court-martial for having told an unflattering story about Italian dictator Benito Mussolini in an address to a Philadelphia civic club. An outpouring of public support and the shrewd attorney Butler engaged—Henry Leonard, an ex–Marine officer who had served with him during the Boxer Rebellion—forced the Hoover Administration to back off, and in the end Butler was allowed to draft his own letter of minimal reprimand. The incident sealed Butler's estrangement from officialdom, and in September, aged just fifty, the Corps' stormy petrel marched noisily into retirement at his own request. In retirement, he continued to lash out at his nemeses: Naval Academy graduates, admirals, the Navy in general, and the "headquarties toadies" who seemed to be leading the Corps.

General Fuller, the new commandant, was a quiet, kindly man affectionately known as Uncle Ben. The Corps' senior officer in length of service as well as position, he had graduated from the Naval Academy in 1889, the same year as the chief of naval operations, Adm. William Veazie Pratt. This fact had figured in his appointment, for Hoover and Secretary Adams anticipated—incorrectly, as it turned out—that the classmates would foster interservice cooperation.

As commandant, Fuller concentrated his efforts on shielding the Corps' already attenuated ranks from the impact of the Great Depression and strengthening its ties to the Navy. In the first of these endeavors he was reasonably successful. Although the Hoover administration prodded Congress to reduce the Corps' enlisted strength from 18,000 in 1930 to 15,350 in 1932, the following year Fuller's testimony to Congress proved instrumental in heading off an administration proposal to cut it to 13,600. Of far greater consequence was the outcome of his efforts to emphasize that the Marines were a component of the naval service and not, as even some of their officers had begun to call them "State Department troops."

Much of the progress in this direction came about through Fuller's encouragement of his energetic deputy, Maj. Gen. John H. Russell, who had returned to duty in 1930 after eight years as high commissioner in Haiti. Appointed assistant to the commandant in February 1933, Russell believed strongly that the future of the Corps lay in the conduct of amphibious operations. Together, he and Fuller made three major contributions to readying it for that role: the formation of the Fleet Marine Force (FMF); the establishment of the Marine Corps Equipment Board; and the sponsorship of studies that produced the *Tentative Landing Operations Manual*.

Fuller had secured the backing of the General Board in reinforcing the Corps' connection to the Navy in 1931. On Russell's suggestion, in 1933 he wrote to Admiral Pratt proposing that the name of the two Marine expeditionary forces be changed to the Fleet Marine Force. Pratt concurred, and Navy Department Order 241 of 7 December 1933 created the FMF. The effect was more than cosmetic. Its charter made the FMF an integral element of the U.S. Fleet, with primary responsibility for the seizure and defense of advanced bases. Fuller declared that the development of this force must be the Corps' top priority. He ordered the Marine Corps Equipment Board activated in late 1933. Its mission was to identify and then persuade the Navy to procure improved landing craft, the need for which had been repeatedly demonstrated. The compilation of the *Tentative Landing Operations Manual*, a distillation of the principles of amphibious warfare, began at the Quantico schools in 1931. While serving as the assistant to the commandant, Russell recommended suspending classes and assigning students and faculty to work on completing the project. Based in part on a pamphlet titled *Joint Overseas Expeditions* recently issued by the Joint Army-Navy Board, the manual appeared in draft form in January 1934. Though not without shortcomings, it provided a firm foundation upon which the Corps could build its amphibious expertise.

Fuller's commandancy also witnessed another of the recurrent proposals to have the Corps absorbed by another armed service. In 1931 Maj. Gen. George S. Simonds, a confidant of Gen. Douglas MacArthur, the Army's chief of staff, prepared a lengthy memorandum arguing that the Army should incorporate the amphibious mission of the Marine Corps. Simonds noted that of all the Western nations, only the United States and Great Britain still maintained separate marine forces, and even the British had taken away the combined arms capabilities of their Royal Marines. The Army, he asserted, could provide the Corps' administrative, supply and schools support, and in the process save the taxpayers a whopping twenty-five million dollars. With the nation engulfed in the worst depression in its history, the Army's argument won immediate favor. However, the Corps' friends rose to the occasion and the legislation died in Congress.

Retiring after a little less than forty-five years' commissioned service in March 1934, Fuller was succeeded by General Russell. Russell's tour, though brief, proved highly productive. Overlooking no opportunity to emphasize the importance of the Fleet Marine Force, Russell even banned the use of *expeditionary*, which he considered old-fashioned, in the title of Marine Corps formations. The withdrawal of Marine forces from Haiti in August 1934 finally freed the Corps from its Caribbean commitments and gave Russell the personnel to begin putting the amphibious doctrine developed at Quantico into practice.

The first large-scale landing exercises since the late 1920s were held from 5 to 10 May 1934. A much more ambitious series of problems, Fleet Landing Exercise (FLEX) 1, took place from 15 January until 15 March 1935. Other FLEXes followed annually until the outbreak of war. On Capitol Hill, Russell achieved an objective that had eluded Lejeune, Neville, and Fuller, persuading Congress to allow the Corps to promote officers on the

In 1941, as it became increasingly probable that the United States would be drawn into the war already raging in Europe and East Asia, the Philadelphia firm of Gum, Inc., introduced two distinctively new series into the sports-centered cavalcade of bubble-gum cards. Well researched and carefully drawn by George Moll, one series was devoted to *America's Army*; the other to *America's Navy*. The latter consisted of sixty-four cards, twenty-two of which featured the Marines. The back of each card carried a detailed description of the activity or scene shown on the front and concluded with the admonition, "Save to get all these picture cards show-ing Uncle Sam's soldiers, sailors, marines, airmen, and civilians in training for NATIONAL DEFENSE."

Left: "*What is a Marine?*" The answer was a member of "the military branch of the U.S. Navy, used for the protection of Uncle Sam's property on land and at sea." Note the scene's clearly Caribbean flavor. Right: "*Turned over for duty.*" This phrase described Marines who, having completed "the full course of study" (a silken euphemism for basic training), were assigned to units "and may be hastily dispatched for duty anywhere on land or at sea." The ship on which this detachment is embarking is a realistic rendition of the *Henderson*, the Corps' principal transport from 1917 through 1941.

Left: "*The Landing Party.*" "When landing duties are necessary," the caption states, "the Marines are first ashore and at the scene of trouble." These Leathernecks are landing the old-fashioned way, from ships' boats rowed by sailors. Right: "*Telling the Marines.*" The back of this card illustrates the insignia that would tell the knowledgeable observer a Marine's rank. The scene is an inspection at sea, with both officer and enlisted rank insignia much in evidence.

Left: "*Pitching Hand Grenades.*" Marines practice lobbing grenades over the crossbar. The high trajectory was supposed to en-sure that the delayed-action fuse exploded before an enemy had time to throw the grenade back. Right: "*Machine-Gun Practice.*" Leathernecks fire a watercooled M2 Browning .50-cal antiaircraft gun at a target being towed two thousand feet behind the aircraft. A device called a sychronizer indicated the range to the target and allowed two or more guns to concentrate their fire.

basis of merit (as determined by selection boards) rather than seniority. Finally, he revitalized the moribund Marine Corps Reserve and instituted the Platoon Leaders Class program of reserve officer training for college undergraduates.

Russell reached the mandatory retirement age in 1936. As his successor he recommended fifty-seven-year-old Brig. Gen. Thomas Holcomb. Other contenders vied for the post, but Russell's long-standing friendship with President Roosevelt guaranteed that Holcomb got the job. It was the first time since 1914 that an officer who had not graduated from the Naval Academy came to head the Corps. But Holcomb, a battalion commander at Belleau Wood and a graduate of both the Army and Navy war colleges, was a thorough professional. Like his predecessors, he assigned top priority to strengthening and training the FMF. And he, too, was an old acquaintance of Roosevelt, whom he had met while the chief executive was a youthful assistant secretary of the navy.

Under Holcomb's leadership the Corps continued to improve its amphibious capabilities. The hands-on experience gathered in the yearly FLEXes was carefully analyzed to refine the doctrine formulated at Quantico. One of the chief difficulties, already identified in the mid-1920s, persisted: the unsuitability of standard ships' boats as landing craft. The problem was solved, largely through the perseverance of the Marine Corps Equipment Board, by the adoption of three specialized craft that satisfied Leatherneck requirements. The first was a troop carrier based on the "Eureka" boat, a shallow-draft, broad-bowed craft

manufactured by Andrew Higgins, a civilian boatbuilder in New Orleans, for use in the Louisiana bayous. Modified in various ways, Higgins' boat became the landing craft, vehicle and personnel (LCVP) of World War II. The success of this project encouraged Higgins to design an amphibian carrier to ferry tanks and wheeled vehicles to a beachhead. The result was the landing craft, mechanized (LCM). The last of the new vehicles also derived from a civilian product, Donald Roebling's "Alligator." An amphibian tractor able to trundle over coral reefs and onto dry land, it entered the Marine Corps' inventory as the landing vehicle, tracked (LVT). The contribution these craft made to victory in World War II would be impossible to exaggerate.

Even before Pearl Harbor, Marines stood toe to toe with the Japanese. When war broke out between China and Japan in 1937, the headquarters of the 2nd Brigade and the 6th Marines deployed to the Shanghai-Tientsin area to reinforce the 4th Marines. This time, the Leathernecks found themselves facing a Japanese adversary determined to break the Western hold on the International Settlements at Shanghai. In one memorable confrontation in the summer of 1940, Chesty Puller, executive officer of the 2nd Battalion, 4th Marines, drew his pistol on a Japanese Army officer who had led a detachment into the American sector to seize some Chinese. The Japanese released their captives and withdrew.

A generation of Marines remembered China duty with tears in their eyes. Although a private earned only twenty-one dollars a month, he could live like a king. Chinese "room boys" shined shoes, washed clothes,

and even cleaned rifles and equipment. A steak in town cost only thirty cents, a bottle of Chinese beer to wash it down—two cents a quart! And then there were the women, White Russian as well as Chinese: beautiful, accommodating and, like everything else, affordably priced.

But the curtain was closing. In September 1939, the German invasion of Poland ignited World War II. France fell to Hitler's armies the following summer. In response to the pleas of British prime minister Winston Churchill, Roosevelt ordered the Marines to lonely, frozen Iceland in the North Atlantic. Earlier, Roosevelt had anticipated using the 1st Marine Division to secure the Azores. Instead, the chief executive decided to send the 1st Provisional Brigade—4,095 Marines formed around the 6th Marines—to relieve the British garrison in Iceland. Landing there on 7 July 1941, the Leathernecks ate unfamiliar English chow and adopted the custom of the rum ration while enduring the unenthusiastic hospitality of the population. An Army brigade began to arrive in August 1941, and by 8 March 1942 the last Marine had departed.

The previous July, Japan had occupied French Indochina. Washington responded to this act of aggression by imposing economic sanctions that set it on a collision course with Tokyo. As war clouds gathered over East Asia, American leaders grew increasingly apprehensive about the defense of the Philippines. On 28 November 1941, the 4th Marines, with its band playing, marched down Bubbling Well and Nanking roads through Shanghai to the docks. The headquarters of the 2nd Brigade and the 6th Marines had already returned home in February 1937. As the fifes and drums played "China Night" one last time, the Leathernecks filed aboard ship. An era had ended.

Worldwide, the Corps numbered just 26,369 enlisted men and 1,556 officers, scarcely more than it had two decades earlier. But they were a hard lot. Few Leathernecks made private first class in one enlistment; most stayed because they had nowhere else to turn in the harsh economic climate of the Depression. The officers were a mix of Naval Academy alumni, distinguished graduates of college and university ROTC programs, and outstanding NCOs selected for officer training. The Leathernecks of 1941 still wore the dishpan helmets of World War I and carried much of the equipment of an earlier era, but the lean interwar years had spawned an earnest and tough Marine Corps ready to wrestle with any adversary.

CHAPTER 10

World War II: South Pacific Campaigns, 1942–1943

A bright, warm sun greeted the occasional Hawaii-based Leatherneck resolute enough to roll out of the sack in time for morning chow on Sunday, 7 December 1941. At the Ewa Mooring Mast Field, near Barbers Point and four miles west of the huge Navy base at Pearl Harbor on the island of Oahu, the startled duty officer of Marine Air Group One (later, MAG 21) saw squadrons of Japanese torpedo planes thunder over the strip, headed in the direction of the base.

Half an hour later, Nakajima fighters strafed the Marine aircraft—parked wing tip to wing tip to prevent sabotage— destroying all forty-seven planes. As the enemy aircraft returned, a new wave of strafing runs by Mitsubishi Zeroes set barracks and hangars afire. Planeless pilots and ground personnel responded with a fruitless fusillade of rifle and pistol fire.

A few minutes earlier, Japanese fighters and torpedo planes had rendezvoused to the northwest of the Hawaiian Islands.

Smoke from burning warships blackens the sky above these Marines deployed on the parade ground outside their barracks at Pearl Harbor on the morning of 7 December 1941. They hope to get a shot at low-flying Japanese aircraft. (National Archives)

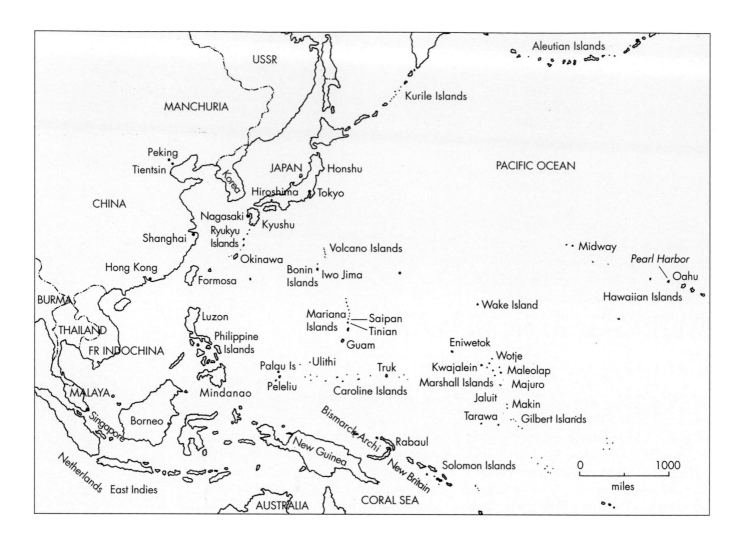

Map 16. The War in the Pacific, 1941–45

They flew off five carriers, part of a task force that had departed the Kurile Islands on 27 November and steamed through the less-transited region of the north Pacific. Except for a few clouds clinging to the mountaintops of Oahu, the attackers had unlimited visibility. At 0753 Cdr. Fuchida Mitsuio signaled his admiral, "Tora! Tora! Tora!" The Japanese had achieved complete surprise, and the attack was on. Fuchida fired a signal flare, and the Japanese torpedo planes converged on the capital ships tied up or at anchor in Pearl Harbor. In minutes, the attackers sank four battleships and damaged four others. Fortunately, the carriers *Enterprise*, *Lexington*, and *Saratoga* were safe at sea.

As bugles and alarms called Marines, soldiers, and sailors to their stations, the smoke from burning ships and buildings billowed skyward. Marines from the barracks and others assigned to the 1st and 3rd Defense Battalions drew rifles and ammunition. Only when the Leathernecks mounted machine guns on the roof of the barracks were they able to shoot down three enemy aircraft. In general, the Japanese encountered little opposition. Marines serving in the ships of the fleet manned antiaircraft batteries to inflict occasional damage on the foe. Fifteen ships tied up at Pearl Harbor had Marine detachments in them. When the battleship *Arizona* blew up and capsized, the commander of her Marine detachment, Maj. Alan Shapley, swam through the debris and burning oil to save a fellow Leatherneck. Pfc. Willard D. Darling's plunge into the harbor to rescue a drowning Navy officer earned him the Navy Cross.

While the Japanese planes returned to their carriers, Marines counted their casualties: 108 dead and another 49 wounded. Officers formed barracks Marines and Leathernecks from the two defense battalions into units prepared to counter an enemy landing, but the Japanese had accomplished their mission and were steaming home. The attack had lasted only 110 minutes; more than 2,403 Americans had died.

As news of the attack reached the Western Pacific, Marines in lonely outposts found themselves surrounded or under siege. More than two hundred Leathernecks stationed in Tientsin and Peking, hopelessly outnumbered and outgunned, received orders to surrender without firing a shot. A garrison of 153 Marines, 271 sailors, and 326 native police on Guam gave up after a short struggle following a Japanese landing on 10 December.

On tiny Wake Island, Maj. James P. D. Devereux's 1st Defense Battalion made an epic stand in the face of impossible odds. Supporting it in the air were twelve F4F Grumman Wildcats of Maj. Paul A. Putnam's VMF-211, which had flown off the *Enterprise* on 4 December. At 0500 on 11 December, Japanese transports escorted by a cruiser attempted to land troops on the island—actually, three islands, located 450 miles from their nearest neighbor. Devereux held his fire until 0615; by then, the light cruiser *Yubari* and six destroyers had closed to within forty-five hundred yards of the beach. Leatherneck shore batteries opened fire, sinking the destroyer *Hayate* and several transports and sending the cruiser limping away. A Marine aviator put down a second enemy destroyer, the *Kisaragi*. Wake's planes also shot down three enemy

bombers and damaged four others. The Japanese withdrew.

But Devereux knew his tiny force was doomed. In Hawaii, a relief force centered on the carriers *Lexington*, *Saratoga*, and *Enterprise* was organized and steamed toward the beleaguered island. Fear of losing the precious carriers prompted their recall and, with them, the last hope for Devereux's garrison. By the seventeenth, Wake was down to four Wildcats; only by cannibalizing damaged planes were ground crews able to get these few into the air. On 23 December, by which date the last Wildcat had been lost, greatly superior Japanese forces succeeded in fighting their way ashore. Realizing that further resistance would be futile, Cdr. Winfield S. Cunningham, the atoll commander, authorized Devereux to lay down his arms. Wake's last, Spartan message to the outside world, "Enemy on island issue in doubt," became a source of grim pride to the American people. Contrary to a story widely believed during the war, however, Devereux had never transmitted a request to "Send us more Japs." As he recalled years later, "Japs were one thing we didn't need any more of."

Wake Island cost the Japanese 820 dead and 330 more wounded, as well as two ships and seven planes. American losses included 49 Marines, 3 sailors, and 70 civilian construction workers killed. Most of the 470 sailors and Marines, 5 soldiers, and 1,146 civilians made prisoner were taken on the *Nita Maru* to Shanghai. En route, Japanese guards beheaded two Marines and three sailors, and abused the other captives. The cruel treatment foreshadowed the bitter struggle to wrest the Pacific from the Empire of Japan. But the little garrison's gallant stand would not be forgotten. Capt. Henry T. "Hank" Elrod, the pilot who sank the *Kisaragi*, was awarded the Medal of Honor—the Corps' first in World War II.

In the Philippines, Marines assigned to the barracks at Olongapo and Cavite mounted out to reinforce the 4th Marines on Corregidor. After years of China duty, most Leathernecks had little respect for the Japanese soldiers they had encountered in Shanghai and Tientsin. But the enemy they faced in the Philippines was cut of the same cloth as the tireless troops who would shortly take Malaya, Singapore, and the Dutch East Indies. Despite a stubborn resistance by the American and Filipino forces, the Japanese closed in on the gaunt defenders. On 29 April 1942—Emperor Hirohito's birthday—a bombardment of Corregidor signaled the beginning of the final push to seize the Philippines. Lt. Gen. Jonathan M. Wainwright—left in command after President Roosevelt ordered the departure of Gen. Douglas MacArthur— directed his forces to lay down their arms on 6 May. Burning his regimental colors, Col. Samuel L. Howard, commander of the 4th Marines, wept as he became the first Leatherneck to surrender an entire regiment.

The Japanese soldier had been taught that to be taken prisoner was dishonorable. His soldier's manual spelled it out for him in no uncertain terms: "To be captured means not only disgracing the Army but your parents. Your family will never be able to hold up its head again. Always save the last round for yourself." To the Japanese,

their captives were dishonored warriors to be used as slave labor. Of the 1,283 Marines captured in the Philippines, 239 died in imprisonment.

The Empire of Japan seemed unstoppable. In the opening months of the war, the forces of Nippon inflicted a series of humiliating defeats on the most powerful nations of the Western World. Hong Kong fell on 25 December 1941. Japanese troops swept down the Malay Peninsula, forcing British and Commonwealth troops onto tiny Singapore; by 15 February 1942 the defenders had hauled down the Union Jack. On 9 March Dutch forces on Java capitulated; by the end of the month, the entire East Indies were in enemy hands.

Although the Japanese attack on Pearl Harbor—"a day that will live in infamy," in the words of President Roosevelt— caught the base's Marine defenders as unprepared as anyone else, the Corps had been practicing its amphibious assault mission for over a decade in the belief that it would one day be tested against Japan. Despite the miserly appropriations and isolationist thinking of the interwar years, by 7 December 1941, the Marine Corps had grown to more than sixty-five thousand men organized into two divisions, thirteen air squadrons, and several defense battalions. The Corps was readier for war than at any time in its history.

In early 1942 two brigades of Marines sailed for Samoa in the South Pacific, the region where strategists assumed that the Japanese would strike next. Instead, the enemy attempted to seize Midway, a tiny American island in the Central Pacific. Taking advantage of a brilliant piece of

Rear Adm. Richmond Kelly Turner (left) and Maj. Gen. Alexander A. Vandegrift were photographed in August 1942 as they planned the amphibious invasion of Guadalcanal. Turner commanded the amphibious force and Vandegrift led the landing force. (National Archives)

code-breaking, U.S. naval forces intercepted the Japanese task force. On 4 June 1942, fifty-two partly obsolete Midway-based Marine aircraft—twenty-five fighters of VMF-221 and twenty-seven dive bombers of VMSB-241—took off to attack the carriers and to defend against inbound strikes. Twenty-three of the intrepid Leathernecks did not return, but their sacrifice helped to set the stage for the great American victory that followed. The next day, eleven of the surviving Marine dive bombers joined in the pursuit of the Japanese. Hit by flak after releasing his bombs at the cruiser *Mikuma*, Capt. Richard E. Fleming crashed his plane into the ship's after turret to earn a posthumous Medal of Honor.

Midway cost the Americans the carrier *Yorktown* and 98 aircraft, but the Japanese lost 4 carriers and 322 planes. Elated with their victory at Midway and in an earlier encounter in the Coral Sea, the Navy's leaders pressed to seize the initiative in the Pacific. In Hawaii, Adm. Chester A.

Nimitz, commander of the Pacific Fleet, proposed sending the 1st Marine Raider Battalion to Tulagi in the Solomon Islands to destroy a Japanese seaplane facility. But in Washington, the Joint Chiefs of Staff—goaded by the Chief of Naval Operations, Adm. Ernest J. King—proposed a much larger operation.

Although the United States and Great Britain had agreed upon a "Germany first" strategy, King argued that U.S. forces should maintain the momentum against the Japanese. By tacit agreement, the war in Europe would remain an "Army show" while the fight in the Pacific rested in Navy hands. Intelligence reports of the construction of a Japanese airfield near Lunga Point on Guadalcanal in the Solomons supported King's argument for offensive action in the South Pacific. Although the Battle of Coral Sea had forestalled a Japanese amphibious assault on Port Moresby, the allied base of supply in eastern New Guinea, completion of the airfield might signal the beginning of a renewed advance to the south. Thus came into being Operation Watchtower, the seizure of Tulagi and Guadalcanal.

At midnight on 6–7 August 1942, officers on the bridge watch of the transport *McCawley* peered anxiously into a murky darkness. In less than three hours, the amphibious force to which the ship belonged hoped to pass undetected through the center of a seven-mile passage between the nearest of the Russell Islands and Guadalcanal. The embarked troops came mostly from the 1st Marine Division, commanded by Maj. Gen. Alexander A. Vandegrift. The core of the division was composed of the ramrod-straight, sunburned Leathernecks who had formed the backbone of the lean interwar Marine Corps; young enlistees—eager to be "first to fight"—filled out its ranks.

Vandegrift had spent thirty-three of his fifty-five years in the Corps. He was by birth a Virginian, the grandson of a Confederate officer who took part in Pickett's Charge, and the general he most admired was Stonewall Jackson, "because he could do so much with so little." Originally Vandegrift had aimed for the Army, hoping to win a commission by competitive examination upon turning twenty-one. When the Army reported no vacancies that year, he accepted his congressman's invitation to take the Corps' test. Banana wars soon began breaking out all over and Vandegrift fought in his share or more of them, serving in the Cuban intervention of 1912; the first Nicaraguan campaign, including the action at Coyotepe; the landing at Veracruz; and the first and second Haitian campaigns. He was badly disappointed that he could not obtain an

assignment "over there" in World War I, but, contrary to his apprehensions, his failure to reach France did not blight his career. In 1928 he commanded a battalion in the brigade sent to China under Smedley Butler, a close personal friend. Seven years later, Vandegrift returned to China to command the elite Legation Guard. From 1937 until his appointment to the 1st Marine Division in November 1941, he acted as assistant to Major General Commandant Holcomb, whom he was expected to succeed at the Corps' helm.

Soft-spoken, self-contained, and unexcitable, preferring compromise to confrontation, Vandegrift offered a leadership style in stark contrast to that of many fire-eating contemporaries. One observer thought he could readily be mistaken for a small-town businessman who taught Sunday school. Vandegrift knew that the Solomons operation would test his skills like no previous assignment. In a letter written to his wife on the day he sailed for the South Pacific, he asked, "When you remember me in your prayers, as I know you will, also ask that I be given the judgment and ability to lead this splendid outfit so that it will accomplish his task with the least possible loss."

When Vandegrift learned of the division's assignment from Vice Adm. Robert L. Ghormley, Commander, South Pacific Force and Area (COMSOPAC), the news came as a shock. Short one regiment, he had expected to spend the winter months in New Zealand. There he planned to train his troops in the tactics of battalion-size and larger units, and absorb sorely needed additions to the division's ranks. Just before the movement to the Solomons, Vandegrift received reinforcements: the 1st Raider Battalion and the 1st Marine Parachute Battalion—units with far fewer men and less firepower than a typical infantry battalion—plus the 2nd Marines (an infantry regiment) and the 3rd Defense Battalion.

While in numbers Vandegrift now had a division, he realized that it lacked the cohesiveness and training of an effective combat force. His overworked staff pleaded for more time, but to little avail; Navy superiors moved D-day back only from 1 August to 7 August 1942. Gen. Merrill B. Twining, then serving as a major on Vandegrift's staff, recalled that Rear Adm. Richmond Kelly Turner—the commander of the amphibious force—carried "a field marshal's baton in his briefcase" and meddled repeatedly in the preparations of the landing plan. His patience at an end, Vandegrift refused to change the plan yet another time. When Nimitz visited the South Pacific later that fall, Vandegrift bent his ear about Turner's irksome interference in operations ashore; Twining believed that Nimitz placed Turner "on a short leash" after that.

The lack of information on the Japanese in the Solomon Islands troubled both Vandegrift and Turner. When the task force left New Zealand on 30 June, Watchtower more resembled a leap of blind faith than a carefully considered and timed example of amphibious professionalism. Reflecting on the frantic preparations for the operation, King provided a droll comment that proved to be the understatement of the campaign: "because of the urgency of seizing and

occupying Guadalcanal, planning was not up to its usual thorough standard."

At 0300 the shrill cry of a bosun's whistle roused the men from their bunks. More than one sleepy Leatherneck most likely muttered the timeless lament: "Gahd! The only people up this time of the night are burglars and bad women!" While the troops wolfed down a heavy pre-assault breakfast, their commanders pondered the formidable task that lay ahead. Combat veterans of World War I led the two infantry regiments: Col. Clifton B. Cates, the 1st Marines, and Col. Leroy P. Hunt, the 5th Marines. Both had commanded companies in France, fought guerrillas in Haiti and Nicaragua, and more recently confronted the Japanese in diplomatic face-offs in China. The division's third infantry regiment—the 7th Marines—had been left behind to defend Fiji. Cates recalled ruefully that his regiment had never even conducted a command-post exercise: "we were short on equipment and short on training . . . maybe we [thought we could] make up in guts what we lacked otherwise." He estimated that more than 90 percent of his regiment had enlisted after the attack on Pearl Harbor; in the 1st Marines, less than 50 percent of the NCOs had any real military experience.

The fifteen ships of Transport Group X-Ray hove to four miles east of Lunga Point, anchoring off Red Beach. Vandegrift ordered the 5th Marines to seize the eighteen-hundred-yard airstrip, backed by dense jungle foliage, and drive seven hundred yards inland. The 1st Marines would pass through them to strike toward a prominent terrain feature, Mount Austen, which

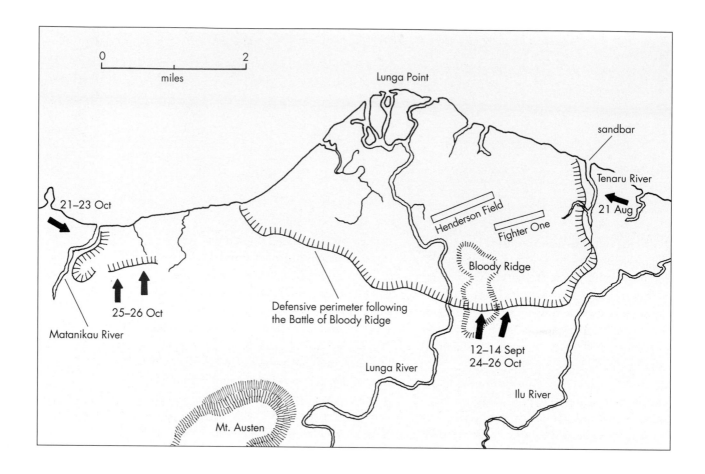

Map 17, left:
The Opening Months
of the Struggle for
Guadalcanal, August–
October 1942

Right: Senior officers of
the 1st Marine Division
following a briefing four
days after the landing on
Guadalcanal: General
Vandegrift (front row, fourth
from left); Col. Pedro A.
de Valle, CO of the 11th
Marines, the division's
artillery regiment (second
from left); Lt. Col. Gerald
C. Thomas, division operations officer (fifth from left);
Col. Clifton B. Cates, CO
of the 1st Marines and,
like Vandegrift, a future
commandant (sixth from
left); and Lt. Col. Randolph
M. Pate, division logistics
officer and another future
commandant (seventh from
left). (National Archives)

overlooked the Japanese airfield. A canny
tactician, Vandegrift believed the Tenaru, a
small, unfordable river on the left flank of the
beachhead, gave him natural protection from
the main body of Japanese troops.

The first landing craft touched down
at 0910. To the Leathernecks' surprise, no
Japanese appeared to resist the landing.
As the troops pushed through the jungle,
supplies began to pour ashore from the
anchored transports. By early afternoon
on 8 August, the 1st and 5th Marines had
overrun both the airfield and the Japanese
encampment with little opposition from
the enemy, apparently dumbfounded by
the audacity of Operation Watchtower.
The Japanese Special Naval Landing Force
battalion—an estimated 430 marines—and
a labor force of some seventeen hundred
Koreans fled inland when the pre-assault
bombardment began the day before. To
the Marines' delight, the enemy left behind
a considerable stockpile of ordnance and
equipment.

On nearby Tulagi, the assistant division
commander, Brig. Gen. William H. Rupertus,
and Transport Group Yoke found that the
Special Naval Landing Force troops there
intended to fight a vicious, no-surrender battle
in defense of the island. Lt. Col. Merritt A.
"Red Mike" Edson's 1st Raider Battalion and
Lt. Col. Harold E. Rosecrans' 2nd Battalion,
5th Marines, landed on Tulagi's south
coast and struck toward the ridge that ran
lengthwise through the island to the native
townsite and government center.

By nightfall Edson had established his
command post in the former British residency.
The Japanese defenders had withdrawn into
a ravine southeast of Hill 281, on Tulagi's
southern tip. Rosecrans' battalion swept
the northern portion of the island and then
moved into position to support Edson along
the crest of Hill 281. As darkness closed in the
Marines anticipated attack by the Japanese
naval infantry.

Throughout the long night, the Japanese
swarmed from hillside caves in repeated,

unsuccessful attempts to penetrate the Raiders' lines. Edson's rules—don't panic, stay in position, count on fellow Marines for support, and avoid indiscriminate firing—kept the Raiders' lines intact. Still, it required heroism to face the Japanese onslaughts throughout the black night. Pfc. Edward H. Ahrens of Company A took on a Japanese patrol single-handedly. Ahrens' company commander, burly Capt. Lewis W. "Lew" Walt, found him at first light, dying from his wounds. Ahrens' foes lay across him in a frozen catafalque of death. In the hand-to-hand combat during the previous night, he had been shot twice and bayoneted three times. Ahrens was honored by a posthumous Navy Cross. By mid-afternoon of 8 August, Japanese opposition on Tulagi had ended.

That night, a cruiser–destroyer force of the Imperial Japanese Navy responded to the American intrusion with a stinging riposte. Adm. Richmond Kelly Turner, the amphibious force commander, had positioned three cruiser–destroyer forces to bar the Tulagi-Guadalcanal approaches. At the Battle of Savo Island the Japanese demonstrated their superiority in night-fighting at this stage of the war, shattering two of Turner's covering forces without loss to themselves. Four heavy cruisers went to the bottom—three American, one Australian—and another lost her bow. As the sun came up over "Ironbottom Sound," Marines watched grimly as Higgins boats swarmed out to rescue oil-coated survivors.

Earlier on the evening of the naval calamity, at a shipboard command con-

ference, Turner announced that Vice Adm. Frank Jack Fletcher, the tactical commander of Operation Watchtower, had obtained Ghormley's permission to withdraw the carriers from the amphibious objective area. Fletcher had already lost one carrier at Coral Sea and another at Midway; he could not risk the loss of a third. After a miserly seventy-two hours off Guadalcanal-Tulagi, he intended to steam away. Turner went on to say that without the covering umbrella of Fletcher's aircraft, he could not guarantee the safety of his ships; he intended to depart as well. Both Vandegrift and his uncommonly able operations officer, Lt. Col. Gerald C. Thomas, left the conference-at-sea visibly stunned.

As promised, Turner withdrew his ships on 9 August. The unloading of supplies ended abruptly, and hulls still half full steamed away. Vandegrift pressed Turner

for a firm estimate on his return, but the taciturn admiral had no answer. The 1st Marine Division had been cast adrift. The hoard of Japanese supplies captured at Lunga Point looked better than ever. When rations fell to two meals a day, hungry Marines ate rice, a varied assortment of canned seafood, and strange edibles courtesy of Emperor Hirohito.

Most of the division's heavy engineering equipment had disappeared with the Navy transports, but the resourceful Marines completed the runway with captured Japanese gear. On 12 August, a Navy PBY-5 amphibian landed to signal the opening of Henderson Field, named in honor of Maj. Lofton R. Henderson, a Marine aviator killed at the Battle of Midway. The PBY departed carrying a load of wounded Marines, the first of more than two thousand to be evacuated by air. Henderson Field became the centerpiece of Vandegrift's strategy: to hold the airstrip at all costs. With it, supplies could come in and wounded could be taken out; no longer must he depend on the unre-liable Navy. The determined Vandegrift instructed his commanders not to conceal their setbacks from the troops. He anticipated no repeat of Wake Island or Corregidor if every Marine did his job.

While Vandegrift's two regiments dug in east and west of Henderson Field, Japanese headquarters in Rabaul, on New Britain, planned a response to this unexpected display of American offensive-mindedness. Although the officers there were surprised by the landing, they were not alarmed. Misled by intelligence estimates of Marine numbers at perhaps two thousand men—one-fifth of their real strength—they believed that a modest force quickly sent could overwhelm the invaders. Buoyed by the optimism of

Imperial General Headquarters, a Japanese journalist proclaimed that the Marines in the Solomons were like "summer insects which have dropped into the fire by themselves."

Confident of victory, Tokyo ordered Lt. Gen. Hyakutake Harukichi's 17th Army at Rabaul to attack the Marine perimeter with a reinforced infantry brigade under Maj. Gen. Kawaguchi Kiyotake. Hyakutake selected a crack infantry battalion from the 35th Brigade—commanded by a veteran of the war in China, Col. Ichiki Kiyono—to land first. Ichiki personally led his men ashore at Taivu Point, east of the Marine perimeter, on the evening of 18 August. A notorious firebrand, Ichiki boasted once that it only took swords and sabers to defeat the Americans. Eleven days after the landing of the Ichiki Detachment, the Kawaguchi Detachment—more than thirty-five hundred troops—would follow. Fortuitously, a heroic

Left: Lt. Dwight Shepler, a Navy combat artist, painted *Fighter Scramble, Guadalcanal*, from sketches he made while observing the frantic efforts of Leatherneck pilots and ground crews responding to a Japanese air attack. The plane parked in the right foreground is an Army Air Force P-38 Lightning, eight of which reached Guadalcanal on 12 November 1942. All the other aircraft are Navy and Marine Corps F4F Wildcats, the mainstay of the Cactus Air Force. (Navy Art Collection)

Bottom Right: Japanese dead of the Ichiki Detachment litter the beach near the mouth of the Tenaru River after the bloody battle on the night of 20 to 21 August 1942. (National Archives)

native scout, Jacob C. Vouza, encountered Ichiki's force as it wove through the jungle toward Henderson Field. Although captured, tortured, and left for dead, the gallant islander escaped and crawled back to the Marine lines to report the enemy formation.

Meanwhile, on 20 August, Vandegrift greeted the arrival of Marine Air Group 23's two squadrons at Henderson Field. A jeep carrier, the *Long Island*, catapulted off nineteen Grumman F4F-4 Wildcat fighters led by Capt. John L. Smith. Twelve Douglas SBD-3 dive-bombers commanded by Maj. Richard C. Mangrum followed. The Marine aviators dubbed Henderson Field "Cactus Base" in radio jargon, and the appellation "cactus" stuck for the remainder of the operation. The arrival of MAG-23 gave Vandegrift's force a much-need sting.

During the night of 20–21 August, Ichiki's troops stormed the Marines' lines in a screaming, frenzied display of the "spiritual strength" which they had been assured would sweep aside their Occidental enemy. As the Japanese charged across the sandbar astride the Tenaru toward the lines of the 1st Marines, Lt. Col. Edwin A. Pollock's 2/1 cut them down. Lt. Col. Lenard B. Cresswell's 1/1 moved upstream on the Tenaru at daybreak, waded across, and assaulted Ichiki's flank. After a mortar preparation, the Japanese tried again to storm the sandbar. A section of 37mm guns sprayed the enemy force with deadly canister shells. By daylight, however, the Japanese still held the coconut grove on the east bank of the river. Pollock's infantrymen moved toward the trees, cutting down Japanese soldiers with well-aimed rifle fire.

Col. Pedro A. del Valle's artillerymen swept the east bank and beyond with their 75mm pack howitzers.

Trapped between the two Marine battalions, Ichiki burned his colors after soaking them in his own blood, and then committed seppuku. Leatherneck mortars and artillery pounded the survivors as they attempted to flee into the jungle. Tanks rolled over the enemy bodies, grinding them into their treads; crocodiles fed on the corpses that clogged the river. Marines counted 777 dead Japanese outside the barbed-wire perimeter; untold numbers of dead and wounded were probably dragged away. The Marines took only 15 prisoners, a grim testimony to the fury of the enemy assault. Leatherneck casualties included 35 killed and another 75 wounded. Reflecting on the defeat, a senior Japanese officer, noting that the attack was sheer folly, remarked that "this tragedy should have taught us the hopelessness of 'bamboo spear tactics.'"

Taking prisoners proved to be risky business. "Dead" and wounded enemies rose up to shoot down Marines or throw a grenade. The ground war in the Pacific began to take on a grim, "no quarter" aspect. In a letter to Holcomb, Vandegrift wrote starkly, "I have never heard or read of this kind of fighting. The wounded will wait until men come up to examine them and blow themselves and the other fellow to pieces with a hand grenade."

While the 1st Marine Division had earned a breathing spell as the Japanese regrouped for another onslaught, the action in the air over the Solomons intensified. Almost every day, Japanese aircraft arrived around

In September 1942, a request from the commandant to send some officers home to provide the nucleus for a rapidly expanding Corps allowed for a shuffle of assignments within the 1st Marine Division on Guadalcanal. Merrill B. Twining, front, became the G3; Henry W. Buse, pictured directly behind him, assumed Twining's post as operations officer in the G3 section. (National Archives)

noon to bomb the perimeter. Marine fighters found the twin-engine Betty bombers easy targets. Zero fighters were another story. Although the Leatherneck Wildcats were a much sturdier aircraft, the Japanese Zeroes' superior speed and better maneuverability gave them a distinct edge in aerial combat. The Leatherneck aviators therefore avoided dogfights wherever possible and attacked by making single firing runs from high-speed dives. Their tactics made the air space over the Solomons dangerous for the Japanese.

From Tulagi, General Rupertus sent 2/5, Edson's Raiders, and the 1st Parachute Battalion back to Guadalcanal to reinforce the main body of the division. In the meantime, the remainder of Kawaguchi's troops—at least, those whose transports had not been sunk by American aircraft—

had also reached the island. Analyzing available intelligence, Vandegrift concluded that the Japanese brigade—now down to approximately three thousand effectives—intended to attack Henderson Field, and he was right. Kawaguchi did intend to attack, and had selected three points for his thrust: against the southeastern face of the perimeter near the Ilu Plain, the western face where the 5th Marines held the line, and the center with his main body. Assembling in the foothills of Mount Austen, Kawaguchi ordered his men to charge down the grassy slopes to burst onto the Lunga Plain only a mile from Henderson Field. Edson correctly predicted the point of attack, and positioned his now-combined Raider-Paratroop force to block it. Del Valle ordered 105-mm howitzers closer to support Edson.

As the Marines readied themselves for the attack, Turner returned bearing both good and bad news. The good news was that he believed he could spirit in a convoy from Samoa and return the 7th Marines to Vandegrift. Through Turner, Ghormley sent the bad news, informing Vandegrift that in the opinion of his staff, naval forces could no longer support the Marines on Guadalcanal. Vandegrift allowed only his operations officer, Col. Gerald C. Thomas, to know of Ghormley's gloomy prediction. Then he ordered Thomas to prepare a contingency plan to withdraw from the perimeter and fight guerrilla fashion at the headwaters of the Lunga River.

The first blow came during the night of 12–13 September, as the Japanese began to probe Vandegrift's lines. At 2100 Kawaguchi attacked Edson's left flank. In desperate hand-to-hand combat, the 840 Raiders and Parachutists held. Eleven more attempts followed in a night that seemed endless. By 0230 Edson could tell Vandegrift

and Thomas: "We can hold!" Kawaguchi had been stopped, but barely. Early in the morning, Vandegrift added 2/5 to Edson's force on the ridge.

Much of the Japanese failure lay in Edson's heroics. Already a legend, Red Mike roamed his battalion's forward perimeter encouraging Marines to hold on. When dawn finally came, the defenders observed hundreds of Japanese bodies strewn over the landscape—almost half the enemy force. Sixty-nine Marines had been killed and 194 wounded; the terrain had a new name: "Bloody Ridge." Edson's force had held the last hill short of the division command post. Japanese stragglers continued to pose a problem, albeit a minor one. The morning after the assault, Marines shot several infiltrators near Vandegrift's headquarters; the division sergeant major himself killed one. The struggle for Bloody Ridge became a moral turning point for the entire Pacific War.

Kawaguchi's defeat prompted Japanese planners to conclude that the campaign to eject the Americans from the Solomons must be accelerated. From Pearl Harbor to Washington, American commanders grew increasingly apprehensive as they scanned decrypted messages that revealed the flow of enemy aircraft, ships, and troops to the Solomons. President Roosevelt noted his "anxiety about the Southwest Pacific" and directed the Joint Chiefs of Staff to "make sure that every possible weapon gets into that area to hold Guadalcanal." The secretary of the Navy, Frank Knox, replied to a journalist's question with a candor not likely to bolster the flagging morale of the beleaguered Marines ashore in the Solomons: "I will not make a prediction, but every man will give a good accounting of himself. There is a good, stiff fight going on—everybody hopes we can hold on."

While the cryptanalysis picture evoked trepidation at the strategic level, Vandegrift's problems defending the perimeter had eased. The 6th Seabee Battalion completed an alternate airstrip, "Fighter One." Turner made good on his pledge to return the 7th Marines, and the transports brought in much-needed supplies. Air operations continued undiminished. Two pioneers of Marine Corps aviation, Brig. Gen. Roy S. Geiger and Col. Louis E. Woods, freed Vandegrift of the burden of managing air defenses. Geiger and Woods tightened procedures, enhanced morale, and began a study of Japanese air tactics to increase the effectiveness of Marine Corps aviation. The efforts of Leatherneck aviators slowed the enemy buildup significantly.

Fearing the landing of additional Japanese artillery, Vandegrift moved to push the western boundary of the perimeter to the Matanikau River. On 24 September Leatherneck units jumped off to make a

Left: Donald L. Dickson, the adjutant of the 5th Marines, painted this scene of the raging fury along Bloody Ridge on the night of 12 to 13 September 1942. (Marine Corps Art Collection)

Bottom Right: A Marine patrol moves out across the Matanikau. (National Archives)

flanking movement from the interior to trap enemy units along the coast. A new battalion, Lt. Col. Chesty Puller's 1/7, found Japanese resistance strong. Much to the dismay of Vandegrift and his staff, Puller's battalion made little progress. Mistaken orders, garbled reports, and a communications failure contributed to friendly casualties of sixty killed and another hundred wounded.

Vandegrift could ill-afford such losses. He had learned the hard way that the Japanese remained on the island in force. In order to prevent them from placing artillery on the sandbar—where it would command his entire perimeter—he ordered another offensive. Two battalions advanced along the coast; three others, including Puller's, pivoted to the left in a hooking maneuver to cross the river and fall on the enemy's right flank and rear. Puller's battalion caught a Japanese unit bivouacked in a ravine, and shattered it with mortar and artillery fire. Two companies of Raiders wiped out an enemy force left behind as a bridgehead in a savage night action punctuated by intense hand-to-hand combat. The classic spoiling operation forestalled Japanese attempts to position their artillery to support an assault on Vandegrift's perimeter. To guard against

a recurrence of the threat, the 5th Marines, now commanded by Red Mike Edson, dug in along the east bank of the Matanikau.

Disease hit the Marines with full force. Hundreds of Leathernecks already harassed by attacks of gastroenteritis and tropical fungus infections were toppled by malaria. Mosquito discipline had been poor, mostly because the men were reluctant to use the antimalarial drug Atabrine, which turned their skin yellow. Many Marines believed that the drug caused impotence. It took a temperature of 103 degrees or higher to earn a ticket to the hospital. Otherwise, Bluejackets and Leathernecks shivered with chills or burned with fever while their buddies nursed them back to health.

Above all else, Vandegrift yearned for the division to be withdrawn to New Zealand. His weary Marines were in desperate need of a rest. The gaunt stares, Atabrine-yellow faces, and blank spaces on unit rosters made him fearful. Meanwhile, Hyakutake planned another attack. Still underestimating Vandegrift's strength—at seventy-five hundred rather than the actual nineteen thousand— the Japanese high command intended to neutralize Henderson Field by naval gunfire.

Under cover of the bombardment, Lt. Gen. Maruyama Masao's 2nd (Sendai) Division would land at night. Hyakutake moved to Guadalcanal to direct the operation in person. Cryptanalysts discovered the main ingredients in the Japanese plan and provided details of the forthcoming attack. But senior officers in Washington remained apprehensive. Returning from a visit to the Southwest Pacific, Gen. Henry H. "Hap" Arnold, the Army Air Force's wartime leader, confided to a friend that "there's another Bataan coming and so you'd better get ready for it."

Vandegrift examined his options carefully. Cactus Air Force provided only a partial solution. Leatherneck aviators performed well in air-to-air combat, but the SBD dive-bombers failed to deter the nightly Japanese destroyer runs. Three times during October the seaplane tender *Nisshin* ran the gauntlet to land material for the Japanese—including eight howitzers and sixteen tanks. It was up to the Navy to control the waters off Guadalcanal, and that had yet to happen.

Vandegrift petitioned for reinforcements, and Ghormley sanctioned his request on 6 October. The 164th Infantry Regiment—the first increment of the Americal Division

—landed at Lunga Point. The fresh soldiers impressed the gaunt, battle-weary Marines—not as a result of their élan, but because of their equipment. Each trooper carried a new semiautomatic M1 Garand rifle, wore new packs, and seemed to have an unlimited supply of Hershey bars. Transports disgorged seventy days of rations. Brisk trading followed until an early afternoon air raid disrupted the bazaar.

In the early morning hours of 14 October, enemy flares illuminated the perimeter as the Japanese began an intense artillery and naval bombardment of Henderson Field. The entire Lunga area shook as the battleships *Kongo* and *Haruna* poured 14-inch shells into the Leatherneck positions. Under cover of the bombardment, Vice Adm. Kurita Takeo hoped to land the rear echelon of the Sendai Division.

Fortunately for the Marines, the Japanese fired mostly armor-piercing rounds left over from naval actions; the shells buried themselves into the ground and did little harm unless scoring a direct hit. Still, many aircraft suffered damage and only seven SBDs could fly the next morning.

Vandegrift knew that a Japanese attack appeared imminent. Expecting the assault to come from the west, he strengthened his forces there at the expense of the defenses to the east. Marines strung additional wire outside the brittle lines of defense and presighted machine guns to cover every approach. But when the Japanese attack came, it was from the south. On the eve of what he and his superiors in Tokyo and Rabaul hoped would be the final ground offensive, the commanding general of the Sendai Division harangued his troops: "The ensuing operation for the capture of Guadalcanal, engaging the attention of all the world, is the decisive battle between Japan and America. . . . If we are not successful . . . not one man should expect to return alive."

In from the jungle east of Bloody Ridge, Maruyama ordered the six thousand men of the Sendai Division forward. The dense foliage offered concealment as the Japanese began their fifteen-mile trek behind Mount Austen on 16 October. Slowed by heavy packs and burdened with artillery shells, the soldiers of Nippon struggled up and down the rain-slicked slopes. The assault began in driblets at the mouth of the Matanikau on 21 October where battalions of the 1st and 5th Marines had dug in. Leatherneck 37-mm guns knocked out Japanese tanks sent to support the infantry. Del Valle's artillery destroyed another three tanks and leveled the advancing infantry. Marine commanders counted more than 650 enemy bodies in front of their lines.

The main attack began at 2130 on 24 October, striking Puller's 1/7 just south of Bloody Ridge and the 3rd Battalion of the 164th Infantry on his left. A regiment of the Sendais hit and then bypassed an outpost thirty-three hundred yards east of Puller's battalion. As the heavens released a torrential downpour, Maruyama's attack force of six infantry battalions became disorganized and failed to mass for the assault. Japanese infantry charged the Leatherneck lines piecemeal. Some shouted, "Maline, you die!" and "Blood for the Emperor!" only to hear a defiant "Blood for Franklin and Eleanor!" in return. As the enemy onslaught began to take on a suicidal aspect, Vandegrift sent Puller an Army battalion as reinforcement. Lt. Col. Herman Hanneken's 2/7, holding a line running eastward from the Matanikau, bore the brunt of the Japanese assault the next night.

Sgt. John "Manila John" Basilone was one reason why the Japanese failed to penetrate the Marine lines. The son of Italian immigrants, Basilone had left a job driving a laundry truck in New Jersey to join the Army in the late 1930s and had been stationed in the Philippines. On the expiration of his enlistment, he opted for the Marines. His exploits earned him the Medal of Honor: "While the enemy was hammering at the Marines' defensive positions," his citation read, "Sergeant Basilone, in charge of two sections of heavy machine guns, fought valiantly to check the savage and determined assault. In a fierce frontal attack with the Japanese blasting his guns with grenades and mortar fire, one of Sergeant Basilone's sections, with its gun crews, was put out of action, leaving only two men able to carry on. Moving an extra gun into position, he placed it in action." Then Basilone "under continual fire, repaired another and personally manned it, gallantly holding his line until replacements arrived." With his ammunition running low and supply lines cut off, Basilone battled his way through hostile lines to resupply the machine-gun section. His actions that day contributed to the virtual annihilation of an entire Japanese regiment. Basilone was offered a battlefield commission but turned it down.

Japanese aircraft appeared over Guadalcanal in increasing numbers on 25 October. Leatherneck pilots flying from Fighter One's strip kept them from providing significant support for the enemy ground forces. Newly arrived Capt. Joseph J. Foss, a

lanky farm boy from South Dakota, became an ace, adding four kills to a like number scored the day previously. By the time Foss left Guadalcanal in January 1943, he had shot down twenty-six enemy aircraft, tying Eddie Rickenbacker's World War I record and earning the Medal of Honor.

While Maruyama prepared a renewed attack, Marine battalion commanders adjusted their positions. An estimated thousand enemy dead lay in front of their lines. Puller had lost only nineteen Marines dead and another thirty wounded. The enemy's new effort also failed, and Maruyama's force melted away into the jungle. Another thousand enemy corpses added to the carnage. Noncombat deaths and illness completed the elimination of the Sendais as an offensive threat.

A final Japanese attack against the western flank of the perimeter on 26 October fared no better. Hanneken's 2/7 held firmly to its anchor on a ridgeline. Another enlisted Marine, Sgt. Mitchell Paige, earned the Medal of Honor on that day: "When the enemy broke through the line directly in front of his position . . . [he] continued to direct the fire of his gunners until all his men were either killed or wounded." Despite the intense enemy fire and the loss of his comrades, Paige "never [ceased] his withering fire against the advancing hordes until reinforcements finally arrived. Then, forming a new line, he dauntlessly and aggressively led a bayonet charge, driving the enemy back and preventing a breakthrough in our lines." Unlike Basilone, Paige accepted his battlefield commission.

After the abortive Japanese attempts to pierce the Marines' lines during October, the primary burden of the defense of Guadalcanal-Tulagi fell to the Navy and Cactus Air Force. The new COMSOPAC commander, Vice Adm. William F. "Bull" Halsey, sent his carrier forces to attack Japanese surface and air units in the Solomons. On 9 November, the Japanese ordered the 38th (Hiroshima) Division ashore at Tassafaronga Point. But in the Naval Battle of Guadalcanal on the night of 14–15 November, most of the force went to the bottom as American aircraft intercepted and sank seven of the eleven troop transports. The naval battle and the successful disruption of the landing of the Hiroshima Division marked the turning point in the campaign for Guadalcanal; no longer could the enemy reinforce his troops ashore with impunity or operate freely in the waters off Guadalcanal. By late November, enemy naval forces in the region had been defeated. Halsey brought welcome gifts to the haggard, malaria-ridden, and exhausted Leathernecks on Thanksgiving Day: turkey dinner with cranberry sauce, and orders to withdraw from the Solomons.

The Army's American Division—already in place—would be joined by the 25th Infantry Division from Hawaii. Instead of returning to New Zealand, the 1st Marine Division would recover and retrain in Australia. On 9 December 1942, the 5th Marines crawled up the cargo nets of the *Hunter Liggett* for transport south. Many were so weak they could scarcely climb aboard. Others collapsed on deck.

Vandegrift paid them a final tribute: "At all times you have faced without flinching the worst that the enemy could do to us and have thrown back the best he could send against us." After visiting the 1st Marine Division cemetery, Vandegrift passed command of ground forces on the Canal to Maj. Gen. Alexander M. Patch of the Americal Division and boarded a plane for Brisbane. Along with Raider commander Red Mike Edson, Vandegrift earned the Medal of Honor for leadership on Guadalcanal. Another Marine Corps officer, Maj. Kenneth D. Bailey, won the medal posthumously for his heroism at Bloody Ridge. Leatherneck losses numbered 1,044 dead, 2,894 wounded, and 55 missing. Navy surgeons recorded over nine thousand cases of malaria. An estimated 25,600 Japanese soldiers died for their emperor out of the 31,400 sent to evict the Americans from Guadalcanal.

A generation of Marines who served on Guadalcanal never forgave the Navy for its lackluster support. During the darkest days on the island, Lt. Col. Merrill Twining resolved to commemorate the larger naval service's benign neglect. He assigned Capt. Donald L. Dickson, a talented artist serving as adjutant of the 5th Marines, to design

an appropriate medal. Eventually cast from a mold prepared in Australia, the "George Medal," as it became known, showed a hand representing the Navy dropping a hot potato in the shape of Guadalcanal into the arms of a grateful Marine. The ribbon of each medal consisted of the herringbone twill of the Leatherneck's utility uniform, supposedly washed in the fetid waters of the Lunga River.

While Marines everywhere basked in the heroic aura earned by the Leathernecks in the Solomons, few realized that a daring mission undertaken almost simultaneously to the launching of Operation Watchtower threatened briefly to tarnish the Corps' image. On 8 August 1942, pressure to show results—however meager—resulted in the dispatch of two companies of the 2nd Raider Battalion under Lt. Col. Evans P. Carlson to attack Makin Atoll in the Gilbert Islands. The gaunt, craggy-faced Carlson, a veteran of the Nicaraguan campaign, was among the Corps' most unorthodox officers. In 1938, he had spent three months with Mao Tse-tung's Eighth Route Army and became enamored with the tactics and esprit de corps of the Chinese communist forces. One result of this experience was

his contribution of the term *gung ho* (pull together)—which would acquire a somewhat derisive connotation—to the Corps' vocabulary. Afterward, he had resigned his commission to undertake a personal crusade for American aid to China. In April 1941, convinced that war was coming, he returned to forest green with a determined belief in the efficacy of guerrilla operations.

Adding to the impetus for the operation was the presence of Maj. James Roosevelt, Carlson's executive officer and the president's son. Landing in rubber boats from the submarines *Nautilus* and *Argonaut* on 17 August, Carlson's raiders found fewer than 70 Japanese rather than the estimated 250. A fierce Japanese counterattack convinced Carlson that he was greatly outnumbered, however, and the Raiders prepared to withdraw. But the rough surf swamped their

rubber boats. Apparently, at this point, Carlson considered surrendering. Then, learning from a prisoner the actual number of Japanese he faced, he renewed his assault on the atoll and blew up an enemy radio station. Reembarking onto the submarines, Carlson discovered to his horror that nine Marines had been left behind in the confusion. Captured by the Japanese, the luckless Leathernecks were beheaded. Despite the mixed outcome of the operation, both Carlson and Roosevelt won Navy Crosses. The raid resulted in the first enlisted Marine Medal of Honor of World War II. Sgt. Clyde Thomason earned his posthumous award by demonstrating exemplary leadership and great personal valor while leading an assault on an enemy position.

During the Guadalcanal campaign, American planners ordered the formation

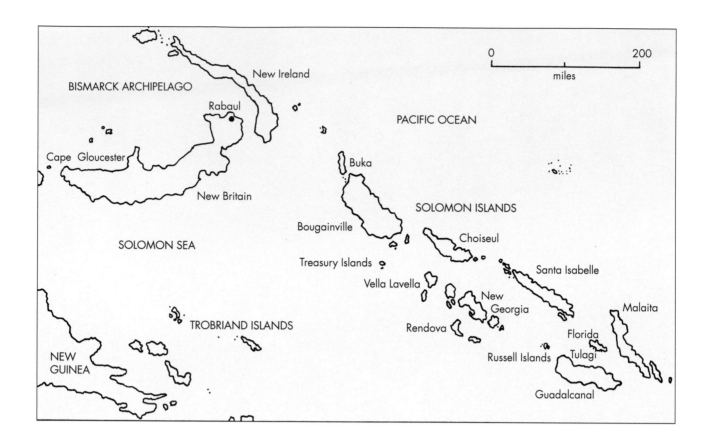

of I Marine Amphibious Corps to include all Leatherneck ground forces in the South Pacific. Vandegrift, newly promoted to lieutenant general, became its commander in July 1943 with the mission of seizing Bougainville in the northern Solomons. In the meantime, Marine units had supported Army troops in the occupation of the undefended Russell Islands in February and landings on fiercely defended New Georgia, midway up the Solomons, in June and July. For his new task, Vandegrift had the 3rd Marine Division for the assault and the Army's 37th Infantry Division in reserve. As a diversion, the 2nd Parachute Battalion under Lt. Col. Victor H. "Brute" Krulak— 725 Marines—would land at Choiseul on the night of 27–28 October 1943. If things went as planned, the Japanese would mistake the battalion for the entire Marine division and reinforce the garrison with troops from Bougainville. As another diversion, the New Zealand 8th Brigade Group landed in the Treasury Islands on 27 October.

Turner and Vandegrift set H-hour for 0645 on 1 November, with the 9th Marines landing on the left and the 3rd Marines (reinforced with the 2nd Raider Battalion) on the right. Naval transports would retire after discharging their cargo, to return with the 21st Marines (the 3rd Marine Division's third infantry regiment) and the 37th Infantry Division. The confused Japanese high command failed to reinforce its meager garrison on Bougainville until it was too late. At the end of the first day, more than fourteen thousand troops and sixty-two hundred tons of supplies had been moved ashore. The only interruptions came from occasional enemy air attacks.

The Leatherneck assault drove the Japanese 23rd Infantry onto the only high ground, renamed "Hellzapoppin Ridge" by the Marines. It took until 18 December for the 21st Marines to wipe out the enemy unit. When the division departed, it had suffered 433 dead and 1,418 wounded. The 3rd Defense Battalion and the Army's XIV Corps remained to garrison the island. A Seabee battalion constructed an airstrip on Bougainville. Beginning on 9 March 1944, the Japanese attempted to regain the area

with six major assaults from the interior over a two-week period, losing 6,843 soldiers in the futile effort.

Most Leatherneck air units continued to operate in the south Pacific as ground elements prepared to participate in the drive to seize the central Pacific from the Japanese. Flying from Henderson Field, Marine aviators—VMF-112, VMF-121, VMSB-144, and VMSB-234—hammered the residual Japanese units that remained. Their operations contributed heavily to the enemy decision to abandon the region. In more than six months of aerial combat,

ninety-four of them lost their lives, but they earned an impressive one-to-three kill ratio against the Japanese pilots.

A number of Marine aviators became aces in the Solomons. The most celebrated following Joe Foss was Maj. Gregory R. "Pappy" Boyington, the hard-drinking, hell-raising commanding officer of the "Black Sheep" of VMF 214. A prewar pilot, Boyington had resigned from the Corps early in 1941 to join the Flying Tigers, a group of American volunteers flying for the Nationalist Chinese against the Japanese. In China, he chalked up his first six victories.

Returning home to rejoin the Corps upon the outbreak of war, he found that his foreign service had made him an object of suspicion and spent a year parking cars before HQMC allowed him back in uniform.

By the time Boyington reached the southwest Pacific, Leatherneck squadrons were equipped with the bent-wing F4U Corsair, the premier American naval fighter of the war. He was then twenty-nine, a relatively advanced age for a fighter pilot. His men called him "Grandpappy" or "Gramps," and reporters settled on "Pappy." Between 16 September 1943 and 3 January 1944, the old man knocked down twenty-two Japanese aircraft; adding his China kills to that number gave him a total of twenty-eight and made him the leading Leatherneck ace of World War II. Forced to bail out of his damaged aircraft after downing two Zeroes during his last mission, he spent the next twenty months as a prisoner of war. Only upon his release did he learn that he had been awarded what everyone thought was a posthumous Medal of Honor.

The third-ranking Marine ace, twenty-three-year-old 1st Lt. Robert M. Hanson, the son of a missionary couple, piloted a Corsair in VMF-215. He ran up the startling score of twenty-five confirmed victories between 1 November 1943 and 3 February 1944, when his plane was hit while attacking a Japanese

flak tower and he crashed into the sea. Of the eleven Leatherneck pilots who earned the Medal of Honor in World War II, nine earned them in the Solomons.

Command of Leatherneck ground forces in the South Pacific had passed to MacArthur, and his Sixth Army staff had alerted the 1st Marine Division, now commanded by Maj. Gen. William H. Rupertus, to its next target in July 1943: Cape Gloucester, at the western end of New Britain. In contrast to the poorly supplied and supported Guadalcanal-Tulagi operation, new equipment and replacements poured into the division. Leathernecks turned in their trusty, time-honored Springfield '03 rifles for new Garand M1s. The temperamental Reising submachine guns went to the surplus pile, replaced by the heavier but reliable Thompson. For the ship-to-shore movement, the Navy provided an impressive array of twenty-four LSTs, fourteen LCMs, and fifteen LCIs. Only the leading battalions in the assault would land from familiar LCVPs, launched from high-speed destroyer transports.

On 26 December 1943, the initial assault waves—composed of 1/7 and 3/7—headed for the beach. Advancing cautiously into thick jungle growing right up to water's edge, the keyed-up Leathernecks found a series of well-constructed but unmanned bunkers. Two additional battalions (1/1 and 1/3) marched seven miles from the main landing site to seize the Japanese airfield. Once ashore, Leathernecks dug into the slimy jungle muck and waited for the Japanese counterattack they knew would come.

Violent winds and heavy rains plagued the attackers. Despite the foul weather, the defenders sought in vain to eject the Marines from the island. A spirited assault against the lines of 2/7 on the night of D-day resulted in more than two hundred dead Japanese. Four times on 2 January 1944, 3/5 and 3/7 tried to cross a formidable obstacle—dubbed "Suicide Creek"—but failed. Finally, three Sherman tanks unlocked the barrier, knocking out the Japanese bunkers that blocked the Marine advance.

Next, the Leathernecks turned to Aogiri Ridge, held by an estimated one thousand well-dug-in defenders. Initial attacks failed, but Lew Walt's 3/5 finally broke through.

The Black Sheep Squadron scrambles at the Turtle Bay fighter strip on Espiritu Santo Island in the New Hebrides, 11 November 1943. (National Archives)

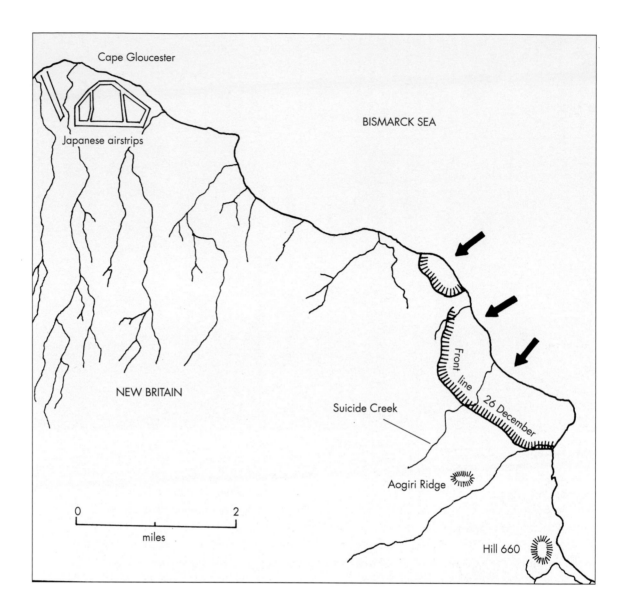

Walt almost individually turned the tide of battle, throwing his weight behind a 37-mm gun to move it into firing position so violently that he dislocated his shoulder. After reaching the crest of the hill, his battalion repulsed five screaming banzai charges during the night of 9–10 January; Aogiri Ridge became "Walt's Ridge."

Only one significant height remained in enemy hands, Hill 660, defended by the Japanese high command's last hope. A Leatherneck battalion swarmed straight up the steep slope on a wide front while another exploited the diversion to approach the position from the rear. Lt. Col. Henry W. Buse Jr.'s 3/7 gained the northwest summit by literally pulling itself up, surprising

the few defenders holding the rearward high ground. By dusk on 14 January, the Leathernecks had tightened their perimeter and beaten off the final, feeble Japanese counterattacks.

Chesty Puller added to his renown at Cape Gloucester. Now the executive officer of the 7th Marines, he prowled the front outside the wire, cheering countless Leathernecks with his jocular, "How's it going, old man?" His fearlessness and seeming invulnerability to Japanese bullets kept many a frightened and exhausted Marine going. To the surprise of Rupertus and the division staff, the enemy began to vanish. Later reports revealed that the Japanese withdrew along the jungle trails

Map 19, left:
The Capture of
Cape Gloucester,
1943–44

Top Right: Kerr Eby
based his *Small Mortar
Loading* from a sketch
he made while with
the Marines slogging
through the mud and
slime of the Eastern
Solomons. (Abbott
Laboratories, Navy
Art Collection)

that led the three hundred miles back to Rabaul, eluding the Leatherneck patrols that pursued them. Attempts by the 5th Marines to outflank the enemy by landing ahead of the retreating columns largely failed. By early February, little combat remained. On 28 April 1944, the 40th Infantry Division relieved the Marines at Cape Gloucester. The offensive had cost 310 Leathernecks killed and another 1,083 wounded.

Without regret, Marines of the 1st Division watched the volcanic cone of Cape Gloucester's Mount Talawe fade into the distance. The campaign to take the island had worn down the division. Malaria and fungal infections were almost epidemic. Optimists believed that the division would return to Australia, where they looked forward to revisiting their old liberty haunts. Instead it took up residence at Pavuvu, the largest of the Russell Islands, forty miles north of the Guadalcanal, to prepare for the next assault. Encamping in a coconut plantation, the division underwent drastic

James Montgomery Flagg painted *The Marines Have Landed* for a recruiting poster early in World War II. The Leathernecks appear wading through the surf, still wearing dishpan helmets and armed with weaponry of the interwar era. (Marine Corps Art Collection)

personnel changes. New Marines joined and combat-experienced veterans rotated home.

The grim contest to wrest the Southwest Pacific from the Japanese had ended. By then MacArthur and his supporters were at loggerheads with the Navy's leadership on how best to bring the Empire of Japan to its knees. MacArthur scored amphibious island-hopping, and in the fall of 1943 was quoted on the front page of the *New York Times*: "Island hopping is not my idea of how to end the war as soon as possible and as cheaply as possible." Just as forthrightly, King called MacArthur's thrust toward the Philippines "absurd." MacArthur was loath to lose his Marines, the amphibious cutting edge of his command. He attempted to flatter Vandegrift by arguing that with the departure of the 1st Marine Division from the Southwest Pacific for the Central Pacific drive, they would simply be "Marines." However, if they remained they would be "MacArthur's Marines." To Washington,

MacArthur thundered his criticism: "By using Army troops to garrison the islands of the Pacific under Navy command, the Navy retains Marine [Corps] forces always available, giving them inherently an army of their own." But Admiral King's wish to get Vandegrift's Marines back under Navy control prevailed.

Despite their severe losses in the South Pacific, senior Japanese commanders remained sanguine in their belief in racial superiority. A communiqué from Hyakutake's headquarters on Rabaul, released during the Guadalcanal campaign, spoke reams about the enemy's unbridled optimism: "Westerners—being very haughty, effeminate, and cowardly—intensely dislike fighting in the rain or mist or dark. They cannot conceive [of the] night as a proper time for battle—though it is excellent for dancing." Hyakutake concluded that "in these weaknesses, lie our greatest opportunity." The long road to Tokyo had barely begun.

CHAPTER 11

World War II: The Central Pacific Drive, 1943–1945

The series of Orange plans developed during the interwar years to guide American strategy in a conflict with Japan envisioned an offensive across the Central Pacific. There the Japanese onslaught had thrown U.S. forces on the defensive for six months following the attack on Pearl Harbor. After the victory at Midway put the war on balance, the enemy threat to the lines of communications to Australia had drawn American resources to the Southwest Pacific—itself a strategically defensive deployment. The turning point came in the grueling struggle for Guadalcanal, where U.S. naval forces defeated the Japanese effort to regain the initiative. American strategists then faced the question of what to do next.

Gen. Douglas MacArthur urged mounting an offensive under his command along the "New Guinea–Mindanao Axis" to liberate the Philippines at the earliest opportunity. Adm. Ernest J. King argued with equal vehemence in favor of launching a drive under naval command through the islands of the Central Pacific: in effect, a revival of the Orange plans. Amphibious forces, spearheaded by fast-carrier task groups, would prevent the Japanese from reinforcing or mutually supporting the links in their far-flung defensive perimeter. The island-hopping campaign also promised to cut Japan's vital supply lines from Southeast Asia and bring the war all the more quickly to the enemy's home waters. In the end, the Joint Chiefs of Staff decided that the United States possessed men and material to support a dual advance and approved both proposals. MacArthur would push up the coast of New Guinea toward the Philippines while the Navy—under Adm. Chester A. Nimitz, Commander-in-Chief, Pacific Fleet—struck across the expanse of the Central Pacific.

Nimitz's forces would be supported by carrier aircraft, MacArthur's by land-based planes. To the displeasure of the Corps' leaders and senior Navy officers, the Joint Chiefs of Staff (JCS) allowed MacArthur to retain the 1st and 3rd Marine Divisions, at least initially. This left only the 2nd and 4th Marine Divisions for V Amphibious Corps in the Central Pacific. But HQMC contemplated the formation of two additional divisions—a 470,000-man Marine Corps by mid-1944. The Army objected, but to no avail; by then, the Corps took all its new recruits from their draft

Opposite: While this World War II recruiting poster might outrage twenty-first-century feminists, it meant just what it said. Every woman who enlisted in the Marine Corps to perform rear-echelon duties, like this sergeant with her clipboard, freed a male Marine to join the fight in the Pacific. At war's end approximately 18,500 women were serving in the Corps. (Marine Corps Art Collection)

boards and thus competed with the Army for manpower.

Originally the Central Pacific offensive was to begin with an attack on the Marshall Islands. As the planning developed, however, strategists concluded that seizure of the more southerly Gilberts would provide needed airfields and anchorages to support the advance north. The Gilberts, a former British protectorate, consisted of sixteen scattered atolls lying across the equator. Betio was the main island in the Tarawa Atoll, and would constitute the first large-scale test of Marine Corps amphibious doctrine against a strongly fortified beachhead. To lead the campaign, Nimitz selected Vice Adm. Raymond A. Spruance, whose command was designated the Fifth Fleet. Rear Adm. Richmond Kelly

Turner headed Spruance's amphibious forces with the ground troops of V Amphibious Corps led by Maj. Gen. Holland M. "Howlin' Mad" Smith, USMC.

A short, thickset, jowly man who wore horn-rimmed glasses and a close-cropped mustache, Smith had been born at Hatchechubbee, Alabama, sixty-one years before. Educated to join his father's law practice, he had escaped the paternal program by obtaining a direct commission in the Corps in 1905. As a junior officer, he saw combat in the Dominican Republic and served in a succession of staff appointments in France during World War I. Between the wars he became increasingly involved in the development of the Corps' amphibious capabilities, holding major commands in the big exercises of 1939–41 and advocating the adoption of the Higgins boat. Admiral Nimitz had personally selected him to command the Marine forces in the Central Pacific. In his outspoken autobiography, Howlin' Mad protested that his sobriquet was unwarranted. "I am not given to sudden, uncontrollable bursts of temper or to bawling out without cause," he insisted. "However, I do speak frankly, freely and emphatically when injustices occur, when official stupidity obstructs plans, or when the brass . . . tries to take liberties with my Marines." To the surprise of many, Smith and the acerbic "Terrible" Turner worked well as a team.

For the assault on the Gilberts— Operation Galvanic—Smith had the 2nd Marine Division, commanded by Maj. Gen. Julian C. Smith, and the 27th Infantry Division, under Maj. Gen. Ralph C. Smith.

On 20 November 1943 the 27th Division's 165th Regimental Combat Team—a New York National Guard outfit—waded ashore at Makin, the northernmost atoll in the Gilberts. Although opposed by fewer than 800 Japanese, it took the 6,470 soldiers—led by overaged officers practicing World War I tactics—four long days to capture the island at a cost of 66 dead. Howlin' Mad Smith began to have his doubts about the effectiveness of Ralph Smith's division.

The real contest for the Gilberts lay 105 miles south of Makin on another tiny atoll of questionable worth: Tarawa. The Japanese had built their defenses on Betio, a palm-fringed islet two miles long and at most half a mile wide at the southwestern corner of the atoll. To hold it, Rear Adm. Shibasaki Keijo had 4,836 men, including 2,619 elite troops of the Sasebo 7th Special Naval Landing Force. Betio bristled with more than five hundred heavy gun emplacements, pill boxes,

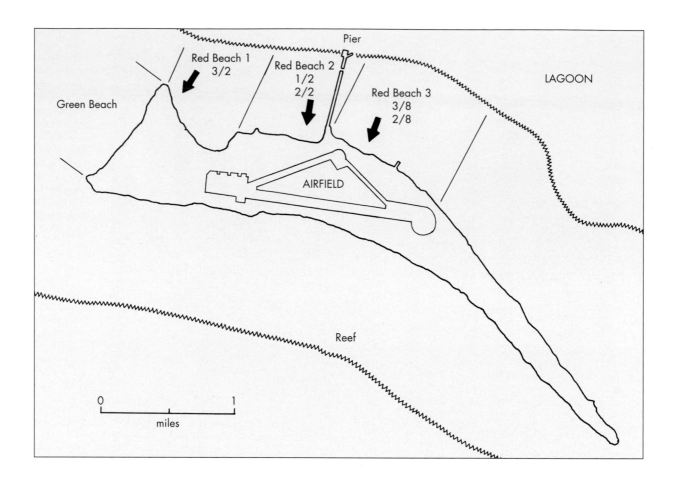

Green Beach

Red Beach 1
3/2

Pier

Red Beach 2
1/2
2/2

Red Beach 3
3/8
2/8

LAGOON

AIRFIELD

Reef

0   1
miles

and blockhouses. Shibasaki bragged that the
Americans could not take the island with
"a million men in a thousand years," and
exhorted his forces to "defend to the last man
all vital areas and destroy the enemy at the
water's edge." The welcome for the landing
forces at Tarawa would be different from that
experienced at Guadalcanal.

The Marines planned to land on the
north shore of the reef. Only LVTs could cross
the barrier, and the landing force had only
one hundred of this new craft, which meant
that the remaining Leathernecks would be
forced to get out and wade ashore if their
boats failed to clear the reef. The pre-D-day
softening up consisted of fifteen hundred tons
of bombs and two thousand tons of naval
ordnance—sufficient, according to the Navy;
not nearly enough, in the opinion of Howlin'
Mad Smith. Turner scheduled H-hour for
0830 on 20 November, then postponed it to
0900 to allow time for silencing the shore
batteries with naval gunfire. Despite the bombardment, the initial assault waves began

taking fire three to four thousand meters from
the beach.

First ashore into the maelstrom of
exploding shells and withering small arms
fire was 1st Lt. William Dean Hawkins and
the Scout-Sniper Platoon, 2nd Marines. A
quarter of an hour ahead of the first assault
wave, the lean Texan six-footer led his
Marines up the seaplane ramp at the end
of Betio's pier. Fighting their way down the
jetty, the platoon used flamethrowers to
torch pier-side shacks concealing machine
gun emplacements. Throughout the day,
Hawkins and his men roamed the seawall
destroying Japanese positions. Riding an
LVT, Hawkins personally destroyed six
machine gun nests; even with two bullets
in his shoulder, he kept fighting to gain a
foothold on the beach for the 2nd Marines.

Concerned that in the smoke shrouding
the island his ships' shells might hit the
landing craft, the commander of the attack
force lifted the bombardment almost twenty
minutes before the first wave touched

down. Thus Shibasaki was given ample time to reposition his troops to oppose the assault. The 2nd and 3rd Battalions, 2nd Marines, and 2/8 hit the beach first, ferried in LVTs. Behind 2/2 the 1st Battalion of the 2nd Marines waded across the reef, just as 3/8 waded in behind 2/8; both battalions incurred heavy casualties from enemy gun emplacements. Once they reached shore the Leathernecks found themselves pinned behind a coconut-log seawall by enemy fire.

After three waves of Marines made it to the beach, the niggardly quota of LVTs had been used up. The remaining assault waves landed on the reef, disgorging their human cargo to be swallowed up in the carnage created by the enemy fire sweeping the lagoon. When the commanding officer of the 2nd Marines became ill prior to the invasion, Lt. Col. David M. Shoup received a spot promotion to colonel and led the regiment in the assault. Although wounded in the leg,

Shoup—a stocky farm boy from Indiana— positioned himself and a makeshift staff next to the pier and directed the action from there. His heroic leadership would be rewarded by the Medal of Honor.

By noon, the assault had stalled. Marines still hugged the narrow beaches and the seawall. Landing craft of all types remained stranded on the reef, piled high with dead and wounded, while reinforcements failed to cross the formidable barrier. Julian Smith asked Holland Smith to release the Corps' reserve, the 6th Marines. Smith passed the urgent request on to Turner, who approved it without hesitation; the battle for the atoll appeared in doubt. Even as the order crackled over the radio nets, Julian Smith ordered 1/8—his divisional reserve—into the fury on the beaches of Tarawa.

As the sun slipped over the horizon, some five thousand Leathernecks had reached shore; another fifteen hundred had been killed

Map 20, Left: D-day on Betio Island, Tarawa Atoll, 20 November 1943

Right: *Landing at Tarawa*, by Richard Gibney, shows the Leathernecks' landing craft heading into the maelstrom. (Marine Corps Art Collection)

or wounded. Fearing the worst, Marines dug into their shallow perimeter to await a long night of Japanese onslaughts. Their thin line of resistance offered no possibility of falling back to regroup; this was a bitter fight to the finish. The pungent smell of decaying bodies clogged the nostrils of both attackers and defenders. Fortunately for the Marines, the pre-assault bombardment had severed Japanese communications, preventing Shibasaki from organizing an effective counterattack.

Any number of fearless Marines contributed to the victory on Tarawa, but correspondent Robert Sherrod credited Hawkins for the ultimate success of the landing. Wounded again on the second day, Hawkins destroyed four more pillboxes before an enemy bullet cut him down for the last time. Hawkins earned one of the four Medals of Honor awarded to Marines for Tarawa—three posthumously—and his citation stands as an epic saga of human bravery in the face of the fiercest odds.

Another Leatherneck who contributed greatly to the success of the landing was the commanding officer of 2/8, Maj. H. P. "Jim" Crowe, a world-class marksman who had

captained the Marine rifle team throughout the 1930s. Instantly recognizable by his pointed red mustache and big swagger stick, he calmly worked his way along the front line. "All right, Marines," he shouted, "try and pick out a target and squeeze off some rounds. You better kill some of those bastards or they'll kill you. You don't want to die, do you? Come on, now, let's

kill some of them!" Although enemy fire usually blanketed anything that moved, Crowe remained untouched. One veteran remembered, "Watching the major was like watching a war movie where the good guys don't get hit." Crowe was awarded the Navy Cross for Tarawa. His luck ran out on Saipan, but he survived the severe wounds he received there and went on to complete forty years in the Corps.

On D+1 Shoup ordered his four battalions to attack to the south. By late afternoon, elements of 1/2 and 2/2 had driven across the airfield and reached the south coast, while 3/2 had secured the western edge of the island. Two new battalions, 1/6 and 1/8, had come ashore, and a battalion of artillery had been emplaced on nearby Bairiki Atoll. As the Leathernecks gained ground, Shibasaki was killed in the shelling of his command post. At 1706 Shoup buoyed the spirits of Turner and Smith with the message: "Casualties many. Percentage dead not known. Combat efficiency—we are winning." A few hours later Col. Red Mike Edson, the division chief of staff, landed and assumed command of all Marines on Betio, allowing Shoup to concentrate on leading his regiment.

The Marines renewed their yard-by-yard advance the next day, eliminating a Japanese strongpoint between Red Beach 1 and Red Beach 2 and, for the first time, inflicting more casualties than they were absorbing. By nightfall they had cleared all except the eastern third of the island. Survivors at the Japanese headquarters sent a final message to Tokyo: "Our weapons have been destroyed and from now on everyone is attempting a final charge." Three times between 1930 and 0400 the remnants of the garrison dashed forward in futile efforts to break through the Marine lines.

Early on the morning of D+3 a fresh battalion, 3/6, moved up to spearhead the advance. It reached the eastern tip of the island around 1200 and at 1330 Julian Smith, who had transferred his headquarters ashore the previous day, declared Betio secure. In seventy-six hours of intense fighting, 984 Marines and 59 Navy men lost their lives; another 2,072 suffered wounds, and 88 Leathernecks were missing. The casualty rate amounted to 19 percent. Only 17 Japanese prisoners were taken—all wounded—plus 129 terrified Korean laborers. An estimated 4,690 Japanese had died for their emperor.

Top Left: The Marine advance up the pier in the opening hours of the assault on Betio inspired Kerr Eby's *Tarawa No. II*. (Abbott Laboratories, Navy Art Collection)

Bottom Left: First Lieutenant William D. Hawkins led the Scout-Sniper Platoon, 2nd Marines, in the first wave at Tarawa. His heroism was instrumental in the success of the assault. (National Archives)

Top Right: Ashore on Tarawa, Marines use all available cover as they push deeper into the Japanese defenses. (National Archives)

Seizure of the Gilberts cost the Navy–Marine Corps team dearly. The casualty figures shocked Americans at home, and supporters of MacArthur—led by the Hearst newspapers—trumpeted that direction of the Pacific war should be vested in him. Less partisan observers concluded that too few Marines had been assigned for the assault, artillery should have been positioned on Bairiki from the beginning, planners should never have gambled on crossing the reef in ships' landing craft, and the Corps had an insufficient number of LVTs available for the operation. Closer to the fighting, Howlin' Mad Smith considered the assault and seizure of the Gilberts a tragic strategic error: "Was Tarawa worth it? My answer is an unqualified: No! From the very beginning the decision of the Joint Chiefs to seize Tarawa was a mistake and from their initial mistake grew the terrible drama . . . resulting in these needless casualties. . . . Tarawa should have been bypassed."

The conquered Gilberts provided sites for much-needed airfields. Four new landing strips appeared following the seizure of Tarawa, and by early 1944 B-24s flew from them in support of further operations against Japan. General Smith asked for at least one Marine aircraft wing (MAW) to support his amphibious corps. The admirals denied his request; the Navy did not want to provide the escort carriers necessary to make a MAW available to the landing force. Thus, Leatherneck flyers remained in the Southwest Pacific until Christmas 1943; only then did squadrons move forward to operate out of airstrips in the Gilberts. The 1st MAW remained in the Solomons until the fall of 1944, when it was deployed to support MacArthur's forces in the liberation of the Philippines.

On 1 January 1944 Lieutenant General Vandegrift replaced Thomas Holcomb, who was approaching the statutory retirement age of sixty-four, as commandant of the Marine

Left: In an obviously staged photograph, Col. David M. Shoup, who commanded the assault forces on the bloody beaches of Tarawa, sits amid Japanese corpses reading Dale Carnegie's *How to Win Friends and Influence People*. The original caption was simply, "We aren't interested in their friendship." (National Archives)

Right: The northern shore of Betio Island, Tarawa Atoll, immediately after the battle. Bodies float in the water beside knocked-out amtracs. (National Archives)

Corps. The succession surprised no one; Holcomb had groomed Vandegrift as the next commandant since the late 1930s. Upon stepping down, Holcomb was awarded his fourth star, thereby becoming the first Marine officer to reach the rank of full general. The Corps that Vandegrift inherited numbered more than 390,000 personnel.

In 1944 the Marine Corps' attention was focused on the Pacific. The war there had become the "Navy's war," and Leathernecks provided the bulk of the Navy's "army" to fight it. Five divisions had been formed, and four air wings joined in support of the forces in the field. The 1st Marine Division was at Cape Gloucester, the 2nd Marine Division recovering and retraining in Hawaii, the 3rd Marine Division preparing to leave Bougainville, the 4th was en route from San Diego to the Central Pacific, and the 5th Marine Division was forming at Camp Pendleton. The Corps was still mostly an all-white, male outfit. But traditional barriers had been broken. The Women Marine Corps Reserve, activated in February 1943, reached its authorized strength of 1,000 officers and 18,000 enlisted personnel in June 1944, and a handful of black Marines, enlisted for the

first time in June 1942, served in service and support units.

The Marshalls were the next step in the struggle to wrest the Pacific from the enemy. Located 620 miles northwest of Tarawa, the Marshalls consisted of more than two thousand small islands and thirty-two atolls scattered over an eight-hundred-square-mile area. The Japanese had held them since World War I. Navy planners recommended simultaneous assaults on Kwajalein Atoll, site of the Japanese headquarters, and several of the other more important atolls. Intelligence reports indicated that the Japanese were constructing airstrips on the islands and there was a seaplane base on Jaluit Atoll. Recalling all too well the high casualties at Tarawa, Smith recommended assaulting Maleolap and Wotje first and then taking Kwajalein. Turner disagreed, causing a predictable outburst from Howlin' Mad: "I don't try to run your ships and you'd better by a goddamn sight lay off my troops!" Although Smith's vituperative analysis proved correct, Nimitz settled the dispute—predictably—in favor of his admirals and Operation Flintlock, the seizure of the Marshalls, went according to the original plan.

Intelligence analysts noted that only Kwajalein appeared to be defended heavily,

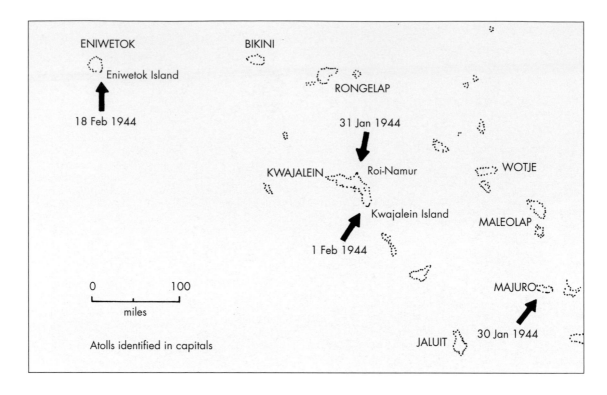

ENIWETOK

Eniwetok Island

18 Feb 1944

BIKINI

RONGELAP

31 Jan 1944

KWAJALEIN

Roi-Namur

WOTJE

Kwajalein Island

MALEOLAP

1 Feb 1944

0   100

miles

MAJURO

Atolls identified in capitals

JALUIT

30 Jan 1944

by an estimated eight thousand Japanese; however, of that number barely twenty-two hundred were combat troops. Prior to D-day Army Air Forces planes from the Gilberts dropped two thousand tons of bombs on the archipelago while Spruance's battleships, cruisers, and destroyers pounded the atolls and islands with thirty-six thousand shells, four times the number expended on Tarawa. Carrier aircraft took control of the skies, destroying every Japanese plane in the Marshalls before D-day. Spruance had an impressive array of three hundred ships and more than eighty-four thousand troops at his disposal. Turner's amphibious force—two new command ships, seven old battleships, eleven carriers, seventeen cruisers, seventy-five destroyers and destroyer escorts, ninety-six transports, twenty-seven cargo vessels, five LSDs, and forty-five LSTs—comprised the heaviest amphibious lift in history to that date.

For his landing force, Smith had only the newly formed 4th Marine Division commanded by Maj. Gen. Harry Schmidt and the 7th Infantry Division under Maj. Gen. Charles H. Corlett. V Amphibious Force also included the 22nd Marines and the 106th Infantry Regiment. The 1st and 15th Defense Battalions tagged along to garrison the Marshalls once the operation concluded. The Army division assigned for the operation to seize the Marshalls came from Hawaii. The 22nd Marines deployed from Samoa while the rest of the 4th Marine Division sailed from Camp Pendleton.

Intelligence estimates indicated approximately three thousand defenders on Roi-Namur, but the islets were not heavily fortified. Only a single pair of 5.5-inch naval rifles covered the approaches to the beach. For the assault, the Marines had three times as many LVTs as at Tarawa. Prior to D-day, Turner's forces occupied undefended Majuro Atoll, two hundred miles southeast of Kwajalein, for use as an advanced base. On D-day, 31 January 1944, the 4th Marine Division would seize Roi and Namur islands in the northern end of the Marshalls; the 7th Infantry Division would storm ashore on Kwajalein in the southern end of the chain. Three months after the initial phase of the operation, the 22nd Marines and the Army's 106th Infantry would seize Eniwetok Atoll in Operation Catchpole.

On D-day the 25th Marines landed on the islets around Roi-Namur; the 14th Marines followed to provide fire support. On

Map 21, left: The Conquest
of the Marshalls, 1944

Right: Bomb-laden Corsairs
of VMF-1 outbound in the
Marshalls, 15 March 1944
(National Archives)

D+1, Col. Louis R. Jones and two battalions of the 23rd Marines assaulted Roi while Col. Franklin A. Hart's 24th Marines came ashore on Namur. H-hour was 1100, an unusual hour caused by delays in coordinating the ship-to-shore movement. On Roi, Leathernecks slaughtered the dazed defenders easily, but on Namur they found the Japanese more determined. The 24th Marines repulsed a banzai attack on the night of D-day, and on the morning of D+2, Smith declared both islets secure. More than 3,563 Japanese had died. Marine casualties numbered 313 killed and 502 wounded.

To the south, soldiers of the 7th Infantry Division landed on Kwajalein on 1 February and completed the conquest of the island four days later. The success of these operations allowed Smith to activate Operation Catchpole, which used the V Corps reserve to take Eniwetok Atoll, 360 miles from Kwajalein in the northwest corner of the Marshalls. On 18 February, after a particularly heavy bombardment, Tactical Group I—the 22nd Marines and the 106th Infantry, commanded by Brig. Gen. Thomas E. "Terrible Tommy" Watson, USMC—stormed ashore to seize the three islands in the atoll.

Once again, a day prior to the landing, Marines emplaced artillery batteries on nearby islets to support the main landings. On the morning of D+2, the 106th Infantry hit the beach in the face of characteristically obstinate resistance. After two days of bitter fighting, the atoll's defenders were overcome. On 22 February, the 22nd Marines seized nearby Parry Island in a fierce battle punctuated by hand-to-hand combat with a well dug-in enemy; thirty-four hundred Japanese troops died and sixty-six chose to surrender. Spruance declared the Marshalls secured on 7 March. Five Marines earned Medals of Honor during the fighting. Operations planners elected to bypass the Japanese bases remaining in the Marshalls. Cut off from resupply and reinforcement by Marine and Navy air attacks, the tiny outposts withered quickly.

MAG-31 began flight operations from the small airstrip on Roi on 15 March and MAG-13 on the twenty-first. That same month, the 4th Base Defense Aircraft Wing set up headquarters on Kwajalein. MAG-22 arrived from Midway to join the units in the Marshalls. A total of ten fighter and four bomber squadrons flew out of the newly acquired airfields. From the spring of 1944 until the end of the war, Leatherneck aviators dropped more than 6,920 tons of bombs on enemy installations on the four main atolls of the Marshalls. Naval gunfire added another 2,340 tons of ordnance to the devastation. Of a Japanese garrison estimated at more than thirteen thousand troops and laborers, more than half died as a result.

The successes in the Gilberts and Marshalls convinced Nimitz that the Fifth Fleet could continue the amphibious advance across the Central Pacific. Sufficient naval forces were available to invade the Marianas while continuing to support MacArthur in his drive toward the Philippines. Nimitz even considered bypassing the Marianas in his eagerness to press on to the home islands of Japan, but the Army—speaking through Hap Arnold—objected. Unexpectedly, considering the ordinary course of Army–Navy wrangling, King agreed with Arnold on the importance of occupying the islands. Arnold viewed the Marianas as airfields for launching B-29 strikes against Japan. The new bombers could carry ten thousand pounds of ordnance to targets fifteen hundred miles distant. King regarded the Marianas as advanced bases in support of the fleet for the final assault on the enemy's homeland.

Convinced, the JCS turned aside MacArthur's argument for putting the full weight of American resources behind the Southwest Pacific drive, and increased the timetable for the war in the Central Pacific. Washington directed Nimitz to bypass Truk and the Carolines and assault the Marianas—Operation Forager—by late spring. The JCS increased MacArthur's force from six Army divisions to twelve, leaving Nimitz with four

Marine and six Army divisions. Both King and Nimitz believed that a landing in the Marianas might force the Japanese fleet to offer battle for the first time since 1942.

Of the fifteen islands in the Marianas, Nimitz's staff considered only Saipan, Tinian, and Guam of importance. In both size and geography, these islands presented a marked contrast to the tiny, flat coral atolls of the Gilberts and Marshalls. Saipan, 13 miles in length, had an area of approximately 72 square miles; Tinian was 50 square miles and Guam, 209. Fields of sugar cane grew on all three, but Saipan and Guam had rugged, wooded interiors—good for defending. As the American drive through the Central Pacific gained momentum, it stimulated Tokyo to reinforce its garrison in the Marianas until, by the late spring of 1944, there were approximately 30,000 Japanese troops on Saipan, 18,500 on Guam, and 9,000 on Tinian. Saipan contained the headquarters of the Japanese Central Pacific Fleet, commanded by Adm. Nagumo Chiuchi. Subordinate to him was Lt. Gen. Saito Yoshitsugu, commanding the Thirty-first Army. Saito had at his disposal 29,662 defenders, including the Yokosuka Special Naval Landing Force. Although the Japanese had the means to mount a mobile defense, they chose to wage a traditional fixed defense at the water's edge.

Spruance as fleet commander retained command of the operation to seize the Marianas. Turner still commanded all amphibious forces under Spruance's Fifth Fleet—a massive armada of more than eight hundred ships and 162,000 soldiers, sailors, and Marines. Smith, newly promoted to

lieutenant general, was designated as commanding general, Expeditionary Forces. Tactically, Howlin' Mad functioned as commanding general of the Northern Troops and Landing Force, which consisted of the 2nd Marine Division under Terrible Tommy Watson, Harry Schmidt's 4th Marine Division; and Ralph Smith's 27th Infantry Division. Far to the east, the 77th Infantry Division rested in strategic reserve in Hawaii. Roy S. Geiger commanded the Southern Troops and Landing Force, composed of Allen H. Turnage's 3rd Marine Division, Brig. Gen. Lemuel C. Shepherd Jr.'s 1st Provisional Marine Brigade, and the 9th and 14th defense battalions. The last two units were to garrison the Marianas once they had been taken.

Since the campaign to seize the Marshalls, HQMC had reduced the size of a division from 19,965 to 17,465 men; however, it had increased the number of flamethrowers, mortars, and tanks, and added an amphibious tractor battalion. The twelve-man infantry squad disappeared in favor of a thirteen-

man variety, composed of three four-man fire teams—one man in each armed with a Browning Automatic Rifle—and a squad leader.

On 11 June, carrier aircraft attacked targets in the Marianas. Two days later, the naval gunfire preparation began. Seven battleships and eleven destroyers hurled fifteen thousand shells onto Saipan; the next day, eight old battleships relieved the modern battleships on the line. Despite the fierce pounding by ships and aircraft, the enemy coastal artillery survived to strike the landing craft as they hit the beaches. The night before the invasion, Tokyo Rose tormented her listeners in the landing force: "I've got some swell recordings for you, just in from the States. You'd better enjoy them while you can, because tomorrow at oh-six-hundred you're hitting Saipan and we're ready for you. So, while you're still alive, let's listen to. . . ."

Two and one-half hours before the actual landing, the 24th Marines and 1/29 conducted a feint off Tanapag Harbor, three miles north of the landing site. Initially, the ruse worked and an enemy regiment deployed to the area, but the main force was not fooled. At 0830 on D-day, 15 June 1944, two divisions of Leathernecks landed abreast on the beaches of Saipan: the 2nd Marine Division on the left, with the 6th and 8th Marines in the assault waves; the 4th Marine Division on the right, with the 23rd and 25th Marines leading. The 27th Infantry Division was held in reserve. Thirty-four LSTs dropped assault waves in seven hundred LVTs.

Within twenty minutes, more than eight thousand Marines were ashore, even though enemy machine-gun and mortar fire raked the landing force when it came within nine hundred yards of the shoreline. Casualties mounted swiftly—five battalion commanders were hit, and 2/6 went through four commanding officers during the first day. A third of the 8th Marines suffered wounds, and Japanese fire killed or wounded 35 percent of the 6th Marines. By dark, twenty thousand Marines had reached shore, at a cost of 10 percent casualties. Undaunted, General Saito voiced his defiance in a message to Imperial Headquarters in Tokyo: "After dark, this division will launch a night attack in force, and expect to annihilate the enemy at one swoop." But he had only thirty-six tanks and fewer than a thousand available infantry to carry out his boast. They did not succeed.

As anticipated, the Japanese fleet came out in a desperate attempt to repel the invasion. It did not succeed either. In the Battle of the Philippine Sea, which exuberant American pilots dubbed the "Marianas Turkey Shoot," the Japanese lost three of their nine carriers and more than four hundred aircraft. When

Spruance broke off the pursuit after sunset on 21 June, the enemy carrier air arm had been reduced to thirty-five planes. By then, there were seventy-eight thousand Americans on Saipan.

Howlin' Mad Smith sent the 27th Division ashore on 22 June, directing the 2nd and 4th Marine Divisions to move aside to allow the National Guard division to fit between them. All three divisions were to jump off in an attack to the north the following morning. Almost immediately, a sag appeared in the center of the advance as the 27th Division— slow and methodical in its tactics—lagged behind the aggressive Leathernecks. Already disappointed in the performance of the 27th Division and its commander, Smith sought the counsel of Turner and Spruance. Both agreed with him that Ralph Smith should be relieved of command. Howlin' Mad lost no time in so doing. Ralph Smith was transferred to a new command in the European Theater and outraged senior Army officers vowed that Army troops would never again be placed under Marine Corps command. Surprisingly, Nimitz, Spruance, and Turner failed to support Holland Smith in the brouhaha that followed. It seemed as though the "Navy–Marine Corps team" existed only when it suited the Navy's purposes. The affair poisoned Army–Marine Corps relations for the remainder of the war, leaving a bitter aftertaste that lingered into the Korean conflict.

Meanwhile, the struggle for Saipan continued. On 25 June, 3/8 and 1/29 captured Mount Tapotchau, the island's dominant terrain feature, after a bitter struggle. A bystander overheard Terrible Tommy Watson exhorting a subordinate to take the height with the encouraging observation that there was nothing on it except some Japs with machine guns and mortars. "Now get the hell up there and get them!" Five days later, the surviving Japanese—military and civilian—poured into the northern end of the island to commit mass suicide. In its final transmission to the embattled garrison, Tokyo continued to ask the impossible: "Because the fate of the Japanese Empire depends on the result of your operations, inspire the spirit of the officers and men and to the very end continue to destroy the enemy gallantly and persistently, thus assuaging the anxiety of our emperor."

The wishful response of the senior surviving Japanese officer on Saipan fore-shadowed the bitter struggles remaining for Marines as they assaulted yet other hellish beaches: "Having received your honorable words, we are grateful for boundless magnanimity of the imperial favor. By becoming the bulwark of the Pacific with 10,000 deaths, we hope to requite the imperial favor." In a final display of devotion, a handful of Japanese troops, led by officers brandishing samurai swords, launched a banzai attack on 7 July. The fanatical force managed to shatter the lines of two battalions of the 105th Infantry

before the artillerymen of 3/10 stopped them in their tracks with fuzes for the howitzer shells cut to explode only fifty-five yards in front of their guns.

At 1615 on the afternoon of 9 July, Turner declared Saipan secured. More than 28,811 Japanese defenders were known to have perished, and countless other charred bodies remained sealed in caves and bunkers. Only 736 prisoners were taken, and 438 of them were Korean laborers. U.S. casualties numbered 3,225 dead, 13,099 wounded, and 326 missing. The loss of Saipan, part of Japan's main line of defense, brought down the Japanese government. American naval forces—spearheaded by Marines—had secured an advanced base close to the home islands of Japan. On 18 July, Prime Minister Tojo Hideki and his cabinet resigned. Six days later, one hundred B-29s flew from Saipan to bomb Tokyo.

On 21 July—"Liberation Day"— Geiger's Southern Force invaded Guam, the southernmost inhabited island in the Marianas. The naval gunfire preparation had begun on 8 July, with six battleships and nine cruisers pummeling the island. Three days later, air strikes added to the destruction of Japanese forces and installations. The landing force faced a total of thirteen thousand

Japanese soldiers reinforced by fifty-five hundred sailors. Charging ashore at 0829 on D-day, Geiger's Marines met stiff resistance at the water's edge from coastal guns that had survived the pre-assault bombardment. Although the Japanese launched a spirited counterattack that night, the Leathernecks held their ground and reached their first objective on the morning of D+1.

On the night of 25–26 July, Lt. Col. Robert E. Cushman Jr.'s 2/9 (attached to the 3rd Marines) beat off no fewer than seven major enemy attacks. More than half of Cushman's command were killed or wounded, and its commander earned a Navy Cross. The commanding officer of Company F, Capt. Louis H. Wilson Jr., like Cushman a future commandant, earned the Medal of Honor. His citation noted that "he and his company fought fiercely in hand-to-hand encounters . . . in a furiously waged battle for approximately ten hours." On 10 August, Geiger declared the island secure. By then, approximately 17,300 Japanese had died. The Americans counted 1,119 dead, 7,122 wounded, and 70 missing.

Two weeks earlier, the 4th Marine Division had invaded Tinian, only three miles southwest of Saipan. The island had been bombarded by air and sea strikes for six weeks before the first Leatherneck stepped ashore. Col. Keishi Ogata, commanding a garrison of 4,700 soldiers and 4,110 sailors, was clearly surprised by the audacious assault. Moving by LVTs directly from Saipan in a shore-to-shore amphibious operation, the Leathernecks landed on 24 July. Although battered by the intense combat to seize Saipan, the 2nd and 4th Marine Divisions took up the assault. The 27th Infantry Division remained on Saipan in reserve. Even though the Japanese attempted to defend the island at the water's edge, Geiger's force quickly established a beachhead. A counterattack at 0200 on D+1 failed to dislodge it. By the end of the day, the 2nd Marine Division had joined the forces ashore and overrun the island's airfield with little difficulty. Commanders declared Tinian secure on 1 August: Marine casualties numbered 1,860. Japanese losses were approximately 6,050 dead and 255 captured, with thousands more believed buried in caves and bunkers.

Eight Leathernecks earned Medals of Honor on Saipan, Tinian, and Guam; only two lived to wear them. An estimated thirty thousand Japanese troops and twenty-two thousand civilians perished in the cauldron of the Marianas. American casualties totaled more than twenty-seven thousand. Three-quarters of them were Marines, again causing MacArthur's supporters to increase their clamor for his elevation to command the entire Pacific War. Just as stridently, Nimitz's supporters continued to back the Navy-Marine drive across the Central Pacific.

Meanwhile, the grim contest to seize the southwest Pacific came to its climacteric. In July 1944 Maj. Gen. William H. Rupertus' 1st Marine Division staged two rehearsals at Cape Esperance in preparation for Operation Stalemate II, the seizure of Peleliu, an island in the Palau group 470 miles east of Mindanao in the southern Philippines. Nimitz favored a landing on Peleliu to provide an air base to support the advance across the central Pacific. Although tropical, Peleliu was not shrouded in jungle foliage. Aerial photographs provided by naval intelligence showed a cover of scrub brush across the island's limestone ridges. But they did not show the hundreds of caves—some natural, some man-made—dotting the island. Even though the number of defenders exceeded that of the landing force, the American commanders hoped the preinvasion bombardment would kill enough Japanese to even the odds. Unknown to General Rupertus, the enemy planned to allow the attackers to seize the beaches and then counterattack. There would be none of

the reckless banzai attacks characteristic of the Guadalcanal campaign. The core of the enemy troops facing the 1st Marine Division was Col. Nakagawa Kunio's 2nd Infantry Regiment, fresh from Manchuria. By the time the amphibious craft entered the waters around Peleliu, Nakagawa had machine guns and mortars sited to cover every avenue of approach to the heart of his defense.

The amphibious force commander, Vice Adm. Theodore S. Wilkinson, elected to bypass the largest island in the Palaus, Babelthuap. Tiny Koror Island, where Pete Ellis had died two decades earlier, was also ignored. Another island in the chain, Angaur, lay nine miles south and four miles west of Peleliu. Believed to be lightly held, it would be secured by the 81st Infantry Division, the landing force reserve for the Peleliu operation. Marine planners conceived a conventional amphibious assault on Peleliu's western shore facing the airfield. Chesty Puller, now commanding the 1st Marines, would strike at the upper fringes of the airfield and then push north. Col. Harold D. "Bucky" Harris would drive with his 5th Marines straight across the airstrip and hold it. Col. Herman Hanneken received orders to land his 7th Marines in the south and overrun that end of Peleliu.

The ten-minute ship-to-shore run proved as perilous as expected. Japanese guns, concealed in caves and protected from the naval bombardment, sank twenty-six LVTs and damaged twice that number. It took until noon for the Marines to establish a firm—albeit shallow and crowded—beachhead. The platoons of Capt. George P. Hunt's Company K, 1st Marines, crossed the beach on the left and faced a coral outcropping honeycombed

with caves and alive with defenders. Despite heavy casualties, Hunt's men worked their way behind the fortifications and rushed the outcrop from the rear to seize the crest. Second Lt. William L. Willis slid down a rope and tossed a smoke grenade into the aperture of a 47-mm gun emplacement, blinding the defenders and allowing one of his Marines to fire a rifle grenade into the position. The exploding ammunition drove the defenders out, clothing ablaze, to be gunned down. But the cost to take Peleliu was high; in two day's time, Hunt's company had only 78 men left out of its original 235. Both Willis and Hunt were awarded the Navy Cross for heroic leadership on Peleliu.

General Rupertus had predicted that Peleliu would be "a short one, a quickie," like Tarawa, "Rough, but fast. We'll be through in three days." He was badly mistaken. Tarawa had been secured in three days; on Peleliu it took the landing force three days to reach the centerpiece of the defense, an intricate network of caves and tunnels honeycombing a cluster of bare, cheerless ridges called the

Umurbrogol. By then it had become evident to most Leathernecks present that Peleliu was not going to be a quickie.

Rupertus, in contrast, remained convinced that if he exerted enough pressure on his regimental commanders and they in turn spurred their subordinates, victory was right around the corner; furthermore, because he wanted victory to belong to the 1st Marine Division alone, he consistently ignored suggestions from his immediate superior, Lieutenant General Geiger, commanding the III Amphibious Corps, to relieve battered Leatherneck units with elements of the 81st Infantry Division. When on 20 September (D+5) Geiger order the 1st Marines out of the line, Rupertus protested that he was certain the fighting would be over in a day or two. By the time the relief was completed on the twenty-third, Puller's regiment had suffered 54 percent casualties. The 7th Marines, withdrawn on 6 October, sustained 46 percent casualties; and the 5th Marines, who remained in action until the sixteenth, 43 percent. The Umurbrogol's surviving defenders were then estimated to number fewer than a thousand. The 321st Infantry Regiment eliminated the last pocket of organized resistance on 27 November (D+73).

Puller came under fire for his performance at Peleliu. His critics, including some within the Corps, charged that his can-do ethic led him to throw Marine lives away in foolhardy attempts to rush positions that should be taken a step at a time. Capt. Everett P. Pope, a Bowdoin College Phi Beta Kappa who earned the Medal of Honor while commanding Company C during the assault on the Umurbrogol, agreed wholeheartedly. "I don't think Chesty Puller was the greatest thing since sliced bread," Pope declared. "He didn't know what was going on, and why he wanted me and my men dead on top of that hill I don't know." On the other hand, Puller's most recent biographer, Jon T. Hoffman, concludes judiciously that "Chesty has gotten a bum rap." Gen. O. P. Smith, assistant division commander on Peleliu, probably would have concurred. "I went over the ground [Puller] captured," Smith remarked, "and I don't see how a human being had captured it, but he did."

Temperatures on the island rose to 115 degrees F and drinking water—often contaminated with rust or oil—ran short. As the fighting continued, critics wondered why Peleliu had not simply been bypassed. African American Marines of the 16th Field Depot volunteered to serve as stretcher bearers, earning the sobriquet, "The black angels of Peleliu." When the last of Rupertus' men left the lines, Peleliu had cost 1,794 dead Americans—including 1,241 Marines—and another 7,800 wounded. Leathernecks

contributed 5,024 of the latter total, along with 117 missing in action. The 1st Marines took the heaviest casualties; in Maj. Raymond G. Davis' 1/1, only 74 men out of almost 500 remained unscathed. Intelligence sources estimated Japanese losses of more than 10,000 while Army and Marine infantrymen took only 302 prisoners. Of the eight Medals of Honor won by Marines on Peleliu, six were earned posthumously by recipients who hurled themselves on enemy grenades.

For more than a year Admiral King had been arguing that American forces should bypass the Philippines and seize Formosa as a base of operations against the Japanese homeland. General MacArthur insisted that the United States was politically and morally obligated to liberate the Philippines at the earliest possible moment. In October 1944, the JCS finally shelved plans to invade Formosa and directed MacArthur to proceed with his campaign through the Southwest Pacific to liberate the Philippines. Nimitz was ordered to assault the islands of Iwo Jima and Okinawa in early 1945.

Code-named Operation Detachment, the seizure of Iwo Jima—an uninhabited and waterless eight square miles of wasteland in the Bonin Archipelago—would provide a base for P-51 fighters needed to escort B-29s flying from the Marianas to strike the Japanese home islands. Only 660 miles south of Tokyo, Iwo Jima was 625 miles from Saipan. The Japanese had completed two airfields on the island and another strip was under construction. Radar installations provided a two-hour warning for Tokyo when B-29s flew past from the Marianas on the way to bomb targets in the home islands. The Japanese called the foul-smelling body of land "Sulfur Island." No source of freshwater existed, and the Japanese garrison collected rainwater in concrete cisterns to sustain itself; by D-day, the enemy force had been on a half ration of water for months.

A once-important factor that American planners no longer needed to take into account was the Imperial Japanese Navy. When MacArthur's troops landed in the Philippines at the end of September, the enemy fleet had come out in a do-or-die attempt to break up the invasion, and in the four interlocking engagements that comprised the Battle of Leyte Gulf, the greatest naval action ever fought, it had died. The remnants of Japanese sea power no longer entered the strategic equation.

D-day for Iwo Jima was scheduled for 19 February 1945; no further delay was possible. Strategists in Washington had set D-day for the invasion of Okinawa for 1 April. After that date, the monsoon season would impede the assault on the Ryukyus. When the Americans launched their assault on the Marianas, the Japanese had begun to strengthen Iwo Jima in earnest. Lt. Gen. Kuribayashi Tadamichi had more than eight months to fortify the island. For the task, Tokyo gave him some twenty-one thousand troops—fourteen thousand Army, seven thousand Navy—plus ample artillery and a tank regiment. Guns ranging from naval rifles to 8-inch coastal artillery—361 in all— covered the approaches from the beaches, and the Japanese constructed hundreds of concrete blockhouses and fortified caves. Kuribayashi planned to destroy the invaders with a positional defense rather than to attempt to stop them at the water's edge. He knew that this was a fight to the finish; no reinforcements or relief seemed plausible. Posters adorning the walls of the bunkers and caves exhorted his troops to die in place: "Once the enemy invades the island, every man must resist until the end, making his position his tomb. Every man must do his best to kill ten enemy soldiers."

Most of Kuribayashi's senior officers seem to have been ignorant of the Japanese defeat at the Battle of Leyte Gulf and continued to believe that the navy would somehow come to their rescue once the assault on Iwo Jima began. On 13 February 1945, a Japanese patrol plane spotted the American task force as it left Saipan. On Iwo Jima, no hysteria followed the report. Most of the defenders knew that the Americans would arrive eventually. But when the news of the sighting reached Tokyo, a mob of Japanese schoolboys toppled Commodore Perry's statue to the ground in a frenzy of anti-Americanism.

Overall responsibility for the operation was vested in Admiral Spruance, commanding the Fifth Fleet. Kelly Turner, recently promoted to vice admiral, remained at the head of the amphibious forces. In an apparent sop to Army critics, Smith became commanding general of the Fleet Marine Force, Pacific, with no tactical control over the landing force. Maj. Gen. Harry Schmidt commanded the V Amphibious Corps, consisting of Graves B. Erskine's 3rd Marine Division, Clifton B. Cates' 4th Marine Division, and Keller E. Rockey's 5th Marine Division. Each infantry battalion had an assault platoon armed with rockets, flamethrowers, and demolition charges. The tank battalions had more flame tanks. Training prior to D-day stressed the assault of fortified positions. Howlin' Mad Smith stunned his commanders and staff with a gloomy estimate of exorbitant casualties; before the battle ended, more than fifteen thousand Americans would lose their lives. Present when Smith made his gloomy prediction, Secretary of the Navy James V. Forrestal exclaimed that "Iwo Jima, like Tarawa, leaves us very little choice except to take it by force of arms, by character, and courage."

Bombers from Saipan and the guns of the fleet blasted Iwo Jima for an incredible seventy-four days—but the immediate pre-D-day shelling lasted only three days. Once again, Howlin' Mad Smith scored the Navy—"not enough!" he growled. He wanted ten days. Task Force 58—which included eight Leatherneck squadrons of Corsairs—steamed to within sixty miles of the Japanese homeland and bombed Tokyo, destroying aircraft that might interfere with the landing on Iwo Jima. When Smith and fellow critics charged that the Navy showed more interest in upstaging the Army Air Forces' B-29 raids on Japan than in continuing to support the amphibious drive, Navy officers countered that the attacks diverted attention from the forthcoming assault.

Nevertheless, the D-day shelling was the heaviest of the Pacific war. Eighty-five minutes of uninterrupted pounding was followed by fighter-bomber runs from Task Force 58, then another intense round of bombardment from the ships offshore. Leatherneck aviators from VMO-4 and VMO-5 flew from makeshift

platforms mounted on the LSTs and helped direct the shelling. The Japanese defenders sustained few casualties because they had burrowed deep underground, but they suffered. A survivor recalled the horror of the bombardment for his captors: "For two days we cowered like rats, trying to dig ourselves deeper into the acrid volcanic dust and ash of Iwo Jima. Never have I felt so helpless, so puny, as I did during those two days. There was nothing we could do; there was no way in which we could strike back."

As his Marines stormed the most terrible beaches in the Corps' history, Smith's prediction of immense casualties—one out of every four assault troops—would be borne out. In a letter to Vandegrift, Smith shared his frustrations and uneasiness on the eve of the landing: "On two separate occasions I protested that naval gunfire is insufficient, with the result that it has been increased to some extent, but not enough, in my opinion, to suffice. I can only go so far. We have done all we can to get ready . . . and I believe it will be successful, but the thought of the probable casualties causes me extreme unhappiness . . . would to God that something might happen to cancel the operation altogether."

At 0330 on 19 February, Leathernecks in the ships of the amphibious force ate what had become the traditional meal before a landing—steak and eggs. Beginning at 0645, battleships and cruisers blasted the landing beaches. A quintet of rocket ships heaped more than five tons of ordnance on the Motoyama plateau. Kuribayashi signaled his superiors that "the violence of the enemy's bombardment is far beyond description." Most observers offshore concluded that

Map 22, left:
The Assault on Iwo Jima,
19 February 1945

Right: A Navy lieutenant,
Howard W. Whalen,
photographed the assault
waves for the invasion of
Iwo Jima. (World War II
Anniversary Committee)

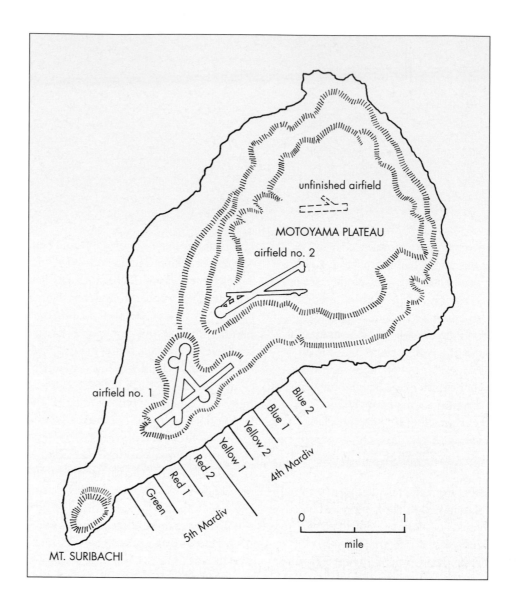

few Japanese could survive the flaming death. "Nobody can live through this," correspondent Robert Sherrod reflected hopefully, "but I know better." The defenders huddled in caves, bunkers, and concrete pillboxes and waited. An awesome armada of death—495 ships of the Fifth Fleet's amphibious force—lay offshore. At 0830, the first assault wave left the line of departure.

At 0902 sixty-nine LVTs—twenty Marines in each—touched down on the southern end of the island: the 5th Marine Division on Green and Red Beaches, the 28th Marines on the left and the 27th Marines on the right; the 4th Marine Division on Yellow and Blue Beaches, the 23rd Marines on the left and the 25th Marines on the right. The 3rd Marine

Division remained offshore as a floating reserve. The 4th Marine Division would drive up the eastern side of Iwo Jima, and the 5th Marine Division would assault up the western flank of V Amphibious Corps' front. There were 482 amtracs in the initial assault, enough to transport eight battalions of infantry. In ten waves at five-minute intervals, nine thousand Marines rushed ashore. The assault divisions had as their initial objectives the enemy airfields and Mount Suribachi—a 556-foot-high extinct volcano at the island's southern tip. Having taken them, they were to turn and attack in line to the north along the island's steep central plateau to its rocky northern beaches, at which the conquest of the island would be complete.

Guns and mortars opened up as the Leathernecks came ashore. Horrified correspondents observed human body parts scattered about in the filthy volcanic ash. Sherrod described it as "a beachhead in hell." Casualties in the first assault battalions soared. Medical personnel attempted to treat the wounded as close to the front as possible. By the time the island was declared secure, 23 doctors and 827 corpsmen would die in the flaming cauldron of Iwo Jima.

Manila John Basilone, recipient of the Medal of Honor at Guadalcanal, rallied his machine gun platoon in 1/27 with characteristic aggressiveness: "Come on, you guys, we got to get these guns off the beach!" That night, Basilone died a warrior's death, struck down by a mortar shell that exploded behind him. His heroism on Iwo Jima earned him a posthumous Navy Cross.

By 1800 the landing force had carved out a beachhead, four thousand yards wide and less than eleven hundred yards deep in the face of the most stubborn Japanese resistance encountered in the war. But more than thirty thousand Marines—six infantry regiments and six artillery battalions—had made it ashore. Late that afternoon, Schmidt and Turner agreed to draw on the force reserve and land most of the 3rd Marine Division. Only the 3rd Marines remained as a reserve now. As the outcome appeared in doubt, Schmidt asked Turner to release the regiment. The amphibious task force commander refused, replying rather tartly that there were sufficient Marines ashore already. Critics

later charged that Turner's decision increased casualties among the landing force. Turner's flawed decision reinforced the arguments of senior Marines that, once the landing force was ashore, the admirals should butt out of the tactical scenario. Almost six hundred Leathernecks lay dead or dying, with survivors clinging to the beachhead. Instead of delivering the expected counterattack under cover of darkness, however, the Japanese stayed in their caves and bunkers. Enemy mortar and artillery shells rained on the narrow beaches throughout the endless night.

On D+1, the 28th Marines under Col. Harry B. Liversedge fought their way, inch by inch, up Mount Suribachi. An estimated sixteen hundred Japanese defenders had burrowed into its sides, concealed in well-camouflaged positions. Another intense naval bombardment preceded the assault. Liversedge's battalions gained only two

hundred yards in that first bloody day. It took four days of bitter fighting to take the height and overrun the adjacent airfield. Hearing Japanese voices coming from fissures in the volcanic rock, Leathernecks poured gasoline into the openings to turn the caves and hideouts into flaming tombs. By then, the combat efficiency of the regiment had declined to less than 75 percent.

At 1015 on 23 February, the 28th Marines took the crest and raised a small flag. Watching from offshore, Secretary of the Navy James V. Forrestal turned to Smith and remarked that "the raising of the flag on Suribachi means that there will be a Marine Corps for the next five hundred years." Two hours later, a larger flag was found and raised on the summit in a more choreographed setting. An Associated Press photographer, Joe Rosenthal, captured the event in a picture that has come to symbolize the valor of the

Corps. Sadly, three of the six Leathernecks who raised the famous flag would not survive the battle for Iwo Jima. The sight of the Stars and Stripes flying over Suribachi disturbed the Japanese defenders. The height was supposed to have been held for two weeks; instead, it had fallen in only three days. But it had cost the 28th Marines 519 men.

By 1 March, the 23rd Marines had been shattered as a combat unit and were replaced by the 24th Marines. Elements of the landing force continued to root out pockets of enemy resistance. Casualties remained high. In one battalion of the 25th Marines, only 150 men remained uninjured out of more than 900 who began the invasion. Of the 24 assault battalion commanders, 19 became casualties. By the end of the second week on Iwo Jima, V Amphibious Corps had sustained more than 13,000 casualties, including 3,000 dead Leathernecks and Bluejackets.

On 3 March 1945, the first U.S. aircraft landed on one of the captured airfields—refurbished and repaired by a Seabee battalion. The Navy C-47 brought in medical supplies and mail, and departed with litters of critically wounded Leathernecks. A day later, the first crippled B-29 landed after a bombing run to Tokyo. By then, the Marines had backed the surviving Japanese into enclaves on the northern coast. On 7 March, units of the 3rd Marine Division conducted a silent predawn attack and effectively wiped out the Japanese tank regiment. By D+19, the Leathernecks finally held the entire plateau. Kuribayashi sent his last message to Tokyo on 16 March: "I humbly apologize to His Majesty that I have failed to live up to expectations. Bullets are gone and water

exhausted. Permit me to say farewell." His body was never found.

On 19 March, two Japanese bombs struck the carrier *Franklin*. Included among the ship's 772 dead were 65 Marines. The blasts knocked two Marine squadrons, VMF-214 and VMF-452, out of the war. The carrier *Wasp* departed the area around the same time, leaving only four squadrons of Leatherneck fighters on the *Bennington* and *Bunker Hill*.

Although the seizure of Iwo Jima was supposed to take no more than four days, it could not be declared secure until 26 March. The final enemy cave was not snuffed out until D+34. An Army regiment came ashore to mop up. More than 22,000 Japanese soldiers had died; fewer than 300 survived the assault. In all, 71,245 Marines landed at Iwo Jima: 5,931 of them were killed and another 13,372 wounded.

There was close to one Leatherneck casualty for every dead Japanese; nearly one in every three Leathernecks ashore was wounded or killed. Howlin' Mad Smith, not easily moved, stood in awe of the toll: "Iwo Jima was the most savage and the most costly battle in the history of the Marine Corps. Indeed, it has few parallels in military history." Nimitz added his postscript to the epic assault: "Uncommon valor was a common virtue." Of the eighty-two Marines who earned Medals of Honor in World War II, twenty-two earned them on Iwo Jima. Among them was Pfc. Jacklyn H. Lucas, 1st Battalion, 26th Marines, the youngest Leatherneck—only six days and seventeen years old—to win the nation's highest award for valor. At the dedication of his division's cemetery, General Erskine

spoke about the human cost to take Iwo Jima: "Victory was never in doubt; its cost was. What was in doubt, in all our minds, was whether there would be any of us left to dedicate our cemetery at the end, or whether the last Marine would be knocking out the last Japanese gunner."

The next order of business was Okinawa. Spruance remained in overall command; Turner continued to head the amphibious force. Code-named Operation Iceberg, the invasion of Okinawa would be the largest of the Pacific war: more than thirteen hundred ships of all types and a landing force of approximately 182,112 men—including 81,165 Marines. Because, for the first time in the Central Pacific drive, Army troops outnumbered Marines, an Army officer was assigned to command the landing force. Lt. Gen. Simon Bolivar Buckner's Tenth Army consisted of two corps: Maj. Gen. John R. Hodge's XXIV Corps (7th, 77th, and 96th Infantry Divisions); and Maj. Gen. Keller E. Rockey's III Amphibious Corps (1st and 6th Marine Divisions). The veteran 1st Marine Division had recovered from Peleliu while the 6th Marine Division, although newly formed, contained a core of veterans from earlier Pacific campaigns. The 2nd Marine Division, rested and re-equipped from the rigors of the Marianas campaign, provided the demonstration force while the 27th Infantry Division formed the reserve. Four air groups joined in the formation of a Marine tactical air force commanded by Maj. Gen. Francis P. Mulcahy. Another eight squadrons of Marine aviators flew from the carriers *Bunker Hill*, *Bennington*, *Essex*, and *Wasp*. By the eve of the invasion, HQMC counted 421,605

Marines in uniform. In addition, 16,017 Navy personnel served in the ranks of the six Marine divisions and four air wings.

Okinawa lay in the center of the Ryukyus, an island chain stretching for more than 790 miles between Japan and Formosa. It offered the amphibians two deep-water bays for the landings and a level interior with at least two large airfields. Only 325 miles from Kyushu, the southernmost of the Japanese home islands, Okinawa measures sixty miles in length and varies in width between two and eighteen miles. One of the forty-seven prefectures of Japan, the island was the home of more than 450,000 people, mostly farmers.

On 26 March 1945, the pre-invasion bombardment began. Rear Adm. Morton L. Deyo's Task Force 54 shrouded Okinawa in a blanket of fire from ten battleships, seven heavy cruisers, three light cruisers, and thirty-two destroyers and destroyer escorts. On the same day, two regiments from the Army's 77th Infantry Division and a Leatherneck reconnaissance battalion landed on the five small islands of the Kerama group, fifteen miles west of Okinawa. This minor adjunct to the main assault to the north served to screen Turner's southern flank and provided a protected anchorage for Spruance's Fifth Fleet.

On 1 April—both Easter Sunday and April Fool's Day—Buckner's landing force stormed ashore, the two corps landing abreast over the Hagushi beaches on the west coast of Okinawa between Yontan and Kadena. The assault was preceded by an attack of five hundred carrier aircraft that strafed and napalmed the landing sites. Soldiers took the southern beaches while Marines seized the

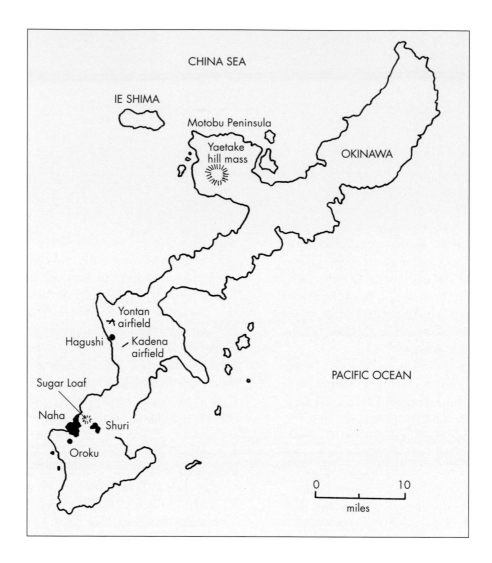

northern beaches. XXIV Corps then wheeled to the south, III Amphibious Corps to the north. The 2nd Marine Division feinted off the southern coast, leading the Japanese to believe that another landing might take place there. Then the veterans of Saipan returned to their ships to become a floating reserve for the remainder of the campaign.

Flawlessly executed, the landing split the island in two. By the evening of L-Day, more than fifty thousand Americans were holding a beachhead three miles wide and over a mile deep. Miraculously, the landing force suffered only twenty-eight men killed and another twenty-seven missing. Lt. Gen. Ushijima Mitsuru, the Japanese commander, hoped to confront the enemy in the south in a final, desperate bid to delay or prevent the impending invasion of the home islands. The slogan he had coined for the 32nd

Army appeared everywhere on the walls of bunkers and barracks: "One plane for every warship. One boat for every ship. One man for every ten enemy. One man for every tank." Ushijima's army consisted of two divisions, the 24th and the 62nd, plus the 44th Independent Brigade, a tank regiment, and artillery units. Two shipping engineer regiments, service units, and the Boeitai—a sort of Okinawan home guard—rounded out his command. Concentrated in the rocky southern third of the island was Rear Adm. Ota Minoru's naval base force. Total Japanese troop strength in the Ryukyus was estimated at more than 155,000 men. On the eve of the invasion, Ushijima expressed optimism in his instructions to subordinates not to oppose the landing; instead the defenders would wait until the Americans were ashore and then pounce on them.

Despite Japanese boasts, soldiers and Marines swept aside the defenders without difficulty during the early stages of Operation Iceberg. XXIV Corps took Kadena on 2 April and commanders declared the airstrip ready to receive planes that night. General Mulcahy established a tactical air command post ashore the same day. Two days later, Maj. Gen. Pedro del Valle's 1st Marine Division cut across the narrow island to the east coast. On 14 April, the 4th Marines attacked the Yaetake Hill mass. Cpl. Richard E. Bush, a squad leader, earned a Medal of Honor in the bitter fighting at Motobu—and lived to wear it. His citation read:

> Rallying his men forward with indomitable determination, Corporal Bush boldly defied the flashing fury of concentrated Japanese artillery fire pouring down from the gun-studded mountain fortress to lead his squad up the face of the rock precipice, sweep over

the ridge, and drive the defending troops from their deeply entrenched position. He fought relentlessly in the forefront of the action until seriously wounded and evacuated with others under protecting rocks. Although prostrate under medical care when a Japanese hand grenade landed in the midst of the group . . . [he] unhesitatingly pulled the deadly missile to himself and absorbed the shattering violence of the exploding charge in his own body.

Meanwhile, on 4 April, XXIV Corps struck to the south against stiffening resistance. Two days later, in a hopeless attempt to disrupt the assault, Tokyo dispatched the remnants of the Japanese fleet. Vice Adm. Ito Seiichi steamed south in the super-battleship *Yamato* in company with nine other warships on a suicidal mission to break up the invasion. On 7 April, the aircraft of Vice Adm. Marc A. Mitscher's Task Force

Map 23, Left: The Campaign for Okinawa, April–June 1945

Top Right: A Navy war artist, Lt. Mitchell Jamieson, captured an almost peaceful scene in *D-Day plus One, Green Beach Two*, on Okinawa. (Navy Art Collection)

Left: Smoke billows from the mouth of an enemy-occupied cave into which Marines have just tossed a satchel charge during the contest for Okinawa. (National Archives)

Right: A flame-throwing tank of the 6th Marine Division douses a Japanese position on Shuri Ridge with napalm. (National Archives)

58 spotted the Japanese force and attacked it, sinking a cruiser and four destroyers. The mighty *Yamato* capsized after being hit by at least sixteen bombs and torpedoes. Less than a tenth of her crew of 2,769 survived the last sortie of the Imperial Japanese Navy.

On the day the *Yamato* sailed, Japanese suicide planes appeared in the skies off Okinawa. An estimated 699 aircraft attacked the invasion force that day—including 355 kamikazes. Two American destroyers, a destroyer escort, and two cargo ships went down. Twelve other vessels suffered damage. The kamikaze raids continued throughout the campaign; for the first time in an amphibious operation, the Navy lost more men killed in action than the Marines or the Army.

On land, the bloody contest continued. In the north, Maj. Gen. Lemuel C. Shepherd Jr.'s 6th Marine Division cleared the Motobu Peninsula. By 12 April—the day of President Roosevelt's death—the advance in the south had ground to a halt. The addition of a third infantry division to the two already in line failed to break the stalemate. On 19 April, the largest single artillery concentration of the Pacific war took place. XXIV Corps amassed 324 guns and fired nineteen thousand shells in an attempt to breach the Japanese defenses—in vain. Leatherneck commanders urged Buckner to land the 2nd Marine Division behind the Japanese line of resistance in an amphibious end-run. Vandegrift, who was visiting the island on an inspection tour, added his support to the idea. Buckner rejected it nonetheless. His decision widened the Army–Marine Corps rift and exacerbated the tensions generated in the Marianas the year before.

Opting for a battle of attrition, Buckner ordered the 1st Marine Division to join the III Amphibious Corps in the south. Both

corps struck toward Naha on 11 May against formidable Japanese resistance. On the thirteenth, Leathernecks began clawing their way up the deadly saddle they called the Sugar Loaf. By 23 May the 6th Marine Division had reached the outskirts of Naha, the island's most populous city; a week later, the 1st Marine Division stormed Shuri Ridge and the ruins of medieval Shuri Castle. Most of Ushijima's troops retreated to the south, joined by hordes of terrified civilians desperately fleeing the falling bombs and shells.

The struggle had shifted in favor of the attackers by the end of May. By then, the Japanese had lost an estimated fifty thousand troops. But the early summer rains began on the twenty-first, turning roads into oozy seas of muck. Filthy water and slime jammed weapons, contaminated wounds, and fouled clothing and food. On 4 June, the 6th Marine Division sealed off the base of the Oroku

Peninsula. The 22nd Marines assaulted the promontory a day later while the 4th Marines executed a skillful shore-to-shore amphibious movement. On the same day, MAG-14 arrived to bring the number of Leatherneck aircraft ashore to more than seven hundred. Maj. Gen. Louis E. Woods relieved Mulcahy as the commanding general of the 4th MAW. On 14 June, units of the 6th Marine Division broke into Oroku village and destroyed the naval defense force. Admiral Ota provided Tokyo with a typical final message: "The naval force is dying gloriously!"

By 17 June, the attacking Americans had shattered Ushijima's army. Discipline gone, Japanese soldiers fought among themselves or turned on the civilian populace in an orgy of pillage and rape. The slippage in Japanese morale was also evident in the seventy-four hundred surrenders—6 percent of the island's garrison. One enemy officer approached the

Left: Two Leathernecks from the 29th Marines share their fighting hole and ponchos with an Okinawan war orphan. (National Archives)

Top Right: Units of the 6th Marine Division advance on Naha, Okinawa's provincial capital, early in June 1945. (National Archives)

Bottom Right: On 14 May 1945, Maj. Gen. Lemuel C. Shepherd Jr. (left) and Gen. Simon Bolivar Buckner observed the intense shelling of Japanese positions near Naha, Okinawa. Shepherd led the 6th Marine Division and Buckner commanded the 10th Army. (National Archives)

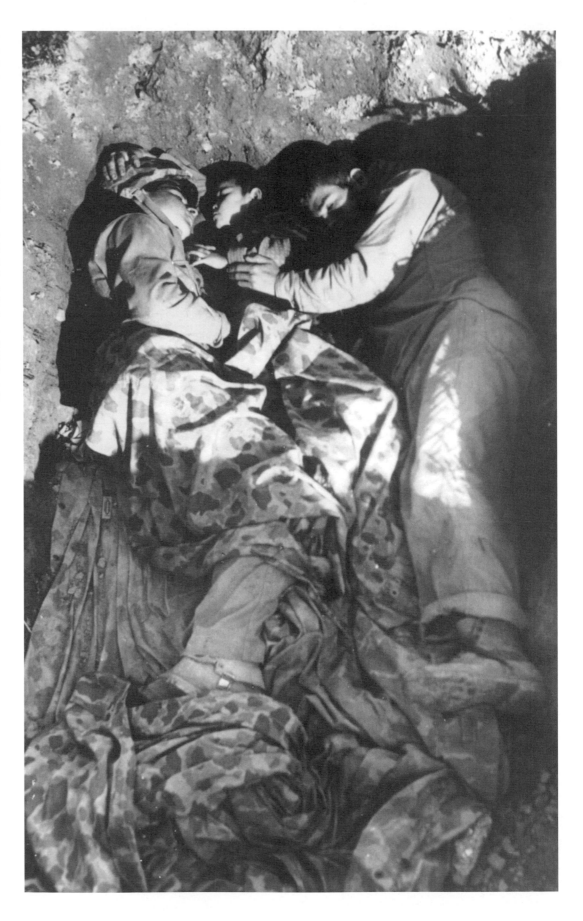

lines of the 7th Infantry Division, dressed only in a loin cloth, and presented his sword. Consulting two dictionaries—one, English-Japanese; the other, Japanese-English—he pronounced solemnly to his captors: "Me vanquished, miserable, dishonorable, depraved."

On 18 June an exploding Japanese shell sent a fragment of coral into General Buckner, killing the landing force commander as he observed an assault by the 8th Marines—brought hurriedly with the 2nd Marine Division in the Marianas. Command of the landing force passed to his deputy, Lt. Gen. Roy S. Geiger, USMC, but only for as long as it took the Army to act. In what must have been the most expeditious personnel action of the war, Army Chief of Staff George C.

Marshall ordered Lt. Gen. Joseph H. "Vinegar Joe" Stillwell of China fame to Okinawa as a replacement for Buckner. Obviously, the Army's leaders had not forgotten the Smith versus Smith imbroglio at Saipan.

Still in command on 21 June, Geiger announced that all resistance on Okinawa had ceased; on the next day, Ushijima committed seppuku. By then MAG-31 was operating out of Yontan and MAG-33 from Kadena. MAG-22 established its headquarters at Ie Shima, and MAG-14 arrived from the Philippines. Thirty-two squadrons of Marine aviators eventually flew in support of the battle for Okinawa.

An estimated 107,539 Japanese and Okinawans died during the eighty-two days of intense combat. The U.S. Navy lost 36 ships sunk and another 243 were damaged—exceeding the losses at Pearl Harbor. Almost 5,000 sailors died—more than the number of soldiers or Marines. More than 3,200 Marines paid the supreme price for victory; another 11,677 Marines wounded added to the grisly total. Altogether, the Tenth Army suffered 65,631 casualties, making Okinawa the most costly campaign of the Pacific war.

Even before the landings on Okinawa, the Joint Chiefs set plans in motion for the invasion of the Japanese home islands. Operation Olympic, the landing on Kyushu, was scheduled for 1 November 1945; three Marine divisions and three air wings would join ten Army divisions in the attack. Operation Coronet, the landing on Honshu, would take place in March 1946; eleven Army divisions and the III Amphibious Corps would provide the assault forces. Even as the guns fell silent on Okinawa, B-29s from island bases were flying twelve hundred sorties a day to turn Japan's wood-and-paper cities into charcoal.

On 26 July, the allies presented the Japanese government with the Potsdam Declaration, which called for unconditional surrender, but Tokyo demurred. As American leaders considered their options, all were painfully cognizant of the fact that an estimated 4.7 million Japanese remained under arms, including 1.5 million stationed in the home islands. U.S. casualties in the planned invasion of Japan were expected to be a minimum of one hundred thousand men. On 16 July the first test of an atomic bomb took place at Alamagordo, New Mexico. On 6 August a B-29 flying from Tinian dropped

a duplicate bomb on Hiroshima; two days later, the Soviet Union declared war on Japan. A second atomic bomb obliterated Nagasaki on 9 August, and a day later the Japanese government sued for peace. On 15 August 1945 the most costly war in the history of the U.S. Marine Corps came to an end.

When the Allied commanders gathered on the deck of the battleship *Missouri* in Tokyo Bay on 2 September, Lieutenant General Geiger represented the thousands of Leathernecks who had paid for the surrender ceremony with their sweat and blood; in a petulant sop to Army–Navy rivalry, Nimitz did not invite Howlin' Mad Smith to the ceremony. Of the almost 500,000 Americans who had worn forest green or jungle camouflage since 7 December 1941, half were serving in the Pacific or in the ships of the fleet on V-J Day. World War II cost the Marine Corps 19,733 dead and 68,207 wounded. Of the 2,270 Marines captured by the Japanese, 1,756 survived. The naval war in the Pacific brilliantly vindicated the dedicated planning by senior Leatherneck officers during the interwar years, many of whom foresaw both war with Japan and a lengthy amphibious campaign as a result.

Not every Marine served in the war in the Pacific. Women Marines filled slots at home, freeing male Marines for assignment to the divisions, air wings, and separate battalions in the Pacific. Traditional commitments in the ships of the fleet, worldwide, continued. A number of Marines with special language skills and backgrounds served with the Office of Strategic Services (OSS)—the forerunner of today's Central Intelligence Agency. Probably the most famous of this group was Peter J.

Ortiz, a Frenchman of Algerian descent born in New York City. While serving in the French Foreign Legion at the beginning of the war, he was taken prisoner by the Germans but managed to escape from his prison camp. After returning to the United States, Ortiz earned a commission in the Marine Corps but was siphoned off quickly for service with the OSS. During a behind-the-lines espionage operation in France, the gallant Ortiz chose to surrender to a Nazi force rather than allow it to destroy the village that had given him sanctuary. He spent the remainder of the war in a prison camp and earned a Navy Cross. Hollywood brought out two movies based on Ortiz's exploits: *13 Rue Madeline*, starring James Cagney; and *Operation Top Secret*, featuring Cornel Wilde. Nonetheless, *The Sands of Iwo Jima* and *Flying Leathernecks* made John Wayne the best-known "Marine" of the war.

CHAPTER 12

The Unification Struggle, Cold War, and Korea, 1945–1953

At the end of World War II, the Marine Corps numbered more than 485,053 men and women. Six divisions and five air wings had served in the Pacific against Japan. After V-J day, the 1st and 6th Divisions deployed to China to disarm Japanese garrisons. A skeletal 2nd Division took up residence at Camp Lejeune as part of the peacetime establishment. The remaining divisions cased their colors. By the summer of 1946, the number of Marines on active duty dropped to 155,000 and the Corps proposed to stabilize its strength at 7,000 to 8,000 officers and 100,000 men, approximately a third of whom would form a Fleet Marine Force (FMF) of two divisions and two air wings.

By that date the Corps, fresh from its greatest triumph, unexpectedly found itself fighting for its life—not on foreign soil but in the halls of Congress. The conflict arose during the Unification Struggle brought about by plans made by the Army's leaders to reorganize the American armed forces to their own institutional advantage. Enthusiastically endorsed by President Harry S. Truman, these plans called for the transformation of the air force, at that time a branch of the

Army, into a separate service; the creation of an umbrella department of defense, with its own secretary, to administer the entire military establishment; and the reduction of the Marine Corps to a force of light infantry units no larger than a regiment, without an air component and with a maximum strength of sixty thousand men. The chief of naval operations, Adm. Chester W. Nimitz, declared indignantly that their adoption would "eliminate the Marine Corps as an effective combat force."

The Army's plan formed the substance of a Senate bill (S. 2044) introduced in January 1946. Well aware of what was coming, Vandegrift had already appointed a strategy board headed by brigadier generals Merritt A. Edson and Gerald C. Thomas to map out the Corps' legislative goals and defenses. They in turn activated two groups of midranking officers to monitor political developments, lobby sympathetic congressmen and journalists, and draft position papers. Among those so assigned were two of the Corps' brightest young men, Lt. Col. Victor H. Krulak—better known as "Brute," the nickname he had received as the smallest (5′ 2″) member of the Naval Academy Class of

1934—and Col. Merrill B. Twining (Naval Academy Class of 1923), both of whom were destined for three stars and consideration for commandant.

On 6 May 1946, Vandegrift appeared before the Senate Naval Affairs Committee to testify on S. 2044. In a highly publicized statement drafted by Krulak and Twining, he declared that the passage of the bill would "in all probability spell extinction for the Marine Corps." Despite the Corps' 170 years of service and all that it should have counted for, the commandant urged Congress to decide its fate purely on the grounds of military effectiveness. "We have pride in ourselves and our past," he continued, "but we do not rest our case on any presumed ground of gratitude owing us from the nation. The bended knee is not a tradition of our Corps." Vandegrift's "bended knee speech" demolished S. 2044. Congress adjourned without acting on the unification question.

When the 80th Congress convened in January 1947, the administration reentered the fray with a bill that was, from the Corps' standpoint, no improvement over its predecessor. The president issued a gag order prohibiting officers from testifying against the measure. Edson thereupon requested immediate retirement in order to be able to tell Congress what he thought of it—which he did, in no uncertain terms. By then, Vandegrift's political action team had concluded that the only way to safeguard the Corps' identity would be to have its functions prescribed by law. The highly effective opposition this group orchestrated to the new bill forced the administration reluctantly to conclude that unification could not be accomplished over the Corps' objections. Yet another bill was therefore introduced, this time including a definition of the services' roles and responsibilities. The section relating to the Marine Corps—206(c)—was written largely by Krulak, Twining, and Lt. Col. James D. Hittle. It defined the Corps as a separate service within the Navy Department—not a branch of the Navy—with the principal responsibility for the development of amphibious doctrine and equipment and the primary mission of "providing fleet marine forces of combined arms, together with supporting arms components, for service with the fleet in the seizure or defense of advanced naval bases and for the conduct of . . . land operations . . . essential to . . . a naval campaign." This legislation passed into law as the National Security Act of 1947. The Corps had achieved a dazzling victory in the fiercest of the many bureaucratic battles in its long history.

One of the arguments that had been advanced for reducing the Corps to light infantry was that the advent of atomic weapons had rendered amphibious assaults obsolete; an enemy with such weapons would vaporize the attackers in their transports before they even reached the beaches. This prospect was also and understandably of concern to the Corps. After witnessing the Bikini A-bomb tests in July 1946, Lt. Gen. Roy S. Geiger, the commanding general of the Fleet Marine Force, Pacific, wrote Vandegrift expressing his opinion "that a complete review and study of our concept of amphibious operations will have to be made."

The commandant responded by convening a Special Board headed by Lt. Gen. Lemuel C. Shepherd Jr. to investigate the

President Harry S. Truman inscribed this photograph of himself and the commandant, Gen. Clifton B. Cates, "with kindest regards," but the chief executive was outraged when Cates and other senior officers urged Marine Corps supporters in Congress to thwart Truman's plans to emasculate the smaller of the naval services. (National Archives)

future of amphibious warfare in the atomic age. The board's report of 16 December 1946 conceded that conventional landings would indeed be impossible against an enemy armed with nuclear weapons. Unlike the Corps' critics, however, the board did not conclude that this finding signaled the end of amphibious operations. Instead, it proposed developing means to make unconventional landings that would deprive the enemy of massed targets for atomic bombs until the attackers were in such close contact that the defenders could not use them without obliterating their own troops as well. The most promising of such means seemed to be transport seaplanes and especially helicopters. As the Corps had none of the latter, the board recommended the immediate organization of an experimental squadron. Vandegrift approved the report three days after receiving it.

Follow-up studies determined that the Corps should concentrate on helicopters, and the Marine Helicopter Experimental Squadron (HMX-1) was activated at Quantico in December 1947. Meanwhile, in a ferment reminiscent of that of 1933–34,

officers assigned to the Marine Corps Schools began to formulate a "New Concept" of what would later become known as "vertical envelopment." The first simulated helicopter assault was made at Camp Lejeune in May 1948. Although only five two-passenger helicopters were available to carry sixty-six Marines ashore from the escort carrier *Palau*, the results buoyed the optimism of the operation's planners. Negotiations were opened with manufacturers for the production of a craft capable of transporting fifteen to twenty combat-loaded Marines for distances up to three hundred miles, and in November the Quantico schools issued a landmark manual in the Amphibious Operations series, *Employment of Helicopters (Tentative)—PHIB 31*. Like the *Tentative Landing Operations Manual* of the preceding generation, it provided the starting point for the development of a doctrine in which the Corps saw the key to its future.

While these events were in progress, a number of changes had occurred on the Corps scene. As Vandegrift approached retirement in late 1947, the choice of his successor quickly narrowed to Cates and

Shepherd. Both had fought at Belleau Wood and commanded divisions in the war against Japan. Deeming their qualifications equal, Truman picked Cates, who was three years older and slightly senior in date of rank. The president announced his decision in an interview with both men, promising Shepherd that "you . . . will have your chance next time"; and he proved as good as his word.

Two significant changes in the Corps' social composition were mandated during Cates' first year as commandant. The passage of the Women's Armed Forces Integration Act on 12 June 1948 required all the services to accept women into their regular as well as reserve components. A month later, a presidential order abolished racial segregation throughout the military. Neither ruling was welcomed by traditionalists within the Corps, and neither had much immediate effect. There were only fifteen hundred African American Marines on active duty, serving in all-black service companies or performing steward's duties, and women regulars were limited to a strength of eleven hundred restricted to chair-borne duty.

In the course of the year, it became apparent that, despite the Corps' success in defining the terms of the National Security Act of 1947, the Truman administration's determination to slash the defense budget put the FMF at peril. The conflict this foreboded crystallized following the appointment of Louis A. Johnson as secretary of defense on 23 March 1949. Johnson viewed the sea services as expensive anachronisms. As he explained to an appalled admiral: "There's no reason for having a Navy and Marine Corps. . . . We'll never have any more amphibious operations. That does away with the Marine Corps. And the Air Force can do anything the Navy can do nowadays, so that does away with the Navy." Johnson's views were similar to those of the chairman of the Joint Chiefs of Staff (JCS), General of the Army Omar N. Bradley, who informed the House Armed Services Committee in October that "I am wondering whether we shall ever have another large-scale amphibious operation. Frankly, the atomic bomb, properly delivered, almost precludes such a possibility."

Under Cates' leadership, the Corps struggled to resist the erosion of its strength and status. Recognizing that in itself the National Security Act provided adequate protection for neither, HQMC sought to underpin it by securing the passage of two additional acts, the most important of which was to make the commandant a statutory member of the JCS. In this position he would have direct access to the secretary of defense and an immediate influence on the formulation of strategic and budgetary policy. The second was to prescribe the strength of the FMF at two divisions, each consisting of six battalion landing teams (BLTs), and two air wings, each of twelve squadrons. The Corps succeeded in marshaling considerable Congressional and public support for both aims. In January 1950, bills were introduced to give the commandant a seat on the Joint Chiefs and to guarantee the Corps' manpower to maintain the FMF at the desired level. Exhausted and confused by four years' fratricide among the armed forces, Congress failed to take action on either proposal.

In the meantime, Secretary Johnson had been busy. In 1948, the FMF had numbered

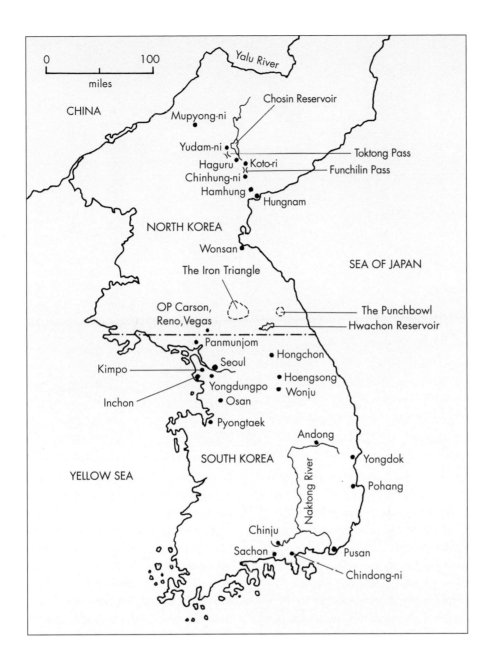

34,086 men organized into eleven BLTs and twenty-three air squadrons. Johnson's first Defense Department budget, for Fiscal Year 1950 (beginning in July 1949), allocated 29,415 men to the FMF, compelling General Cates to reduce the number of BLTs to eight; that same year, the secretary decommissioned eleven of the FMF's twenty-three air squadrons. In testimony to Congress in October, Cates asserted that "it appears . . . that the power of the budget, the power of coordination, and the power of strategic direction . . . have been used to destroy the operating forces of the Marine Corps." But worse was to follow. In early June 1950 Secretary

Johnson announced that the budget for Fiscal Year 1951 would cut the FMF to 23,952 men in six BLTs and twelve squadrons. The announced retrenchment meant a drop in the enlisted ranks from 78,715 men to 67,025. In response to the reductions, planners prepared to reduce infantry regiments to only two battalions with just two platoons in each rifle company. Artillery batteries anticipated reduction to four howitzers each, rather than the customary six. Senior officers concluded ruefully that when the pruning had reached fruition, the 1st Marine Division would resemble a World War II regimental landing team. Three weeks later, on 25 June 1950,

eight divisions of the Communist North Korean People's Army, spearheaded by 150 Soviet-made T-34 tanks, crossed the 38th Parallel and invaded South Korea. At that time, HQMC counted only 74,279 Marines on the muster rolls.

The ill-equipped Republic of Korea (ROK) forces, lacking armor and heavy artillery, proved no match for the attackers. Seoul, the country's capital, fell on 28 June. By that date President Truman had decided that although the United States had no treaty obligation to defend South Korea, its role as the leader of the Free World required it to do so. The Soviets were staging one of their recurrent boycotts of the United Nations, which made it possible for the American delegation to obtain passage of a resolution condemning the invasion as an act of aggression and calling on member nations to aid in repulsing it. Command of U.S.—and, a few days later, UN forces—was vested in Gen. Douglas MacArthur.

In the frantic, opening days of a war, which had taken Washington policy makers unaware, no one seemed to have time for Cates. Senior Army and Air Force officers on the staff of the JCS even suggested leaving the Marines off the troop list for Korea. Nevertheless, the commandant continued to press his case for Leatherneck participation in the conflict. On 1 July the chief of naval operations, Adm. Forrest C. Sherman, offered MacArthur a brigade of combat-ready Marines. MacArthur, who had learned the value of Marines in the South Pacific, immediately asked the JCS to assign the unit to his command. Even before the JCS received MacArthur's enthusiastic response, Cates had ordered the commanding general at Camp Pendleton to place the 1st Marine Division on alert for possible deployment.

On 2 August, Brig. Gen. Edward A. Craig's 1st Provisional Marine Brigade marched ashore at Pusan, on the southeastern tip of the Korean peninsula. At the time of the Communist invasion, there were only 27,656 men serving in FMF units, but on 19 July 1950, President Truman authorized the call-up of the Marine Corps Reserve. Eventually, more than 35,000 men answered the call to the colors—many of them veterans of World War II.

Brig. Gen. Edward A. Craig (right) commanded the 1st Provisional Marine Brigade in the Pusan perimeter and then served as assistant division commander of the 1st Marine Division. Here he is seen conferring with Col. Chesty Puller outside Seoul following the Inchon invasion. (National Archives)

In Korea, the events of the intervening month had been little less than catastrophic. Three understrength U.S. Army divisions, hurriedly deployed from occupation duty in Japan, displayed the effects of soft living. Without mines and effective antitank weapons, the poorly trained GI's barely managed to slow the Communist advance. By the end of July, however, U.S. forces (now organized as the Eighth Army, under the command of Lt. Gen. Walton H. Walker) had established a leaky perimeter around Pusan. Another American division had entered the lines since the invasion, increasing the Army total to four. The Eighth Army also included five ROK divisions, but these lacked the heavy armaments to stand up against the North Korean divisions hammering Walker's thinly held fifty-mile front.

The Marine brigade was built around Lt. Col. Raymond C. Murray's 5th Marines, a single battalion of artillery from the 11th Marines, and Brig. Gen. Thomas J. Cushman's MAG-33. The lean and determined Craig, who had once served as an aide-de-camp to John A. Lejeune, laid out the parameters of the desperate situation to his troops in no uncertain terms just prior to departing from California: "It has been necessary for troops now fighting in Korea to pull back at times, but I am stating now that no unit in the brigade will retreat except on orders from an authority higher than the 1st Marine Brigade. You will never receive an order to retreat from me."

Craig's 6,534 cocksure Leathernecks exuded a confidence not shared by senior Army officers and officials within the Department of Defense, but the Leathernecks surprised their enemy. Used to confronting the dispirited ranks of the ROK Army or the out-of-shape troops in the American Army divisions deployed hurriedly from Japan, the invaders found to their alarm and dismay that the Marines fought and fought well. Marines were easy to distinguish on the battlefield because, unlike the other forces in the United Nations command, the Marines wore camouflaged covers on their helmets and leggings instead of high-top boots. More importantly, they refused to give ground no matter the odds, and they always carried their dead and wounded from the battlefield. A British liaison officer in Pusan observed the small force of Marines—still carrying the weapons and equipment of World War II—and recorded a glimmer of optimism: "If Miryang is lost, Taegu becomes untenable and we will be faced with a withdrawal from Korea. I am heartened that the Marine Brigade will move against the Naktong salient tomorrow. These Marines have the swagger, confidence, and hardness that must have been in Stonewall Jackson's Army of the Shenandoah. They remind me of the Coldstreams at Dunkerque. Upon this thin line of reasoning, I cling to the hope of victory."

Ground troops were not the Corps' only contribution to the struggle. Marine aviators sailed from San Diego on 12 July. MAG-33 began the transit across the Pacific in the escort carrier *Badoeng Strait*. When Craig's brigade landed at Pusan, VMF-214 began flight operations from the carrier. One of the first helicopter rescues of the war occurred within a week. First Lt. Gustave F. Lueddeke picked up Capt. Vivian M. Moses of VMF-323 after enemy ground fire downed

the latter's Corsair. The dauntless Moses volunteered for another mission the following day and was again shot down. This time, he drowned in a rice paddy after being thrown from his aircraft. MAG 33 flew 1,511 sorties while deployed in the Pusan area, 995 of them in support of ground troops. An Army officer, envious of the close air support enjoyed by the Marines, remarked that "we have to have air support like that or we might as well disband the infantry and join the Marines."

On the day the Marines landed, North Korean attacks threatened to break through the southern sector of the Pusan perimeter. Many commanders feared the fall of Pusan and an American Dunkirk. On 3 August, the Marine brigade was attached to the 25th Infantry Division as part of Task Force Kean, replacing the badly mauled 24th Infantry Division at the southern

end of the perimeter. Walker hoped that with the support of the Marines he could launch the first UN offensive of the war, break the back of the North Korean 6th Division, and retake Chinju. Walker ordered the Leathernecks to seize the enemy-held ridges near Chindong and advance south to Kosong and west to Sachon until they reached Chinju. Although the reductions in manpower following World War II had left Craig's battalions with only two rifle companies and a weapons company, 65 percent of his NCOs and officers were veterans of the war against Japan.

The UN offensive went amiss almost from the beginning as uncoordinated Army and Marine units became lost and attacked the wrong objectives. North Korean soldiers, infiltrating the columns of refugees, snarled the lines of communications. Hundred-degree-plus temperatures felled many of the unacclimated U.S. troops. The first success for the Leathernecks came on 11 August when the artillerymen of 1/11 blasted a convoy of the North Korean 83rd Motorized Rifle Regiment. Marine Corsairs strafed the enemy as they attempted to flee. Although the Marines were diverted to counter a new crisis before reaching Sachon, they had blunted the enemy's assault on the southern face of the perimeter. Intense combat continued through the remainder of a scorching August. Once again, Craig's Marines prevented a North Korean breakthrough across the Naktong. Reluctantly, on 4 September, Walker released the brigade to MacArthur, who had plans of his own for it. In thirty-eight days of fighting, the token force of Leathernecks had inflicted

more than 10,000 casualties on the invaders while suffering only 902 of their own (172 killed, none captured).

Meanwhile, the Corps came under attack from a new quarter. On 29 August, in reply to a letter from a congressman urging that the commandant should be included in the JCS, President Truman wrote: "For your information the Marine Corps is the Navy's police force and as long as I am President that is what it will remain. They have a propaganda machine that is almost equal to Stalin's." Both letters appeared in the newspapers on 5 September. The furor they provoked was so great that the next day Truman tendered two handsome apologies, the first in a letter to the commandant and the second in a personal appearance at the annual convention of the Marine Corps League. "I sincerely regret the unfortunate choice of language . . . in my letter of 29 August," the president told General Cates. "I am profoundly aware of the magnificent history of the United States Marine Corps."

A new chapter was about to be added to that history. From the opening days of the war, MacArthur had been convinced that an amphibious landing behind the Communist front would turn the tide of battle in favor of the UN forces. MacArthur reasoned that an amphibious assault at Inchon, the port city of Seoul, would cut the supply lines to the enemy forces besieging the Pusan perimeter and liberate the South Korean capital and its important airfield at Kimpo. Only twenty-five miles from Seoul, the seaport was part of the vital network connecting the capital and the airfield with the road and rail system across the Han River.

Left: Leatherneck flight crews load rockets onto the Corsairs of VMF-323 aboard the *Badoeng Strait* off the west coast of Korea in September 1950. The escort carrier supported the Inchon invasion. (National Archives)

Bottom Right: The exhaustion of a rifle company commander, Capt. Francis I. "Ike" Fenton, during a period of intense combat along the Naktong was recorded by David Douglas Duncan, one of the great photographers of the twentieth century and himself a Marine veteran of World War II. At the time the photograph was taken, more than half of Fenton's men had been killed or wounded and the remainder were running out of ammunition. The company held its position. (Copyright David Douglas Duncan. Harry Ransom Humanities Research Center, The University of Texas at Austin.)

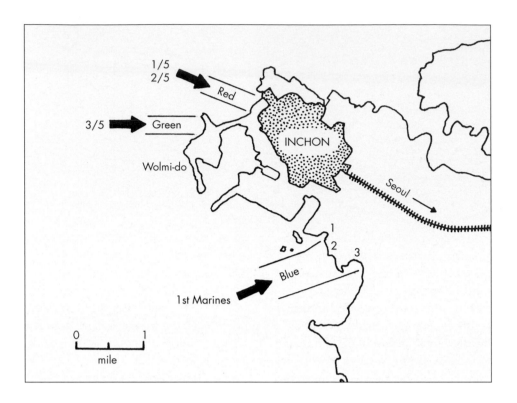

Map 25, Left: The Inchon Invasion, 14 September 1950

Right: Navy combat artist Herbert C. Hahn's meticulous panorama, *Inchon*, shows the evening assault. At center, landing craft converge on Red Beach. The tip of Wolmi-do, with five LSTs drawn up on Green Beach, appears at right. In the background are the causeway connecting the island to Inchon and palls of smoke rising over the city. Destroyers firing in support of the landing and an LST stand offshore. (Navy Art Collection)

MacArthur's intelligence officers estimated that the North Korean garrisons in the area consisted of only 2,200 second-rate troops, and 21,500 better-trained and equipped soldiers around Seoul.

Few persons outside his staff shared MacArthur's enthusiasm. Inchon offered an assortment of an amphibian's worst nightmares: a narrow channel that was easily mined and twisted its way through extensive mud flats; a high sea wall; an island (Wolmi-do) blocking the harbor entrance; and the most extreme tidal range in the world—thirty-two feet. Because of the tidal conditions, there was only one day during the month of September—the fifteenth—on which an amphibious assault was remotely feasible. To add a final complicating factor, MacArthur's planners concluded that Wolmi-do would have to be secured before a landing could be made at Inchon itself, and that both operations could not be carried out on the same tide. This meant that more than eleven hours must elapse between the attack on Wolmi-do, made on the morning tide, and the landing at Inchon, which would go in on the evening tide, with just ninety-nine minutes of daylight remaining.

Faced with these daunting circumstances, MacArthur chose to gamble on the element of surprise. In the end, he had to exploit his enormous prestige and formidable rhetorical skills to persuade the Joint Chiefs to approve the operation. "We shall land at Inchon," he intoned in his characteristically majestic manner, "and I shall crush them!" Even then, the most that dubious Navy and Marine commanders would concede was that the invasion was "not impossible."

With the support of Shepherd, then commanding FMFPac, MacArthur asked for the 1st Marine Division for the task. The Joint Chiefs approved his request; the 1st and 7th Marines received orders to deploy to South Korea with sufficient replacements and attachments to build up the division to a strength of more than twenty-four thousand men. Whereas the 5th Marines had been manned by FMF troops in the skeletonized units already at Camp Pendleton when the conflict broke out, the 1st Marines were filled out by scouring posts and stations worldwide. To constitute the division's third infantry regiment, the 7th Marines, HQMC ordered almost the entire 6th Marines from Camp Lejeune to the West Coast. Units simply

exchanged designations and colors. BLT 3/6, on duty with the Sixth Fleet, steamed directly from the Mediterranean to become 3/7 in Korea. Unfortunately, the 7th Marines did not arrive in time for Operation Chromite—the invasion of Inchon—and only marched ashore to join the 1st Marine Division on 21 September 1950. Maj. Gen. O. P. Smith, a lean, white-haired fifty-six-year-old, commanded.

Many of the Leathernecks came armed with World War II combat experience. Decades later Brig. Gen. Edwin H. Simmons, a regular officer then commanding a company of the 1st Marines, recalled that "from a tactical point of view, it was the best division I ever served in. The quality of the men was superb." Chesty Puller, Simmons' regimental commander, added a rousing postscript to the briefing his officers received on the upcoming operation. "You young people are lucky," he growled. "We used to have to wait every ten or fifteen years for a war. You get one every five years! You people have been living by the sword. By God, you better be ready to die by it!"

MacArthur assigned the 1st Marine Division, along with the 7th Infantry Division, to X Corps, to be commanded his chief of staff, Maj. Gen. Edward M. Almond, USA. More than one Leatherneck questioned MacArthur's choice of a commander when he could have employed the more experienced Shepherd. Senior Marines suggested that the decision was yet another example of Army–Marine Corps rivalry.

To support the operation, the 1st Marine Air Wing left El Toro, California, on 1 September with MAG-12 (three squadrons of aircraft). By the time of the landing, there were six aircraft carriers off the west coast of Korea, and some of them contained squadrons of Marine aircraft. On the first day of Operation Chromite, the Corsairs of VMF-323 and VMF-214 hit the island of Wolmi-do. At 0630 on 15 September, Lt. Col.

Robert D. Taplett's 3/5 stormed ashore on the island. The surprised enemy offered little opposition. As Taplett's Marines advanced to the high ground, they shot down scattered North Korean troops and collected dazed and deafened prisoners. Grenades and satchel charges quickly reduced the lightly manned caves and pillboxes. Less than sixty minutes after H-hour, a Marine from Company G raised a flag from a shattered tree stump atop the island's highest hill. Taplett declared the island secured at 1100 and requested permission to strike down the causeway connecting Wolmi-do with Inchon. Smith declined the aggressive Taplett's offer because the remainder of the division was still aboard ship waiting for the evening high tide.

Aboard the flagship *Mount McKinley*, MacArthur saw the flag go up over Wolmi-do. To the officers around him on the bridge, he said, "That's it. Let's get a cup of coffee." To the fleet, he radioed: "The Navy and Marines have never shown more brightly than this morning." Taplett's Leathernecks counted 180 dead North Koreans, estimated that another 100 lay entombed in caves and bunkers, and displayed 136 dejected captives. Not a single Marine had been killed and only 18 were wounded.

Late that afternoon, Murray and the remaining two battalions of his 5th Marines landed over Red Beach, a stretch of seawall located squarely on the Inchon waterfront. Puller's 1st Marines came ashore on Blue Beach, three miles south of the downtown area, in hopes of encircling the port district. As the Leathernecks stormed ashore, fires from the old Asahi Brewery, railroad yards, and factories on the outskirts of the city lit the sky.

Left: The moment General MacArthur saw the Stars and Stripes that 3/5 raised over Wolmi-do, shown in this photograph, he was certain that the Inchon invasion was a success. (National Archives)

Top Right: After 3/5 secured Wolmi-do early on D-day, the remainder of the 5th Marines came ashore on Red Beach in the late afternoon when the high tide returned. They are shown here scrambling up scaling ladders and over the sea wall into Inchon. (National Archives)

Bottom Right: Amtracs carry Chesty Puller's 1st Marines toward Blue Beach at Inchon. (National Archives)

Although a handful of North Koreans from the 226th Rifle Regiment offered a short, sharp fight, most of the enemy on the high ground surrounding Inchon opted to surrender. By D+1 (16 September), the Leathernecks had punched through the outskirts of Inchon and left the mopping up to ROK marines. The North Korean command's decision to commit only a single infantry regiment to the defense of Inchon allowed MacArthur to take the port cheaply. Allied losses on D-day numbered only 22 dead and 174 wounded; the following day saw only 3 dead and 21 wounded. On 18 September, soldiers of the 7th Infantry Division filed ashore, followed by the 7th Marines.

Smith ordered Murray's 5th Marines to seize Kimpo airfield, then cross the Han River and march up its right bank to Seoul. Puller's 1st Marines were to punch straight up the Seoul-Inchon highway, seize Yongdungpo on the Han opposite Seoul, and ford the river to link up with the 5th Marines entering Seoul from the north. While waiting to jump off, the Leathernecks of 1st Lt. H. J. "Hog Jaw" Smith's Company D spotted six T-34 tanks approaching their lines accompanied by an estimated two hundred enemy soldiers. Waiting until the enemy had closed to point-

blank range, the Marines fired every weapon at their disposal at once. Five accompanying M26 Pershing tanks contributed to the carnage. In seconds, all of the T-34s began to burn and the corpses of North Korean infantry littered the road. Eight Corsairs of VMF-214 inundated another file of T-34s with napalm. The first round of the battle of Seoul had gone to the UN forces, spearheaded by Marines.

In the following days, the battle toughened. Although the North Koreans had lightly garrisoned the capital city with headquarters and service troops, thousands of seasoned soldiers besieging the Pusan perimeter hurried to meet the assault on their rear. With their arrival, North Korean strength around Seoul approached that of the invasion force. Nevertheless, the enemy proved unable to organize an effective defense of the capital. Kimpo airfield and Yongdungpo fell to the Leathernecks. Assaulting Marines found only two under-strength and demoralized North Korean regiments defending the airfield. Most enemy soldiers had been issued white civilian clothing so that they could meld easily into the civilian noncombatants clogging the roads to the south.

MAG-33 occupied the airfield on 19 September. Between 7 September and 9 October, four Leatherneck F4U squadrons—two flying from carriers and two operating out of Kimpo—flew 2,163 sorties in support of X Corps. VMF[N]-542 flew another 573 deadly nighttime bombing missions.

Puller's 1st Marines found themselves tangling with a regiment of the North Korean 18th Division. The fracas ended in a wild fight between Capt. Robert H. Barrow's Company A and at least a battalion of enemy troops. Barrow, a future commandant, dug his men in beside a dike on Yongdungpo's riverfront. At 2100 on 21 September, the North Koreans attacked behind five T-34 tanks. As the tanks rumbled up the street parallel to the dike, Barrow's Marines replied coolly with 3.5-inch rocket fire to stall the advance. The riflemen of Company A, fighting from deep holes, drove back five separate enemy attacks during the night; before dawn, the enemy force abandoned its assault. Barrow's Marines counted 310 dead North Koreans.

On 24 September the battle for Seoul began in earnest. The 1st Marines crossed the Han in amtracs to join Murray's 5th Marines in the struggle for the capital. By then, the 5th Marines had reduced the crack North

Korean 25th Brigade to near impotence. The commander of Murray's Company I, Capt. Robert A. McMullen, suffered his seventh wound in two wars. Puller added to his personal legend, appearing wherever the fighting was fiercest with his trademark pipe clenched between his teeth and a crumpled utility cap on his head (he disliked wearing a helmet). A corporal recalled that "whenever he saw a Marine walking away from the front, whether for ammo or to an aid station or whatnot, Puller would frown at him with a hard, unfriendly stare. When he saw one of us going toward the front, for any reason, he'd wave and smile and call, 'How things doin', old man?'"

By 27 September American flags fluttered from many of Seoul's shattered buildings. North Korean defenders began an abrupt withdrawal from the city, pursued by Col. Homer L. Litzenberg's 7th Marines, who had circled around the capital from the north. Litzenberg's seizure of Uijongbu on 3 October marked the end of the Inchon-Seoul campaign, a masterstroke of amphibious strategy costing fewer than two thousand Leatherneck casualties.

During the same period, the Eighth Army broke out of the Pusan Perimeter and drove

Left: Marines spring from their landing craft, and an LST beaches herself at Inchon on D-day, 15 September 1950. (National Archives)

Right: Marine tanks and South Korean forces, apparently including armed civilians, round up North Korean troops in Seoul on 26 September 1950. (National Archives)

north. On 26 September, the 1st Cavalry Division, leading the advance from the south, linked up with elements of X Corps at Osan, thirty miles below Seoul. By the beginning of October, the UN command had taken more than 125,000 prisoners; eight of the approximately fourteen enemy divisions in South Korea had been destroyed, and the others were fleeing north in disorder. As an effective fighting force, the North Korean Army had ceased to exist. To the surprise of senior Marine commanders, MacArthur did not order the Leathernecks to rejoin the main body of UN forces following the amphibious landing at Inchon; he had another mission for them.

On 1 October, two days before withdrawing the 1st Marine Division from combat, MacArthur called on all North Korean forces to surrender unconditionally. On the day of his appeal, two events transpired that augured grave consequences for the conduct of the war: the South Korean 3rd Infantry Division crossed the 38th Parallel into North Korea, a penetration authorized by President Truman and the JCS; and Communist China's premier, Chou En-lai, warned that "the Chinese people would not

supinely tolerate . . . seeing North Korea savagely invaded by the imperialists." Earlier, Chou had told India's ambassador that if U.S. troops crossed the 38th Parallel, China would enter the war. In the aftermath of victory at Inchon, however, no one took the threat of Chinese intervention seriously. With the enemy on the ropes, American policy makers became beguiled by the possibility of seizing the moment to do more than merely defend South Korea.

A new and more ambitious aim became official on 7 October, when the UN General Assembly adopted a U.S.-sponsored resolution establishing the objective of reunifying the entire Korean peninsula under an "independent and democratic government." Thus MacArthur eyed the Yalu River, the boundary between North Korea and the Chinese province of Manchuria, as the limit of advance for UN forces. Ignoring the warnings from Communist China, MacArthur ordered the 1st ROK Corps, 1st Cavalry and 24th Infantry Divisions, and the British Commonwealth Brigade to advance up the east side of Korea and across the 38th Parallel. The ROK II Corps maneuvered in the center of the peninsula while the ROK

Capital and 3rd Divisions advanced along the west coast. At the same time, MacArthur sought a repeat of his success at Inchon.

MacArthur's strategy called for Smith to reassemble the 1st Marine Division at Inchon by 7 October, then travel by Navy transport around the Korean peninsula for a landing at Wonsan, North Korea's major port. Rapidly advancing ROK troops captured Wonsan just three days later, eliminating the need for an amphibious assault. MAG-12 moved from Kimpo to Wonsan and began flight operations immediately. After waiting on board their transports while the Navy cleared the harbor of mines, the Marines filed ashore on 26 October. Smith ordered the 1st Marines to clear the area around Wonsan of enemy stragglers and infiltrators. The 5th and 7th Marines began the drive north to Hamhung and Hungnam in preparation for the advance by UN troops to the Yalu. MacArthur envisioned an easy push to the border, with little opposition from the dispirited North Koreans.

Smith did not share MacArthur's optimism. The possibility of Chinese intervention worried the normally imperturbable Leatherneck. MacArthur's orders required the Marine division to advance inland from Hungnam north and west, traveling seventy-eight miles along a single road through narrow valleys between steep mountains to Yudam-ni near the Chosin Reservoir. From the reservoir, it was only seventy miles to the Chinese border. Tactically, MacArthur's plans made little sense. Advancing in a column of infantry battalions along the mountainous road denied the Leathernecks the opportunity to maintain links with friendly units; nearly eighty miles of rugged terrain separated them from the soldiers of the Eighth Army to the west.

Litzenberg's 7th Marines led the column, followed by Murray's 5th Marines and Puller's 1st Marines. A savvy, hard-driving officer, Litzenberg ordered heavy patrols to scour the hilltops along his flanks. Marine Corsairs flew continuous cover for the regiment, and the battalion of 105-mm howitzers in support of the 1st Marines blasted the terrain to their front. On 1 November the 1st Cavalry Division encountered large numbers of Chinese troops in the Eighth Army's sector. The following day, Smith learned that an ROK division operating near Hamhung had reported taking several prisoners claiming to belong to the 124th Division of the Chinese People's Liberation Army. At midnight on 2 November, the forward companies of the 7th Marines made contact with elements of the 124th Division. Gen. Lin Pao, the veteran commander of China's Fourth Field Army, had deployed his Ninth Army Group, one hundred thousand troops organized in ten divisions, across the border from Manchuria.

The enemy attack began with bugle calls, green flares, and the screeching of whistles. Litzenberg's Marines held their ground and the Chinese left the field in disarray. Captured documents and the number of enemy dead—662 in front of one Leatherneck battalion alone—suggested that the Marines had mauled at least two of the three Chinese regiments that had attempted to stall the division's advance. Despite Smith's cautionary reports to X Corps headquarters, his orders to advance to the Yalu remained unchanged.

For the next five days, the 7th Marines fought through a series of strongpoints manned by the 124th Division along the way to the plateau on which lies the Chosin Reservoir. By 13 November, advanced elements of the Marine division had entered Hagaru-ri, a sizeable town at the southern end of the reservoir. Although Smith had not reached his objective, he ordered the 7th Marines to halt in the vicinity of Hagaru-ri until the 5th Marines joined them and Puller's 1st Marines could report the main supply route to the rear had been secured.

Despite the reports of Chinese units reaching his headquarters in Tokyo, Mac-Arthur refused to alter his plan for an advance to the Yalu. Earlier, he had opined that Communist forces could not or would not launch a counteroffensive; he even predicted victory by Christmas. MacArthur's unbridled optimism meant a further advance to the north for the weary column.

In mid-November, the weather grew increasingly colder. A piercing wind from the wastes of Siberia swept the four-thousand-foot-high Chosin Plateau. Streams iced over, as did the reservoir. Surgeons treating wounded men in frigid hospital tents were appalled to find that blood froze to their gloves. On 23 November, Smith sent the 5th

and 7th Marines forward to Yudam-ni. Both regiments made the fourteen-mile trek in two days, fighting through lightly held Chinese roadblocks. On 27 November, the 5th Marines began the fifty-five-mile march from Yudam-ni to Mupyong-ni—the next leg of MacArthur's drive to the Yalu. A starless and moonless night engulfed the weary Marines as they shivered and ached in the −20 degree cold.

As the Leathernecks bedded down in a tight perimeter, dire news reached Smith's headquarters at Hagaru-ri. Units throughout the Eighth Army reported a major Chinese offensive in progress. Entire UN divisions had either halted or been forced to give ground; ominously, some units—notably, ROK outfits—had been routed and had fled the battlefield. On the night of 27–28 November, the Marine division came under attack all along the route from Chinhung-ni to the perimeter at Yudam-ni. "If they'd hit us with everything they had that first night," Murray recalled, "I don't think we could have killed them fast enough." By the morning of the twenty-eighth, the division found itself facing the prospect of annihilation.

The Marines confronted an estimated eight Chinese divisions. Moving under cover of darkness, the enemy had slipped

Left: Capt. William E. Barber (left) earned the Medal of Honor while commanding Company F, 7th Marines, in the defense of Toktong Pass. Lt. Col. Raymond G. Davis (right) earned the nation's highest award for heroism for leading 1/7 across the frozen hills of North Korea to break the Chinese siege of the vital pass. (*Leatherneck* [November 1990] and *Officer Review* [November 1998])

Right: David Douglas Duncan captured some of the most memorable images of the retreat from the Chosin Reservoir. Writing of this scene, he recalled the wind, "shrieking and wild," that swept out of Manchuria. "That wind was like nothing ever known by the trapped Marines, yet they had to march through it." (Copyright David Douglas Duncan. Harry Ransom Humanities Research Center, The University of Texas at Austin)

through the hills undetected to envelop the Marine main supply route. Chinese tactics stunned the UN forces. Usually Chinese units deployed in columns of battalions and rushed their opponent's lines in night attacks with utter disregard for their losses. Other than infantry mortars, the Chinese possessed few supporting arms. But Leatherneck artillery and close air support kept the Communists off the high ground to lessen the threat.

Smith understood all too well that his division held four separate perimeters from Chinhung-ni north to Yudam-ni. He ordered the 5th and 7th Marines to break out and join him at Hagaru-ri, after which the division would withdraw to Koto-ri and Chinhung-ni. Initially, the retreating regiments had to make their way through high, bitterly cold Toktong Pass halfway between Hagaru-ri and Yudam-ni. Litzenberg ordered Capt. William E. Barber's F/2/7 to guard the pass and prevent the Chinese from establishing a roadblock. Underscoring the gravity of the situation, he reinforced Company F with heavy machine guns and 81-mm mortars.

At 0230 on 28 November, a battalion of the Chinese 59th Division hurled itself at Barber's lonely outpost. Although the enemy troops overran three of its positions during the night, Company F still held the pass at daybreak. The Leathernecks had lost 20 men killed and 54 wounded, while an estimated 450 dead Chinese littered the terrain in front of them. Air drops provided munitions to keep the surrounded Marines going in the face of superior numbers. Hit in the hip on the second day of the assault, Barber, who had been decorated for heroism and wounded twice on Iwo Jima, commanded his company from a stretcher. His gallantry at Toktong Pass earned Barber the Medal of Honor.

The Marines felt the cold during the endless night, but the attacking Chinese—ill-clothed for winter weather and shod in sneakers—suffered far worse. Back in Yudam-ni, the 5th and 7th Marines faced a situation similar to Barber's. After attempts to shatter both regiments failed, the Chinese concentrated on holding the high ground in front of the Marines. On 30 November, Litzenberg and Murray decided to risk a breakout. Carrying their wounded and with their vehicles and artillery, the Marines began to fight their way down the fourteen miles of the main supply route across Toktong Pass to Hagaru-ri. Taplett's 3/5 led the advance and broke the encirclement by nightfall on 3 December. Meanwhile, Lt. Col. Raymond G. Davis' 1/7 began a desperate night march across the barren landscape toward Barber's

perimeter at Toktong Pass. At first light, an air strike and mortar fire cleared the way for 1/7 to join Barber's company in the pass; only 82 Leathernecks of the original 240 in F/2/7 could walk. Like Barber, Davis earned the Medal of Honor.

The squadrons of MAG-33 supported the beleaguered riflemen with air strikes from Wonsan and Yongpo, near Hungnam. VMF-214 and VMF-323, flying from Navy carriers, added to the power of the air–ground team. VMO-6 flew artillery-spotting missions. Parachute drops from Marine Corps and Air Force transports kept the weary columns supplied with food and ammunition: eight hundred thousand pounds at Hagaru-ri and more than a million at Koto-ri. Even boxes of PX goods came

fluttering down in the parachute drops; when the irrepressible Puller learned that one such parcel contained packages of condoms, he supposedly snarled: "What the hell do they think we're doing to these Chinese?"

With Toktong Pass relieved, the retreat could begin. The 5th and 7th Marines fought their way through the Chinese encirclement with Lt. Col. Harold S. Roise's 2/5 acting as rear guard. Finally, seventy-nine hours after setting out, units of Murray's 5th Marines reached the Hagaru-ri perimeter. The Leathernecks brought along all of their equipment, except for eight 155-mm howitzers abandoned after their diesel-powered prime movers ran out of fuel. The new arrivals joined a scratch force that had fought the two Chinese divisions to a

Left: Col. Charles Waterhouse's *The Chosin Few* evokes the cold and misery of the 1st Marine Division's epic attack from another direction in the frozen countryside surrounding the Chosin Reservoir. (Copyright Charles Waterhouse)

Right: Chesty Puller commanded the 1st Marines during the Chosin Reservoir campaign. Informed that his outfit was surrounded by Chinese troops at Koto-ri, he supposedly growled, "Fine, that will make it easier to kill them." (National Archives)

standstill. By the time the retreating Marines arrived, engineers had the Hagaru-ri airstrip in operation. Transport aircraft flew supplies and ammunition in and casualties out. More than three thousand disabled Marines left via the air pipeline, along with a thousand wounded and frostbitten soldiers from the 7th Infantry Division, which had been cut to pieces on the eastern side of the Chosin Reservoir.

The breakout of the two regiments from Yudam-ni buoyed Smith's confidence. He and his staff now began planning in earnest for the withdrawal of all Leathernecks from Hagaru-ri. Refusing to call the division's retrograde movement a retreat, Smith referred to the maneuver as an attack to the rear. Down the main supply route he intended to take the survivors of assorted Army units, ROK stragglers, and 235 Royal Marines of 41 Independent Commando. Smith waited two days before setting out, allowing the 5th and 7th Marines to rest and eat warm food. Five hundred replacements, many of them previously wounded men, returned from hospitals in Japan.

On the starry, bitterly cold night of 6 December, a Chinese division slammed into the 5th Marines at Hagaru-ri. Fire discipline and heavy use of supporting arms paid dividends; hundreds of Chinese fell in the worst slaughter of the Chosin Reservoir campaign. The next night, eight hundred Chinese soldiers jumped Maj. Francis Fox Parry's 3/11. Parry deployed his artillerymen as infantry to beat off the attack. When a second Chinese assault stalled his column, Parry's Marines unlimbered their howitzers and fired point-blank into the onrushing horde; the time-fuzed shells exploded as close

as forty-five yards in front of the guns. In another action that evening, a Chinese unit hit the division's command post. Headquarters Marines, walking alongside their vehicles, took the attackers under fire as a Corsair from VMF(N)-513 made strafing runs to within yards of the road. By then, the 7th Marines had reached Puller's perimeter at Koto-ri.

On 7 December, the 5th Marines set fire to all supplies and ammunition remaining at Hagaru-ri. Then they, too, joined the weary column marching away from the reservoir. The grim procession stretched for more than eleven miles. Six squadrons of Marine

Corsairs wheeling above the force made any Chinese attempt to interfere with it suicidal. More than ten thousand men and in excess of a thousand vehicles made it down the main supply route; Smith's commanders reported 7 missing Leathernecks and Bluejackets, 103 killed, and 506 wounded.

The 1st Marine Division, with assorted attachments and stragglers, now numbered over fourteen thousand men. Before the division pulled out of Koto-ri, General Shepherd flew in with the intention of accompanying it on its breakthrough to the sea, but Smith persuaded him not to add to the worry of having a three-star Marine killed or captured to all those he already carried. Chesty Puller put Maggie Higgins, the courageous woman war correspondent, on Shepherd's plane for the flight out, despite her protests—delivered with a vehement profanity that startled even the usually unflappable Puller—that she wanted to stay with the

troops. Smith then ordered the division on the road for the last leg of the withdrawal, through Funchilin Pass to the perimeter at Chinhung-ni, which was being held by Puller's 1st Battalion. Litzenberg's regiment moved out first and in two days of hard fighting narrowed the gap to just six miles. The two battalions with Puller at Koto-ri formed the rear guard. Their fifty-two-year-old colonel circulated among his men, encouraging young Leathernecks by his outrageous assurance: "You're the 1st Marine Division," he growled, "and don't you forget it. We're the greatest military outfit that ever walked on this earth. Not all the Communists in hell can stop you. We'll go down to the sea at our own pace and nothing is going to get in our way. If it does, we'll blow hell out of it." The 7th Marines took the point and fought its way south to the pass. Lt. Col. Donald M. Schmuck's 1/1 advanced from Chinhung-ni to seize Hill 1081 overlooking Funchilin Pass. A swirling snowstorm and −14 degree temperatures aided Schmuck's Leathernecks as they mounted Hill 1081 apparently unseen by the shivering Chinese and took the enemy bunkers in savage, hand-to-hand fighting.

By nightfall on 10 December, elements of the Marine division were flowing easily from Koto-ri to Chinhung-ni. The lack of serious opposition made it obvious that the Marines had bested the Chinese forces. American correspondents, waiting to interview the

arriving Marines, were astonished to learn that the Leathernecks had never doubted their ability to break out from the reservoir. In the early hours of 12 December, the Marines and stragglers boarded ships for Pusan.

The Chosin Campaign cost the Corps 4,418 casualties, including 718 dead. Not included in that number were those Leathernecks suffering from illness, frostbite, or intestinal problems caused by eating frozen C-rations. American intelligence estimates put Chinese losses at a staggering 37,500, with 25,000 killed—more than 50 percent of the troops engaged. Perhaps 35–40 percent of the enemy casualties resulted from the close air support furnished by Leatherneck Corsairs, close air support hitherto unequaled in warfare. The Leatherneck aviators offered a tuneful tribute to their faithful Corsairs:

> Up in Korea 'midst rocks, ice, and snow,
> The poor Chinese Commie is feeling
> so low,
> As our Corsairs roar by overhead,
> He knows that his buddies will all soon
> be dead.
>
> Lin Pao went way up to cold Koto-ri,
> His prize Chinese Army in action to see,
> He said that his soldiers no battle
> could lose,
> But all that he found was their hats
> and their shoes.

O. P. Smith deserved all of the praise heaped on him. Unlike the overly confidant MacArthur and his fawning subordinates, Smith foresaw what might happen and endeavored all along to be ready for the

Left: Weary Marines gather the bodies of other American Marines, British Royal Marines, and U.S. Army and Republic of Korea troops for a mass burial at Koto-ri, 8 December 1950. (National Archives)

Bottom Right: David Douglas Duncan took this photograph on 9 December 1950 with the thermometer reading 40 degrees below zero. When Duncan asked this half-frozen young Leatherneck what he wanted if he could have any wish, the Marine replied, "Just give me tomorrow." (Copyright David Douglas Duncan. Harry Ransom Humanities Research Center, The University of Texas at Austin)

worst, even while obeying orders with which he disagreed. By smashing the Chinese Ninth Army Group, the resourceful Marine had saved not only his division but also the port of Hungnam and probably the entire X Corps. The Marines had destroyed no less than seven Chinese divisions. Marching out of the Chosin Reservoir in the swirling snow of a subzero North Asian winter, the half-frozen Leathernecks gave their fellow UN troops and the American people a badly need morale boost. Chesty Puller emerged with his fifth Navy Cross—the greatest number ever awarded to a single individual—and his first star, although he had been selected for promotion to brigadier general before the Chosin campaign.

Christmas Day 1950 found the 1st Marine Division at Pusan, bivouacked in the same bean patch where the 1st Provisional Brigade had encamped six months before. There, the Leathernecks—ostensibly in reserve for the Eighth Army—thawed, showered, and removed the lice from their clothing. Thirty-four hundred replacements swelled the division's ranks. By then, U.S. war aims had come full circle. No longer did Washington policy makers dream of unifying Korea under a pro-Western government. From now on, the fight would continue simply to preserve the prewar status quo.

On New Year's Day 1951, Chinese forces launched their second major offensive of the war. Twenty-one Chinese and twelve North Korean divisions struck south. Several ROK divisions were overrun, and Seoul fell on 4 January. The Eighth Army's new commander, Gen. Matthew B. Ridgway—Walker having died in a jeep wreck on 23 December—placed his troops along a defense line running from Pyongtaek to Wonju. Ridgway ordered Smith's Marines—bolstered by another eighteen hundred replacements—to deal with North Korean guerrillas operating behind his lines, harrying a triangular area on the east coast between Pohang, Andong, and Yongdok. While UN forces engaged in pitched battles against the Chinese and North Korean troops farther to the north, the Leathernecks patrolled rice paddies and hunted down small bands of Communist irregulars.

Grimmer work began anew on 11 February 1951, when Ridgway attached the 1st Marine Division to Maj. Gen. Bryant E. Moore's IX Corps in the center of the peninsula. Ten days later the Leathernecks jumped off as part of two successive operations Ridgway dubbed "Killer" and "Ripper." This time, the UN command sought not to gain ground in the north but to expel Chinese forces from South Korea. Ridgway hoped to force the Communist armies to mass, thus making them easy targets for artillery and air strikes. Instead, the Chinese withdrew slowly in front of the Marines for the next four weeks. Rough terrain and wet weather gave the Leathernecks their greatest problem. By 14 March, the 1st Marine Division had driven past Hoengsong and now brushed up against an enemy hill defense replete with bunkers. By then, UN forces had outflanked the Communists, recapturing Seoul that same day.

Still determined, Communist forces organized for a new offensive that the UN command expected in the so-called Iron Triangle between Chorawon, Pyonggang,

and Kumhwa. In anticipation of the enemy offensive, Ridgeway ordered the Marines to advance to a new phase line, "Kansas," above the 38th Parallel. On 8 April the 7th Marines—now commanded by Col. Herman R. Nickerson Jr.—was among the first of the Eighth Army units to recross the 38th Parallel. Three days later, the simmering conflict between Truman and MacArthur reached a dramatic climax when the president relieved the general as UN Commander and replaced him with Ridgway. Lt. Gen. James A. Van Fleet assumed command of the Eighth Army.

By late April, the Marine division had fought its way north to the Hwachon Reservoir, just above the 38th Parallel. On the night of 22–23 April, the Chinese counterattacked. A human torrent poured over the ROK division on the left of the Marines. Within minutes the South Korean

lines broke as terrified soldiers fled south, leaving a ten-mile-wide gap in the Eighth Army's front. At daybreak Chinese troops were surging past the Marine division's dangling flank. To divert the tide General Smith committed his division reserve, the 1st Marine Regiment, and deployed the 7th Marines to form a new front angling back to the left rear. On the other side of the gap, the U.S. 24th Infantry Division reacted in similar fashion, refusing and reinforcing its right flank. With the Eighth Army's entire line under heavy attack, however, Van Fleet directed both units to fall back. Meanwhile, American and British forces took position to stem the advance of the Chinese who had moved through the gap, and in a few days a firm new front was established twenty miles below the old line. On 26 April, the crisis past, Smith relinquished command of the

Landing Zone, Korea, by Col. H. Avery Chenoweth, USMCR (Ret.), depicts HRS-1 helicopters of HMR-161 ferrying Marines to the front. The artist served as an infantry platoon leader in Korea in 1951. (Marine Corps Art Collection)

division to Maj. Gen. Gerald C. Thomas, a distinguished Leatherneck who had worn forest green since World War I. Chesty Puller rotated home in May. Korea was Puller's last war. He retired a lieutenant general in 1955.

The beginning of June found the 1st Marine Division approaching the Yanggu and the Soyang river valley. Chinese forces occupied the series of ridges overlooking the large valley, named the "Punchbowl" by the Leathernecks. Hill 1316, a sizeable enemy ammunition and supply center, lay directly to its front. The terrain dominated the Iron Triangle, the Communist ammunition and supply center, and Thomas expected a hard fight. Reinforced with the ROK 1st Marine Regiment, the division hammered at the approaches of Hill 1316 and the southern rim of the Punchbowl in an offensive that took most of June but denied the area to the enemy. For the next six months, Communist forces attempted in vain to retake the contested ground.

Chinese and North Korean losses in the first year of the war stunned leaders in both nations, and on 10 July 1951 cease-fire talks began; they would drag on for two long years. From the outset, the Communists appeared unwilling to bargain in good faith. In a bid to apply military pressure at the bargaining table, General Van Fleet ordered the Marines back into the line on 27 August. This time, the Leathernecks prepared to seize the enemy-held hills on the north side of the Punchbowl. In contrast to the earlier stages of the conflict, Communist forces now appeared on the battlefield supplied with ample artillery, mortars, machine guns, and ammunition. More ominously for the Leathernecks, much

of their Marine close air support disappeared. The Air Force demanded and obtained operational control of all fixed-wing aircraft in the theater, with the result that Marine riflemen on the ground received less support. On 20 September Van Fleet called a halt to the offensive, concluding that casualties were running too high. Nevertheless, the Leathernecks held the northern rim of the Punchbowl.

In that same month, Helicopter Transport Squadron (HMR)-161 arrived with the new Sikorsky HRS-1 helicopter, a five-passenger craft with a top speed of ninety knots. HMR-161 demonstrated its utility on 13 September by transporting 18,848 pounds of rations to infantry battalions on the forward edge of the battle area and evacuating seventy-four wounded men on the return trip. A few days later, HMR-161 transported the entire divisional reconnaissance company to the top of Hill 884. Old-timers scoffed, but a Marine who did not have to climb a thousand feet with a full pack arrived fresh and ready to fight. The hopes that the Corps' prewar planners had pinned on the helicopter had not been misplaced.

After September 1951, the war in Korea settled into a positional conflict reminiscent of World War I. Leathernecks and UN soldiers constructed bunkers on the reverse slopes of the steep hills while Communist forces dug tunnels into the hillsides. Patrol actions and small attacks dominated the next twenty-two months. While not as intensive as the opening phases of the war, these months accounted for 40 percent of the division's total casualties. Thomas did what he could to relieve the boredom of the outpost war.

On 10 November 1951, at exactly noon, he ordered every weapon in the division—from rifle to heavy artillery—to fire a single round in one tremendous thunderclap to celebrate the Marine Corps' birthday.

On 23 March 1952, the division—now commanded by Maj. Gen. John T. Selden—moved from the Punchbowl area to a stretch of front along Korea's west coast. Its mission was to defend the vital corridor to Seoul, Kimpo, and Inchon. Between 26 and 29 March, the Chinese made one last, desperate attempt to take a series of Marine outposts called Carson, Reno, and Vegas. These names were inspired by the realization that holding the positions would be a gamble, which proved the case. Though Carson breasted the enemy tide, the Chinese overran the other two outposts. Lew Walt's 5th Marines quickly recovered Vegas, but Reno remained in Communist hands. By the time the fighting died down, Marine casualties totaled 1,015 men; Chinese losses were estimated to be twice that number.

Aerial combat, pitting Leathernecks against Communist pilots, occurred only infrequently. The first encounter took place on 21 April 1951 when two aviators of VMF-312 flying from the *Bataan*, Capt. Phillip C. DeLong and 1st Lt. Harold Daigh, were jumped by four North Korean Yaks. Daigh shot down one enemy aircraft immediately while DeLong—a World War II ace with eleven kills—destroyed two others. Daigh damaged the fourth Yak, sending it limping home. A little more than six months later, on 4 November 1951, Capt. William F. Guss, a Marine aviator flying an F-86 Sabrejet on exchange duty with the U.S. Air Force,

downed the first of twenty-six MiGs that would fall to Leathernecks in the course of the war. The Corps' only ace of the Korean War, Maj. John F. "Handsome Jack" Bolt Jr., downed six MiG-15s between May and July 1953 while on exchange duty with the 51st Fighter Interceptor Wing. Two other Marines flying with the Air Force each scored three confirmed victories: Maj. Alexander J. Gillis and Maj. John H. Glenn, the latter of whom would gain celebrity as America's first astronaut. Another Leatherneck pilot was already a celebrity: thirty-four-year-old reserve Capt. Ted Williams, the Boston Red Sox baseball star. Recalled to active duty in 1952, Williams flew thirty-nine combat missions in the same squadron as Glenn.

Joseph Stalin's death on 5 March 1953 probably encouraged Communist China to end a conflict it knew it could not win. The incoming Eisenhower administration's thinly veiled threats to go nuclear also appear to have influenced enemy thinking. The war ended with the signing of a truce—not a peace—at Panmunjon on 27 July 1953. By that date, 4,267 Marines had lost their lives in Korea, and another 21,744 suffered wounds—twice the total for World War I. These figures represented approximately 18 percent of the overall total of 136,913 American casualties. Forty-two Leathernecks earned the Medal of Honor—26 of them posthumously. Only 227 Marines were captured out of a total of 7,190 U.S. personnel, a ratio of 1:570 versus 1:150 for the U.S. Army. Leathernecks in captivity demonstrated an 87 percent survival rate versus 62 percent for American soldiers. The 1st MAW pilots flew 127,496 sorties and lost 436 aircraft. Army and Air Force partisans opposing the Corps as a separate service or with a combined arms capability had to admit that the Marine performance in Korea—both ground and air units—had been far superior to that of the Eighth Army and X Corps. In Korea, the Marines could not claim to have been among the "first to fight," but few could dispute their claim to have been "the best." Hanson Baldwin's terse comment in one of his columns for the *New York Times* spoke reams about Marine Corps esprit and professionalism: "The Marines were ready."

CHAPTER 13

The Vietnam War, 1954–1975

A s the war in Korea ground to its unsatisfactory conclusion, the Marine Corps faced cuts in both manpower and dollars. President Truman's budget for Fiscal Year '54 called for a reduction in the number of Leathernecks from 248,000 to 225,000. The following year, the administration of President Dwight D. Eisenhower reduced the size of the Corps even further to 205,000 men and women. In January 1952 the 3rd Marine Division was activated at Camp Pendleton, and in August 1953 it deployed to Japan as a strategic reserve for the winding down of the Korean War. In 1955 the 1st Marine Division left Korea and returned to Camp Pendleton while the 1st MAW deployed to Japan. An infantry regiment left the 3rd Marine Division when it redeployed to Okinawa and became the main component of the 1st Marine Brigade at Kaneoe Bay, Hawaii. The 2nd Marine Division remained at Camp Lejeune, North Carolina, where it had been since the end of World War II.

On 31 December 1955 General Shepherd retired. The Eisenhower administration accepted his recommendation for a successor: Randolph McCall Pate, fourth in seniority among the Marine lieutenant generals. Lacking the extensive combat command experience of his immediate predecessors, Pate brought a new style of leadership and executive management to the Corps' highest post; in the process, he created more controversy than the Marine Corps had experienced since the ouster of Maj. Gen. Commandant George Barnett in 1920.

When Eisenhower's secretary of defense, Charles E. Wilson, decreed that all officers serving in the Washington area would work in mufti, Pate—a traditionalist—embellished the edict by requiring his officers to wear a hat. The new commandant made such anachronisms as swagger sticks almost mandatory for all officers and senior NCOs. Many officers close to Pate suggested that he suffered from mental lapses that affected his judgment. Nevertheless, Pate survived a serious controversy surrounding a tragedy involving the Corps' time-honored method of recruit training.

Leatherneck élan during the Korean War remained in the memories of most citizens in the mid-1950s. But a tragedy at Parris Island cast a pall of gloom over the Corps' leadership and the tradition of tough military

Opposite: This propaganda poster typified the optimism prevalent during the early years of the deployment of U.S. forces in Vietnam. It exhorts the citizenry to stand up to the Communists, and reads: "The Viet Cong must leave South Vietnam." (Marine Corps Art Collection)

M. Shoup, who had earned the Medal of Honor at Tarawa, as the Corps' twenty-first commandant.

Shoup's highest priority was increasing the combat readiness of the FMF. While this was a goal with which all Marines could agree, the new commandant's often abrasive manner and impatience with what he considered outmoded traditions—swagger sticks, for one—raised many hackles, especially among the Corps' old guard. Years later Col. Robert D. Heinl Jr. blustered to one of the authors of this book that "Shoup was Eisenhower's way of getting even with the Marine Corps." During the Shoup era, the Navy reconfigured the escort carriers *Boxer* and *Princeton* as amphibious assault ships (LPHs), and construction began on a new class of LPH with the *Iwo Jima*. The trusty M1 rifle was replaced by the M14, which fired the standard 7.62 NATO cartridges. Because one in four of the new M14 rifles contained a feature allowing fully automatic fire, the Browning Automatic Rifle went to the surplus pile. A new machine gun, the M60, replaced the .30 caliber of World War II and Korean War vintage. His critics notwithstanding, Shoup could take credit for overseeing the entire replacement of the Corps' arsenal of infantry weaponry; it would not happen again for another three decades.

In late 1962, intelligence reports revealing the construction of missile sites in Cuba brought the United States and the Soviet Union dangerously close to nuclear war. During the crisis, units from the 2nd Marine Division reinforced the naval base at Guantánamo Bay to near regimental strength. The remainder of the division sortied at sea between Florida and Cuba, the 2nd MAW deployed to Florida and Puerto Rico, and the 5th MEB steamed from Southern California to join the gigantic armada in the Caribbean. Army units moved to southern ports in anticipation of an invasion of Cuba. As tensions heightened, President John F. Kennedy's firm resolve forced the Soviet leadership to remove the offensive missiles from Cuba.

On 1 January 1964 Wallace M. Greene Jr., a graduate of the Naval Academy Class of 1930, succeeded Shoup as commandant. Greene had earned a reputation as a polished, proficient, hard-working officer whose extensive staff service made him well qualified to uphold the Corps' interests in the tumult of interservice rivalries. More of an internationalist than his predecessor, Greene did not share Shoup's misgivings over U.S. involvement in trouble spots worldwide.

In April 1965 disputing factions in the presidential elections in the Dominican Republic appeared to threaten U.S. lives and property. Learning that opponents of the elected government had taken control of Santo Domingo, President Lyndon B. Johnson ordered U.S. troops into the capital city. Clearly, Johnson feared that another Cuban-style Communist dictatorship might be about to emerge in the Caribbean. In the waters nearby stood the 6th Marine Expeditionary Unit, composed of BLT 3/6 and HMM 264. U.S. ships began to evacuate American nationals at 1300 on 27 April. That evening, the first Leathernecks filed ashore. The next day all of 3/6 occupied Santo Domingo. The U.S. force increased rapidly; on 30 April, a brigade of the 82nd Airborne arrived and the remaining elements of a Marine expeditionary brigade—BLT 1/6 and BLT 1/8—flew in along with the headquarters of the 4th MEB. BLT 1/2 was held offshore in reserve. As the government of the Dominican Republic regained control, a multinational peacekeeping force from several Latin American nations replaced the American military and naval contingents.

Just as the political turmoil in Latin America seemed to be settling down, a troubled area thousands of miles from Latin America had already begun to test the resolve of the U.S. government and its populace like no other conflict in its history. For a decade the conflict engulfed the Marine Corps. The nations of Southeast Asia seemed to embody the "domino theory" of the 1950s and 1960s. Communist insurgencies, inspired by the governments of China and the Soviet Union, fed on the seedbeds of political and economic discontent. In the British colony and then commonwealth nation of Malaya, British and Malayan forces spent more than a decade suppressing a Communist terrorist movement that had taken root among the Chinese minority. The Kingdom of Thailand was confronted by no fewer than three insurgent groups, two of them Communist-inspired. Across the border in Laos, Communist instigators from North Vietnam proselytized the native population to foment an insurgency—the Pathet Lao—against the royalist government. The governments of the United States and Soviet Union became increasingly involved in support of the factions in Laos to the point of actually coming to loggerheads over the tiny, landlocked nation. A Marine

helicopter squadron was sent to Thailand in 1961 because of the worrisome situation in Laos. Then, on 17 May 1962, an entire Marine Expeditionary Unit (MEU) deployed to northeast Thailand in a show of force to intimidate Pathet Lao forces and their North Vietnamese supporters. The deployment was brief. On 1 July, Leatherneck units began to withdraw, and by the end of the month were all out of Thailand. Both the United States and the Soviet Union agreed to disengage from the controversy in Laos, but the former merely began a series of covert operations in support of the royalist government while the latter funneled its support for the Pathet Lao through Hanoi. Yet the real potential for trouble lay across the Annamite Mountains in the two Vietnams.

A former French colony, Vietnam had been split in two following an unsuccessful attempt by Ho Chi Minh, the charismatic leader of the Viet Minh—a Communist-controlled popular front fighting for liberation from French colonial rule—to unify the three colonies encompassing Vietnam (Cochin China, Annam, Tonkin) under the Communist banner. In the north, Ho held sway with the Lao Dong (Worker's Party) controlling a Marxist government. In the south, Ngo Dinh Diem led a presumably democratic government. In fact, the government of South Vietnam was riddled with corruption, and the Catholic Diem enjoyed little support from the primarily Buddhist population.

U.S. involvement in the troubled Vietnams began almost immediately after the Geneva Accords of 1954 divided the country to separate the warring factions. Convinced that Communist-inspired insurgencies would engulf the region, the United States organized the Southeast Asian Treaty Organization (SEATO), a defensive alliance composed of Great Britain, France, Australia, New Zealand, Pakistan, Thailand, and the Philippines. Later that year President Eisenhower ordered economic aid to the Diem government and the establishment of the Military Assistance and Advisory Group (MAAG), Vietnam, which in 1962 became the U.S. Military Assistance Command, Vietnam (MACV). From the beginning, Marines served in MAAG-Vietnam and MACV.

On 2 August 1954 Lt. Col. Victor J. Croizat became the first senior Marine Corps advisor or *co-van* (trusted friend) to the Vietnamese Marine Corps. On 24 October of that year, President Eisenhower promised U.S. assistance to the Diem government in the face of aggression from the North Vietnamese. Soon U.S. military advisors began training South Vietnamese forces, replacing French instructors. When the People's Republic of China signed an agreement providing economic aid to North Vietnam on 7 July 1955, the political and military situation in Vietnam became increasingly worrisome. By 1960 MAAG-Vietnam had grown from 327 advisors to 685; that same year, Hanoi announced the formation of the "National Front for the Liberation of South Vietnam" under its aegis. On 1–2 November 1963 Diem was overthrown and assassinated in a coup d'état. The leaders of the coup had the tacit approval of the United States, which, while deploring the murders, welcomed a change in leadership. Contrary to American expectations, South Vietnam drifted into

anarchy as competing factions wrestled for power, and a Communist-inspired infra-structure gained support among the rural populace.

In 1964 the United States instigated a series of covert activities—code-named Plan 34A—aimed at deterring North Vietnamese aggression. South Vietnamese commandos infiltrated into North Vietnam and South Vietnamese Navy patrol boats launched raids against the coastline of the Communist north. Plan 34A put the United States and North Vietnam on a collision course.

On 2 August North Vietnamese torpedo boats launched an attack on the U.S. destroyer *Maddox* cruising in the Tonkin Gulf. Two days later the *Maddox* and another U.S. destroyer, the *Turner Joy*, reported a similar attack. Both ships were steaming in international waters. On 5 August, President Johnson ordered a series of retaliatory air strikes from the carriers *Constellation* and *Ticonderoga*. BLT 2/3, which had just arrived in the Philippines from Okinawa for training, reembarked for a hurried transit to Vietnamese waters. Eventually an entire MAB joined the amphibious force. Into the fall the force cruised up and down the Vietnamese coast, waiting for an expected order to land the landing force. At least twice Leathernecks drew ammunition and prepared to go ashore but were subsequently ordered to stand down. By the Marine Corps' birthday, the Leathernecks had returned to Okinawa.

Ashore in South Vietnam, however, the deadly struggle intensified. On 1 November, Viet Cong (VC; literally "Vietnamese Communist") units fired mortar shells at the U.S. compound at Bien Hoa, inflicting

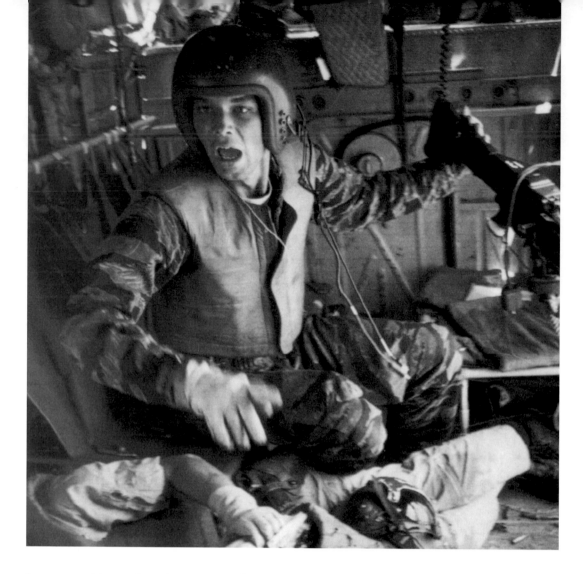

heavy casualties on American personnel and destroying a number of aircraft. On 24 December a bomb exploded outside a billet housing U.S. advisors in Saigon, killing and wounding a number of Americans. By the beginning of 1965 more than twenty-three thousand U.S. military personnel were serving in Vietnam, but the situation worsened. On 7 February Viet Cong units attacked a U.S. barracks at Pleiku in the Central Highlands. President Johnson ordered another series of retaliatory air raids on the north. Three days later VC sappers bombed an enlisted barracks at Qui Nhon, and President Johnson ordered yet another air strike. By 2 March, a bombing offensive aimed at North Vietnam— Operation Rolling Thunder—was under way. Meanwhile, in the south, the deteriorating military situation around Danang became increasingly alarming. Many believed that South Vietnam's second most populous city might fall into insurgent hands.

Danang was more than the commercial hub of an estimated quarter-million Vietnamese. Its huge airfield supported a multitude of activities: Vietnamese Air Force; U.S. Air Force; and the South Vietnamese airline Air Vietnam. The headquarters of Military Region I was located within the air base defensive perimeter. Intelligence estimates indicated the presence of at least six thousand Viet Cong in the immediate vicinity of Danang. MACV's commander, Gen. William C. Westmoreland, requested the dispatch of a Marine unit to secure the vital Danang airfield. U.S. Ambassador Maxwell D. Taylor gave his reluctant approval, despite his conviction that American servicemen could not adapt to the fighting endemic to the jungles and rice paddies of Southeast Asia.

Commander-in-Chief, Pacific (CINC-PAC), Adm. Ulysses S. Grant Sharp, vehemently disagreed: "The Marines," he snapped, "have a distinguished record in

When *LIFE* photographer Larry Burrows snapped this picture LCpl. James Farley, the crew chief of chopper Yankee Papa 13, was shouting to his gunner, "My gun is jammed. Cover your side. I'll help these guys." Earlier that day HMM-163 had deployed from Danang to carry a South Vietnamese battalion into action. Yankee Papa 3 was disabled by enemy fire at the landing zone, and YP 13 took on its copilot and crew chief, both of whom were badly wounded. Farley attempted to extricate the helicopter's pilot, who was pinned in his seat, bloody, unconscious, and perhaps dead, but heavy fire forced YP 13 to lift off before he had succeeded. Despite Farley's best efforts, the copilot, here lying beside the door, died in the air. The crew chief survived, and another helicopter rescued YP 3's pilot, who was still alive. This photograph appeared on the cover of *LIFE* for 16 April 1965. (Getty Images)

counter-guerrilla warfare." Lt. Gen. Victor H. "Brute" Krulak, the Corps' counterinsurgency expert, then commanding the Fleet Marine Force, Pacific, was generally believed to have provided the stimulus—if not the actual words—to Sharp's pithy response. Westmoreland's request passed from CINCPAC to the Pentagon, and then to the White House, where it received swift approval from President Johnson.

By 8 March 1965, Task Force 76 with the embarked troops of the 9th MEB lay off the coast of South Vietnam; Brig. Gen. Frederick J. Karch, a dapper, mustached officer with a fondness for camouflage ascots and shoulder holsters, commanded. At 0902 the first Leathernecks from 3/9 landed at Red Beach just north of Danang. Heavily laden Marines, sweating in the tropical heat and humidity, were greeted not by armed and menacing Viet Cong but by a beaming mayor. Accompanying this gentleman were scores of beautiful Vietnamese girls wearing white *ao dais* over black silk trousers, each carrying a basket of flower garlands to present to the men who had come to protect them. Even before BLT 3/9 came ashore, approximately thirteen hundred Marines were already in Vietnam, either in a helicopter squadron or in the antiaircraft missile battalion poised to protect the Danang airstrip from air attack. In the two days following 3/9's landing, BLT 1/3 arrived by air from Okinawa. Karch ordered 1/3 to provide security for the airstrip, and directed 3/9 to take up defensive positions on Hill 327, the terrain dominating the skyline to the west of Danang.

The buildup continued rapidly. On 10 April, a squadron of Marine F-4s—VMFA-

531—arrived and established its base alongside the Vietnamese Air Force and U.S. Air Force contingents on the Danang airstrip. A day later BLT 2/3—diverted from a routine deployment from Thailand to the Philippines—came ashore. On 14 April another BLT (3/4) arrived by air from Hawaii and took up defensive positions at Phu Bai near the ancient capital of Hue.

Meanwhile, someone in Saigon with an ear for historical punctilio suggested that the term *expeditionary* might remind the Vietnamese of the hated French *Corps d'Expéditionnaire*; thus, "9th Marine Expeditionary Brigade" became "9th Marine Amphibious Brigade." The appellation stuck, and when the III Marine Expeditionary Force replaced the 9th MEB (or 9th MAB) on 6 May, it became III Marine Amphibious Force or III MAF. And so it remained for the remainder of the Vietnam War and well into the 1980s.

On 11 May the 1st MAW established its headquarters alongside the busy airstrip at Danang. Four days earlier the 3rd MAB had landed fifty-seven miles south of Danang and established a base near an unnamed beach called "Chu Lai," supposedly General Krulak's name rendered in Mandarin Chinese.

On 13 June 1965, the *New York Times* reported that twenty "major government upheavals" had occurred in South Vietnam since the fall of Diem. Policy makers wondered just how the United States could support a regime in Saigon that could not gain the legitimacy required to earn the support of the populace. Opting for a military solution, the buildup of free-world forces accelerated as Westmoreland predicted that the Army of the

Republic of Vietnam (ARNV) was nearing collapse. By early June MACV counted two Army, one Australian, and seven U.S. Marine Corps infantry battalions; on 22 June Westmoreland asked Washington to increase his numbers of U.S. battalions to thirty-three; instead, the JCS approved an increase to forty-four battalions of American infantry. MACV claimed that with these battalions in 1965 it could prevent South Vietnam from losing the war; with an additional twenty-four battalions in 1966, it could begin winning the war. Four days after his request, Westmoreland received authorization to commit U.S. troops in combat. On 12 July 1st Lt. Frank S. Reasoner of Company A, 3rd Reconnaissance Battalion—a former enlisted Marine who won an appointment to the U.S. Military Academy—earned the first Leatherneck Medal of Honor in the Vietnam War. He was killed by enemy fire as he attempted to come to the aid of his wounded radio operator after being ambushed while on patrol deep in Viet Cong–controlled territory.

On 30 July 1965 General Westmoreland gave Maj. Gen. Lewis W. Walt, the commander of III MAF, operational control of all U.S. forces in I Corps. The corps' area embraced the five northernmost provinces of South Vietnam, containing a civilian population of twenty-six million people. A Leatherneck battalion, 3/4, operated out of Phu Bai just south of Hue; the 3rd Marines were west and north of Danang; 9th Marines south of the city; and the 4th Marines at Chu Lai, far to the south. The 1st MAW counted four air groups in-country: MAG-12 with A-4s at Chu Lai; MAG-11 with F-4s at Danang; MAG-16 at Danang with helicopters; and MAG-36 at Chu Lai, also with rotary-wing aircraft.

Coincident with Walt's Marines taking to the field with the full panoply of traditional Leatherneck air support, his troops drew

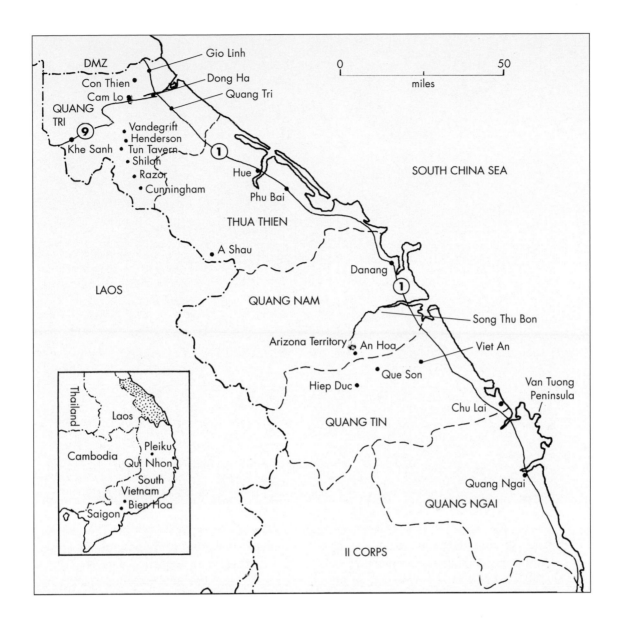

heavy fire not only from the ellusive enemy but also from American journalists. On 3 August a company of the 9th Marines swept through a village on the Cam Do River six miles southwest of Danang. On taking small-arms fire, the Leathernecks responded with a fusillade of rifle, machine-gun, and mortar fire. Sweeping through the village, the company suffered casualties from surprise firing devices or booby traps and deadly *punji* stakes—sharpened bamboo spikes dipped in excrement. As the Marines put the torch to the VC-controlled village, CBS reporter Morley Safer reported the attack, tearfully intoning that "if these people weren't VC-sympathizers before, they certainly are now!" The *Chicago Daily News* chimed in:

"[Marines] have killed or wounded a number of Vietnamese civilians and burned dozens of homes in the dirtiest war Americans ever had to fight." From that time until the end of U.S. military involvement, members of the Fourth Estate appeared increasingly to relish reporting accounts of what it believed to be untoward conduct by allied forces—especially Americans—in the increasingly controversial war in Southeast Asia.

On 18 August, the first large-scale Marine offensive of the war began. Intelligence reports indicated the presence of the two-thousand-man-strong 1st VC Regiment on the Van Tuong Peninsula, fifteen miles south of Chu Lai. Col. Oscar F. Peatross—a veteran of Carlson's Raiders of World War

II fame—led his 7th Marines ashore on the peninsula in a combination amphibious and heliborne assault that decimated the enemy force. The Marines counted 964 VC dead while losing only 51 Marines killed and 203 wounded by the time Operation Starlite ended on 24 August. Unimpressed, Westmoreland criticized Walt and his senior commanders for their unwillingness to leave coastal enclaves and move into the hinterland. Westmoreland and his staff thought III MAF preoccupied with the Corps' sacrosanct amphibious doctrine and its jealously guarded prerogatives with regard to fixed-wing close air support. From Hawaii, Krulak remained an invidious guardian of the Corps' amphibious fiefdom and the sanctity of its close air support. Senior Air Force officers longed to gain operational control of Leatherneck fixed-wing aviation. Westmoreland eventually accepted their argument, and in 1968 the fixed-wing assets of the 1st MAW were subordinated to the

"mission direction" of the Seventh Air Force. In practice, the consequence of the change proved slight. The Air Force might have won a doctrinal victory, but the great majority of 1st MAW's missions continued to be flown in support of Marines on the ground.

By the end of 1965, Westmoreland and the senior members of his staff stood poles apart from Walt and his commanders. Their differences extended from doctrinal issues to overall strategy. Influenced perhaps by Krulak, Walt believed strongly that his Marines should provide a shield behind which the South Vietnamese government could gain strength and earn the confidence of the rural populace. Krulak—fond of quoting the ancient Chinese military sage Sun Tzu—knew all too well that that the VC infrastructure would wither and die only when the rural populace accepted the Saigon regime. "Winning their hearts and minds" became an often-repeated phrase

In *Vietnam Episode, I Corps Area*, Robert Benney painted a scene of intense combat with numerous casualties. Some of the wounded are being loaded on the then-venerable UH-34 Seahorse helicopter at right. A CH-46 Sea Knight approaches carrying a palette of supplies, center, followed by a UH-1 Huey with pods of rockets visible outboard its skids. Above and to the left of the Huey, an F-4 Phantom begins a bombing run. A veteran of the Abbott Labs' World War II combat artist program, Benney also served with the Marines in Vietnam. (Marine Corps Art Collection)

at senior levels of command; however, to the Marine in the bush it translated simply as "grab them by the balls, and their hearts and minds will follow!" For his part, Westmoreland remained scornful of his Marines' penchant for endearing themselves to the peasantry or promoting "civic action." He continued to argue for a strategy of attrition to defeat the Communists. Simply stated, friendly forces would kill more Viet Cong or North Vietnamese Army (NVA) troops than could be replaced; sadly, that concept proved flawed almost from the outset. In South Vietnam, Viet Cong cadres emptied the villages of all healthy males, ages seventeen to thirty-five, in Communist-controlled areas; South Vietnamese authorities did the same in cities and the villages where they held sway. In North Vietnam, draft-eligible young men were inducted into the NVA on turning seventeen.

Despite the criticism from chair-bound detractors in Saigon and Washington, Walt's Marines put their theories into practice. Near Phu Bai 3/4 combined a squad of Leathernecks with a platoon of locally recruited Vietnamese militia to operate at the village and hamlet level. As the unit became woven into the life of the village, people began to trust first them and then the government of South Vietnam. The concept expanded quickly until Combined Action Platoons or CAPs operated throughout I Corps. The idea proved to be one of the most successful innovations of the Vietnam War.

Notwithstanding the increasing number of free-world forces in Vietnam and Marines in I Corps, enemy units continued to harass

Leatherneck installations without hindrance. On 27 October, VC sappers demonstrated their ability to infiltrate the heavily guarded lines of even rear-area cantonments. Crawling through the protective wire and minefields surrounding the Corps' helicopter base at Marble Mountain, just south of Danang, the VC took out twenty-four aircraft and damaged twenty-three others. That same night VC sappers infiltrated the airstrip at Chu Lai, blowing up four and damaging six of MAG-12's A-4s.

The following month, Army of the Republic of Vietnam (ARVN) units abandoned the town of Hiep Duc in Quang Tin Province, allowing easy entrance for enemy units to the two district capitals of Viet An and Que Son in the Que Son Valley. In Operation Harvest Moon, the first joint ARVN-USMC operation of the war, three ARVN battalions deployed into the area to find and fix major enemy units. When significant contact was made, Task Force Delta—the 7th Marines plus 2/1 (the Special Landing Force)—under Brig. Gen. Jonas M. Platt would enter the fray.

Operation Harvest Moon began on 8 December. Two of the ARVN battalions made contact almost immediately and were decimated by a sizable VC main force unit. Platt ordered in two of his battalions by helicopter, and before long the entire task force had entered the action. B-52 bombers flying from Guam dropped their first payloads in support of ground forces in Vietnam during Operation Harvest Moon. Platt's Leathernecks lost 45 killed and 218 wounded before the Viet Cong melted into the jungle. The Marine and ARVN units reported that they had killed over a thousand VC.

By the beginning of 1966 Westmoreland had his 44 battalions in the field, but intelligence officers reported 110 enemy battalions in South Vietnam; ominously, 27 of the Communist battalions were composed of North Vietnamese Army regulars. MACV increased its requirements to win the war: by the end of 1966, it wanted 162 ARVN, 74 U.S., and 23 other battalions in-country. Alarmed, Secretary of Defense Robert S. McNamara agreed, even though the new requirements meant a U.S. troop strength of four hundred thousand. As he requested approval for the new troop levels from President Johnson, McNamara predicted that a thousand American servicemen would be killed in action each month.

In February General Walt traveled to Washington for a series of conferences. In a surprise move, President Johnson promoted Walt to lieutenant general. Senior military planners urged the immediate call-up of

reserves in order to provide the manpower for the widening war. But the president and his advisors demurred because of domestic political considerations and urged other sources to provide forces. On 1 March the 5th Marine Division was reactivated and the personnel strength of the Marine Corps jumped from 190,000 to more than 278,000.

General Walt returned to I Corps to face an uprising of militant Buddhists opposed to the Saigon regime. The upheaval brought the pacification effort in the northern provinces to a halt. Meanwhile, Westmoreland and the MACV staff grew increasingly fearful that major North Vietnamese units planned an offensive far to the north along the Demilitarized Zone (DMZ) near the border with Laos. Special Forces camps along the Laotian border fell to enemy units in the early spring. At Westmoreland's insistence, 1/1 occupied the old Civilian Irregular Defense Group camp at Khe Sanh along Highway 9

Left: Marines engaged in Operation Harvest Moon advance across a rice paddy toward a tree line that has been blasted by an A-4. (National Archives)

Right: Maj. Gen. Lewis W. "Lew" Walt, the first commander of III MAF, discusses the progress of Operation Harvest Moon with the commander of Company E, 7th Marines. (National Archives)

leading from Dong Ha to the Laotian border just below the DMZ. Walt believed that the battalion would find nothing, and it returned to confirm his estimate.

Westmoreland continued to insist that the NVA would attack across the DMZ and again urged Walt to position a battalion north of Dong Ha. The battalion again found nothing of significance on 30 May, and a second battalion sent into the area in June also came up empty-handed. This time, however, the 4th Marines established a patrol base at Dong Ha. Then ARVN units in the area reported the capture of a North Vietnamese claiming to be from the 324B Division. The prisoner told his interrogators that his entire division had crossed the DMZ into South Vietnam.

In response to this information, Task Force Delta was activated with three infantry battalions and an artillery battalion. Dong Ha grew quickly into a sizeable logistical

support area. Intelligence officers opined that the 324B Division was somewhere to the north of Dong Ha. Quickly making contact with the enemy force, the Leathernecks of Task Force Delta slammed into the NVA unit. Operation Hastings III lasted from 15 July until 3 August, ultimately involving eight thousand Marines and three thousand ARVN troops. More than eight hundred North Vietnamese regulars lost their lives in Hanoi's attempt to establish a foothold in the northernmost provinces of South Vietnam.

Walt and Westmoreland continued to disagree, the former asserting that the NVA only diverted attention from the pacification program, and the latter insisting that the two NVA divisions poised just above the DMZ posed a real threat to I Corps. In August 1/4 moved west from Dong Ha to Cam Lo and almost immediately encountered the NVA on a ridge to the north. By then, ample intelligence reports indicated that the 341st

NVA Division had crossed the DMZ to join forces with the 324B Division. In response, III MAF initiated Operation Prairie. By the time its four phases concluded in May 1967, the threat to the northern provinces appeared to have subsided. By then, Westmoreland had lost confidence in Walt's Leathernecks. He shared his concerns in a secret message to the chief of staff of the Army on 22 January 1968: "The military professionalism of the Marines falls far short of the standards that should be demanded by our armed forces. Indeed, they are brave and proud, but their standards, tactics, and lack of command supervision throughout their ranks requires improvement in this national interest. I feel

somewhat insecure with the situation in Quang Tri province, in view of my knowledge of their shortcomings. Without question, many lives would be saved if their tactical professionalism [was] enhanced."

In June 1967 General Walt was called home to become assistant commandant of the Marine Corps. At the time and for some years thereafter, he remained convinced that the war could be won. Lt. Gen. Robert E. Cushman Jr. succeeded him in command of III MAF. In September Secretary McNamara's representatives—the Pentagon "whiz kids" so despised by senior officers charged with fighting the war—met with Westmoreland to unveil an anti-infiltration barrier to be

Left: Company G, 4th Marines, moves up a rugged slope in pursuit of North Vietnamese regulars during Operation Hastings (15 July–3 August 1966) two miles below the DMZ. A heavy artillery and mortar barrage preceded the assault, but the Leathernecks still encountered a well-fortified enemy. (National Archives)

Bottom Right: Larry Burrows photographed these wounded Marines awaiting a medevac helicopter on Mutters Ridge in northern I Corps on 5 October 1966. The bloodied gunnery sergeant at left had just bid a reluctant farewell to the corpse of his company commander. During the nine years Burrows worked in Vietnam he was awarded the Overseas Press Club's annual Robert Capa Gold Medal "for the best published photographic reporting from abroad requiring exceptional courage and enterprise" no fewer than three times. Capa had been killed while photographing the French Indo-China War in May 1954. Burrows' turn came in February 1971, when a helicopter carrying him and several other journalists was shot down over Laos. (Getty Images)

constructed across the DMZ. The product of sophisticated but misguided technology, the barrier would consist of sophisticated sensors, mines, and a new defensive wire featuring razor-sharp edges. Senior officers from Vietnam to the Pentagon proclaimed the concept preposterous. General Greene flatly opposed the project and made no secret of his misgivings. The secretary of defense ended all criticism by simply forbidding public comment from the uniformed services.

As Marines installed the barrier, Westmoreland urged Cushman to reinforce the battalion positioned at Khe Sanh. But by late fall 1967 the monsoon rains had struck

northern I Corps with a vengeance. The dirt roads in Quang Tri Province turned into impassible quagmires, and the heavy cloud cover made aerial supply for Khe Sanh increasingly difficult. On 13 December III MAF alerted the 3rd Marine Division that intelligence sources indicated a force of four NVA regiments in the vicinity of Khe Sanh. In response the headquarters of the 26th Marines joined the battalion at Khe Sanh and the base was reinforced with 3/26.

In the rice paddies and hamlets farther to the south, the pacification effort so assiduously emphasized by the Marines since 1965 experienced difficulty balancing reverses with

Left: *Red Assault*, by the noted artist and illustrator John Groth, depicts a Marine force closing in on a Viet Cong hamlet west of Da Nang in January 1967. Groth was present during the operation. (Marine Corps Art Collection)

Bottom Right: Leathernecks of Company M, 7th Marines, move to board helicopters that will transport them to search an area for NVA troops spotted the evening before. (National Archives)

successes. Idealistic American interlopers found it difficult to accept the Confucian maxim that "the writ of the emperor does not extend beyond the village gate." Soldiers and Leathernecks alike failed to comprehend the complicated political structure of Vietnam, with its twisting maze of nepotism. Western-oriented intelligence officers refused to believe that the half-starved Communist combatants, most suffering from malaria and other diseases, would be willing to continue to fight on forever against seemingly hopeless odds.

Cushman commanded all free-world forces in I Corps—except, of course, the ARVN troops. To the south, the Americal Division held sway in Quang Ngai and Quang Tin provinces. The veteran 1st Marine Division operated throughout Quang Nam Province while the 3rd Marine Division maneuvered in Thua Thien and Quang Tri provinces in the north. The latter had deployed to the two northernmost provinces in October. Approximately eighty thousand South Vietnamese troops also served in I Corps. Together, troop lists in South Vietnam counted seventy-three allied infantry battalions in the five northernmost provinces of South Vietnam.

The 9th MAB maintained its headquarters on Okinawa as CINCPAC's strategic reserve. Components to form a nominal Marine Amphibious Unit rotated out of Vietnam, becoming part of the 7th Fleet's Special Landing Force, and deployed by sea to the waters off South Vietnam. On 1 April 1967 CINCPACFLT ordered the activation of a second amphibious ready group; thus, two special landing forces were available to support the operations of the Seventh Fleet. But in reality they were used to reinforce existing operations in the III MAF area of operations—although sent ashore infrequently to participate in combat operations in II, III, and IV Corps. Each special landing force contained a battalion landing team and a medium helicopter squadron.

At the end of the year 81,249 of the 298,498 Marines in uniform were serving in Vietnam: 21 of the Corps' 36 infantry battalions, 14 of its 33 fixed-wing squadrons, and 13 of its 24 helicopter squadrons. No other U.S. armed service contributed such a large percentage of its forces to the Vietnam War. Career Marines returned for second tours—later, some would begin third tours.

Meanwhile, the Johnson administration had been considering a replacement for General Greene, whose tenure at the Corps' helm was approaching its end. In the forefront of the contenders stood the generals most symbolic of Leatherneck participation in the war, Walt and Krulak. But although both of them called in every marker in their favor, the Oval Office and Pentagon chose an officer far removed from the conflagration in Southeast Asia. On 1 January 1968 Greene's chief of staff, Lt. Gen. Leonard F. Chapman Jr. became the twenty-fourth commandant of the Marine Corps. An artilleryman, Chapman had commanded a battalion in World War II and served with distinction in a variety of subsequent assignments. He would lead the Corps through some of the most trying times in its long history.

In the spring of 1967, Pentagon staffers concluded that a new rifle, the M16 firing the standard-NATO 5.56 cartridge, offered advantages over the M14 because of its high volume of fire at short ranges. Never before had a military organization so dependent upon the prowess of skirmishing infantry conducted such a wholesale change in its basic weaponry in the middle of a war. Veterans and rookies alike grumbled, and then swore vehemently as the M16 demonstrated a proclivity to jam. Journalists found the grist for their mills with endless reports taken from disgusted and confused soldiers and Marines. Only when troops learned to keep the chambers meticulously clean with the aid of wire-bristle bore brushes did the acrimony subside. But up and down the chain of command, the ill-timed adoption of the M16 was ridiculed as yet another of McNamara's innovations run amok.

More ominous considerations plagued commanders than balky M16s, however, including a buildup of NVA forces in Quang Tri Province. Cushman had already responded by positioning all three of the 3rd Marine Division's infantry regiments in the northernmost provinces of I Corps. Enemy activity in the northwest corner of Quang Tri increased in intensity. NVA rockets, mortars,

Left: Marines from the Special Landing Force check Viet Cong bodies during Operation Deckhouse VI in February 1967. (National Archives)

Right: Combat artist John Steel's *Mass for the Fallen* shows a Catholic chaplain holding Mass in remembrance of fallen Marines. (Navy Art Collection)

Left: A wounded Leatherneck from Company F, 4th Marines, is lifted out of heavy foliage during Operation Choctaw, conducted in the summer of 1967 just south of the DMZ. When the terrain prevented a landing by medevac helicopters, injured Marines were often taken out of the field in this fashion. (National Archives)

Right: The personal anguish of the Vietnam War is mirrored in this photograph of a Marine bowing his head in grief on learning that a close friend was killed during Operation Hickory near the DMZ in May 1967. (National Archives)

and artillery pounded ARVN and Marine installations at Gio Linh and Con Thien. Leatherneck patrols made heavy contact with NVA units near Khe Sanh and Hill 861. The 3rd Marines joined an ARVN force to clear the area south of the Ben Hai River of enemy troops. Westmoreland and his staff suspected an enemy offensive in the offing, but no one imagined the scope and intensity of Tet 1968.

Since the Army's epic encounter in the Ia Drang Valley in late 1965, U.S. forces had proven themselves superior in every major encounter with either Viet Cong or NVA units. The enemy appeared to be reeling under the weight of American firepower and logistical superiority. Confidence prevailed from MACV to CINCPAC to the White House. In response to the perceived threat in the north, Westmoreland ordered the 101st Airborne and 1st Air Cavalry divisions into the two northernmost provinces. Intelligence

reports revealed the 325C and 304th NVA divisions massing outside Khe Sanh, and the 308th and 341st NVA divisions menacing Camp Carroll and the Rockpile closer to Dong Ha. The headquarters of the 3rd Marine Division moved to Dong Ha and Cushman sent 2/26 to Khe Sanh to give Col. David E. Lownds all of his organic battalions.

On 2 January 1968 a patrol from Khe Sanh ambushed an NVA reconnaissance party, killing a regimental commander. Later in the month, a fusillade of rocket and mortar fire impacted on the base, setting off its ammunition dump and fuel farm. Cushman sent in 1/9 to reinforce the 26th Marines and, with a sense of diplomacy, asked for the loan of an ARVN ranger battalion. Two more batteries of 105-mm howitzers reinforced the artillery already at Khe Sanh. The base's defenders also gained solace from the knowledge that the Army's 175-mm

Left: John Olson, a combat photographer for *Stars and Stripes*, captured this poignant scene of wounded Marines loaded on a tank for evacuation from Hue during the bloody fighting during Tet 1968. (Copyright John Olson)

Right: Company D, 5th Marines, moves through the streets of battle-scarred Hue during the Tet Offensive of 1968. Desperate fighting to drive out or kill the NVA invaders destroyed much of the city. (National Archives)

gun battalion at Camp Carroll could fire in support of the outpost.

As expected, the Viet Cong announced a truce for the Tet holiday, 27 January–3 February, in celebration of the Vietnamese Lunar New Year. South Vietnam followed with its own cease-fire scheduled for thirty-six hours around 29 January. The enemy offensive probably began in earnest on the night of the government's cease-fire, when rockets and mortars hit military installations at Danang; the next night, Chu Lai received similar treatment. Communist forces throughout the country hoped to confine allied military units in their cantonments, keeping them huddled behind sandbagged walls or in bunkers while they attacked provincial and district capitals to discredit and disrupt the South Vietnamese government and the pacification program. No less than six NVA divisions had entered

the two northernmost provinces of I Corps. On 31 January two regiments of NVA joined Viet Cong units in Hue, Vietnam's third largest metropolitan center, and seized most of the city.

Just to the south of Hue stood the only friendly force available: Task Force X-Ray, with three battalions of Leatherneck infantry to defend the base at Phu Bai and keep Highway One open between there and Danang. Regimental Landing Team 27 arrived from Camp Pendleton to take over the 5th Marines' sector south of Danang and the veteran regiment moved north to recapture the ancient capital. The 1st Battalion, 1st Marines, marched from Phu Bai to attempt to breach the Citadel. On 4 February 2/5 arrived from Quang Nam Province to join in the house-to-house fighting, but after a week of intense urban combat, both battalions were spent. On 12 February 1/5 moved on the

A combat photographer captured a Leatherneck clambering through the rubble of Hue. For most Marines, pitched battles in an urban setting were an anomaly after months of fighting in the paddies of the lowlands. (National Archives)

Citadel with ARVN and South Vietnamese Marine units; it took another twelve days of bloody combat to rid the ancient fortress of the invaders.

U.S. Marine losses numbered 142 killed and 857 wounded. During their brief occupation of the city, NVA and VC death squads executed more than 5,000 Vietnamese civilians considered ideological threats to the Communist revolution. Finally, on 2 March, the battle for Hue was declared over. Three Marine Corps and thirteen Vietnamese battalions had destroyed an estimated eight to eleven NVA battalions in one of the bitterest confrontations of the war. The beautiful, ancient capital lay in ruins and many of its inhabitants dead in the rubble or in makeshift graves dug by their executioners.

Farther to the north, NVA forces laid siege to Khe Sanh. Colonel Lownds had more than six thousand men at his disposal, but an estimated fifteen thousand NVA were poised outside their position. Journalists, many of whom came no closer to the siege than the bars of their hotels in Saigon, demonstrated a fondness for comparing the Leathernecks' situation to that of the beleaguered French at Dien Bien Phu in 1954. President Johnson, growing increasingly concerned, required the Joint Chiefs of Staff to sign a memorandum "guaranteeing" that Khe Sanh would not fall. As they had done at Dien Bien Phu, the Communists practiced classic seventeenth-century siegecraft, pushing a complex network of trenches ever closer to the base's perimeter and shelling its interior. The difference was that at Khe Sanh they never succeeded in closing the defenders' airstrip or breaking into their positions.

On 6 February mortar and artillery shells signaled an NVA assault on the camp of the Civilian Irregular Defense Group at Lang Vei, between Khe Sanh and the Laotian border. The NVA took the camp, riding through its gates in Soviet-built PT-76 amphibious tanks. Only half the estimated five hundred defenders escaped, most fleeing with an assortment of refugees to Khe Sanh. Arriving from Saigon, Westmoreland excoriated everyone in sight at III MAF headquarters: more air support for the 1st Air Cavalry Division from Leatherneck fixed-wing aviation assets! Why was Lang Vei not reinforced? On the heels of his stormy visit, MACV announced the opening of an MACV forward command post in the northern provinces of I Corps. Its operational control included the 3rd Marine Division, 101st Airborne Division, and 1st Air Cavalry Division; however, the new headquarters was under the operational control of III MAF. Westmoreland's dictum suggested that he had little confidence in the Marines to prevent a takeover of the northern provinces by the NVA.

On 1 April Operation Pegasus began, an offensive by the 1st Air Cavalry Division, the 1st Marines, and four ARVN battalions aimed at reestablishing overland communications with Khe Sanh. Eleven days later journalists prodded by senior Army officers gleefully reported the "relief" of Khe Sanh by units of the 1st Air Cavalry Division. At the remote outpost, however, no one registered particular joy simply because they never considered themselves in danger of being overrun. During the seventy-seven days the siege was calculated to have lasted,

Khe Sanh's defenders had lost 205 killed and 1,668 wounded. Enemy casualties were estimated at between 10,000 and 15,000. At a White House ceremony, a greatly relieved Johnson presented the Presidential Unit Citation to Colonel Lownds for the 26th Marines' gallant defense of Khe Sanh; then he awarded Lownds a Navy Cross and a Bronze Star to the regimental sergeant major.

The Tet offensive shattered the VC infrastructure in the hamlets and villages—which had taken the Communists years to build—and decimated enemy forces. An estimated fifteen thousand VC and NVA were killed; communists—both in the north and south—experienced a number of surprises. To their bitter disappointment and chagrin, ARVN forces did not desert or defect; the people did not rally to the communists but instead looked on in horror at the senseless massacre of innocent civilians; and the people not rise up against the Saigon regime. Yet the military defeat was lost in the wake of an obvious political disaster. Millions of Americans watched their television screens in horror as Viet Cong stormed the U.S. Embassy in Saigon and NVA units raised the flag of North Vietnam over the Citadel of Hue. President Johnson announced that veteran politician Clark Clifford would replace the ineffectual McNamara as secretary of defense on 1 March. Gen. Creighton W. Abrams relieved Westmoreland, who was named Chief of Staff of the Army.

Then, on 31 March, Johnson surprised the nation and the world with the announcement that he would not seek reelection. The president also announced a partial suspension of the bombing of North Vietnam. But his hope that the two concessions would bring the Communists to the peace table was disappointed. The enemy merely took comfort from his pronouncement and the subsequent American political turmoil. When the Communist Party of South Vietnam met for its 9th Conference in July 1969, its leaders reaffirmed what they had learned the year before, that "the internal contradiction between the U.S. rulers and . . . the American people was the greatest weak point of the Americans at this time."

In the wake of the Tet Offensive, III MAF units pressed their counteroffensive along the DMZ. An enemy force attacked Dong Ha between Highway One and Route 9; then, on 29 April, an ARVN regiment locked horns with a sizable NVA unit. Lt. Col. William Weise's 2/4 entered the fray against the main body of the enemy force. Beginning on 1 May, the battalion attacked the fortified village of Dai Do. The commanding officer of Company G, Capt. M. Sando Vargas Jr., fought off several successive enemy counterattacks that night despite being seriously wounded. Capt. James E. Livingston led Company E through intense fire to support Vargas. Although wounded as well, Livingston joined Vargas to lead the two companies in an assault through the village. By then Livingston had suffered another wound. Both Livingston and Vargas earned Medals of Honor for their heroism at Dai Do.

At a press conference in Washington on 10 June, Westmoreland admitted that the war could not be won because of "our national policy of not extending the war." In other words, he blamed the refusal of politicians to allow the military to apply the full fury of America's war-making potential against North Vietnam. Thus began the argument that civilians in Washington had tied the hands of American fighting men in Southeast Asia. Many senior officers believed strongly that the only way to bring the conflict to a conclusion in favor of South Vietnam and its supporters was to take the ground war to the north; but by then, antiwar sentiment in the U.S. precluded the adoption of such a strategy. The presidential election that fall made it clear that the American public wanted out of Vietnam. Republican candidate Richard M. Nixon promised a plan to end the war without surrendering while Democrat Hubert H. Humphrey suggested that if he

were elected, the United States would simply pull out of the conflict.

By the end of 1968 it was obvious that the Marine Corps had been in Vietnam too long. An aura of permanency prevailed in many cantonments. At Danang, the headquarters of III MAF, 1st MAW, and the 1st Marine Division were air conditioned and—except for the sandbags surrounding them and armed sentries in profusion—appeared not unlike similar installations outside Vietnam. Marines in rear areas ate in mess halls that provided meals just as tasty and varied as back home; even Leathernecks in the bush found the dismal diet of C-Rations varied with B-Rations, extra canned fruit and juices, and something new and tasty—the long-range patrol ration. Infantry companies were helilifted out of the paddies and jungles for a "breathing spell" at a mini-R & R center at White Beach astride the sparkling Pacific waters near Danang. There, for a few brief hours, weary Marines could drink all the cold beer or soda they wanted and gorge themselves on steak and shrimp without worrying about being in someone's gun sight. Once each tour, a Marine might travel to Hawaii to meet his wife, or to some exotic Pacific city in search of rest,

relaxation, and "horizontal refreshment." From the time the first Marine marched ashore, senior officers demonstrated a determined effort to separate their men from the depravity usually accompanying any army in the field. Liberty in the populated areas was only authorized near the end of the Marine Corps' deployment in Vietnam. But troublesome trysts with local prostitutes occurred nonetheless, and substance abuse accompanied the dilemma for commanding officers. Young Marines, especially, responded to the enticing and lurid refrains: "Hey, Marine, you want boom-boom?" or "Hey, Marine, you want smoke a joint?" without considering the consequences.

The war had become a routine, and many Marines grew indifferent to its persistent problems and challenges. ARVN units continued to perform inconsistently according to the whims of both commanders and weary Vietnamese troops who saw no end to the conflict. Returning Leathernecks found themselves attacking and seizing the same old terrain. Grave cynicism replaced the idealistic and anti-communist motivation of 1965, for few believed that the South Vietnamese—with their corrupt political machinery and mostly lackluster armed forces—could manage

without the Americans. Ethnic slurs peppered the daily speech of Marines—officer as well as enlisted—and the sad commentary heard in infantry units, "a dead Gook is a Viet Cong," rang true more often than not.

Leatherneck commanders were forced to deal with increasingly frequent racial and drug-related incidents. Troops found a simple solution when faced with an unpopular officer or NCO: a fragmentation grenade tossed into a billet in the dark of night. "Fragging," as it was called, became yet another dark aspect of the Vietnam War that made the days long

for Leatherneck commanders. But the endless war continued as friendly forces continued to win every battle even though Washington and Saigon appeared to be working together in order to lose the war; political opponents in the United States, growing more militant and gaining support, became increasingly persuasive. On the battlefield Marine Corps commanders found more and more that "Viet Cong" units consisted largely of NVA regulars. U.S. and allied victories had taken a deadly toll among the insurgents.

All told, 33,938 Marines were killed or wounded in Vietnam in 1968. Among the latter was twenty-three-year-old 2nd Lt. Lewis Burwell Puller Jr., Chesty Puller's only son. Young Puller was a platoon leader in the 2nd Battalion of his father's old regiment, the 1st Marines. Arriving in-country in August, he had already seen considerable combat when on 11 October his company staged a cordon-and-search operation at a village identified as a Viet Cong stronghold. Moments after exiting his helicopter, Puller unwittingly detonated a booby-trapped 105-mm howitzer shell. Miraculously, he did not lose consciousness, and afterwards he realized that the pink mist that briefly enshrouded him was produced by the vaporization of his legs, both of which had been torn off close to his torso. He had also lost most of his left hand, his right thumb and little finger, and much of his buttocks. In World War II or Korea he would have died within hours, but the intervening advances in military medicine enabled him to survive. The first time Chesty saw him, in an Air Force hospital outside Washington, he wept.

Terrible wounds psychological as well as physiological notwithstanding, young Puller seemed to make a model recovery. In the years following his entry into civilian life, he graduated from law school, fathered a child, served as an attorney in the Veterans Administration and the Department of Defense, and made an unsuccessful bid for Congress. After his political defeat, however, the despair he had been denying overwhelmed him and he spiraled into acute alcoholism. A bungled suicide attempt provided a wake-up call and, with the help of Alcoholics Anonymous and his devoted wife Toddy, Puller fought his way back to sobriety. In 1991 he published an absorbing, courageously candid autobiography, *Fortunate Son*, which won a richly merited

Pulitzer Prize. Of Chesty he wrote, "He had been a wonderful father and I was fortunate to be his son; but it had not been easy living in his shadow." Sadly, Puller's rehabilitation was not lasting. He relapsed into alcoholism, and on the afternoon of 11 May 1994 he put a bullet through his head. "To the names of the victims of the Vietnam War," Toddy Puller told the press, "add the name of Lewis B. Puller."

Late in 1968 intelligence sources reported NVA units hard at work to reopen infiltration routes from Laos into Quang Tri and Thua Thien provinces. An estimated two NVA infantry regiments, supported by an artillery regiment and an engineer regiment, had moved along the border facing the A Shau and Da Krong valleys southwest of Quang

Tri and west of Hue. The commanding general of the 3rd Marine Division ordered Col. Robert H. Barrow's 9th Marines to interdict and destroy NVA units infiltrating into the northernmost provinces of I Corps. Thus began one of the most successful allied operations of the Vietnam War.

In early 1969, construction began on three fire support bases (FSB) to support Operation Dewey Canyon: Shiloh, Razor, and Cunningham. Barrow positioned his headquarters and five batteries of artillery on FSB Cunningham; 1/9 helilifted into Shiloh while 3/9 occupied FSBs Henderson and Tun Tavern; 2/9 operated out of FSB Vandegrift farther to the north. On 25 January, 3/9 assaulted three landing zones on a ridge sixty-six hundred yards southwest of FSB Razor.

On 10 February Barrow moved 1/9 from FSBs Vandegrift and Shiloh to a new FSB, Erskine, along with a 105-mm howitzer battery to support it. Increasingly evidence pointed to a heavy enemy buildup of supplies and material just across the border into Laos in apparent anticipation of a major thrust into South Vietnam in the vicinity of Route 922. The usual truce for the Vietnamese Tet holiday went in effect on 16 February, followed by the usual number of expected violations. At 0345 NVA forces assaulted FSB Cunningham. Although the attackers penetrated the position's defensive perimeter, the Leathernecks succeeded in ejecting them.

Between 18 and 22 February, the heaviest fighting of Operation Dewey Canyon occurred. First Lieutenant Wesley L. Fox's Company A bore the brunt of the onslaught and the veteran Marine—commissioned from the ranks after a sixteen-year career—

earned the Medal of Honor. Although wounded with all of the other members of his headquarters group, Fox continued to command his company. He personally led an attack that captured a large bunker complex. Fox was "wounded again in the final assault . . . refused medical attention, established a defensive posture, and supervised the preparation of casualties for medical evacuation." Fox's citation concluded that his "indomitable courage, inspiring initiative, and unwavering devotion to duty in the face of grave personal danger inspired his Marines to such aggressive action that they overcame all enemy resistance."

During Operation Dewey Canyon, Marine aircraft flew 461 fixed-wing close air support missions, dropping more than two thousand tons of ordnance on enemy positions. MAG-36 and MAG-30 flew over twelve hundred helicopter sorties in support of the 9th Marines and ARVN units. Colonel Barrow's supporting artillery fired more than 134,000 rounds. U.S. and South Vietnamese forces suffered 130 dead and 920 wounded while NVA units lost an estimated 1,617 dead. The amount of enemy ordnance seized stunned even the most optimistic planners.

Much farther to the south intelligence officers at the headquarters of the 1st Marine Division and III MAF took pains to sift every grain of evidence in the closing months of 1968 to determine if Communist forces planned another large offensive. While no major indications surfaced to suggest an offensive of the magnitude of Tet 1968, enemy troop movements and contact reports pointed towards a series of coordinated attacks in Quang Nam Province around the

A Viet Cong captive awaits his fate as an ARVN interpreter studies documents found on him. As the number of VC combatants dropped through attrition, especially after Tet 1968, Marines increasingly encountered an enemy similar to this one: barefoot, attired only in shorts, and nearly emaciated as a result of operations denying him access to native foodstuffs. (National Archives)

time of the lunar new year. On 17 January 1969 the 7th Marines captured a signals officer from the headquarters of Group 44—Communist headquarters in the region—who indicated that a winter-spring offensive was in progress. Two weeks later the same regiment captured two NVA claiming to be in the 21st Regiment, who also reported a major offensive in the making. ARVN forces also detected signs of an enemy offensive brewing. Then, just before the Tet holiday, an ARVN unit clashed with an enemy battalion south of Hill 55, killing forty-nine NVA. The two prisoners taken claimed to belong to the 36th NVA Regiment, apparently moving out of its rainy-season sanctuary in the southern end of the province. The 5th Marines in the An Hoa basin reported elements of at least two NVA regiments in their area along with several Viet Cong units.

On 23 February, a squad-sized patrol from Capt. Paul K. Van Riper's Company M, 7th Marines, spotted an NVA force west of Danang. An hour later another patrol observed an enemy unit through a Starlight scope. With an artillery fire mission in progress, two squads from the 3rd Platoon went out to ambush the force. A sweep of the area at first light revealed that M/3/7 had surprised an NVA mortar company. By daylight, Company M found itself engaged with a sizeable enemy force. In a day punctuated by heavy hand-to-hand fighting—often in clouds of tear gas—the Leathernecks counted thirty NVA killed and took another three prisoners; the following day, another nine enemy soldiers died. Near Danang, a rocket ignited 240,000 gallons of JP4 aviation fuel at the 1st MAW fuel farm and

another rocket struck the ARVN ammunition dump near III MAF headquarters.

By then the remainder of Lt. Col. Francis X. Quinn's 3/7 had entered the intense fighting that erupted with the onset of the long-awaited enemy offensive. Thick stands of bamboo and dense growths of elephant grass prevented observation and provided good cover for the enemy units. The intense heat and humidity taxed the Marines heavily. Individual heroism became commonplace in 3/7 during its fierce encounter with the NVA force. One Marine, LCpl. Lester W. Weber, a machine-gun squad leader in Company M, earned a posthumous Medal of Honor in some of the most savage combat recorded by Leathernecks of the Vietnam War. In the words of his citation: "Weber's platoon came under heavy attack from concealed hostile soldiers. He reacted by plunging into the tall grass, successfully attacking one enemy and forcing eleven others to break contact." Then, "upon encountering a second NVA, [Weber] overwhelmed him in fierce hand-to-hand combat. Observing two other soldiers firing upon his comrades from behind a dike, Weber ignored the frenzied firing of the enemy and raced across the hazardous area and dived into their position." He landed beside the two NVA. Wresting an AK-47 assault rifle from one, he beat them both to death with it. "Although by now the target for concentrated fire from hostile riflemen, Weber remained in a dangerously exposed position to shout words of encouragement to his emboldened companions. As he moved forward to attack a fifth enemy soldier, he was mortally wounded."

As Company M continued to attack, the remaining units of 3/7 joined in pursuit

of the enemy. Early in the afternoon of 24 February Capt. Fred T. Fagan led Company K across the highway leading from Danang and intercepted a sizeable NVA force. In a sweep of the area the following morning, Company K discovered numerous enemy bodies and took several prisoners. Later one of the POWs was identified as an NVA regimental commander. Interrogation of the haughty captive revealed that the enemy hoped to hurt 3/7 badly enough to draw

the remainder of the 1st Marine Division into the paddies west of Danang. There at least two NVA regiments and an assortment of Viet Cong units would spring the trap. The enemy plan fell apart during the period 22–28 February, when 3/7 tore up the enemy task force and took its commander captive. Throughout I Corps, U.S. and allied units responded to the enemy offensive by repulsing every attempt to breach their positions.

In March Lt. Gen. Herman Nickerson Jr. relieved Cushman in command of III MAF. Three months thereafter President Nixon's "Vietnamization" plan went into effect. This scheme called for U.S. forces to conduct a phased withdrawal during which increased training and equipment turnovers would (supposedly) enable the South Vietnamese armed forces to shoulder the burden of defending their country by themselves. By 31 August the first increment of twenty-five thousand Americans—including several Leatherneck units—would depart Vietnam.

Even as the Oval Office announced the American retrenchment, the grim struggle in the paddies and jungles continued unabated. On 9 March, the depleted ranks of the 141st NVA Regiment chanced a daylight crossing of the Arizona Territory in hopes of slipping undetected across the Song Thu Bon to attack the headquarters of 1/7 on the north bank. Observed by elements of both 1/5 and 1/7, the survivors of the abortive post-Tet offensive of 1969 were decimated by a rain of artillery shells fired by batteries from the 11th Marines and ordnance from 1st MAW aircraft. Leathernecks found 292 enemy bodies littering the rice paddies on the south side of the Song Thu Bon. Nevertheless, Communist headquarters merely inserted another NVA regiment into the fray. In the early summer, the 90th NVA Regiment began operations in the Arizona Territory west of the An Hoa Combat Base, but elements of the 5th Marines killed an estimated 320 NVA from the new unit before the first rains of the fall monsoon fell.

In the early fall the White House announced another troop withdrawal, which included two Marine regiments and a division headquarters. Almost as if Hanoi worked in concert with the American withdrawal, significant encounters with NVA forces fell markedly. By the fall of 1969, most enemy contact consisted of terrorist acts carried out by VC guerrillas.

On 9 March 1970 XXIV Corps and III MAF exchanged positions, with the latter displacing to a new headquarters astride Red Beach. III MAF's last commanders, lieutenant generals Keith B. McCutcheon and Donn Robertson, controlled for the most part only U.S. forces in Quang Nam Province. The era of the multibattalion operations had ended. The residual Leatherneck force concentrated on providing protection for populated areas. In September 1970 the 7th Marines stood down and prepared to return to Camp Pendleton; the 5th Marines followed in February 1971. This left Col. Paul X. Kelley's 1st Marines as the only Leatherneck ground combat force in-country. It would be up to the South Vietnamese to continue the struggle.

As the Americans prepared to depart, South Vietnamese forces prepared to launch their first independent, large-scale operation. Lam Son 719, staged in early 1971, envisioned a large-scale spoiling operation across the border into the enemy sanctuaries in Laos from Quang Tri Province. U.S. advisors were pointedly excluded from the foray, as were any American ground forces. Leathernecks from the 1st Marine Division provided security along Highway 41 for the ARVN units, and Marine Corps aviators flew some helicopter support missions. Otherwise, the operation was Vietnamese in its entirety—and it became a disaster very quickly. The South

Vietnamese troops proved no match for the communist forces who outnumbered and outmaneuvered them. The disaster of Lam Son 719 foreshadowed the military future of South Vietnam.

On 14 April 1971 the colors of III MAF, the 1st Marine Division, and 1st MAW were cased; 3rd MAB became the senior Marine Corps unit in Vietnam. But even this residual force was scheduled to depart by midsummer; all combat operations on the part of U.S. forces would cease on 7 May. The only Leathernecks remaining in-country would be the guards at the U.S. Embassy in Saigon and the consulate in Danang, advisors to Vietnamese Marine units, and personnel assigned to the Air and Naval Gunfire Liaison Company (ANGLICO) that supported allied forces other than Marines.

Veterans of the lingering war wondered just how long it would take the North Vietnamese to attempt to overrun the south now that the Americans had left. In the spring of 1972 NVA forces in divisional strength struck across the DMZ and from Laos into the northernmost provinces. Farther to the south another NVA force attacked from Cambodia into the Central Highlands. In Quang Tri Province NVA forces quickly overran ARVN units astride the DMZ and occupied the old Leatherneck bases in the area; before long, the flag of North Vietnam flew over the provincial capital of Quang Tri City. As South Vietnamese forces rallied to repel the invader, the U.S. responded with naval gunfire and close air support—but no ground troops other than advisors.

Closer to the intense combat along the DMZ, a lone Marine officer provided one of the most courageous acts of the war and succeeded in blunting the NVA attack. Capt. John W. Ripley, an advisor to a Vietnamese Marine battalion, single-handedly emplaced more than five hundred pounds of explosives on the Dong Ha bridge over the Cua Viet River. As he swung hand-over-hand across the beams supporting the bridge, Communist forces on the other side of the river took him under fire. An enemy column with an estimated two hundred tanks approached, hoping to cross the bridge and continue the assault into the northern provinces. Barely returning to safety on the south side of the bridge, Ripley detonated his charges and collapsed the center span of the bridge into the river. Timbers on both sides burned for a week. For this act of consummate heroism,

Thirty-two-year-old Capt. John Ripley, shown here in the uniform of the Vietnamese Marine Corps, served two tours during the conflict. He earned the Navy Cross, Silver Star, two Bronze Stars with combat "V," and Purple Heart. Although wounded several times, he refused to report the injuries because it would result in his removal from the field. The Republic of Vietnam awarded him the Distinguished Service Order and Cross of Gallantry with Gold Star. (Courtesy Mary Ripley)

Ripley was awarded the Navy Cross; many of his contemporaries felt that he deserved the Medal of Honor.

By fall, South Vietnamese units and their American advisors had beaten off the invasion. President Nixon's clear threat to resume hostilities was not lost on the leadership in Hanoi. When Communist negotiators walked out of the Paris peace talks, the United States resumed the bombing of the north, including Hanoi, and for the first time mined Haiphong harbor. However confident North Vietnam appeared to be, its leaders knew they could expect a much tougher Nixon now that he had trounced Democratic-hopeful George S. McGovern in the presidential election. On 27 January 1973 the Paris Peace Accords were signed, ending American participation in the Second Indochina War. Within the next month, 591 American POWs—including 26 Marines—returned home; earlier, 9 Leathernecks had escaped captivity, 3 were exchanged, and 8 died in captivity. Another 105 Marines remained on the MIA list while 2 were listed as simply "unaccounted for." Capt. Donald G. Cook, captured in 1964, died in captivity; he earned a posthumous Medal of Honor for his unflagging courage in the face of hopeless odds and extreme peril.

The final chapter in the Marine Corps' involvement in the Southeast Asian struggle occurred two years later. On 12 April 1975 CH-53 helicopters from HMH-462 and HMH-463 evacuated Americans, selected government officials, and foreign nationals from the Cambodian capital of Phnom Penh in Operation Eagle Pull; five days afterwards, the Khmer Rouge entered the city in triumph. Later in the month, South Vietnamese began to flee their country as North Vietnam launched an all-out conventional invasion. During 29–30 April more than nine thousand people were evacuated from beleaguered Saigon by Marines flying helicopters from ships of the Seventh Fleet in Operation Frequent Wind. On 30 April Saigon fell to the NVA. As President Nguyen Van Thieu fled, doubtless he carried with him President Nixon's letter of 14 November 1972, which stated: "You have my absolute assurance that if Hanoi fails to abide by the terms of the agreement it is my intention to take swift and retaliatory action." But by the time of the Communist offensive in 1975, Nixon had left office in disgrace; his successor, Gerald R. Ford, and a feckless Congress chose to sit on the sidelines as a ruthless Communist takeover of South Vietnam ensued.

The longest war in the Corps' history had ended on a sour note. Casualty figures listed 13,095 Leathernecks killed in action during the divisive conflict. Another 88,594 suffered wounds, of whom 51,392 required hospitalization. Fifty-seven Marines—and a Navy chaplain and 3 hospital corpsmen serving with Leatherneck units—earned Medals of Honor, 46 of them posthumously.

CHAPTER 14

The New Breed, 1976–2000

The Vietnam War took a heavy toll on the Marine Corps, sapping its strength and morale like no conflict before. Recruiters experienced difficulty filling enlistment quotas and often met their required numbers with young men and women who did not meet the Corps' usual high standards. Some recruits came straight from courtrooms and jails, as judges grew fond of offering sentences of military service in lieu of incarceration. Career Marines, both officers and NCOs, found their days long and dark. Civilian officials appeared to take an intrusive role in military and naval affairs. Barracks lawyers, assisted by liberal-minded attorneys, found it easier to thwart the system. Conscientious commanding officers did their best, but at times it was difficult to carry on. Congressional critics convinced themselves that better living quarters for junior enlisted Marines would attract high-quality recruits. Instead, the dormitories or "military motels" that replaced the traditional barracks only made it more difficult for commanders to control their troops. Libertarians in and out of uniform contributed to the growing malaise by providing seemingly insurmountable legal hurdles in the face of rising incidences of petty thievery, racially motivated assaults, and drug and alcohol abuse of an unparalleled scale. Many career Marines left the Corps rather than face a new generation of recruits who seemed unpatriotic, apathetic, and unwilling or incapable of accepting the traditional Leatherneck code of toughness and discipline.

Shortly after the Vietnam War ended, the strength of the Marine Corps dropped to less than two hundred thousand men and women. Yet historical commitments overseas, at home, and in support of the fleet remained. In traditional "can-do" fashion, senior Leathernecks ignored what was happening outside the gate and applied themselves to day-to-day problems. Shortages in the ranks resulted in many units reverting to cadre status. More than one grizzled Marine muttered: "We've done so much for so long with so little, we can now do everything with nothin'."

On 1 January 1972 Gen. Robert E. Cushman Jr. became the commandant and thus inherited the social and political problems accompanying the postbellum stand-down. Just as during the retrenchments following previous conflicts, critics declared

We don't promise you a rose garden

THE MARINES ARE LOOKING FOR A FEW GOOD MEN.

NAVMC 7141 PCN 103 012019 00

that the Marine Corps had become an expensive anachronism unsuited to the defense needs of the United States. Officials within the office of the secretary of defense, some members of the congressional armed services committees, and analysts at the prestigious Brookings Institute united in calling for a drastic restructuring of the Corps. Following the debacle in Southeast Asia, many pundits concluded that America's military orientation lay in the direction of Western Europe and the armor-heavy defense of NATO. The Corps' expertise in amphibious warfare and light-infantry structure appeared irrelevant to the post-Vietnam defense posture.

Cushman addressed the Corps' critics in much the same strident fashion as his predecessors: "We are pulling our heads out of the jungle and getting back into the amphibious business. . . . We are redirecting our attention seaward and reemphasizing our partnership with the Navy and our shared concern in the maritime aspects of our national strategy." The commandant provided figures sure to delight congressional watchdogs: the Marine Corps provided 15 percent of the nation's ground divisions and 12 percent of the tactical air forces with only 3.6 percent of the defense budget. While the Navy supported the Corps by launching the first two multipurpose amphibious assault ships (LHAs), the *Tarawa* and *Saipan*, and promising to build seven more, it instead cut the program to five; at the same time, the number of amphibious ships was reduced by half. In response to the extreme shortage of amphibious shipping, naval planners proposed—and Congress approved—the

deployment of a series of container ships holding the large quantities of heavy equipment and supplies necessary to sustain the operations of a forward-deployed Marine amphibious brigade. Strategically located throughout the world, the container ships supposedly would make up for the shortage of amphibious ships in the fleet.

Opponents of amphibious operations also found the grist for their mills in an incident in Southeast Asia. On 12 May 1975 a Cambodian gunboat fired across the bow of the container ship SS *Mayaguez* as she crossed the Gulf of Siam en route from Hong Kong to Bangkok. A Khmer Rouge—Cambodian Communist—boarding party took over the defenseless vessel and directed it to an anchorage near Koh Tang, an island thirty-five miles from the Cambodian coast. Then, unknown to American officials, the captors moved the crew of the *Mayaguez* to the port of Sihanoukville. After meeting with his National Security Council, President Gerald R. Ford ordered a rescue mission.

The directive to "do something" passed through channels to the Seventh Air Force at Nakon Phanom, Thailand. With no amphibious forces within easy steaming distance of Koh Tang, 2/9 (reinforced with Company D, 1/4) in Okinawa boarded Air Force transports for a hurried flight to Utapao, Thailand. From this huge, joint Thai-U.S. air base on the Gulf of Siam, Air Force CH-53 and HH-53 helicopters lifted off on 15 May to seize the *Mayaguez* and rescue its crew.

Sixty-nine Marines from Company D boarded the *Mayaguez* after being off-loaded from the destroyer escort *Harold*

E. Holt. Scrambling aboard the container ship in a cloud of tear gas at 0550 on 15 May, Leathernecks found the merchant ship deserted. As America prepared to flex its military might, the government of Cambodia realized its tenuous position and began the diplomatic overtures to release the civilian crew of the merchant vessel. Nonetheless, at sea in the Gulf of Siam and in Thailand, U.S. forces began a complicated rescue mission.

A raid on Koh Tang began at 0600 on the same day. Led by Lt. Col. Randall W. Austin, 2/9 assaulted the little island in the face of devastating ground fire from its defenders. The landing force had no way of knowing that Cambodian authorities had already released the crew of the *Mayaguez* and that they were aboard their ship steaming south to Singapore. The Americans suffered heavy casualties. Of the first two helicopters to approach the eastern end of the island, intense ground fire downed one, killing seven Leathernecks, two Navy corpsmen, and the Air Force copilot. Three more Marines died as they attempted to swim from the wreckage. The second helicopter made it to the beach but with its tail rotor shot off. The survivors formed a defensive perimeter and fought off repeated Cambodian attacks throughout the day.

On the other side of Koh Tang, anti-aircraft fire damaged one helicopter full of Marines; it limped back to Thailand. Five more helicopter loads of Marines landed, one carrying the battalion command group. Strikes from Air Force fighters and mortar fire from 2/9 drove the Cambodians into the jungle. Additional Leathernecks stormed ashore, and shortly after noon two of the

three groups on the ground had linked up. By then, 225 Americans were on the island. With news of the crew's release, evacuation of the force began. By 1800 the small detachment on the eastern side of Koh Tang had departed for Thailand. Two hours later, a helicopter lifted out the last of the Leathernecks positioned on the western side of the island.

The number of casualties disturbed some members of Congress. Of the fifteen Air Force helicopters involved, ground fire downed three and damaged ten. Forty-one American servicemen died in the brief engagement or in an associated helicopter crash in Thailand. Three Leathernecks were reported missing; although declared killed in action at the time of the extraction from the island, an independent investigator discovered years later that the luckless trio had been captured by the Khmer Rouge and subsequently executed. Politically, the action alarmed critics primed to storm the barricades after the divisive experience of the Vietnam War. Some commentators suggested that the flawed response underscored the limitations of amphibious warfare.

Meanwhile, internal problems plagued the Corps, whose claim to be able to mold a man and a Marine out of any boy, regardless of his education or background, came under scrutiny. On 6 December 1975 drill instructors (DI) allowed fellow recruits to beat Pvt. Lynn E. McClure unconscious with pugel sticks. When McClure died three months later from head injuries, depot superiors chose to punish senior officers in the chain of command rather than the DIs themselves. Even before the outcry over the incident had subsided, a Parris

Marines from Company D, 4th Marines, board the SS *Mayaguez* from the destroyer escort *Harold E. Holt*, 15 May 1975. (National Archives)

Island DI accidentally shot a recruit during marksmanship training. Reacting to these embarrassments was the responsibility of a new commandant, Gen. Lewis H. Wilson, the Corps' last World War II Medal of Honor recipient on active duty, who succeeded Cushman on 1 July 1975. Wilson seized the initiative by directing a talented subordinate, Lt. Gen. Robert H. Barrow, to recommend long-term corrective measures.

The result of the Barrow initiatives, approved by Wilson, saw a sharp increase in the number of officers involved in recruit training. Recruiters were challenged to increase the numbers of high school graduates. Only after a recruit completed boot camp successfully did a recruiter receive credit for his or her accession. Old-timers decried these measures, charging that the

Corps had taken a step backwards by diluting traditional NCO prestige. Others applauded them, noting that brutalities in basic training did little to improve the military potential of recruits. The far-reaching changes, coupled with a succession of enlightened senior officers at the two recruit depots, resulted in a rapid abatement of abuses. Equally important, commanders throughout the Corps noted a significant improvement in the quality of the Marines completing recruit training. The need for "a few good men [and women]" remained, as Leatherneck service obligations worldwide continued just as they had for Marines of earlier eras.

Barrow took the helm of the Corps on 1 July 1979. As Wilson's handpicked successor, few expected bold innovations from him. Instead most observers thought he would continue existing programs to increase the combat efficiency of the Corps. Both officers enjoyed good relations with Congress and the Oval Office. A courtly, soft-spoken officer whose Louisiana drawl belied a tough and determined Marine, Barrow charmed bureaucrats in the Pentagon and members of Congress alike.

Although President Jimmy Carter chose not to respond with military means immediately after the seizure of the U.S. embassy in Teheran by Iranian revolutionaries in November 1979 or after the Soviet invasion of Afghanistan the following December, an unsuccessful attempt to rescue the American hostages in Iran—Operation Blue Light—took place in the spring of 1980. On 24 April Marine aviators piloted eight RH-53D helicopters from the aircraft carrier *Nimitz* in an attempt to liberate the U.S. citizens held captive in the Iranian capital. When three of the helicopters experienced mechanical failure, the on-scene commander of the rescue mission ordered the operation aborted at its staging area two hundred miles south of Teheran. Unfortunately, on departing the site, a helicopter collided with one of the transports, killing five airmen and three Marines. Critics suggested that both crises underscored the limitations of military power—including amphibious force—in the complicated world of the 1980s. Others scored the Carter Administration for not taking more decisive action earlier. But in the subsequent presidencies of Ronald Reagan and George H. W. Bush, the Corps had ample opportunity to demonstrate the utility of amphibious forces.

On 25 May 1982 the 32nd Marine Amphibious Unit (MAU) departed North Carolina. Like similar MAUs before it, the 32nd would cross the Atlantic and join the Sixth Fleet in the Mediterranean. During the six-month deployment, the MAU expected to participate in an amphibious exercise in Portugal and otherwise enjoy the fine liberty of the region. The disintegrating political situation in Lebanon changed these plans. On 6 June 1982 the MAU arrived at Rota, Spain. That same day, Israeli forces invaded southern Lebanon to drive the troops of the Palestine Liberation Organization (PLO) away from their borders. As conditions in Lebanon deteriorated in the wake of the Israeli incursion and the lives of foreign nationals appeared threatened, the government of Lebanon appealed to the international community for assistance in evacuating the innocent bystanders first, and then the fighters of the PLO.

Lebanese military units brought several hundred civilian evacuees to a small port ten miles north of Beirut. From there, the 32nd MAU was to escort them to safety aboard merchant ships lying offshore. Expecting the worst, the Marines landed on 25 August only to find a pleasant seaside resort populated by sunbathers, water skiers, and wind surfers. Most of the vacationing Lebanese seemed oblivious to the heavy fighting to the south. More than six thousand refugees of all nationalities passed through the MAU checkpoint. On 30 August PLO leader Yasir Arafat himself was escorted through the processing station. By 1 September the last of the PLO forces had departed, and on 10 September the MAU left Lebanon to resume its normal deployment schedule. Once again its peaceful routine would be short-lived.

The assassination of Lebanon's president-elect on 8 September plunged the country deeper into turmoil. Eight days later Lebanese Christian militiamen entered two of the PLO refugee camps and massacred more than eight hundred Palestinians. Under these explosive circumstances, the Lebanese government requested the return of the multinational peacekeeping force, including U.S. Marines. On 22 September the 32nd MAU hurriedly left Naples to take up positions around the Beirut International Airport. It joined a greatly enlarged multinational force of twenty-two hundred Italian and French troops already in Lebanon. The Marines filled sandbags, dug bunkers, and fought tedium while performing a unique mission called "presence."

There were some tense moments, but for the most part the Marines had to contend with nothing worse than boredom and minor discomfort brought on by unusually chilly weather in late fall. The 32nd MAU counted only twenty serious "incidents" during its stay ashore, and on 29 October 1982 it was relieved by another MAU. The Marines patrolled the village of Hay-es-Salaam adjacent to the airstrip. In typical Marine fashion the locale became "Hooterville"—just as the tiny village hard against the airstrip at Danang had become "Dogpatch." And just as Vietnam came to be known to a generation of Marines as simply "'Nam," Beirut became "the Root." A succession of MAUs rotated in and out of Lebanon after completing the customary six-month deployment stint.

Tensions heightened considerably on 18 April 1983 when terrorists bombed the U.S. embassy in Beirut. Marines from the MAU supplemented the normal security

guard. As a cordon of concrete and barbed wire grew increasingly tighter around the Marine perimeter, Leathernecks received orders to allow no one to enter without specific authority. A determined corporal demonstrated that when a Marine receives an order, he carries it out to the letter. Stopping an approaching limousine at rifle point, the Marine waved away the driver's protests: "But this is the president of Lebanon." The obdurate sentry remained unimpressed: "I don't give a f— who he's the president of; my orders say nobody's coming through." The incident demonstrated anew to Leatherneck commanders that "presence" drew heavily on the patience of their young Marines.

On 23 May 1983 the 24th MAU deployed ashore to the international airport. Throughout the long summer the Leathernecks patrolled the streets and alleys surrounding the airport. Presently, as the uneventful weeks passed, Marines could be observed jogging around the airport perimeter. The cuisine improved substantially over the initial diet of field rations; by then the MAUs had their own galley in operation ashore. The deployment in Lebanon grew alarmingly routine. In early fall, however, the MAU issued warnings to its subordinate units to be wary of cars rigged with explosives attempting to breach its perimeter.

Sunday, 23 October, promised to be a fine day for the Leathernecks and Bluejackets of the MAU. Commanders ordered a delayed reveille for 0600, with a modified holiday routine to follow. The MAU mess hall scheduled brunch for 0800–1000, with an afternoon holiday picnic of hot dogs and hamburgers. As the sun rose over the hills

dominating the skyline above Beirut, a sentry observed a yellow Mercedes truck circling the parking lot that separated the MAU compound from the airport. Then the vehicle sped away down the road to Beirut.

At approximately 0622, the truck reappeared, crossed the parking lot, and crashed through the wire barricade separating the parking lot from the building housing three hundred sleeping servicemen. Detonating his lethal cargo in the lobby, the Arab suicide driver set off an explosive charge equal to twelve thousand pounds of TNT and collapsed the building in one huge thunderclap. In a moment, 241 Americans died, including 220 Marines, the highest single-day loss since D-day at Iwo Jima. Twisted corpses dangled from cracks in the collapsed building, some missing legs or upper torsos, and blood dripped from the concrete support columns.

Once the shock wore off at home, the Oval Office and Pentagon took several well-aimed salvoes from critics of the Reagan administration's policy in Lebanon. Armchair tacticians demanded disciplinary action against those in the chain of command whose apparent negligence contributed to the tragedy. Their accusations were countered by the personable and patrician Gen. Paul X. Kelley, who had become the Corps' twenty-eighth commandant on 1 July 1983. An eloquent speaker, Kelly had commanded both a battalion and a regiment in Vietnam and served a tour with Britain's tough Royal Marines. He took immediate steps to diffuse criticism of his Leathernecks. In a widely reported interview, he recalled meeting an injured Marine in the intensive care ward at a military hospital in Germany: "[He was] in a critical condition with more tubes going in and out of his body that I have ever seen. When he heard me say who I was, he grabbed my camouflage coat, went up to the collar, and counted the stars. He squeezed my hand, and then attempted to outline words on his bed sheet. When what he was trying to write was not understood, he was given a piece of paper and pencil, and then he wrote 'Semper Fi.'"

Kelley requested the appointment of an independent commission to investigate the tragedy. Ultimately, a panel headed by Adm. Robert L. Long, USN (Ret.), examined the ingredients culminating in the disaster. The Long Commission's conclusions faulted senior military commanders and their civilian superiors for not providing an adequate explanation of the dubious mission of "presence." Clearly, not everyone down the chain of command understood exactly what it meant.

The Long Commission found that a specific set of rules for countering terrorist attacks had not been prepared or promulgated, despite numerous examples by extremist Arab factions determined to achieve political objectives through terrorism and intimidation. Finally, the commission blamed both the MAU and BLT commanders for failing to initiate proper precautions to protect their troops, and recommended that the secretary of defense take whatever administrative or disciplinary action he deemed appropriate. But in his testimony on Capitol Hill, Kelley argued that reasonable and prudent defensive measures had been taken; there was no way to predict the attack or adequately defend against it.

Yet the survivors carry the heaviest burden. Father George W. Pucciarelli, the 24th MAU's chaplain, provided a poignant recollection:

Three years have passed since that morning. Not a day goes by when I don't think of that moment and the long hours that followed. . . . When I think of the Marines who died in Beirut, I always think of one man, who for me has come to memorialize all the fine young men who died there. This Marine, trapped deep within the building, had survived the blast itself. . . . His left arm had been cut up badly and bled profusely. His legs were pinned in the fallen debris. Yet in his entrapment he found that he could still move his right arm. He took out a bandage in an effort to stop the bleeding. It was hopeless. He next reached into his wallet and withdrew photographs of his wife and children. He placed them on a ledge in front of him—and in this way, remembering his family, he died.

As Americans mourned the loss of their servicemen in Beirut, events in the eastern Caribbean demanded yet another deployment of Marines. On 19 October, the prime minister of Grenada was murdered in a military coup d'état. As the island nation drifted into anarchy, the Organization of Eastern Caribbean States requested U.S. military assistance. President Reagan and his advisors had two concerns: first, the presence of seven hundred Americans on the island, including a large number of students at St. George's University Medical School; secondly, the Cuban-sponsored construction of a military-capable airfield at Point Salines on the southern tip of the island, along with whatever else Cuban dictator Fidel Castro had in mind for the future of Grenada.

A request from the Joint Chiefs of Staff to the Commander-in-Chief, Atlantic

(CINCLANT), Adm. Wesley L. MacDonald, for an operational plan resulted in the formulation of a typical amphibious assault on the island. The 22nd MAU had sortied on 18 October 1983 from North Carolina for a routine deployment to the Mediterranean. Additional assets from the 2nd Marine Division would join the 22nd MAU in Grenada by air. These arrangements did not satisfy the JCS: its chairman, an Army general, and the chief of staff of the Army were supported by the Air Force member in calling for a different plan. Anxious to demonstrate the utility of the Army's new ranger battalions, this triumvirate insisted on a joint service venture. The result was an overly complicated amphibious–airborne assault fraught with communications and coordination problems of unparalleled scale—so great, in fact, that following the operation Congress dictated major changes in the conduct of joint service operations.

The 22nd MAU consisted of BLT 2/8, HMM-261, and a service support group. At 2200 on 22 October the amphibious task force received orders to turn toward

Grenada. CINCLANT estimated that the Grenadian People's Revolutionary Army (GPRA) numbered approximately twelve hundred men, reinforced with a militia of two to five thousand men and an armed police force of three to four hundred. In addition, six hundred armed Cubans, including several military advisors, were engaged in the construction of a large airfield at Point Salines. The JCS placed Vice Adm. Joseph Metcalf III, the commander of the Second Fleet, in overall command of the operation. Metcalf notified the MAU's commander, Col. James P. Faulkner, that the main operation would be conducted by Army paratroop and ranger units in a daring airborne assault, with the Marines remaining in reserve. Nevertheless, the MAU continued to plan for an amphibious or heliborne assault on the island. During the hours of darkness on 23 October, liaison officers from CINCLANT arrived with a draft operations order for the assault. The amphibious task force, TF 124, received the mission of seizing the Pearls airport and the port of Grenville, both located on the windward, or Atlantic, midsection of the

A Marine UH-1N "Huey" helicopter from the amphibious assault ship *Guam* prepares to touch down at Pearls Airport on Grenada on 25 October 1983, the first day of Operation Urgent Fury. Its door gunner is equipped with an M60D machine gun. A troop-carrying CH-53 Sea Stallion approaches at right while recently landed Marines move out. (Defense Visual Information Center)

island. Army Rangers and units of the 82nd Airborne Division would land by parachute and secure the airfield at Point Salines.

D-day was set for 25 October; Metcalf directed that no landings take place before 0400. A SEAL team, dropped into the Pearls area to reconnoiter the beach earlier, reported conditions to be marginal at best for an amphibious landing. After the first two rifle companies had been helilifted ashore, perhaps the remainder of the MAU could come ashore in landing craft. In a fitting and sentimental touch to the scenario, Navy superiors changed the movie schedule for that evening aboard the *Guam* to show John Wayne in the epic *Sands of Iwo Jima*. Reveille came all too quickly at 0100. The landing force wolfed down the traditional breakfast of steak and eggs, and then drew ammunition for the assault.

The first helicopters lifted off the *Guam* at 0315. The CH-46s carrying the Marines and the AH-1 Cobra gunships escorting them totaled twenty-one aircraft in the first wave. The Leathernecks landed without resistance or mishap just south of the airfield. Scattered but ineffectual resistance marked the remainder of the deployment ashore. Meanwhile, Company F was helilifted into the Grenville area and faced little or no opposition as the Marines secured the town and port. To the surprise of the landing force, most Grenadians welcomed them as liberators from the harsh rule of the Marxist military council and pointed out members of the GPRA attempting to flee in the guise of civilians.

As the Leathernecks consolidated their position in the Pearls area, the rangers at

Point Salines encountered stiff resistance. At 1405, two reinforced battalions of the 82nd Airborne landed at Salines to support a ranger battalion locked in combat with Cuban troops. As the pockets of resistance diminished, the rangers and paratroopers took control of the airfield and evacuated the American students from the St. George's University Medical School.

The BLT commander, Lt. Col. Ray L. Smith, took up a position ashore in the Pearls/Grenville area with his two remaining rifle companies. Company G landed on the western side of the island to lift the siege of the governor-general's residence. As the Marines burst into Government House, they found the governor-general, Sir Paul Scoon, his wife, and nine other civilians—all eager to accept evacuation to one of the ships offshore.

Shortly thereafter, Metcalf alerted Colonel Faulkner that he had just learned the True Blue Campus was only one of two campuses of the St. George's University Medical School; approximately two hundred additional students occupied an annex at Grand Anse, on the southeast side of the island. To support a rescue effort, the MAU provided nine CH-46s and four CH-53s to transport the rangers in and the evacuees out.

As the tropical sun broke over the island on the morning of 28 October, most of its residents found themselves under the control of the armed forces of the United States or nearby Caribbean nations. Then Metcalf alerted the MAU of the possibility of Cuban—or even North Korean—forces occupying the small island of Carriacou, just north of Grenada. He ordered an amphibious landing there for 1 November. Once ashore the Marines found that local GPRA members had lost all desire to engage in combat; most had shed their uniforms and were attempting to mingle with the townspeople. No Cubans or North Koreans were found.

A total of 590 U.S. citizens were evacuated from Grenada along with 80 foreign nationals who requested protection. Eighteen U.S. servicemen died and 116 suffered wounds or injuries; the casualty figures included 1 Marine dead and 6 wounded. The U.S. force accounted for 707 Cubans, including 24 killed and 59 wounded. Forty-five members of the GPRA were killed. As additional elements of the 82nd Airborne arrived, the Leathernecks returned to their ships. By the afternoon of 2 November the MAU was ready to resume its journey to the Mediterranean.

Three years later Marines participated in the Reagan Administration's aerial strike against suspected terrorist facilities in Libya, Operation Eldorado Canyon. Senior U.S. officials had long concluded that the sites harbored those responsible for recent attacks against Americans. Most damning was a signal intelligence intercept from Libya to the terrorist group in Germany responsible for the bombing of a Berlin discotheque crowded with off-duty U.S. servicemen. On 11 April 1986 F-111s flying from bases in Great Britain and F-18s catapulted from the carriers *America* and *Coral Sea* bombed targets in the North African nation. Leatherneck aviators from VMFA-314 and VMFA-323 flying F-18s participated in the airstrike.

The Marine Corps entered the last half of the 1980s burdened by a variety of troubles. Leathernecks assigned to the embassy in Moscow became embroiled in a scandal over allegations that two of their number allowed KGB agents to prowl sensitive areas of the embassy building in exchange for sexual favors from comely comrades. Another embassy Leatherneck faced charges of succumbing to blackmail after an affair with a Soviet woman. Although the Naval Investigative Service appeared to have bungled the investigations, the unproven charges tarnished the Corps' image and its splendid record of providing security for U.S. embassies worldwide.

Whenever Leathernecks appear to be in disarray, civilian authorities find it easy to intervene in their affairs. In this case, the authority was an activist secretary of the Navy—James H. Webb Jr. A former Marine himself, Webb had graduated from the Naval Academy in 1968. As an infantry platoon leader in Vietnam, he earned the Navy Cross and suffered wounds that resulted in his medical discharge. Still passionately devoted to the Corps, he decided that the Leathernecks needed a commandant able to restore the warrior spirit and toughness he remembered from his stint as a Marine. Ignoring the recommendation of Kelley and other senior officers, Webb opted for a different type of commandant.

The selection of Lt. Gen. Alfred M. Gray to be the twenty-ninth commandant of the Marine Corps in 1987 surprised most members of the Corps, not least Gray himself. Many applauded the change. An impression current in some quarters held that Kelley and the coterie of lieutenant generals around him had become military bureaucrats, too remote from Marines in the field. Al Gray was expected to bridge the gap. More than thirty years a Marine, he had carried a rifle as a teenaged private first class in the Korean War. Tough, tobacco-chewing, and plain-speaking, he now found himself the champion of much of the Marine Corps. Perceiving an overall softness pervading the ranks, Gray promised more realistic training. He disparaged such hallowed traditions as jogging in tennis shoes—preferring forced marches—and spit and polish: "I don't give a shit how you look. I care how you are!" he once exclaimed to an audience of bemused young Leathernecks. Gray also emphasized special operations, and MEUs whose components had completed the prerequisite training became entitled to the suffix SOC—Special Operations Capable. Despite his gruff exterior, Gray was by no means an anti-intellectual. Under his leadership the Quantico schools were reorganized to form the Marine Corps University.

Yet Kelley left a modernized Marine Corps prepared to fight on the battlefields of the 1990s and beyond. Sophisticated personal equipment added to the lethality of the Leatherneck infantryman. The basic quality of the individual Marine improved markedly during his tenure, from an enlisted force composed almost totally of high school graduates to a better-educated officer corps. New aircraft appeared to replace the aging warhorses of the Vietnam era. The light-armored vehicle entered the inventory, and the eight-wheel, thirteen-ton chassis offered a variety of configurations to provide ground commanders with an enhanced flexibility in maneuver warfare. Navy planners forged ahead with the development of air-cushioned landing craft that could provide an over-the-horizon assault capability with a range of at least two hundred miles. By 1986, the Navy had christened the final two of the thirteen maritime prepositioning ships (MPS). Combat loads to support MAB-level operations were in place aboard MPS shipping in Diego Garcia and Guam; shore-based equipment and supplies had been positioned in Norway.

The U.S. naval contingent in the Persian Gulf grew markedly during the Iran-Iraq War of 1980–88. On 14 April 1988 the frigate *Samuel B. Roberts* struck an Iranian mine; only Herculean efforts by her gallant crew kept the ship afloat. A special force of Leathernecks, Marine Air-Ground Task Force 2–88, collaborated with Navy forces in Operation Praying Mantis to destroy the Iranian oil-drilling platforms in the gulf. The sites had been used for military purposes such as providing support for Iranian speedboat attacks against neutral shipping.

Even as the Soviet Union began to unravel, events in other parts of the world demanded the presence of Marines. The administration of President George H. W. Bush had grown increasingly impatient with events in Panama—especially the arrogance of its president, Gen. Manuel Antonio Noriega. Mounting evidence revealed him at the center of a major drug-dealing operation. When the Panamanian strongman refused to allow his elected successor to take office, the United States reinforced its garrison in the Canal Zone with additional forces—including Marines.

On the steamy night of 16 December 1989 armed members of the Panamanian Defense Force (PDF) halted a Marine officer

and his three companions at a roadblock. They were off duty, dressed in civilian clothing, and en route to a dinner gathering. When the PDF thugs attempted to drag the unarmed Americans from the car, the driver sped away. The burst of small-arms fire that followed killed the Marine officer. At about the same time, an American Navy officer was beaten by the PDF and his wife threatened with sexual assault. From the perspective of the Oval Office, Noriega and his band of thugs had overstepped the limits of Yankee patience.

On Wednesday, 20 December, President Bush ordered an invasion of Panama to capture Noriega, destroy the forces loyal to him, and protect American lives and properties. By then, an additional seven thousand soldiers and Marines had joined the almost thirteen thousand U.S. troops already in the Canal Zone. The forces that carried out Operation Just Cause came mainly from the U.S. Army, but they included

a detachment of seven hundred Marines. The Leathernecks were ordered to seize the Bridge of the Americas spanning the canal and the Arraijan Tank Farm. The latter facility was a strategic fuel storage area in the jungle located approximately two miles from Howard Air Force Base, a U.S. cantonment on the outskirts of Panama City. The Marines assaulted residual positions held by Noriega supporters, neutralized PDF facilities, and provided roadblocks. Noriega was eventually apprehended, brought to the United States for trial, and subsequently imprisoned.

After the intervention in Panama, Leatherneck forces continued to remain on watch throughout the world. On 1 August 1990, the 13th MEU (SOC)—unit designations having changed from "amphibious" back to "expeditionary"—was in Philippine waters. Ostensibly deployed for routine training ashore and a port visit, the force had been employed in assisting the Filipino people in earthquake relief. The 22nd MEU stood off

Liberia ready to evacuate American citizens should civil unrest topple the government of that West African nation. Elsewhere, the 24th and 26th MEUs continued predeployment workup training while the 11th MEU practiced special-operations skills. None of these and other peacetime training missions and deployments suggested that almost the entire operating forces of the Marine Corps would soon deploy to the Persian Gulf.

An hour after midnight on 1–2 August 1990, three Iraqi divisions crossed the border into the small, oil-rich sheikdom of Kuwait. A special-operations division landed by helicopter in Kuwait City and by the end of the next day had taken the capital hostage. Within twenty-four hours of the invasion, the Iraqis had positioned forces on the border of Saudi Arabia. By 7 August, even before the United Nations had granted approval or before a coalition of concerned nations had been formed, Secretary of Defense Richard B. Cheney directed JCS Chairman Gen. Colin L. Powell to alert military, naval, and air units for possible deployment to the Persian Gulf. For the Marine Corps, this meant 1st MEB in Hawaii, the 7th MEB on the West Coast, and the 4th MEB on the East Coast. On 10 August Gen. H. Norman Schwarzkopf, commander-in-chief, Central Command (CENTCOM), requested the three MEBs in the Persian Gulf. Operation Desert Shield, the defense of Saudi Arabia, commenced. The 7th MEB deployed by air from Twentynine

Palms, California, and arrived at Al Jubayl, Saudi Arabia, on 14 August. Meanwhile, the ships of Maritime Prepositioning Ship Squadron (MPS)-2 had steamed from its anchorage at Diego Garcia in the Indian Ocean. The squadron carried the supplies and heavy equipment for thirty days of MEB operations. The 7th MEB was followed by the 1st MEB from Hawaii, and on 26 August MPS Squadron-3 arrived from Guam to marry up with the 1st MEB. Meanwhile, the 4th MEB sailed from North Carolina on 17 August.

On 2 September, the I MEF assumed command of all Marines in the theater of operations. The force was led by Lt. Gen. Walter F. Boomer, who had been decorated for heroism as an advisor to the South Vietnamese Marines during the 1972 Easter offensive. By 6 September I MEF consisted of the 1st Marine Division, 3rd Marine Aircraft Wing, and 1st Force Service Support Group. The Joint Chiefs of Staff gave CENTCOM operational control of all Marine forces ashore. By November 1990, more than forty-two thousand Marines—nearly one-fourth of the Corps' active-duty strength—had

deployed to the Persian Gulf. Of that total thirty-one thousand were ashore in I MEF while the 4th MEB and 13th MEU (SOC) sortied offshore to provide CENTCOM with a formidable amphibious capability.

On 8 November, President Bush announced an anticipated increase of U.S. forces in the region by more than two hundred thousand men and women. For the Marine Corps, this meant the deployment of II MEF from the East Coast and the 5th MEB from California. In his characteristically outspoken manner, Gray explained his personnel situation to a group of bemused journalists: "We now have four kinds of Marines: those in Saudi Arabia; those going to Saudi Arabia; those who want to go to Saudi Arabia; and those who don't want to go to Saudi Arabia, but are going anyway!"

Five days after President Bush revealed the quantum increase of U.S. forces into the troubled region, a selected call-up of reservists began. As weekend warriors—many with skills honed in previous conflicts—answered the call to the colors, the first of a series of amphibious exercises in the region com-

menced with Operation Sea Soldier. Clearly, this seaborne posturing was intended to offer Iraqi dictator Saddam Hussein a snapshot of what might happen if Iraq persisted in its aggression. On 1 December the 5th MEB steamed to the Gulf from Southern California to join the rapid buildup of military, air, and naval might in the region.

The next contingent of Leathernecks scheduled for the Persian Gulf was II MEF, consisting of the 2nd Marine Division, 2nd MAW (later absorbed by the 3rd MAW), and 2nd Force Service Support Group. The fly-in echelon began on 9 December with a lift rate of one thousand troops per day and was completed on 15 January 1992. Maritime Prepositioning Squadron 1 steamed

from the East Coast on 14 November and reached Al Jubayl on 12 December. By then it was determined that sufficient command-and-control and aviation elements existed in the theater, and the headquarters of the II MEF remained in North Carolina. By 15 January approximately eighty-four thousand Marines—half of the Corps' active-duty strength—had deployed to the Persian Gulf. Sixty-six thousand (including a thousand women) served ashore in I MEF units while the remaining eighteen thousand Leathernecks floated offshore in the 4th MEB, 5th MEB, and 13th MEU (SOC). This total approached that of Marines in Vietnam during the peak year of 1968 and exceeded the number landed at Iwo Jima in 1945. But Operation Desert

Shield drew rapidly to a close. Iraq indicated no willingness to abide by a UN resolution calling for its withdrawal from Kuwait, nor did Saddam Hussein demonstrate undue concern over the crippling oil embargo.

The Iraqi leadership appeared to be putting their faith in an illusionary anti-Western coalition of their Arab brothers. Libya and Iran blustered, and Jordan's King Hussein eschewed joining the coalition against Iraq, but the remaining Arab nations in the region fell into line with nations worldwide willing to resort to arms to free Kuwait. The UN deadline for the evacuation of Kuwait came and went on 15 January with no lessening of the bellicose rhetoric from Iraq. Operation Desert Storm was about to commence with the air-war phase.

On 17 January, Air Force F-117 Stealth fighter-bombers, Navy Tomahawk Cruise Missiles, Army Apache helicopters, and Navy–Marine Corps fighter-attack aircraft eliminated the Iraqi command-and-control systems. During the first twenty-four hours of the air war, Coalition aircraft flew two thousand sorties and dropped twenty-five

hundred tons of ordnance. After the first day of intense air activity, CENTCOM reported the loss of only four aircraft. In response to the bombardment, Iraq fired lethal Scud missiles at targets in Israel and Saudi Arabia. The United States then positioned Patriot ground-to-air missile units in theater to counter the threat. Leaders in the Arab countries joined their counterparts in nations worldwide in condemning the Iraqi attacks on civilian targets; the coalition of nations intent on forcing Iraq to abandon Kuwait remained intact. The air war continued unabated for more than a month. Meanwhile, the first ground action took place.

After nightfall on 29 January three Iraqi divisions rolled toward the Saudi border to deliver what was meant to be a major spoiling attack. Along the coast the 5th Mechanized Division intended to break through the Arab contingents forming Joint Forces Command-East and seize the town of Ra's al Khafji. Inland the 3rd Armored Division would penetrate the coalition front along the boundary between the Arabs and I MEF and wheel to the east and capture Al

Mish'ab, a port twenty miles below Khafji.
Farther inland the 1st Mechanized Division
would cover the Iraqis' western flank by
attacking the Marine outposts in the vicinity
of Umm Hujul.

Two of the Iraqi divisions soon came
to grief. A Marine recon team discovered
the advance of the 3rd Armored Division
and called for air strikes that eliminated it
from the play. The 1st Mechanized Division
achieved surprise but was beaten back by
a combination of ground and air action at
a cost of eleven Marines dead—tragically,
all from friendly fire. The 5th Mechanized
Division had better luck and was able to
scatter the thin screen of coalition forces
above Khafji and occupy the town.

I MEF could easily have responded to the
incursion, but military etiquette dictated that
the honor of liberating Khafji be reserved for
the Saudis, supported by Leatherneck artillery
and air power. Nevertheless, the Corps was
represented on the ground. Two Marine recon
teams were in Khafji when it was overrun.
The senior NCO, Cpl. Charles Ingraham,
reached a courageous decision quickly. Rather
than join in the retreat, the Leathernecks

climbed to a rooftop where they could call
in fire for a counterattack. They remained
undetected, and their fire directions proved
instrumental in the town's recapture two days
later. Concurrently, the 4th and 5th MEBs
conducted Exercise Sea Soldier IV off Oman,
and the 13th MEU (SOC) executed Operation
Sting, an amphibious raid on the Iraqi-
occupied island of Maradim. Although enemy
forces had abandoned the site, Marines seized
large stocks of material.

By then CENTCOM had settled on its
campaign plan—an end-run by the XVIII
Airborne Corps and VII Corps around the
desert flank of the four hundred thousand
Iraqi troops dug in above the Saudi frontier.
The XVIII Airborne Corps would swing wide
to reach the Euphrates and prevent the Iraqi
Army in Kuwait from being withdrawn or
reinforced; VII Corps' armor and mechanized
infantry would destroy it. Initially, Army
planners proposed to assign I MEF a secondary role in this operation. Boomer did not
take that news kindly, protesting that the
Marines should be permitted to strike toward
Kuwait City. Schwarzkopf concurred, and
later, when his staff suggested still another

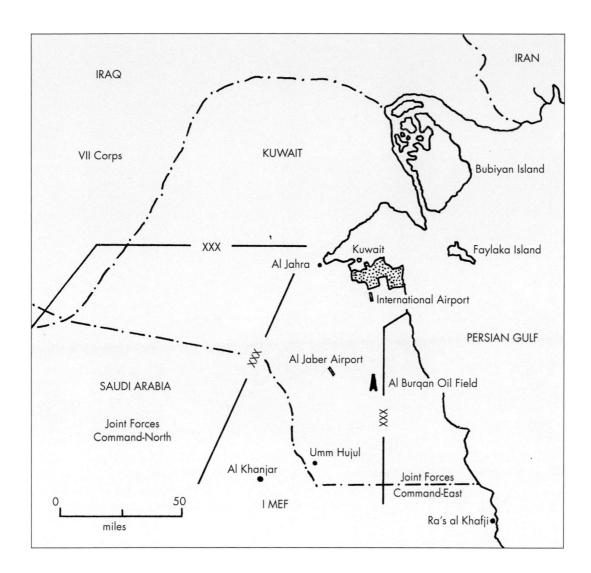

mission for I MEF, he snarled: "Stop screwing with the Marines."

Boomer and his staff made plans to attack northeastward into Kuwait on both sides of Umm Hujul with I MEF's divisions in line: the 1st Marine Division (Maj. Gen. James M. Myatt) on the right, and the 2nd Marine Division (Maj. Gen. William Keys) on the left. The 2nd Armored Division's Tiger Brigade, attached to I MEF for the campaign, would cover the Leathernecks' left flank. To support the advance, the Marine logistics command, headed by Brig. Gen. Charles C. Krulak, built an 11,280-acre, mostly underground supply base in the Saudi desert; Krulak christened it Al Khanjar, Arabic for "dagger." The idea of complementing the offensive with an amphibious assault was finally dropped in early February because the Navy lacked an adequate mine-clearing capability.

Encouraged by the Iraqis' poor showing in the January battles, Boomer counted on reaching Kuwait City in three days. CENTCOM planners, in contrast, believed that the Marines would merely absorb the Iraqis' attention while the Army's two corps enveloped them. Accordingly, I MEF and most of the XVIII Airborne Corps were scheduled to attack on the opening day of the ground war; VII Corps would not jump off until the next day.

On 14–15 February, I MEF opened its new command post near Al Khanjar. While the air war continued to pound Iraq, elements of the Leatherneck divisions conducted screening operations and probed the Iraqi obstacle belts along the border. Four days later, both divisions began moving to final positions in preparation for the ground assault. Deception operations and tests of

Iraqi defenses continued. Ground operations in Operation Desert Storm began at 0400 on 24 February 1991. Many steeled themselves for reports of heavy casualties. Concerns over Iraq's chemical and biological weapons capability weighed heavily on the minds of commanders at all levels.

I MEF units spearheaded the attack toward Kuwait City, with the Arab joint forces' commands to their left and right following a day later. Leading elements of both Marine divisions breached the obstacle belts and penetrated into Kuwait at first light. Keys' Leathernecks moved forward to the inspiring strains of "The Marines' Hymn," played at full volume from the loudspeakers of an Army psychological warfare unit attached to the Tiger Brigade. Combined-arms task forces from the 1st Marine Division captured the Al Jaber airfield, which had become an Iraqi fire base and command

center, and reached the Al Burqan oil field. The invading Marines took twenty-one Iraqi tanks and more than four thousand POWs while suffering one Marine killed and nine wounded, and damage to three tanks and one light armored vehicle. In the 2nd Marine Division's zone, the 2nd Light Armored Infantry Battalion screened for the 6th and 8th Marines and the Tiger Brigade. Losing only one dead and eight wounded in the daring thrust, 2nd Marine Division units reported the capture intact of an entire Iraqi tank battalion and forty-five hundred POWs, including a brigade commander. At the same time 3rd MAW flew 671 sorties in support of I MEF. Leatherneck aviators struck elements of six Iraqi divisions and reported the destruction of 40 tanks, 121 vehicles, 3 antiaircraft artillery sites, and 4 missile sites. Offshore, the 5th MEB sent Regimental Landing Team 5 ashore to constitute a

Left: Marine gunners fire 155-mm shells from an M-198 howitzer at Iraqi positions inside Kuwait on 20 February 1991. (Defense Visual Information Center)

Bottom Right: Leatherneck tankers perform maintenance on their M-60A1 main battle tanks deep inside Kuwait on the afternoon of 27 February 1991. On the ground between the tanks are mine-clearing plows and rollers. (Department of Defense Still Media Records Center)

reserve force for I MEF. By nightfall Boomer's troops were nearly halfway to Kuwait City.

The Marines' breathtaking breakthrough took CENTCOM planners by surprise. They had not expected I MEF to do more than fix the Iraqis in place until VII Corps slammed into their flank. Instead, the Marines were obviously well on the way to driving the Iraqis out of the theater of operations. At 1300 Schwarzkopf ordered VII Corps to begin its attack that afternoon, a day ahead of schedule.

The next morning Leathernecks found the northern horizon shrouded by dense black smoke pouring from oil wells the enemy had set ablaze. Shortly after sunrise, the Iraqis exploited the situation to launch their first and last counterattack. Two mechanized brigades, about 250 vehicles altogether, charged out of the smoke cloaking the Al Burqan oil

field toward the 1st Marine Division. At one point, Iraqi armor approached to within four hundred yards of General Myatt's command post, but by midday the enemy thrusts had been repulsed. The division also cleared the remnants of the Iraqi defenders from the Al Jaber airfield. An estimated eighty enemy tanks and one hundred other destroyed vehicles dotted the desert while more than two thousand prisoners added to the burgeoning bag of dispirited Iraqi soldiers opting to throw down their arms rather than face annihilation. The 2nd Marine Division enjoyed equal success, destroying 248 tanks and taking forty-five hundred prisoners. In support of the operation, the 3rd Marine Aircraft Wing flew 460 sorties. Offshore, the 4th MEB conducted an amphibious demonstration designed to convince the

Iraqi leadership that a heliborne assault was imminent. Gunfire from the battleship *Missouri* added to the illusion. At 2000, after approximately forty hours of ground combat, the Iraqi Army began to retreat from Kuwait.

On the third day of the ground war, 26 February, elements of the 1st Marine Division assaulted the Kuwait International Airport. By the time Iraqi forces in the area surrendered late that afternoon, 250 of their T-55 and T-62 tanks had been destroyed. Friendly personnel and equipment losses remained remarkably low. The next day, the division consolidated positions around the airport and paved the way for Arab forces to enter Kuwait City. At the highest levels, it was deemed politically correct to allow units from Arab nations in the coalition to be the first to enter the Kuwaiti capital. Units of the 2nd Marine Division remained in blocking positions near Al Jahra. There they would join with Kuwaiti resistance forces to assist another contingent of Arab forces moving on Kuwait City.

At 0800 on 28 February, just four days into the ground offensive, President Bush ordered a cease-fire. The costs to the opposing sides in Operation Desert Storm were ridiculously lopsided. The forces of I MEF destroyed 1,040 tanks, 608 armored personnel carriers, 432 artillery pieces, and 5 missile sites and captured more than 22,308 POWs. Despite the somber predictions at home of heavy casualties, Marine commanders reported only 5 dead and 48 wounded in the four days of combat. An estimated 1,510 Iraqi troops had been killed by Leatherneck units. The 3rd MAW lost 2 aircraft during the ground offensive, and 4 fixed-wing aircraft and 1 helicopter prior to its opening. During Operation Desert Storm, Marines earned two Navy Crosses, eight Distinguished Service Medals, fourteen Silver Stars, and twenty-one Distinguished Flying Crosses. The Marine Corps had validated its strict code of professionalism and élan, and Al Gray earned the credit for preparing his Marines to fight in a high-tech war in the 1990s.

The coalition's war aim, the liberation of Kuwait, had been achieved more quickly and economically than seemed possible. Some

observers faulted President Bush for not carrying the war to Baghdad and toppling Saddam Hussein, but that would have fragmented the coalition, whose Arab leaders were already uneasy about the mood in their own capitals. Saddam's days appeared to be numbered, in any event.

Iraq is inhabited by three distinct groups: the Kurds, a non-Arabic people in the north, comprising about 20 percent of the population; Sunni Muslims concentrated in the so-called Sunni Triangle north and west of Baghdad, constituting another 20 percent; and Shiite Muslims, forming the remaining 60 percent. Saddam, himself a Sunni, chose his principal lieutenants from that sect. The Kurds had long aspired to independence, or at least autonomy, while the Shiites dreamed of ending the Sunnis' political predominance. At the close of the war both groups launched revolts. Unfortunately, Saddam remained powerful enough to crush them. By the end of March a third of the Kurdish population was streaming toward the country's forbidding northern frontiers. Iran admitted more than a million refugees, but Turkey,

with restive Kurds of its own, halted half a million at the border.

On 7 April the United States—to an extent indirectly responsible for the Kurds' plight—began airdropping supplies to them. British Prime Minister John Major then proposed expanding the scope of Operation Provide Comfort, as the air drops had been named, by deploying an international ground force to create safe havens for the Kurds inside Iraq. President Bush concurred and on 10 April the United States, Great Britain, and France announced the imposition of a no-fly zone for Iraqi military aircraft north of the 36th Parallel. The dispatch of eleven thousand American and nine thousand Western European troops followed. The U.S. contingent included the 26th MEU (SOC). The Iraqis chose not to interfere, and by mid-July the ground force had withdrawn. The air umbrella remained in place for more than a decade.

A second no-fly zone policed by the same three nations, this one south of the 32nd (later extended to the 33rd) Parallel, was established a year later to discourage Saddam's

Left: Marines roll into Kuwait International Airport in light armored vehicles on 27 February 1991, the final full day of Operation Desert Storm. A CH-53 Sea Stallion helicopter appears at right. (Defense Visual Information Center)

Right: The commanding officer of the 1st Battalion, 1st Marines, Lt. Col. Michael D. Fallon, took this photograph of some of his Leathernecks in "Mopp" (chemical protective) suits atop a dug-in Iraqi tank at Kuwait International Airport on 27 February 1991. (U.S. Naval Institute Photo Archives)

continued persecution of the Shiites in the Tigris-Euphrates delta. The new air patrol was designated Operation Southern Watch. Operation Provide Comfort was renamed Operation Northern Watch in 1997, at which time France dropped out. Leatherneck aviators participated in both watches. F/A-18 Hornet strike fighters routinely flew patrols in support of Southern Watch from carriers in the Persian Gulf, and KC-130 aerial refuelers were held in readiness at Incirlik, Turkey, Northern Watch's base, to support the helicopters standing by to rescue airmen downed inside Iraq. Later in the decade AV-8B Harrier II STO/VL (short take off/vertical landing) attack aircraft from amphibious ready groups made occasional appearances over the south-ern no-fly zone and a squadron of EA-8B Prowler electronic warfare aircraft was based at Incirlik. The

remnant of Saddam's air force never contested these activities, but the target-acquisition radar of Iraqi SAM sites and antiaircraft artillery sometimes locked on coalition aircraft, which responded by launching antiradiation missiles at the offending positions. Despite years of trying, the Iraqis failed to shoot down a single plane.

Gen. Carl E. Mundy relieved Gray as commandant of the Marine Corps in July 1991. A graduate of Auburn University who earned his commission through the Platoon Leaders Class program, Mundy had grown up knowing that he wanted to be a Marine. In Vietnam he had served as the executive officer of 3/26 and on the staff of III MAF. As commandant he emphasized the Corps' long-established partnership with the Navy in the conduct of littoral warfare, the presumptive employment of both services now that the collapse of the Soviet Union had ended the Cold War. Equally notable was his success in maintaining the strength of the Corps at 174,000 personnel, a considerable achievement in an era of aggressive budget cutting. His calm, deliberate manner proved helpful in smoothing some of the feathers ruffled by Al Gray. When Mundy retired four years later, President Clinton told him, "Of all the general officers I have worked with, you were the one I knew was always telling me exactly what you believed."

Yet not all of Mundy's initiatives were successful. Every commanding officer knows the enormous financial and emotional difficulties that young Marines inflict on themselves through marriage at an early age. Mundy, planning to eliminate that situation and the complications it caused, announced that the Marine Corps would no longer accept married recruits. To Mundy's surprise and chagrin, Secretary of Defense Les Aspin pilloried his decision as "antifamily" and overruled him. The embarrassed commandant was forced to recant his edict.

During the 1990s the Corps became involved in an ill-starred attempt at nation building and two major peacekeeping operations. The former took place in Somalia, where in 1991 long-time dictator Mohammed Siad Barre was overthrown in a bloody civil war. His downfall plunged the country into anarchy as the warlords of the most powerful of the clans that composed Somali society jockeyed to succeed him. By the summer of 1992 a million and a half people were in danger of starvation; three hundred thousand had already succumbed. When the dimensions of the tragedy became known, the United States, the United Nations, and private aid organizations sent food and medicine pouring into Somalia. The immediate result was to demonstrate that without troops to safeguard distribution centers and convoys most of the supplies intended for the starving would end up in the hands of armed thugs. Late in November 1992 the United States volunteered to commit forces, and the United Nations accepted its offer. The first U.S. troops—Navy SEALs and force recon Marines, followed by elements of the 15th MEU (SOC)—went ashore at Mogadishu on 9 December. Other units, Army as well as Marine, quickly joined them; by year's end 12,500 American military personnel were serving in Somalia. A Marine lieutenant general, Robert B. Johnson, commanded what soon became United Task Force (UTF) Somalia.

Moving swiftly, American, Canadian, and Western European troops occupied Mogadishu and nine designated distribution centers well ahead of schedule. The security they established around these sites almost extinguished what a Marine officer called "Somalia's extortion economy," and within days convoys were flowing smoothly to the famine belt. Ironically, the operation's very success antagonized the clan gunmen, who concluded that the foreign forces represented a threat to their status and their livelihood. Snipers began firing at Marine patrols, which not only fired back but also confiscated weapons' caches. On one occasion helicopter gunships reduced the compound housing a warlord's arsenal to rubble. As Marine Maj. Gen. Anthony C. "Tony" Zinni, UTF Somalia's director of operations, put it: "The

Opposite: A Marine combat patrol moves out during Operation Provide Comfort, a follow-on operation to Desert Storm intended to protect the Kurds in northwestern Iraq. (Defense Visual Information Center)

training. During the night of 8 April 1956 an inexperienced drill instructor marched the seventy-four recruits of Platoon Seventy-One into the murky waters of Ribbon Creek on an unauthorized punishment hike. Six Marines drowned. The drill instructor, SSgt. Matthew C. McKeon, admitted that he had been drinking. The outcry following the deaths suggested to many observers that the Corps' senior leadership had lost control. To regain command and to prevent future training accidents, HQMC ordered the creation of a recruit training regiment at both depots, with their commanding officers reporting directly to an inspector-general of recruit training at HQMC.

Leatherneck commitments overseas remained significant. In the summer of 1958 competing factions in the Lebanese presidential election brought that Middle Eastern nation close to anarchy. Troops from nearby Syria loomed menacingly, exacerbating the situation, and the government of Lebanon asked that the United States and Great Britain intervene. A sizable force of Marines was present in the Mediterranean at the time: BLT 1/8 aboard ships just north of Malta, BLT 3/6 at sea between Athens and Crete, and BLT 2/2 steaming between Cyprus and Beirut. The headquarters of the 2nd Provisional Marine Force was in the area, ostensibly to conduct an amphibious exercise in Sardinia.

At 1330 on 15 July 1958, BLT 2/2 stormed ashore in full battle regalia across a Lebanese beach filled with soft-drink peddlers and gawking sunbathers. At 0730 the following morning BLT 3/6 joined it and the two forces marched toward Beirut. Two days later, BLT 1/8 filed ashore and BLT 2/8 arrived by air. A British brigade landed in Jordan and the U.S. 24th Airborne Brigade from Germany joined Marine forces in Lebanon on 19 July. Despite predictions to the contrary, the Lebanese went to the polls without incident on 31 July. On 18 October, the last of the Leathernecks departed; five days later, the president-elect took office.

Widespread misgivings over Pate's style of managerial leadership notwithstanding, President Eisenhower reappointed him to a second two-year term on 1 January 1958. Increasingly, however, Pate angered his civilian superiors. The Corps' two hundred thousand men and women absorbed one-fourth of the Navy Department's budget. Critical of the ballooning military-industrial complex, Eisenhower sought reductions. Citing congressional authority for three divisions and three wings, Pate opposed the lower manpower figures the administration favored. As Pate's second term of office approached its end in 1959, senior officials looked for a team player to replace him.

Lt. Gen. Merrill Twining, a brilliant planner and dedicated staff officer, appeared to be the odds-on favorite. But Eisenhower sought a dramatic shift in direction for the Marine Corps in the nomination of the next commandant. Twining's role in orchestrating the defeat of the Army's attempt to emasculate the Marine Corps during the defense unification squabble after World War II era remained in the memory of the president and his staff. The press release on 11 September 1959 stunned naval circles. The administration had bypassed Twining, four other lieutenant generals, and several senior major generals to select Maj. Gen. David

Somalis will test you, and if they do, you've got to snap their garters pretty smartly."

When U.S. troops first deployed to Somalia, the government pledged that they would be withdrawn by 20 January 1993. The humanitarian crisis had in fact been overcome by that date, but the troops remained. "Mission creep" had set in. UN secretary general Boutros Boutros-Ghali implored the United States to keep its soldiers and Marines in Somalia until a multinational UN force could be assembled to replace them, and Washington agreed to delay their departure. The last Marine unit did not leave Mogadishu until 24 April. A few days later Johnson transferred command to a Turkish general. Four thousand U.S. soldiers remained in Somalia.

By then the ground rules had changed. On 26 March the UN Security Council passed a resolution that not so subtly changed the objective of the operations in Somalia from famine relief to nation building. This project envisioned marginalizing the warlords by disarming the clans. As might have been expected, the warlords bridled. The ensuing violence climaxed on the streets of Mogadishu on 3 October, when a detachment of four hundred U.S. Army Rangers and Delta Force commandos was ambushed on the way to arrest a warlord believed responsible for the massacre of twenty-four Pakistani

peacekeepers. Eighteen Americans were killed and seventy wounded.

Shocked by the costliest day's fighting for U.S. forces since the Vietnam War, the Clinton administration announced that the troops in Somalia would be reinforced immediately and withdrawn in six months. The last transport left Mogadishu on 24 March 1994. Two amphibious ready groups lay offshore with embarked MEUs ready to intervene in case of need, but the evacuation proceeded peacefully.

The Americans' departure left ten thousand third-world peacekeepers in Somalia. These contingents stuck it out for almost a year before being evacuated by UN Combined Task Force United Shield between 27 February and 3 March 1995. Meticulously planned and executed under the orders of Tony Zinni, a lieutenant general now, the operation involved twenty-three ships from six nations and thirty-five hundred U.S. and Italian Marines. The two nations' Leathernecks secured a perimeter from which the peacekeepers were withdrawn. Hoping to avoid bloodshed, Zinni ordered his men to ignore the potshots roving Somali gunmen loosed in their direction, but when the firing became too persistent he gave U.S. Marine snipers a concise counterorder: "Take them out." There were no friendly casualties. In the best tradition of Leatherneck leadership, Zinni was the last to leave the beach.

Marine Sniper, Mogadishu, Somalia, 1993, by Col. Peter M. "Mike" Gish, USMCR, shows a Leatherneck from the 15th MEU during a dawn raid on a gang headquarters. (Marine Corps Art Collection)

Both peacekeeping operations occurred in the Balkans. The outburst of nationalism throughout Eastern Europe following the collapse of the communist dictatorships was all the fiercer for having been so long suppressed. Of the six so-called republics that had formed the Serb-dominated federation of Yugoslavia, no fewer than four—Bosnia-Herzegovina, Croatia, Macedonia, and Slovenia—declared independence in 1991. Macedonia was the only one whose secession the intransigent Serb (later Yugoslav) president Slobodan Milošević did not oppose with force. Western diplomacy halted the fighting in Croatia and Slovenia within a few months, but Milošević refused to relinquish Bosnia-Herzegovina, which included a substantial Serbian population. Instead, the Yugoslav Army and the Bosnian Serbs undertook a barbaric campaign of "ethnic cleansing"—a euphemism for expropriation, arson, murder, and rape—directed against Bosnia's Muslim population. Neither economic sanctions, the deployment of peacekeepers, nor the expulsion of Yugoslavia from the United Nations succeeded in altering Milošević's policy.

In 1993 the North Atlantic Treaty Organization (NATO) initiated two more forcible measures in which Leathernecks became engaged: the imposition of a no-fly zone over Bosnia-Herzegovina, Operation Deny Flight, to protect the peacekeepers and deprive the Yugoslavs of air support; and a naval blockade of the Adriatic, Operation Sharp Guard, to prevent munitions from reaching Yugoslavia by sea. The conduct of Deny Flight was for the most part peaceful, although on a handful of occasions NATO planes, including Marine Hornets based at Aviano, Italy, attacked targets that threatened the peacekeepers or the air patrols.

The amphibious ready groups that rotated in and out of the Adriatic also spent a generally quiet three years, but in June 1994 a U.S. Air Force officer had reason to be very glad that one was there. On the second of that month, Capt. Scott O'Grady ejected near Banja Luka, Bosnia, when a Serbian SAM hit his F-15C Fighting Falcon while on an Operation Deny Flight patrol. After six dangerous days' hide-and-seek with Serbian search parties, O'Grady was extracted by a Marine TRAP (tactical recovery of aircraft and personnel) team from the 24th MEU (SOC) embarked on the *Kearsarge.* The airman was picked up without incident, but the helicopters' return flight attracted appreciable ground fire, happily inaccurate. Recalling his ordeal O'Grady said, "The real heroes in this story are the Marines. They trained and prepared for the mission with what they had, and when the call came, they unhesitatingly went into harm's way. When your back's to the wall, you want someone who'll do whatever it takes. From personal experience, I can tell you, 'Send in the U.S. Marines.'"

After four fitful years, the Bosnian conflict suddenly came to a close. In August 1995 Serb mortar shells bloodied a crowded marketplace in the city of Sarajevo. World famous as the site of the 1994 Winter Olympics, Sarajevo had become a symbol of Bosnia's agony. The attack on it spurred NATO to take its most vigorous action to date, a sustained bombing campaign, Operation Deliberate Force, which commenced on 30 August. A dozen all-weather F/A-18D Hornet two-seaters from Marine Fighter Attack Squadron (All Weather) (VMFA [AW])-533 joined in the sorties flown from the NATO base at Aviano, Italy, as did ten Prowlers from Marine Tactical Electronic Warfare Squadrons VMAQ-1 and VMAQ-3 and Harriers operated amphibious ready groups from the *Kearsarge* and the *Wasp* in the Adriatic. A total of 3,515 strikes were launched against 338 targets over a period of seventeen days, with a time-out for talks. Coupled with a ground offensive by the Bosnian Muslims and their Croatian allies, the air attack brought the Serbs to the bargaining table. In November Milošević and the presidents of Bosnia-Herzegovina and Croatia reached an agreement that restored peace to the region. The contested republic was transformed into a union of two self-governing components, one populated largely by Muslims and Croats, and the other by Serbs. Yugoslavia withdrew its troops from both, and the UN peacekeepers were replaced by a stronger NATO force.

The Balkan peace was short-lived. Before the disintegration of Yugoslavia, the Serbian province of Kosovo enjoyed autonomy. Milošević had put an end to this arrangement, revoking the province's autonomy and steadily increasing the Serb government's sway over its primarily ethnic Albanian population. By 1996 these measures had provoked the formation of a resistance movement, the Kosovo Liberation Army. The Serbian army and paramilitary organizations responded two years later by undertaking another brutal wave of ethnic cleansing, this time aimed at the Kosovar Albanians.

Still horrified by what had happened in Bosnia, the United States and the Western European nations reacted to this new provocation by an aerial show of force and round-the-clock diplomacy. Neither had any effect, and on 23 March 1999 NATO went to war for the first time in its fifty-year history by authorizing air strikes against Yugoslavia. Within hours, the U.S. Senate approved American participation. Operation Allied Force opened with an attack on the Serbian air defense system on the evening of the twenty-fourth.

The air campaign lasted seventeen days. During that period the number of NATO aircraft involved increased from 400 to 1,050. U.S. Air Force, Navy, and Marine planes constituted 70 percent of the total force, flew 50 percent of its 38,000 sorties, and delivered 80 percent of its ordnance. Allied command of the air was virtually absolute—only one aircraft was lost—and targets were carefully selected to minimize civilian casualties. The Aviano-based Prowlers of VMAQ-2 protected strike aircraft throughout the conflict by jamming enemy radar and communications. Together with their compatriots in VMAQ-4 and VMAQ-1, who reached the scene later, they logged some 460 sorties in the course of the offensive. Four Harriers from the *Nassau* amphibious ready group struck targets in Yugoslavia on 15 April, and on 28 May two squadrons of F/A-18D Hornets, VMFA (AW)-533, and VMFA (AW)-332, arrived from Marine Corps Air Station, Beaufort, South Carolina, to enter the fray.

The cease-fire terms that Milošević finally accepted called for the withdrawal of his forces from Kosovo, the restoration of the province's autonomy, and the introduction of fifty thousand UN peacekeepers. The first to reach the U.S. occupation zone was Battalion Landing Team 3/8 of the 26th MEU from the *Kearsarge* ready group. This nasty little conflict was Milošević's last hurrah. Turned out of office in 2000, he was subsequently handed over to the UN War Crimes Tribunal at The Hague. He died of a heart attack during his trial.

At the same time that it was participating in the complicated operations in Somalia and the Balkans, the Marine Corps continued to perform its traditional mission of protecting American (and associated) lives imperiled by war or disorder in unruly places of the world. Seven such rescues took place in the nineties: at Mogadishu, Somalia, in 1991; Bujumbura, Burundi, in 1994; Monrovia, Liberia, and Bangui, Central African Republic, in 1996; Tirana, Albania, and Freetown, Sierra Leone, in 1997; and Asmara, Eritrea, in 1998. In every case, Marines evacuated endangered U.S. and foreign nationals by air without loss to themselves or those they rescued. Only in Tirana was there scattered firing, and the only casualty was an Albanian who had the misfortune to be observed aiming a shoulder-fired missile at a Marine helicopter. Leatherneck units also participated in the restoration of democracy in Haiti, where only the last-minute capitulation of the military dictatorship averted a full-scale invasion (1994), and supported Australian peacekeepers in helping to stabilize the fragile new nation of East Timor (1999, 2000).

As in the past, Marines provided humanitarian aid to victims of natural and man-made disasters. On the evening of 29 April 1991 Cyclone Marian roared ashore in Bangladesh, killing 131,000 people and causing catastrophic damage. An amphibious ready group with the 5th MEB embarked, en route home from the Gulf War, was diverted to the scene. With the help of U.S. Army and Air Force planes, Marines, and sailors distributed 4,500 tons of desperately needed supplies. Local officials credited Operation Sea Angel with saving thirty thousand lives. Later in the decade Leathernecks were among the American forces deployed to aid refugees from the Rwandan civil war (1994), flood victims in Kenya (1998) and Mozambique (2000), and survivors of an earthquake in Turkey (2000). Closer to home they helped the homeless after hurricanes and severe storms in Puerto Rico (1999), Central America (1999), and Venezuela (2000) and fought forest fires in Idaho (2000).

In 1995 Gen. Charles C. "Chuck" Krulak succeeded Carl Mundy to become the Corps' thirty-first commandant. Best known for his brilliant performance as chief of I MEF's advanced logistics in the Gulf War, Krulak was a graduate of the Naval Academy Class of 1964. He had served two tours in Vietnam, commanding a rifle platoon and two rifle companies and emerging with a Silver Star, three Bronze Stars, and two Purple Hearts. Even before 9/11, Krulak anticipated that in the future Marines would face the challenge of "asymmetrical" warfare—struggles in which an enemy unable to compete with U.S. forces in a conventional conflict would seek to circumvent rather than engage them and accept action only in circumstances chosen to neutralize American technological supremacy: urban areas, for example. The result would

be what Krulak styled a "three-block war," one in which the same Marine unit might find itself providing humanitarian assistance, keeping the peace, and fighting a battle within the same three-block area on the same day.

To help prepare for such conflicts, Krulak established the Marine Corps Warfighting Laboratory at Quantico, a center meant to reprise the role the Quantico schools had played in the development of amphibious doctrine seventy years earlier in readying the Leathernecks for the battlefields of the twenty-first century. He also increased the rigor of the Corps' already rugged recruit training program and introduced a capstone event called the Crucible, a grueling, virtually

sleepless, forty-four-hour exercise carefully designed so that it can be completed only through teamwork. Finally, Krulak supported the development of a new generation of hardware, including the revolutionary tilt-rotor MV-22 Osprey, able to operate as both a helicopter and a fixed-wing aircraft, and an amphibious assault vehicle capable of carrying a rifle squad ashore from over the horizon and serving as an armored fighting vehicle once it reached land.

On 1 July 1999 Gen. James L. Jones Jr. accepted the Corps' battle color from Krulak in the traditional change of command ceremony at Eighth and Eye. The son of a retired Marine colonel working abroad,

Like their nineteenth-century forebears, modern Marines are often called to the aid of American citizens abroad. On 15 March 1997 Leathernecks airlifted from the amphibious assault ship *Nassau* form a defensive perimeter around the American embassy housing compound in Tirana, Albania, to safeguard the evacuation of U.S. nationals after widespread rioting led to the collapse of the Albanian government. (Defense Visual Information Center)

Jones had spent his boyhood in Paris and joined the Marines after taking a bachelor's degree at the Georgetown University School of Foreign Service. In Vietnam he served as a rifle platoon leader and company commander, winning the Silver Star and Bronze Star. As commandant, Jones focused on maintaining and enhancing the capabilities of the Corps' operating forces. He found this no easy task in an era of aggressive budget cutting, but his native diplomacy and the Congressional contacts he had made during previous Washington tours enabled him to obtain the appropriations needed to fund the Corps' personnel and programs. One of the most important of the latter ran into trouble in 2000 when two of the first four production-model Ospreys crashed, killing everyone on board. Although investigations revealed that one crash was the result of pilot error and the other of a mechanical failure unrelated to tilt-rotor technology, the disasters caused many skeptics to conclude that the Osprey was a turkey in disguise. To demonstrate his confidence in the new aircraft, Jones took a highly publicized flight in one—accompanied by his wife.

The Marine Corps that entered the new millennium had changed dramatically from the one that came home from Vietnam. In the early 1970s, senior Marines concluded that the Corps could not isolate itself from the political and socioeconomic turmoil outside the gate. A generation of Leathernecks may recall with little fondness the required attendance at human relations seminars ("hum-rel" in the vernacular of the day) designed to create awareness of the needs and fears of women and minorities. Hum-rel has

come and gone, but the number of minority Marines and women in positions of authority has increased. On 27 April 1979 veteran aviator Frank E. Peterson became the first African American Marine to be selected for general officer rank; he retired as a lieutenant general. Women now serve in Marine security detachments at U.S. embassies worldwide and fill a wide variety of positions throughout the Corps. Women deployed with force service support groups during operations Desert Shield and Desert Storm. No longer is it necessary to maintain separate organizations at posts and stations for "WMs." And the pejorative term "BAMs" (Big-Assed Marines) has slipped into the dustbin of the Corps' history after more than four decades of insulting usage. On 15 May 1985 Gail M. Reals became the first woman Marine to win a brigadier general's stars in competition with male Marines. First Lieutenant Sarah Deal qualified as a helicopter pilot in 1995, making her the Corps' first female aviator. Carol A. Mutter retired as a lieutenant general in 1998. Frances C. Wilson served first as a major general as the commandant of the Industrial College of the Armed Forces and earned another star when she became the president of the National War College.

Meanwhile, Saddam Hussein continued to cause problems. Militarily, Saddam never recovered from the Gulf War; the no-fly zones were not the only checks on his freedom of action. The continuation of the UN economic and military sanctions imposed before the war deprived him of the means to reequip his armed forces, and the cease-fire terms required him to destroy his existing stocks of weapons of mass destruction (WMD), to desist from developing other WMDs, and to cooperate with UN inspectors dispatched to monitor and verify both procedures. Hobbled as he was, however, Saddam remained a force for regional instability. On three occasions between 1994 and 1996 he instigated troop movements that appeared to presage an invasion of Kuwait or the Kurdish Autonomous Zone. The Clinton administration responded to two of these deployments by rushing forces to the region, amphibious ready groups leading the way, and to the third by launching forty-four cruise missiles at air defense sites in southern Iraq. Each time, Saddam's spokesmen protested that he had merely been holding maneuvers.

Then, in 1998, Saddam hit upon the tactic that would become the proximate cause of his downfall: a refusal to cooperate with the UN weapons inspectors. In December of that year, the coalition reacted to the Iraqi suspension of official contacts with the inspectors by a four-day air offensive, Operation Desert Fox. The Hornets of VMFA-312 shared in the sorties made from the carrier *Enterprise* on the seventeenth, striking all their assigned targets. Altogether American and British forces flew 650 attack sorties and launched 415 cruise missiles. Analysts estimated that the incoming ordnance scored 70 to 80 percent hits, but Saddam was not moved to mend his ways. As one of his lackeys bragged afterward, Iraq could absorb endless numbers of cruise missiles. By the close of the decade many Americans, some destined to hold influential positions in the administration of President George W. Bush, had reached the conclusion that something would have to be done about Saddam Hussein. The Marines would be there when it was.

CHAPTER 15

The War on Terror, 2001–

On the morning of Tuesday, 11 September 2001, nineteen Islamic terrorists seized control of four airliners over the northeastern United States, and the world changed. Between 0848 and 0905, two of these aircraft flew into the Twin Towers of the World Trade Center; a third crashed into the Pentagon at 0939; and the fourth, whose brave passengers rose against the hijackers, plowed into a field in Pennsylvania at 1003. In little more than an hour, approximately 2,830 Americans had been killed, more than in the attack on Pearl Harbor. The United States was at war.

There was only one terrorist organization capable of mounting an operation of such complexity: al-Qaeda—"the base"— a shadowy, supranational network founded in 1994 by a fanatical Saudi visionary named Osama bin Laden. Bin Laden's aims were simple but sweeping. They included the elimination of Western influence throughout the Muslim world, the destruction of Israel, and the enforcement of the most stringent interpretations of Islamic law. These goals were agreeable to the Taliban, the fundamentalist party that had taken power in Afghanistan in 1996, and al-Qaeda,

bankrolled by bin Laden's personal fortune, became a state within a state.

The world at large first became aware of al-Qaeda in August 1998, when it exploded bombs at the American embassies at Nairobi, Kenya, and Dar-es-Salaam, Tanzania, killing or wounding more than thirteen hundred people. The Clinton administration responded by launching cruise missiles at al-Qaeda training camps in Afghanistan and a chemical plant in the Sudan believed to be linked to the organization. Bin Laden was unharmed. The Central Intelligence Agency had been tracking him ever since. By 2001 he was considered a deadly threat to the United States, but no one had foreseen what form that threat would take.

On 16 September, five days after the attack on America, President George W. Bush called on the Taliban to close al-Qaeda's training camps and surrender bin Laden. As expected, the Taliban declined to comply with the president's demands. American bombs and missiles began to fall on Afghanistan on 7 October.

The prospect of war with Afghanistan alarmed many commentators, who cited the success of the (U.S.-supported) guerrilla war

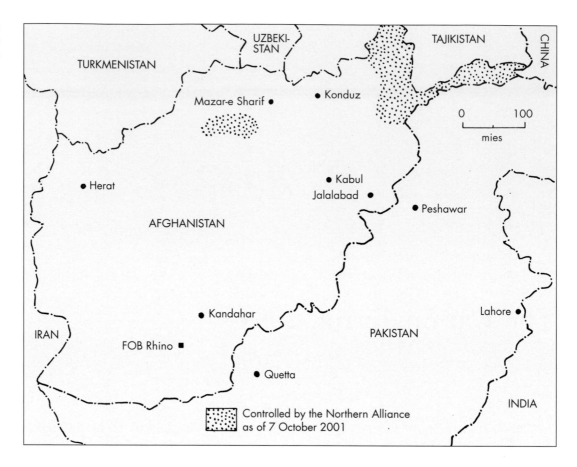

Konduz

Mazar-e Sharif ●

0   100

mies

● Herat

● Kabul
Jalalabad
● Peshawar

AFGHANISTAN

● Kandahar

Lahore ●

IRAN

PAKISTAN

FOB Rhino ■

● Quetta

INDIA

Controlled by the Northern Alliance
as of 7 October 2001

that had compelled the Soviet Union to withdraw from the country after occupying it from 1979 to 1989. But the United States did not intend to invade Afghanistan. An anti-Taliban army was already on the scene. It belonged to the Northern Alliance, which had lost a civil war to the Taliban but retained control of roughly 10 percent of the country. The Taliban's forces were about twice as numerous and much better armed. Nevertheless, the CIA, whose agents had been in contact with the Northern Alliance for years, assured President Bush that with the assistance of American air power it could overcome the Taliban. While the CIA provided greenbacks and guidance, special forces would supply ground controllers for precision-guided smart bombs that could even the military odds. Pakistan granted the United States the prerequisite base rights.

Assuming that the plan worked, the Marine role in Operation Enduring Freedom seemed destined to be slight. There were no Leatherneck attack squadrons aboard the carriers on station at the beginning of the conflict, and the only mission foreseen for the 15th MEU (SOC), which reached the Arabian Sea in the *Peleliu* amphibious ready group in September, was to rescue aviators and dispose of aircraft downed in hostile territory.

The call to perform such a mission was not long in coming. On the evening of 19 October Army Rangers and special forces carried out two heliborne raids deep inside Afghanistan. On their return a Black Hawk crashed at a staging area on Pakistan's disputed frontier. The other raiders evacuated the killed and injured, but the wrecked aircraft remained in place. The Marines were to extract or destroy it. Their first attempt to reach the scene was turned back by heavy ground fire. Pakistan then announced that it was sending troops to secure the site. Upon the Leathernecks' return, their officers were met by a polite Pakistani major who offered them cups of tea in chipped china served from a silver tray. Nylon straps were fastened around the Black Hawk, and a CH-53 lifted it into the sky.

Marines began to play a more active part in the war a few days later, when the carrier *Theodore Roosevelt* arrived on station and the Hornets of VMFA-251 flew their first strikes over Afghanistan. By this time CENTCOM had begun to consider enlarging the Marines' mission. While the Northern Alliance had responded enthusiastically to the American overtures, substantial anti-Taliban forces had yet to emerge in the south. The commitment of even a modest number of U.S. troops—not small special operations teams but a ground combat unit—might encourage the Taliban's enemies to take the plunge, and the Leathernecks were the only ground combat unit in the neighborhood. At the end of October Brig. Gen. James N. Mattis assumed command of a new formation, Task Force 58, consisting of the *Peleliu* and *Bataan* amphibious ready groups, the latter of which was summoned from the Mediterranean with the 26th MEU (SOC) embarked. Mattis' orders were to plan a series of raids into southern Afghanistan.

In the course of the planning process, a new concept arose. The impact would be much greater, it was reasoned, if instead of making intermittent raids the Marines established a permanent presence. The site selected for what became forward operating base (FOB) Rhino was a compound with its own airstrip in the Afghan countryside one hundred miles south of Kandahar. Built as a hunting lodge for the chief of staff of the United Arab Emirates, it had been one of the locations raided on 19 October.

FOB Rhino was occupied by elements of the 15th MEU (SOC), carried in C-130 transports from Pakistan, on 25 November.

The Marines' entry was unopposed; a SEAL team had been operating from the base since the twenty-first. Fourteen hundred Marines, including Mattis, were on the ground within a week. By then the war had gained momentum. Bad weather and the usual unforeseen circumstances had imposed a two- to three-week delay on the insertion of special forces teams into northern Afghanistan. As a consequence, the emphasis of air operations did not switch from strategic to tactical bombing until the end of October, but on 5 November the Northern Alliance launched an offensive before which the Taliban simply dissolved. When Northern Alliance forces entered Kabul, the Afghan capital, on 13 November, they had occupied half the country in little more than a week.

In the south things did not progress quite so smoothly. The Southern Alliance that had coalesced in November was halted outside Kandahar, the Taliban's spiritual center, on 3 December. Even so, aerial reconnaissance reported numerous vehicles, presumably filled with fleeing Taliban, leaving the city westbound on Route 1. Marines from FOB Rhino were sent to investigate. They found only a trickle of traffic, but on the evening of 7 December two companies rather grandiloquently designated Task Force Sledgehammer destroyed three truckloads of Taliban. The first vehicle was riddled by automatic weapons fire when its occupants responded to a summons to hold up their hands by a display of assault rifles; the second and third were obliterated by five-hundred-pound bombs after the Leathernecks called in an airstrike.

The Southern Alliance had entered Kandahar earlier that day, and on the tenth a

column rolled out of Rhino with orders to seize the international airport ten miles west of the city. Detachments from both the 15th and 26th MEUs, both SOC, took part in the advance. They occupied their objective without undue incident on 14 December. The next day they were set to work constructing a temporary prison capable of holding up to three hundred Taliban and al-Qaeda detainees. The facility accepted its first inmates on 18 December. John Walker Lindh, the American Taliban, was among its alumni. Regrettably, Osama bin Laden eluded capture.

Hamid Karzai, the Southern Alliance leader who had negotiated the surrender of Kandahar, assumed office as Afghanistan's interim prime minister on 22 December. Although die-hard Taliban remained at large, this event as much as any other signified the close of the basically conventional war in Afghanistan. FOB Rhino was evacuated on 3 January 2002. The 101st Airborne Division relieved the Leathernecks in control of Kandahar International Airport on the nineteenth, and the last elements of the 26th MEU (SOC) returned to the *Bataan* amphibious ready group on 8 February.

In terms of hours spent in combat, the Leathernecks' contribution to the outcome of the Afghan war was negligible, but in this case combat was a misleading measure.

A CH-46 helicopter from HMM-365 drops Marines from the 26th MEU (SOC) onto a remote mountaintop in Afghanistan during operations against the Taliban and al-Qaeda in January 2002. (Defense Visual Information Center)

Simply by their presence the Marines had encouraged the uncertain to join the Southern Alliance and inspired the irresolute to desert the Taliban, both for the same reason: the demonstration the Marines provided of America's commitment to the war. As the noted historian Norman Friedman concluded in his study of the conflict, "the Marines, who came from the sea, were an absolutely essential element in the victory in southeastern Afghanistan."

But Afghanistan was only the first round in the war on terror. In his State of the Union address on 19 January, President Bush asserted that Iran, Iraq, and North Korea constituted an "axis of evil" that could not be allowed to threaten the United States "with the world's most destructive weapons." Of the three states so stigmatized, the president's advisors viewed Iraq as the prime candidate for "regime change," shorthand for the overthrow of Saddam Hussein. No one questioned the desirability of expelling the Iraqi dictator from the international scene. As the events of the decade since the Gulf War left no doubt, he was an incorrigible troublemaker. Some suspected that, despite the lack of evidence, so unsavory an individual must have ties to al-Qaeda. Others predicted that the installation of a democratic government in Iraq would stimulate the growth of democracy throughout the Arab world. What really galvanized the administration, however, was the conviction that Saddam Hussein retained weapons of mass destruction and was intent on acquiring more. The need to eliminate Saddam's WMDs constituted the president's principal rationale for going to war.

After the fall of Baghdad, the failure of a painstaking search to uncover any WMDs made it embarrassingly evident that the intelligence analysis upon which the administration acted was in error; yet despite the harsh criticism that revelation provoked, it was a reasonable error. Most of Saddam's own generals were certain that he retained secret stores of WMDs. In the 1980s, Saddam had repeatedly used chemical agents against the Iranians and the Kurds. Following the Gulf War, UN weapons' inspectors obtained inventories of the existing stockpiles of such weapons. Iraq claimed that these stockpiles had since been destroyed, but there remained a significant shortfall between the quantity of weapons the inspectors could verify had indeed been destroyed and the totals shown on the inventories. What had become of the difference? It appeared unlikely that the discrepancy was simply an accounting error.

Of course, Saddam could have allayed American anxieties at any time by ordering Iraqi authorities to cooperate fully with the inspectors. This he declined to do, even after President Bush announced that in the future the United States would follow a preemptive strategy: faced with an obvious and imminent danger, it would not wait to be attacked; it would strike first. Saddam's refusal to come clean about his supposed WMDs stemmed from his belief that Iran, not the United States, was the major threat to his regime. So long as no one knew whether he possessed WMDs, or so he reasoned, the uncertainty posed a powerful deterrent to Iran. To dispel the uncertainty would destroy the deterrent. His policy, therefore, was to keep the world guessing.

Although Bush did not finally abandon hope of a diplomatic solution until December 2002, he had begun to investigate his military options a year earlier. In November 2001 he asked Secretary of Defense Donald W. Rumsfeld to review the Pentagon's contingency plan for a conflict with Iraq. Rumsfeld had not liked what he found. The secretary of defense was fiercely dedicated to what he called the "transformation" of the American armed forces from heavy formations configured to defeat Soviet armor in Central Europe to a lighter, more nimble but—thanks to advances in military technology—even more deadly force prepared to intervene anywhere in the world. The plan for war with Iraq, OPLAN 1003–98, called for the deployment of more than four hundred thousand troops, which would take six months, including a lengthy bombing campaign preceding the ground attack. Rumsfeld deemed both the force level and the time span excessive, products of the military mindset he was determined to reform. Accordingly, he instructed CENTCOM's new commander, Army general Tommy Franks, to develop a plan for employing a much smaller force in a much faster-paced campaign that would showcase transformation in action. The result was so light that in December 2002 Franks' land forces commander, Lt. Gen. David McKiernan, persuaded Rumsfeld to commit additional troops. In the end the total allocated to enter Iraq was fixed at 285,000, which was 100,000 fewer than projected by OPLAN 1003, but there was no guarantee that this number would actually set foot in the country. To reduce the time devoted to the buildup, the land attack was to begin before

all the formations assigned to it had reached the theater. If the war had been decided before they did so, their deployments could be cancelled. This was, in fact, what came to pass. Eventually 170,000 troops crossed the border into Iraq. Unfortunately, the number of troops sufficient to win the war proved insufficient to preserve the peace.

Pentagon and CENTCOM planners completed what was thought to be the final war plan by January 2003. It envisioned an attack begun by four divisions, roughly a third of the force involved in Desert Storm. The 3rd Infantry Division and the 1st Marine Division would strike north from Kuwait to lead V Corps and I MEF in the march on Baghdad. The 4th Infantry Division and the 1st (UK) Armoured Division would push south from Turkey to link up with the Kurdish militia and advance on Mosul and Kirkuk. At the last moment, however, Turkey refused to allow coalition land forces to enter its territory. The 4th Infantry Division remained aboard transports in the eastern Mediterranean, where CENTCOM believed its presence would tie down several Iraqi divisions, and the British division was reassigned to the southern front.

The forces available to Saddam Hussein to oppose the coalition were only a shadow of those he had fielded for the Gulf War. The Iraqi Army consisted of seventeen divisions vice the forty of 1991: eleven infantry, three mechanized, and three armored, all understrength and unmotivated, with heavy weapons that were for the most part obsolete and ill maintained. On paper, it numbered three hundred thousand; in reality, at most two hundred thousand. U.S. forces regarded

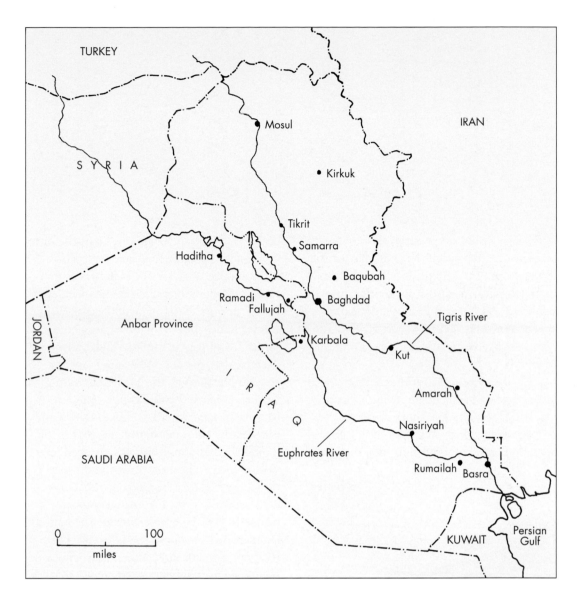

these units, in a metaphor much in vogue at the time, as no more than speed bumps. In contrast, the five divisions of Saddam's elite Republican Guard, sixty thousand strong, were expected to put up a good fight, but the Republican Guard suffered from some of the same material deficiencies as the regular Army. U.S. intelligence largely discounted the Saddam Fedayeen (Saddam's Martyrs), a paramilitary organization created in 1994 to serve as the first responder in the event of another Shiite revolt. Weapons caches were awaiting its members in Ba'ath Party headquarters throughout the country. In 2003 the Shiites, badly burned in their last uprising, refrained from a repeat. Nevertheless, the Fedayeen would play a much more important role in the war than anyone had foreseen.

Whatever illusions were entertained in Baghdad, realistically there was never any question about the outcome of the conflict. The only question was how messy the coalition's victory would be. There were three chief concerns: that Saddam would use WMDs; that he would order his army to set fire to Iraq's oil fields, as it had to Kuwait's; and that as U.S. forces neared his capital, he would withdraw the Republican Guard into the city to wage a bitter, block-by-block defense that would transform Baghdad into Stalingrad on the Tigris. American troops felt certain that sooner or later Saddam would "slime" them with chemical and biological weapons, and, aside from communications aspiring to dissuade Iraqi officers from obeying orders to use WMDs, there was not much they could do about it. By moving fast enough they might be able to avert the destruction of the oil fields and to prevent the Republican Guard from retiring into Baghdad. As General Franks emphasized, speed would be of the essence. No one took his prescription more seriously than the Marines.

On the evening of 17 March 2003 after weeks of vainly attempting to obtain a new UN resolution authorizing the use of force against Iraq, President Bush gave Saddam Hussein and his sons forty-eight

The commander of I MEF, Lt. Gen. James T. Conway, uses an Abrams tank as a rostrum to address Regiment Combat Team 7 at Camp Coyote, Kuwait, on 13 February 2003, a few weeks before the opening of Operation Iraqi Freedom. (Defense Visual Information Center)

hours to leave Iraq. To no one's surprise, the ultimatum was ignored. There were then some 260,000 U.S. service members in the theater of operations. That figure included I MEF, approximately 61,000 Leathernecks serving under the command of Lt. Gen. James T. Conway in the 1st Marine Division (Reinforced), the 3rd MAW, 1st Force Service Support Group, the MEF Engineer Group, and Task Force Tarawa. The 1st Marine Division numbered 22,200 men and women, the latter in assignments that made it unlikely they would become engaged in close combat. The most powerful division the Corps had ever sent into battle, it was organized into three regimental combat teams (RCTs), 1, 5, and 7, formed around the regiments whose numerals they bore. Each RCT consisted of three infantry battalions reinforced by a light armored reconnaissance battalion, an artillery battalion, a detachment of amphibious assault vehicles (AAVs) for river crossings, and a company or more of engineers. In addition, RCT-5 and RCT-7 included a tank battalion. RCT-1 had only a tank company, but its advance was screened by the 1st Reconnaissance Battalion. This formidable force was commanded by Maj. Gen. James N. Mattis, who had gained a second star since the Afghan cam-paign. Conway's other ground combat unit, the 2nd MEB (TF Tarawa), consisted of 5,100 troops from II MEF under Brig. Gen. Richard F. Natonski. Its RCT-2 included three infantry battalions, an artillery battalion, a light armored reconnaissance company, and a company each of AAVs and tanks. The 3rd MAW, commanded by Maj. Gen. James F. Amos, included 340 attack aircraft—rotary and fixed-wing—plus numerous support elements.

A future commandant, Conway had led BLT 3/2 through operations Desert Shield and Desert Storm. In *One Bullet Away,* a brilliant evocation of a young officer's experience in Afghanistan and Iraq, Nathaniel Fick wrote that "Conway looked like a gene-ral should: tall, tanned, and white-haired, with a deep voice that was both soothing and authoritative. . . . [He] commanded instinctive respect." Optimistic and unflappable, Conway cared deeply about his Marines. A small unit leader called on to brief him on an un-usually dangerous mission was surprised by Conway's interest in ascertaining that there was a realistic extraction plan in case things went wrong. That did not mean he shunned the graveyard humor the Corps cultivates. "Officers," he concluded one briefing, "please don't go get yourselves killed. It's very bad for unit morale."

If Jim Conway looked like a general, Jim Mattis—slight, thin-faced, bespectacled—looked like a no-nonsense high-school teacher. In his case, appearances were mis-leading. A salty field soldier, serious student of military history, and confirmed bachelor, Mattis had devoted his life to the Corps. He enjoyed the unusual distinction of having commanded every troop unit from a platoon to a division, including a battalion in Desert Shield and Desert Storm. It was probably inevitable, given the resulting alliteration, that his Marines would nickname him "Mad Dog," but they smiled when they said it. "Mattis is kinetic," Nate Fick declared. "The troops who knew him from Afghanistan loved him, and everybody else loved him

by reputation. Stars on a collar can throw a barrier between leader and led, but Mattis's rank only contributed to his hero status. Here was an officer, a general, who understood the Marines, who, in fact, was one of them." In Iraq, Mattis' call sign was Chaos. His Marines thought that was really cool.

Chaos was what Mattis aimed to create behind Iraqi lines. There was perhaps no one more completely attuned to Franks' desire for the forthcoming campaign to be characterized by speed of execution. Mattis intended for the 1st Marine Division to charge forward as fast and as far as possible, maintaining momentum without paying undue attention to what was happening beyond its flanks or to its rear. The objective—the objective espoused by Fuller, Liddell Hart, and the other theorists of mechanized warfare in the 1930s—was not to destroy the enemy but to paralyze him by stunning his high command so badly that its decisions never regained touch with strategic reality. To help achieve the prerequisite mobil-ity, the 1st Marine Division would move "logistics light." No one, regardless of rank, was permitted more personal gear than a private. Everyone would sleep on the ground, and everyone would eat only two MREs (meals ready to eat) a day. The 3rd MAW's C-130s would keep the division's four thousand vehicles supplied with fuel; if no airfield was available, they would land on the highway.

At the time President Bush presented his ultimatum to Saddam Hussein, the pre-sumptive invasion of Iraq was scheduled to open with air and missile strikes at 2100 (local time) on 21 March. The ground attack would commence at 0600 the next morning.

Well before that date, however, coalition ground forces were active in Iraq. Starting on the evening of 19 March, American, British, and Australian special forces supported by U.S. Army Rangers took control of Iraq's western desert to prevent it from being used as a launching site for Scud missiles aimed at Israel, as it had in 1991.

While these operations were in progress, the ground assault was moved ahead, first to 0600 on the twenty-first and then to 2030 on the twentieth. Both changes were the result of misapprehensions. The first followed the discovery that some wells in the Rumaila oil field were burning. This intelligence caused CENTCOM to fear that the Iraqis were about to torch the whole complex. In fact, only seven wells had been set on fire, apparently as a tactical measure to decrease visibility, and no preparations had been made for a general conflagration. The second change was made after a CIA officer advised Mattis that a brigade, perhaps two, of modern, Soviet-made T-72 tanks from the Republican Guard's Medina Division had moved south to meet the Marines. Although the report proved unfounded, Mattis had no choice but to take it seriously. Higher headquarters approved his request to attack early, and moments after Marine engineers blasted a hole in the berm along the Iraqi frontier, Col. Joseph F. Dunford Jr.'s RCT-5 became the first major ground combat unit to enter Iraq. Operation Iraqi Freedom had begun.

The first item on the Leathernecks' agenda was to secure the Rumaila oil fields and their attendant installations. RCT-5's task was twofold: to seize the twelve vital gas and oil separation platforms (GOSPs) and to shield the left flank of Col. Steven Hunter's RCT-7, which followed it into Iraq the next morning, from the brigade of T-72s. By noon, RCT-5 had seized the GOSPs, easily overcoming the scattered resistance encountered; it was becoming evident that the T-72s were imaginary; and the Iraqi division positioned to defend the oil fields was beginning to dis-integrate. A few hours later RCT-7 took its key objective, a pumping and control station that handled the output of more than 300 of Rumaila's 454 active wellheads—14 percent of the world's oil supply. The Marines named it the Crown Jewel. The capture of the station was entrusted to C/1/7, which had been rehearsing the operation for six months. That they met no opposition was a disappointment to the young Leathernecks. They had been looking forward to the occasion to demonstrate their prowess.

These attacks were carried out in conjunction with the 1st (UK) Armoured Division, which had been attached to I MEF after being switched south. Rather incongruously for a division identified as armored, the British formation included 3 Commando Brigade, Royal Marines. The 15th MEU (SOC) was attached to 3 Commando Brigade for the commencement of the campaign. The Royal Marines entered action on the twenty-first, when 40 and 42 Commandos, battalion-sized units, were helilifted from British warships to occupy the Fao peninsula, which constitutes Iraq's sole direct access to the Persian Gulf. At the same time, coalition special forces secured the main tanker loading terminal twenty-five miles offshore,

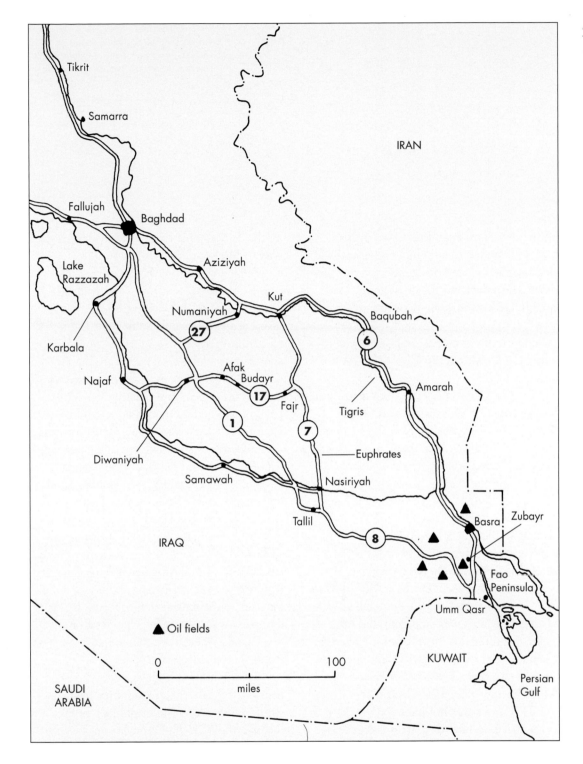

Tikrit

Samarra

IRAN

Fallujah

Baghdad

Lake
Razzazah

Aziziyah

Kut

Numaniyah

Baqubah

27

6

Karbala

Najaf

Afak
Budayr

Amarah

17

Fajr

Tigris

1

7

Diwaniyah

Euphrates

Samawah

Nasiriyah

Tallil

Basra

Zubayr

8

IRAQ

Fao
Peninsula

Umm Qasr

▲ Oil fields

KUWAIT

0   100

miles

SAUDI
ARABIA

Persian
Gulf

and the 15th MEU (SOC) advanced overland to seize Umm Qasr, the country's
only deep-water port. Although sporadic
fighting flickered on for several days, by
nightfall the peninsula was effectively
under coalition control.

The next day Royal Marines relieved
their American counterparts at Umm Qasr

and the latter proceeded to their next
objective, the naval base at the river port of
az Zubayr on the Shatt el-Arab, thirty miles
to the northwest. The naval base was taken
without opposition on the twenty-third, the
same day RCT-5 and RCT-7 handed over
their positions in the oil fields to the British.
The two Marine units then raced west to take

up the march on Baghdad. Other British forces joined the remaining Leathernecks in clearing Zubayr and on the morning of the twenty-fifth declared the city secure. The British had also thrown a cordon around Basra, Iraq's second-largest city, and the situation in the southeast appeared well in hand. On 27 March the 15th MEU (SOC) rejoined I MEF.

By then U.S. forces were deep inside Iraq. On the twenty-first, as RCT-5 and RCT-7 charged into the oil fields, two other columns opened the offensive against the Iraqi capital. The Army's 3rd Infantry Division advanced up the Euphrates Valley. To its right came TF Tarawa and, behind Tarawa, Col. Joseph W. Dowdy's RCT-1. Ordinarily, a Marine division in the attack would leave one of its three regiments in reserve, but Mattis put all of them on line once the crossing at al Nassryria took place. "Doctrine," he liked to say, "is the last resort of the unimaginative." Moreover, Mattis was confident that his troops would honor the injunction he sent to all hands on the eve of war: "Demonstrate to the world there is 'No Better Friend, No Worse Enemy,' than a U.S. Marine."

TF Tarawa was not intended to take part in the drive on Baghdad. Its mission was to secure I MEF's lines of communications. At the moment, it had two immediate objectives: to relieve the Army in control of the bridge at Tallil and to seize two bridges at an Nasiriyah. RCT-5 and RCT-7 would use the Route 1 bridge at Tallil. RCT-1 would cross the Route 7 bridges at Nasiriyah and push toward Kut, where in World War I an overambitious division of the British Indian Army had been captured

by the Turks. This route was the shortest way to Baghdad.

But it was not the way Mattis meant to go. The advance on Kut was a feint. At the beginning of the war, five Iraqi Army divisions were echeloned along the Tigris on the Leathernecks' right flank. None was considered a cause for concern. To the 1st Marine Division's front, however, were two units of the Republican Guard, the Baghdad Division at Kut and the al Nida Armored Division at al Aziziyah. These formations were definitely a cause for concern. By threatening Kut, RCT-1 would pin down the Baghdad Division. RCT-5 and RCT-7 would proceed up Route 1, turn east at the intersection of Route 27, cross the Tigris at Numaniyah, thereby isolating the Baghdad Division, and strike north on Route 6 to engage the al Nida Division. RCT-1, having reached the gates of Kut, was to execute a smart about-face and fall back to the intersection of Route 17. At that point it would swing away west on the first leg of a wide circuit that would bring it to Route 6 on the heels of RCT-7.

Meanwhile, miles beyond the Leathernecks' left flank, the 3rd Infantry Division would move along the Euphrates, break through the Karbala Gap between the city of Karbala and Lake Razzazah, and attack Baghdad from the southwest. As in the Gulf War, the Army's operations officially constituted the main effort. Franks assigned the Marines to provide the supporting effort. Their job was to make the Army's job easier. But, as in the Gulf War, they would do far more.

By the morning of 23 March, RCT-1 had covered eighty of the three hundred

miles to Baghdad. At times the Humvees of the 1st Recon Battalion, screening its right flank, hurtled along at sixty miles an hour. Yet easy as it seemed, the advance had already revealed the two tribulations that would plague Marines throughout the war: sand and sleeplessness. Iraq's powder-fine sand infiltrated everything, including lungs, where the dried vegetable matter it included triggered allergies and caused infections. Leathernecks' eyes watered, their noses ran, and they coughed up knots of yellow phlegm. Most recovered from "the crud" in a week, but the more susceptible suffered all the way to Baghdad. Sleep deprivation was equally unavoidable in an advance that soon became a rolling traffic jam. Officers often

went thirty-six hours without sleep and were pleased to average four hours a day. In the 1st Recon Battalion, Marines kept awake by nibbling instant-coffee crystals straight from the can. But there was no remedy for either of these afflictions, and otherwise everything was going well. No one had reason to suspect that 23 March would be the American forces' worst day of the war.

Things began to go wrong about 0600, when a serial of the 507th Maintenance Company, a component of an Army Patriot missile battalion, blundered into Nasiriyah. By the time the captain in command realized he was far off course and turned around, it was too late. Only four of the detachment's eighteen vehicles escaped from the city. They

Map 31, left:
Nasiriyah

Right: The Saddam
Canal Bridge at
Nasiriyah, the
seizure of which
sparked one of the
sharpest actions
in the march
on Baghdad.
(Defense Visual
Information Center)

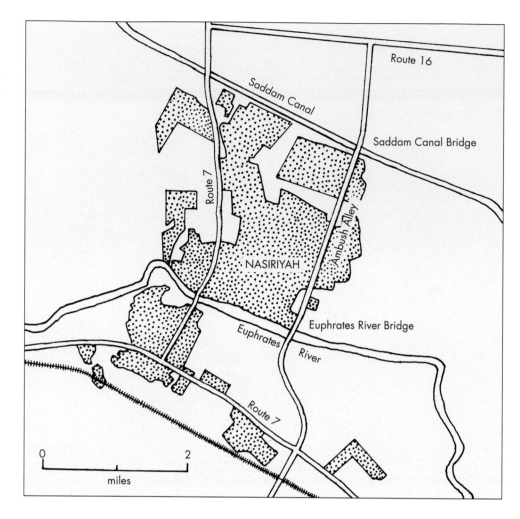

soon encountered RCT-2's tank company leading TF Tarawa on its way to seize the bridges, and the 507th's excited captain announced that some of his people had been left behind. Pressing forward with three tanks, the Marines located ten soldiers, half of them wounded. Of the serial's thirty-three members, nine had been killed and eight captured. The latter included a pretty, petite blonde destined to become the most famous female in the American armed forces: Pfc. Jessica Lynch.

This development put a new face on matters. The Leathernecks knew that the Iraqi 11th Infantry Division was stationed at Nasiriyah, but it had not been expected to present many problems. The Leathernecks did not know that the Fedayeen and foreign volunteers anxious to join in a *jihad* (holy war) against the infidels had begun pouring into the city on the twenty-second. Nor were

they aware that the 11th Division had not self-demobilized as completely as anticipated. Nevertheless, it was clear that someone intended to fight for Nasiriyah.

Lt. Col. Ricky Grabowski's 1/2 was charged with capturing the bridges. A city of four hundred thousand, Nasiriyah straddles an island formed by the Euphrates to the south and the Saddam Canal to the north. There are two sets of bridges at Nasiriyah, one on the west side of the city and one on the east. TF Tarawa's objective was the eastern pair. These bridges, two-and-a-half miles apart, were connected by a four-lane concrete highway that the Marines dubbed Ambush Alley. Because his mission was to seize the bridges, not to secure Ambush Alley, Grabowski reasoned that this was a roadway best avoided.

Delayed by more than its share of the usual misunderstandings, 1/2 moved forward

around midmorning. Bravo Company, supported by three tanks, crossed the bridge across the Euphrates and turned right to detour around Ambush Alley. Alpha Company took charge of the bridge, and Charlie Company crossed it to follow Bravo through Nasiriyah. Bravo Company did not get far. While cutting across a field with a deceptively firm-looking surface, its vehicles—tanks included—became hopelessly stuck. Bravo Company had gone just far enough that Charlie Company found no trace of it. Charlie's commander reasoned that the most likely explanation for Bravo's disappearance was that it gone up Ambush Alley after all. He decided to do the same, and Charlie's eleven AAVs sped through Nasiriyah and across the Saddam Canal Bridge. Despite a rain of rocket-propelled grenades (RPGs), only one vehicle, the last in line, was damaged, and it kept going.

Dismounting, the Leathernecks found themselves under intense fire from artillery, mortars, machine guns, RPGs, and automatic rifles. The 11th Division had deployed three battalions at the northern end of the canal bridge, and C/1/2 had driven right into them. In the two hours that ensued it fought what was perhaps the most desperate action involving Marines in the Iraq War. The company's worst moment came when it was strafed and bombed by two U.S. Air Force A-10 Thunderbolts cleared to attack by a Marine forward air controller who was not aware of any friendly forces north of the canal. By the time relief arrived, Charlie Company had lost eighteen dead and seventeen wounded; but it had held the bridge. Back at the Euphrates, Alpha and Bravo companies had been engaged in a sharp little firefight of their own.

The next move belonged to Col. Joe Dowdy, the commander of RCT-1, which had come up during the action and was waiting to cross the bridges. To do so, it would have to pass through RCT-2, but Dowdy's attempts to coordinate the movement were consistently frustrated by a failure in communications. RCT-1 and RCT-2 belonged to different MEFs, and their radios had different cryptological settings. Somehow the need, demonstrated in many exercises, to ensure that East Coast Marines and West Coast Marines were able to communicate had been overlooked. The only way Dowdy could talk to anyone in RCT-2 was in person. This limitation presented obvious problems. Dowdy knew that 1/2 had secured the bridges, but he also knew that no one had secured Ambush Alley. RCT-1 included 950 vehicles. Of this number, 250 were armored. Granted that they should be able to take care of themselves, what about the other 700? Dowdy did not relish the thought of committing them to what might become a shooting gallery two-and-a-half miles long.

After deliberating with his staff, Dowdy decided that RCT-1 would blast through Nasiriyah at first light the next morning. Before first light, he changed his mind. Only the armored vehicles would brave Ambush Alley. Their soft-skinned compatriots would make a day-long detour around the city. Sorting out the change took time, and it was late afternoon before the 2nd Light Armored Reconnaissance Battalion became the first unit of RCT-1 to enter Nasiriyah. Moving under cover of an artillery barrage, it reached the Saddam Canal Bridge without being the target of a single shot. At this juncture Dowdy received a confusing report that RCT-2 was in action with insurgents somewhere inside the city, so he halted his units' movement while he tried to discover what was happening. He also learned that he had visitors. Conway and Mattis had become concerned about the holdup at Nasiriyah. RCT-5 and RCT-7

were rapidly advancing up Route 1. RCT-1 was supposed to cover their right flank, which meant that it must keep more or less abreast of them. After twenty-four hours at Nasiriyah, it had fallen behind. Conway came forward to investigate the situation in person. Mattis sent his assistant division commander, Brig. Gen. John F. Kelly, to do the same.

Conway and Kelly told Dowdy that there could be no more delays. RCT-1 must push through Nasiriyah. Following his meeting with Kelly, Dowdy adopted a new tactic. One battalion, 3/1, would be sent forward to picket Ambush Alley—that is, establish a strongpoint at every intersection—while the rest of RCT-1, soft-skinned vehicles and all, passed along it. The battalion entered the city around midnight. Ambush Alley had been picketed an hour later, and Dowdy's convoy, miles in length, began to flow through Nasiriyah. No vehicles were lost. Every now and again a Fedayeen with an RPG appeared at the mouth of an alley, but 3/1's pickets were delighted to gratify his desire for martyrdom before any harm had been done. The end of the convoy cleared the city around 1400 on 25 March, a day behind schedule. Still unsure about Dowdy's appreciation of the situation, Mattis told Kelly to remain with RCT-1.

It was now D+5, and the contours of the war had become clear. The cheering crowds that American intelligence had led the troops to expect were seldom in evidence. The civilian population, while not hostile, was reserved. In contrast, the estimate of the Iraqi Army proved correct. Few of Saddam's soldiers were disposed to die for him. U.S. forces had yet to make ground contact with the Republican Guard. The drubbing its

Medina Division gave two squadrons of Army attack helicopters on the twenty-fourth indicated that it should be taken seriously, but the U.S. playbook provided for that. Everyone had expected the Republican Guard to hang tough.

The surprise was the Fedayeen. Despite their dismissal by CENTCOM planners, these virtually untrained irregulars had emerged as the principal opposition to the advance through southern Iraq. By professional standards, the Fedayeen and the jihadists who hastened to join them were extremely amateurish. They did not handle their weapons well, they had little grasp of tactics, and they lacked leadership. Their encounters with U.S. forces in the field invariably ended in their destruction or flight. "This is the perfect war," declared 1/7's Sgt. Maj. Henry Bergeron. "They want to die, and we want to kill them." On the other hand, the Fedayeen could slow movement through urban areas, where the environment partly offset the U.S. technological advantage and they could shelter in structures they correctly assumed the Americans would respect. At Samawah a captured Iraqi captain told his interrogators that if U.S. forces wanted to take the city quickly all they had to do was destroy the schools and mosques. Even after a city was taken, the Fedayeen did not give up. Neither I MEF nor V Corps could spare troops to garrison every settlement in its wake. Once the combat units passed, the Fedayeen returned to threaten the Americans' ever-lengthening lines of communications. V Corps headquarters was already worried.

One of the points on which the Fedayeen converged was ad Diwaniyah, a city on Route 17 a few miles west of Route 1. Nearing the intersection, 3/5 ran into an uncharacteristically sophisticated ambush. Weapons Company's Combined Anti-Armor Platoon was caught in a killing zone, unable to move forward because the battalion's tanks were blocking the road and raked by machine-gun, RPG, and automatic rifle fire. The platoon's leader was twenty-eight-year-old 1st Lt. Brian R. Chontosh, an ex-enlisted Marine from Rochester, New York. Quickly sizing up the situation, Chontosh directed the driver of his Humvee to go through a breach in the berm behind which the Iraqis were entrenched. Inside the berm the vehicle came under fire from a machine-gun emplacement. Chontosh reacted by ordering his driver to head straight for the gun, and the Humvee's gunner silenced it with a burst of .50-cal machine-gun fire. Chontosh then instructed the driver to steer into the Iraqi entrenchment. There he sprang from the vehicle and, followed by his two Marines, began fighting his way along the trench. When his rifle ran out of ammunition, he drew his pistol; when his pistol was empty, he picked up an Iraqi rifle; and when that rifle had been emptied, he picked up another. In the meanwhile, one of his men handed him an Iraqi RPG launcher, and he fired it into a knot of enemy fighters. In the course of his onslaught, Chontosh cleared two hundred yards of trench, killing upwards of twenty Iraqis and wounding several more. "I was just doing my job," he said later. "I did the same thing every other Marine would have done." Chontosh was awarded a Navy Cross.

That afternoon, U.S. forces throughout southern Iraq were enveloped in a fierce

sandstorm that turned the world a surrealistic orange. Winds gusted up to forty-five miles an hour and visibility dropped to twenty-five yards. Despite the difficulties these conditions created, Leathernecks and soldiers continued to push forward. By the evening of 25 March their leading elements were two-thirds of the way to Baghdad. The storm ended on the twenty-seventh, and late that day RCT-5 seized "the elbow" where Route 1 intersects Route 27, the point at which the forces pushing up the former were to make their surprise turn toward the Tigris. Within hours an unhappy Mattis ordered RCT-5 to fall back thirty miles. He did not want to leave it in a position that might signal the Leathernecks' intentions, because the advance had been called to a halt.

A day earlier, the 3rd Infantry Division's hard-charging commander, Maj. Gen. Buford Blount, had reluctantly concluded that he needed to halt and resupply before the final drive on Baghdad. Meanwhile, Lt. Gen. William Wallace, V Corps' commander, and General McKiernan had grown increasingly apprehensive over the Fedayeen threat to U.S. supply lines. The 3rd Infantry Division's call for a halt served as a catalyst. Early on the twenty-seventh, McKiernan flew from Kuwait to meet with Wallace and Conway. Conway agreed that it would desirable to suspend the offensive for a few days to establish firmer control of the rear areas. In Qatar General Franks, clearly dubious, deferred to McKiernan's judgment. At midday, an operational pause of unspecified duration was announced.

Humvees of Company D, 1st Light Armored Reconnaissance Battalion, an element of RCT-5, in the driving sandstorm that blanketed U.S. forces on 25 March 2003. This photograph was taken on the twenty-sixth. The storm lifted the next day. Some of the vehicles are armed with TOW (tube-launched, optically tracked, wire-guided) missile launchers. (Defense Visual Information Center)

In the following days I MEF and V Corps concentrated on securing their lines of communications. V Corps committed its reserve, three airborne brigades, to suppress Fedayeen activity in the cities in its rear. Mattis sent battalions from RCT-7 and RCT-1 east and west along Route 17 to break up the Fedayeen at Afak, al Budayr, Fayr, and Diwaniyah. TF Tarawa, which had declared Nasiriyah secure on the twenty-seventh, and the 1st (UK) Armoured Division acted to solidify coalition control in the southeast. U.S. air power continued to pummel the Republican Guard divisions in the path of the arrested advance, with the 1st MAW averaging about 315 sorties a day.

On 29 March Mattis requested permission to advance to the Tigris so his Marines would have water available to wash their vehicles in the event of a chemical attack. Conway approved the request, and on 31 March RCT-5 recaptured "the elbow" at the junction of Routes 1 and 27. By then the 3rd Infantry Division had been resupplied, and Blount was as eager as Mattis to resume the offensive. On 1 April McKiernan formally ended the pause. For commanders and troops anxious to get on with the war, this was welcome news.

Later that day RCT-1 neared the outskirts of Kut, setting the stage for the most dramatic personnel action in the history of the Marine Corps since World War II. At that point, the feint by which Mattis planned to paralyze the Baghdad Division was virtually complete. After some skirmishing meant to strengthen the impression that an attack on Kut was imminent, RCT-1 would drop back to join the division for the approach

to Baghdad. Such at least was the plan; but outside the city, General Kelly decided that the plan could be changed for the better. Kelly had come to believe that RCT-1 had little to fear from the defenders of Kut. In that case, there was no need for it to make a time-consuming, 170-mile detour before resuming its march north. It could simply skirt the city. This would save at least twenty-four hours, a serious consideration in a campaign that stressed speed. Kelly had detected a development U.S. intelligence had missed. RCT-1's feint had not pinned the Baghdad Division to Kut after all. On 30 March it had pulled back to the capital, leaving the city to be defended by an army infantry division approximately 60 percent understrength. Still, there was always the Fedayeen.

When Kelly explained his thinking to Dowdy, the colonel was aghast. In his opinion the idea of entering Kut was a thoroughly bad one, likely to entangle RCT-1 in a costly action of the sort TF Tarawa had fought at Nasiriyah. Burly, broad-shouldered Joe Dowdy loved his regiment, "the first of the first," Chesty Puller's old regiment, and he loved his Marines. To date RCT-1 had lost only a single Marine killed in action, and Dowdy was determined not to lose any others without good cause. In the end, it was agreed that RCT-1 would test the city's defenses to see how strong they really were. The decision as to whether the Leathernecks could penetrate them at an acceptable cost would rest with Dowdy.

On 3 April Dowdy led two battalions into Kut. They were soon engaged in a brisk firefight during which one of his Marines was not surprised to see the colonel risk his

life to shove an Iraqi family to cover. Soon it was time for Dowdy to make his choice. The counsel he was receiving from outside the city was not helpful. Kelly encouraged him to push ahead; the division staff advised him to pull back. The Fedayeen seemed to be out in force. Dowdy decided that passing through Kut was not an intelligent option. He withdrew.

RCT-1 reached Numaniyah on 4 April after a detour that took only about half the projected thirty-six hours, but Dowdy's career was over. Dissatisfied with what he considered the colonel's lack of drive, Kelly had recommended relieving him of command, and a helicopter was waiting to carry him to Mattis' headquarters. Mattis was calm and sympathetic. After a brief conversation, he told Dowdy that his excessive caution would cause needless casualties and informed him

that he was relieved of command. Dowdy appealed to Mattis to reconsider, but the division commander made it clear that his decision was final. He proceeded to ask Dowdy to unload his pistol and give him the cartridges. Dowdy replied that he did not intend to shoot himself, and Mattis let the matter drop. Col. John A. Toolan Jr., the division operations officer, was named to command RCT-1. Dowdy completed the campaign as an observer in a P-3 reconnaissance plane. He was retired at his own request in 2004. Toolan and the other RCT commanders later became generals, and both Kelly and Mattis gained an additional star. In an address to a civic club in 2005, Dowdy said that he had never regretted his decision at Kut.

Meanwhile, American forces had continued their drive northward. On 2 April, the 1st Marine Division reached the Tigris and the 3rd Infantry Division surged through the Karbala Gap. The Leathernecks' advance was led by RCT-5's 2nd Tank Battalion, which had no difficulty seizing the bridge at Numaniyah. RCT-7 crossed the river the next day and turned north behind RCT-5. There was now only one obstacle between the Marines and Baghdad. The al Nida Division of the Republican Guard remained at Aziziyah, directly in their path. Despite U.S. air strikes, the division was believed to be 80 percent combat effective. Until now the Leathernecks had engaged army formations whose performance was, with occasional exceptions, as poor as predicted, and the Fedayeen, whose ardor was offset by their incompetence. The outcome of a clash with Saddam's elite was therefore a matter of more than mild interest.

As expected, the al Nida Division put up a fight for Aziziyah. The little battle that resulted was sharp but one-sided. There was simply no way an Iraqi division, however brave and dedicated, could withstand the combination of airpower, firepower, armor, and enterprising infantry the 1st Marine Division could bring to bear against it. As plumes of smoke roiled into the sky and the air filled with the crackle of machine guns and the thud of incoming ordnance, one young Leatherneck marveled, "This is like *Full Metal Jacket*." Earlier in the day Conway had told Mattis that if he saw the chance, "go for it." Mattis, who had come forward to observe the engagement, saw the chance. Although the Republican Guard and the Fedayeen were still fighting, it was clear that they could not seriously impede the division's advance. Baghdad was just fifty-five miles to the north.

Mattis directed RCT-5 to plan on reaching it the next day.

Accordingly, 2nd Tanks led RCT-5 into the outskirts of the Iraqi capital on the afternoon of 4 April. Hours earlier advanced elements of the 3rd Infantry Division had entered the Baghdad International Airport on the opposite side of the city. To all appearances, a perfectly coordinated pincers had closed on the capital. Once again, as in the Gulf War, the Leathernecks' performance had exceeded their brief. In recognition of that fact, McKiernan met Conway at Numaniyah to establish the ground rules for the end game at Baghdad. The Tigris was designated the operational boundary between V Corps and I MEF. The occupation of the city west of the river would be carried out by the Army; to the east, by the Marines.

Mattis had planned for RCT-5 to continue north and then wheel west around the outskirts of Baghdad before attacking to the southwest while RCT-7 followed Route 6 to attack to the northwest. To carry out its part, RCT-5 would have to cross the Diyala River, which flows in a generally southerly direction along the eastern edge of the city before emptying into the Tigris. Throughout 5 April, the day on which the Army made its first "thunder run"—armored raid—into Baghdad, RCT-5 looked for a practicable site to bridge the Diyala north of Route 6. None was found. The search continued on the sixth with no better result. Mattis had to abandon his idea of an attack from the north.

RCT-7 had reached the scene earlier that day and found two bridges still standing in its front: a narrow steel footbridge and a four-lane, concrete structure promptly designated

Opposite: Marines of Company D, 1st Light Armored Reconnaissance Battalion, guard Iraqis captured during the action with the al Nida Division at Numaniyah on 2 April 2003. (Defense Visual Information Center)

the Baghdad Bridge. Iraqi engineers had blown a ten-foot-wide hole in the footbridge's flooring and dropped the Baghdad Bridge's fifty-foot center span, but the Leathernecks believed they could make use of both. Mattis ordered RCT-7 to attack the next morning. Upstream, the 1st Tank Battalion would attempt to repair another bridge. RCT-1, which had caught up with the division, would attack across the Diyala in its AAVs. There was an extra element of risk in this maneuver: it was not known whether all the vehicles were still watertight. The crews were told to keep the top hatches open so they could get out if their vehicles began to sink.

Carrying a metal gate and planks to throw across the gap, 3/4's Company K rushed the footbridge at first light on 7 April. The Marine positions along the river

were being shelled by Iraqi artillery, but the infantry once entrenched on the far bank had departed and Kilo crossed the bridge without loss. Company I followed and the two units established a bridgehead. At the Baghdad Bridge, two tanks provided covering fire while the 8th Engineer Battalion positioned a collapsible bridge across the missing span. A minefield at the end of the bridge was cleared, and 3/4 led the division into eastern Baghdad. 1st Tanks and RCT-1's AAVs also crossed the river without difficulty. Some hardy Iraqi infantrymen opposite RCT-1 held their ground until the first AAVs breasted the Diyala. A prisoner, still shocked, explained, "When we saw the tanks floating across the river, we knew we could not win." By nightfall, seven battalions had entered Baghdad. General Franks visited Iraq for the first time that day. After conferring with General Conway he made a brief address to the troops. "I just want you to know," he said, "that if I had a son, I'd want him to be a Marine."

The occupation of Baghdad took little more than two days. For the most part, resistance was light. Before crossing the Diyala, division headquarters had divided East Baghdad into three sectors, one per RCT, which had in turn been subdivided into infantry battalion areas. RCT-5 and the remainder of the division entered the city on the eighth, and the next morning Conway told Mattis to give the Leathernecks their head. By nightfall, all Iraqi military and

governmental facilities between the Diyala and the Tigris were in Marine hands.

The Leathernecks' advance also produced an image that, more graphically than any other, symbolized the fall of Saddam Hussein. On reaching Firdos (Paradise) Square, tankers found that an enthusiastic crowd had looped a rope around an eighteen-feet-high bronze statue of Saddam Hussein and was vainly attempting to pull it off its pedestal. Cpl. Edward Chin of Bravo Company 1st Tanks, secured a cable from a tank retriever around the statue's neck, and the vehicle began to tug on it. For a moment, nothing happened; then, slowly at first, the statue toppled forward, face down. The head broke off and

some Iraqis happily rolled it away. Filmed by American television, the event was seen live by millions of viewers around the world, including President George W. Bush. Saddam Hussein's near quarter-century of rule over Iraq had ended. Regime change was a reality.

Despite that reality, the fighting around Baghdad was not quite over. On the afternoon of 9 April the CIA relayed rumors that Saddam had been sighted at Almilyah Palace, on the edge of the city, and 1/5 was sent to investigate. Subsequently, its objectives were expanded to include the seizure of a nearby mosque, where Saddam was also supposed to have been seen, and a local Ba'ath Party headquarters. By the time these missions were accomplished on the morning of the tenth, one Marine had been killed and twenty-two wounded. Fedayeen casualties were estimated to number at least one hundred dead. No trace was found of Saddam Hussein.

The 1st Marine Division was also called on to establish an American presence at a potential trouble spot. The spot was Tikrit, Saddam Hussein's hometown and a likely rallying point for his followers. Mattis gave the job to Kelly, who hurriedly organized the division's three light armored reconnaissance battalions (LARs), a company of truck-mounted infantry, and a smattering of other troops into a task force he named Tripoli. The Leathernecks set out for Tikrit, one hundred miles to the north, on 12 April. The operation paid an unexpected dividend the next day. At Samarra, three-quarters of the way to Tikrit, an Iraqi policeman directed the 3rd LAR to a house in which the surviving American POWs were being held: five soldiers from the 507th Maintenance Company and two

Army helicopter pilots who were shot down on 24 March. TF Tripoli occupied Tikrit after the perfunctory firefight on 14 April. Kelly's troops soon restored order, and the city was close to calm when they relinquished it to the newly arrived 4th Infantry Division between 19 and 21 April.

By then the 1st Marine Division had left Baghdad and begun the move to its occupation zone in southern Iraq. Most observers assumed that the war was effectively over; sooner or later Saddam Hussein would be run down, and otherwise all that needed to be done was a little mopping up. As had been the case in the earlier war with Iraq, coalition casualties were remarkably light in relation to the magnitude of the operations in which they had been incurred. Leatherneck losses totaled 310—54 dead and 256 wounded, two-thirds of whom belonged to the 1st Marine Division. It had never been intended for the Marines to remain long in Iraq after the close of hostilities, and the final elements of I MEF returned home in October.

On 1 May President Bush flew to the aircraft carrier *Abraham Lincoln* and, in a speech delivered before a huge banner proclaiming MISSION ACCOMPLISHED, declared that major combat operations in the Iraq were at an end. With the notable exception of the two battles for Fallujah, those words were true enough; but, contrary to the conclusion they invited, the war in Iraq was by no means at an end. Only six weeks after the president's speech Gen. John P. Abizaid, the incoming CENTCOM commander, told reporters that coalition forces had become the target of "a classic guerrilla-type campaign." The conventional war that U.S. troops won so handily had been succeeded by a vicious insurgency U.S. policy makers had failed to foresee.

Washington's key assumptions about postwar Iraq proved to have been wishful thinking. Perhaps most fundamental was the expectation that the infrastructure of the Iraqi state and society would survive regime change, or, as then–National Security Advisor Condoleeza Rice observed in retrospect, "the institutions would hold." In other words, government ministries would continue to function; the army and police, purged of committed Ba'athists, would provide security; and, after wartime damage had been repaired, existing facilities would generate electricity, furnish potable water, treat sewage, and, in general, perform the vital tasks upon which urban populations depend. Thus, once the Iraqis organized their own democratic government, which it was supposed would take no more than two months, coalition forces could begin to withdraw. The Pentagon anticipated that most American troops would be out of the country within a year.

None of these projections was realized. Unable to absorb even a glancing blow, Iraq's fragile infrastructure not only swooned but resisted resuscitation. Municipal services became mostly a memory. The police possessed neither the resources nor the will to cope with the insurgency, and on 23 May L. Paul Bremer III, the American diplomat appointed to supervise the recovery of Iraq, dissolved the army, convinced that it would be preferable to build a new force from scratch. This meant that some 175,000 U.S. and U.K. troops became solely responsible for maintaining order throughout a nation

the size of California with a population of twenty-four million. Especially in Baghdad, the inability of American forces to police every neighborhood and jump-start public utilities undermined their prestige during the critical, opening months of the occupation, when Iraqi attitudes remained fluid. No doubt Ba'athist bitter-enders, fanatical Fedayeen, and disgruntled Sunnis would have launched an insurrection in any event; but the fact that coalition forces were so thin on the ground emboldened them and encouraged jihadists and al-Qaeda operatives to cross the country's porous borders from Syria and Iran.

The consequence was a pernicious, decentralized insurgency in which the U.S. technological advantage was minimized and most U.S. casualties were inflicted by simple roadside bombs, soon to become infamous as IEDs—improvised explosive devices. Neither the deaths of Saddam Hussein's sinister sons Uday and Qusay in a shoot-out with members of the 101st Airborne at Mosul on 23 July nor the capture of Saddam himself in a "spider hole" on a farm near Tikrit on 13 December lessened the violence. Fortunately, the insurrection was largely confined to the Sunni Triangle defined by Baghdad, Tikrit, and Ramadi. Of Iraq's eighteen provinces, twelve remained more or less tranquil. Convinced that the insurgency could be countered without committing additional forces, American authorities chose to maintain existing troop levels while re-creating the Iraqi army and invigorating the police so that together they could assume the responsibility for their country's security. In the meanwhile, U.S. servicemen could look forward to revisiting Iraq. When the Marines' new commandant, Gen. Michael W. Hagee, was asked if the Corps was prepared to rotate troops through the country for years, he said simply, "We are prepared to do anything."

Quick-witted and composed, with a natural, unaffected manner that won many friends, Mike Hagee had become the Corps' thirty-third commandant in January 2003. He was the seventh successive Vietnam veteran to occupy that post. In the usual order of events, Jim Jones would have retained the post for another six months, but in September 2002 he had been appointed Supreme Allied Commander, Europe (SACEUR) and Commander, U.S. European Command (COMUSEUCOM), positions no Marine had ever held. Like all wartime commandants, Hagee was obliged to divide his attention between enhancing the Corps' capability to fight the war actually in progress and preparing it to fight the wars of the future—in addition, of course, to the inevitable budgetary battles. Measures to ready Marines for duty in Iraq ranged from an intensive, thirty-day desert training exercise to classes on Arabic culture. Especial attention was given to developing means to counter the greatest tactical threat Marines faced in Iraq, the IED. After a Marine squad was accused of murdering an Iraqi civilian, Hagee made one of his frequent visits to the country to underscore his declaration that, if the allegation was true, such conduct was unacceptable and those who engaged in it would be held accountable.

In a remark redolent of Clausewitz, Hagee told an interviewer that he believed the battlefield of the future would be much like the battlefield of the present, full of uncertainty, chaos, friction, and fog. That did not mean he believed that battles would be fought the same way. Under his leadership, the Corps explored the tactical concept rather opaquely entitled "distributed operations," which aimed to exploit advances in communications technology to allow units to "distribute" their components over a much greater area than they would have traditionally occupied. Progress was also made in developing doctrine and techniques for the employment of the MV-22 Osprey, and the decision was made to contribute a Marine contingent to the Special Operations Command, which dated back to 1987 but had been assigned increased responsibilities for the prosecution of the war on terror in 2002. Finally, Hagee overlooked no opportunity to remind lawmakers that a substantial supplemental appropriation would be required to replace the equipment the Corps was wearing out in Iraq.

On 20 March 2004 the 1st Marine Division relieved the 82nd Airborne Division in al Anbar Province, the cradle of the Sunni insurgency. Conway still commanded the MEF. Mattis retained command of the 1st Marine Division, and half of his eighteen thousand troops were veterans of the march on Baghdad. Iraq's largest province, encompassing approximately a third of the country, Anbar extends from the central Euphrates to the Syrian border. Fallujah, its second most populous and probably most hostile city, was the base of Abu Musab al Zarqawi, the chief of al-Qaeda operations in Iraq. A week after the Marines assumed responsibility for the province, four American employees of Blackwater Security Consulting, driving west from Baghdad, followed Route 10 into Fallujah. They did not come out alive. Three quarters of the way through the city, their SUVs were riddled by a hail of automatic weapons' fire. The Americans' bodies were mutilated, burned, and dismembered, and the charred remnants of two corpses were suspended from the overhead girders of a bridge spanning the Euphrates. Fallujan photographers recorded the scene, complete with crowds of jubilant Iraqis.

Outraged by the atrocity, American civilian and military leaders from Baghdad to Washington urged I MEF to take immediate action to punish the perpetrators. To their consternation, the Marines demurred. No U.S. troops had been stationed inside Fallujah in more than six months. The paratroop battalion assigned to oversee the city had operated from a base two miles to the west, only sending daily patrols into Fallujah's mean streets. Plans called for the Marine battalion that replaced it to do the same. In time, senior Leathernecks hoped to persuade two new Iraqi Army battalions stationed on the edge of the city to participate in the patrols. To attack into an unfamiliar urban area with a quarter-million inhabitants seemed to Conway and Mattis guaranteed to generate needless casualties, especially among innocent civilians. They were overruled. On 2 April, I MEF received written orders to occupy Fallujah.

Two days later the Marines converged on the city. Three battalions were committed to the attack: one from the north of Route 10, which runs generally east to west through Fallujah, and two from the south. Opposing them were an estimated five hundred hard-core insurgents and a thousand amateurs. Each little group fought its own battle, firing quick bursts at the Marines and taking refuge in the nearest house or shop, most of which were ready-made little fortresses, with cement walls and flat, parapet roofs. In this case, the absence of a central command was probably to the insurgents' advantage because it gave them the flexibility to exploit their local knowledge and spared them the mistake of trying to hold any particular line. These circumstances and their disregard of death notwithstanding, they were unable to interrupt the Leathernecks' advance. On 8 April Colonel Toolan, the officer in tactical command of the offensive, told Mattis that the city would be secured within seventy-two hours.

In the meantime, however, the insurgents had played their trump card: the media. Early in April they had invited al-Jazeera, the Arab satellite television network, to send a news team into Fallujah. During the fighting, al-Jazeera's crew filmed its most arresting footage in the city's hospitals. The bloody, heartrending scenes it collected were viewed around the world. Exaggerated reports of civilian casualties—six hundred dead and a thousand wounded—provoked speculation that the Marines were applying excessive force. The predictable protests followed, both at home and abroad. Soon Bremer and Abizaid, who had agreed that the Marines should go into Fallujah, agreed that to let them go farther might throw the country into chaos. On the evening of 8 April, Conway was instructed to cease offensive operations against the city. Nothing was said of Ramadi, the provincial capital, where a large-scale uprising on 6 April had embroiled 2/4 in heavy fighting that lasted until the surviving insurgents melted away five days later. The difference was there were no Arab television crews in Ramadi. Conway put it succinctly: "Al-Jazeera kicked our butts."

While events in Fallujah attracted international attention, Leathernecks were conducting operations throughout Anbar Province. One of many unheralded incidents took place on 14 April at Husabayah, near the Syrian border, where Cpl. Jason L. Dunham became the first Marine to receive the Medal of Honor since the Vietnam War. A razor-thin, twenty-two-year-old six-footer from the little town of Scio, New York, Dunham had extended his enlistment so that he could serve a full tour with 3/7 in Iraq. His squad was inspecting civilian vehicles for weapons in an area from which an RPG had been fired. As Dunham approached a Toyota SUV the driver leaped out and grappled with him. They went down in a heap, and two of Dunham's comrades ran to help him. "No, no, no!" he shouted. "Watch his hand!" A moment later the Iraqi released the grenade Dunham had been the only American to see. Dunham covered it with his helmet and body. He was mortally wounded, with two grenade fragments in his brain. The other two Marines were also wounded but, as a result of his selfless action, survived. So, briefly, did the Iraqi. Although bleeding from the torso, he stood up and began to run away. A fourth Marine put twenty-five rounds into him. Jason Dunham lived long enough to be transported to the National Naval Medical Center at Bethesda, Maryland. The Corps provided airline tickets for his parents to fly

to his side. It soon became evident that his condition was hopeless, and on 22 April the Dunhams made the agonizing decision to remove his life-support systems. Mike Hagee, who regularly visited wounded Marines in Bethesda, pinned a Purple Heart on his pillow before he died, and Mrs. Dunham cried on the commandant's shoulder.

At Fallujah the Marines were initially given to understand that the offensive had merely been put on hold. There was never a cease-fire. As the days passed and the nominally twenty-four-hour delays multiplied, the Leathernecks maintained and improved their positions; endured mortar, rocket, and rifle fire; conducted patrols deep into the city; deployed sniper teams that picked off armed men at ranges up to six hundred yards; sent a task force to suppress insurgent activity along the road to Baghdad; and remained confident that they would be allowed to resume the offensive. Finally, on 24 April, it became clear that an advance would not be authorized. As of that date, thirteen Marines had been killed in action at Fallujah.

Two days later a thirty-nine-man patrol became heavily engaged inside the city. By the time it regained friendly lines, one Marine had been killed and seventeen wounded. That afternoon Conway gave the order to initiate the controversial experiment called the Fallujah Brigade. Earlier in the month he had been approached by a retired Iraqi officer, Col. Mohammed Latif, with an intriguing proposition. If the Marines would withdraw from Fallujah and provide the funding, Latif and officers of his choosing would organize an Iraqi force of five or six hundred men that would restore order in the city. Latif made an

excellent impression, his political credentials were impeccable—seven years in jail under Saddam—and his proposal represented what was from an American perspective the ideal solution to the impasse: Iraqis policing Iraqis. The only question, a big one, was whether Latif could pull it off.

In the end, Latif could not. He dutifully organized the Fallujah Brigade. On 10 May, the date the last Marine unit withdrew from the city, he arranged for Mattis to pay a peaceful if very tense call on the mayor, and for a few weeks the incidence of IEDs discovered in the vicinity declined. Thereafter the situation deteriorated precipitously. The insurgents interpreted the Marines' departure to evidence that the city had fought them off. The Fallujah Brigade's failure to respond to a mortar attack on its compound cost Latif whatever authority he had briefly exercised.

He had been commuting from Baghdad; after mid-July he simply stayed home. His successor limited his contact with the Marines to paydays. In August the commanders of the two Iraqi battalions outside the city were kidnapped and killed. Aside from occasional Marine air strikes on terrorist safe houses, the insurgents' sway over Fallujah was absolute and undisturbed.

Perhaps inspired by events in al Anbar, an ambitious young Shiite cleric, Muqtadr al Sadr, launched his second rebellion against the central government on 5 August. The son of a popular clergyman murdered on Saddam's orders in 1993, al Sadr had attracted a fanatical following by castigating the infidel occupation of Iraq and proceeded to recruit a personal militia he named the Mahdi Army. His first uprising had taken place in April. The U.S. 1st Armored Division had put it down by the end of the month, but Bremer allowed al Sadr to retain his freedom in return for calling upon his adherents to stop fighting. Now al Sadr was at it again. This time the outbreak was confined to Najaf, al Sadr's stronghold and the capital of the province of the same name. The task of dealing with it was assigned to the 1st Battalion, 4th Marines, later reinforced by the 2nd Battalion of the 7th Cavalry. Once again, al Sadr was driven into a corner, and once again and for the same reasons the civilian leadership in Baghdad let him go free; but that leadership was no longer American. Bremer's administration had formally transferred power to an Iraqi interim government on 28 June. The leading political figure in Iraq was now the new prime minister, Iyad Allawi, a London-trained neurosurgeon who had been active in the exile opposition to Saddam.

If Allawi felt that forbearance was indicated in regard to al Sadr, he did not feel the same way about the situation in Fallujah. In August he shut down al-Jazeera's Iraq bureau, and the following month he dissolved the Fallujah Brigade. He also undertook high-profile talks with the city's insurgent leaders. Presumably, these exchanges were intended to demonstrate that Allawi was a man of moderation, but the tough rhetoric that counterpointed them showed he was really not interested in a negotiated settlement.

Washington agreed that the time had come to act. Around the middle of September, the Marines outside Fallujah became convinced that they would finally get the go-ahead. They were not disappointed. Orders to subdue the city reached I MEF on 6 November.

By that date many of the Leathernecks who had participated in the first battle of Fallujah had rotated to other assignments. They included Conway and Mattis. I MEF was now commanded by Lt. Gen. John F. Sattler, and the 1st Marine Division by Maj. Gen. Richard F. Natonski, who had commanded TF Tarawa in 2003. In preparing for the operation, the Marines surmised that the insurgents would expect them to attack from the same locations that they had before. Obviously, it would be in their interest to frustrate that expectation. As finalized, the division's plan projected an assault from the north with six battalions on line on a front three miles wide. Thanks to the generous support of Joint Task Force headquarters in Baghdad, no fewer than thirteen battalions

were assembled: six Marine, three Army, three Iraqi, and one British. Altogether, they numbered approximately twelve thousand troops. The attack was entrusted to four Marine battalions, 3/1, 1/3, 3/5, and 1/8, and two medium sized task forces, the 2/2 Infantry and the 2/7 Cavalry, the latter of which had fought beside the Marines at Najaf. One of the Iraqi battalions would take part in a curtain raiser. Afterward all three, untrained in urban warfare, were to follow the Marines and occupy the area they had cleared. A battalion of Britain's famed Black Watch was deployed to safeguard communications between Fallujah and Baghdad. The remaining battalions formed a cordon around the city.

Operation Phantom Fury, soon renamed Operation al Fajr—"dawn" in Arabic—began at dusk on 7 November, when the 36th Iraqi Battalion, supported by the 3rd Light Armored Reconnaissance Battalion, set out to seize the hospital on the west bank of the Euphrates opposite the city proper and the two bridges nearby. These objectives were quickly secured. The attack from the north was launched twenty-four hours later. The civilian population of Fallujah had heeded Allawi's warnings. Of the city's 250,000 residents, fewer than 30,000 remained. On the other hand, the number of defenders had doubled, to approximately a thousand insurgents and two thousand enthusiasts.

An artillery bombardment preceded the ground assault. Despite its decision to bring Fallujah under control, Baghdad restricted the application of force. The Marines were authorized to hit fewer than twenty of the two hundred targets they had carefully identified. Once the battle was under way, the use of artillery, often directed by UAVs—unmanned aerial vehicles carrying infrared cameras that could penetrate the dark—became more lavish. When the fighting ended Leatherneck gunners and mortar men had fired fourteen thousand rounds and the 3rd MAW had flown 540 strikes. Nearly half of Fallujah's thirty-nine thousand buildings were damaged or destroyed.

The fury of the attack seems to have stunned the insurgents. The Marines reached Route 10 on 10 November, several days ahead of schedule. Resistance stiffened as they pushed into the southern half of the city. The sticky business of house-to-house fighting demanded a high order of heroism. Twenty-five of forty-six men in a platoon of 1/8 became casualties on a single day. Later in the battle, twenty-five-year-old Sgt. Rafael Peralta, a Mexican-born naturalized citizen serving in 1/3, was mortally wounded and fell to the floor of a room occupied by several other Marines. Seconds later an enemy grenade dropped among them. Without hesitation, Sergeant Peralta seized the grenade and thrust it beneath his body, saving the lives of his comrades. In a letter to his brother and sister on the eve of the offensive, he wrote: "We are going to defeat the insurgents. Watch the news, it's going to be all over. Be proud of me, bro, I'm going to make history."

Veterans of the April battle thought that the enemy displayed more tactical sophistication this time around. Leathernecks also noted with professional approval that when an insurgent was hit in the open, his comrades nearly always tried to drag him to cover. In the end, of course, there was no cover left. On the afternoon of 14 November the Marines completed the occupation of Fallujah, although pockets of resistance remained. The last sizable action occurred on the sixteenth, when two dozen insurgents fought to the death in a compound that proved to have been the headquarters of Abu Musab al Zarqawi. Zarqawi himself had decamped.

Approximately a thousand insurgents and jihadists were killed and eleven hundred captured. U.S. casualties numbered 70 dead and 651 wounded. On a trestle of the bridge above which pieces of the Blackwater contractors' blackened bodies had been suspended in March, someone had painted the Arabic words: "Fallujah—Graveyard of the Americans." On another, nearby trestle, an unknown member of the 3rd Battalion, 5th Marines, painted

THIS IS FOR
THE AMERICANS
OF BLACKWATER

THAT WERE
MURDERED HERE
IN 2004.
SEMPER FIDELIS.
3/5
(DARK HORSE)
P.S. FUCK YOU.
911

"Dark Horse" is the nickname of 3/5. The battalion commander ordered the postscript to be painted over.

While the Iraq insurgency constituted by far the Corps' largest overseas involvement after the fall of Baghdad, it was not the only one. Between July and October 2003 Leathernecks participated in peacekeeping and humanitarian operations in Liberia, Senegal, and Sierra Leone. The following spring they were among the units deployed to Afghanistan to support Hamid Karzai's government against a resurgence of the Taliban. Another contribution to the war on terror was made by Marine missions sent to help train their counterparts in

Chad, Colombia, Djibouti, Georgia, and the Philippines. Leathernecks also provided assistance to victims of the great southeast Asian tsunami in 2004, as they would to the survivors of Hurricane Katrina on the U.S. Gulf Coast in 2005.

I MEF rotated home in March 2005. Its place in Anbar Province was taken by II MEF, which consisted of the 2nd Marine Division, the 2nd MAW, and the 2nd Force Support Service Group. The insurgency persisted. II MEF did not fight any pitched battles à la Fallujah during its year in Iraq, but it conducted ten named operations of varying scale and duration intended to disrupt insurgent activities. The most productive, Operation Steel Curtain, took place in November. In the seventeen days it spanned, Marines killed 140 insurgents and detained 256 suspects.

When I MEF returned in the spring of 2006, Iraq had apparently made major strides toward democracy. Despite insurgent threats against anyone who dared participate, from 60 to 70 percent of the nation's eligible

voters had turned out to cast their ballots at three elections within a year: in January 2005 to seat a transitional assembly to draft a new constitution; in October to ratify that constitution; and in December to choose a regular national assembly. The Shiites, Sunnis, and Kurds all fielded one or more of their own parties for a third of them. No one won an absolute majority, which greatly complicated matters, but in May 2006 prime minister designate Nouri al-Maliki, deputy leader of one of the principal Shiite parties, was able to present his cabinet to the assembly. For the first time in its history, Iraq possessed a genuinely representative government.

Unfortunately, the hopes to which these developments gave rise were blighted when, on 22 February 2006, al-Qaeda bombs shattered the Golden Mosque at Samarra, one of Shiite Islam's holiest shrines. The outrage was intended to inflame the sectarian tensions ever present in Iraqi society, and it succeeded all too well. In the following months the hostilities that had begun as an insurrection against foreign forces showed ominous signs of morphing into a civil war as Sunni and Shiite extremists targeted each other's communities. The death of Abu Musab al Zarqawi, mortally wounded by a U.S. air strike in June 2006, had no more lasting effect than the capture of Saddam Hussein. During the following month, the deadliest to date, 3,400 Iraqis, the majority civilians, fell victim to acts of sectarian violence. By then the conflict in Iraq had lasted nearly as long as World War II; U.S. casualties numbered 21,000, including 2,000 dead, and opinion polls revealed that most Americans believed

that war was going badly and favored bringing the troops home.

The midterm elections of November 2006, generally regarded as a referendum on President Bush's pledge to "stay the course" in Iraq, cost his party control of both houses of Congress. This setback notwithstanding, the administration remained committed to the goal of establishing a stable, democratic Iraq. On 10 January 2007 Bush stunned his critics by announcing his intention to send a "surge" of 21,500 additional troops to that country: 17,500 to Baghdad, where 85 percent of the acts of violence in Iraq occurred, and 4,000 to Anbar Province. For its part, the Maliki government agreed to concentrate more forces in the capital and rescind the rules of engagement that had barred U.S. forces from entering certain neighborhoods. If the surge proved successful, it would give the Iraqi

government time to gain political traction and implement measures, such as an equitable distribution of the country's oil revenues, designed to reconcile the Sunni population to the new Iraq.

A day following the president's bombshell, Secretary of Defense Robert M. Gates, who had replaced Donald Rumsfeld in December, announced that he planned to ask Congress to expand U.S. ground forces by 92,000 troops, including 27,000 Marines, over a five-year period. The increase was required to ease the strain of long deployments in the war on terror. The Corps' share would give it an authorized strength of 202,000, the greatest since the Vietnam War.

The contrast between the reception these initiatives received from the public, the press, and the political opposition could hardly have been more extreme. The expansion of the

Left: An Abrams tank from the 3rd Battalion, 2nd Marines, secures the streets of al Ubaydi, a village in al Anbar Province, during Operation Matador, 12 May 2005. The operation was undertaken to disrupt the flow of foreign terrorists across the border from Syria. (Defense Visual Information Center)

Right: This young Marine from 2/3 was photographed on patrol in Haqlaniyah, Anbar Province, on 20 December 2006. He is carrying his M16A2 at the ready. His night-vision goggles are folded over his helmet. (Defense Visual Information Center)

Army and Marine Corps, already espoused by many members of Congress, met with widespread bipartisan support. The troop surge encountered a firestorm of criticism, but on Capitol Hill the Democratic majority could do no more than deplore and denounce it. The Army's foremost counterinsurgency expert, Gen. David Petraeus, a paratrooper with a Princeton Ph.D., assumed command of Multinational Force–Iraq in Baghdad on 10 February. By that date, the surge had apparently scored its first success. On 13 January Muqtadr al Sadr ordered his Mahdi Army not to oppose coalition forces and personally went into hiding. In August he extended the stand-down for another six months. Not all of his adherents heeded his orders, but the majority obeyed.

Even before the surge was announced, the 25,000 Marines operating in Anbar Province found the security situation changing in their favor. During the summer of 2006 al-Qaeda had gone too far. The acts of terror with which it sought to maintain control of the province boomeranged. Rather than being intimidated, the Anbaris were outraged. In September a group of sheiks met at Ramadi to form the al-Jazeera Council, which began working with U.S. forces to expel al-Qaeda from the city. Other tribes soon joined the movement, and Anbar Awakening (Sahawah al Anbar) took shape in October. The sheiks who rallied to it not only raised their own tribal levies but also urged their followers to enlist in the Iraqi Army and police.

U.S. forces supported these developments. Backed by American firepower, the Anbaris had regained control of their capital by March 2007, when President Maliki visited the city.

In the following months the process was repeated throughout the province. Between October 2006 and October 2007 the number of terrorist attacks in Anbar plunged from 1,350 a month to fewer than 100. Military personnel and newsmen familiar with the old Anbar were astonished at the transformation. Taking a veteran journalist to buy kebabs at an open-air restaurant in downtown Ramadi, a Marine officer assured him, "It's safer than London or New York." Soon a story made the rounds that lance corporals were complaining they didn't have anybody to shoot. At least for the moment, what had been the most violent province in Iraq had become one of the most peaceful. Moreover, the example set there spread. In the spring of 2007 Anbar Awakening was renamed Iraq Awakening, and at the close of the year there were approximately three hundred communal and regional awakening councils counting some seventy thousand fighters in Sunni areas throughout the country.

Indeed, as 2007 approached an end, some Marines felt that Iraq was becoming too peaceful. Among them was Jim Conway, who had succeeded Mike Hagee to become Commandant of the Marine Corps a year earlier. To Conway it seemed that his Marines would be wasted performing garrison duty in Anbar Province. In October he proposed that as soon as the situation permitted they should be shifted to Afghanistan, where a NATO force, predominantly American, was contending with a resurgent Taliban. "That's why young Americans join the Marine Corps—to fight for their country," he said. "I think if there's fighting going on, we need to be there." The 25,000 U.S. troops engaged in Afghanistan included only a few hundred Marines, but Conway believed that the Corps' expeditionary capabilities made it well suited for the conflict. Early in December Secretary Gates ruled that the time was not ripe for such a redeployment. Barely a month later, however, the Pentagon announced that 3,200 Marines would be sent from the United States to Afghanistan for seven months to offset, in part, a shortfall of 7,500 troops in the NATO forces there. Although spokesmen were careful to specify that this was an "extraordinary, one-time" deployment, some old hands wondered if it signified that the Corps had gotten its nose into the tent.

Meanwhile, the surge had achieved impressive results. In the course of the buildup the number of troops involved was increased to 30,000, raising U.S. end strength in Iraq to 165,000. But the change went far beyond force levels. Petraeus brought new concepts of counterinsurgency to Baghdad. Previously, the strategic priority had been to train the Iraqi Army. Now it was to secure the Iraqi population, beginning in Baghdad. Previously, the Army units at Baghdad had conducted patrols and raids from enclaves—forward operating bases—to which they returned once their mission was completed. Localities that had been cleared were turned over to Iraqi forces, which often proved unable to hold them. Now U.S. and Iraqi units operating from a score of joint security stations and combat outposts established throughout Baghdad maintained a permanent presence. The object became not merely to clear but to control and retain.

The first phase of the Baghdad Security Plan, the elimination of terrorist havens within the capital, had been largely accomplished when the last of the troops committed to the surge reached Iraq in June. The second phase, the disruption of al-Qaeda infrastructure in the "belts" encircling Baghdad, was launched on the fifteenth of that month. This offensive (Operation Phantom Thunder) was succeeded in August by another (Operation Phantom Strike) designed to prevent al-Qaeda driven from Baghdad and the belts from regrouping outside the city. Terrorist strongholds in Diyala and Salah ad-Din provinces, to the north of Baghdad, were targeted by a third offensive, Operation Phantom Phoenix, which opened in January 2008.

Overall acts of violence, which had increased steadily since the bombing of the Golden Mosque in early 2006, reached a peak in June 2007 as al-Qaeda responded to the American offensive. Then, as the tide turned, they declined dramatically. By late December attacks on coalition forces and Iraqi civilians had fallen 60 percent. The influx of Iranian weapons noted in the spring also decreased sharply. Of course, these gains came at a cost. Offensives are seldom inexpensive. With 899 U.S. troops killed in action, 2007 was the deadliest year ever in Iraq, but as al-Qaeda capabilities deteriorated, American casualties dwindled. The number of deaths in December (23) was the lowest of any month in the conflict, with the single exception of February 2004.

Yet all these gains were reversible. As Petraeus cautioned at year's end, it was not time for victory dances in the end zone. The future conduct of Muqtadr al Sadr and the Iranians were only two of the uncertainties

facing American leaders. President Maliki's predominantly Shiite government looked askance at the awakening councils, fearful that the Sunni tribal levies might revert to rebellion, and some U.S. officials worried that these apprehensions might prove justified unless the government showed itself willing to recognize and reward the councils' contribution to the fight against al-Qaeda. Presumably worse yet, the Iraqi parliament had failed to enact legislation calculated to bring about the political reconciliation upon which the ultimate success of the surge would depend. Skeptics charged that the time the surge had bought had been wasted.

The reality was more nuanced. Although the government had yet officially to adopt the majority of the measures U.S. policy makers considered essential to promoting the unity of Iraq, it had actually begun to implement some of the most important of them—sharing oil revenues, for example. There were also indications that the Bush administration was preparing to launch another surge, this time diplomatic, early in 2008. If such a surge achieved anything approaching the success of its military predecessor, the long struggle in Iraq might be brought to a satisfactory conclusion.

In the meantime, a succession of top-level appointments had shattered the glass ceiling that kept senior Marines from holding major commands outside the Corps. As far back as 1991, Gen. Joseph P. Hoar was selected to head CENTCOM, thereby assuming the responsibility for all the armed services' operations in an area extending from Egypt to Pakistan and Kazakhstan to Kenya. Another Leatherneck, Tony Zinni, preceded Tommy Franks in the same post. Jim Jones' appointment as SACEUR in 2002 gave him command of NATO's European as well as American forces, and in September 2005 Gen. Peter M. Pace succeeded Air Force general Richard Myers as the senior serving officer in the U.S. armed forces, chairman of the Joint Chiefs of Staff (JCS), a body on which the Marine Corps was not even represented at the time of Pace's birth. The son of Italian emigrants and a graduate of the Naval Academy Class of 1967, Pace had served with distinction in a variety of assignments, most recently as vice chairman of the JCS from September 2001. He also possessed solid combat credentials from service in Vietnam and Somalia.

Unfortunately, Pace was destined to be a single-term chairman. As the time for his reappointment drew near, congressional leaders warned Secretary Gates that in view of the six years Pace had spent in the Pentagon, his confirmation hearings would become an acrimonious inquest into the whole course of the war in Iraq. In June 2007 Gates announced that, for this reason alone, he would advise the president not to renominate Pace. Adm. Mike Mullen was subsequently named to the post. The ceremony marking Pace's retirement and the change of command took place at Fort Myer, Virginia, on 1 October. Afterward Pace drove to the Vietnam Memorial Wall, where he left his four-star insignia and a note that read: "For Guido Farinaro, USMC. These are yours—not mine! With love and respect, your platoon leader, Pete Pace."

Just as the Marine Corps changed dramatically in 1898 as a result of the Spanish-American War and embraced the new responsibilities that followed in the Caribbean and East Asia, again in 1917 after the U.S. entered World War I, and in 1941 when America was thrust into World War II, so had the Corps changed dramatically as a result of the war on terror. Chesty Puller, never at a loss for a suitable and snappy rejoinder—after being apprised of the major commitments levied on his beloved Corps in support of the wars of the twenty-first century, or that women Marines served in combat service support units in these conflicts—might have snarled: "Old Corps, New Corps, it doesn't make a damn bit of difference!" But as a crusty gunnery sergeant told one of the authors of this volume, then a flush-cheeked PFC with the sand of Marine Corps Recruit Depot, San Diego, still in his boondockers: "Son, the Old Corps was yesterday!"

Suggestions for Further Reading

Selections from the source material used by the authors appear listed by chapter. In addition, the authors recommend the following materials that cover the entire panorama of the Marine Corps' history.

Alexander, Joseph H. *A Fellowship of Valor: The Battle History of the United States Marine Corps.* New York: Harper-Collins, 1997.

Clark, George B. *Legendary Marines of the Old Corps.* Pike, NH: The Brass Hat, 2002.

Heinl, Robert Debs, Jr. *Soldiers of the Sea: The United States Marine Corps, 1775–1962.* Annapolis, MD: Naval Institute Press, 1962.

Millett, Allan R. *Semper Fidelis: The History of the United States Marine Corps.* New York: Macmillan, 1980.

Millett, Allan R., and Jack Shulimson, eds. *Commandants of the Marine Corps.* Annapolis, MD: Naval Institute Press, 2004.

Moskin, J. Robert. *The U.S. Marine Corps Story.* New York: McGraw-Hill, 1977. 3rd edition, Boston: Little, Brown, 1992.

Simmons, Edwin Howard. *The United States Marines: A History*, 3rd ed. Annapolis, MD: Naval Institute Press, 1998.

Chapter 1: Marines through the Ages

Field, Cyril. *Britain's Sea Soldiers: A History of the Royal Marines*, 2 vols. Liverpool: Lyceum, 1924.

Marini, Alfred J. "Parliament and the Marine Regiments," *Mariner's Mirror* 62 (February 1976): 39–45.

Nihart, Brooke. "Amphibious Operations in Colonial North America." In *Assault from the Sea: Essays on the History of Amphibious Warfare*, edited by Merrill L. Bartlett, 46–50. Annapolis, MD: Naval Institute Press, 1983.

Rodgers, William L. *Greek and Roman Naval Warfare.* Annapolis, MD: Naval Institute Press, 1964.

Chapter 2: The Continental Marines, 1775–83

Fowler, William W., Jr. *Rebels under Sail: The American Navy during the Revolution.* New York: Scribner's, 1976.

McCusker, John J., Jr. "The American Invasion of Nassau in the Bahamas," *American Neptune* 25 (July 1965): 189–217.

Smith, Charles R. *Marines in the Revolution: A History of the Continental Marines in the American Revolution, 1775–1783*. Washington, DC: Government Printing Office, 1975.

Symonds, Craig L. "The American Naval Expedition to Penobscot, 1779," *Naval War College Review* 24 (April 1972): 64–71.

Chapter 3: The Early Years, 1798–1820

Alexander, Joseph H. "Swamp Ambush," *Military History* 14 (March 1998): 38–44.

Bartlett, Merrill L. "Court-Martial of a Commandant," *U.S. Naval Institute Proceedings* 111 (June 1985): 64–72.

London, Joshua E. *Victory in Tripoli: How America's War with the Barbary Pirates Established the U.S. Navy and Shaped a Nation*. New York: Wiley, 2005.

Chapter 4: The Era of Archibald Henderson, 1820–59

Bartlett, Merrill L. "Danang, 1845," *Naval History* 3 (Fall 1989): 55–57.

Bauer, K. Jack. *Surfboats and Horse Marines: U.S. Naval Operations in the Mexican War, 1846–1849*. Annapolis, MD: Naval Institute Press, 1969.

Dawson, Joseph G., III. "With Fidelity and Effectiveness: Archibald Henderson's Lasting Legacy to the Marine Corps," *Journal of Military History* 62 (October 1998): 727–53.

Simmons, Edwin H. "The Secret Mission of Archibald Henderson," *Marine Corps Gazette* 52 (November 1968): 66–67.

Sprague, John T. *The Origins, Progress, and Conclusion of the Florida War*. New York: Appleton, 1848.

Chapter 5: Marines in Blue and Gray, 1859–65

Donnelly, Ralph W. *The Confederate States Marine Corps: The Rebel Leathernecks*. Shippensburg, PA: White Mane, 1989.

Johnson, Robert Underwood, and Clarence Clough Buel, eds. *Battles and Leaders of the Civil War*. 4 vols. New York: Century, 1884, 1887–88.

Robinson, Charles M., III. *Hurricane of Fire: The Union Assault on Fort Fisher*. Annapolis, MD: Naval Institute Press, 1998.

Sullivan, David M. *The United States Marine Corps in the Civil War*. 4 vols. Shippensburg, PA: White Mane, 1997–2000.

Tucker, Spencer. *A Short History of the Civil War at Sea*. Wilmington, DE: Scholarly Resources, 2002.

Chapter 6: At Sea in the Postbellum Years, 1865–98

Castel, Albert, and Andrew C. Nahm. "Our Little War with the Heathen," *American Heritage* 19 (April 1968): 18–23, 72–75.

Holden-Rhodes, J. F. "The Adventures of Henry Clay Cochrane," *Marine Corps Gazette* 66 (November 1982): 69–70; (December 1982): 14–15; 67 (January 1983): 32–33; (February 1983): 46–47; (March 1983): 50–51; (April 1983): 54–55.

Shulimson, Jack. *The Marine Corps' Search for a Mission, 1880–1898*. Lawrence: University Press of Kansas, 1993.

———. "U.S. Marines in Panama, 1885." In *Assault from the Sea: Essays on the History of Amphibious Warfare*, edited by Merrill L. Bartlett, 107–20. Annapolis, MD: Naval Institute Press, 1983.

Chapter 7: Colonial Infantry, 1898–1917

Butler, Smedley D., with Lowell Thomas. *Old Gimlet Eye: The Adventures of Smedley D. Butler*. New York: Farrar & Rinehart, 1933; reprint: Quantico, VA: Marine Corps Association, 1981.

Cosmas, Graham, and Jack Shulimson. "The Culebra Maneuver and the Formation of the Marine Corps' Advance Base Force, 1913–14." In *Assault from the Sea: Essays on the History of Amphibious Warfare*, edited by Merrill L. Bartlett, 121–32. Annapolis, MD: Naval Institute Press, 1983.

Langley, Lester D. *The Banana Wars: An Inner History of the American Empire, 1900–1934*. Lexington: University Press of Kentucky, 1983.

Sweetman, Jack. *The Landing at Veracruz*. Annapolis, MD: Naval Institute Press, 1968.

Chapter 8: Over There, 1917–18

Bartlett, Merrill L. "Leathernecks, Doughboys, and the Press," *Naval History* 7 (October 1993): 46–53.

———. *Lejeune: A Marine's Life, 1867–1942*. Columbia: University of South Carolina Press, 1991; reprint: Annapolis, MD: Naval Institute Press, 1996.

Clark, George B. *Devil Dogs: Fighting Marines of World War I*. Novato, CA: Presidio, 1999.

Coffman, Edward M. *The War to End All Wars: The American Military Experience in World War I*. Madison: University of Wisconsin Press, 1986.

Thomason, John W. *Fix Bayonets!* New York: Scribner's, 1926; reprint: Quantico, VA: Marine Corps Association, 1978.

Chapter 9: Between the Wars, 1919–41

Ballendorf, Dirk Anthony, and Merrill L. Bartlett. *Pete Ellis: An Amphibious Warfare Prophet, 1880–1923.* Annapolis, MD: Naval Institute Press, 1997.

Bartlett, Merrill L. "Ouster of a Commandant," *U.S. Naval Institute Proceedings* 106 (November 1980): 60–65.

Clark, George B. *With the Old Corps in Nicaragua.* Novato, CA: Presidio, 2001.

Millett, Alan R. "Assault from the Sea: The Development of Amphibious Warfare between the Wars—the American, British, and Japanese Experience." In *Military Innovation in the Interwar Period,* edited by Williamson Murray and Alan R. Millett, 50–95. New York: Cambridge University Press, 1976.

Williams, Robert H. *The Old Corps: A Portrait of the U.S. Marine Corps between the Wars.* Annapolis, MD: Naval Institute Press, 1982.

Chapter 10: World War II: The South Pacific Campaigns, 1942–43
Chapter 11: World War II: The Central Pacific Drive, 1943–45

Alexander, Joseph H. *Storm Landings: Epic Amphibious Battles in the Central Pacific.* Annapolis, MD: Naval Institute Press, 1997.

Frank, Richard B. *Guadalcanal.* New York: Random House, 1990.

Gordon, John W. "General Thomas Holcomb and 'The Golden Age of Amphibious Warfare,'" *Delaware History* 21 (Fall–Winter 1985): 256–70.

Jones, Wilbur D., Jr. *Gyrene: The World War II United States Marine.* Shippensburg, PA: White Mane, 1998.

Spector, Ronald H. *Eagle against the Sun: The American War with Japan.* New York: Macmillan, 1985.

Chapter 12: The Unification Struggle, Cold War, and Korea, 1945–53

Alexander, Joseph H., and Merrill L. Bartlett. *Sea Soldiers in the Cold War: Amphibious Warfare, 1945–1991.* Annapolis, MD: Naval Institute Press, 1995.

Hoffman, Jon T. *Chesty: The Story of Lieutenant General Lewis B. Puller, USMC.* New York: Random House, 2001.

Keiser, Gordon W. *The U.S. Marine Corps and Defense Unification.* Washington, DC: National Defense University Press, 1982.

Owen, Joseph R. *Colder Than Hell: A Marine Rifle Company at Chosin Reservoir.* New York: Ballantine, 1996.

Russ, Martin. *The Last Parallel: A Marine's War Journal.* New York: Rinehart, 1957.

Chapter 13: The Vietnam War, 1954–75

Caufield, Matthew P. "India Six," *Marine Corps Gazette* 53 (July 1969): 27–31.

Miller, John G. *The Bridge at Dong Ha*. Annapolis, MD: Naval Institute Press, 1989.

Shulimson, Jack, ed. *The U.S. Marines in Vietnam*. 11 vols. Washington, DC: Government Printing Office, 1977–1997.

Spector, Ronald H. *After Tet: The Bloodiest Year in Vietnam*. New York: Macmillan, 1993.

Chapter 14: The New Breed, 1976–2000

Frank, Benis M. *U.S. Marines in Lebanon, 1982–1984*. Washington, DC: Government Printing Office, 1987.

Gordon, Michael R., and Bernard E. Trainor. *The Generals' War: The Inside Story of the Conflict in the Gulf*. Boston: Little, Brown, 1995.

Spector, Ronald H. *Grenada, 1983*. Washington, DC: Government Printing Office, 1987.

Trainor, Bernard E. "Amphibious Operations in the Gulf War," *Marine Corps Gazette* 78 (August 1994): 56–60.

Chapter 15: The War on Terror, 2001–

Fink, Nathaniel. *One Bullet Away: The Making of a Marine Officer*. Boston: Houghton-Mifflin, 2005.

Friedman, Norman. *Terrorism, Afghanistan, and America's New Way of War*. Annapolis, MD. Naval Institute Press, 2003.

Gordon, Michael R., and Bernard E. Trainor. *Cobra 2: The Inside Story of the Invasion and Occupation of Iraq*. New York: Pantheon, 2006.

West, Bing. *No True Glory: A Front Line Account of the Battle for Fallujah*. New York: Bantam, 2005.

West, Bing, and Ray Smith. *The March Up: Taking Baghdad with the 1st Marine Division*. New York: Bantam, 2003.

Index

Combined Action Platoons (CAPs), 343
commerce raiding, 20
Confederacy, 22, 30
Confederate Army, 95
Confederate Congress legislation, 95, 109
Confederate States Marine Corps: Charleston campaign, 103–5; duties of, 102–3; formation of, 94–95; merger with Army, 108–9; Mississippi River operations, 97, 100, 102; Mobile, defense of, 118; officers in, 91, 95–97; Richmond, defense of, 106–7; security responsibilities of, 103; special operations, 105–6; Tucker's Naval Brigade, 116–17; uniform example, 109
Confederate States Marine Corps companies: A, 97, 100, 106; B, 97, 98, 100; C, 97–98, 100, 105–6, 118; Camp Beall (Drewry's Bluff), 98–100, 102, 103, 106–7, 112; D, 102; E, 102, 111, 116, 118; F, 102
Confederate States Naval Academy, 100
Confederate States of America, 91, 118
Confederate States ships: *Alabama*, 94; *Atlanta*, 102; *Chickamauga*, 103; *Chicora*, 105; *Gaines*, 110; *Jamestown*, 97, 98; *Macon*, 111; *McRae*, 97, 102; *Morgan*, 110, 118; *Nashville*, 118; *North Carolina*, 112; *Patrick Henry*, 97, 100; *Raleigh* (ironclad), 112; *Selma*, 110; *Shenandoah*, 103; *Sumter*, 97, 103; *Tallahassee/Olustee*, 103; *Tennessee*, 110–11; *Virginia* (ironclad), 97–98
Confederate States squadrons and brigades: Charleston Squadron, 102, 116; James River Squadron, 97, 98, 105–6, 116, 118; Mobile Squadron, 102, 110, 118; Tucker's Naval Brigade, 116–17
Congress, 98
Constellation, 36, 38, 43
Constellation (carrier), 337
Constitution, 37, 40, 47–48, 49, 50, 55
Continental Marines: *Alliance* and *Sybil* engagement, 30–31; amphibious operations, 19, 23–24; *Bonhomme Richard* and *Serapis* engagement, 26; Charleston campaign, 29–30; commandant of, 15; daily rations, 16; Delaware River battles, 21, 31; enlistment duration proposal, 14–15; final battles of Revolution, 30–31; founding of, 13–15; institutional integrity of, 19–20; Lake Champlain, control of, 20–21; losses of, 22, 31; Mississippi River operation, 22–23; New Providence Island raids, 16, 17–19, 20, 23–24; Penobscot expedition, 19, 26–29; security responsibilities of, 22; success of, 31; troop strength, 20, 31; *Trumbull* and *Watt* engagement, 11–13, 30

Continental Marines units: 1st battalion, 14; 2nd battalion, 14
Continental Navy: commerce raiding, 20; decentralization of, 19–20; founding of, 13; losses of, 22, 26; recruitment difficulties, 20; ships, sale of, 31; ships of, 20, 21–22, 30; troop strength, 20; Whitehaven raid, 24–26
Contreras, Mexico, 77
Conway, James T.: Anbar Province, 430; Baghdad, advance to, 422, 423; Baghdad operations, 425, 427; command of, 412, 413; as commandant, 440; Fallujah, 431–32; Nasiriyah delays, 420; troop shift to Afghanistan, 440–41
Cook, Donald G., 370
Coolidge, Calvin, 220
Coral Sea, 382
Corinto, Nicaragua, 167, 168, 222
Corlett, Charles H., 276
Cornwallis, Charles, 29
Coronet, Operation, 301
Corregidor, Philippines, 238
Corsair, F4U, 260, 277, 287, 310, 311, 313, 316, 317, 319, 323
corvus, 2
Coyotepe, Nicaragua, 168
Craig, Edward A., 308, 309, 311
Crane, Stephen, 145, 146, 147
Creek War, 66–67
Cresswell, Lenard B., 246
Croatia, 399, 400
Croix de Guerre, 190, 197, 200
Croizat, Victor J., 337
Crowe, H. P. "Jim", 272–73
Croyable (France), 34, 36
Crucible, 402
Cuba: Cuzco Well, 145–46; Grenada operations, 379, 381, 382; Guantánamo Bay, 144, 145, 147, 165, 219, 335; Havana, 10, 141; interventions in, 161–62, 165, 167, 180, 203; missile crisis, 335; Negro Rebellion, 167; Santiago, 144–47; Spanish-American War, 139, 141, 143–47; steamer incident, 94; Sugar Intervention, 180; U.S. protection of, 147
Cukela, Louis, 192
Culebra, Puerto Rico, 170, 219
Cullam, David, 24
Cumberland, 98
Cunningham, Alfred A., 169, 201–3, 217
Cunningham, Winfield S., 237
Cunningham fire support base, 365
Curtis Jenny, 208, 210
Cushman, Robert E., Jr.: challenges to existence of Corps, 371, 373; as commandant, 371;

Guadalcanal: aviation operations, 246–47, 249, 254, 255; Bloody Ridge, 248; Fighter One, 242, 249, 254; George Medal, 256; Henderson Field (Cactus Base), 244–45, 246, 247, 251, 252–53, 259; Japanese attacks, 245–46, 248, 252–55; Japanese attacks, plans for, 248–49, 251; losses at, 246, 248, 250, 254, 256; malaria, infections, and diseases, 250, 251; medal for service at, 256; naval battle, 255; naval support, withdrawal of, 243–44, 248, 256; perimeter expansion, 249–51; prisoners' behavior, 246; reinforcements, 251–52; Savo Island, Battle of, 243; seizure of, 239–42; Thanksgiving Day, 255; Tulagi, 239–40, 241–46; turning point, 248, 255, 267; withdrawal from, 255–56

Guadalupe Hildago, Treaty of, 81

Guam, 147, 152, 237, 278, 281–82, 283, 383

Guam, 381

Guantánamo Bay, Cuba, 144, 145, 147, 165, 219, 335

Guayacanas, Dominican Republic, 178

Guaymas, Mexico, 74, 75

Guerrière (Britain), 47

Gulick, Louis M, 224

Gunboat No. 6, 40

Gunboat No. 9, 41

gung ho, 257

gunnery duels, 3–4

gunnery sergeant, 139

Gus, William F., 330

Hagee, Michael W., 430, 432, 440

Hague, 30

Haiti: atrocities in, 210; cacos pacification, 174–77, 207–10; Fort Berthol, 175; Fort Capois, 175; Fort Dipité, 175; Fort Rivière, 175–77; Fort Selon, 175; Garde d'Haiti, 221; Gendarmerie d'Haiti, 177, 221, 228; interventions in, 179, 203, 401; Mirebalais, 208; pirate activity, 36–37; Port-au-Prince, 208, 209; revolutions in, 174; self-government potential, 221; troops stationed in, 217; withdrawal from, 231

Halifax, Nova Scotia, 14

Hall, John, 36

Halls of the Montezumas, 81

Halsey, William F. "Bull", 255

Hamilton, William, 26, 29

Hampton Roads, Virginia, 93, 97–98

Hancock, 22

hand salute, 44

Hanneken, Herman, 208–9, 253, 254, 283

Hanoi, Vietnam, 370

Hanson, Robert M., 260–61

Harbord, James G., 186, 187, 190, 191, 192

Harding, Warren, 217, 218

Harold E. Holt, 373–74

Harpers Ferry, Virginia, 89–90

Harris, Harold D. "Bucky", 283

Harris, John, 67, 69, 88, 91, 92, 107–8

Hart, Franklin A., 277

Hartford, 121–22

Haruna (Japan), 252–53

Harvest Moon, Operation, 343

Hastings, Operation, 345, 346

Hatcheelustee Creek, Florida, 67

Hatteras Islet, North Carolina, 91

Havana, Cuba, 10, 141

Havre de Grace, Maryland, 94

Hawaii, 147, 219–20, 235–37, 238

Hawkins, William Dean, 270, 272

Hayate (Japan), 237

Hay-es-Salaam, Lebanon, 377

Headquarters Marine Corps (HQMC): Division of Operations and Training (DOT), 213; focus of, 213; location of, 35, 38–39

Heinl, Robert D., Jr., 228, 335

helicopters: AH-1 Cobra, 381; Apache, 389; Black Hawk, 406; CH-46, 381; CH-53, 370, 373, 374, 381, 406; *Employment of Helicopters (Tentative)—PHIB 31*, 305; HH-53, 373, 374; MV-22 Osprey, 402, 403, 430; promise of use of, 305; RH-53D, 376; Sikorsky HRS-1, 328, 329; vertical envelopment, 305. *See also* U.S. Marine Corps squadrons, helicopter

Henderson, Archibald: as acting commandant, 57; career of, 59; chain of command, sanctity of, 59; as commandant, 59–61; as *Constitution* commander, 55; court martial of Wharton, 56; death of, 88; election-day riots, 84–85; enlisted men, life of, 60; family of, 61; Mexican War, 76; officers, quality of, 59–60; Quallah Battoo action, 65; rank of, 120; recruitment efforts, 60; Seminole War, 66–68, 69

Henderson, Lofton R., 244

Henderson, Richard, 96, 97, 117

Henderson Field (Cactus Base), 244–45, 246, 247, 251, 252–53, 259

Henley, John D., 40

Herbert, Hilary A., 120, 138

Heywood, Charles (father), 74

Heywood, Charles (son): advanced base mission, 149; Civil War, 98, 111; as commandant, 135; expansion of Corps, 138, 147, 149; Panamanian intervention, 133–34; promotion of, 149; reforms under, 135–36; retirement of, 160; Spanish-American War, 143

North Carolina, 112

North Korea, 409. See also Korea

North Korean military units: 6th Division, 310; 18th Division, 317; 25th Brigade, 317; 83rd Motorized Rifle Regiment, 311; 226th Rifle Regiment, 316; North Korean People's Army, 308, 318

North Korean Yaks, 330

North Vietnam, China's support for, 337

North Vietnamese Army (NVA): 21st Regiment, 366; 36th Regiment, 366; 90th Regiment, 368; 141st Regiment, 368; 304th Division, 354; 308th Division, 354; 324B Division, 345; 325 C Division, 354; 341st Division, 345, 347, 354; attrition strategy to defeat, 343; in Viet Cong units, 362

Northern Alliance, 406, 407

Northern Watch, Operation, 396

Norway, 383

Nueva Segovia Province, Nicaragua, 223–28

Numaniyah, Iraq, 424, 425

O'Bannon, Presley N., 41–43

Ocotal, Nicaragua, 223

Office of Strategic Services (OSS), 301–2

Oglethorpe, James, 7

O'Grady, Scott, 399

oil fields: defense of, 203; Iraq, 411, 412, 414, 415

Okinawa, 285, 286, 293–301

Olongapo, Philippines, 160, 238

Olustee/Tallahassee, 103

Olympic, Operation, 301

Oman, 390

One Bullet Away (Fick), 413

Orange, 31

Ortiz, Peter J., 301–2

Osborne, William, 39

Osborne, William S., 40

Osprey, MV-22, 402, 403, 430

Ota Minoru, 294, 297

P-51 fighters, 285

Pace, Peter M., 442–43

Pacific campaigns: amphibious operations, 258, 265, 267, 274, 276–77; atomic bombs, 301; aviation operations, 276–78; Betio Island, Tarawa Atoll, 268, 269–74, 275; Cape Gloucester, New Britain, 261–63; Catchpole, Operation, 276, 277; Coronet, Operation, 301; Detachment, Operation, 285–93; division size and weapon systems, 279; Forager, Operation, 278–83; Galvanic, Operation, 268–74; Gilbert Islands, 268–74; Iceberg, Operation, 293–301; island-hoping campaign, 265, 267; Iwo Jima, 285–93; Japanese islands, invasion of, 301; Japanese victories, 238; Leyte Gulf, Battle of, 286; losses during, 273–74, 291, 293, 300–301; Makin Atoll, Gilbert Islands, 256–57, 269; malaria, infections, and diseases, 250, 251, 263; Mariana Islands, 278–83; Marshall Islands, 268, 275–78; Midway, 238–39, 267; naval support for, 287; Okinawa, 285, 286, 293–301; Olympic, Operation, 301; Pavuvu, Russell Islands, 263, 265; Pearl Harbor, 235–37, 238; Peleliu, 283–85; planning operations for, 214–15, 217; prisoners of war, treatment of, 237–38; readiness of Marines for, 238; Saipan, 279–81; Stalemate II, Operation, 283–85; troop strength, 267–68, 275; Wake Island, 237–38; Watchtower, Operation, 239–56; weapon systems, 252, 261. See also Solomon Islands

Pacific Squadron, 69, 70, 71, 74

Pacificador Province, Dominican Republic, 178

Paige, Mitchell, 254, 256

Pakistan, 406

Palau, 305

Palestinian Liberation Organization (PLO), 376–77

Palo Alto, Mexico, 75

Palos, 122, 123, 124, 125

Panama, 133–34, 160–61, 383–84

Panama Battalion, 162, 164, 167–68

Panama Canal treaty, 160–61

Panama City, New Granada, 81

Panamanian Defense Force (PDF), 383–84

Panmunjon, truce at, 331

Paris Peace Accords, 370

Parris Island, South Carolina, 184–85, 333–34, 374–75

Parry, Francis Fox, 323

Parry Island, Marshall Islands, 277

Passamaquoddy, Nova Scotia, 13–14

Patapsco, 38

Patch, Alexander M., 256

Pate, Randolph McCall, 243, 333, 334

Pathet Lao, 336

Patrick Henry, 97, 100

Patriots' War, 44, 45–46

Pavuvu, Russell Islands, 263, 265

pay for Marines, 35, 63, 233–34

PBY Catalina, 244

Peace Establishment Act, 56

Pearl Harbor, 235–37, 238

Peatross, Oscar F., 341–42

Pegasus, Operation, 357–58

About the Authors

MERRILL L. BARTLETT served more than twenty years as a Marine, including two tours in the Vietnam littoral. His other overseas assignments took him to Thailand, Japan, and at sea with the Marine detachment in the heavy cruiser *Newport News* (CA 148). For his final posting, Lt. Col. Bartlett recruited for the Marine Corps and taught history at the U.S. Naval Academy, where he earned the William P. Clements Award as outstanding military educator (1979). The "Merrill Bartlett Prize" in history was established at the Academy to honor the occasion of his retirement in 1983. He is the author or co-author and editor or co-editor of seven books on naval history, and he has written more than a hundred published essays and book reviews as well. Two of his essays, both appearing in the U.S. Naval Institute *Proceedings*, won the Colonel Robert D. Heinl Jr. Memorial Prize in Marine Corps History (1981, 1987).

JACK SWEETMAN is the author, coauthor, translator, editor, and coeditor of ten books and many shorter pieces in the fields of naval and military history. He served as a company commander in the U.S. Army and was a Ford Fellow at Emory University, where he earned his Ph.D. For many years contributing editor of *Naval History* magazine, he is a recipient of the Alfred Thayer Mahan Award for Literary Achievement and a Fellow of the Royal Historical Society. He lives in Orlando, Florida.

THE NAVAL INSTITUTE PRESS is the book-publishing arm of the U.S. Naval Institute, a private, nonprofit, membership society for sea service professionals and others who share an interest in naval and maritime affairs. Established in 1873 at the U.S. Naval Academy in Annapolis, Maryland, where its offices remain today, the Naval Institute has members worldwide.

Members of the Naval Institute support the education programs of the society and receive the influential monthly magazine *Proceedings* and discounts on fine nautical prints and on ship and aircraft photos. They also have access to the transcripts of the Institute's Oral History Program and get discounted admission to any of the Institute-sponsored seminars offered around the country. Discounts are also available to the colorful bimonthly magazine *Naval History*.

The Naval Institute's book-publishing program, begun in 1898 with basic guides to naval practices, has broadened its scope to include books of more general interest. Now the Naval Institute Press publishes about seventy titles each year, ranging from how-to books on boating and navigation to battle histories, biographies, ship and aircraft guides, and novels. Institute members receive significant discounts on the Press's more than eight hundred books in print.

Full-time students are eligible for special half-price membership rates. Life memberships are also available.

For a free catalog describing Naval Institute Press books currently available, and for further information about joining the U.S. Naval Institute, please write to:

Member Services
U.S. NAVAL INSTITUTE
291 Wood Road
Annapolis, Maryland 21402-5034
Telephone: 800.233.8764
Fax: 410.571.1703
Web address: www.usni.org